GOD
TONIC

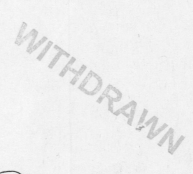

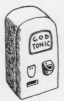

THE STORY OF
JEZEBEL
AND HER TURBULENCE WITH
THE PROPHETS OF ISRAEL

Design & Production: Jordan Shiveley
Art Direction: Tom Kaczynski

Uncivilized Books
P.O. Box 6534
Minneapolis, MN 55406
USA
uncivilizedbooks.com

First Edition, July 2017

10 9 8 7 6 5 4 3 2 1

ISBN 978-1-941250-16-7

DISTRIBUTED TO THE TRADE BY:
Consortium Book Sales & Distribution, LLC.
34 Thirteenth Avenue NE, Suite 101
Minneapolis, MN 55413-1007
cbsd.com, Orders: (800) 283-3572

Printed in CANADA

ELIJAH BRUBAKER

THE STORY OF JEZEBEL
AND HER TURBULENCE WITH THE PROPHETS OF ISRAEL

A SATIRIC RECOUNTING OF THE PIOUS STRUGGLE OF ELIJAH, ELISHA AND JEHU AS THEY FIGHT FOR THE IMMORTAL SOULS OF THEIR PEOPLE BASED ON THE BEST SELLING BOOK **THE BIBLE** WRITTEN BY GOD

Uncivilized Books

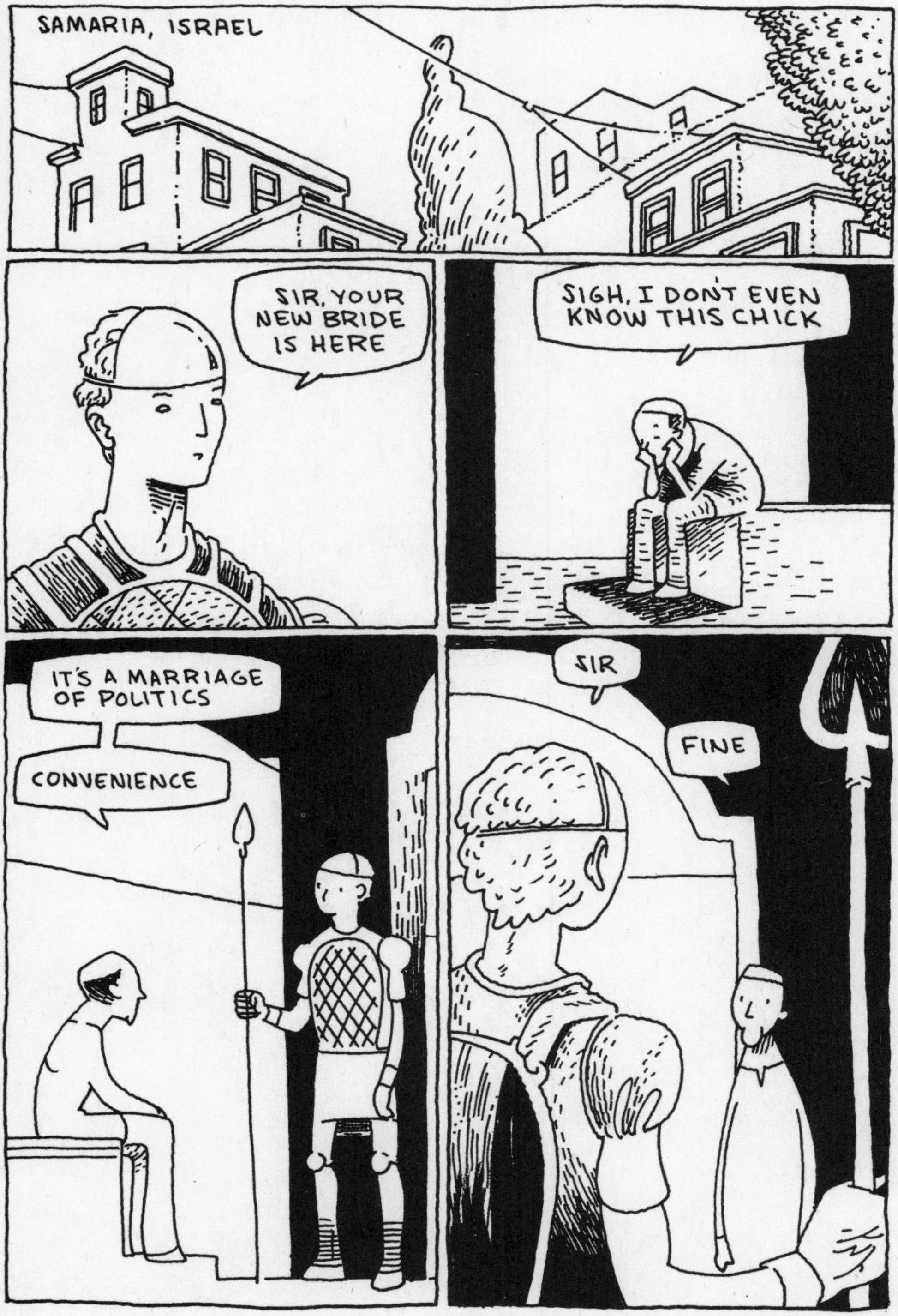
SAMARIA, ISRAEL
SIR, YOUR NEW BRIDE IS HERE
SIGH, I DON'T EVEN KNOW THIS CHICK
IT'S A MARRIAGE OF POLITICS
CONVENIENCE
SIR
FINE

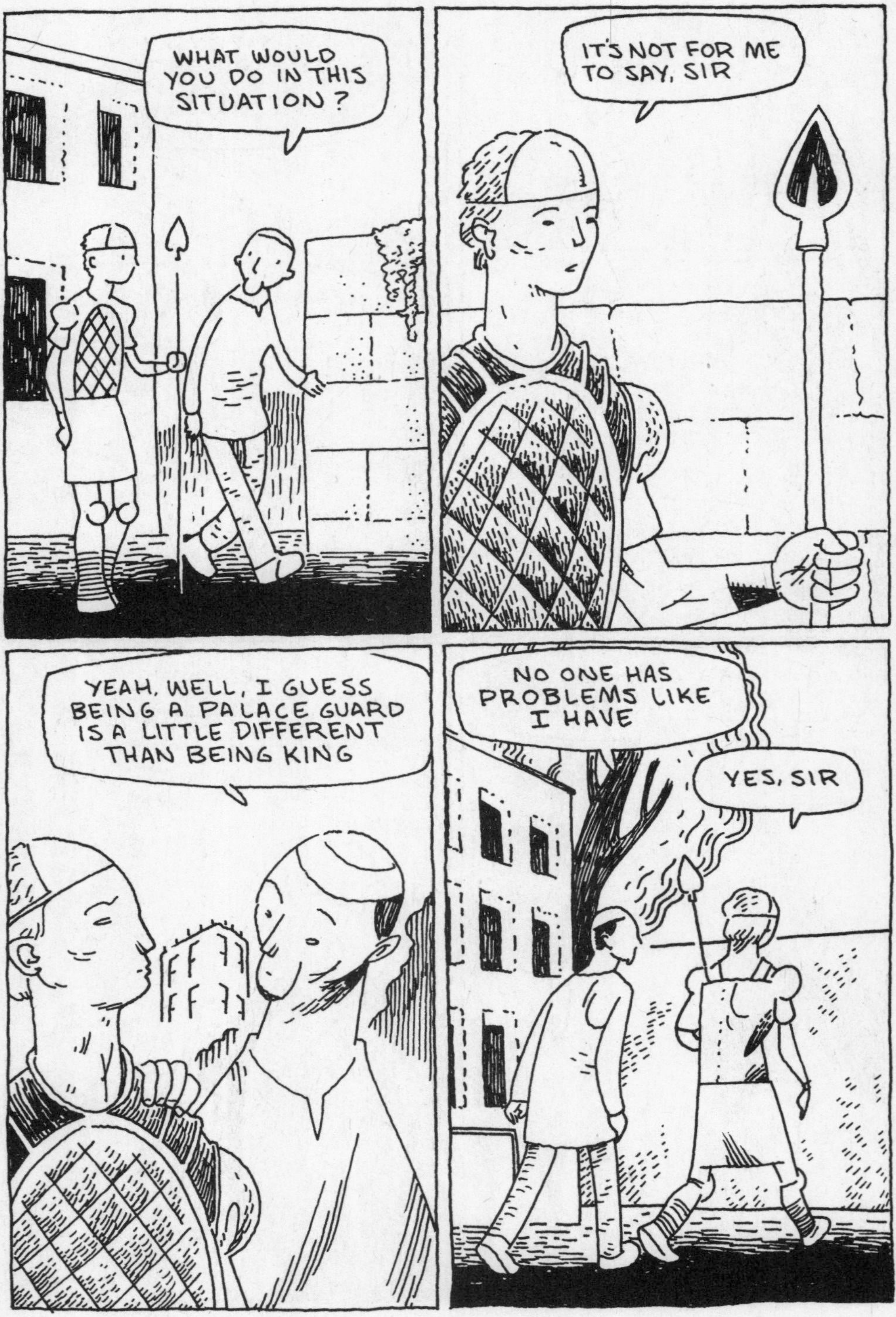
WHAT WOULD YOU DO IN THIS SITUATION?
IT'S NOT FOR ME TO SAY, SIR
YEAH, WELL, I GUESS BEING A PALACE GUARD IS A LITTLE DIFFERENT THAN BEING KING
NO ONE HAS PROBLEMS LIKE I HAVE
YES, SIR

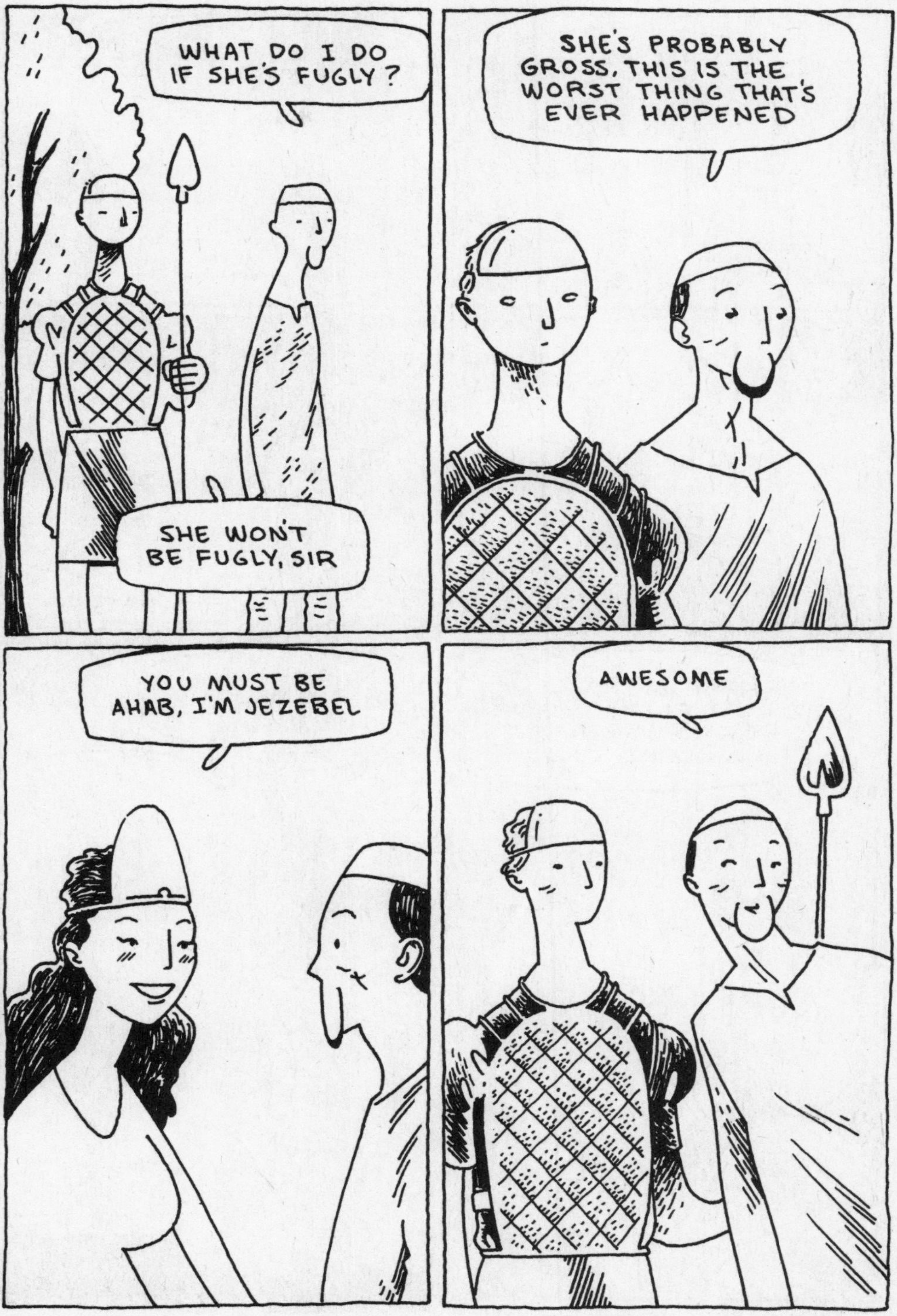
WHAT DO I DO IF SHE'S FUGLY?
SHE WON'T BE FUGLY, SIR
SHE'S PROBABLY GROSS, THIS IS THE WORST THING THAT'S EVER HAPPENED
YOU MUST BE AHAB, I'M JEZEBEL
AWESOME

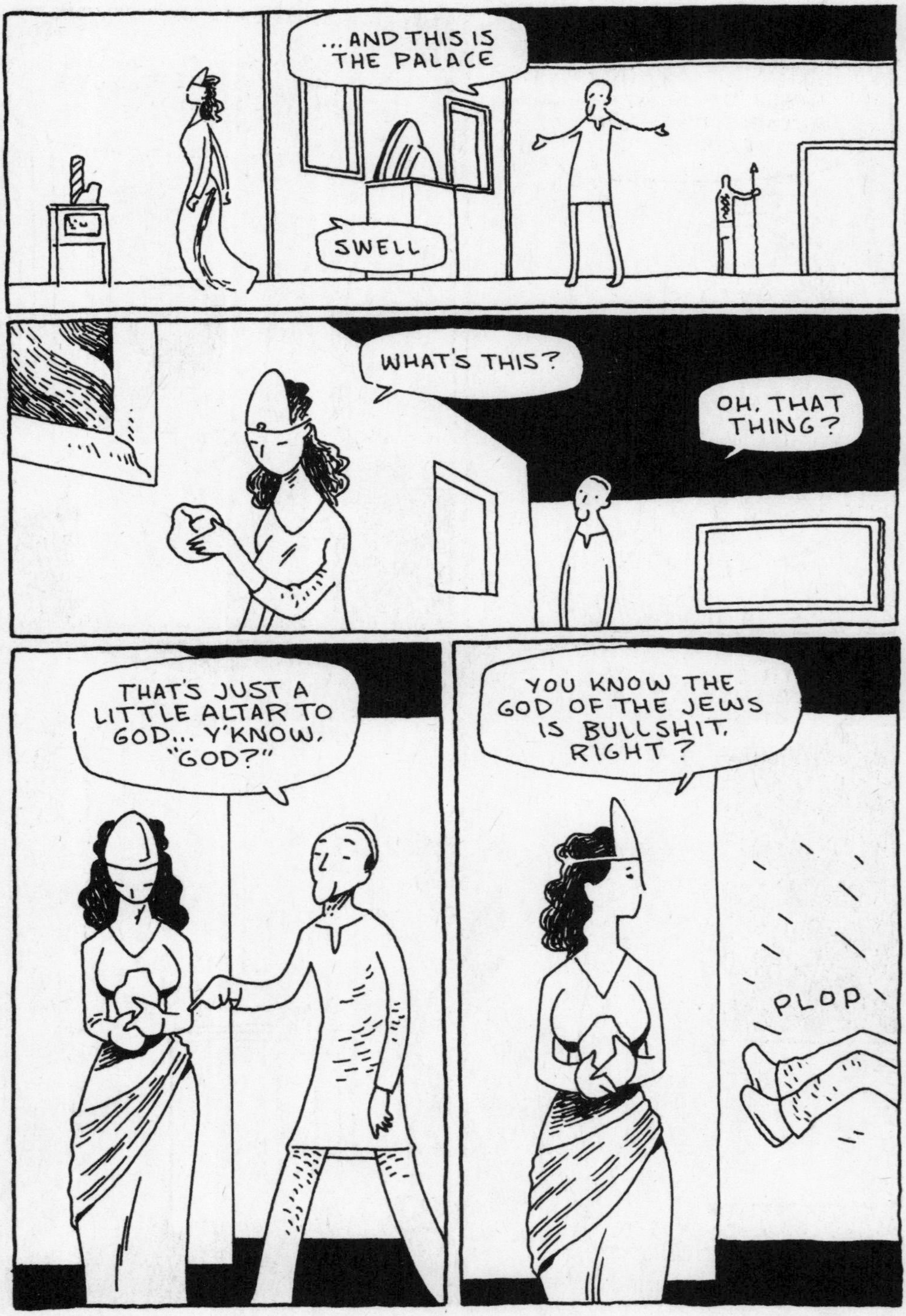
...AND THIS IS THE PALACE
SWELL
WHAT'S THIS?
OH, THAT THING?
THAT'S JUST A LITTLE ALTAR TO GOD... Y'KNOW, "GOD?"
YOU KNOW THE GOD OF THE JEWS IS BULLSHIT, RIGHT?
PLOP

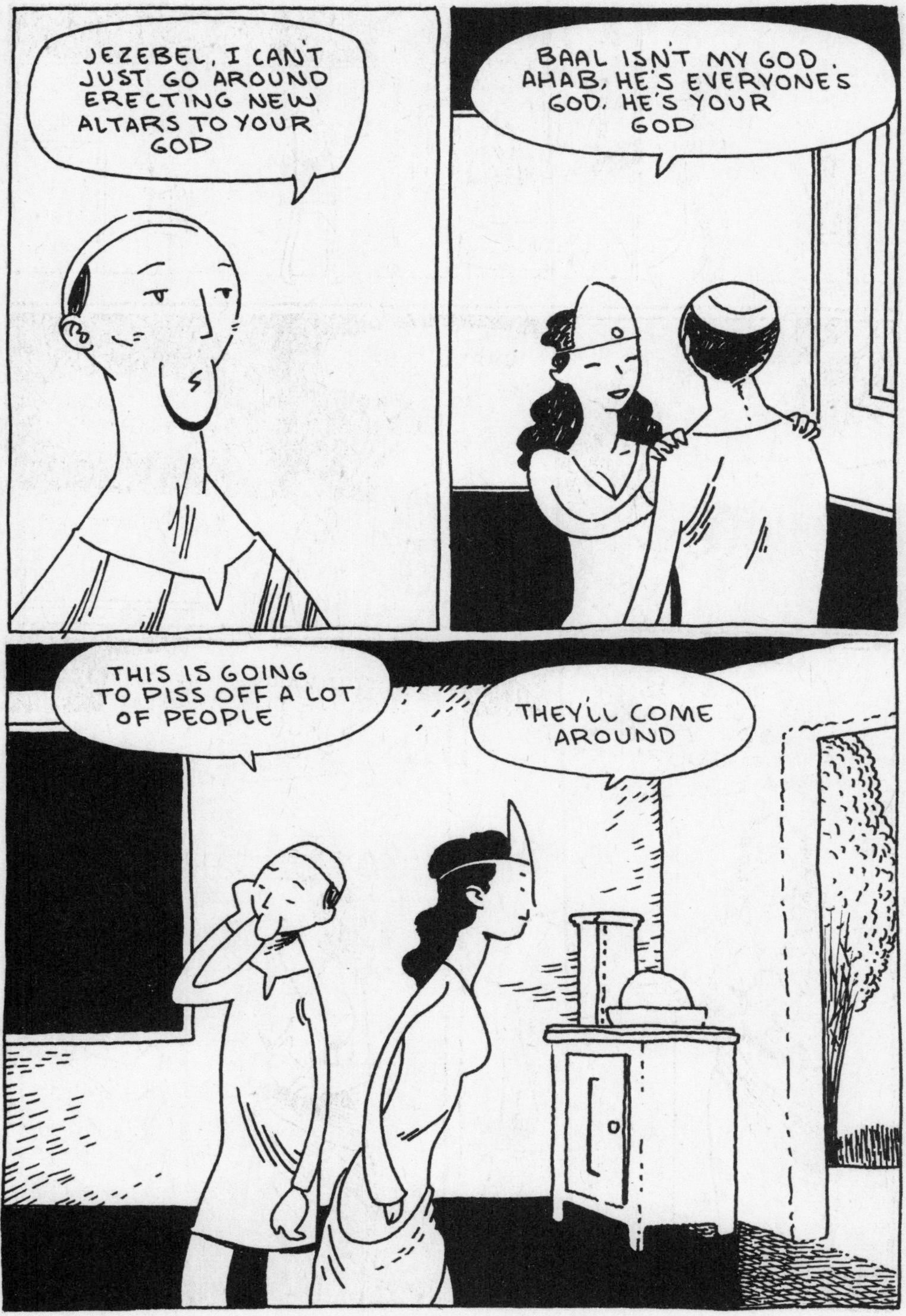
JEZEBEL, I CAN'T JUST GO AROUND ERECTING NEW ALTARS TO YOUR GOD
BAAL ISN'T MY GOD. AHAB, HE'S EVERYONE'S GOD. HE'S YOUR GOD
THIS IS GOING TO PISS OFF A LOT OF PEOPLE
THEY'LL COME AROUND

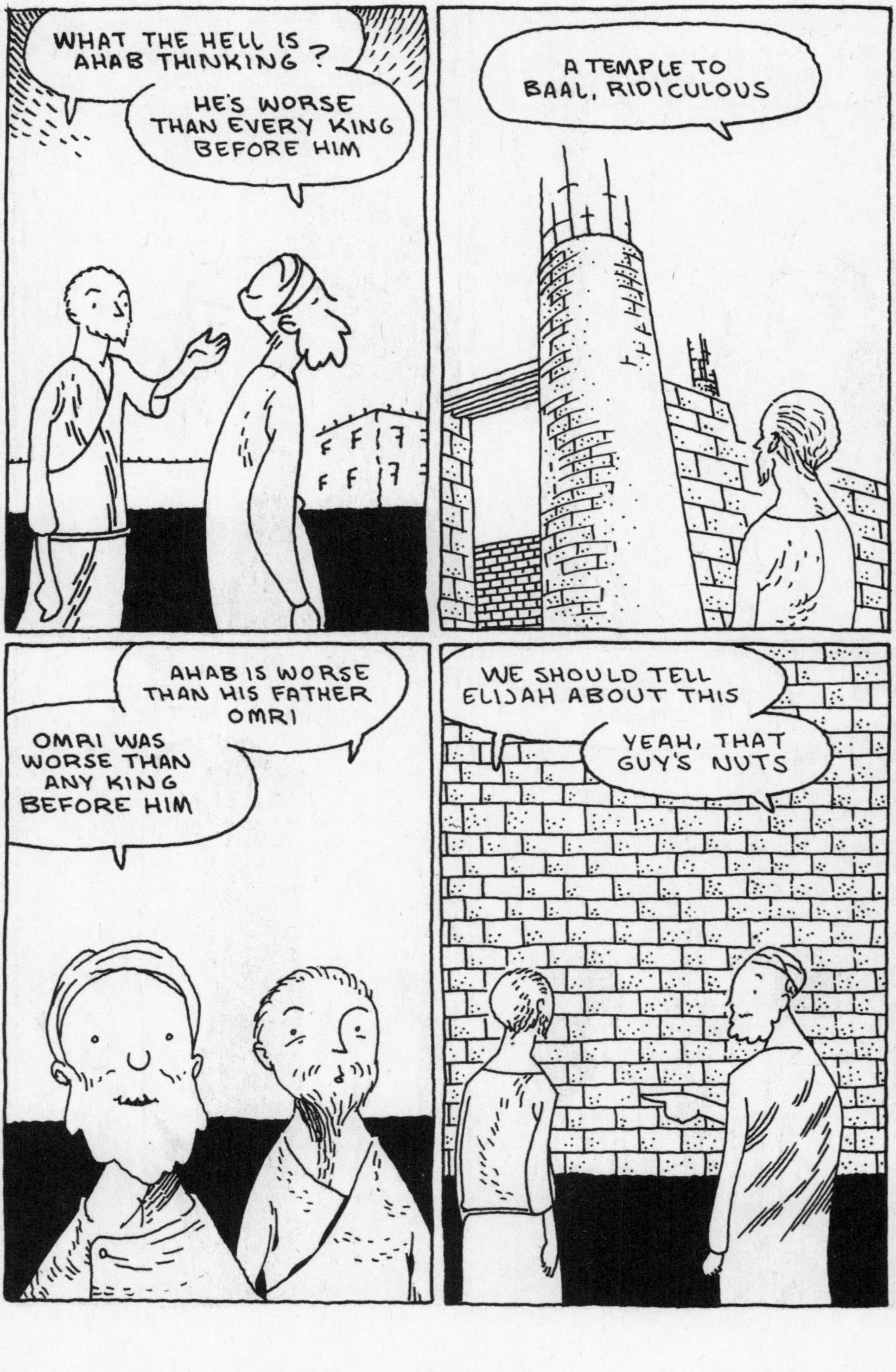
WHAT THE HELL IS AHAB THINKING?
HE'S WORSE THAN EVERY KING BEFORE HIM
A TEMPLE TO BAAL, RIDICULOUS
AHAB IS WORSE THAN HIS FATHER OMRI
OMRI WAS WORSE THAN ANY KING BEFORE HIM
WE SHOULD TELL ELIJAH ABOUT THIS
YEAH, THAT GUY'S NUTS

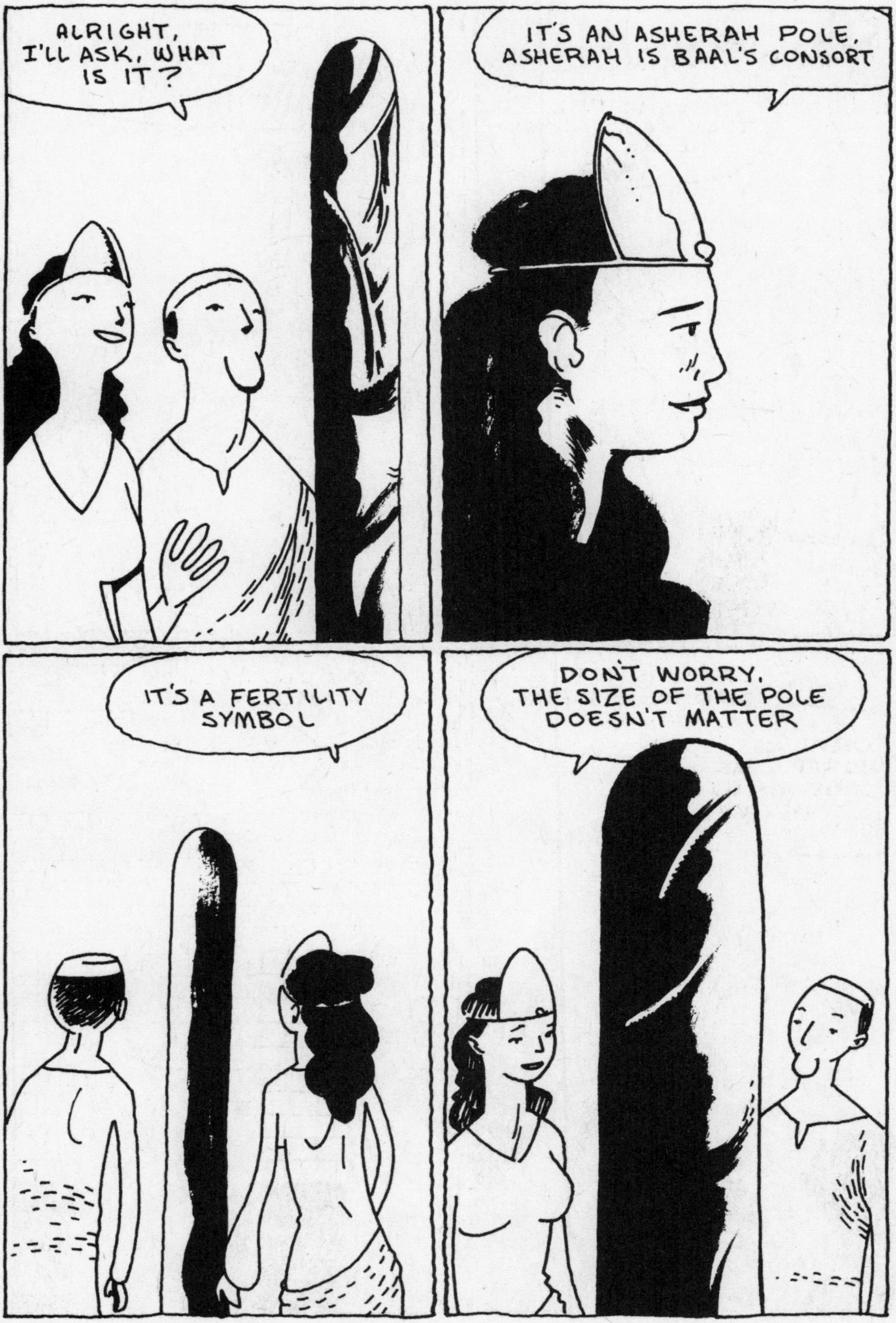
ALRIGHT, I'LL ASK, WHAT IS IT?
IT'S AN ASHERAH POLE, ASHERAH IS BAAL'S CONSORT
IT'S A FERTILITY SYMBOL
DON'T WORRY. THE SIZE OF THE POLE DOESN'T MATTER

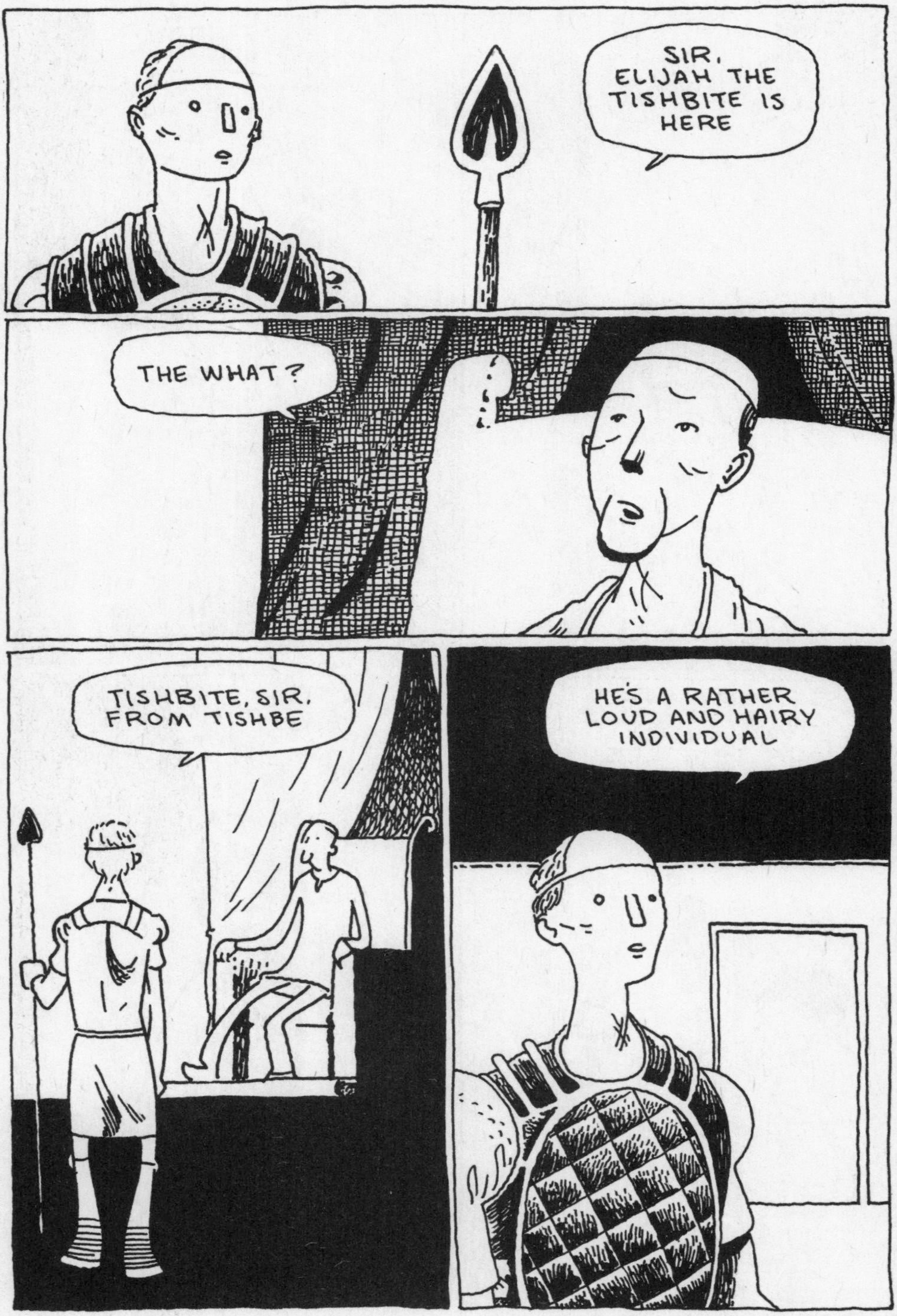
SIR, ELIJAH THE TISHBITE IS HERE
THE WHAT?
TISHBITE, SIR, FROM TISHBE
HE'S A RATHER LOUD AND HAIRY INDIVIDUAL

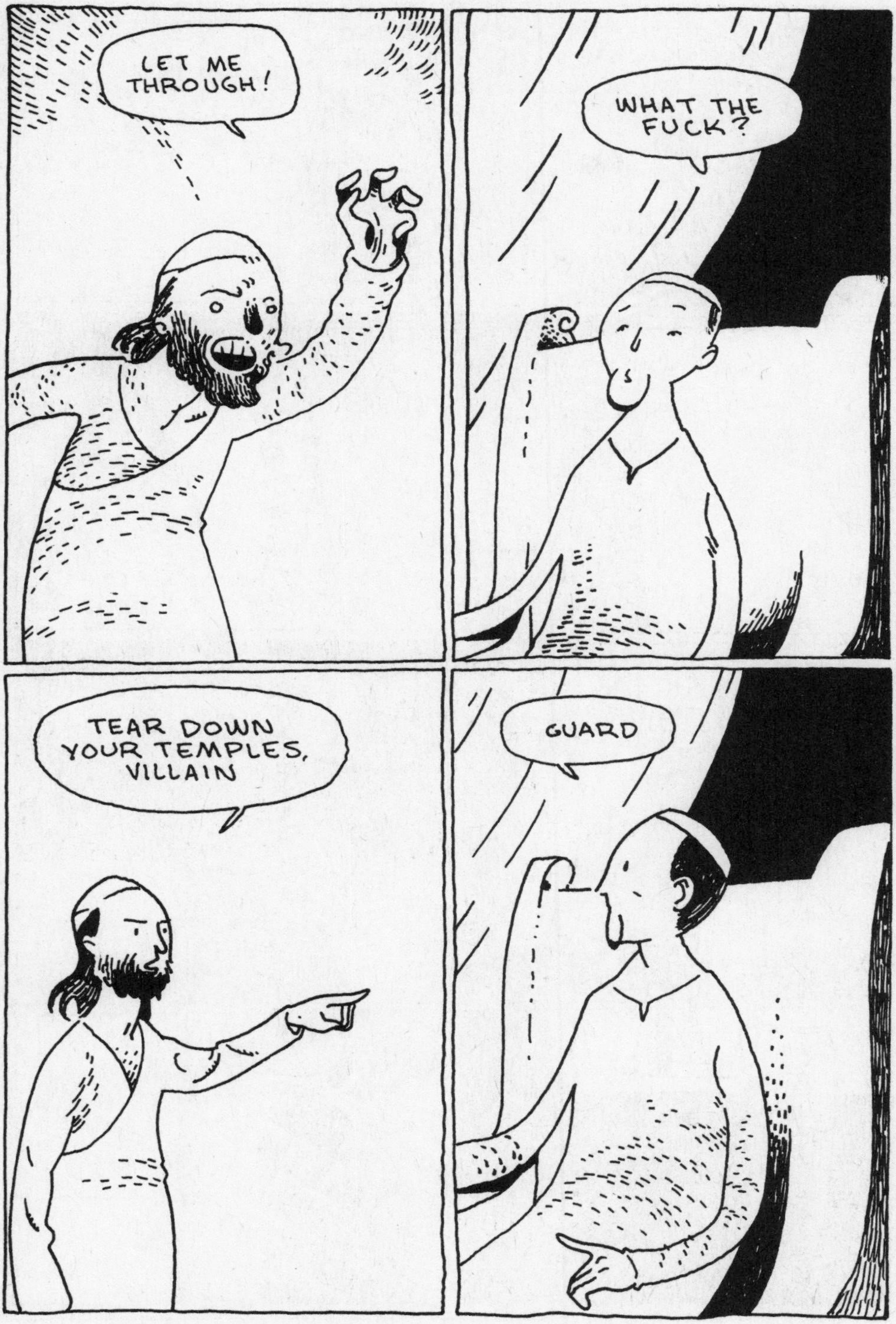
LET ME THROUGH!
WHAT THE FUCK?
TEAR DOWN YOUR TEMPLES, VILLAIN
GUARD

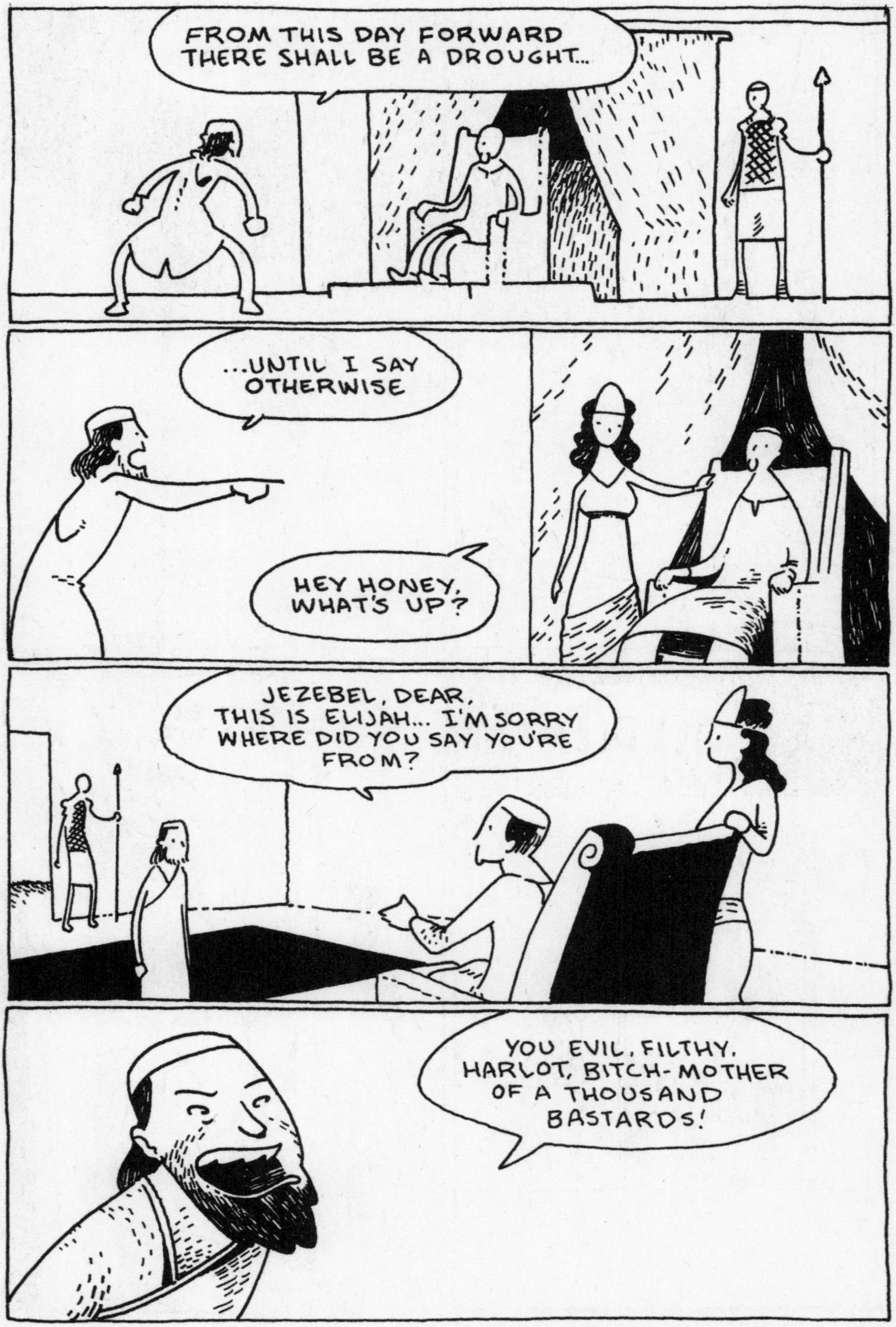
FROM THIS DAY FORWARD THERE SHALL BE A DROUGHT...
...UNTIL I SAY OTHERWISE
HEY HONEY, WHAT'S UP?
JEZEBEL, DEAR, THIS IS ELIJAH... I'M SORRY WHERE DID YOU SAY YOU'RE FROM?
YOU EVIL, FILTHY, HARLOT, BITCH-MOTHER OF A THOUSAND BASTARDS!

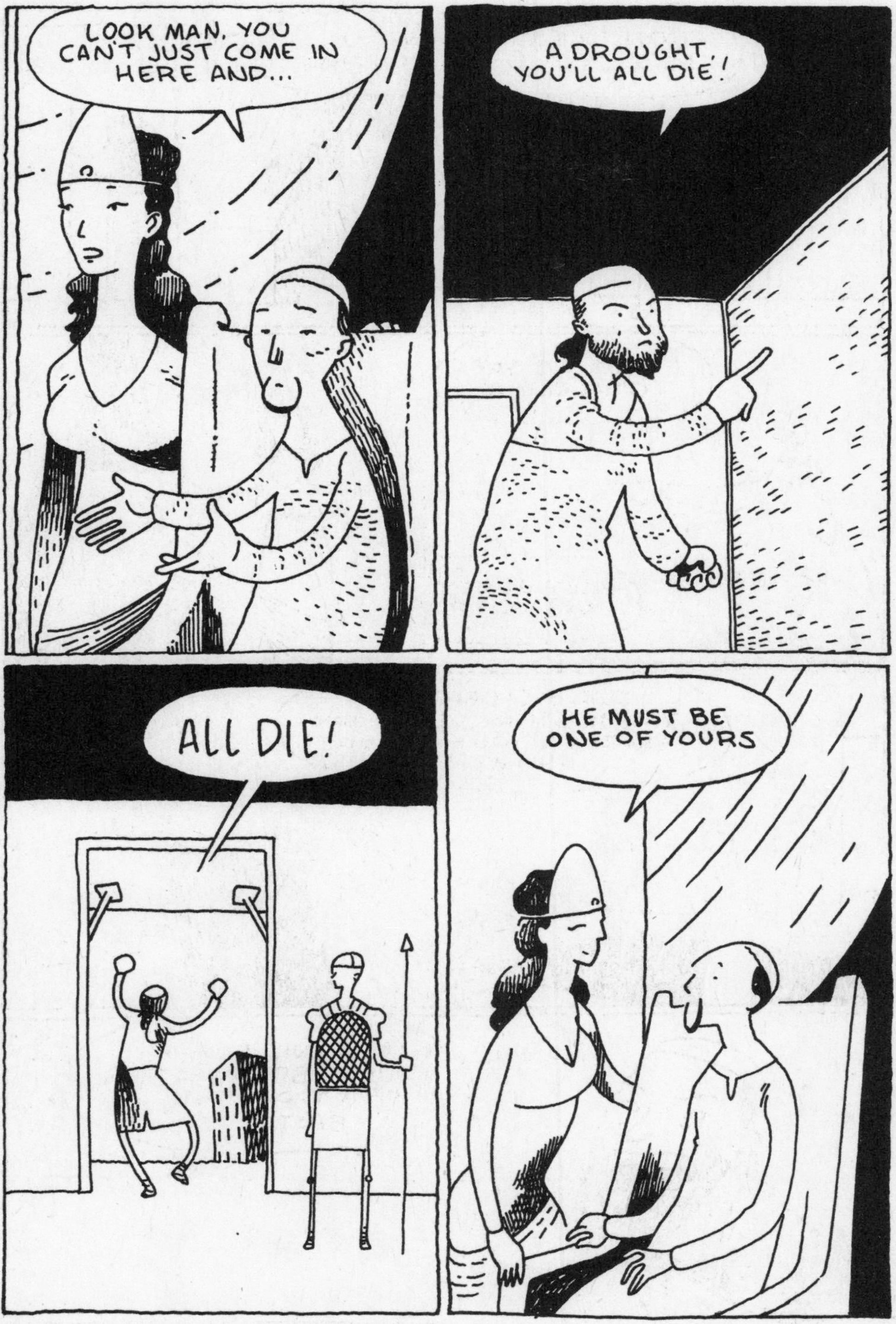
LOOK MAN, YOU CAN'T JUST COME IN HERE AND...
A DROUGHT, YOU'LL ALL DIE!
ALL DIE!
HE MUST BE ONE OF YOURS

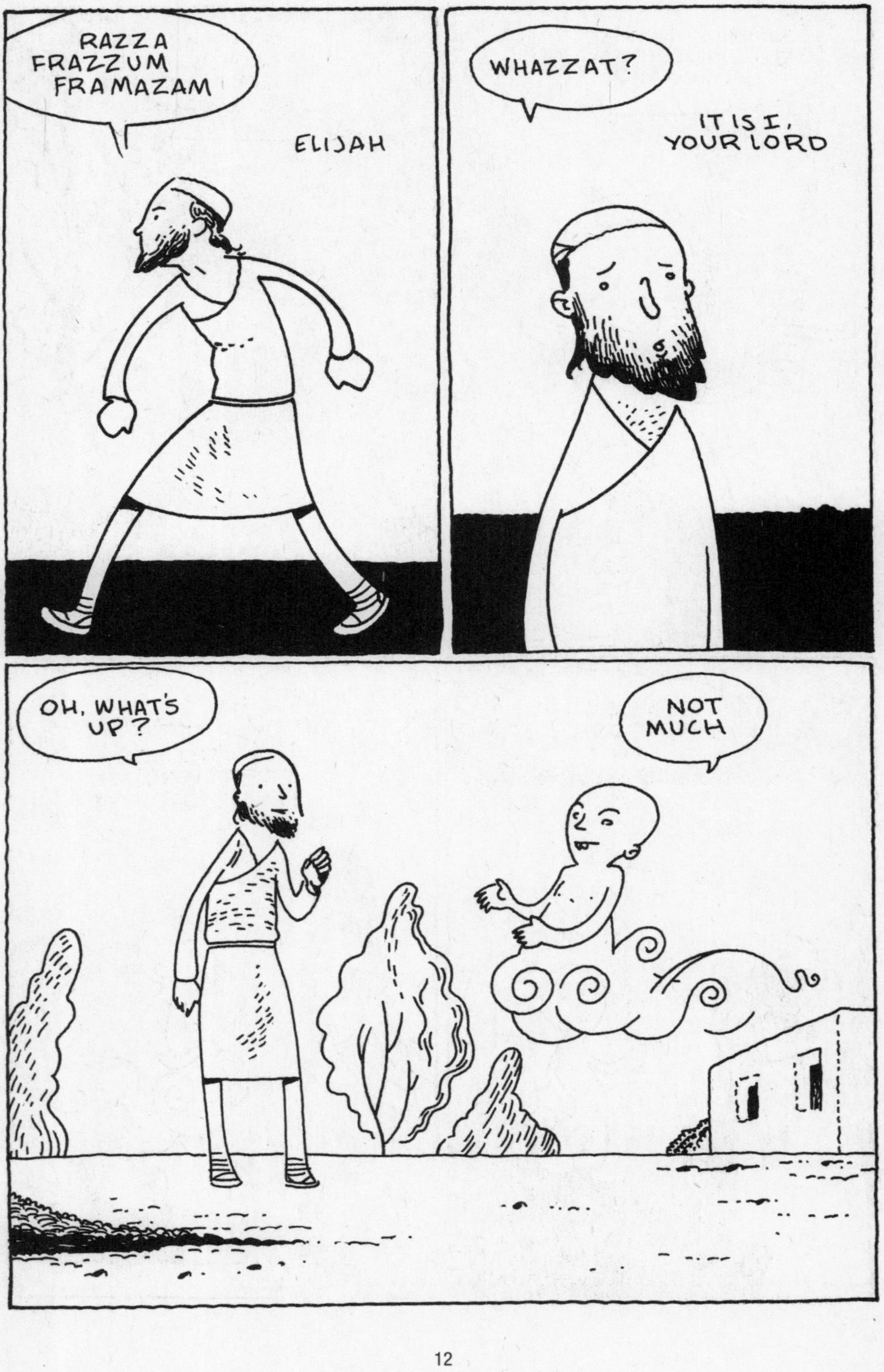
RAZZA FRAZZUM FRAMAZAM
ELIJAH
WHAZZAT?
IT IS I, YOUR LORD
OH, WHAT'S UP?
NOT MUCH

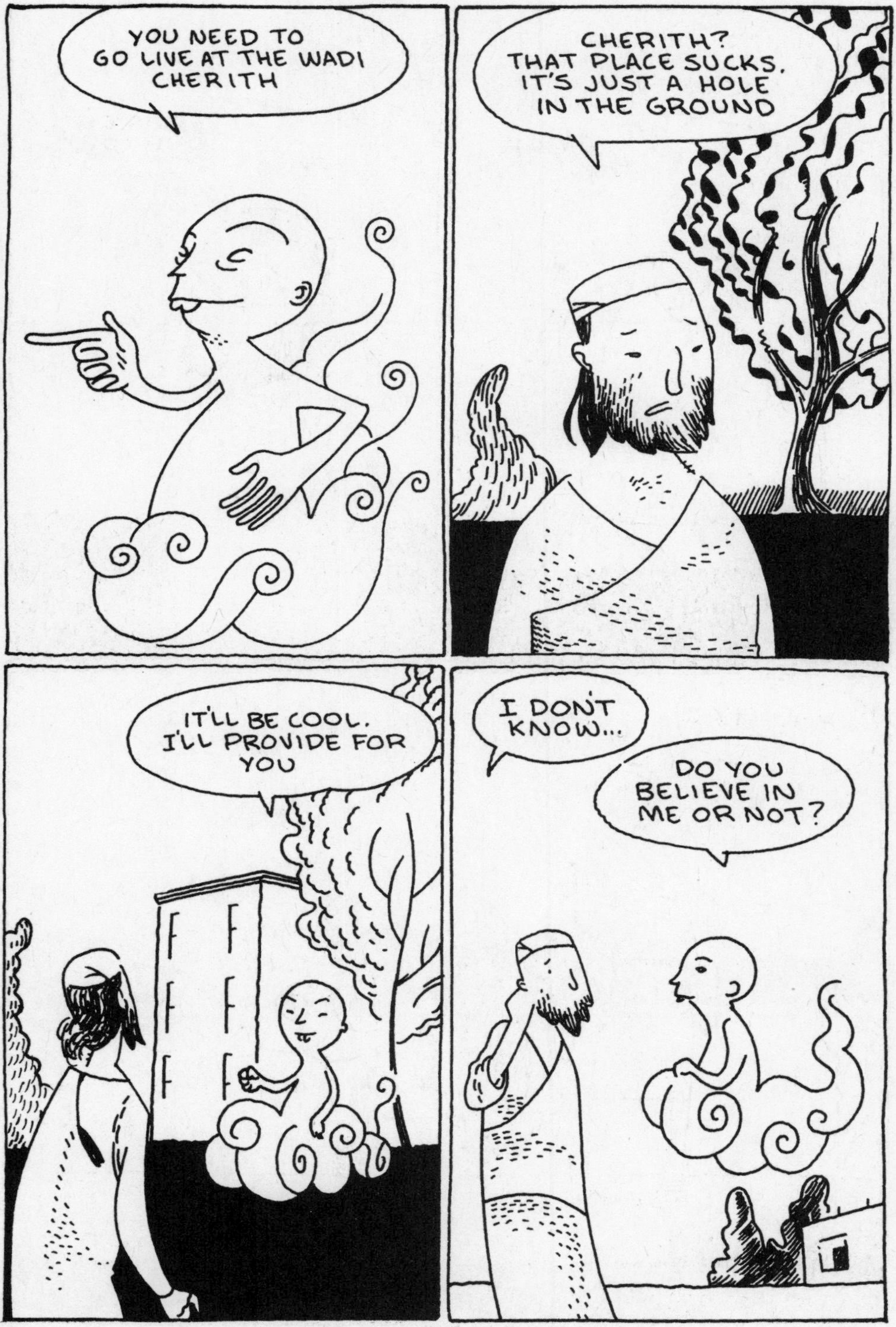
YOU NEED TO GO LIVE AT THE WADI CHERITH
CHERITH? THAT PLACE SUCKS. IT'S JUST A HOLE IN THE GROUND
IT'LL BE COOL. I'LL PROVIDE FOR YOU
I DON'T KNOW...
DO YOU BELIEVE IN ME OR NOT?

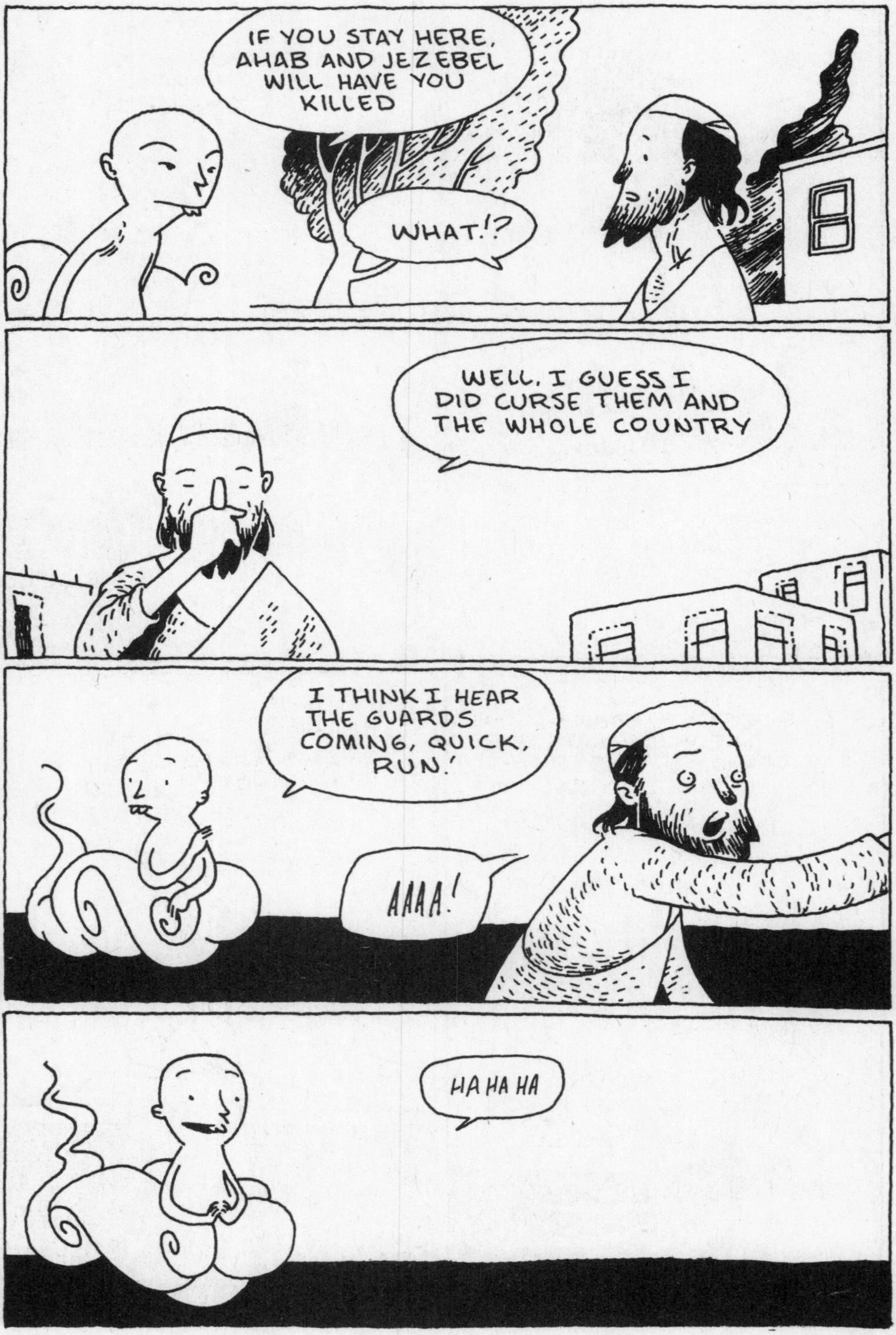
IF YOU STAY HERE, AHAB AND JEZEBEL WILL HAVE YOU KILLED
WHAT!?
WELL, I GUESS I DID CURSE THEM AND THE WHOLE COUNTRY
I THINK I HEAR THE GUARDS COMING, QUICK, RUN!
AAAA!
HA HA HA

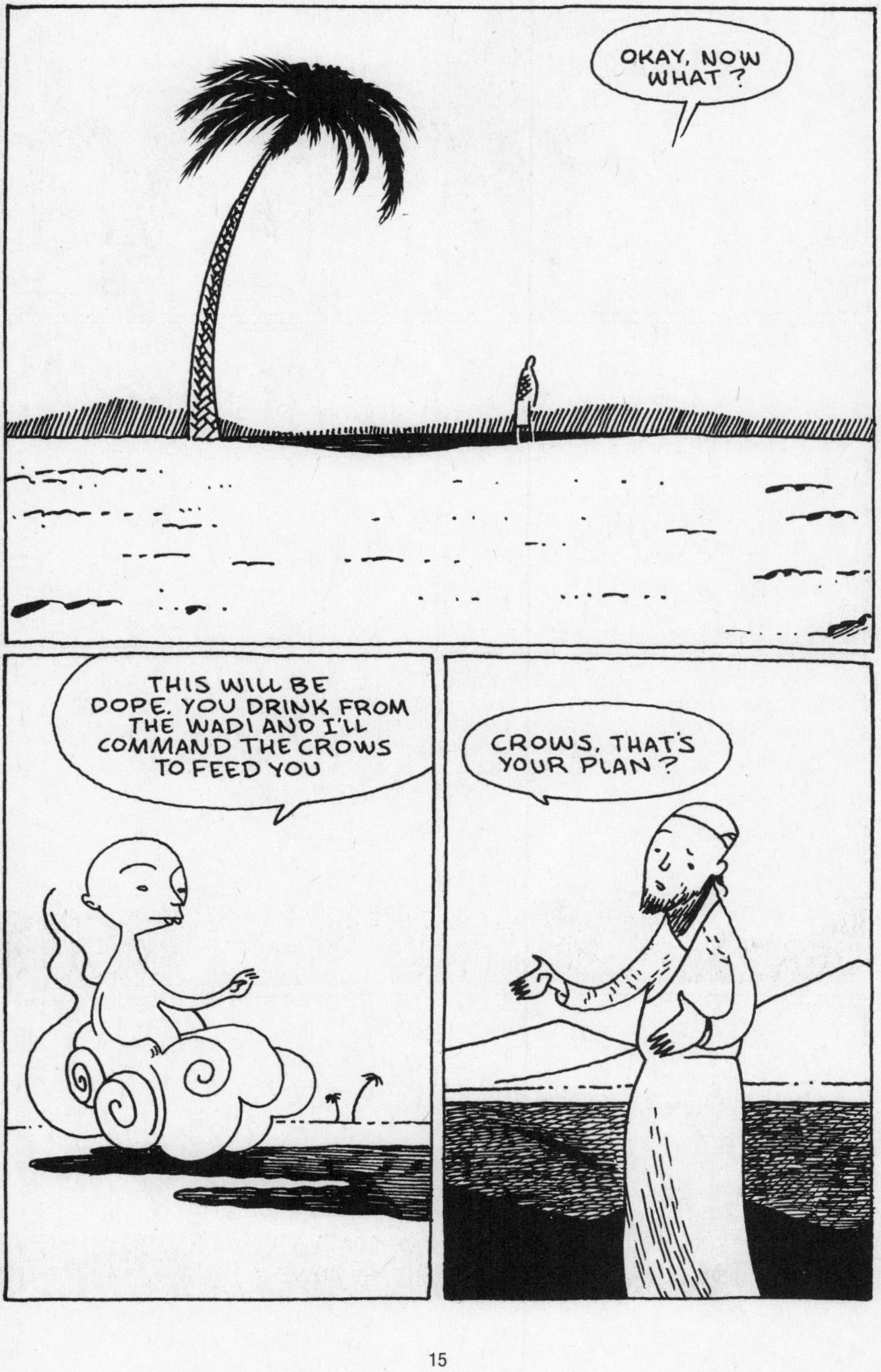
OKAY, NOW WHAT?
THIS WILL BE DOPE. YOU DRINK FROM THE WADI AND I'LL COMMAND THE CROWS TO FEED YOU
CROWS. THAT'S YOUR PLAN?

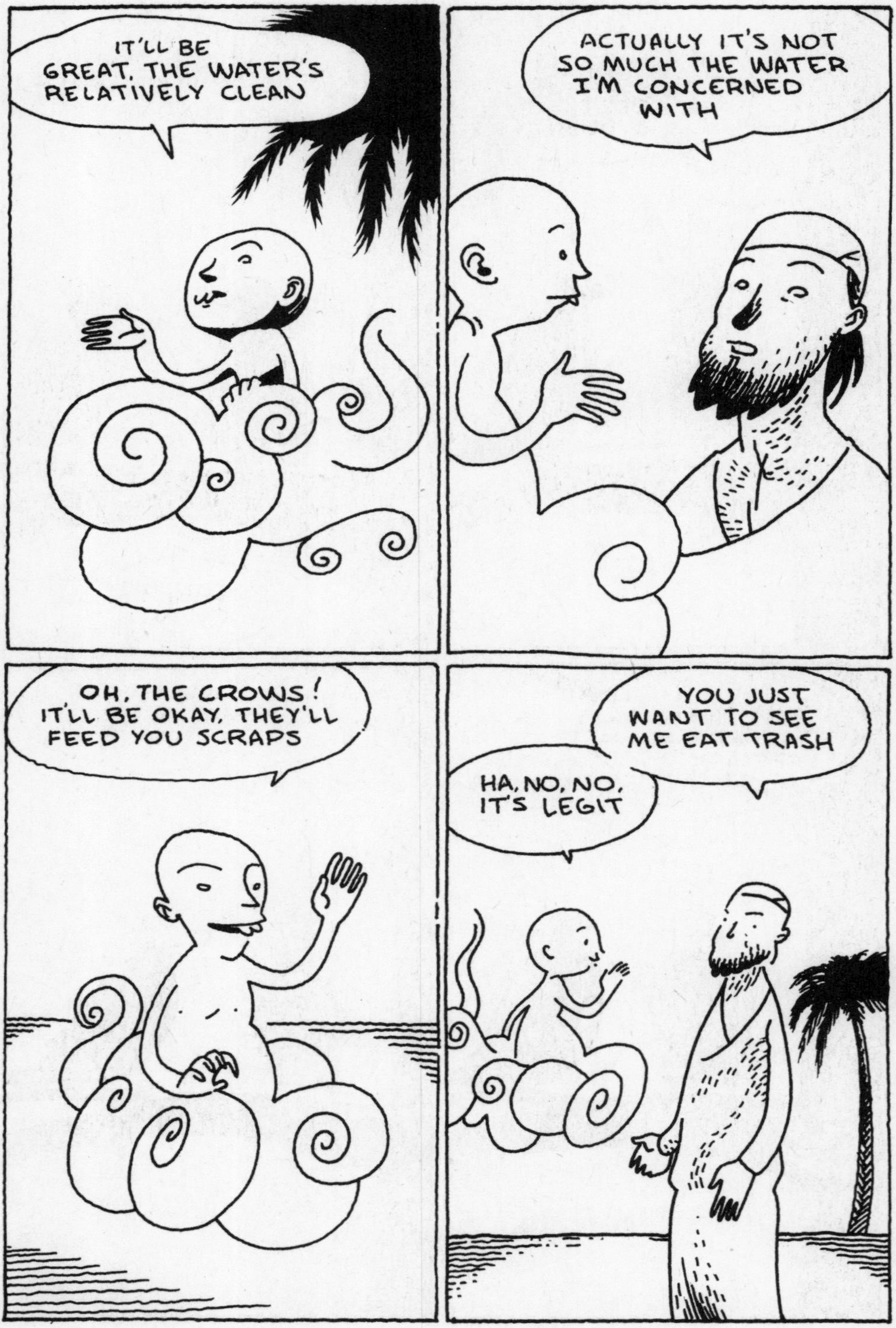
IT'LL BE GREAT. THE WATER'S RELATIVELY CLEAN
ACTUALLY IT'S NOT SO MUCH THE WATER I'M CONCERNED WITH
OH, THE CROWS! IT'LL BE OKAY. THEY'LL FEED YOU SCRAPS
YOU JUST WANT TO SEE ME EAT TRASH
HA, NO, NO, IT'S LEGIT

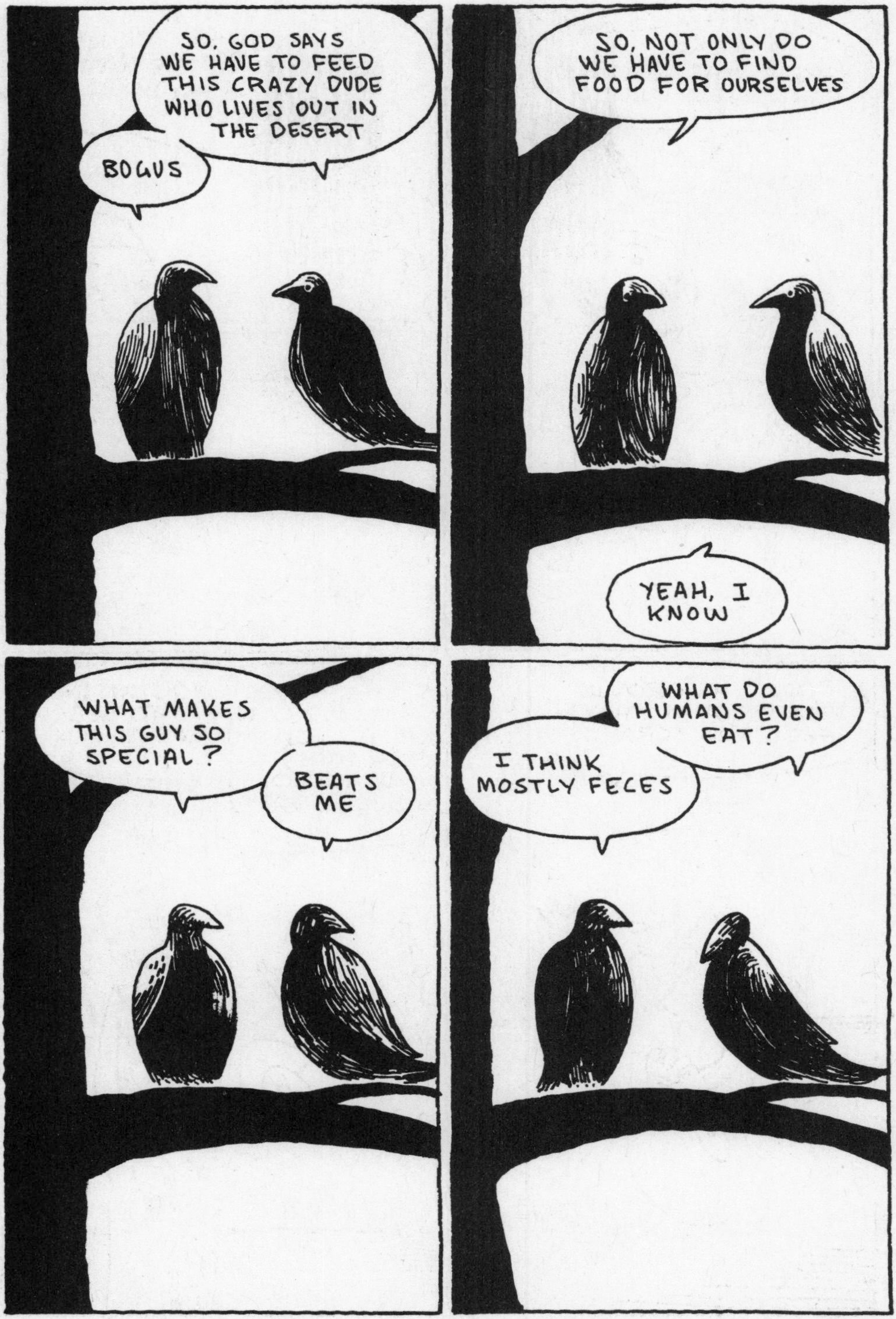
SO, GOD SAYS WE HAVE TO FEED THIS CRAZY DUDE WHO LIVES OUT IN THE DESERT
BOGUS
SO, NOT ONLY DO WE HAVE TO FIND FOOD FOR OURSELVES
YEAH, I KNOW
WHAT MAKES THIS GUY SO SPECIAL?
BEATS ME
WHAT DO HUMANS EVEN EAT?
I THINK MOSTLY FECES

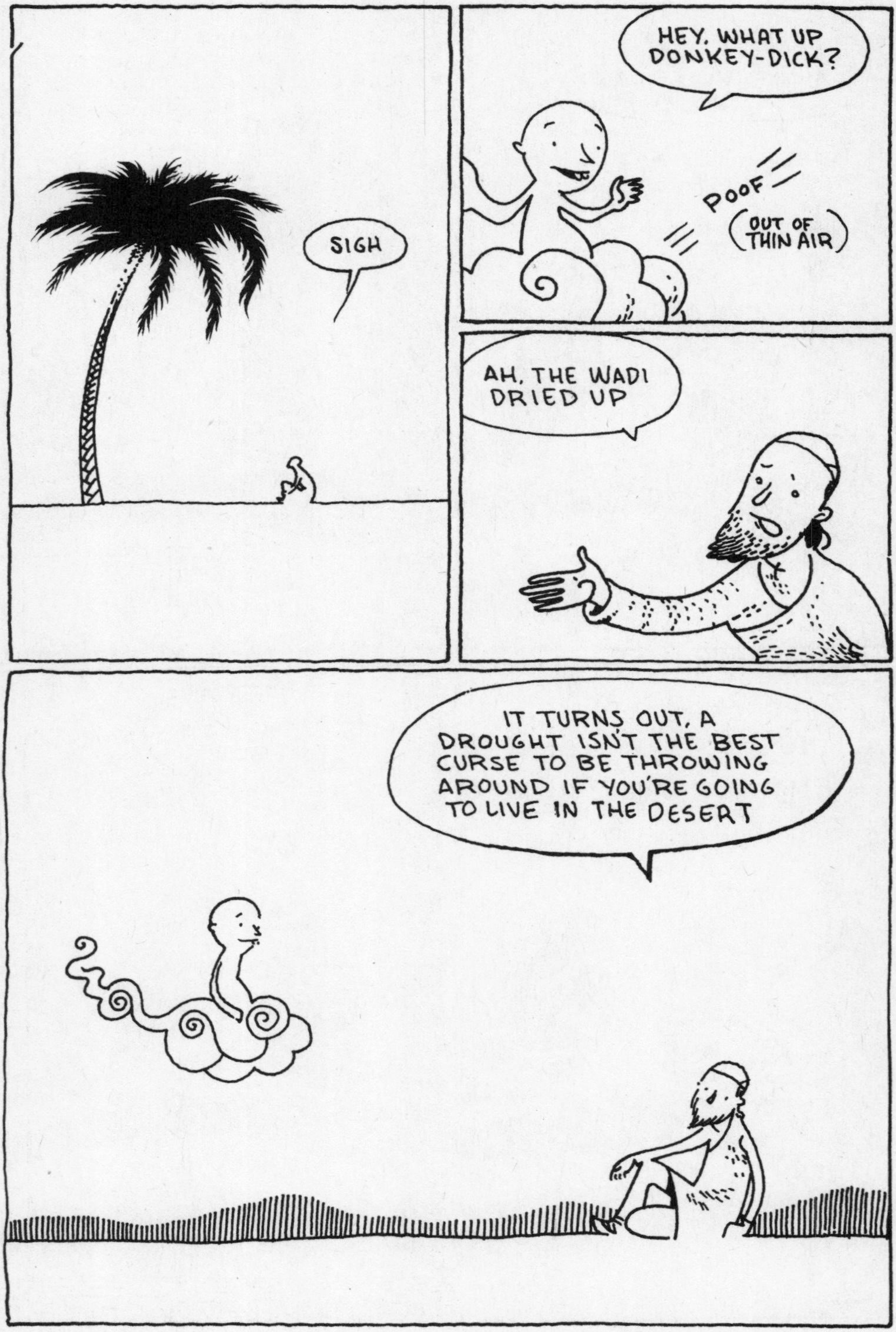
SIGH
HEY. WHAT UP DONKEY-DICK?
POOF
(OUT OF THIN AIR)
AH, THE WADI DRIED UP
IT TURNS OUT, A DROUGHT ISN'T THE BEST CURSE TO BE THROWING AROUND IF YOU'RE GOING TO LIVE IN THE DESERT

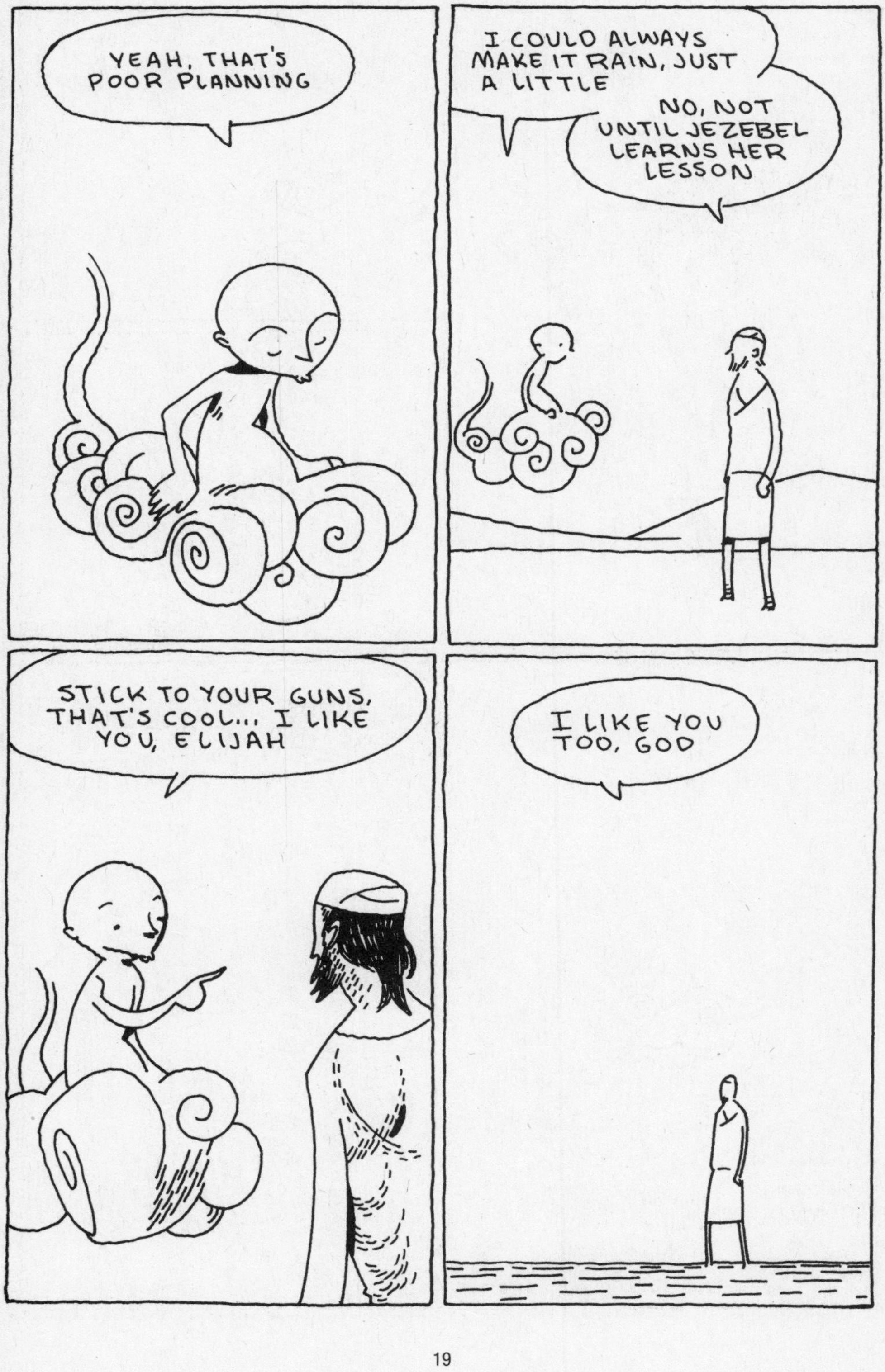
YEAH, THAT'S POOR PLANNING
I COULD ALWAYS MAKE IT RAIN, JUST A LITTLE
NO, NOT UNTIL JEZEBEL LEARNS HER LESSON
STICK TO YOUR GUNS, THAT'S COOL... I LIKE YOU, ELIJAH
I LIKE YOU TOO, GOD

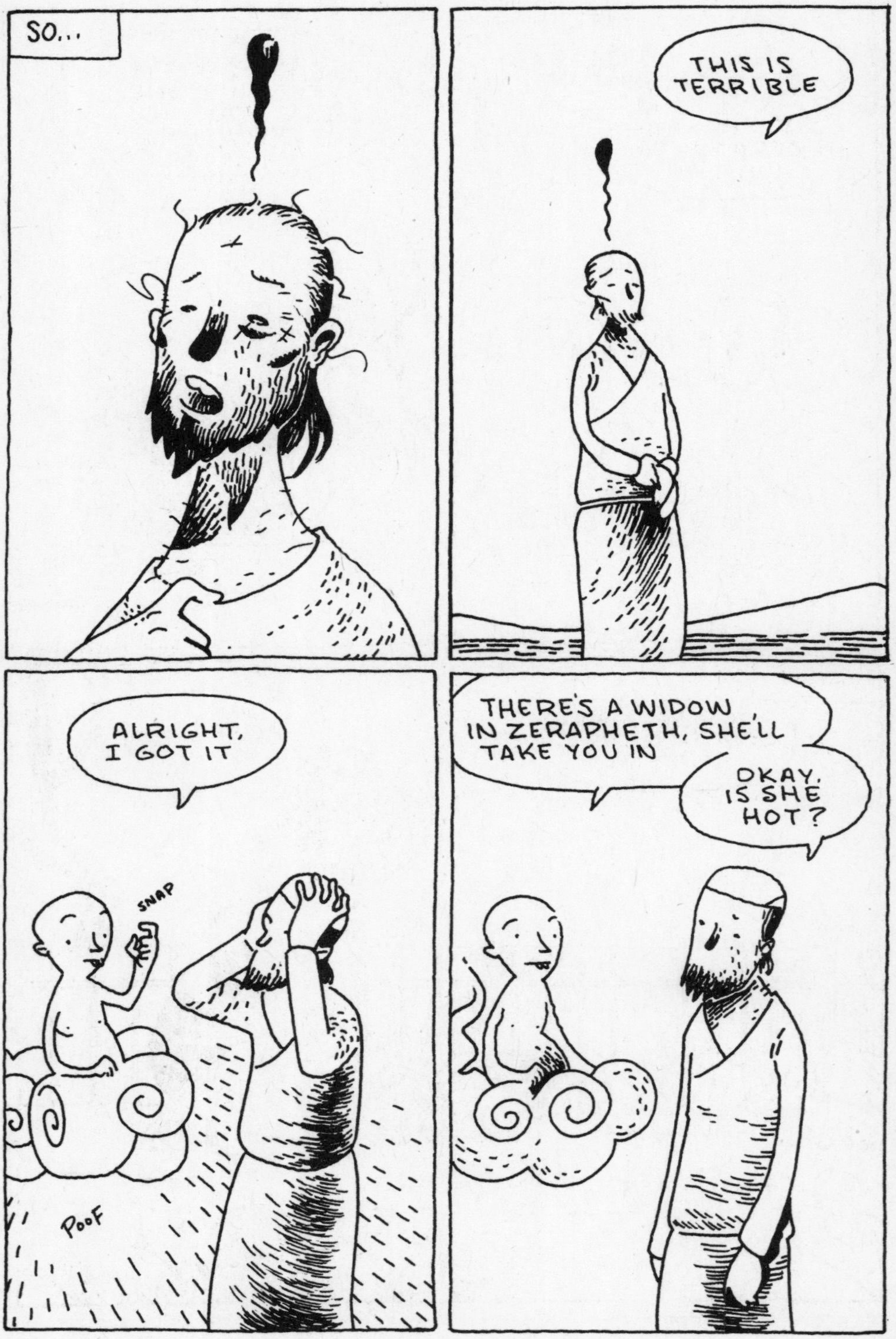
SO...
THIS IS TERRIBLE
ALRIGHT, I GOT IT
SNAP
POOF
THERE'S A WIDOW IN ZERAPHETH, SHE'LL TAKE YOU IN
OKAY. IS SHE HOT?

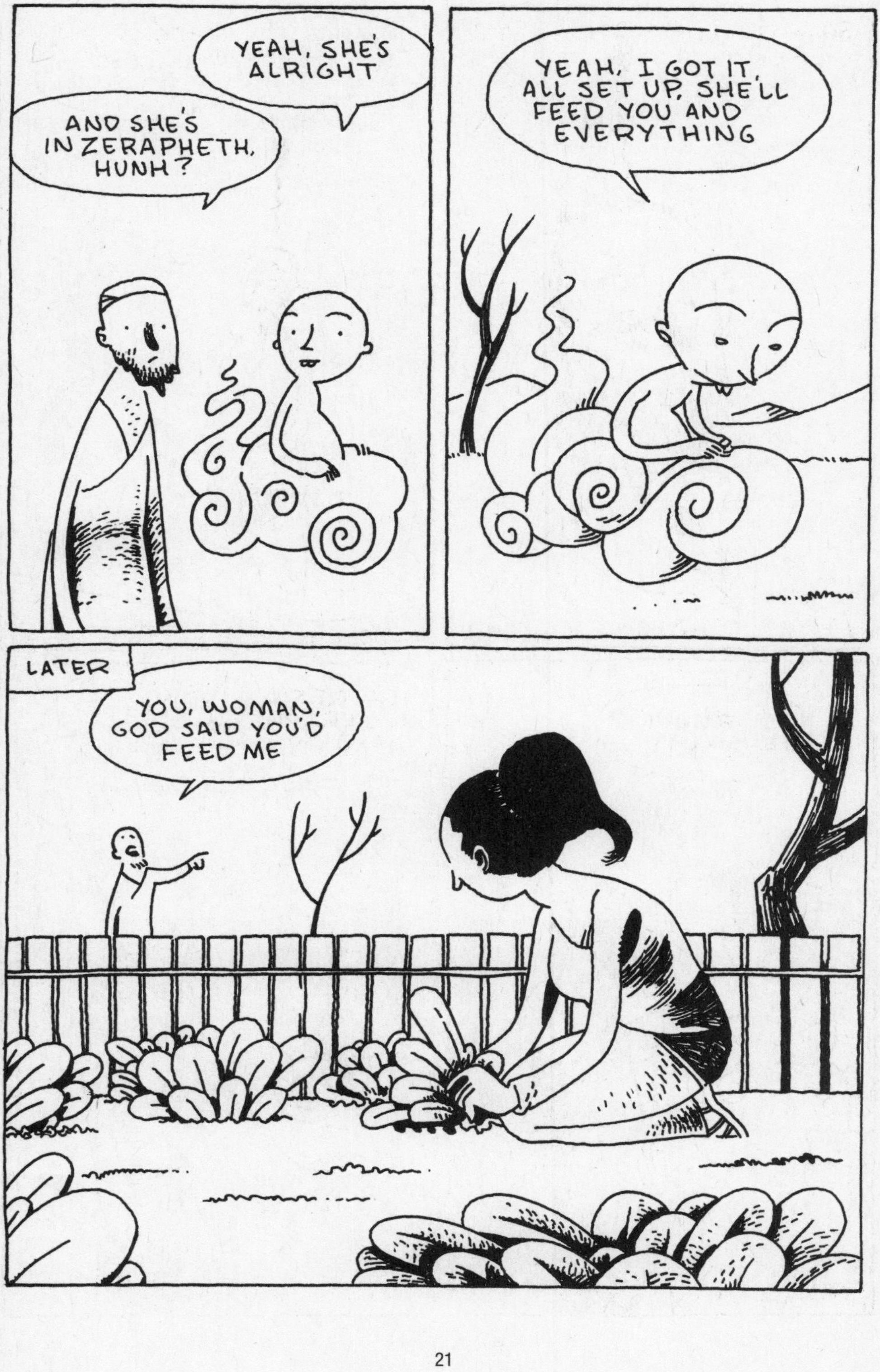
YEAH, SHE'S ALRIGHT
AND SHE'S IN ZERAPHETH, HUNH?
YEAH, I GOT IT, ALL SET UP, SHE'LL FEED YOU AND EVERYTHING
LATER
YOU, WOMAN, GOD SAID YOU'D FEED ME

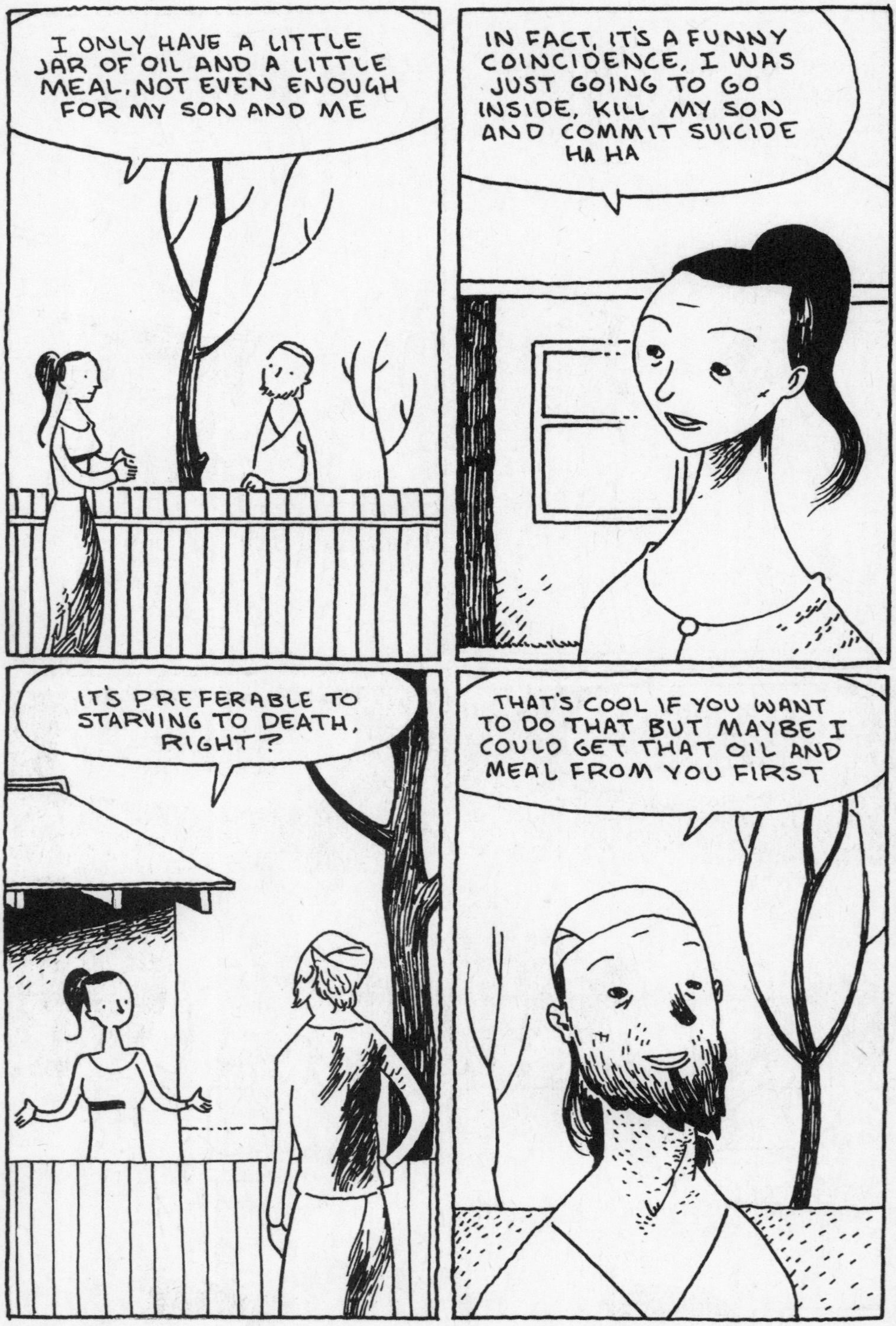

I ONLY HAVE A LITTLE JAR OF OIL AND A LITTLE MEAL, NOT EVEN ENOUGH FOR MY SON AND ME
IN FACT, IT'S A FUNNY COINCIDENCE, I WAS JUST GOING TO GO INSIDE, KILL MY SON AND COMMIT SUICIDE HA HA
IT'S PREFERABLE TO STARVING TO DEATH, RIGHT?
THAT'S COOL IF YOU WANT TO DO THAT BUT MAYBE I COULD GET THAT OIL AND MEAL FROM YOU FIRST

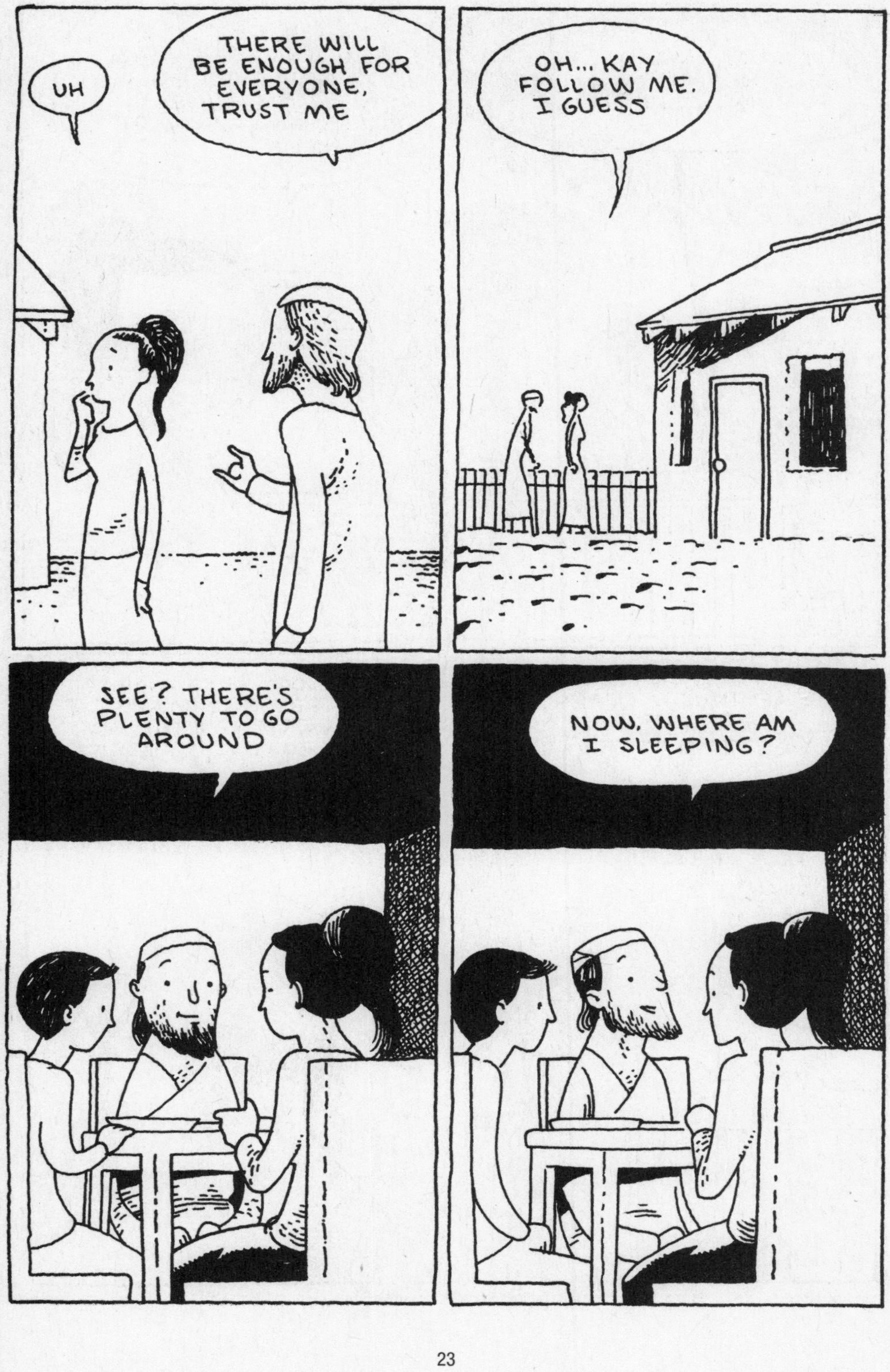
UH
THERE WILL BE ENOUGH FOR EVERYONE, TRUST ME
OH... KAY FOLLOW ME. I GUESS
SEE? THERE'S PLENTY TO GO AROUND
NOW, WHERE AM I SLEEPING?

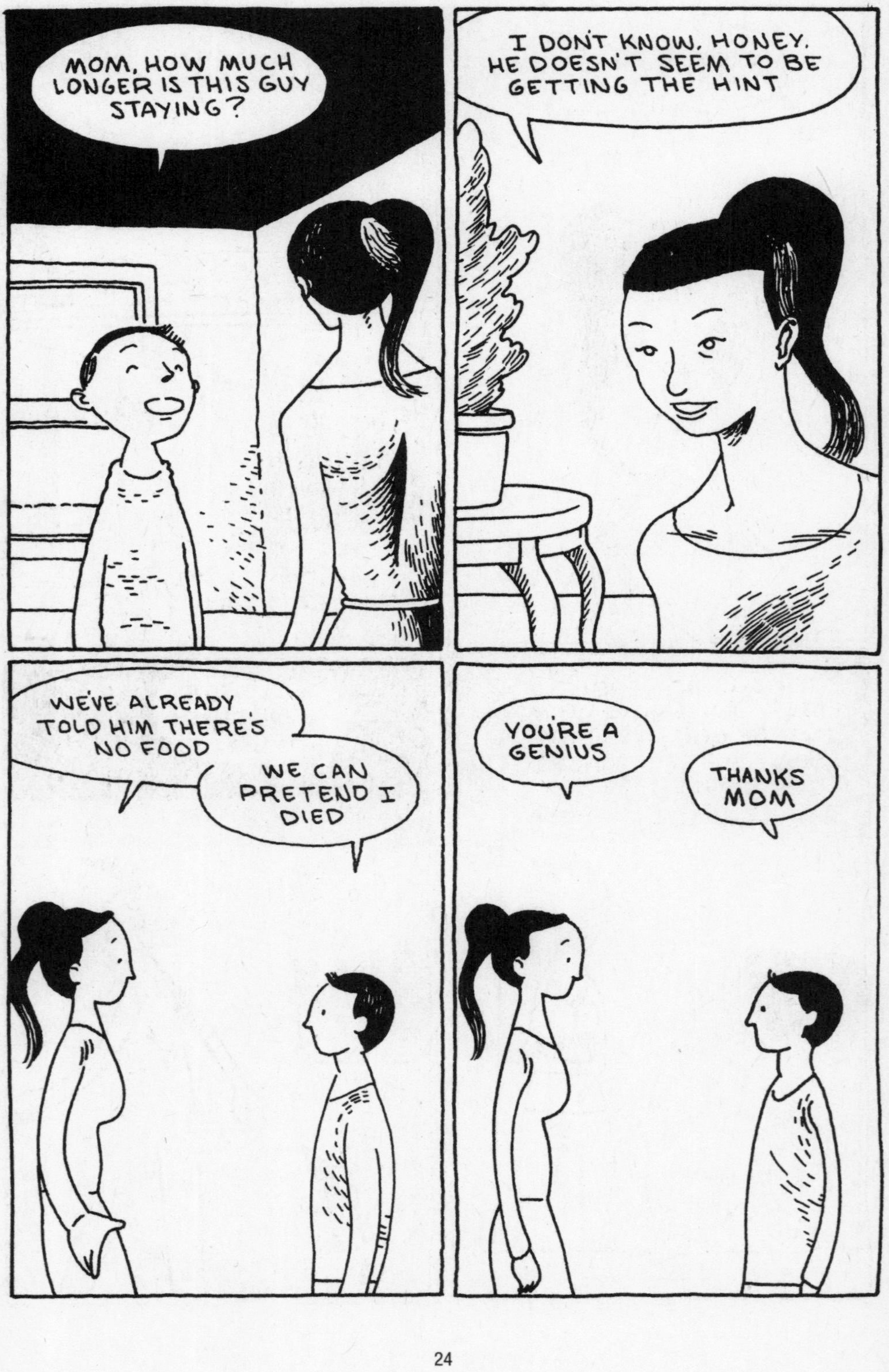
MOM, HOW MUCH LONGER IS THIS GUY STAYING?
I DON'T KNOW, HONEY. HE DOESN'T SEEM TO BE GETTING THE HINT
WE'VE ALREADY TOLD HIM THERE'S NO FOOD
WE CAN PRETEND I DIED
YOU'RE A GENIUS
THANKS MOM

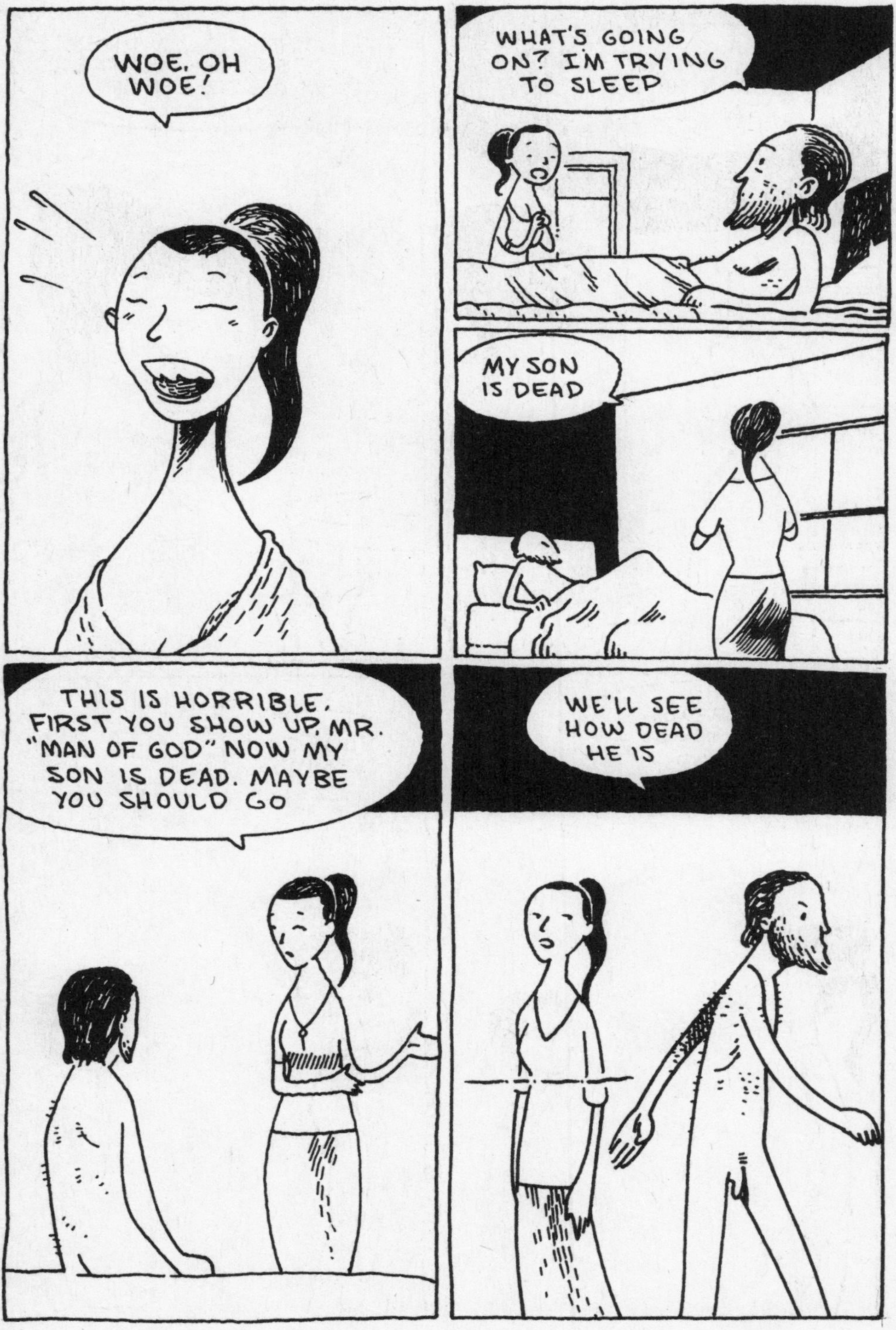
WOE, OH WOE!
WHAT'S GOING ON? I'M TRYING TO SLEEP
MY SON IS DEAD
THIS IS HORRIBLE. FIRST YOU SHOW UP, MR. "MAN OF GOD" NOW MY SON IS DEAD. MAYBE YOU SHOULD GO
WE'LL SEE HOW DEAD HE IS

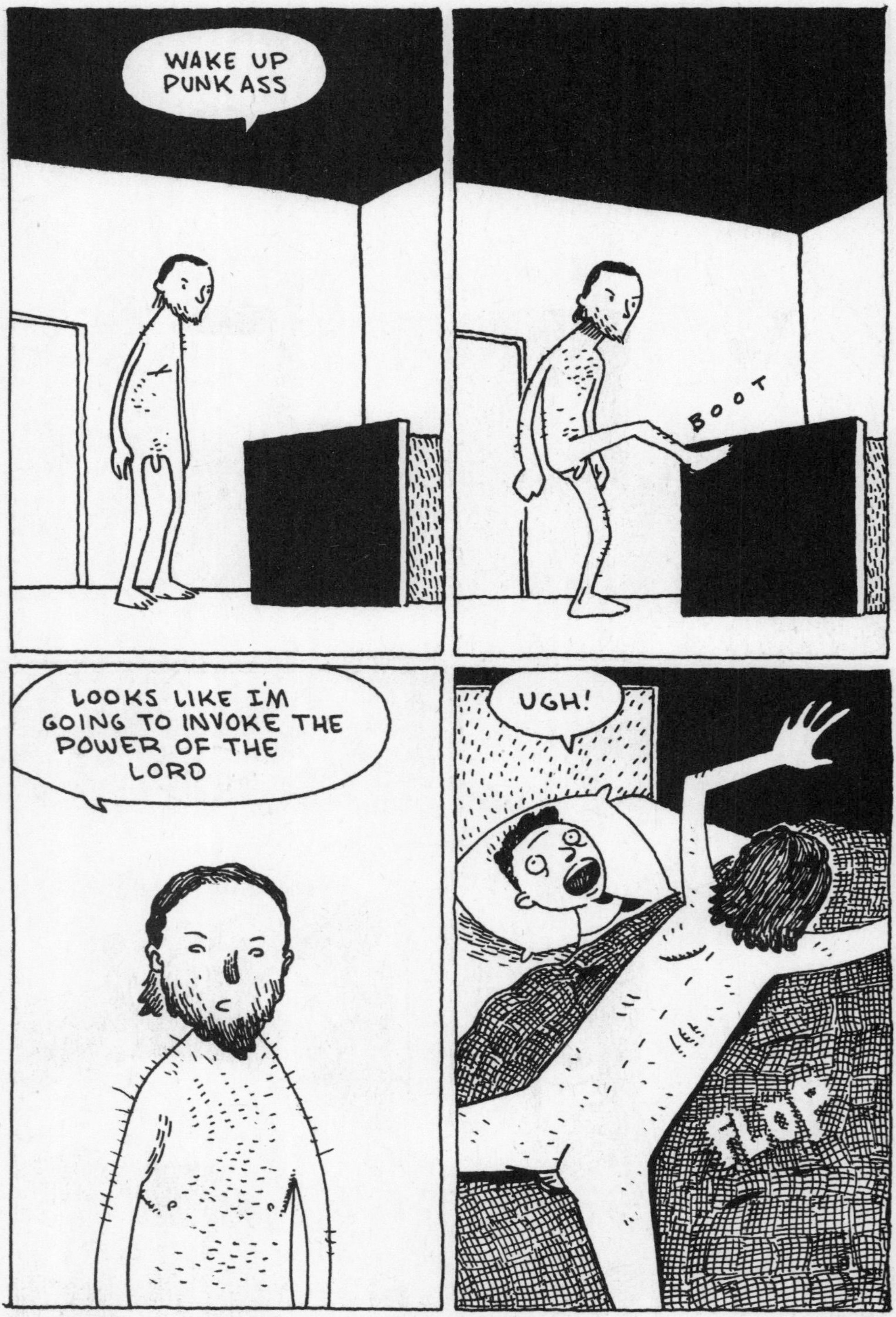
WAKE UP
PUNK ASS
BOOT
LOOKS LIKE I'M GOING TO INVOKE THE POWER OF THE LORD
UGH!
FLOP

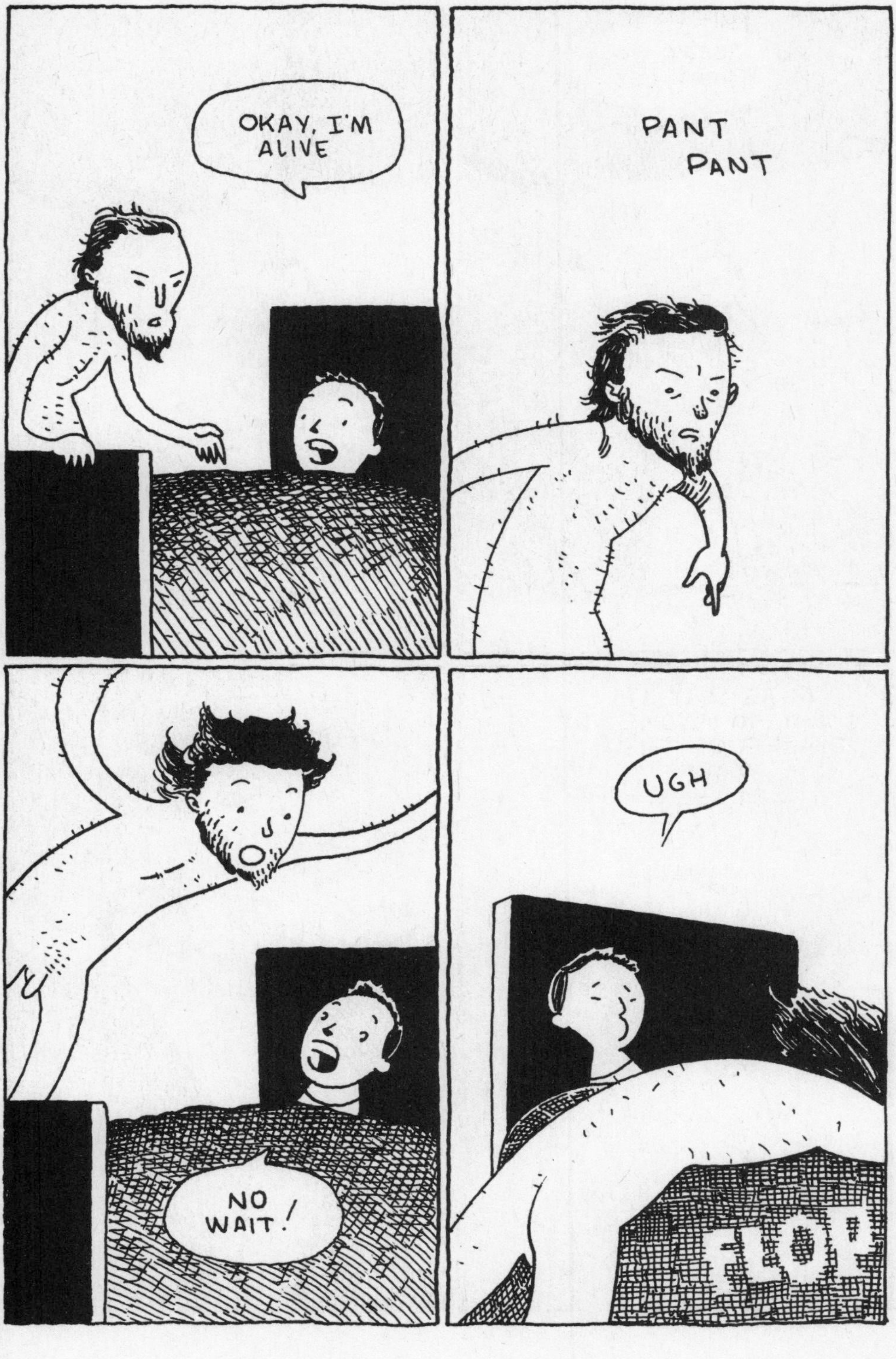
OKAY, I'M ALIVE
PANT PANT
NO WAIT!
UGH
FLOP

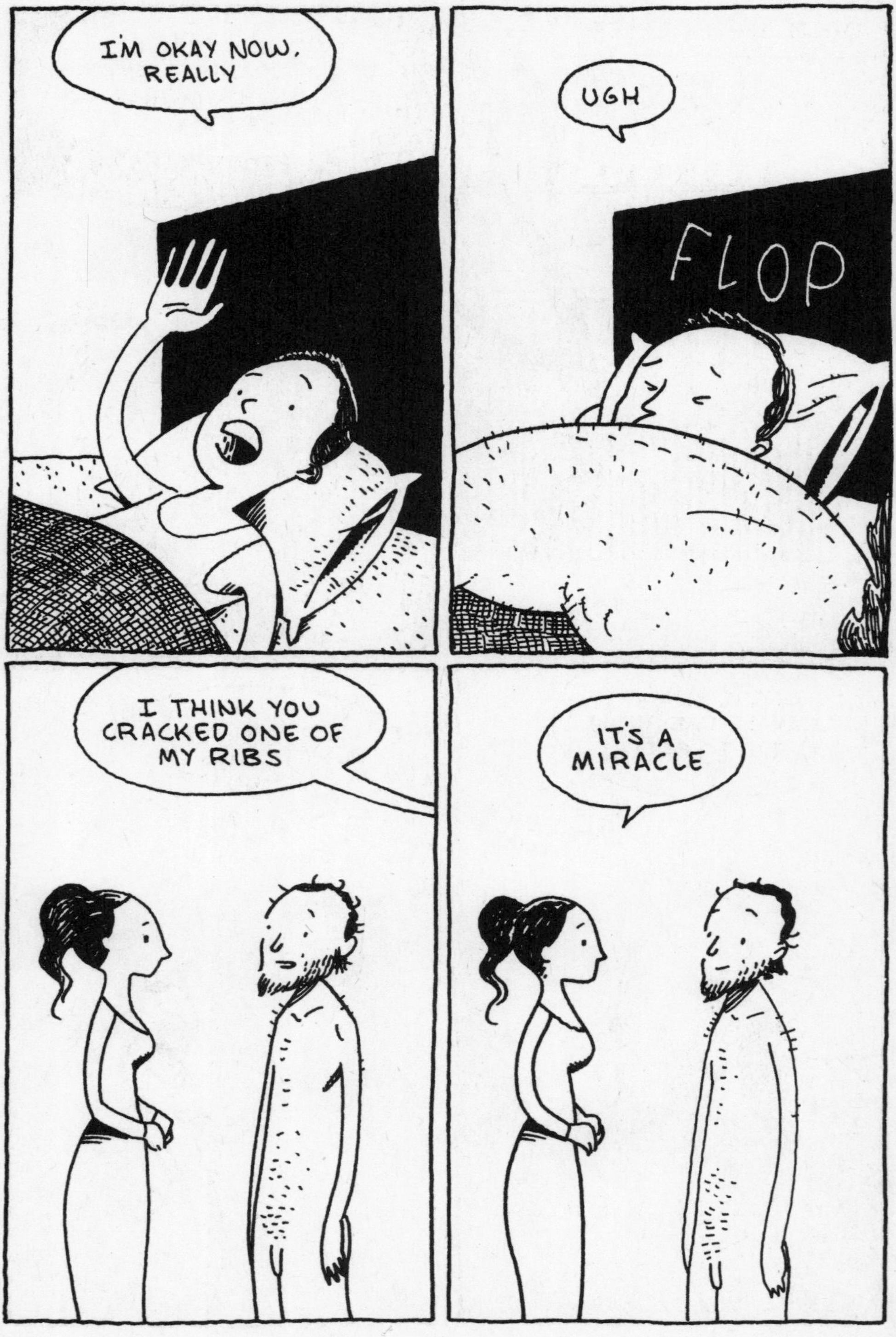
I'M OKAY NOW, REALLY
UGH
FLOP
I THINK YOU CRACKED ONE OF MY RIBS
IT'S A MIRACLE

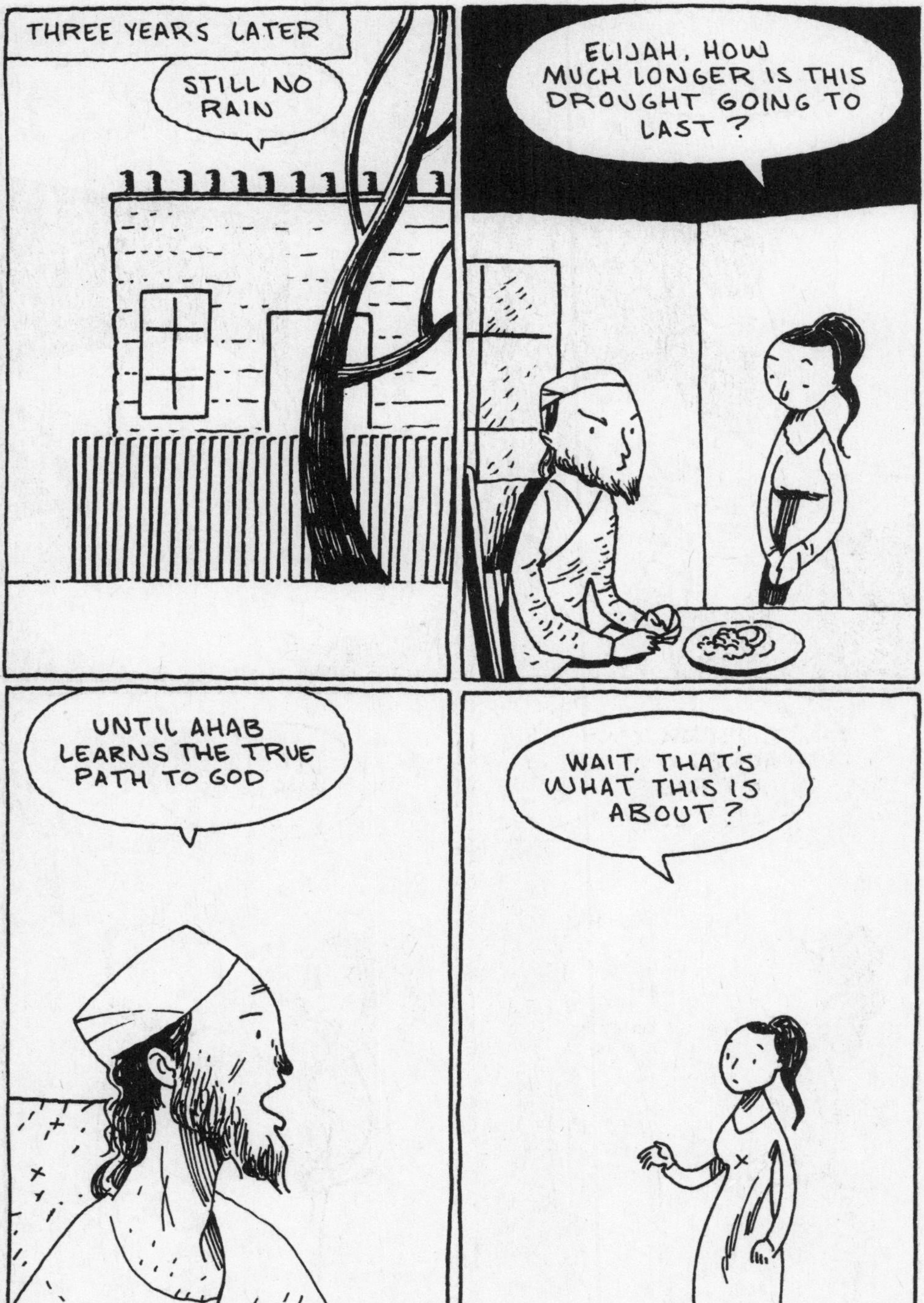
THREE YEARS LATER
STILL NO RAIN
ELIJAH, HOW MUCH LONGER IS THIS DROUGHT GOING TO LAST?
UNTIL AHAB LEARNS THE TRUE PATH TO GOD
WAIT, THAT'S WHAT THIS IS ABOUT?

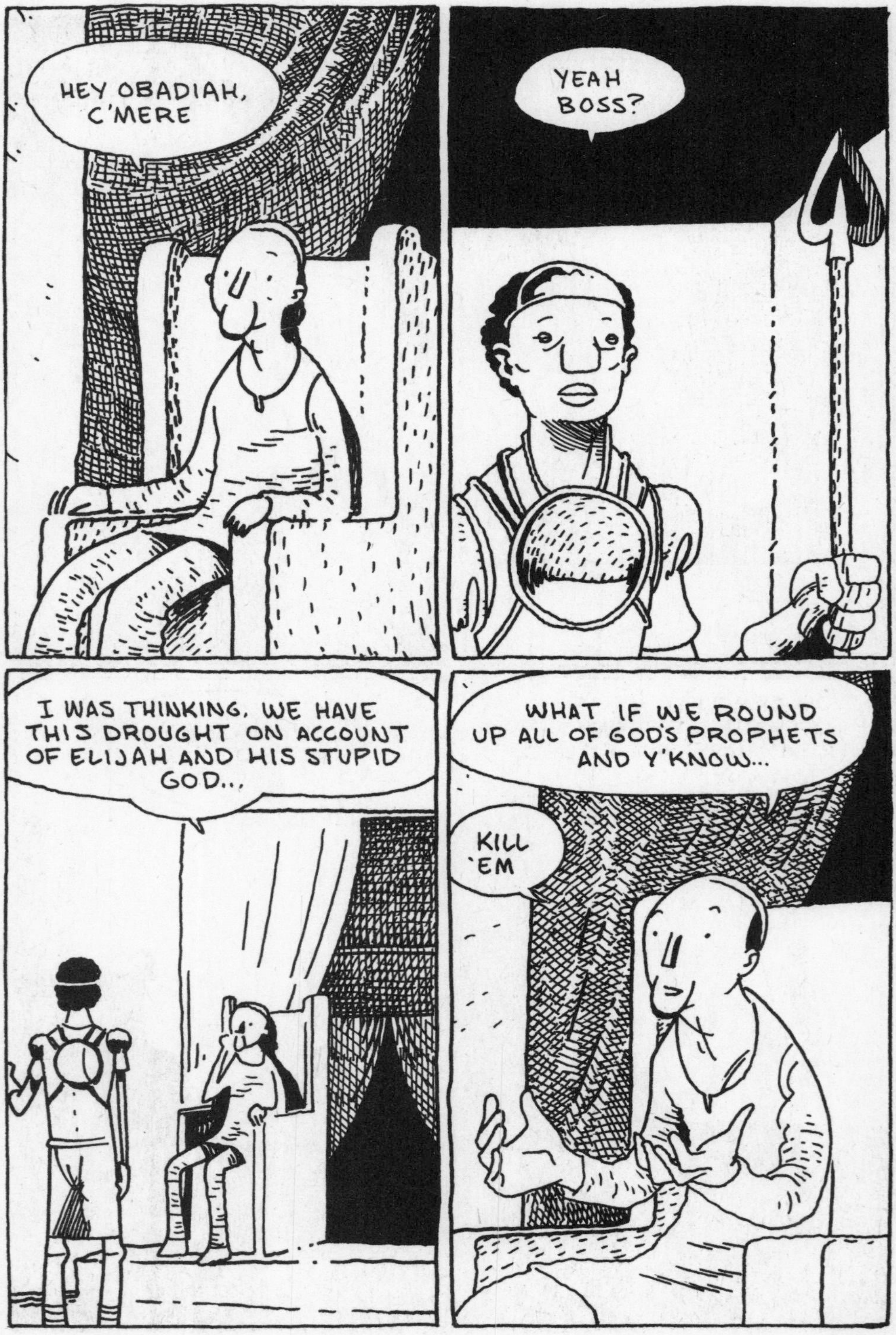
HEY OBADIAH, C'MERE
YEAH BOSS?
I WAS THINKING. WE HAVE THIS DROUGHT ON ACCOUNT OF ELIJAH AND HIS STUPID GOD...
WHAT IF WE ROUND UP ALL OF GOD'S PROPHETS AND Y'KNOW...
KILL 'EM

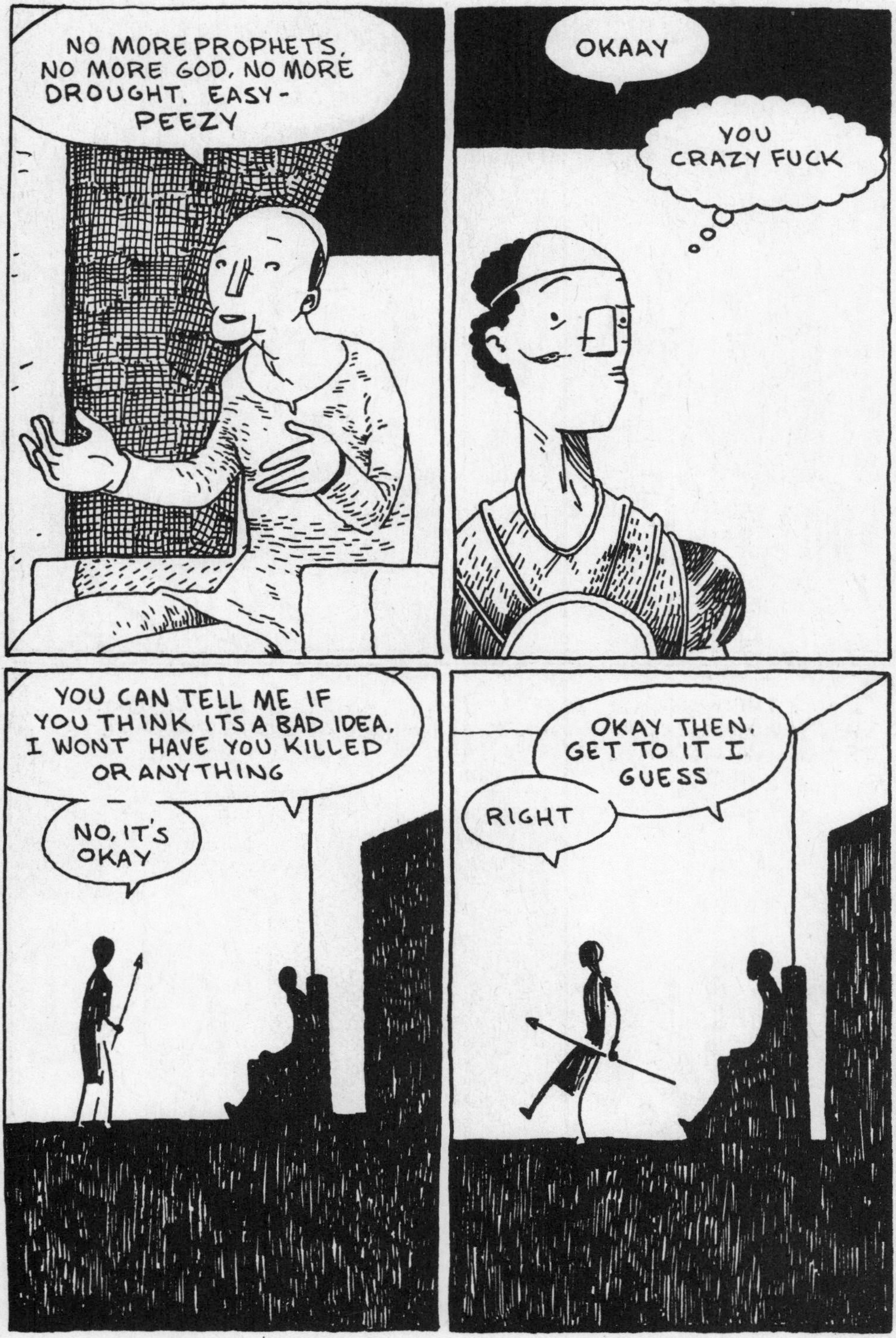
NO MORE PROPHETS, NO MORE GOD, NO MORE DROUGHT. EASY-PEEZY
OKAAY
YOU CRAZY FUCK
YOU CAN TELL ME IF YOU THINK ITS A BAD IDEA. I WONT HAVE YOU KILLED OR ANYTHING
NO, IT'S OKAY
OKAY THEN. GET TO IT I GUESS
RIGHT

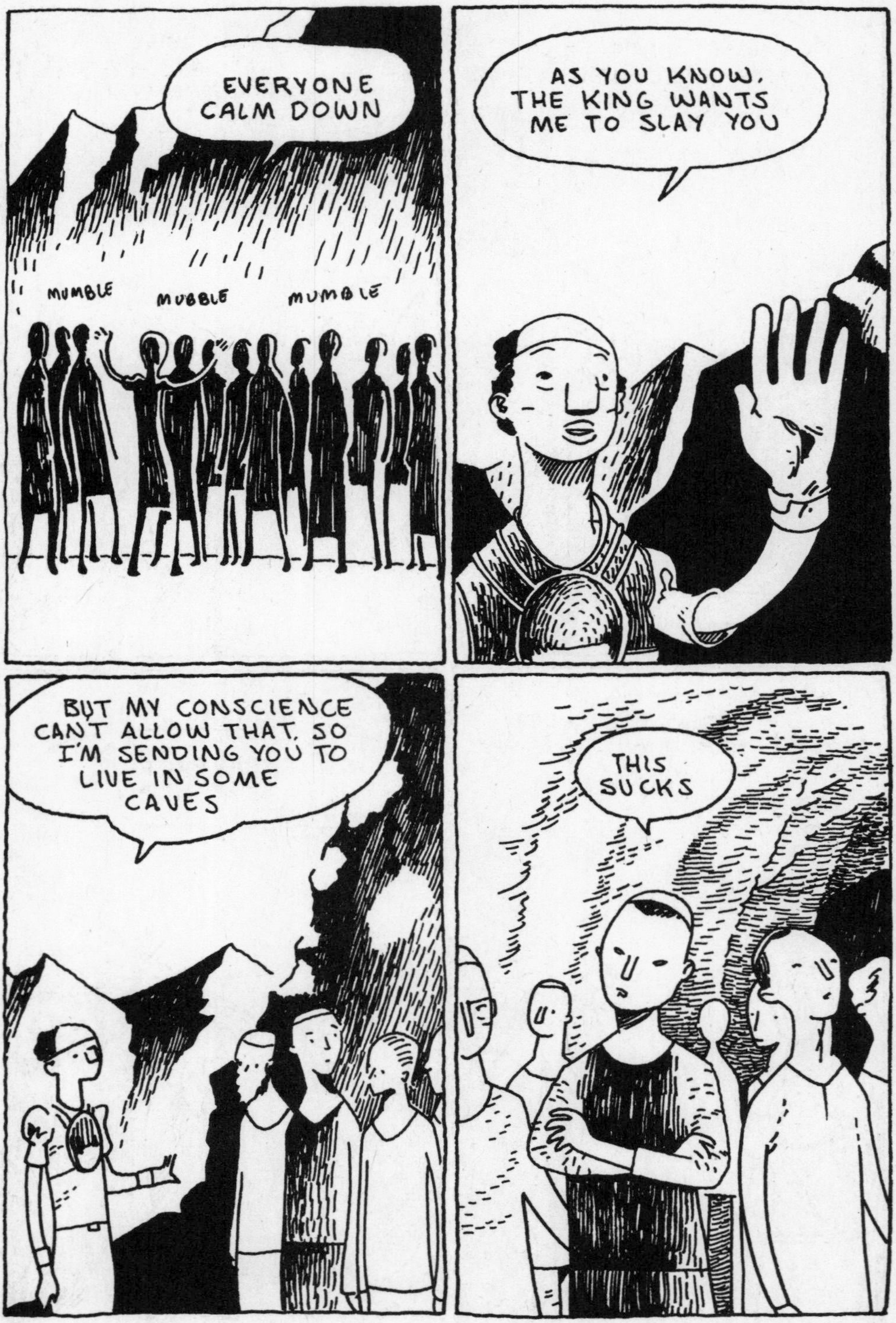
EVERYONE CALM DOWN
MUMBLE
MUBBLE
MUMBLE
AS YOU KNOW, THE KING WANTS ME TO SLAY YOU
BUT MY CONSCIENCE CAN'T ALLOW THAT, SO I'M SENDING YOU TO LIVE IN SOME CAVES
THIS SUCKS

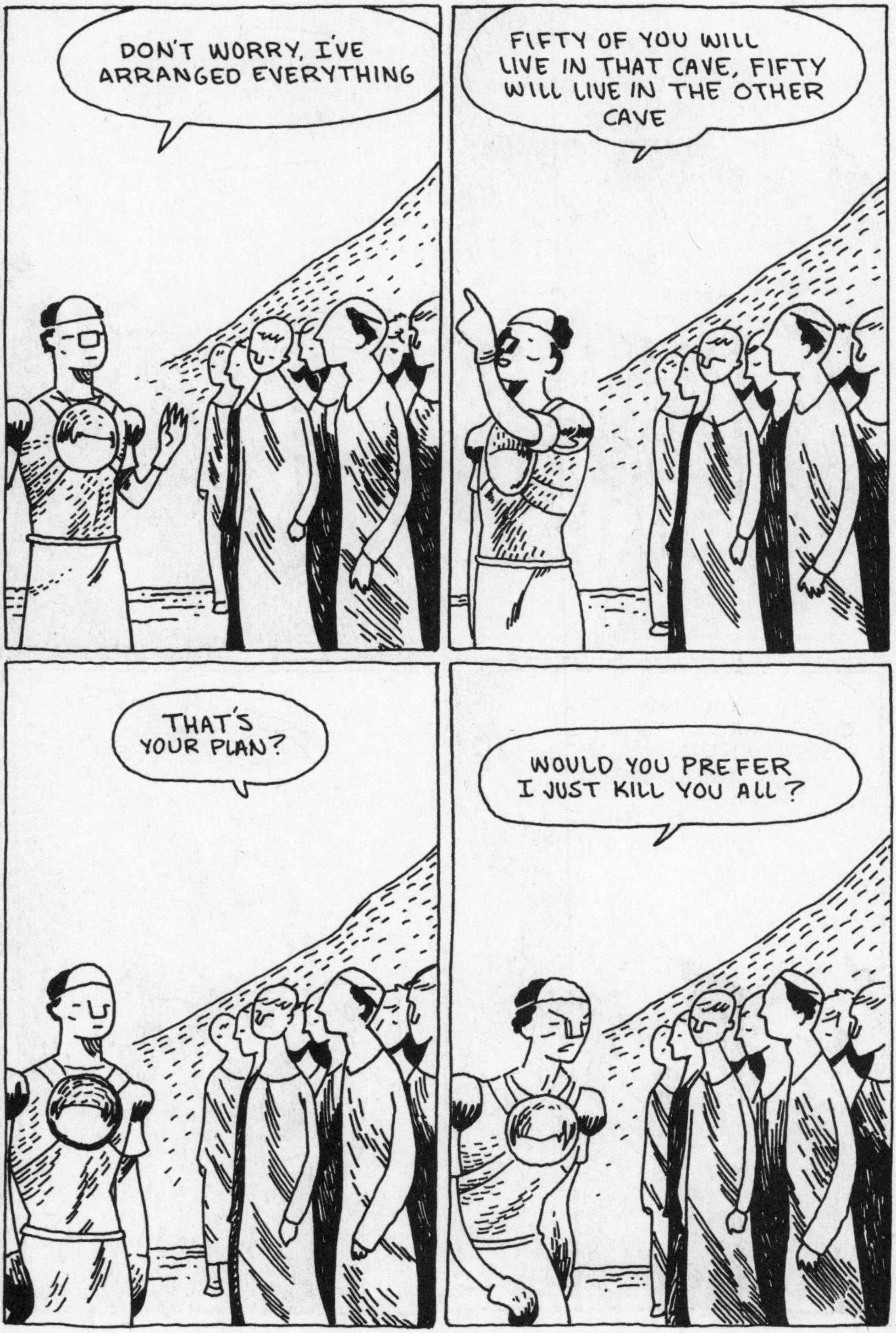
DON'T WORRY, I'VE ARRANGED EVERYTHING
FIFTY OF YOU WILL LIVE IN THAT CAVE, FIFTY WILL LIVE IN THE OTHER CAVE
THAT'S YOUR PLAN?
WOULD YOU PREFER I JUST KILL YOU ALL?

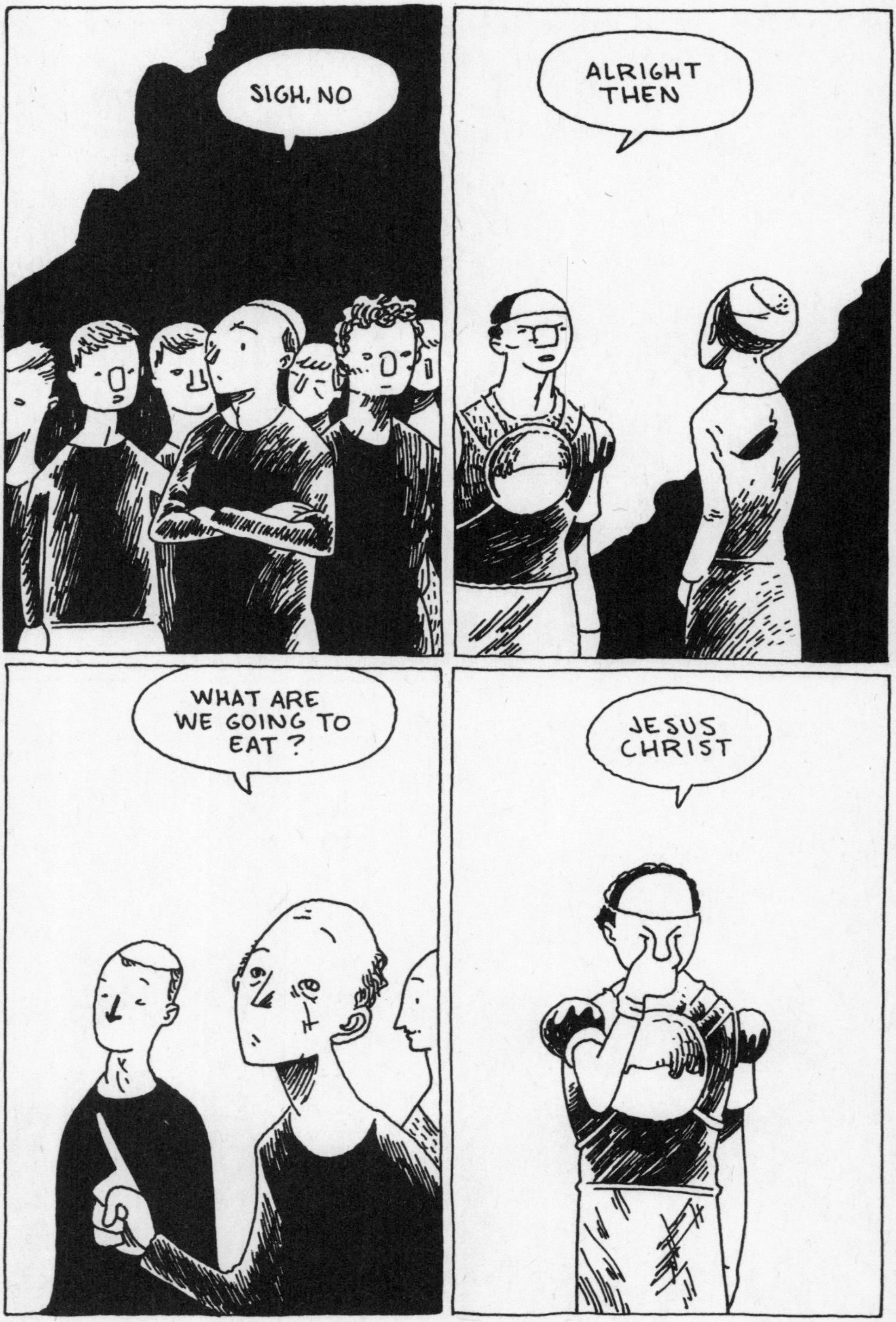
SIGH, NO
ALRIGHT THEN
WHAT ARE WE GOING TO EAT ?
JESUS CHRIST

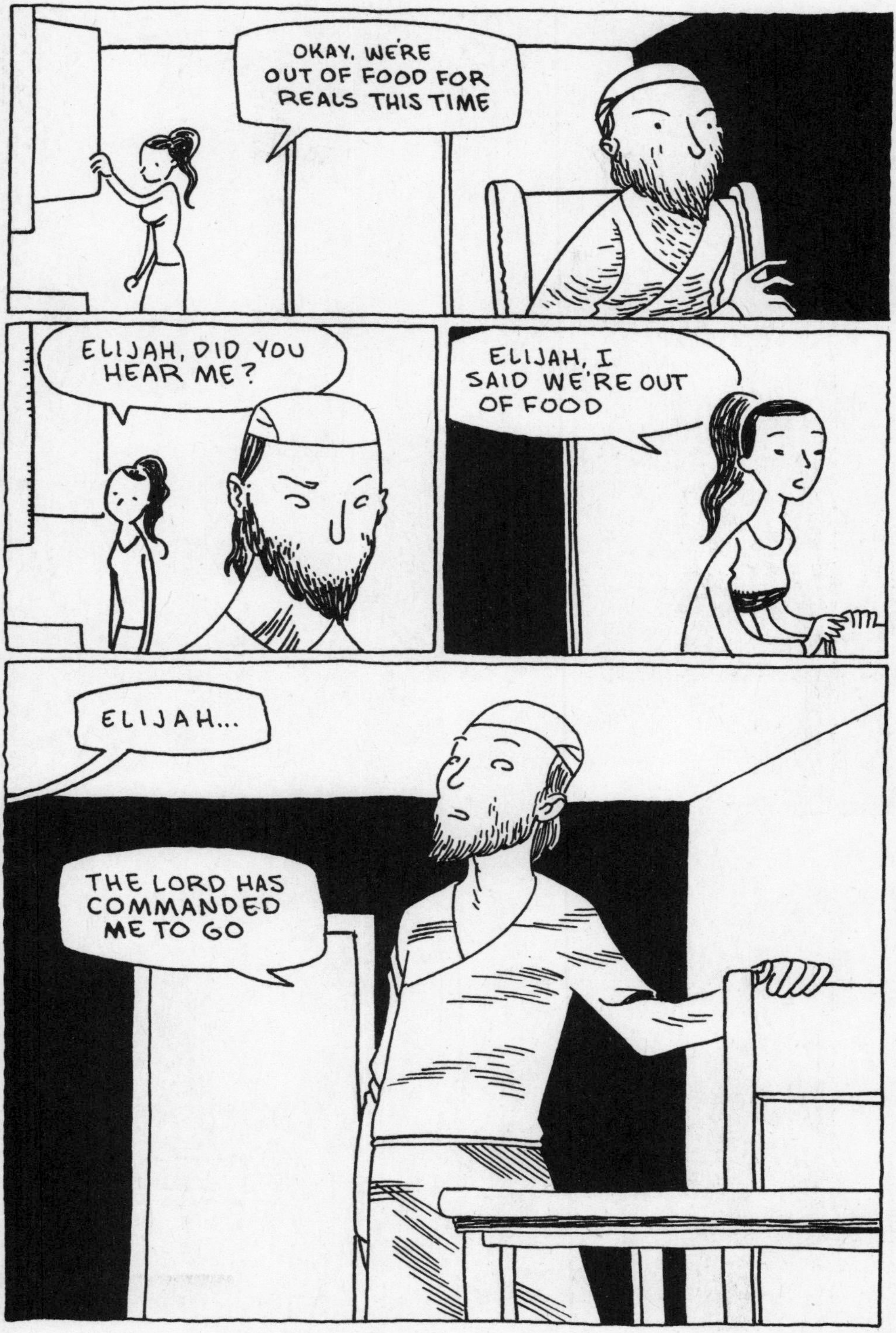
OKAY. WE'RE OUT OF FOOD FOR REALS THIS TIME
ELIJAH, DID YOU HEAR ME?
ELIJAH, I SAID WE'RE OUT OF FOOD
ELIJAH...
THE LORD HAS COMMANDED ME TO GO

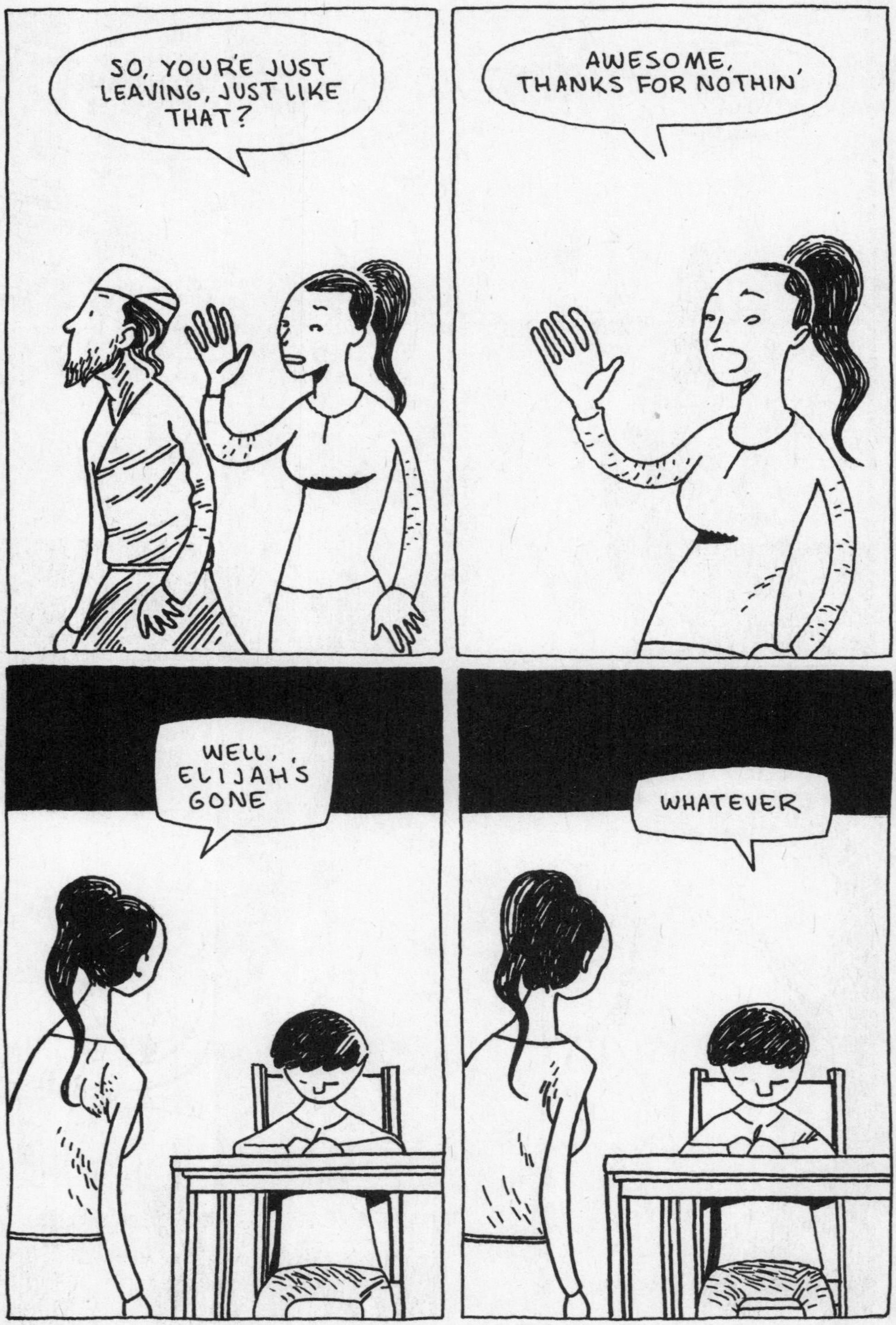
SO, YOU'RE JUST LEAVING, JUST LIKE THAT?
AWESOME, THANKS FOR NOTHIN'
WELL, ELIJAH'S GONE
WHATEVER

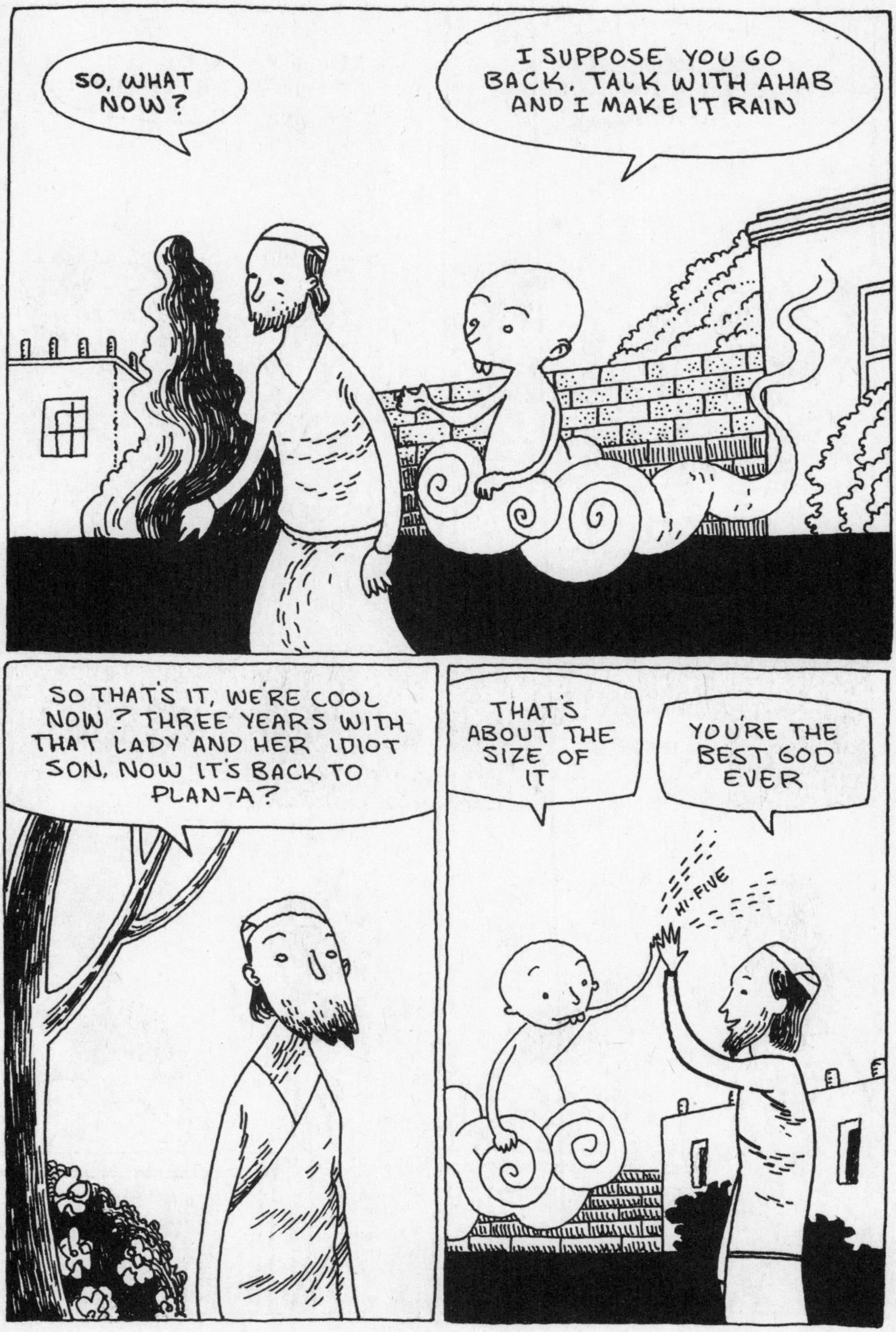
SO, WHAT NOW?
I SUPPOSE YOU GO BACK, TALK WITH AHAB AND I MAKE IT RAIN
SO THAT'S IT, WE'RE COOL NOW? THREE YEARS WITH THAT LADY AND HER IDIOT SON, NOW IT'S BACK TO PLAN-A?
THAT'S ABOUT THE SIZE OF IT
YOU'RE THE BEST GOD EVER
HI-FIVE

THIS DROUGHT IS KILLING US
WE NEED TO HEAD OUT AND FIND A PATCH OF GRASS. ANYTHING TO FEED THE CATTLE
TAKE SOME MEN AND SEARCH THAT WAY, I'LL DO THE SAME, THIS WAY
JACKASS

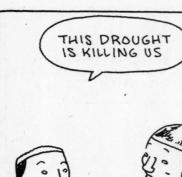

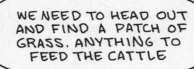

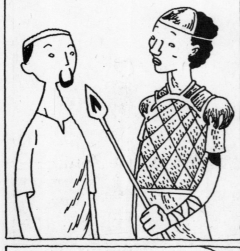

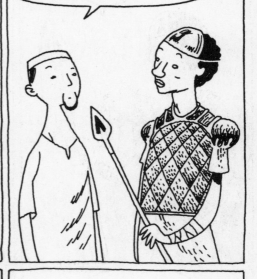

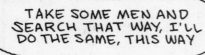

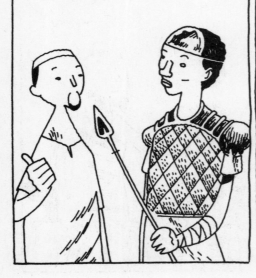

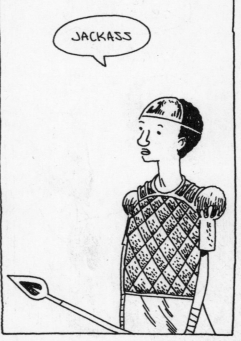

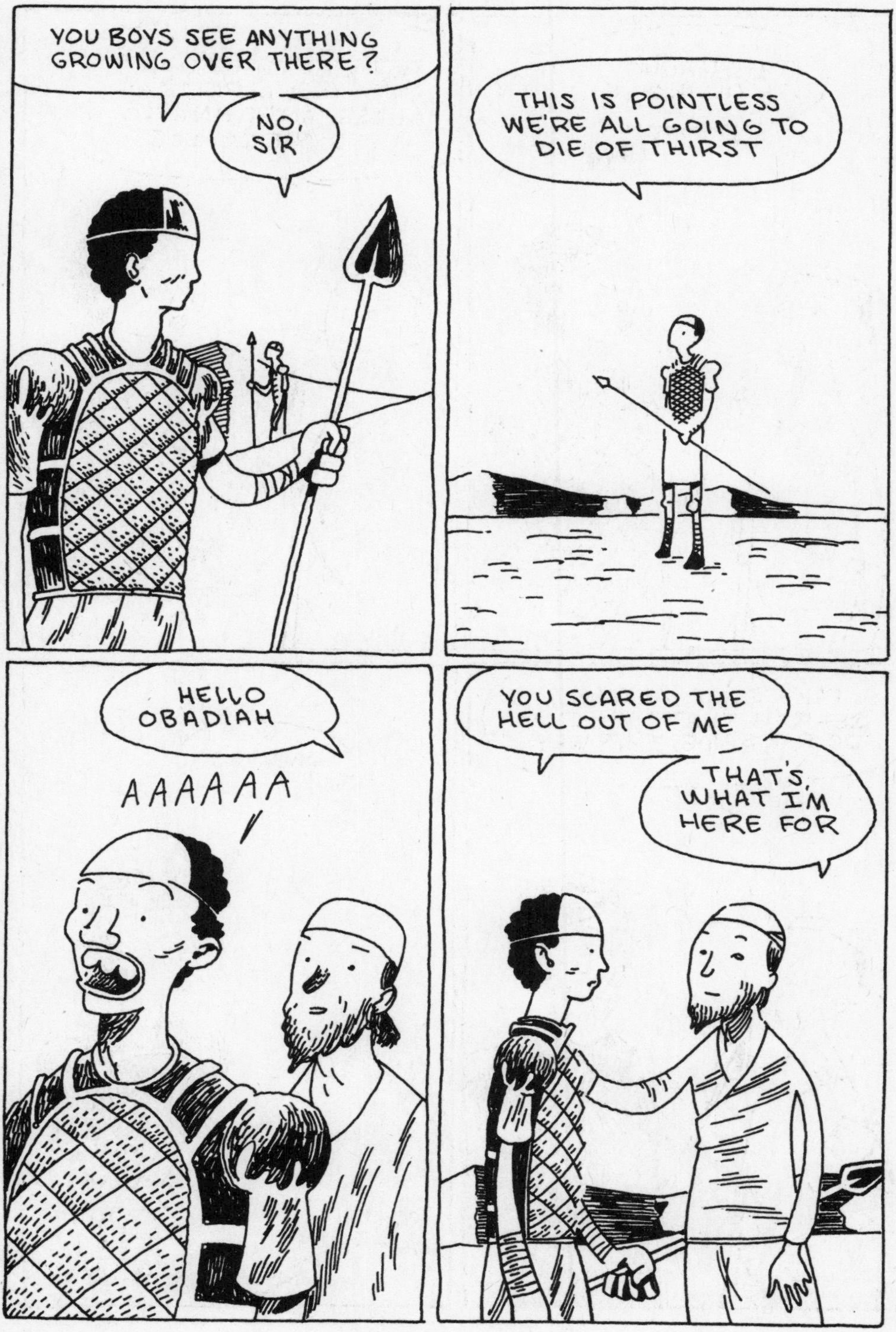
YOU BOYS SEE ANYTHING GROWING OVER THERE?
NO, SIR
THIS IS POINTLESS WE'RE ALL GOING TO DIE OF THIRST
HELLO OBADIAH
AAAAAA
YOU SCARED THE HELL OUT OF ME
THAT'S WHAT I'M HERE FOR

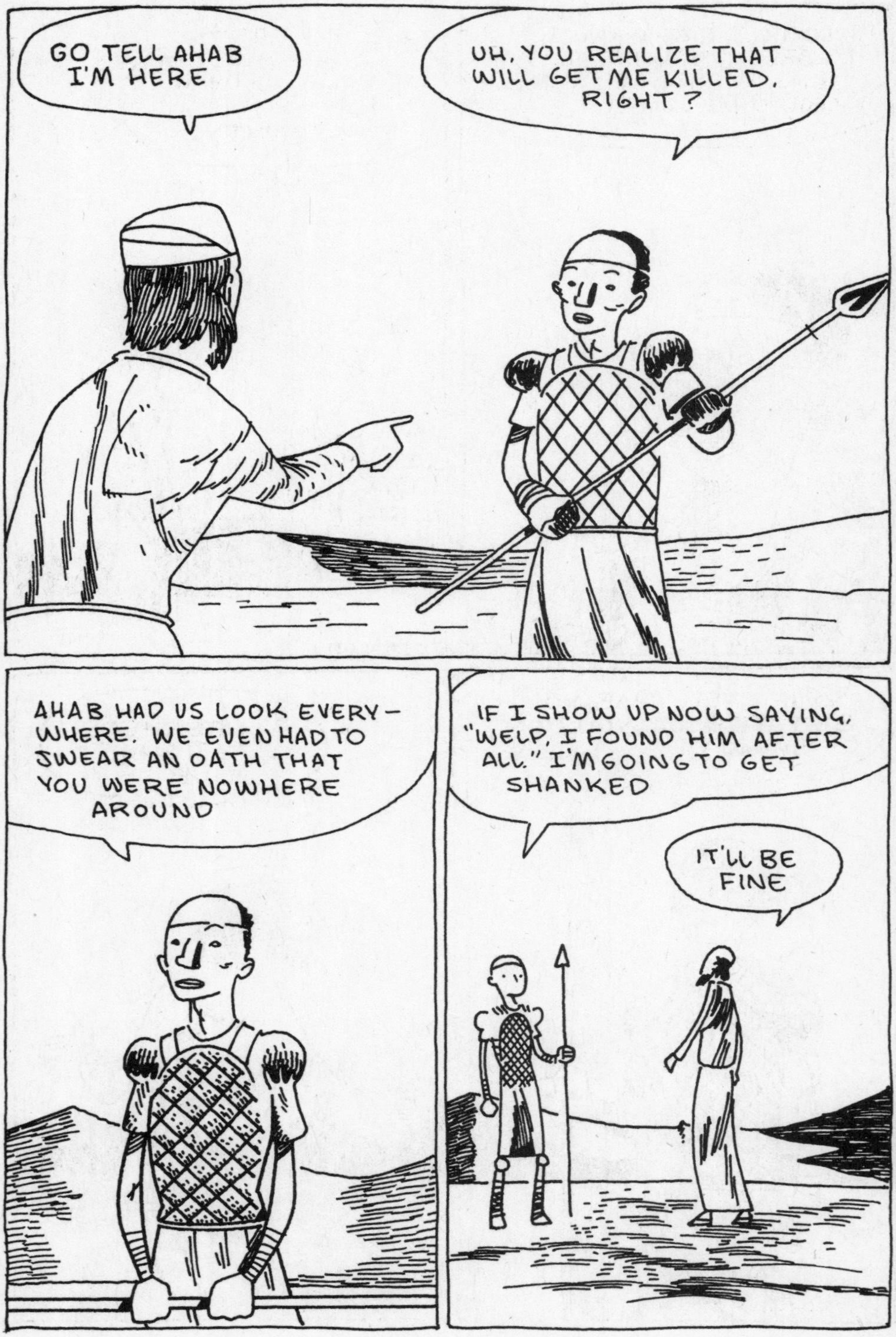
GO TELL AHAB I'M HERE
UH, YOU REALIZE THAT WILL GET ME KILLED, RIGHT?
AHAB HAD US LOOK EVERY-WHERE. WE EVEN HAD TO SWEAR AN OATH THAT YOU WERE NOWHERE AROUND
IF I SHOW UP NOW SAYING, "WELP, I FOUND HIM AFTER ALL." I'M GOING TO GET SHANKED
IT'LL BE FINE

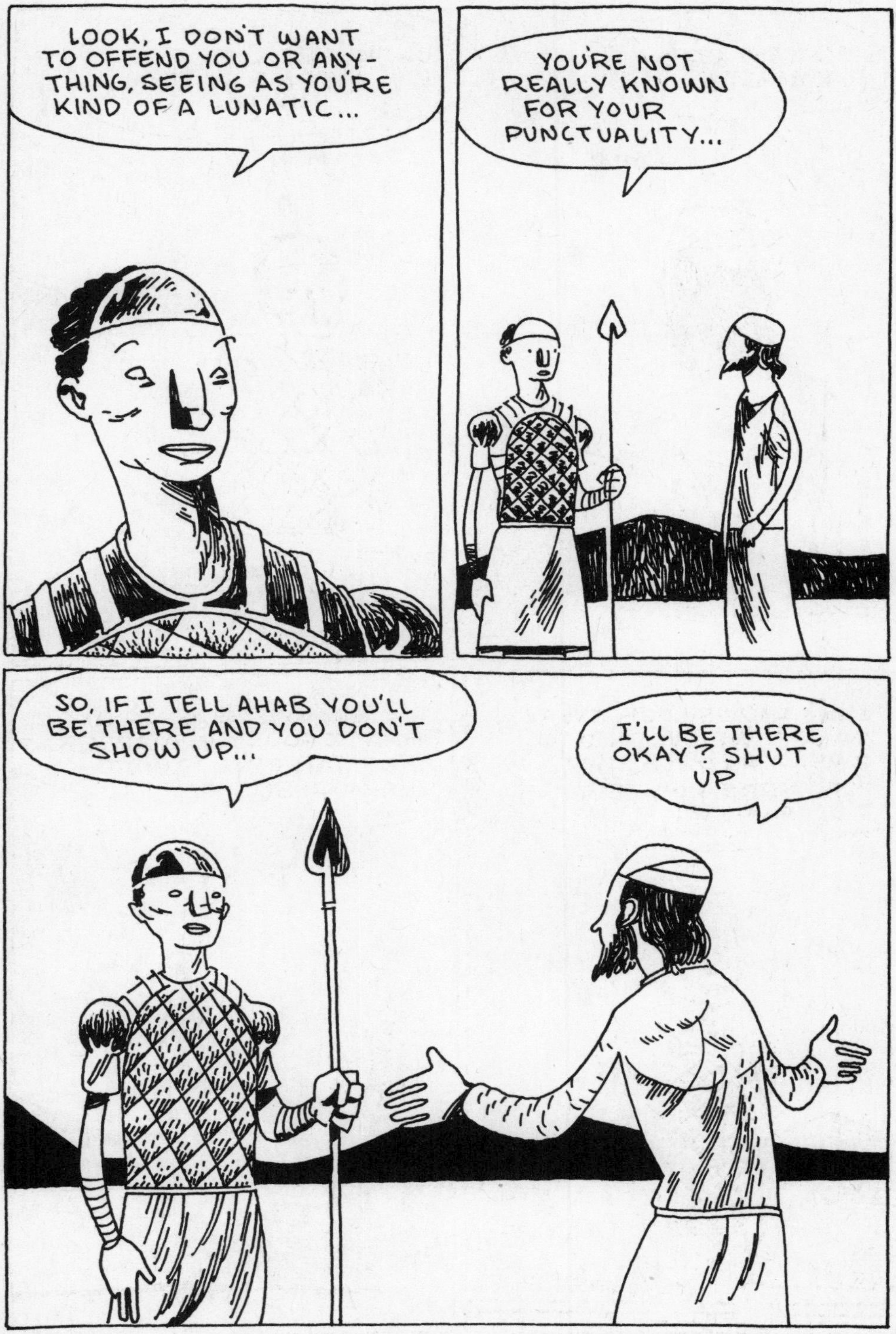
LOOK, I DON'T WANT TO OFFEND YOU OR ANY-THING, SEEING AS YOU'RE KIND OF A LUNATIC...
YOU'RE NOT REALLY KNOWN FOR YOUR PUNCTUALITY...
SO, IF I TELL AHAB YOU'LL BE THERE AND YOU DON'T SHOW UP...
I'LL BE THERE OKAY? SHUT UP

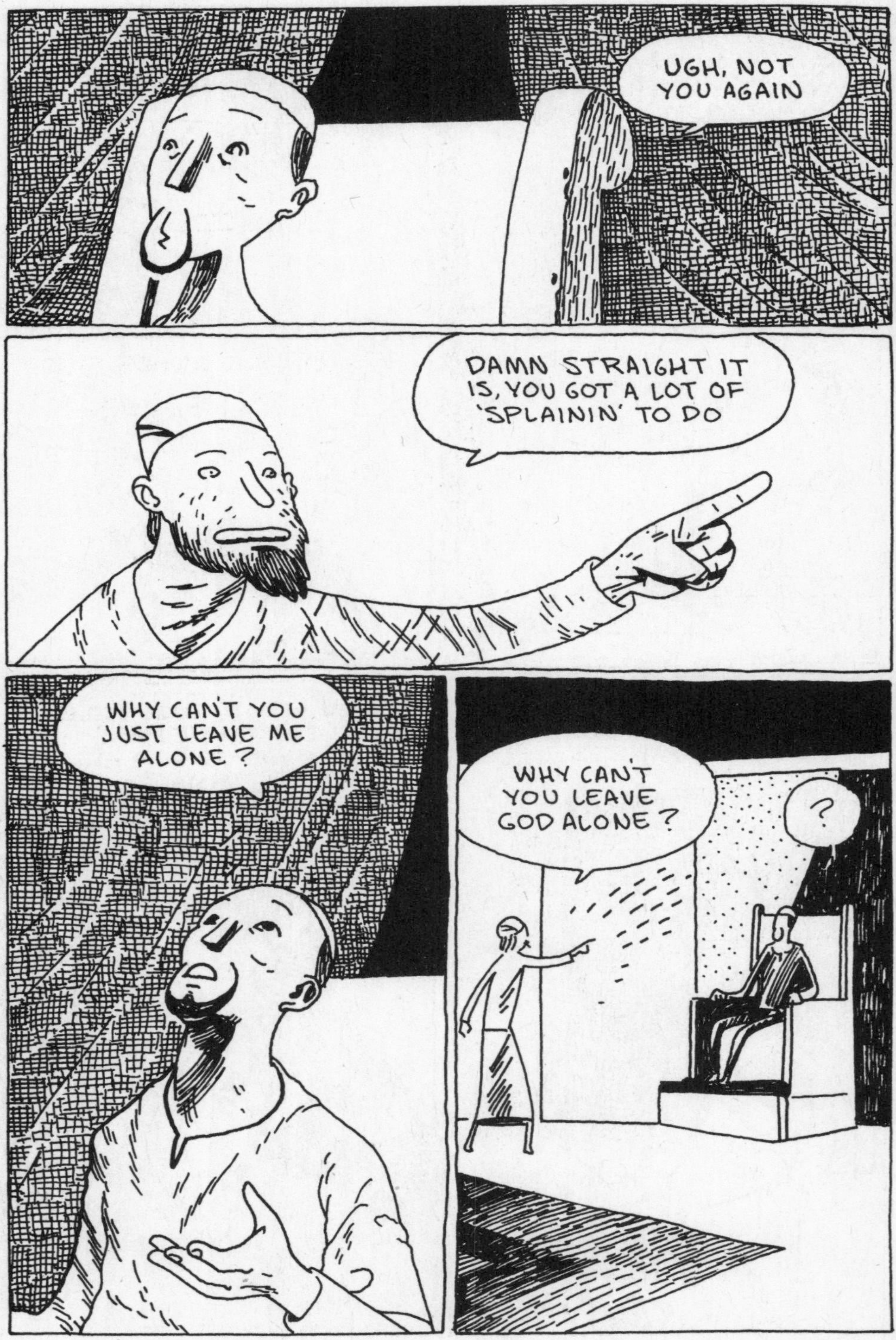
UGH, NOT YOU AGAIN
DAMN STRAIGHT IT IS, YOU GOT A LOT OF 'SPLAININ' TO DO
WHY CAN'T YOU JUST LEAVE ME ALONE?
WHY CAN'T YOU LEAVE GOD ALONE?
?

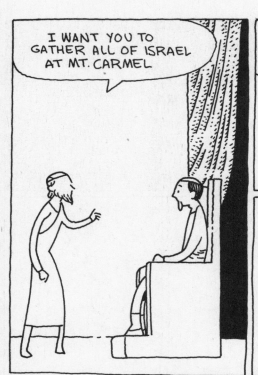

I WANT YOU TO GATHER ALL OF ISRAEL AT MT. CARMEL

ON ONE SIDE, WE'LL HAVE ALL THE PROPHETS OF BAAL AND ASHERAH

ON THE OTHER SIDE, WE'LL HAVE ME, GOD'S LAST PROPHET

WELL, YOU'RE NOT REALLY THE LAST OF GOD'S PROPHETS

YOU WANT TO QUIBBLE OVER STUPID DETAILS OR YOU WANT TO DO THIS THING?

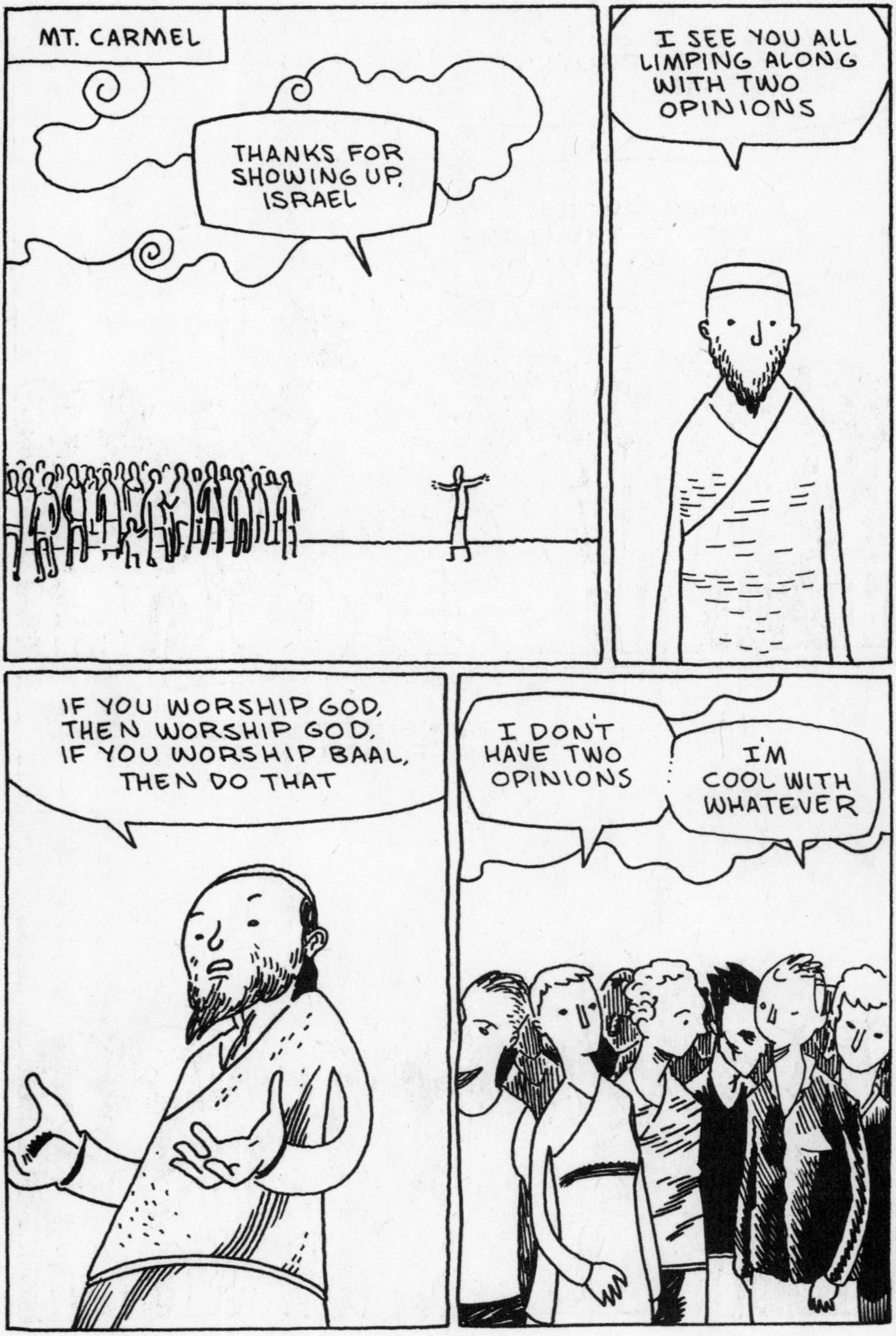
MT. CARMEL
THANKS FOR SHOWING UP, ISRAEL
I SEE YOU ALL LIMPING ALONG WITH TWO OPINIONS
IF YOU WORSHIP GOD, THEN WORSHIP GOD. IF YOU WORSHIP BAAL, THEN DO THAT
I DON'T HAVE TWO OPINIONS
I'M COOL WITH WHATEVER

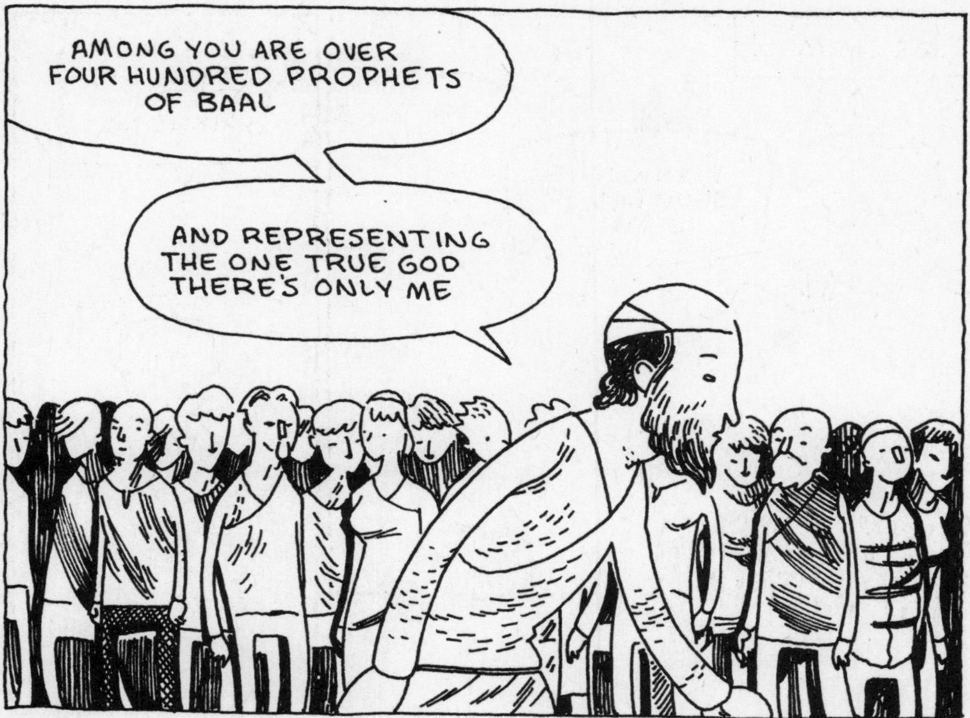
AMONG YOU ARE OVER FOUR HUNDRED PROPHETS OF BAAL
AND REPRESENTING THE ONE TRUE GOD THERE'S ONLY ME

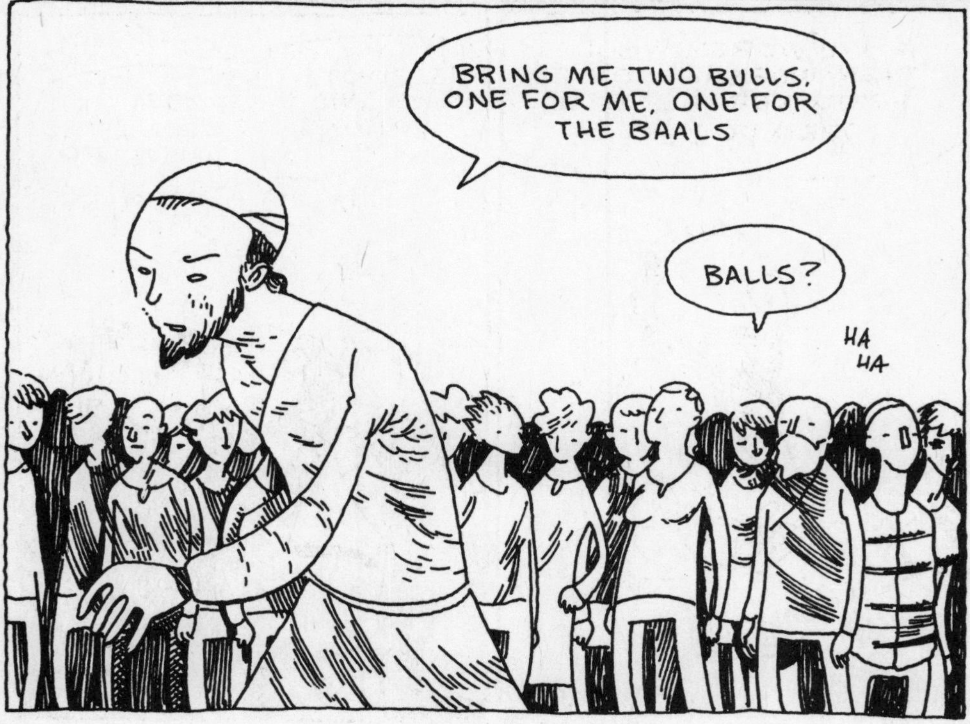
BRING ME TWO BULLS, ONE FOR ME, ONE FOR THE BAALS
BALLS?
HA HA

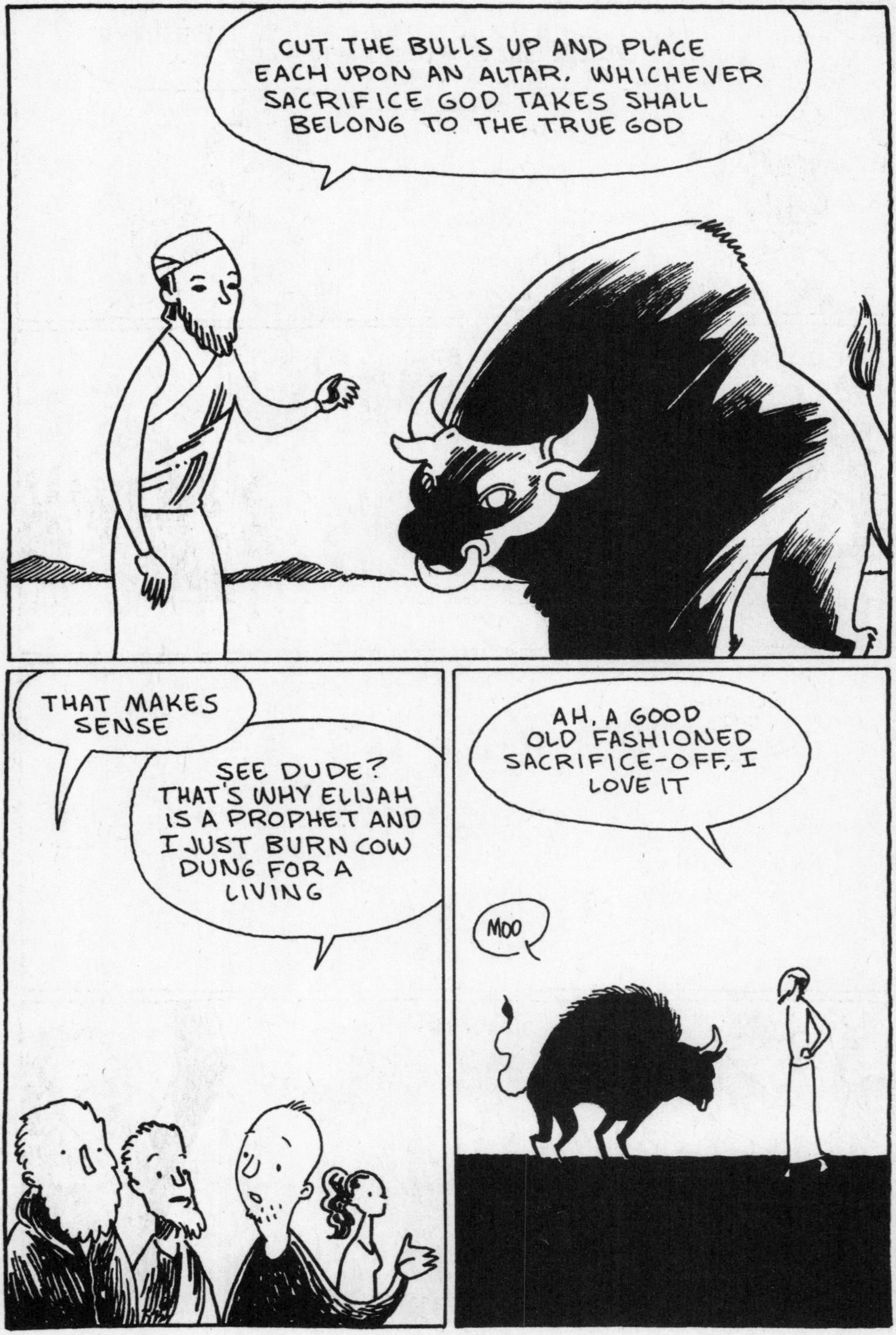
CUT THE BULLS UP AND PLACE EACH UPON AN ALTAR. WHICHEVER SACRIFICE GOD TAKES SHALL BELONG TO THE TRUE GOD
THAT MAKES SENSE
SEE DUDE? THAT'S WHY ELIJAH IS A PROPHET AND I JUST BURN COW DUNG FOR A LIVING
AH, A GOOD OLD FASHIONED SACRIFICE-OFF, I LOVE IT
MOO

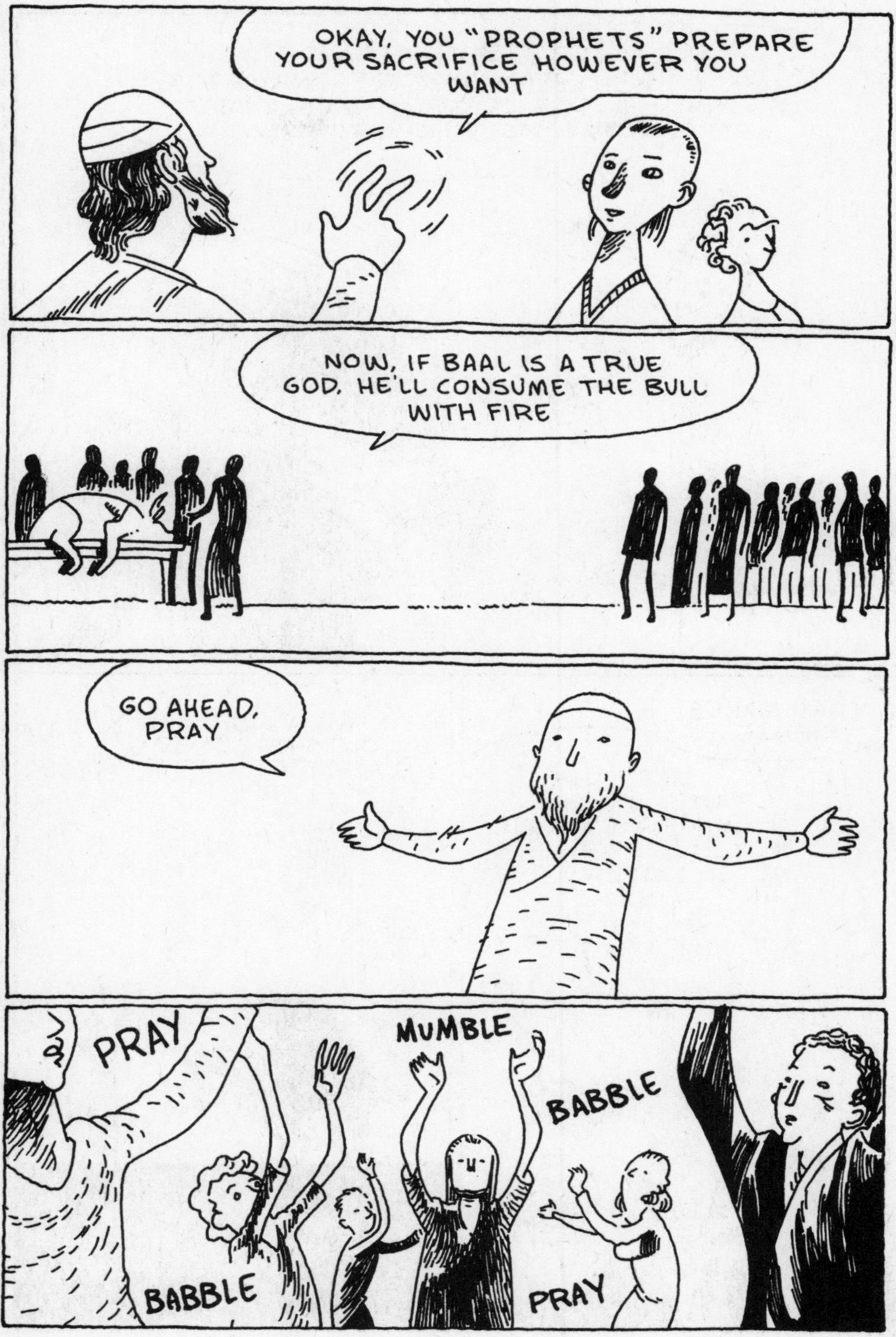

OKAY, YOU "PROPHETS" PREPARE YOUR SACRIFICE HOWEVER YOU WANT
NOW, IF BAAL IS A TRUE GOD, HE'LL CONSUME THE BULL WITH FIRE
GO AHEAD, PRAY
PRAY
MUMBLE
BABBLE
BABBLE
PRAY

WHATS THE MATTER DUMBASSES? IS BAAL DEAF, PERHAPS HE'S SLEEPING?
YOU NEED TO PRAY LOUDER TO WAKE HIM UP

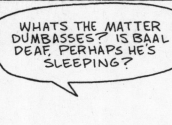

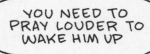

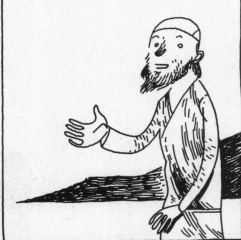

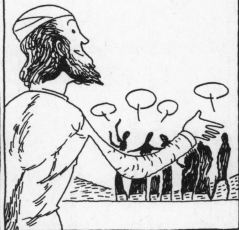

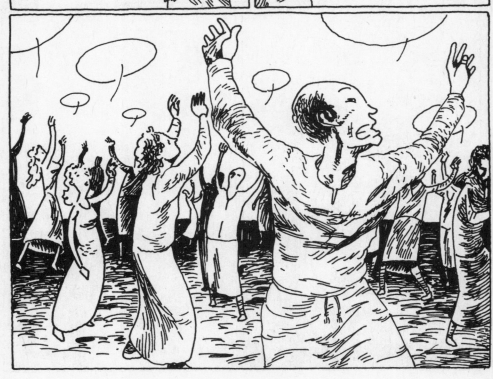

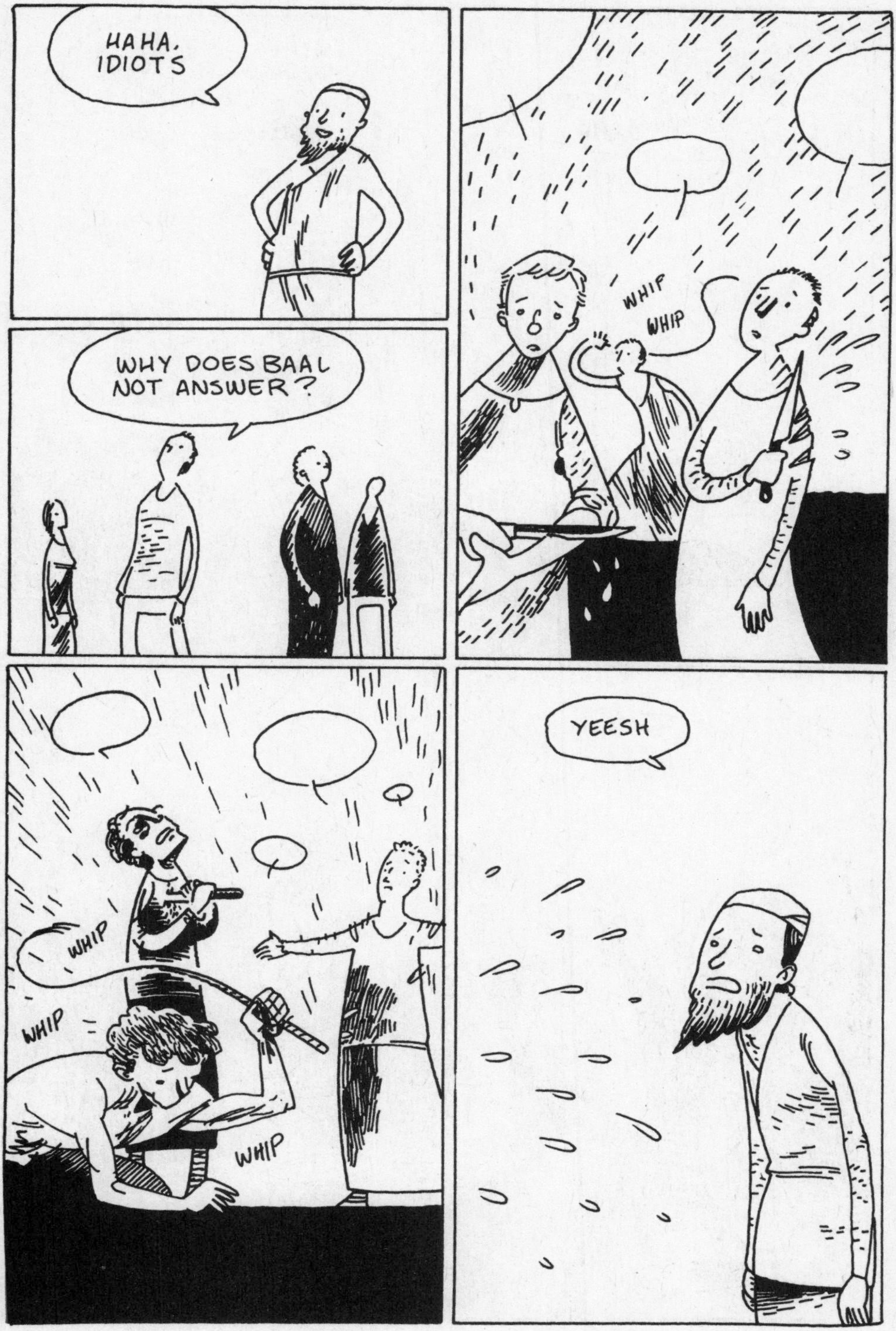

HAHA, IDIOTS
WHY DOES BAAL NOT ANSWER?
WHIP
WHIP
WHIP
WHIP
WHIP
YEESH

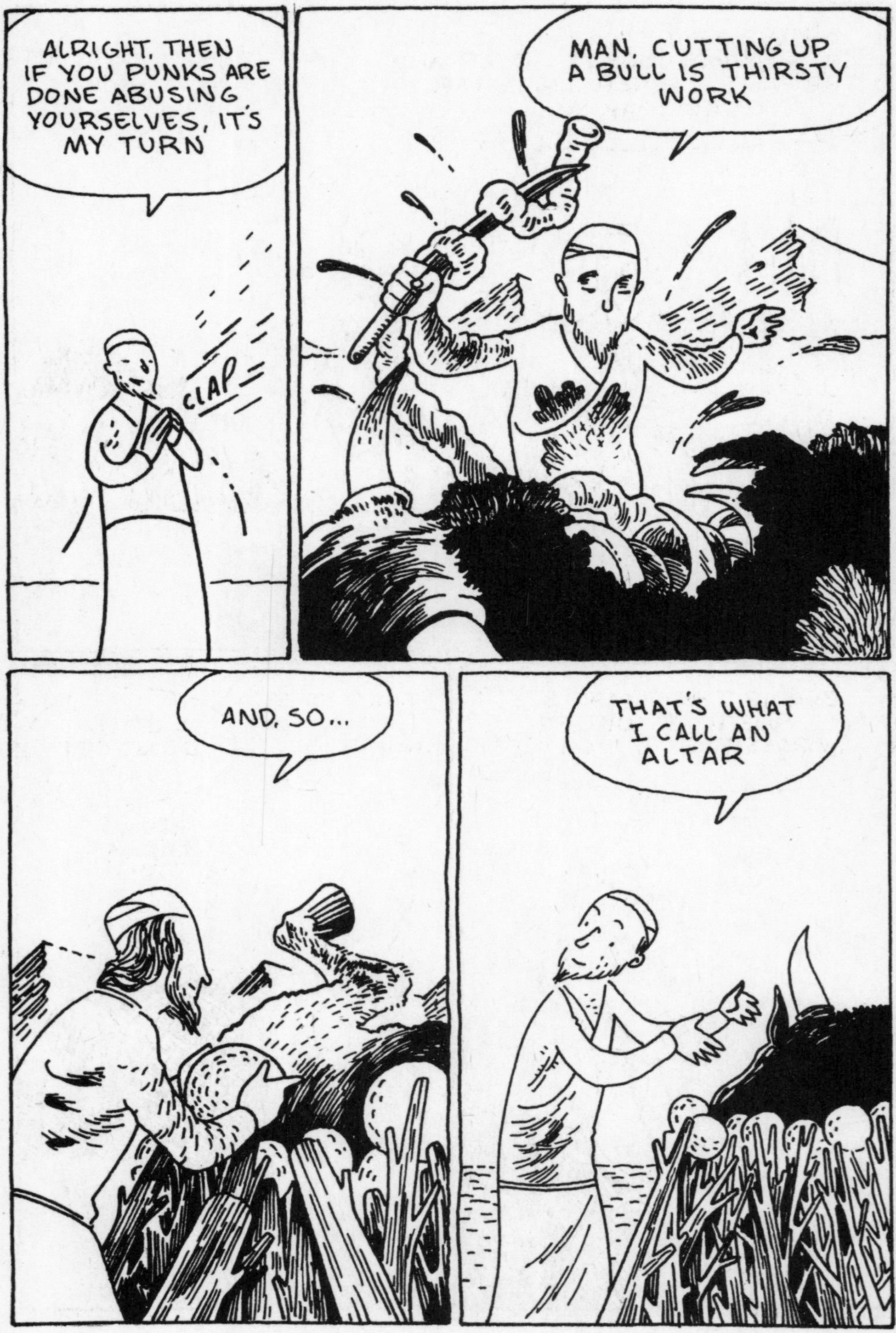
ALRIGHT. THEN IF YOU PUNKS ARE DONE ABUSING YOURSELVES, IT'S MY TURN
CLAP
MAN. CUTTING UP A BULL IS THIRSTY WORK
AND, SO...
THAT'S WHAT I CALL AN ALTAR

HERE'S WHAT I WANT YOU TO DO, GET A COUPLE JUGS OF WATER AND THROW IT ALL OVER THE ALTAR. A REAL SOAKING
BUT IF THE ALTAR IS WET, IT WILL BE IMPOSSIBLE TO LIGHT
THAT'S THE PLAN NUMBSKULL
I STILL DONT GET IT

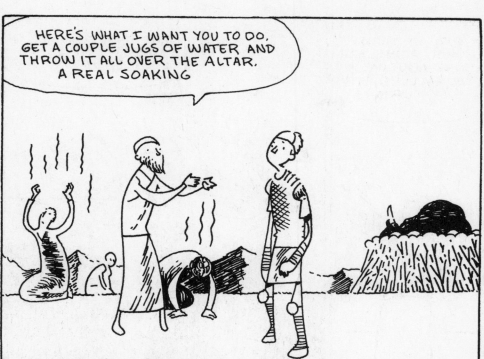

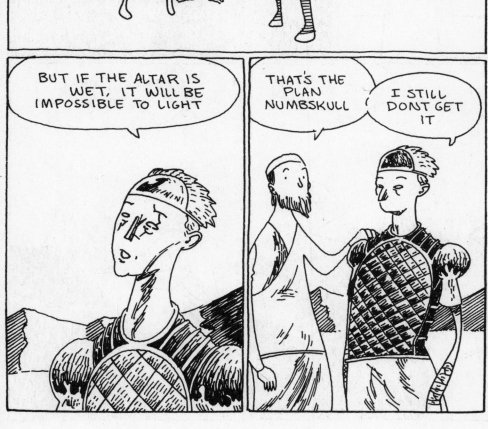

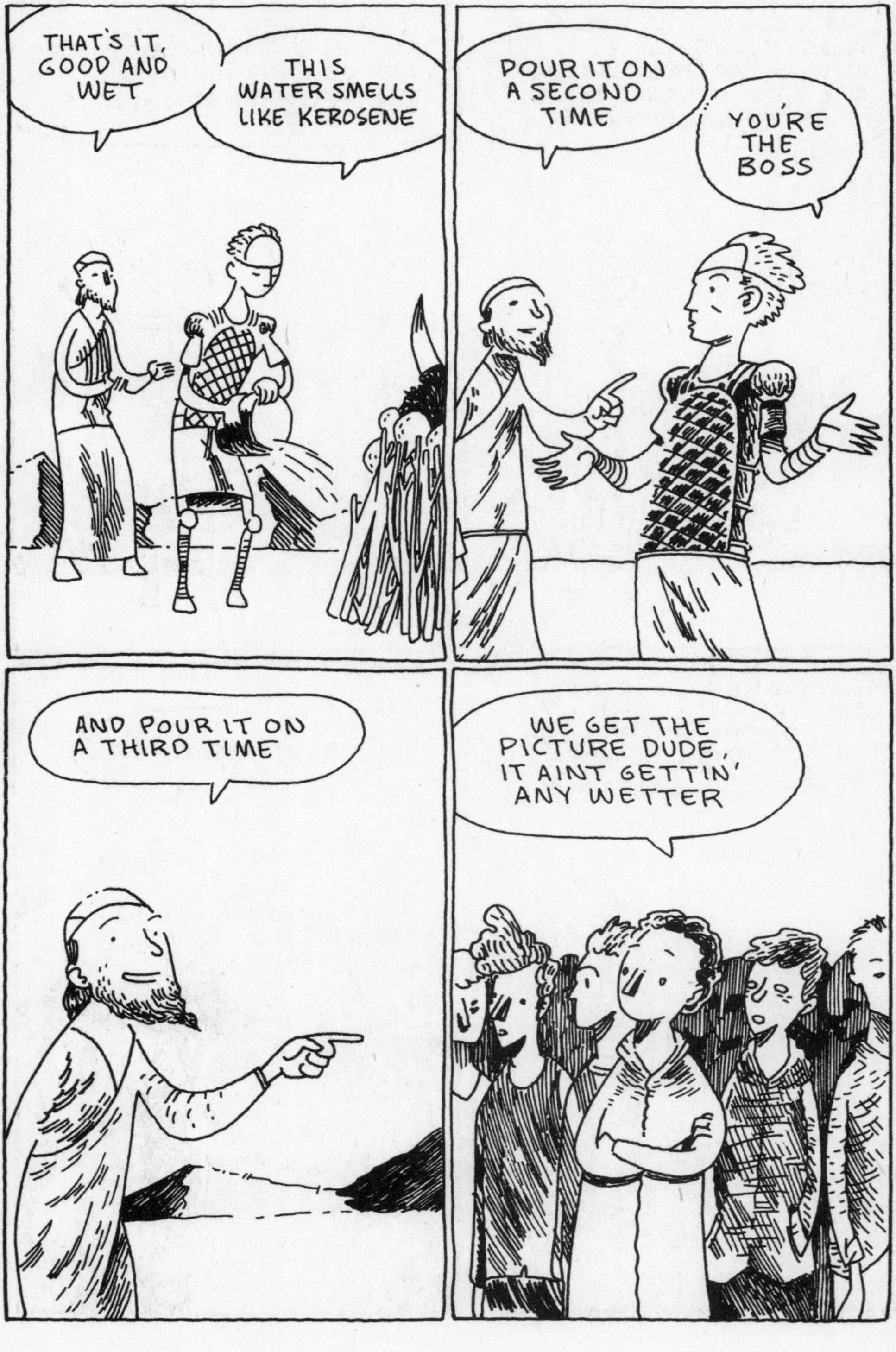
THAT'S IT, GOOD AND WET
THIS WATER SMELLS LIKE KEROSENE
POUR IT ON A SECOND TIME
YOU'RE THE BOSS
AND POUR IT ON A THIRD TIME
WE GET THE PICTURE DUDE, IT AINT GETTIN' ANY WETTER

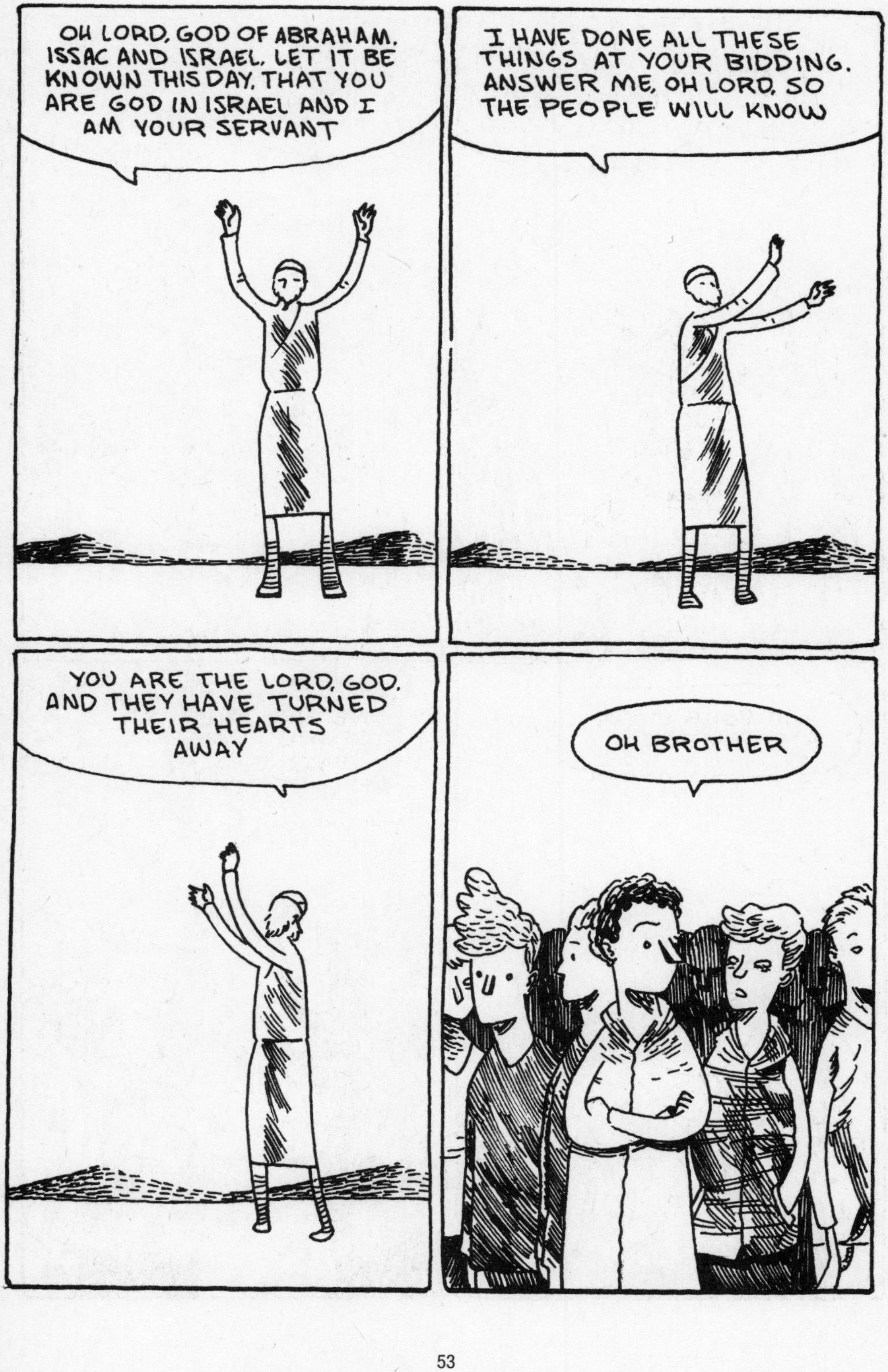
OH LORD, GOD OF ABRAHAM, ISSAC AND ISRAEL, LET IT BE KNOWN THIS DAY, THAT YOU ARE GOD IN ISRAEL AND I AM YOUR SERVANT
I HAVE DONE ALL THESE THINGS AT YOUR BIDDING. ANSWER ME, OH LORD, SO THE PEOPLE WILL KNOW
YOU ARE THE LORD, GOD, AND THEY HAVE TURNED THEIR HEARTS AWAY
OH BROTHER

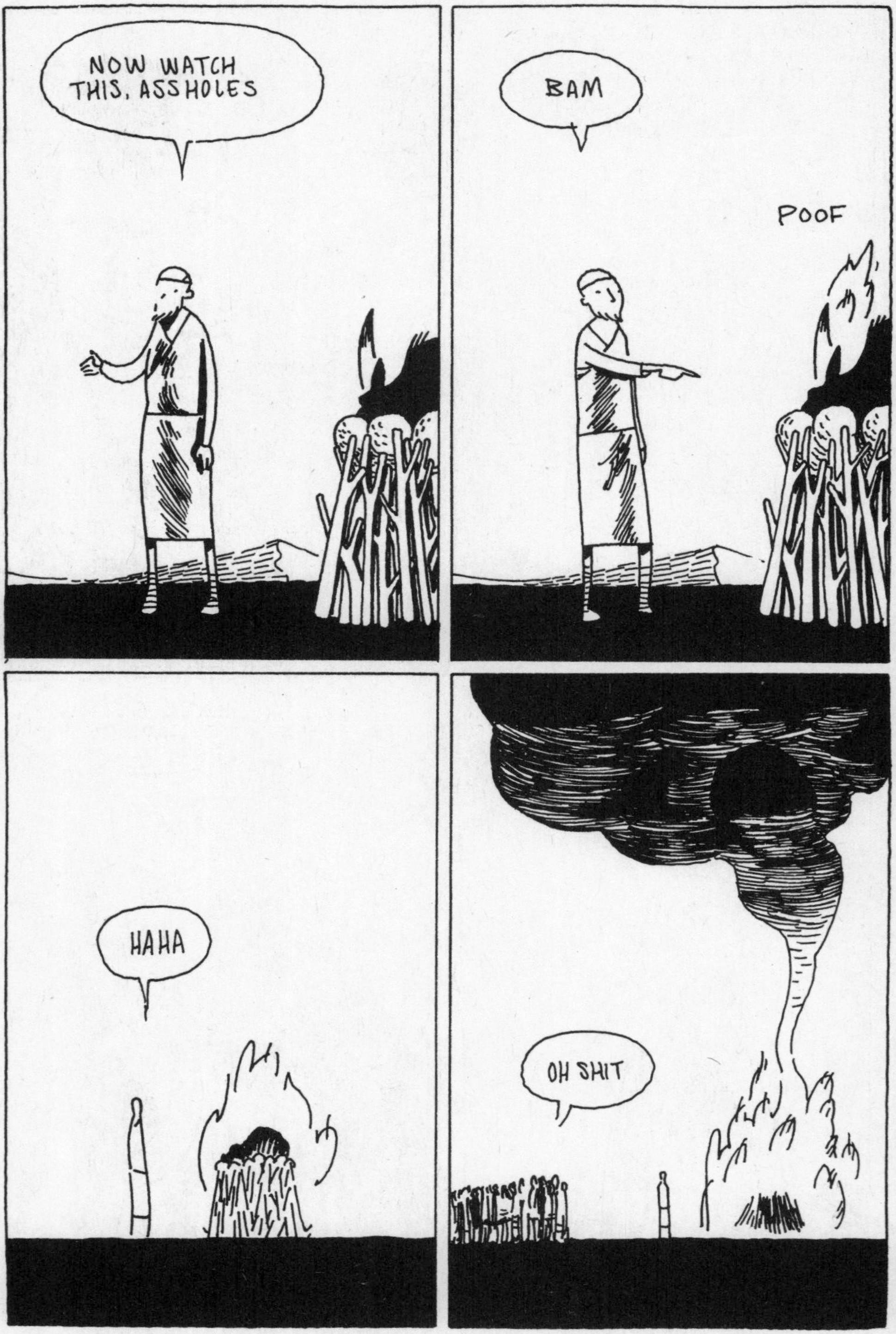
NOW WATCH THIS, ASSHOLES
BAM
POOF
HAHA
OH SHIT

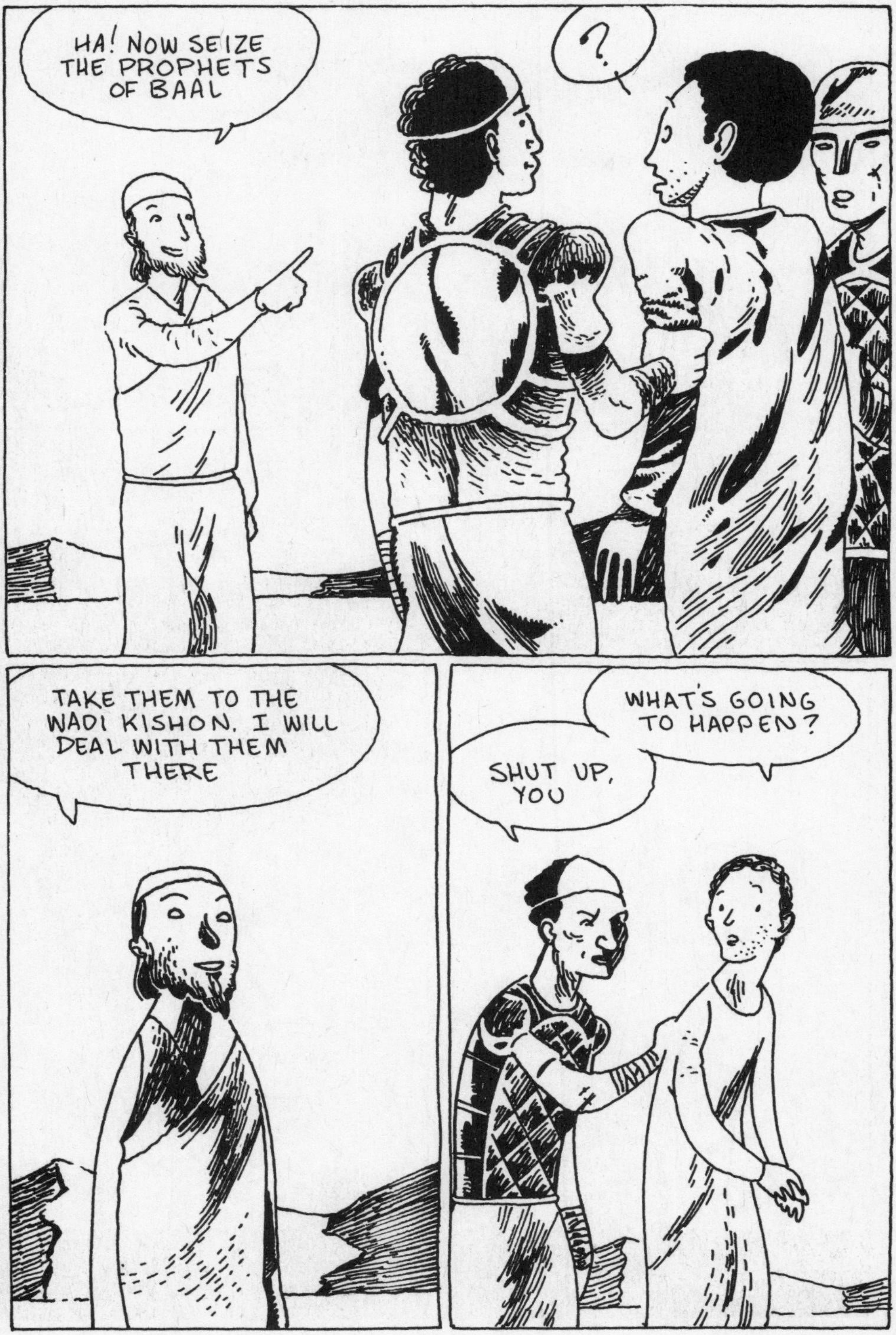
HA! NOW SEIZE THE PROPHETS OF BAAL
?
TAKE THEM TO THE WADI KISHON. I WILL DEAL WITH THEM THERE
WHAT'S GOING TO HAPPEN?
SHUT UP, YOU

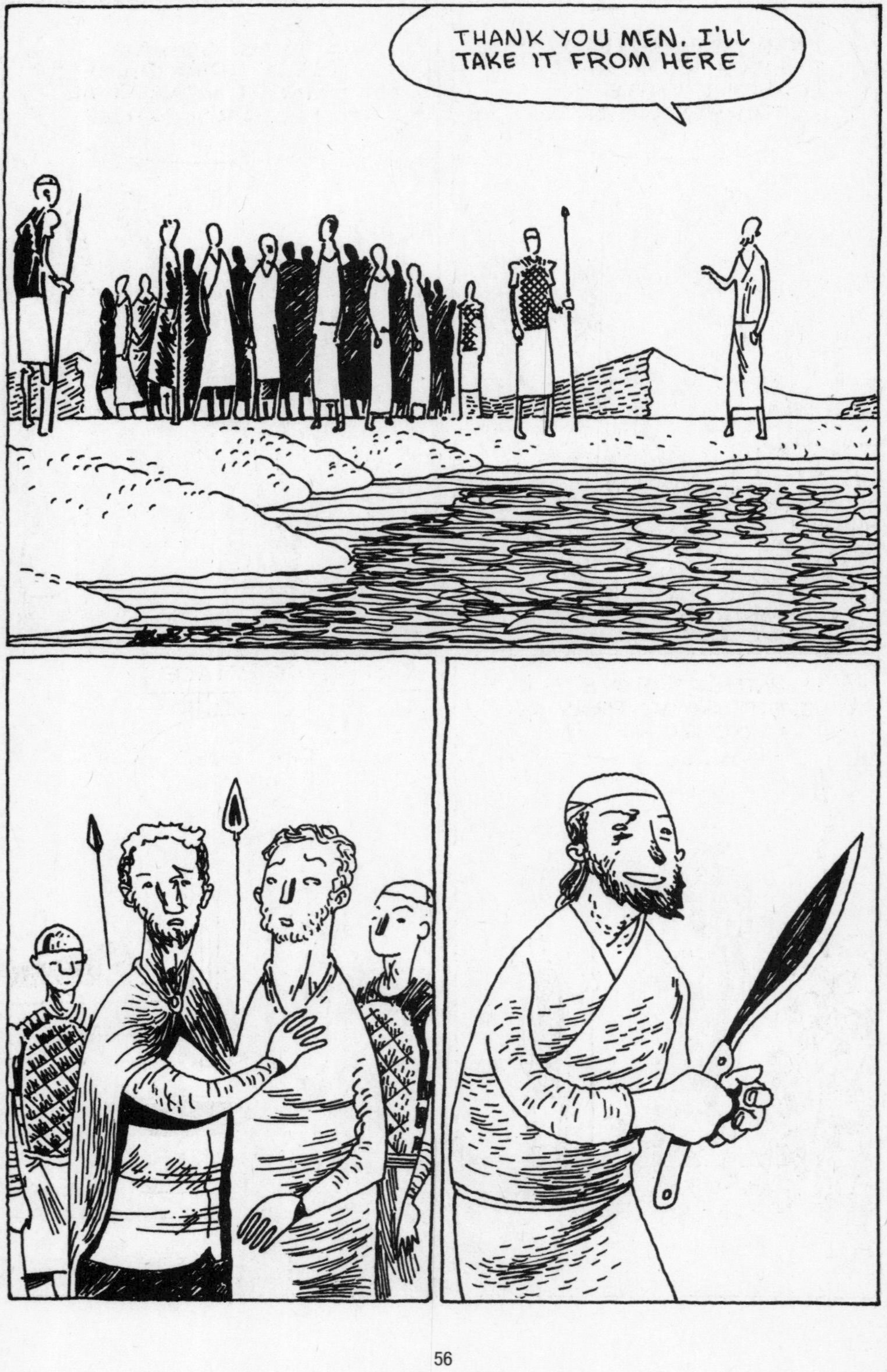
THANK YOU MEN. I'LL TAKE IT FROM HERE

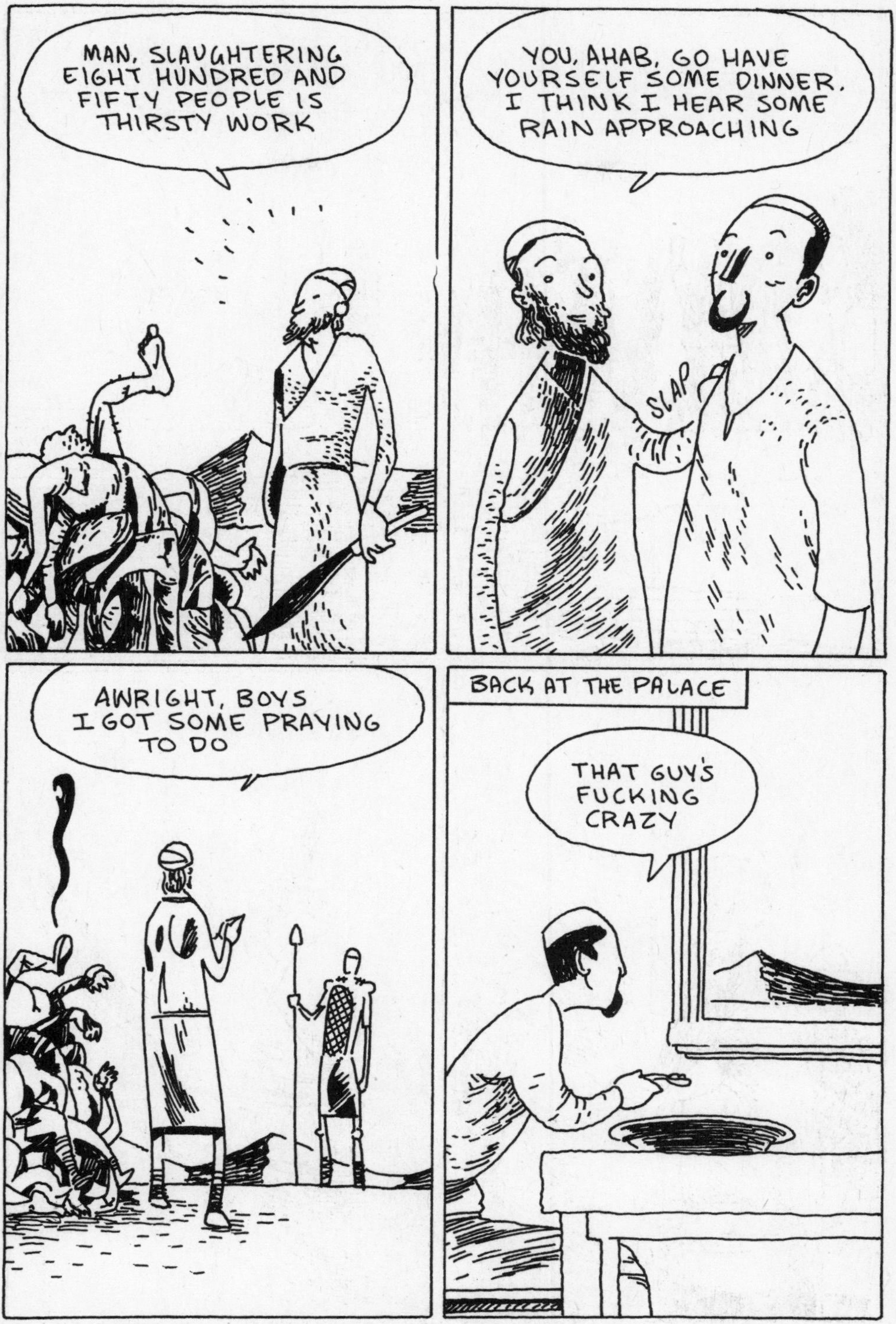
MAN, SLAUGHTERING EIGHT HUNDRED AND FIFTY PEOPLE IS THIRSTY WORK
YOU, AHAB, GO HAVE YOURSELF SOME DINNER. I THINK I HEAR SOME RAIN APPROACHING
SLAP
AWRIGHT, BOYS I GOT SOME PRAYING TO DO
BACK AT THE PALACE
THAT GUY'S FUCKING CRAZY

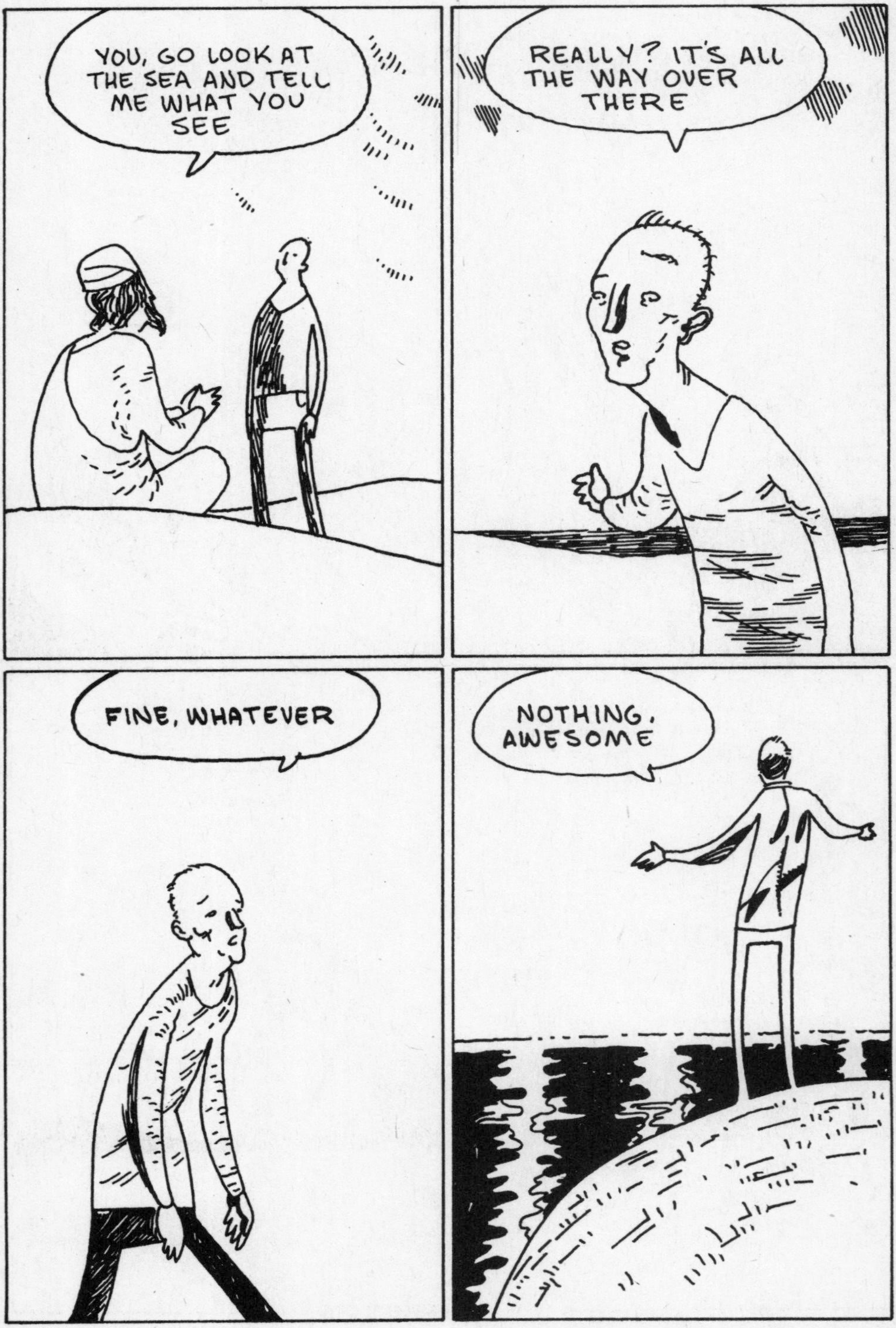
YOU, GO LOOK AT THE SEA AND TELL ME WHAT YOU SEE
REALLY? IT'S ALL THE WAY OVER THERE
FINE, WHATEVER
NOTHING, AWESOME

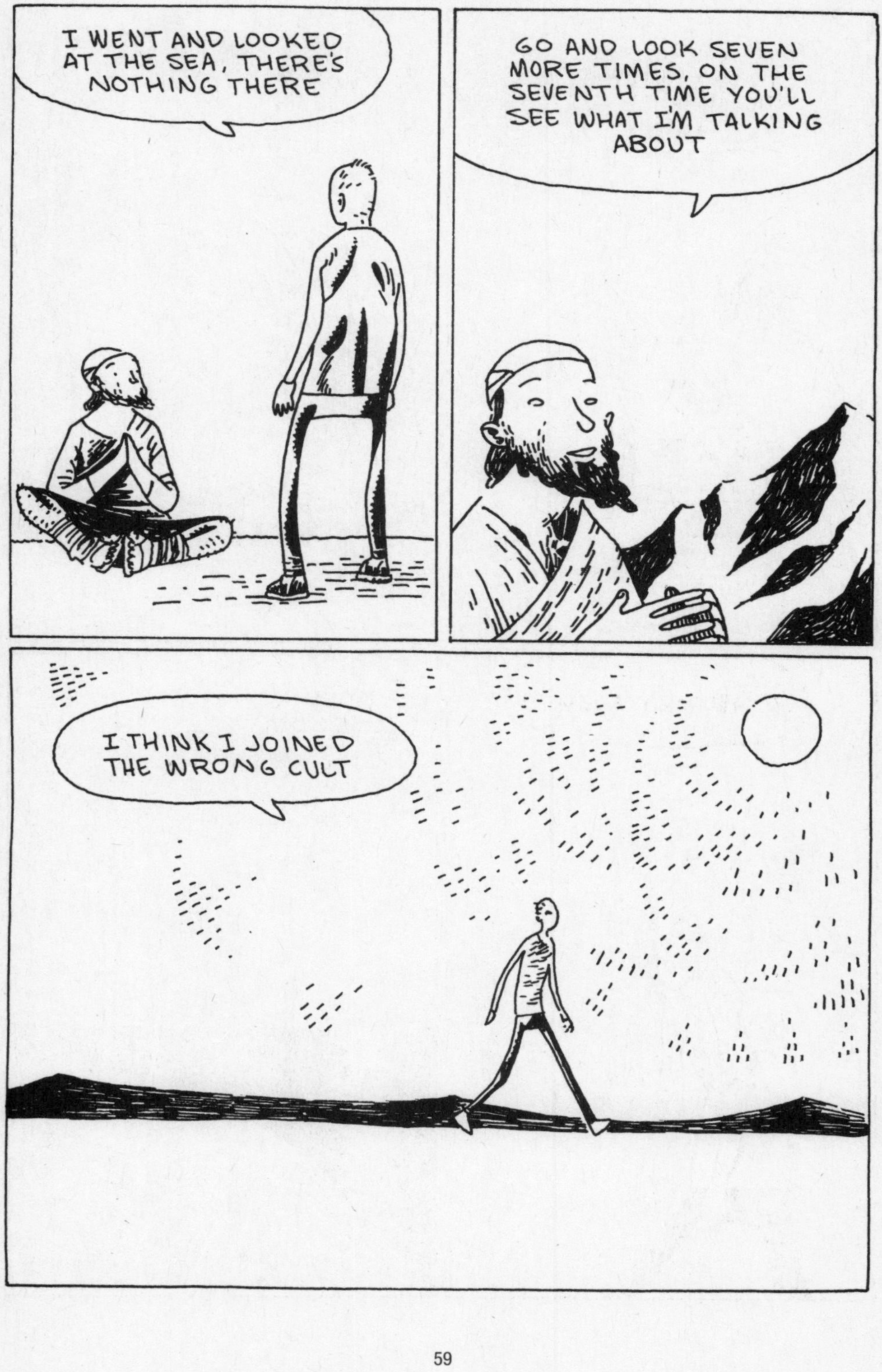
I WENT AND LOOKED AT THE SEA, THERE'S NOTHING THERE
GO AND LOOK SEVEN MORE TIMES, ON THE SEVENTH TIME YOU'LL SEE WHAT I'M TALKING ABOUT
I THINK I JOINED THE WRONG CULT

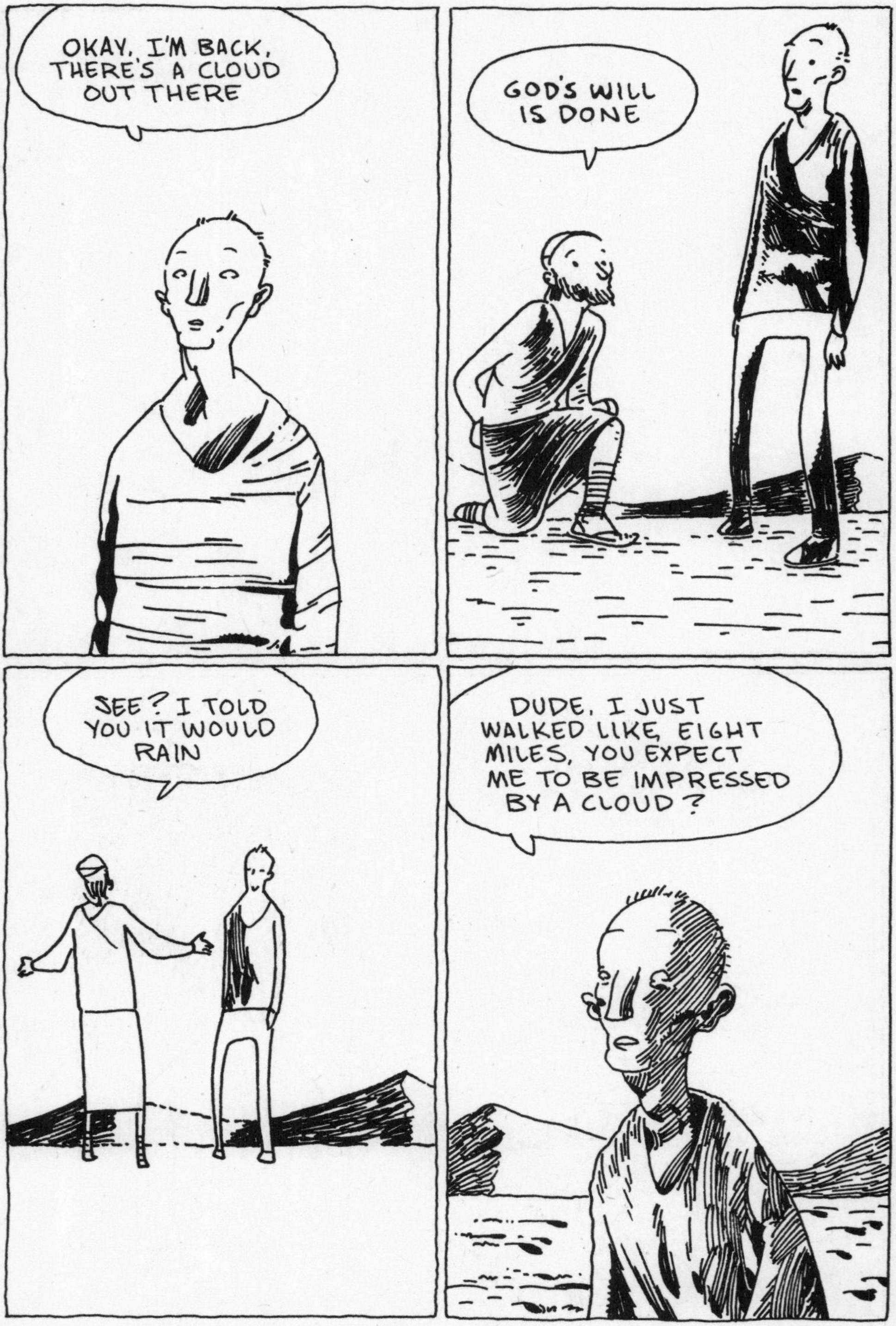
OKAY, I'M BACK, THERE'S A CLOUD OUT THERE
GOD'S WILL IS DONE
SEE? I TOLD YOU IT WOULD RAIN
DUDE, I JUST WALKED LIKE, EIGHT MILES, YOU EXPECT ME TO BE IMPRESSED BY A CLOUD?

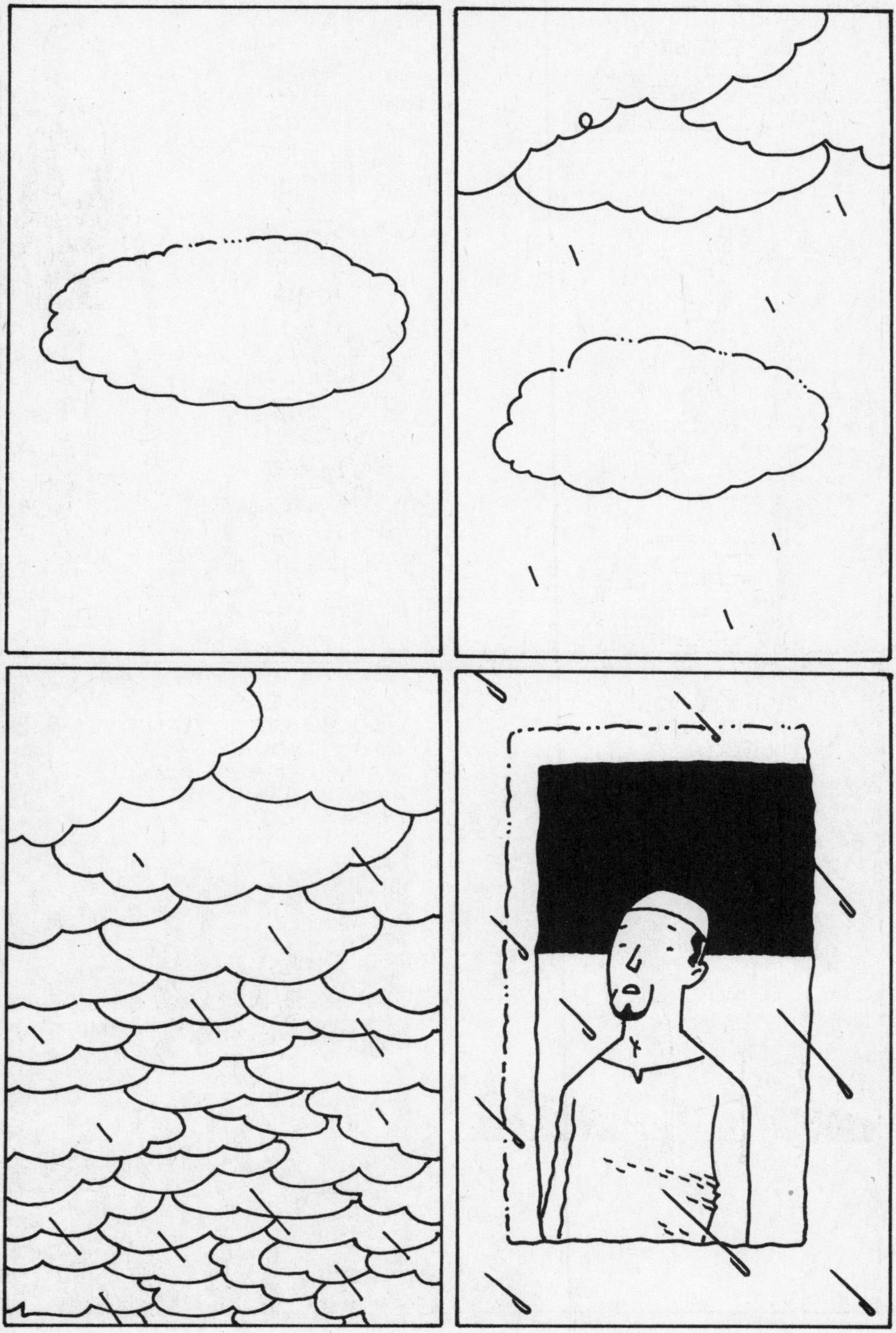

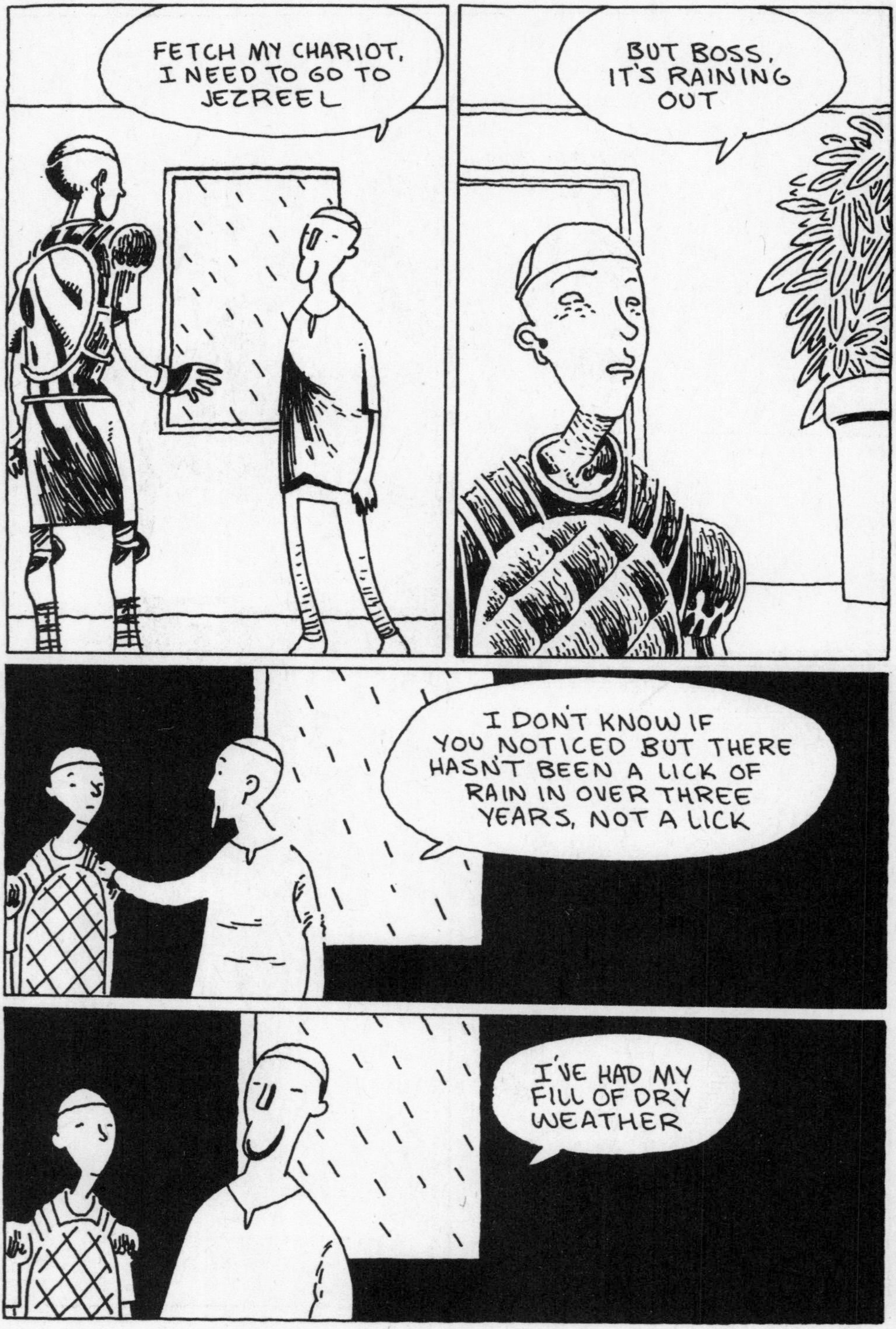
FETCH MY CHARIOT, I NEED TO GO TO JEZREEL
BUT BOSS, IT'S RAINING OUT
I DON'T KNOW IF YOU NOTICED BUT THERE HASN'T BEEN A LICK OF RAIN IN OVER THREE YEARS, NOT A LICK
I'VE HAD MY FILL OF DRY WEATHER

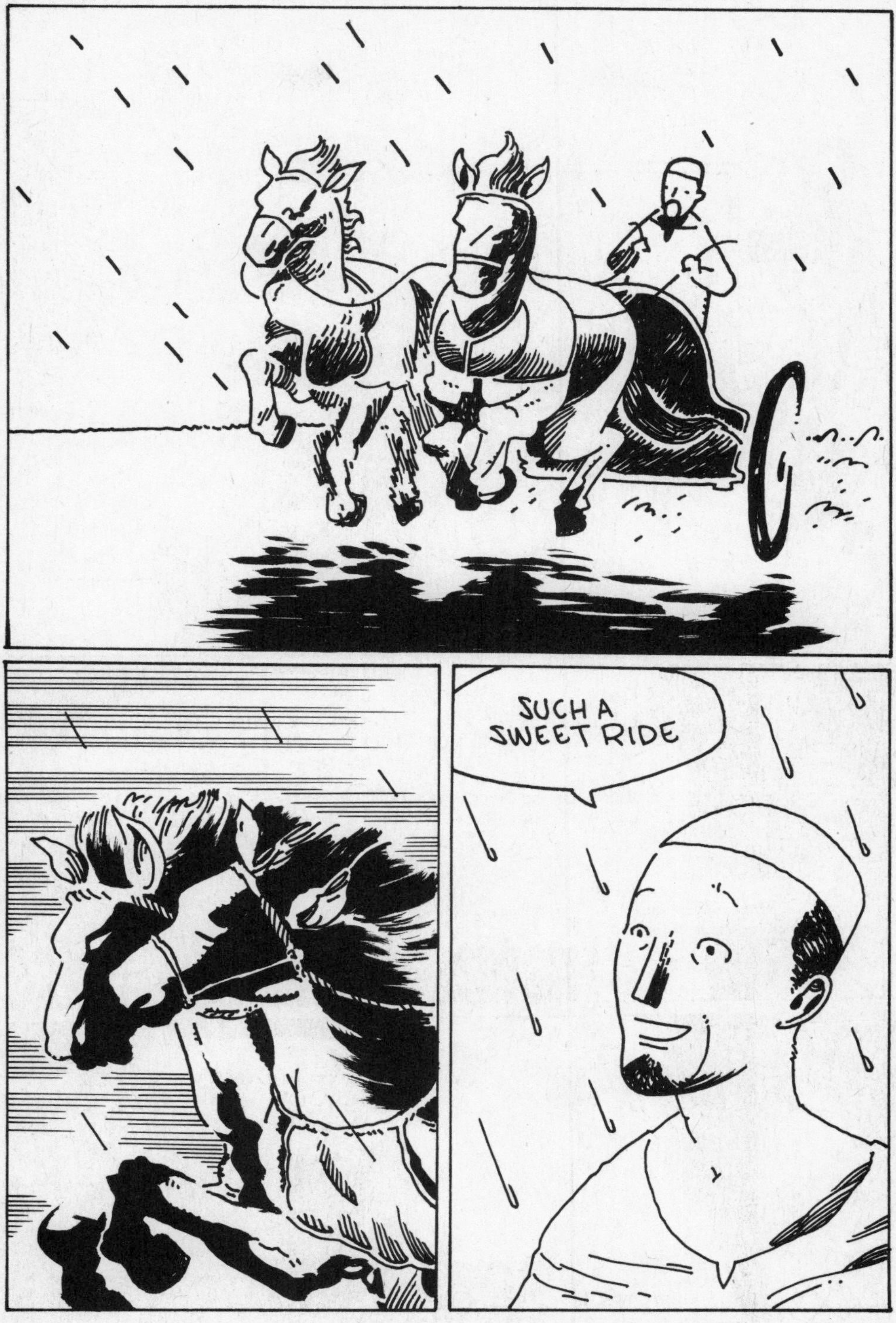
SUCH A SWEET RIDE

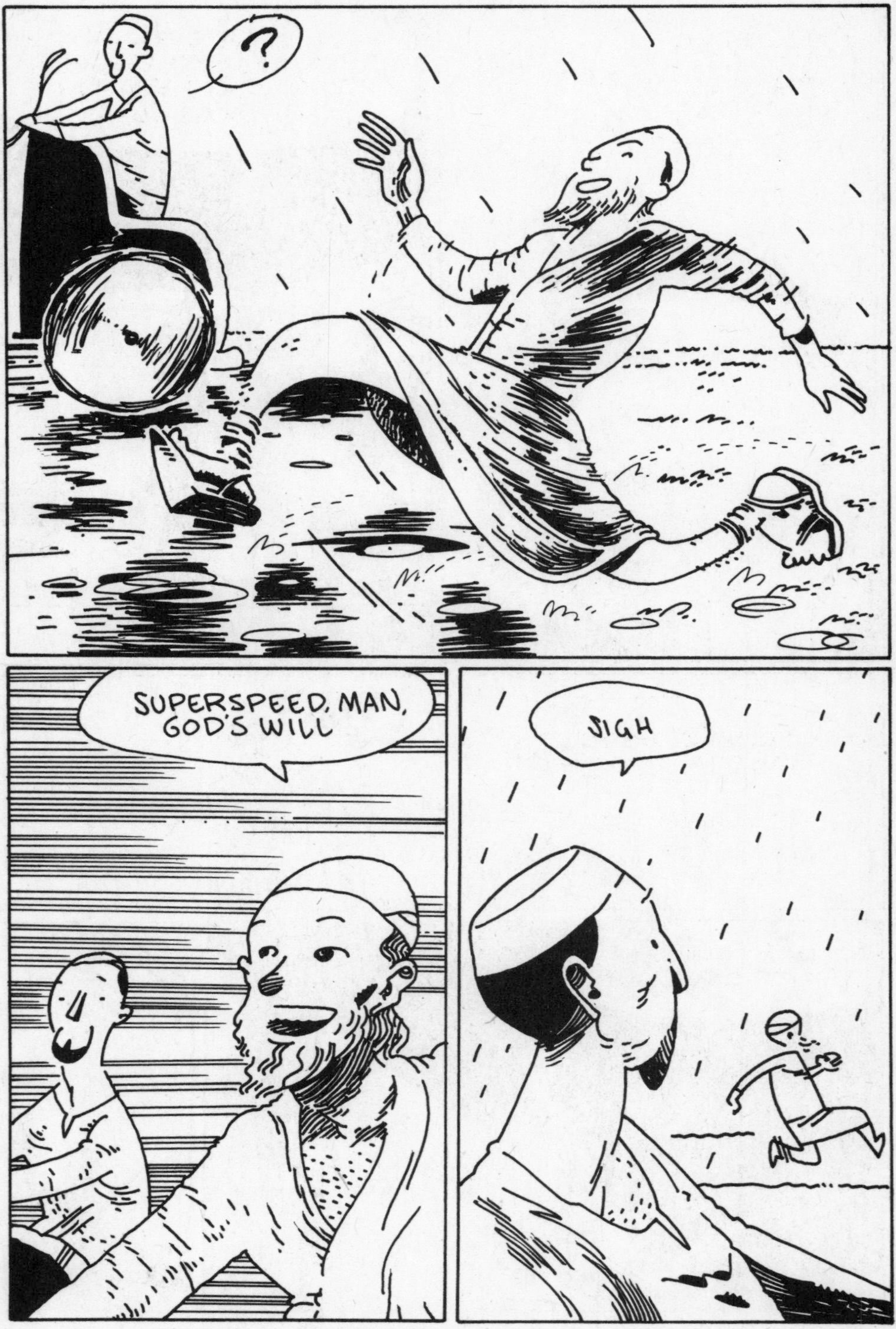
?
SUPERSPEED, MAN, GOD'S WILL
SIGH

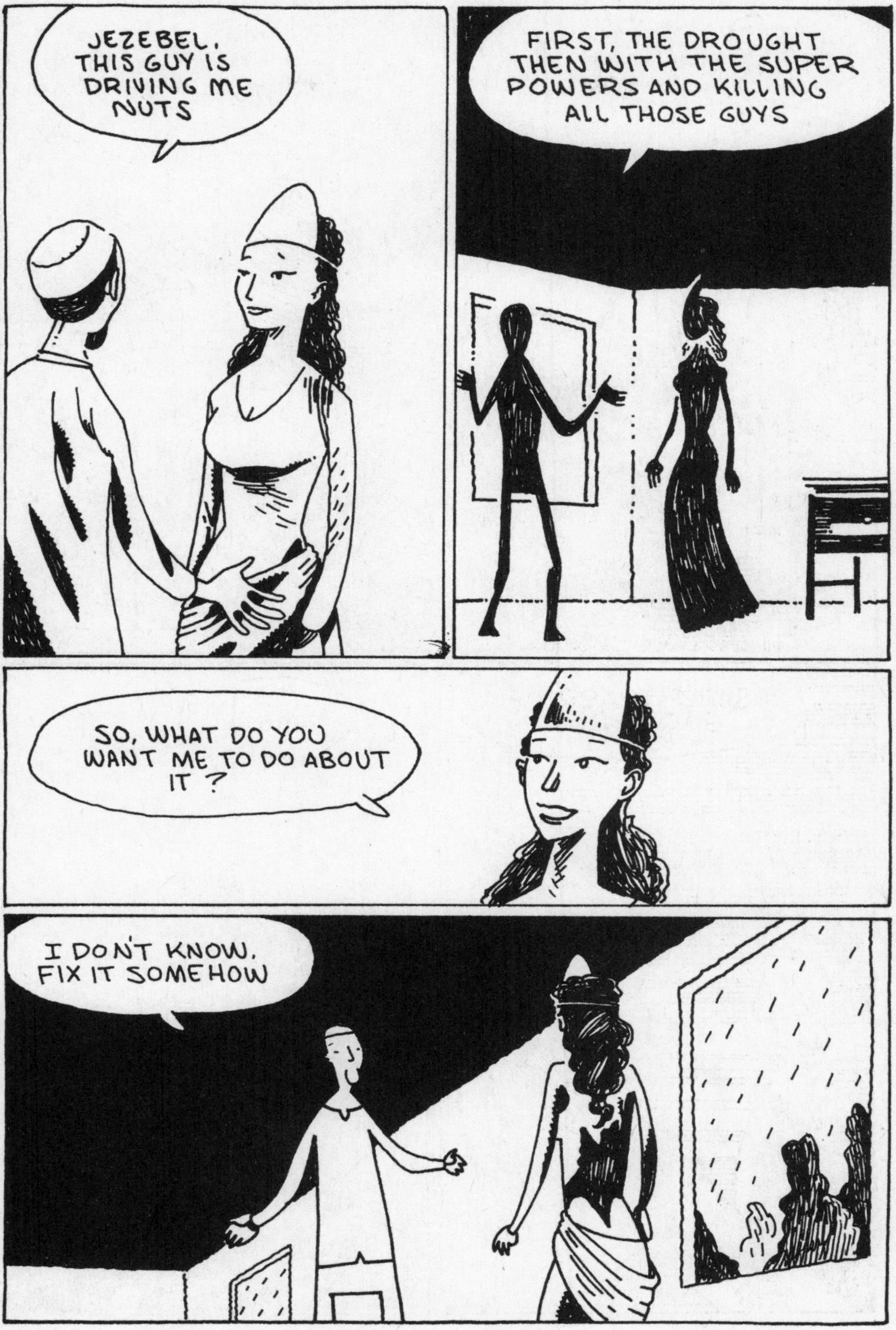
JEZEBEL. THIS GUY IS DRIVING ME NUTS
FIRST, THE DROUGHT THEN WITH THE SUPER POWERS AND KILLING ALL THOSE GUYS
SO, WHAT DO YOU WANT ME TO DO ABOUT IT ?
I DON'T KNOW. FIX IT SOMEHOW

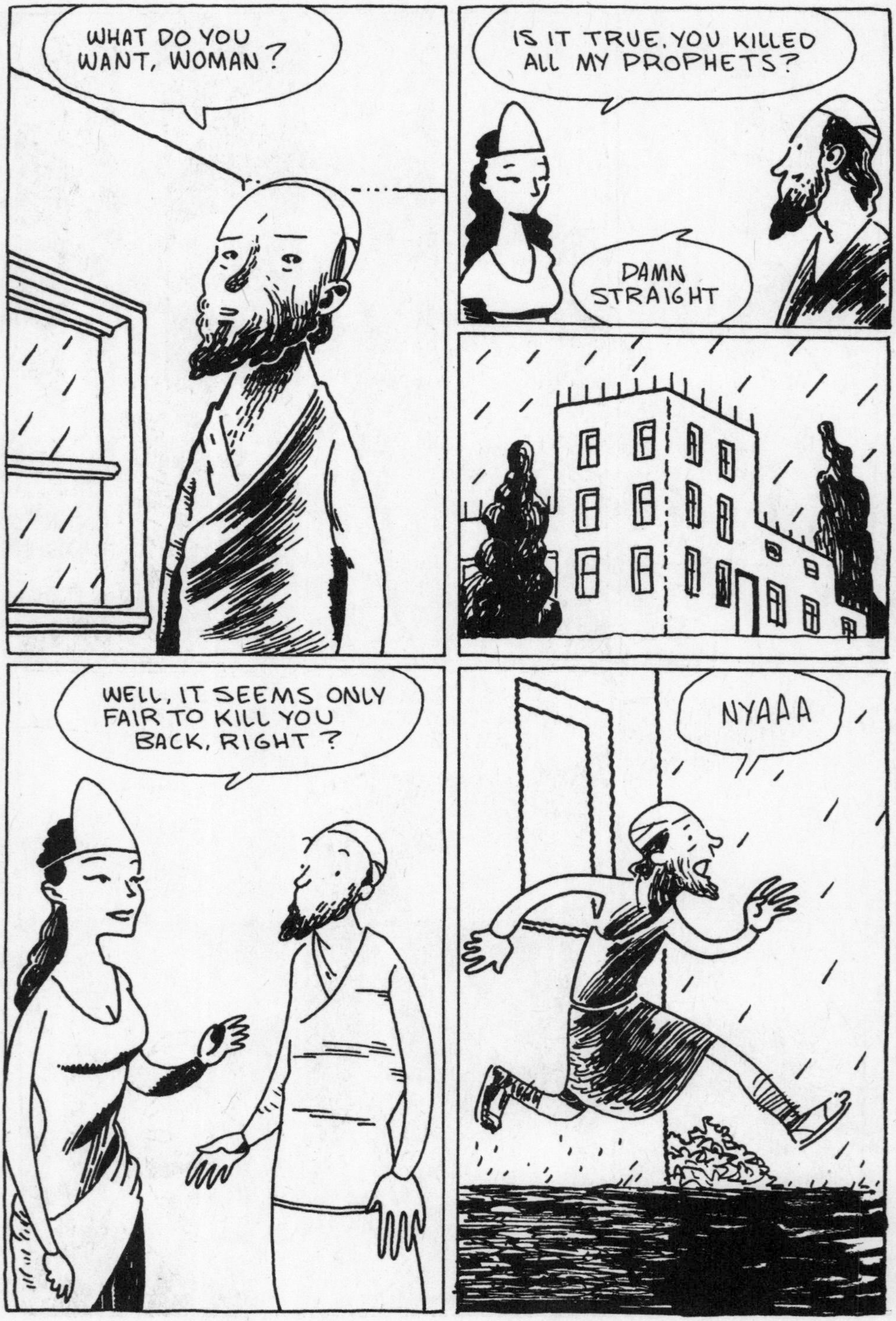
WHAT DO YOU WANT, WOMAN?
IS IT TRUE, YOU KILLED ALL MY PROPHETS?
DAMN STRAIGHT
WELL, IT SEEMS ONLY FAIR TO KILL YOU BACK, RIGHT?
NYAAA

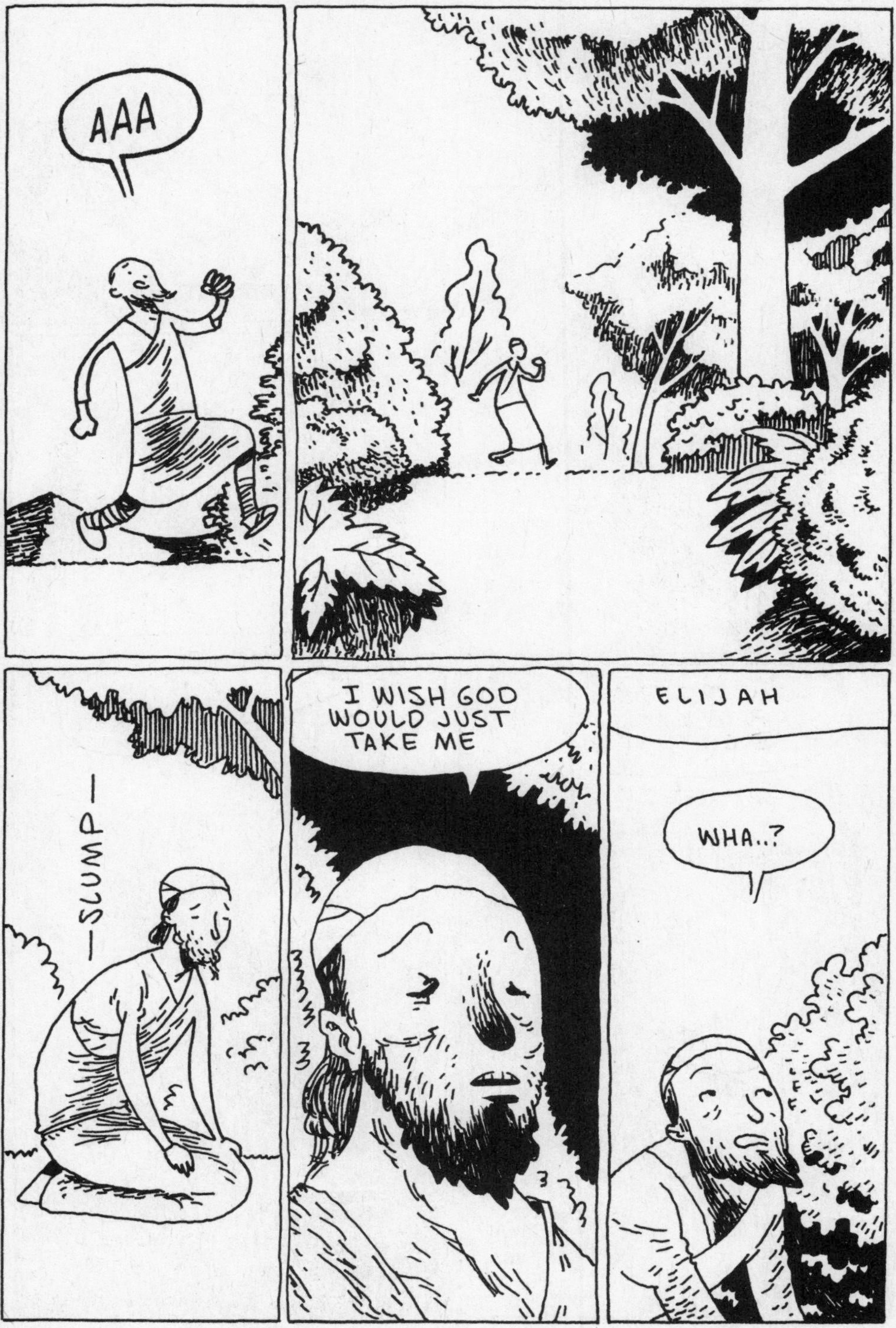
AAA
—SLUMP—
I WISH GOD WOULD JUST TAKE ME
ELIJAH
WHA..?

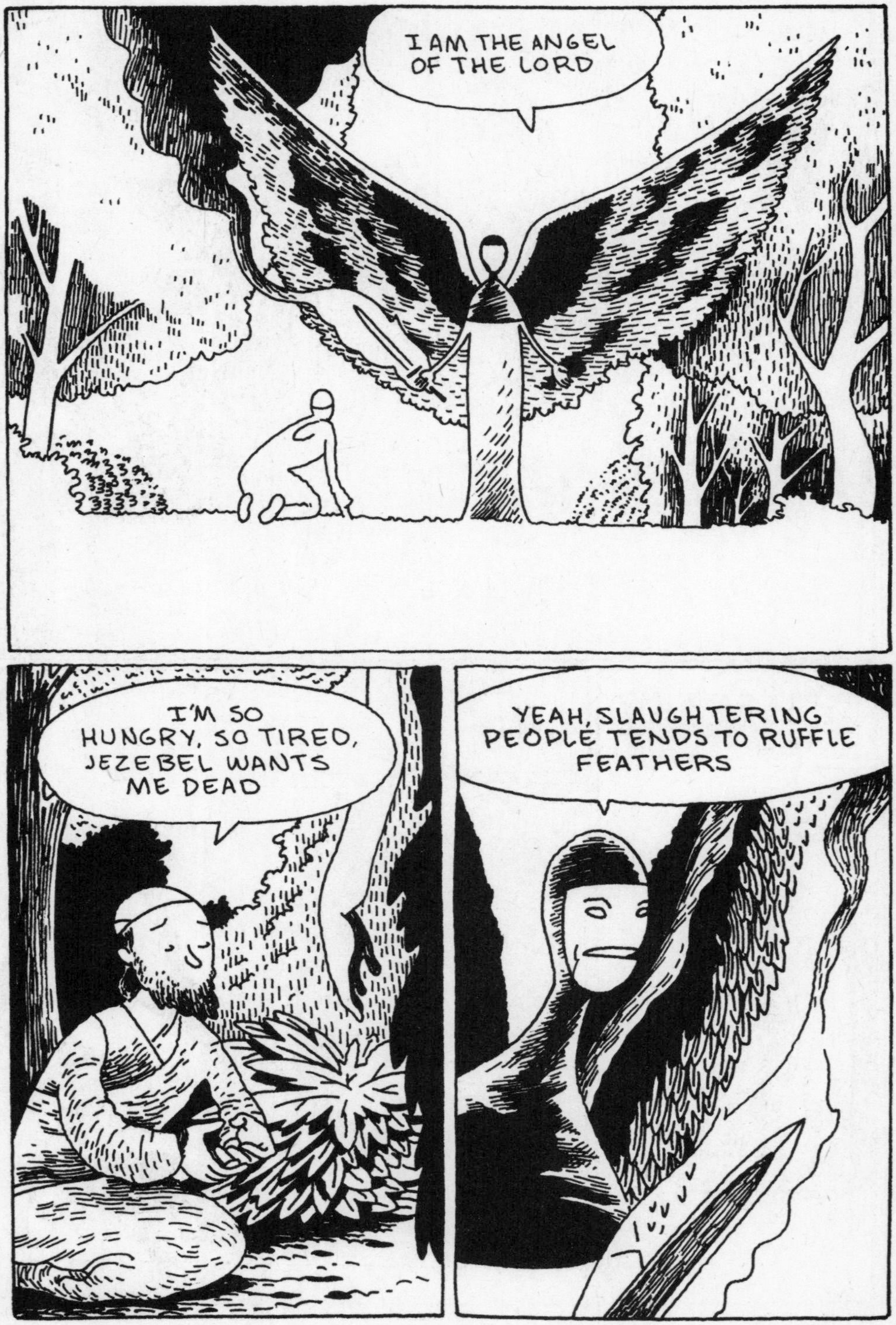
I AM THE ANGEL OF THE LORD
I'M SO HUNGRY, SO TIRED, JEZEBEL WANTS ME DEAD
YEAH, SLAUGHTERING PEOPLE TENDS TO RUFFLE FEATHERS

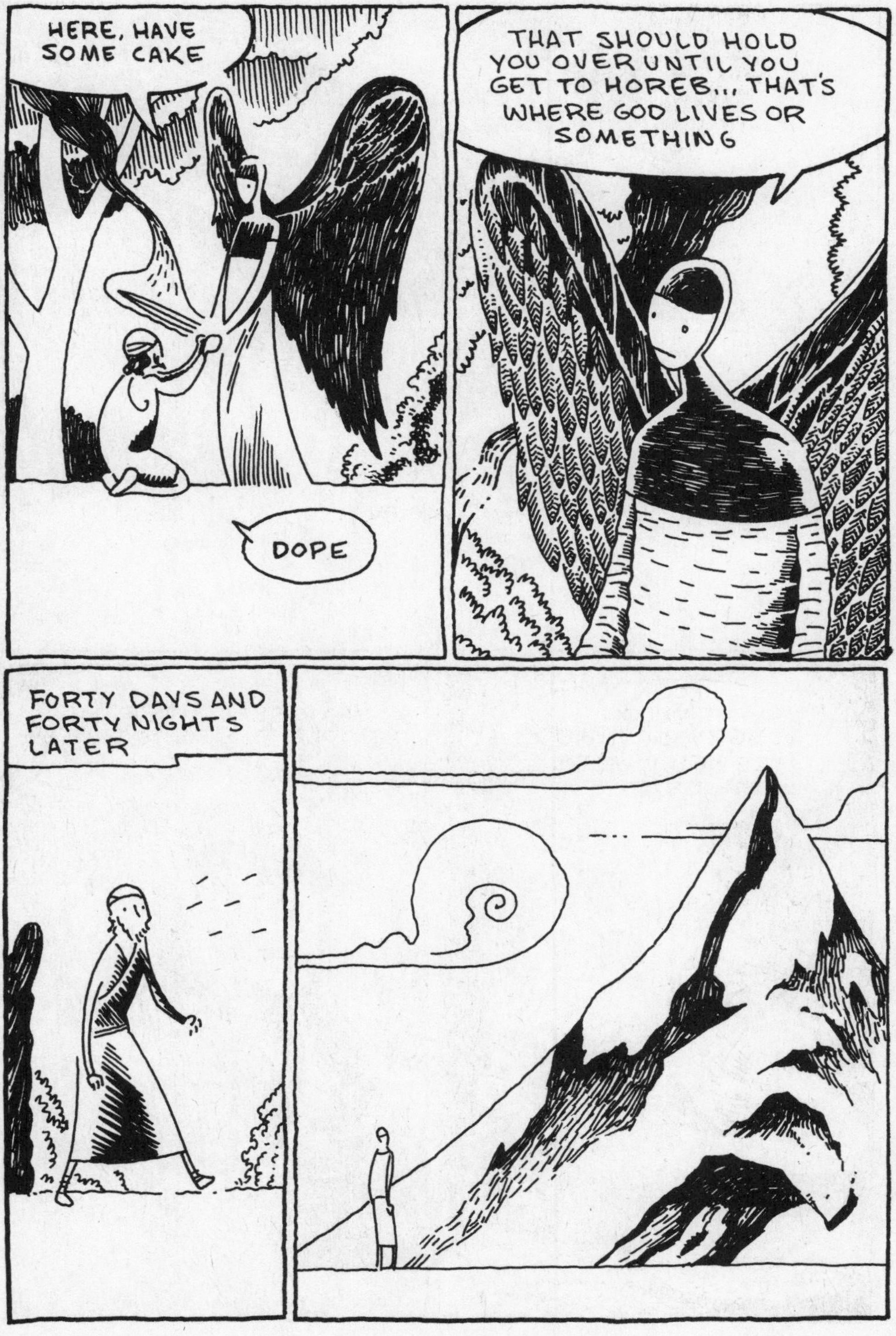
HERE, HAVE SOME CAKE
DOPE
THAT SHOULD HOLD YOU OVER UNTIL YOU GET TO HOREB... THAT'S WHERE GOD LIVES OR SOMETHING
FORTY DAYS AND FORTY NIGHTS LATER

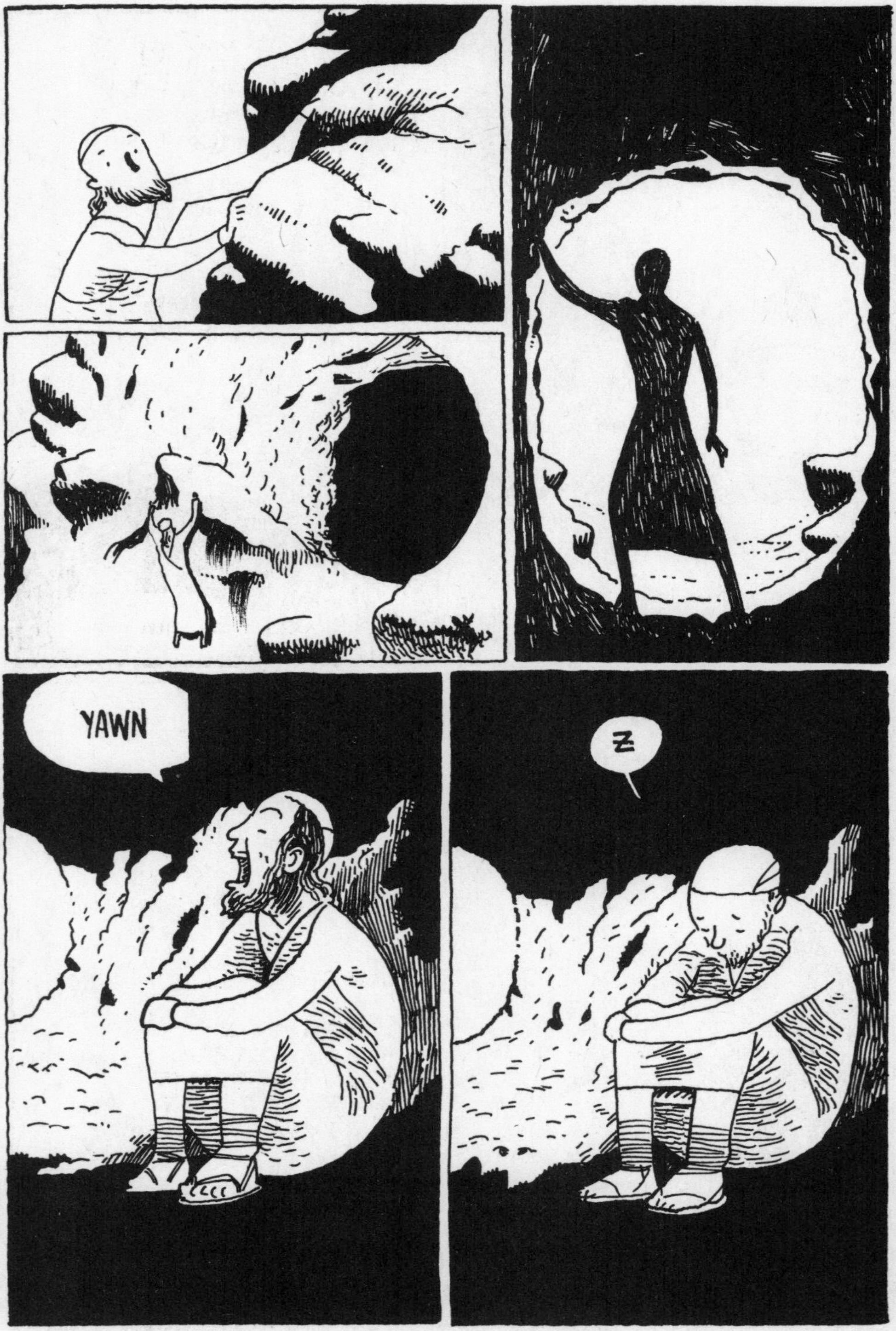
YAWN
Z

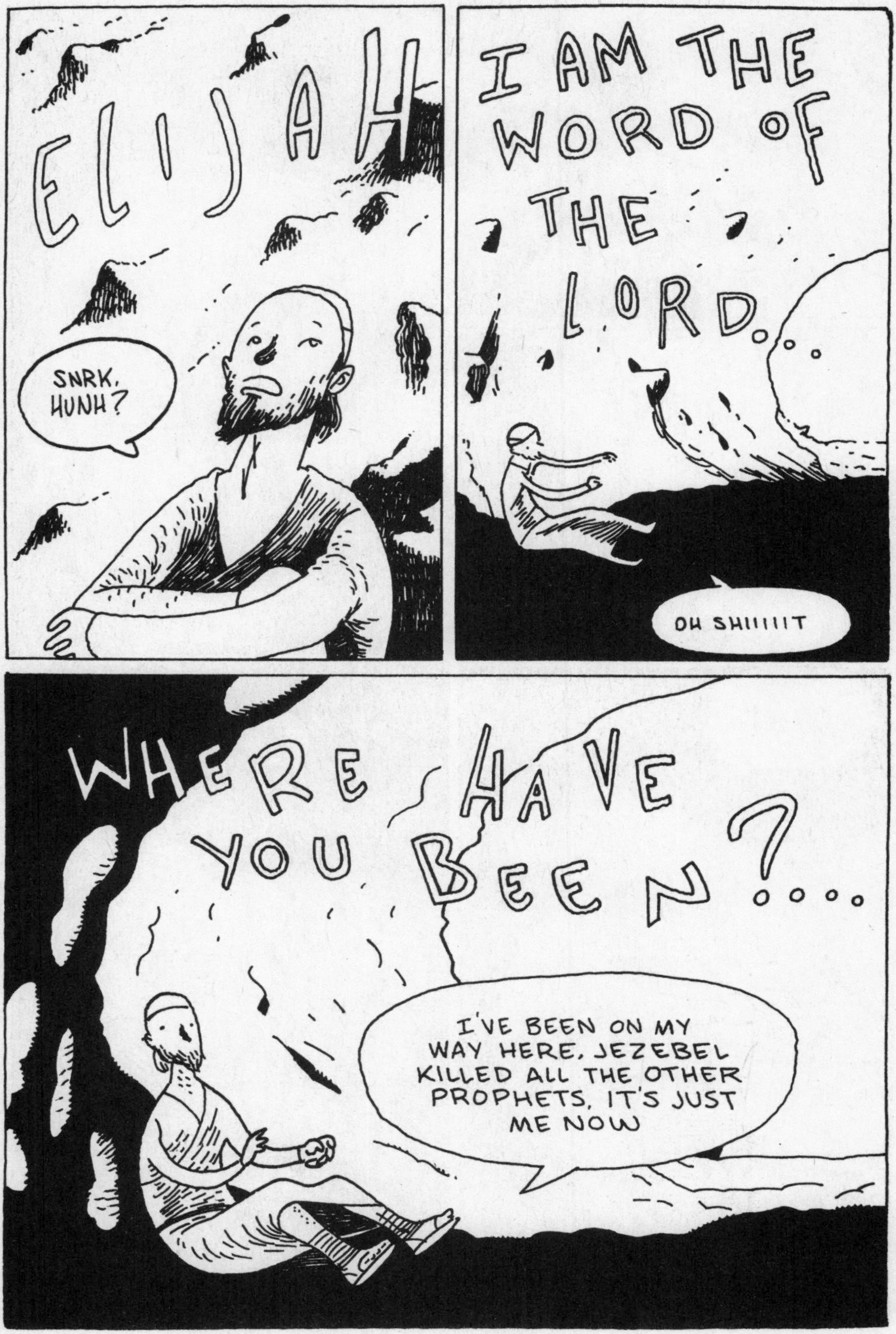
ELIJAH
SNRK, HUNH?
I AM THE WORD OF THE LORD...
OH SHIIIIIT
WHERE HAVE YOU BEEN?....
I'VE BEEN ON MY WAY HERE, JEZEBEL KILLED ALL THE OTHER PROPHETS, IT'S JUST ME NOW

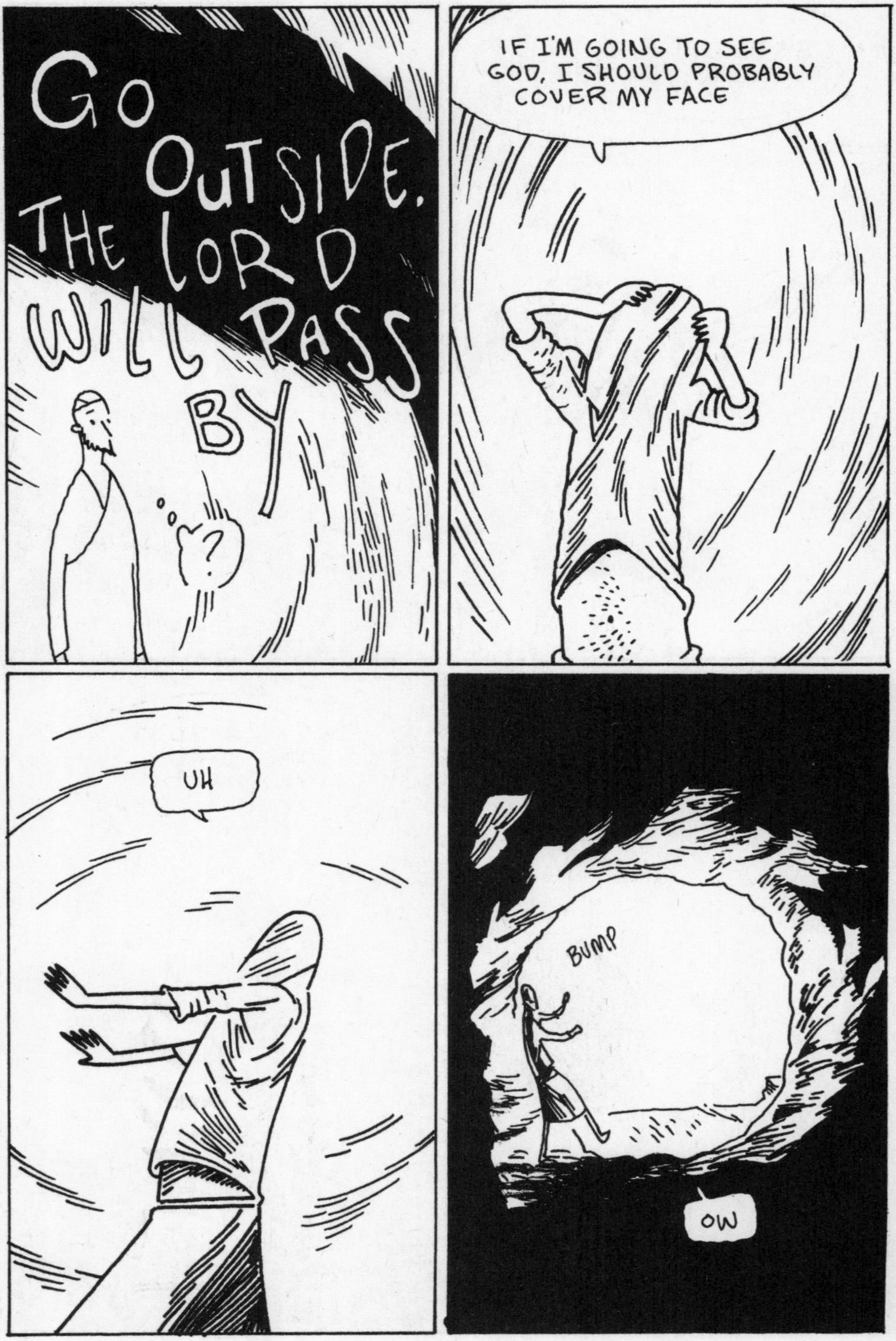
GO OUTSIDE. THE LORD WILL PASS BY
?
IF I'M GOING TO SEE GOD, I SHOULD PROBABLY COVER MY FACE
UH
BUMP
OW

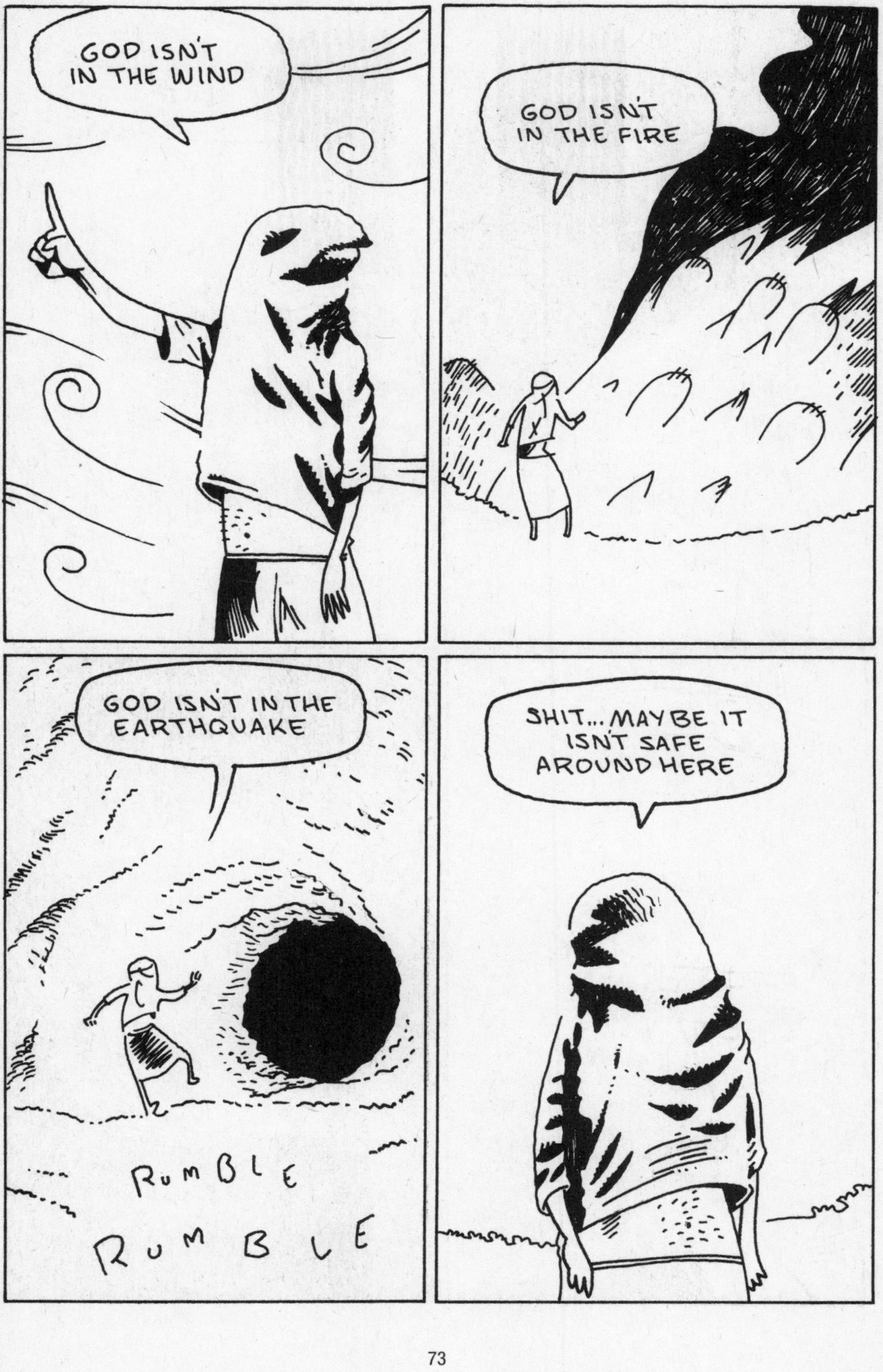
GOD ISN'T IN THE WIND
GOD ISN'T IN THE FIRE
GOD ISN'T IN THE EARTHQUAKE
RUMBLE
RUMBLE
SHIT... MAYBE IT ISN'T SAFE AROUND HERE

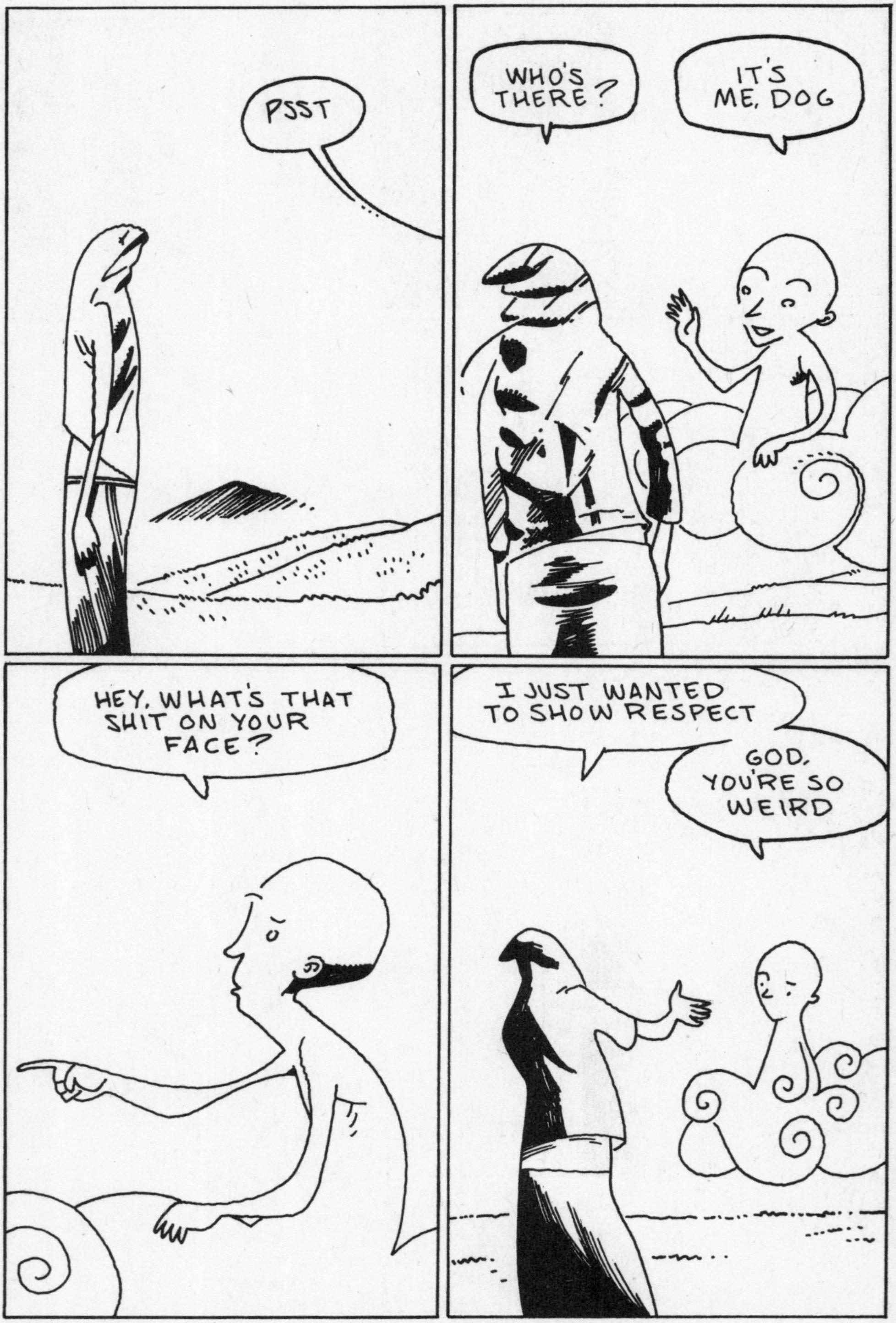
PSST
WHO'S THERE?
IT'S ME, DOG
HEY, WHAT'S THAT SHIT ON YOUR FACE?
I JUST WANTED TO SHOW RESPECT
GOD, YOU'RE SO WEIRD

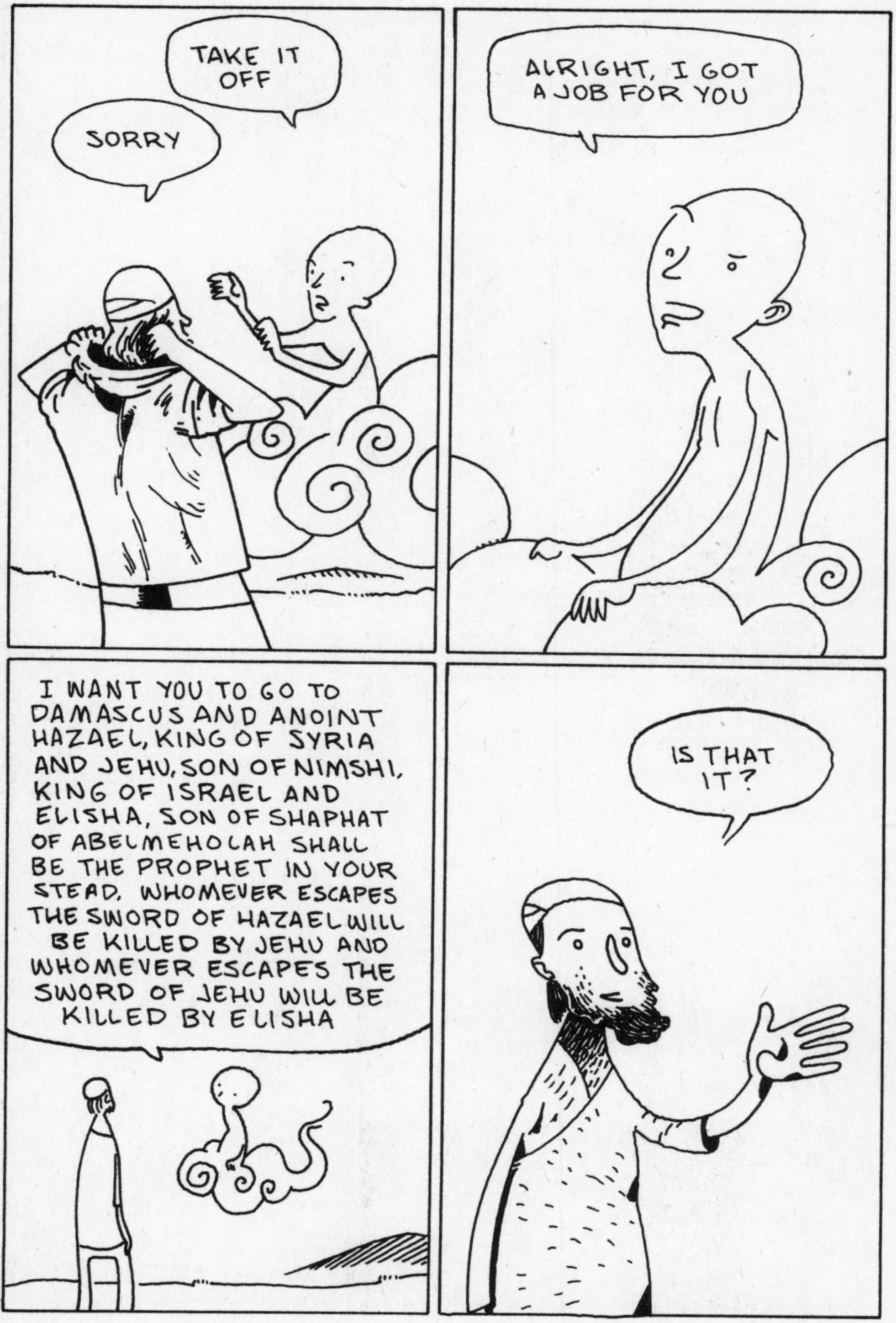
TAKE IT OFF
SORRY
ALRIGHT, I GOT A JOB FOR YOU
I WANT YOU TO GO TO DAMASCUS AND ANOINT HAZAEL, KING OF SYRIA AND JEHU, SON OF NIMSHI, KING OF ISRAEL AND ELISHA, SON OF SHAPHAT OF ABELMEHOLAH SHALL BE THE PROPHET IN YOUR STEAD. WHOMEVER ESCAPES THE SWORD OF HAZAEL WILL BE KILLED BY JEHU AND WHOMEVER ESCAPES THE SWORD OF JEHU WILL BE KILLED BY ELISHA
IS THAT IT?

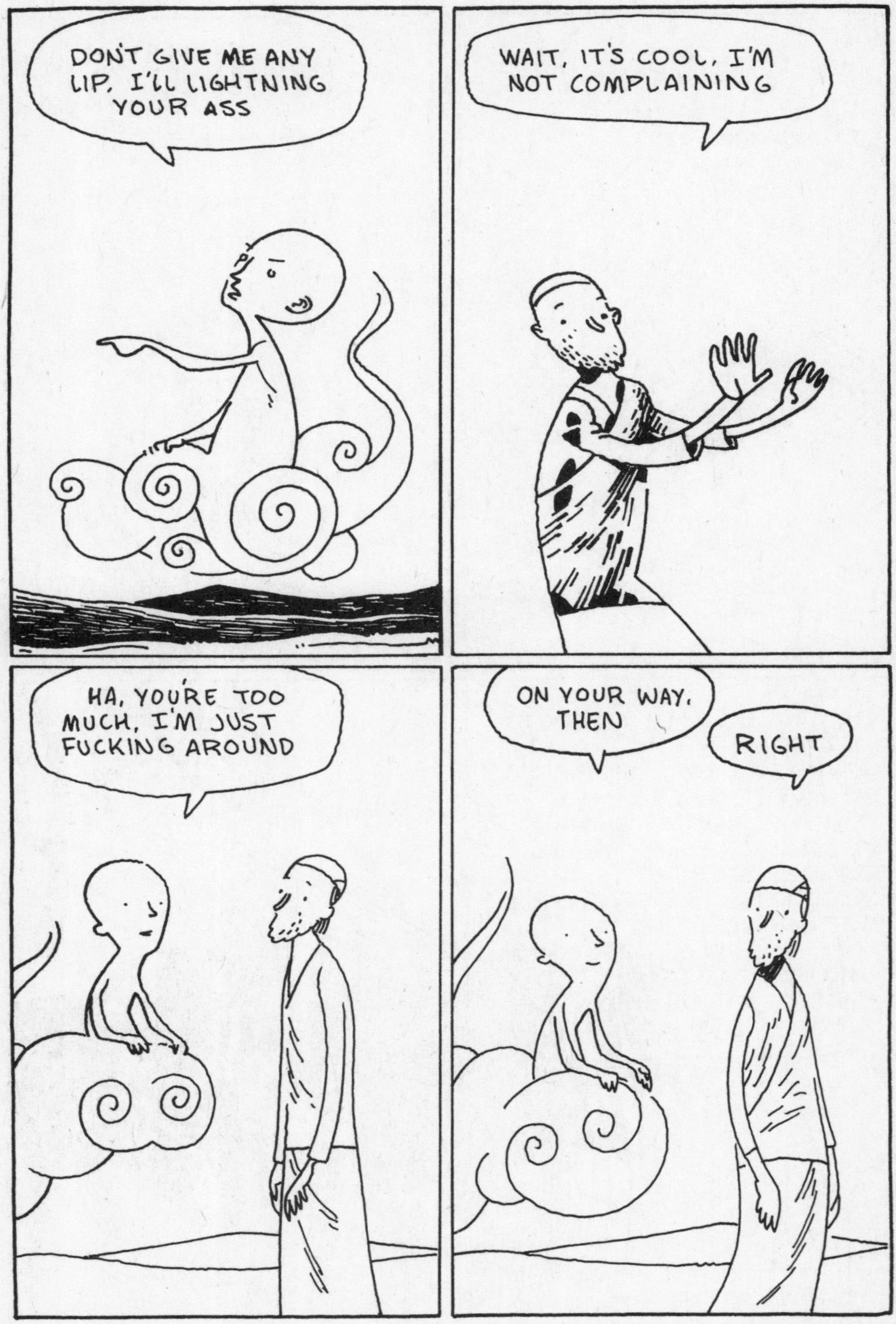
DON'T GIVE ME ANY LIP. I'LL LIGHTNING YOUR ASS
WAIT, IT'S COOL, I'M NOT COMPLAINING
HA, YOU'RE TOO MUCH, I'M JUST FUCKING AROUND
ON YOUR WAY, THEN
RIGHT

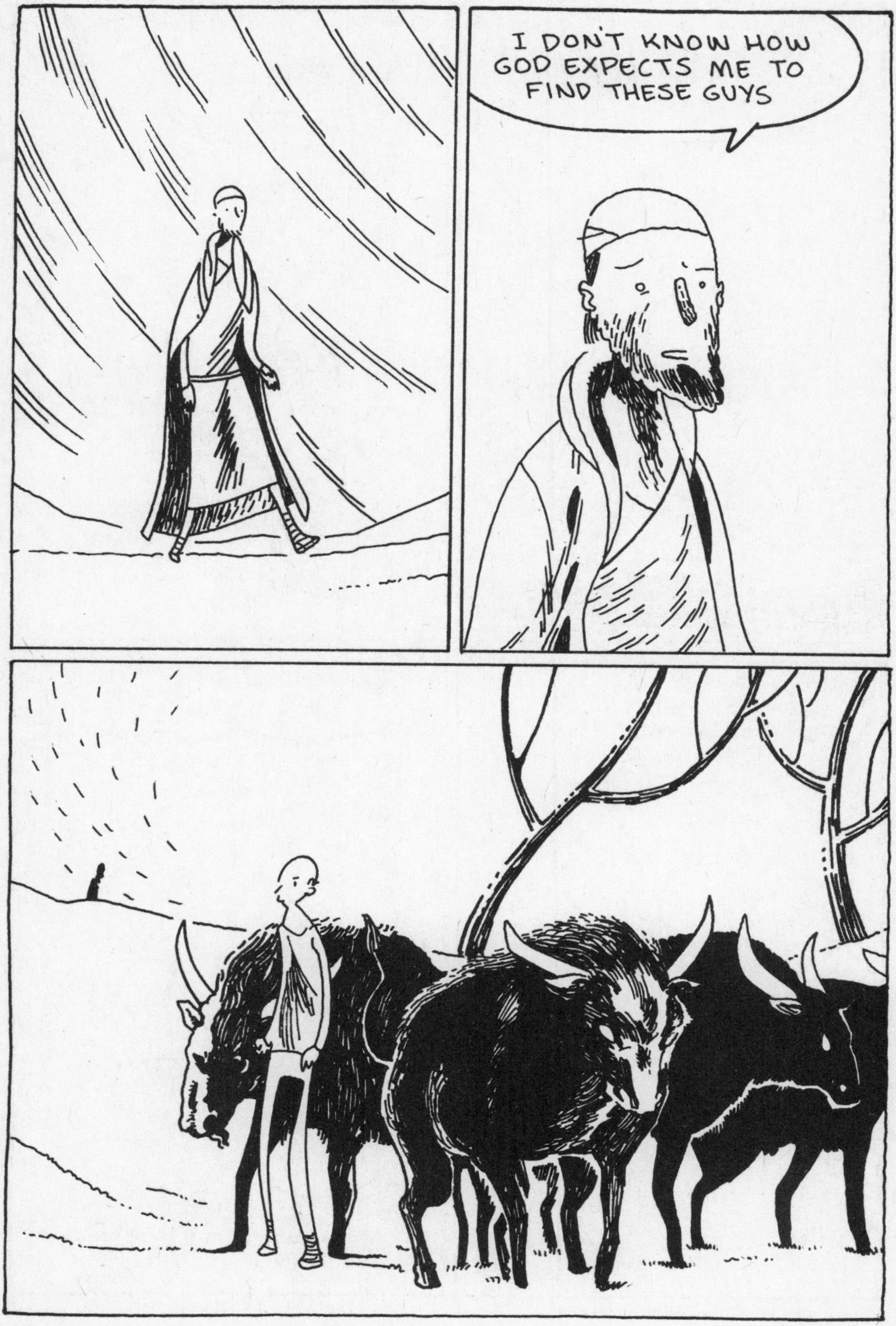
I DON'T KNOW HOW GOD EXPECTS ME TO FIND THESE GUYS

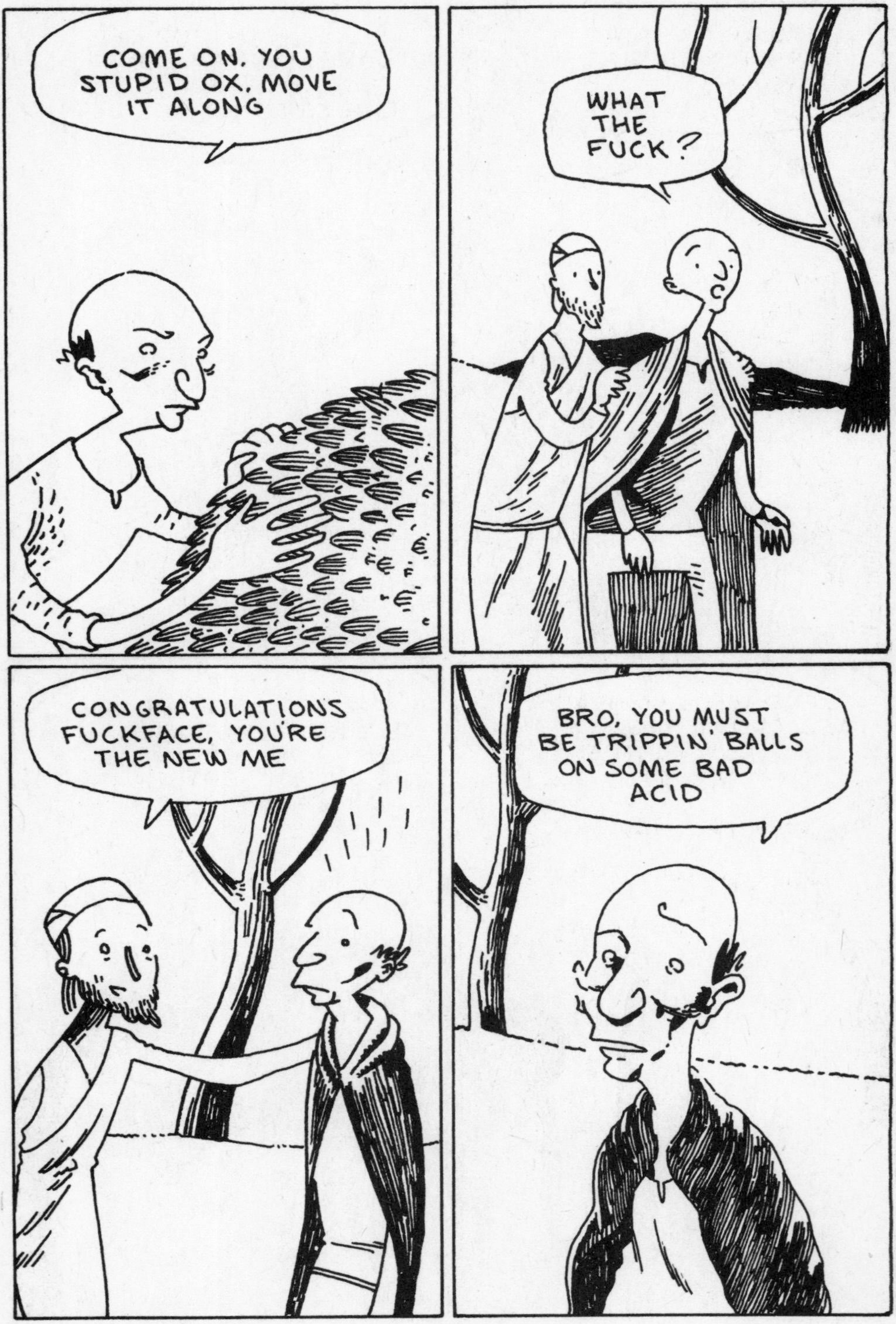
COME ON. YOU STUPID OX. MOVE IT ALONG
WHAT THE FUCK?
CONGRATULATIONS FUCKFACE, YOU'RE THE NEW ME
BRO, YOU MUST BE TRIPPIN' BALLS ON SOME BAD ACID

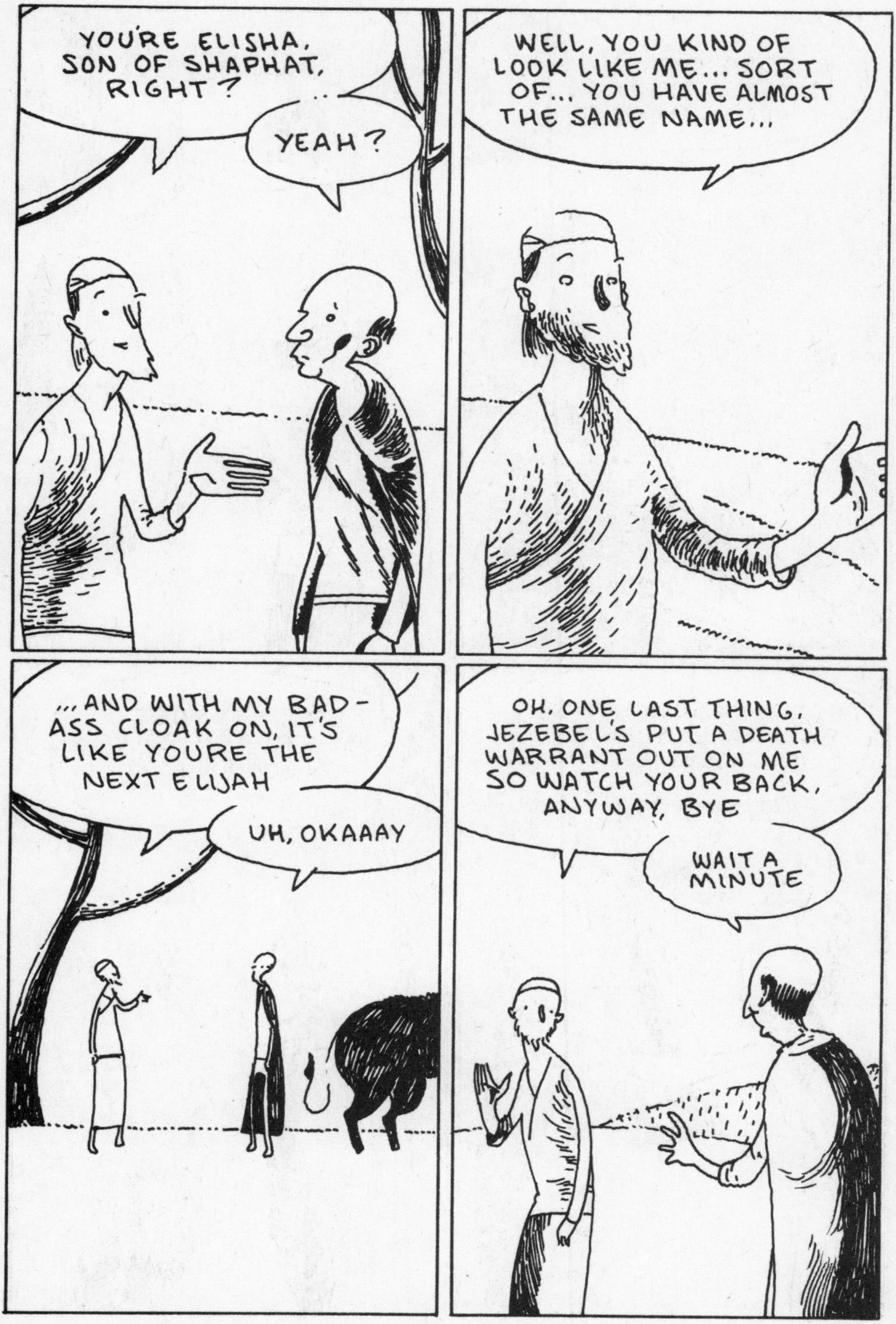
YOU'RE ELISHA, SON OF SHAPHAT, RIGHT?
YEAH?
WELL, YOU KIND OF LOOK LIKE ME... SORT OF... YOU HAVE ALMOST THE SAME NAME...
...AND WITH MY BAD-ASS CLOAK ON, IT'S LIKE YOURE THE NEXT ELIJAH
UH, OKAAAY
OH, ONE LAST THING, JEZEBEL'S PUT A DEATH WARRANT OUT ON ME SO WATCH YOUR BACK, ANYWAY, BYE
WAIT A MINUTE

I WANT TO GO WITH YOU BUT FIRST I GOTTA SAY GOOD-BYE TO MY MOM AND POPS

UH

...SO, THIS GUY CAME OUT OF THE DESERT, PUT HIS CLOTHES ON ME AND SAID IT WAS GOD'S WILL

BUT SON, WITHOUT YOU TO PLOW THE FIELD, HOW WILL WE EAT?

THE OXEN

SNAP

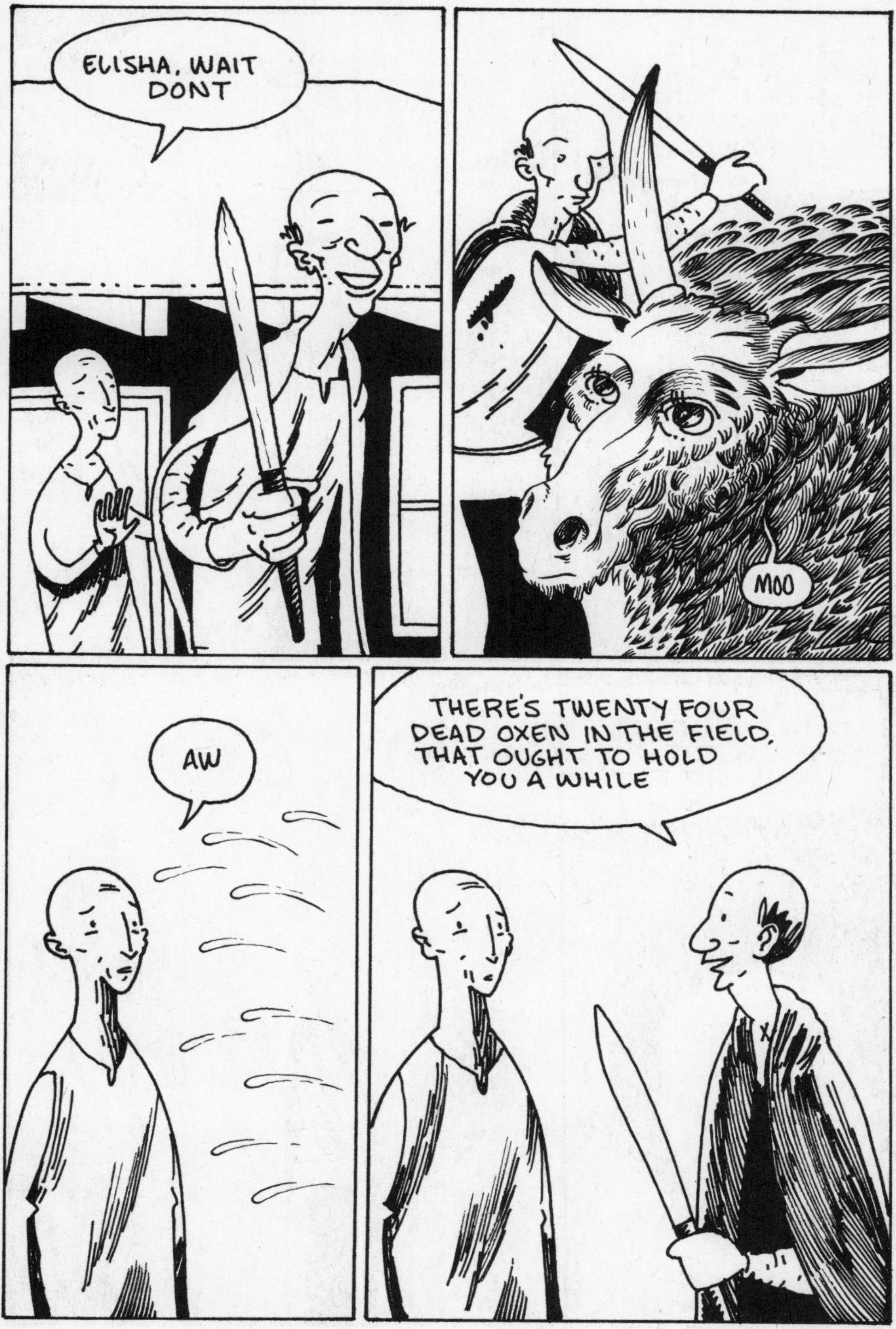
ELISHA, WAIT
DONT
MOO
AW
THERE'S TWENTY FOUR DEAD OXEN IN THE FIELD, THAT OUGHT TO HOLD YOU A WHILE

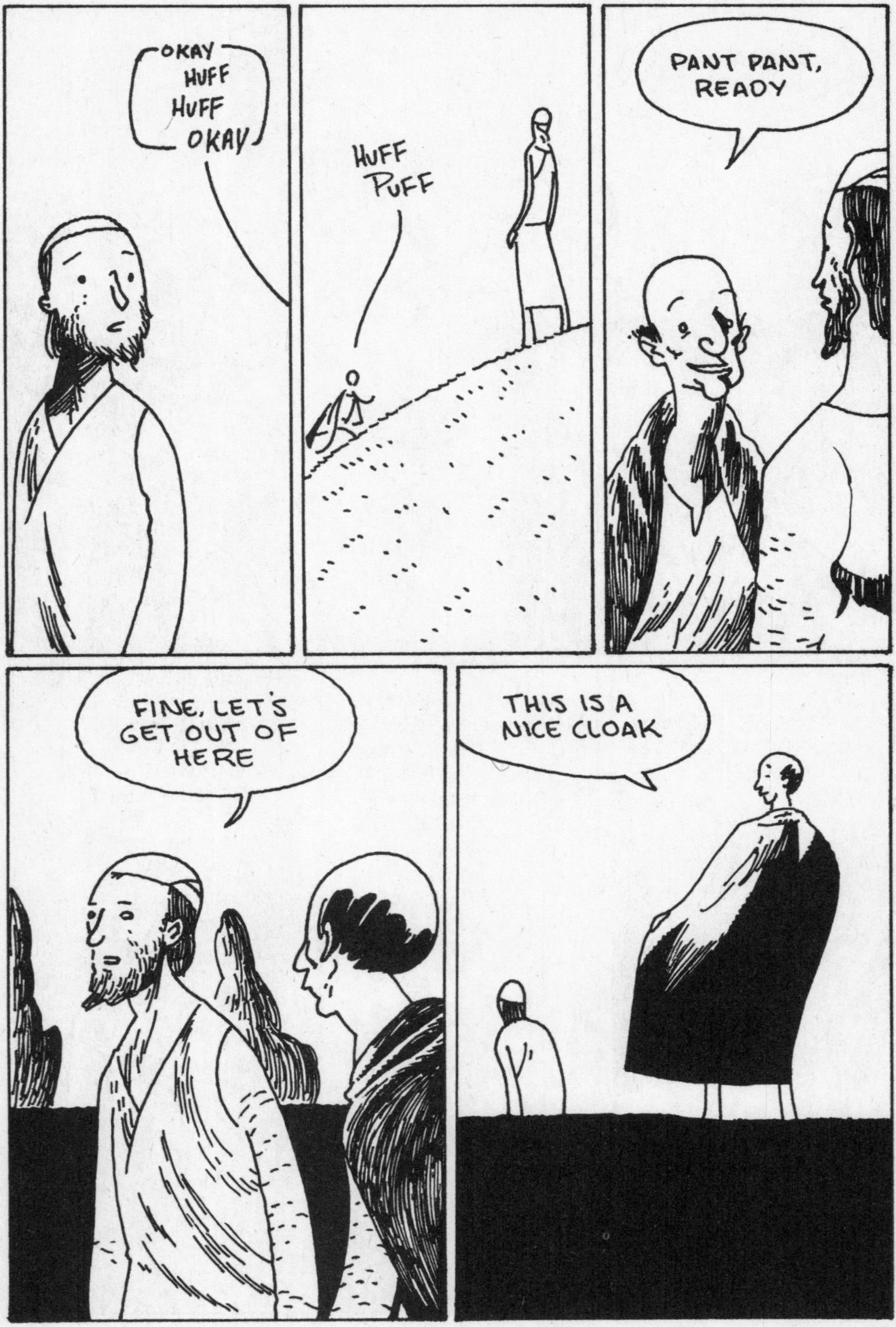
OKAY
HUFF
HUFF
OKAY
HUFF
PUFF
PANT PANT,
READY
FINE, LET'S
GET OUT OF
HERE
THIS IS A
NICE CLOAK

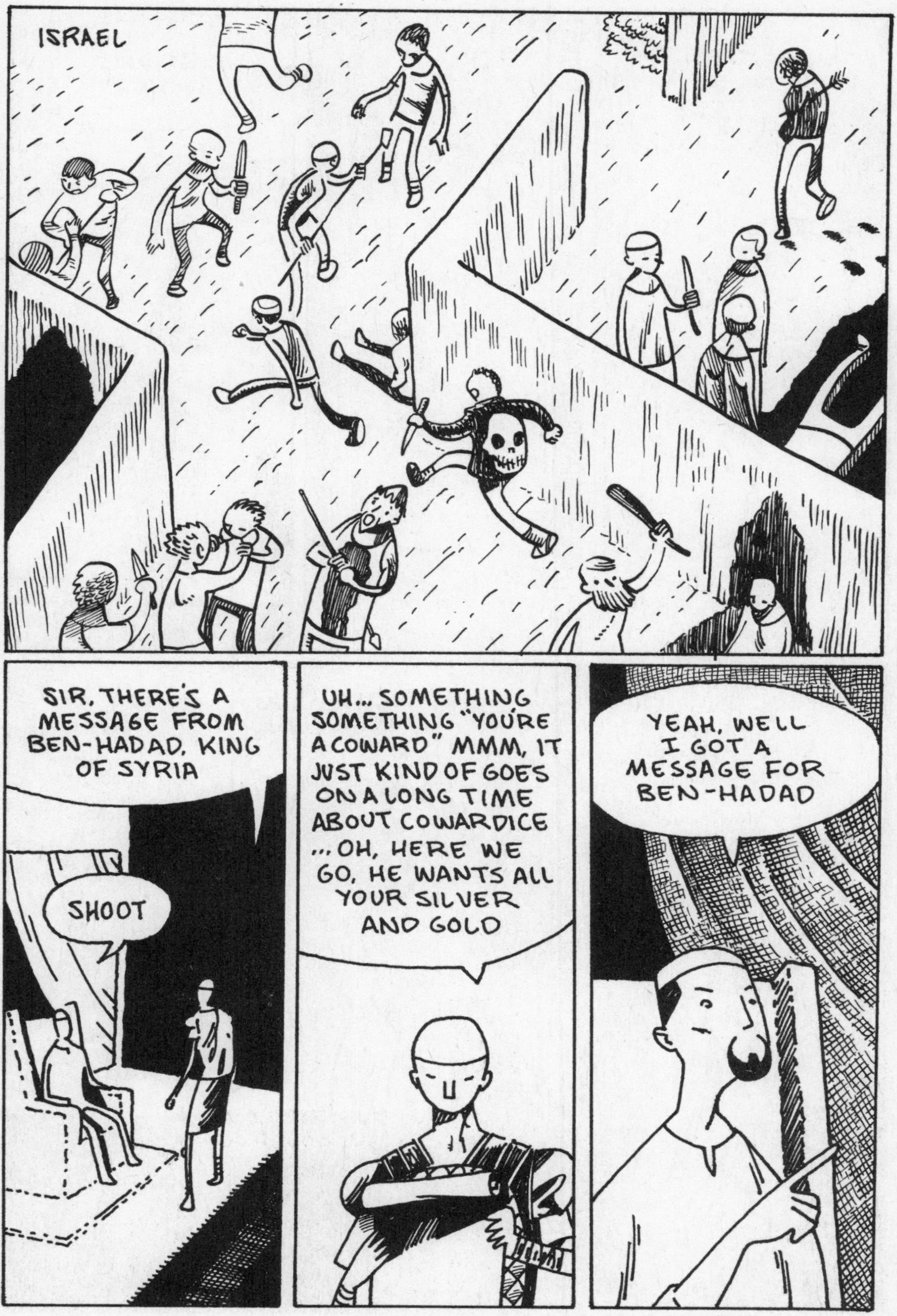
ISRAEL
SIR, THERE'S A MESSAGE FROM BEN-HADAD, KING OF SYRIA
SHOOT
UH... SOMETHING SOMETHING "YOU'RE A COWARD" MMM, IT JUST KIND OF GOES ON A LONG TIME ABOUT COWARDICE ...OH, HERE WE GO, HE WANTS ALL YOUR SILVER AND GOLD
YEAH, WELL I GOT A MESSAGE FOR BEN-HADAD

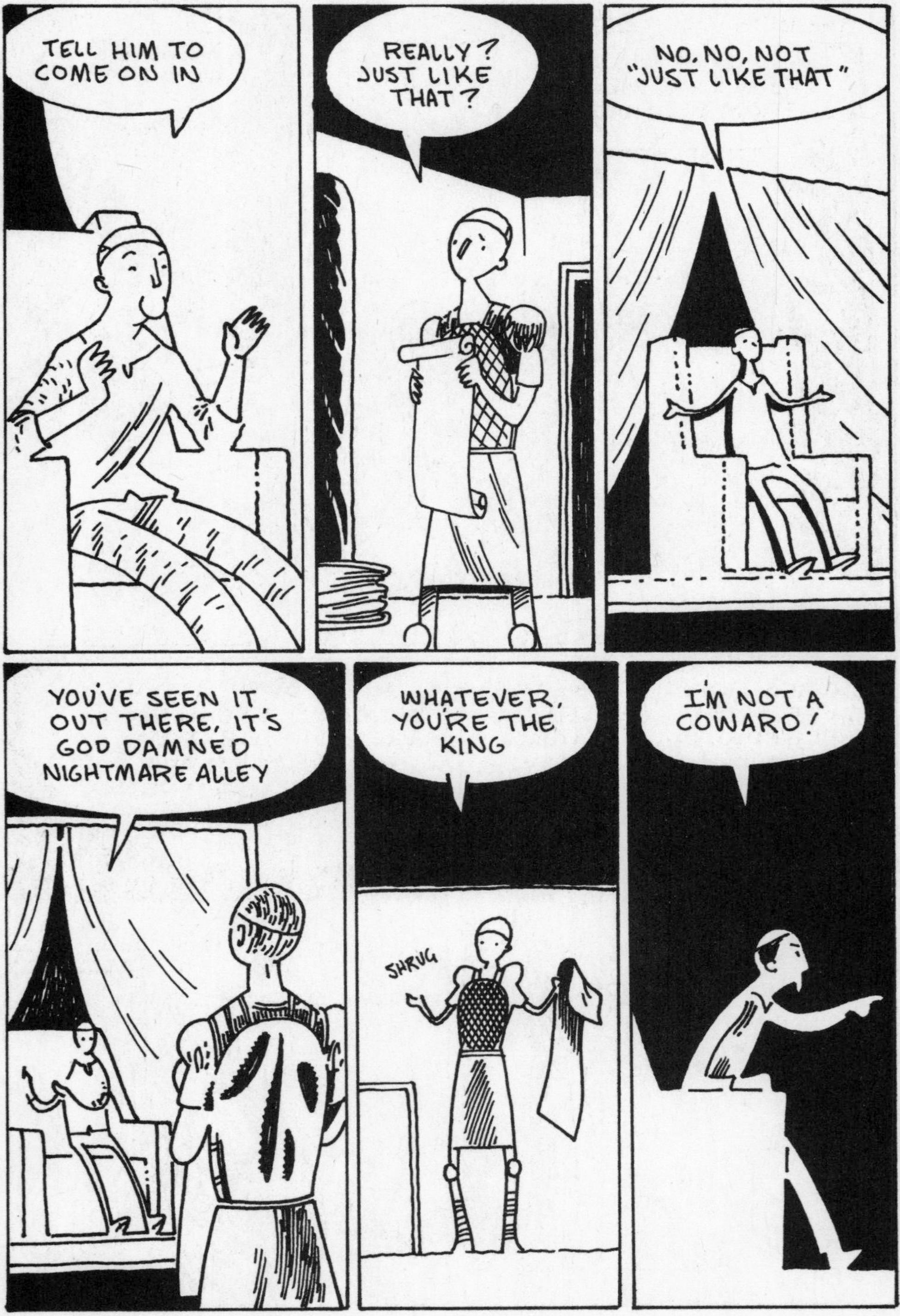
TELL HIM TO COME ON IN
REALLY? JUST LIKE THAT?
NO, NO, NOT "JUST LIKE THAT"
YOU'VE SEEN IT OUT THERE, IT'S GOD DAMNED NIGHTMARE ALLEY
WHATEVER, YOU'RE THE KING
SHRUG
I'M NOT A COWARD!

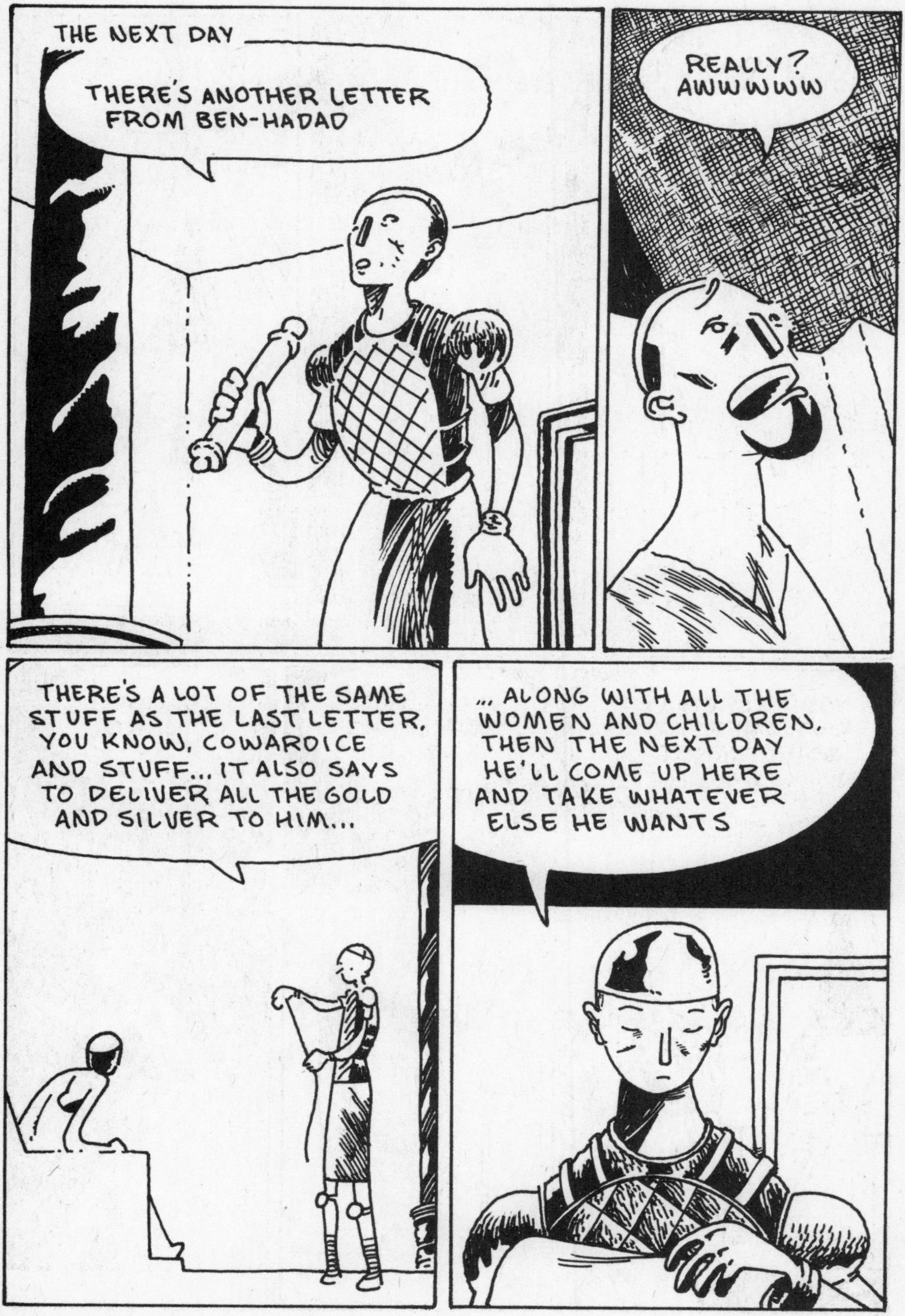
THE NEXT DAY
THERE'S ANOTHER LETTER FROM BEN-HADAD
REALLY? AWWWWW
THERE'S A LOT OF THE SAME STUFF AS THE LAST LETTER. YOU KNOW, COWARDICE AND STUFF... IT ALSO SAYS TO DELIVER ALL THE GOLD AND SILVER TO HIM...
... ALONG WITH ALL THE WOMEN AND CHILDREN. THEN THE NEXT DAY HE'LL COME UP HERE AND TAKE WHATEVER ELSE HE WANTS

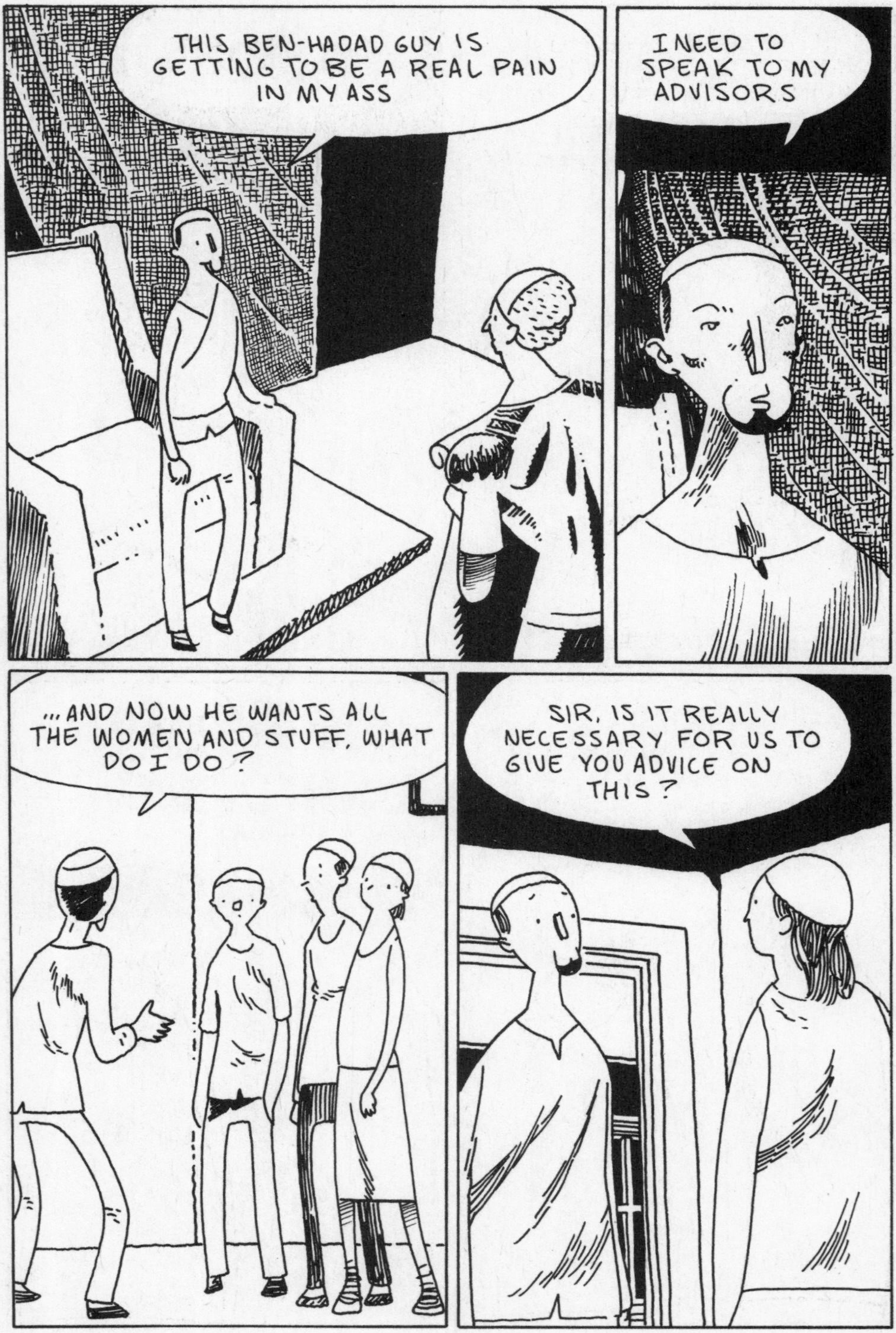
THIS BEN-HADAD GUY IS GETTING TO BE A REAL PAIN IN MY ASS
I NEED TO SPEAK TO MY ADVISORS
...AND NOW HE WANTS ALL THE WOMEN AND STUFF, WHAT DO I DO?
SIR, IS IT REALLY NECESSARY FOR US TO GIVE YOU ADVICE ON THIS?

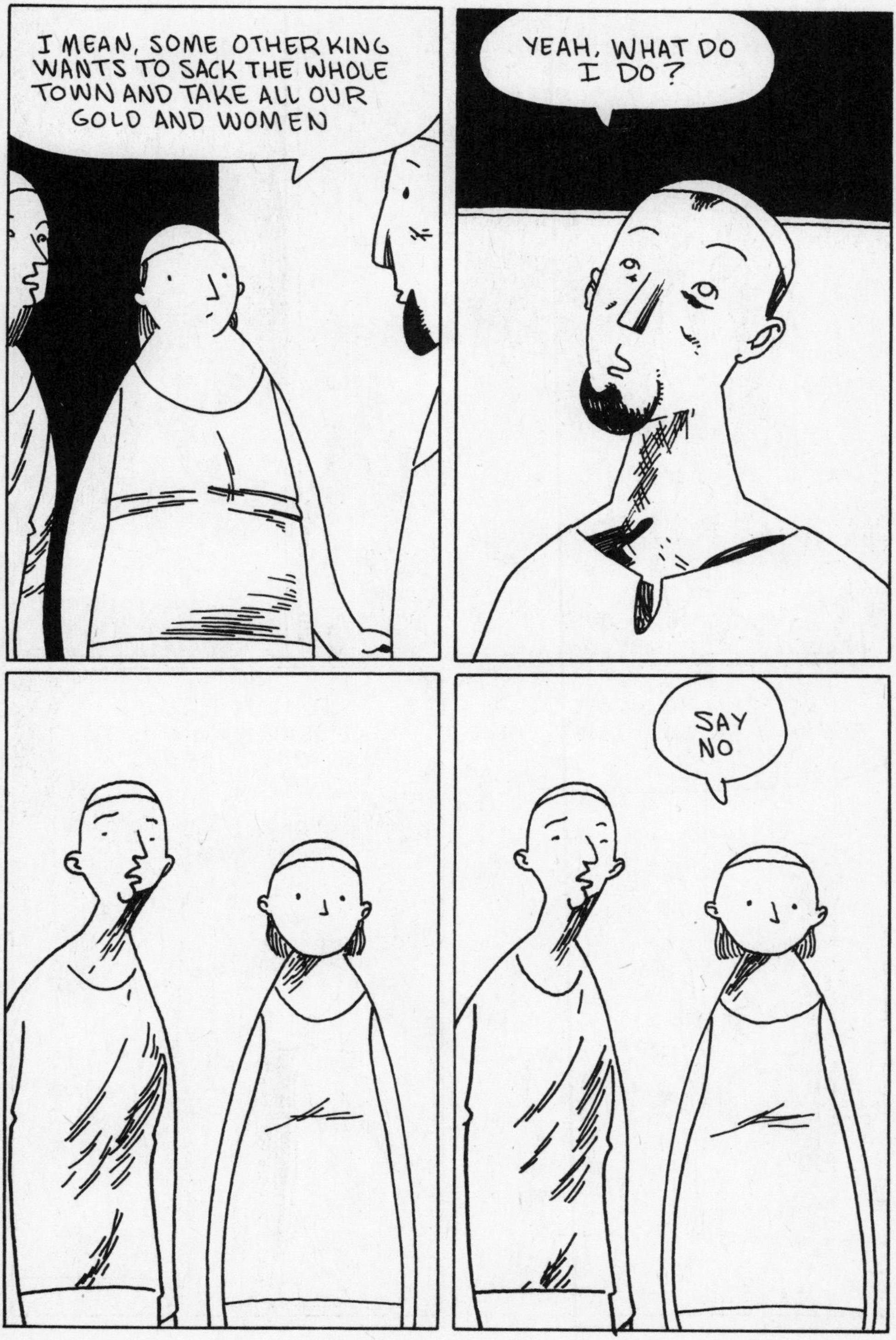
I MEAN, SOME OTHER KING WANTS TO SACK THE WHOLE TOWN AND TAKE ALL OUR GOLD AND WOMEN
YEAH, WHAT DO I DO?
SAY NO

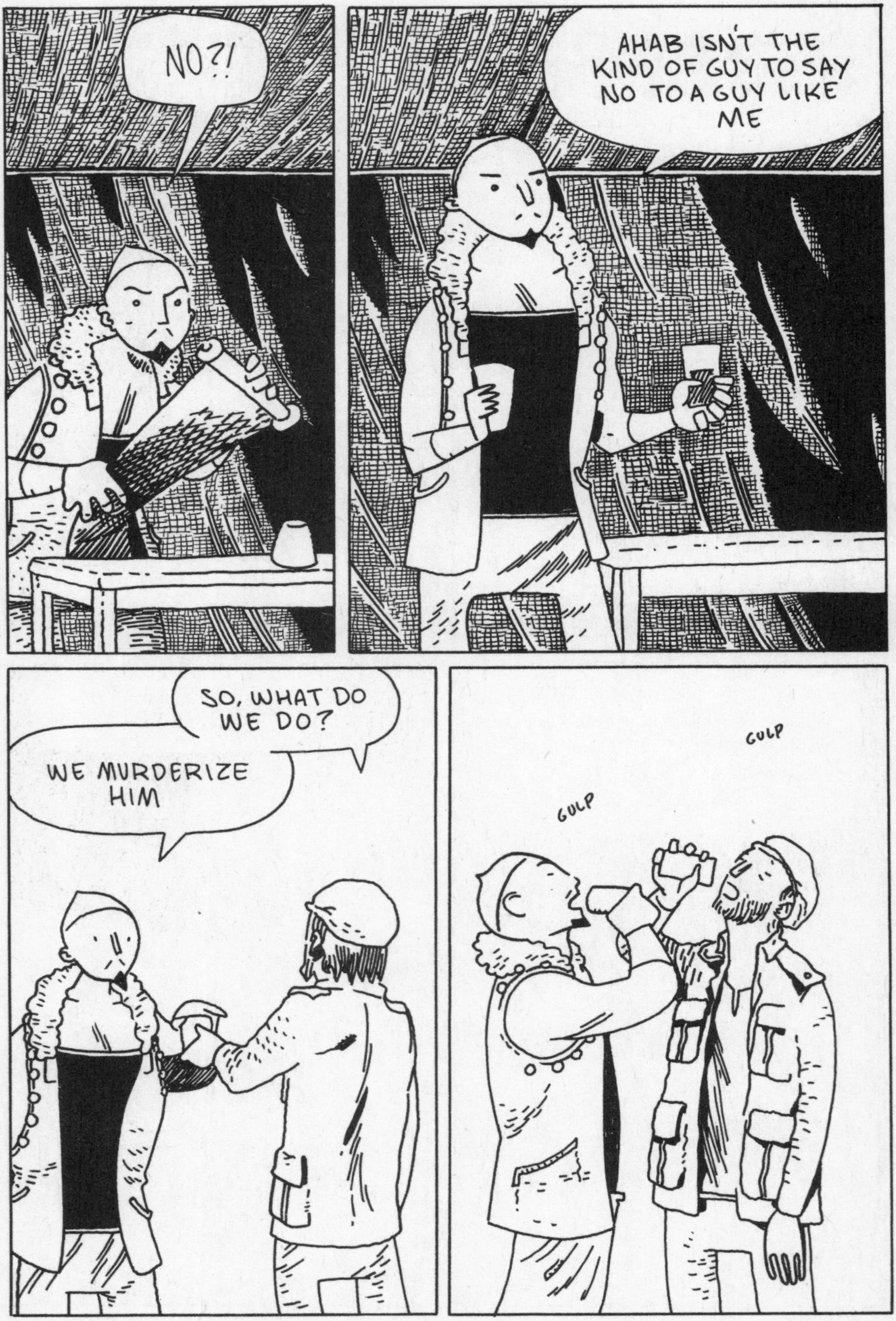
NO?!
AHAB ISN'T THE KIND OF GUY TO SAY NO TO A GUY LIKE ME
SO, WHAT DO WE DO?
WE MURDERIZE HIM
GULP
GULP

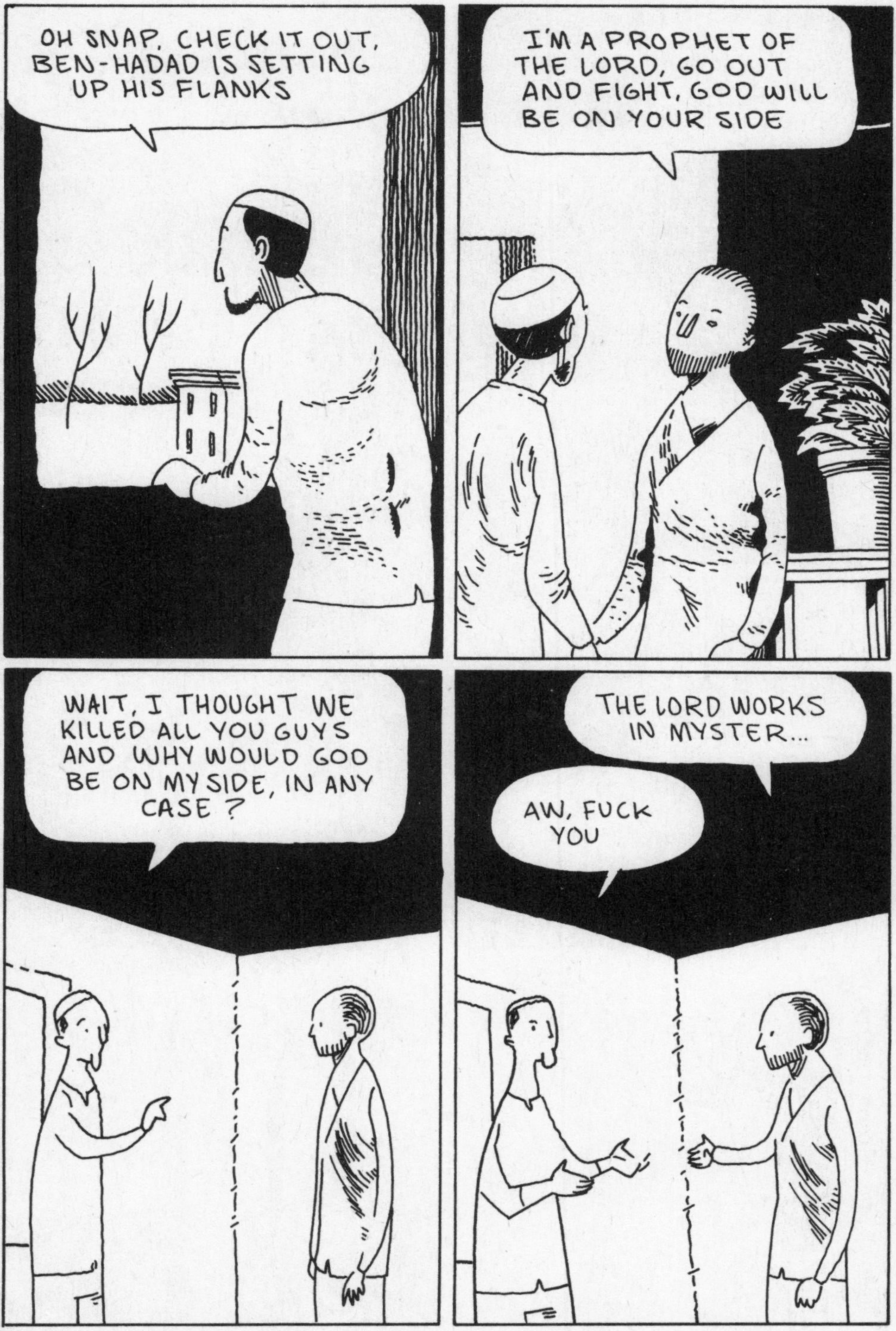
OH SNAP, CHECK IT OUT, BEN-HADAD IS SETTING UP HIS FLANKS
I'M A PROPHET OF THE LORD, GO OUT AND FIGHT, GOD WILL BE ON YOUR SIDE
WAIT, I THOUGHT WE KILLED ALL YOU GUYS AND WHY WOULD GOD BE ON MY SIDE, IN ANY CASE ?
THE LORD WORKS IN MYSTER...
AW, FUCK YOU

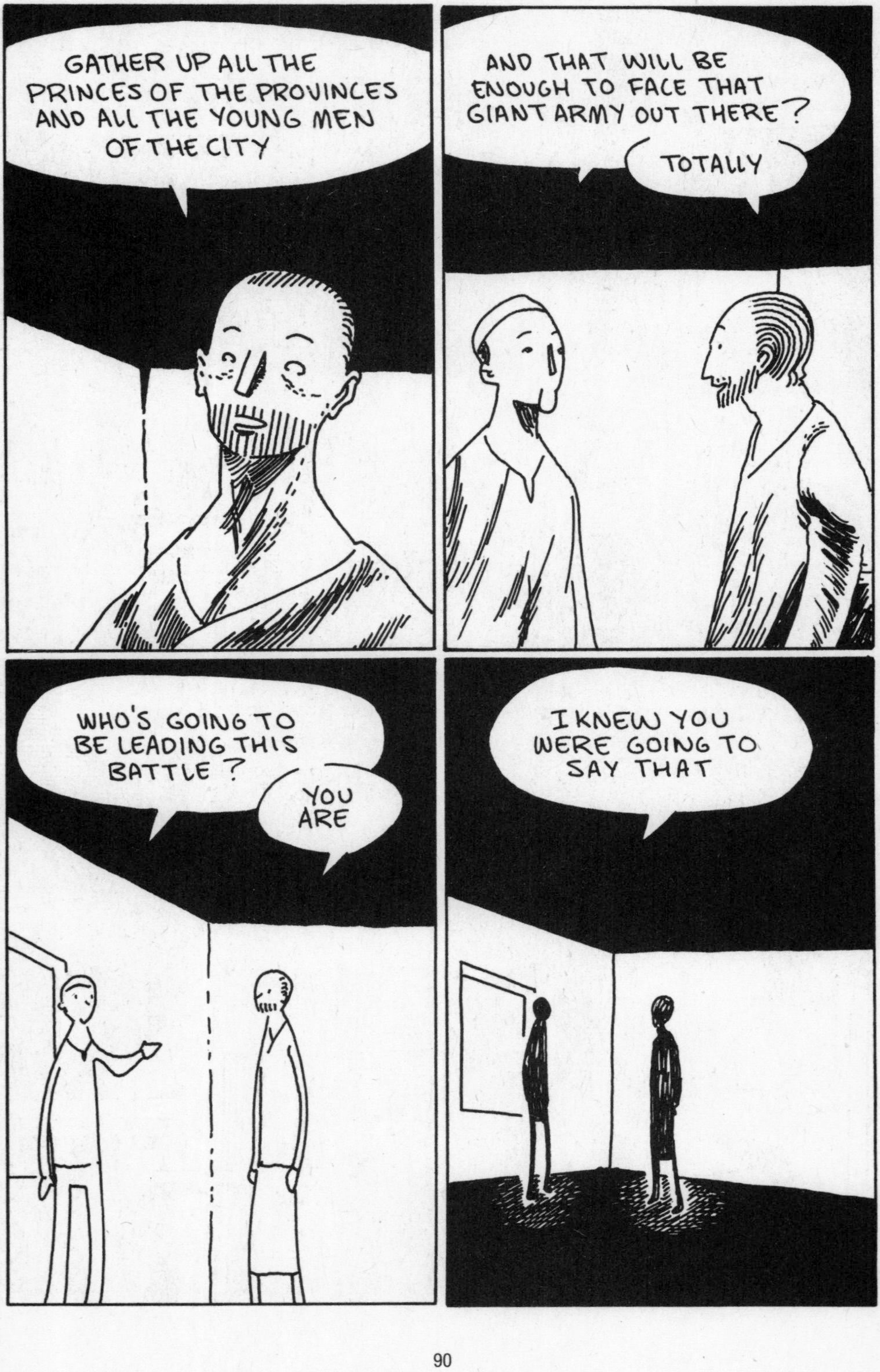
GATHER UP ALL THE PRINCES OF THE PROVINCES AND ALL THE YOUNG MEN OF THE CITY
AND THAT WILL BE ENOUGH TO FACE THAT GIANT ARMY OUT THERE?
TOTALLY
WHO'S GOING TO BE LEADING THIS BATTLE?
YOU ARE
I KNEW YOU WERE GOING TO SAY THAT

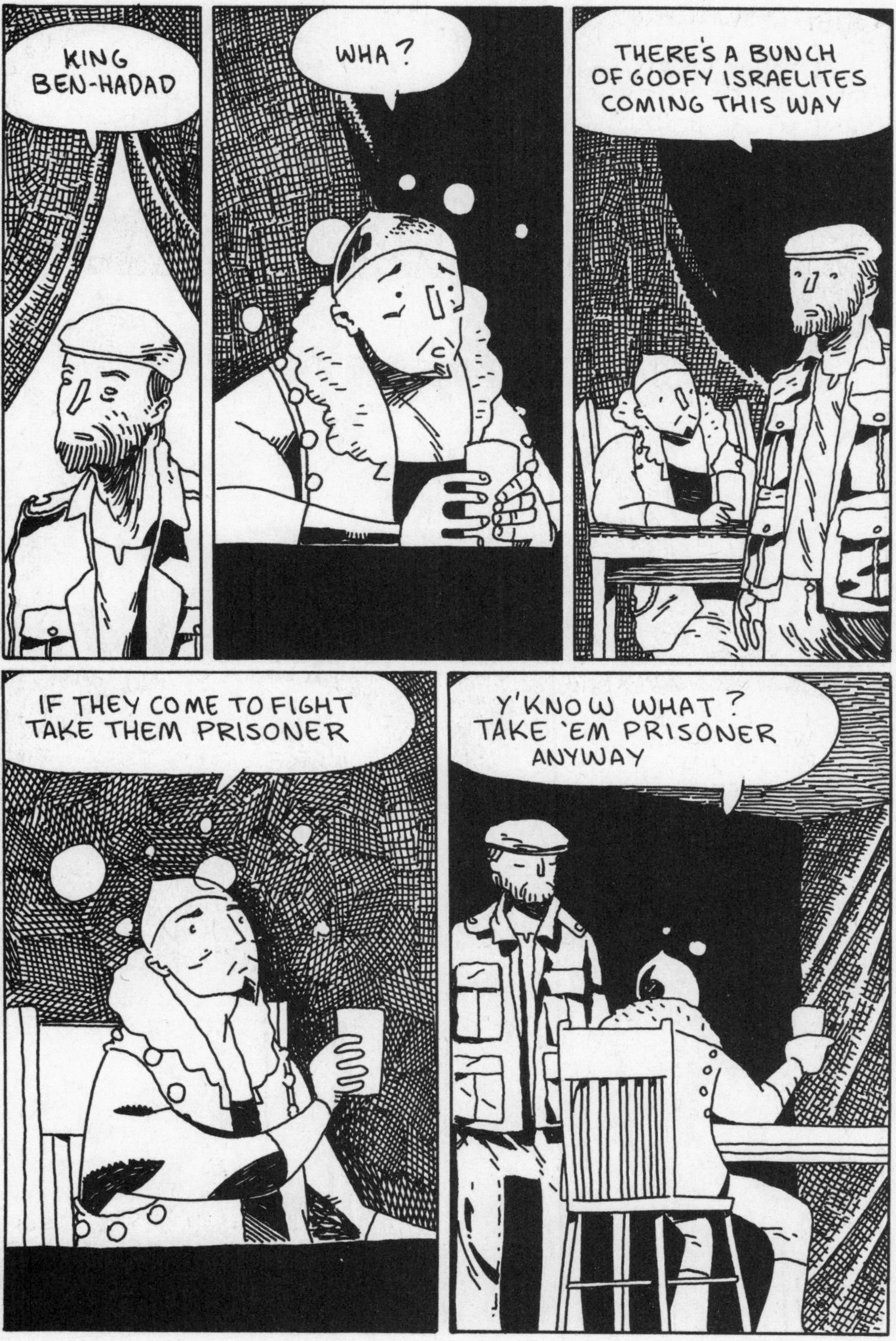
KING BEN-HADAD
WHA?
THERE'S A BUNCH OF GOOFY ISRAELITES COMING THIS WAY
IF THEY COME TO FIGHT TAKE THEM PRISONER
Y'KNOW WHAT? TAKE `EM PRISONER ANYWAY

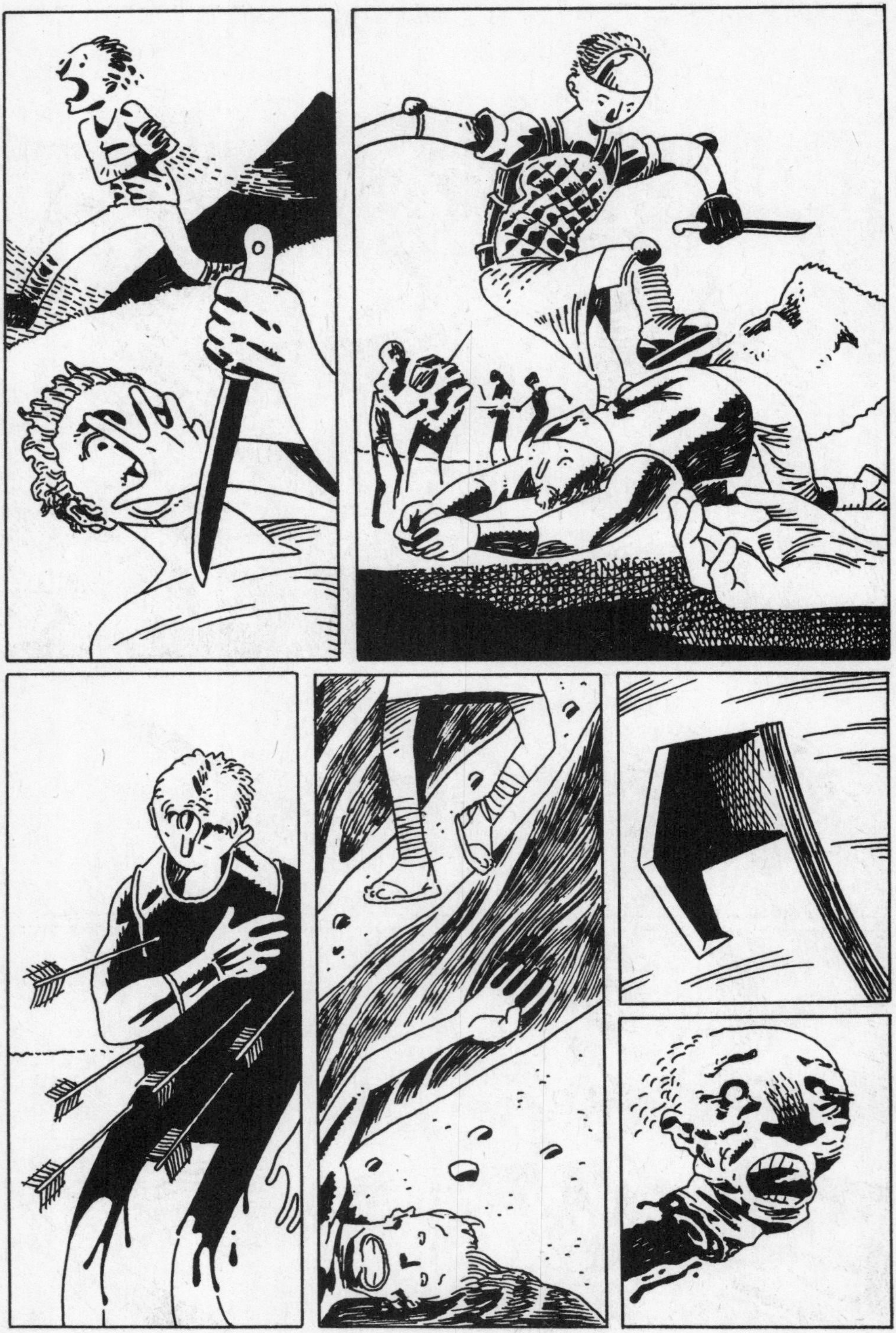

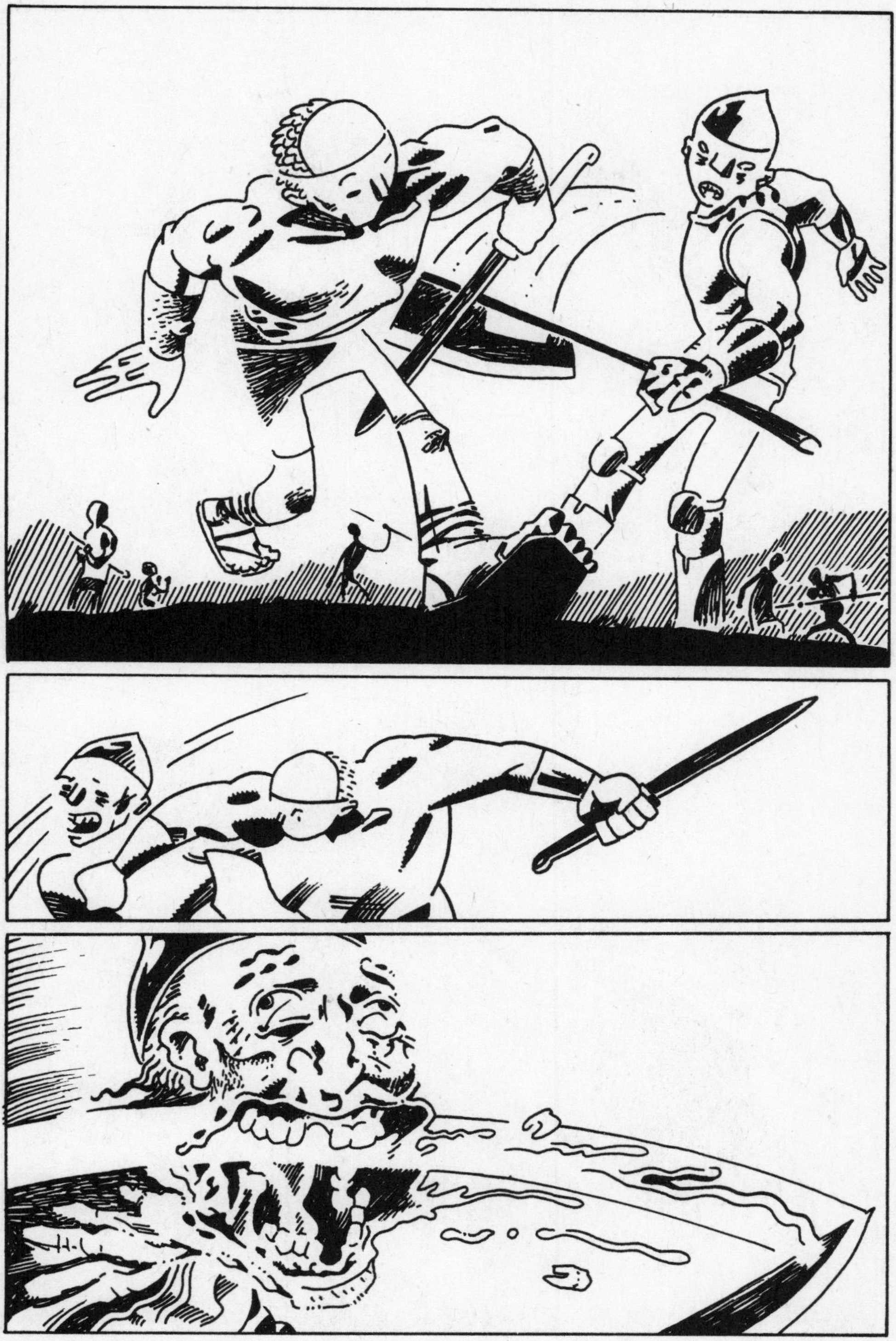

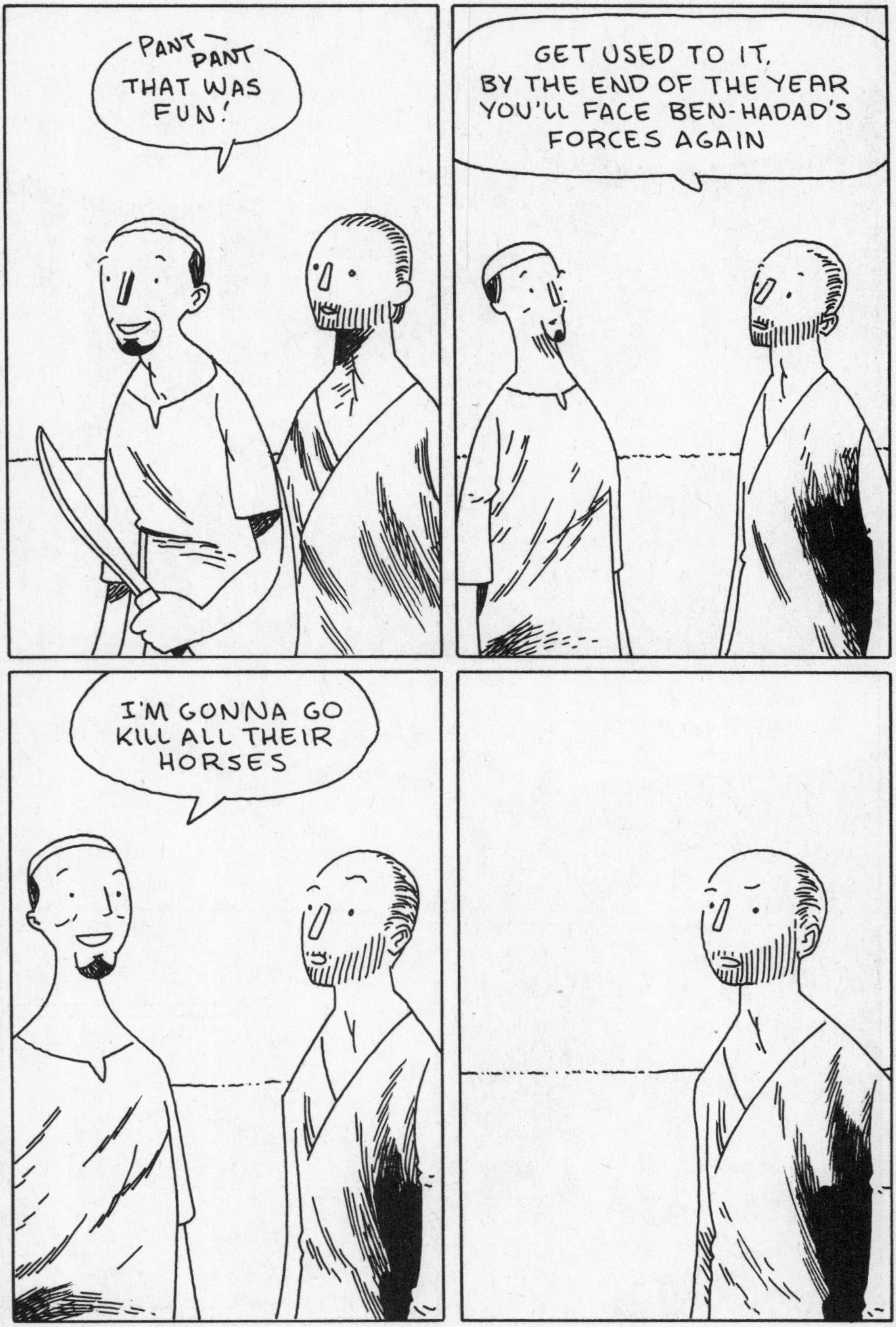
PANT—PANT
THAT WAS FUN!
GET USED TO IT, BY THE END OF THE YEAR YOU'LL FACE BEN-HADAD'S FORCES AGAIN
I'M GONNA GO KILL ALL THEIR HORSES

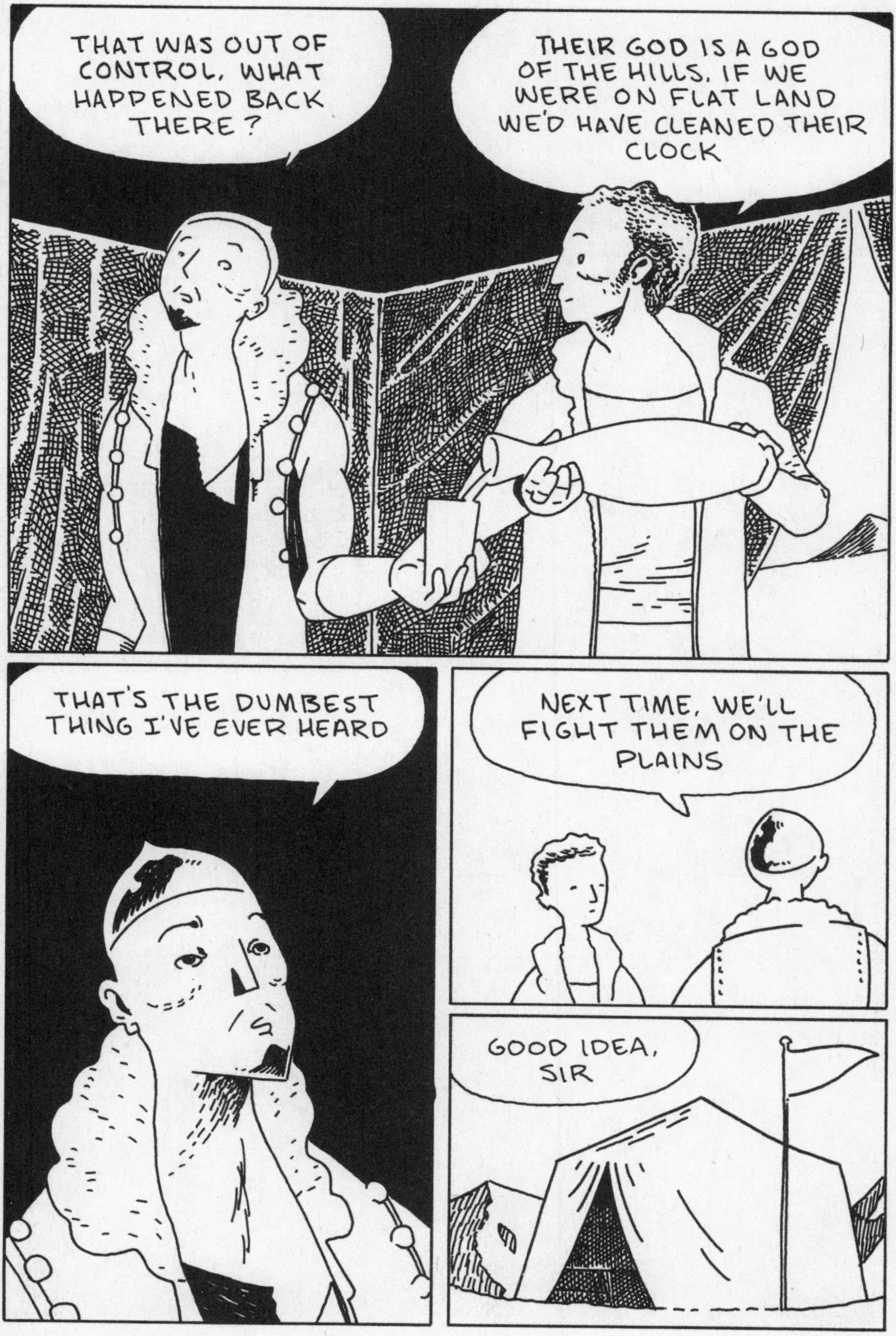
THAT WAS OUT OF CONTROL. WHAT HAPPENED BACK THERE?
THEIR GOD IS A GOD OF THE HILLS. IF WE WERE ON FLAT LAND WE'D HAVE CLEANED THEIR CLOCK
THAT'S THE DUMBEST THING I'VE EVER HEARD
NEXT TIME, WE'LL FIGHT THEM ON THE PLAINS
GOOD IDEA, SIR

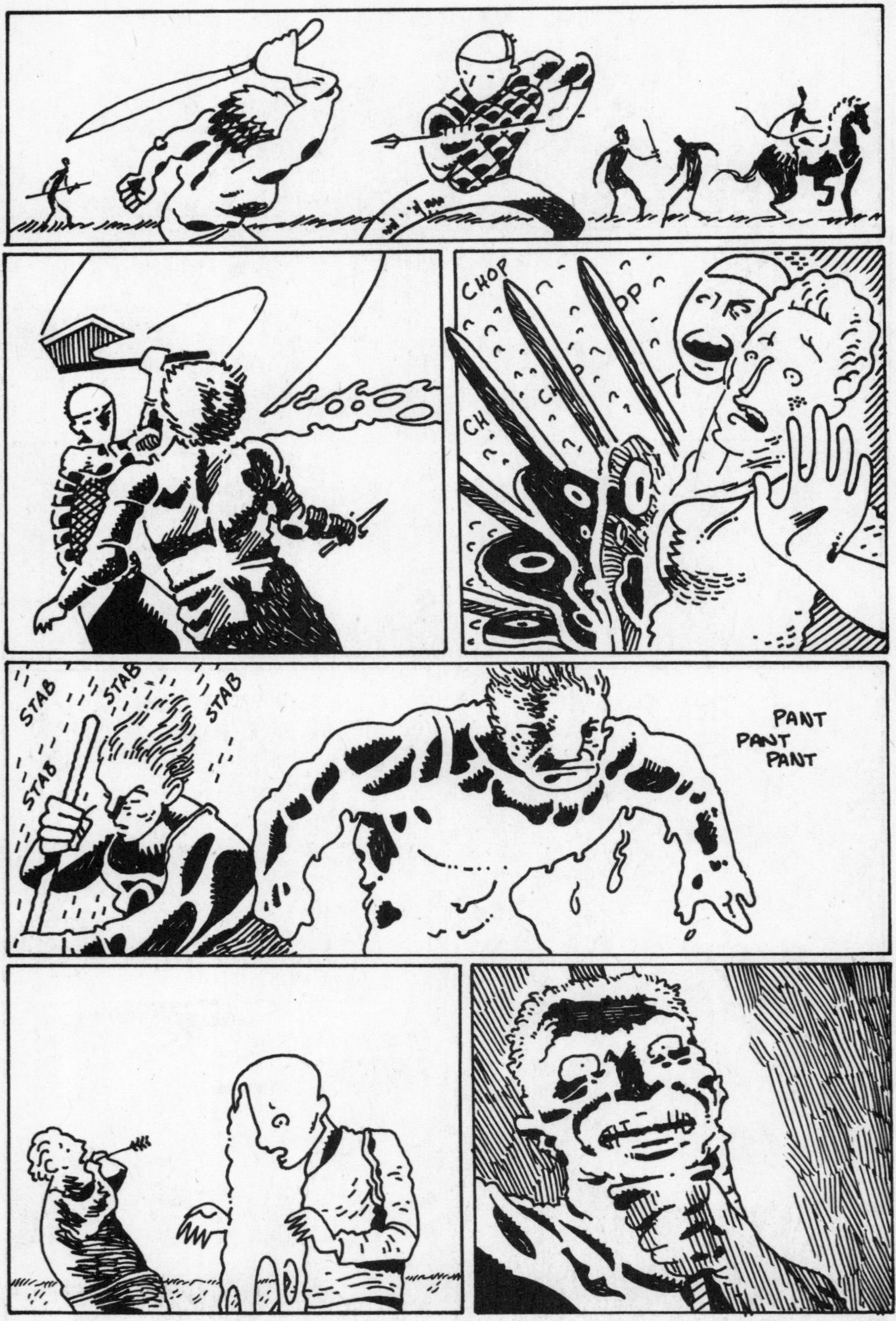
CHOP
CH
CH
PP
STAB
STAB
STAB
STAB
PANT
PANT
PANT

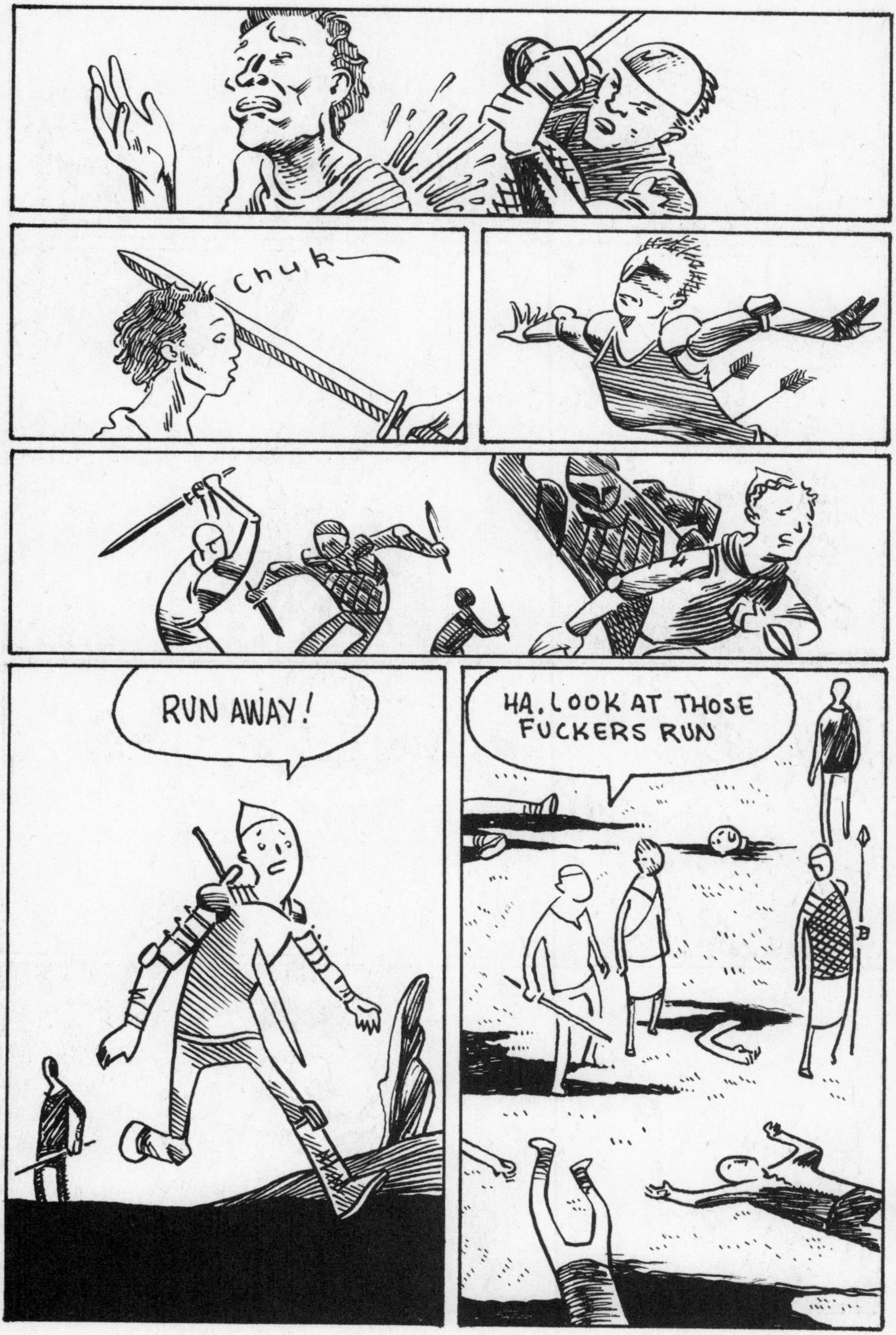
Chuk—
RUN AWAY!
HA. LOOK AT THOSE FUCKERS RUN

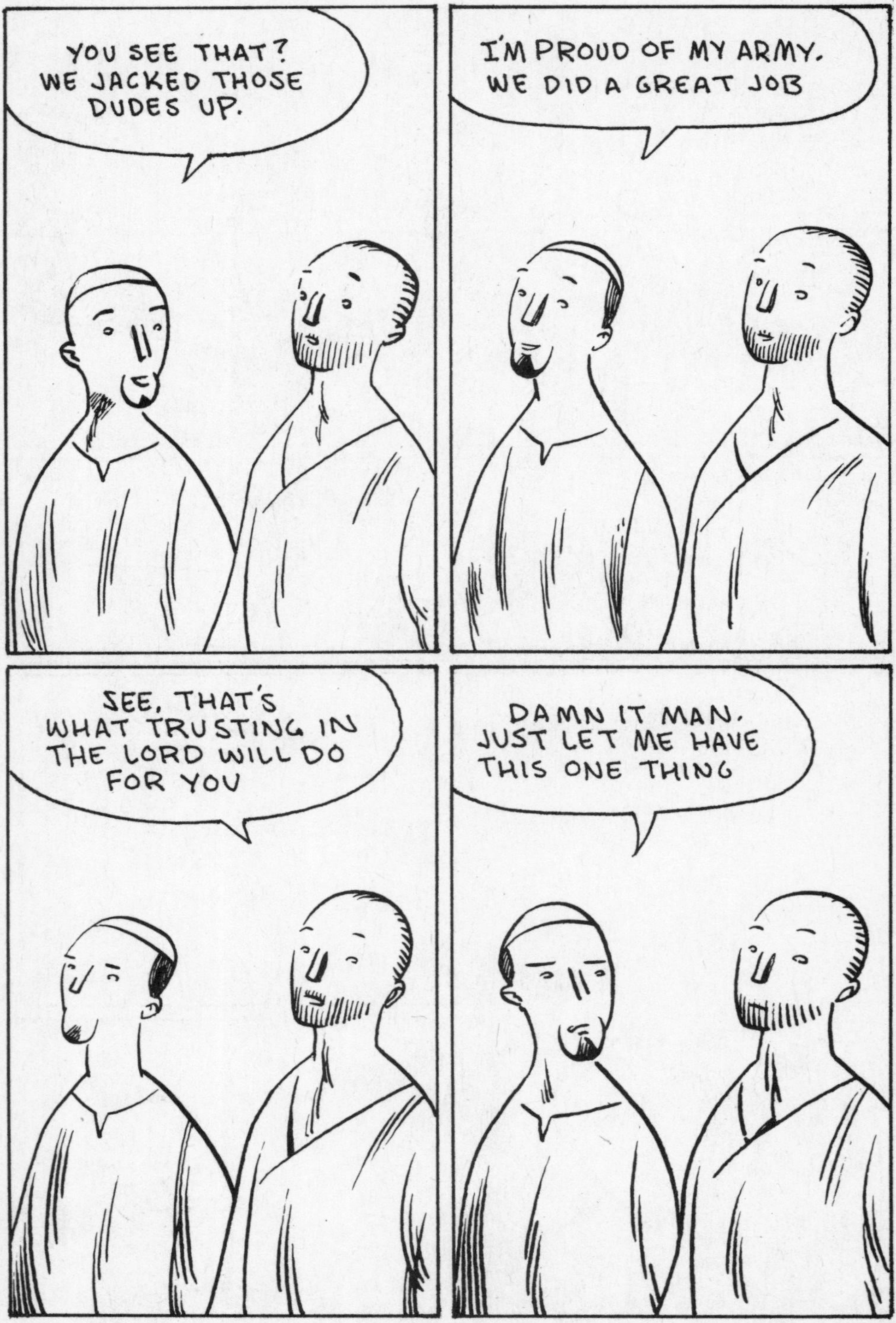
YOU SEE THAT? WE JACKED THOSE DUDES UP.
I'M PROUD OF MY ARMY. WE DID A GREAT JOB
SEE, THAT'S WHAT TRUSTING IN THE LORD WILL DO FOR YOU
DAMN IT MAN. JUST LET ME HAVE THIS ONE THING

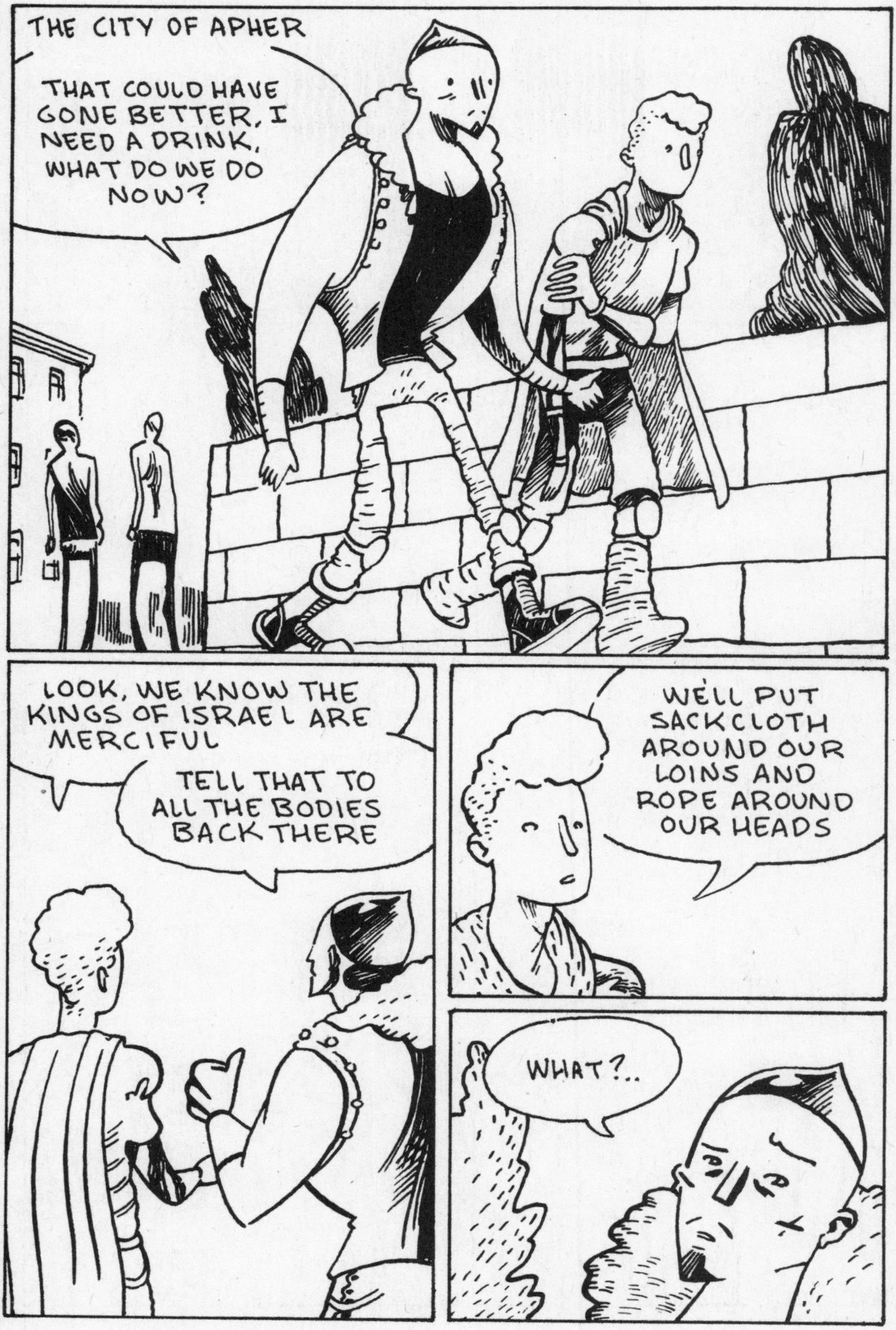
THE CITY OF APHER
THAT COULD HAVE GONE BETTER, I NEED A DRINK. WHAT DO WE DO NOW?
LOOK, WE KNOW THE KINGS OF ISRAEL ARE MERCIFUL
TELL THAT TO ALL THE BODIES BACK THERE
WELL PUT SACKCLOTH AROUND OUR LOINS AND ROPE AROUND OUR HEADS
WHAT?..

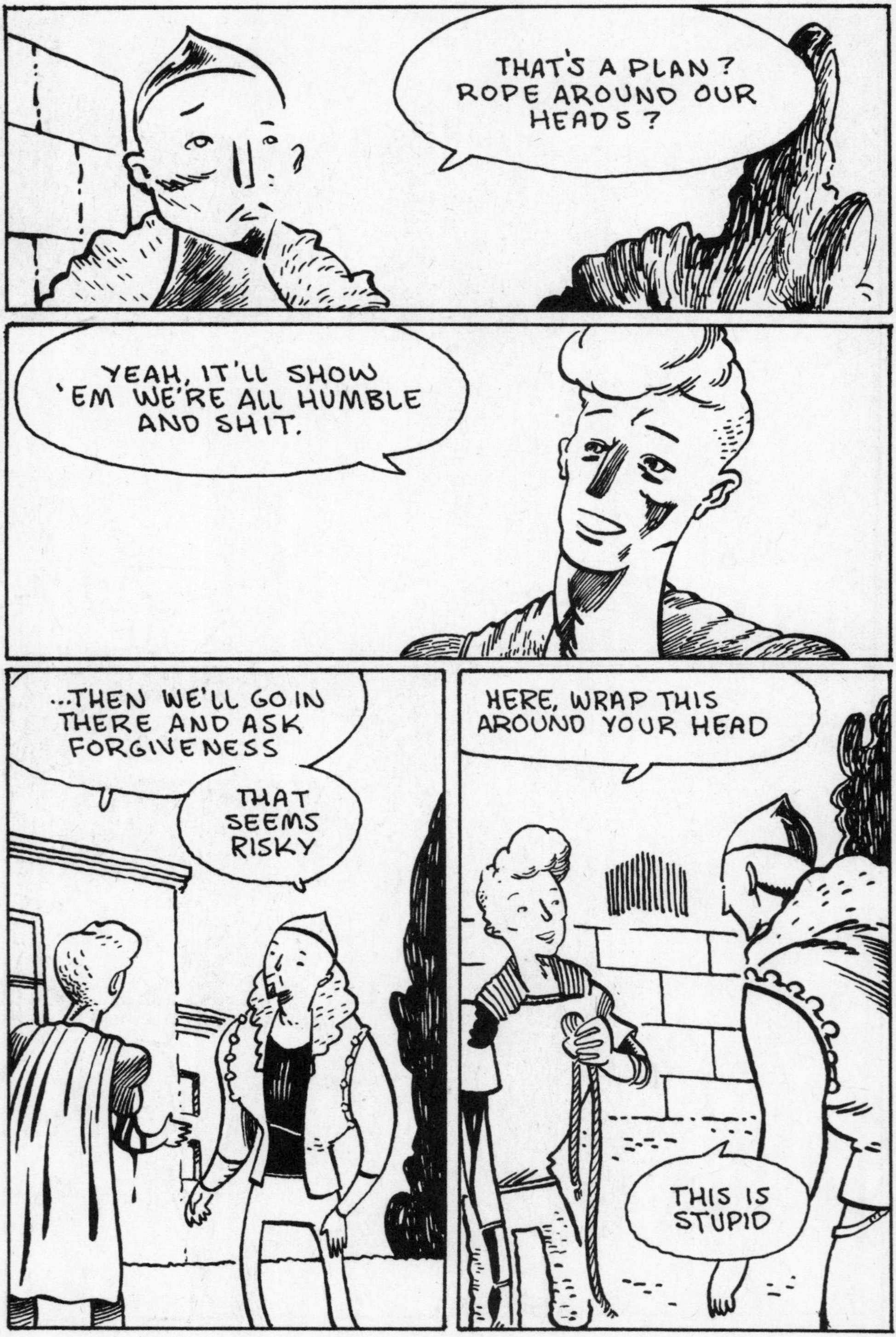
THAT'S A PLAN? ROPE AROUND OUR HEADS?
YEAH, IT'LL SHOW 'EM WE'RE ALL HUMBLE AND SHIT.
...THEN WE'LL GO IN THERE AND ASK FORGIVENESS
THAT SEEMS RISKY
HERE, WRAP THIS AROUND YOUR HEAD
THIS IS STUPID

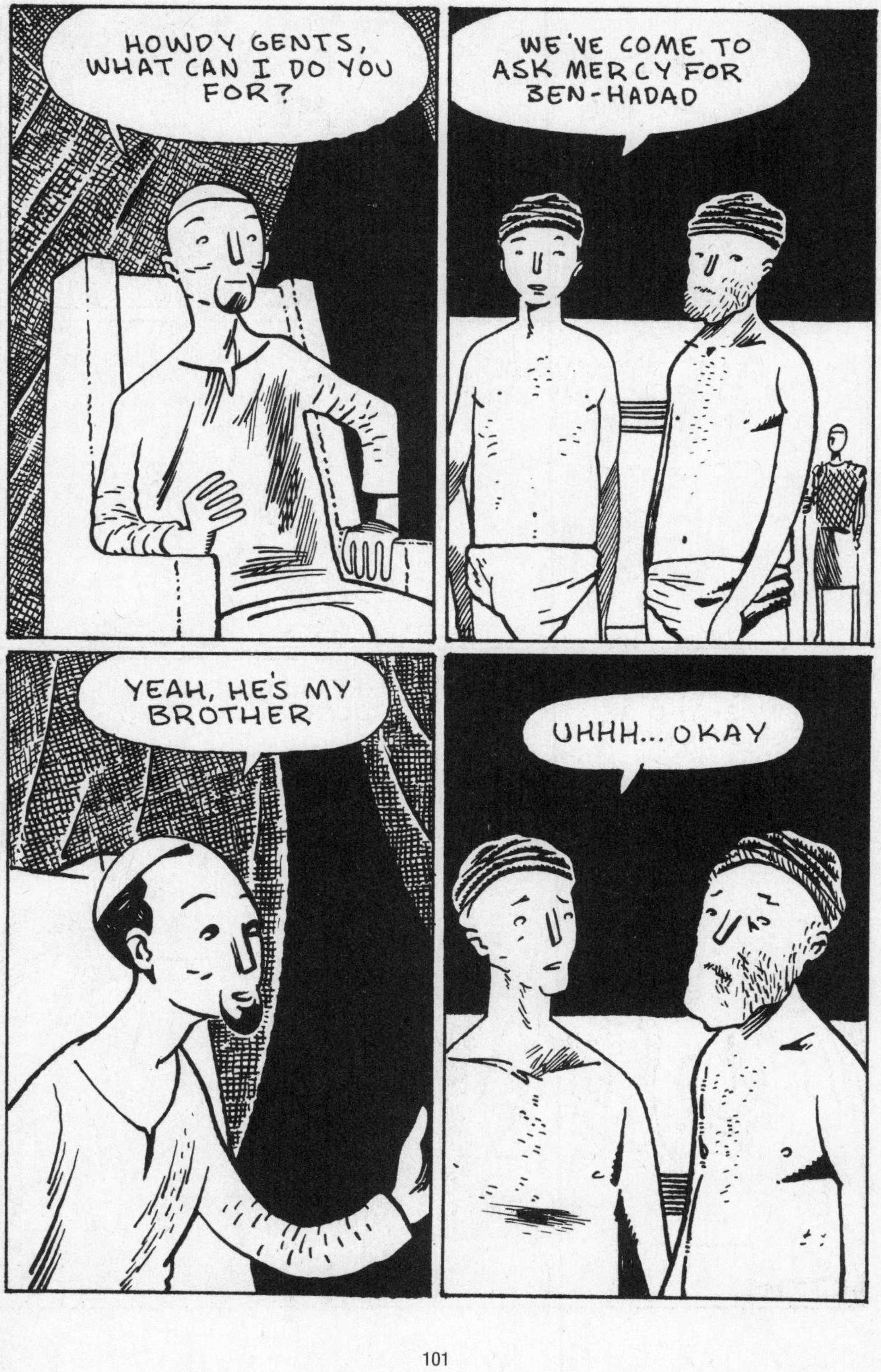
HOWDY GENTS, WHAT CAN I DO YOU FOR?
WE'VE COME TO ASK MERCY FOR BEN-HADAD
YEAH, HE'S MY BROTHER
UHHH... OKAY

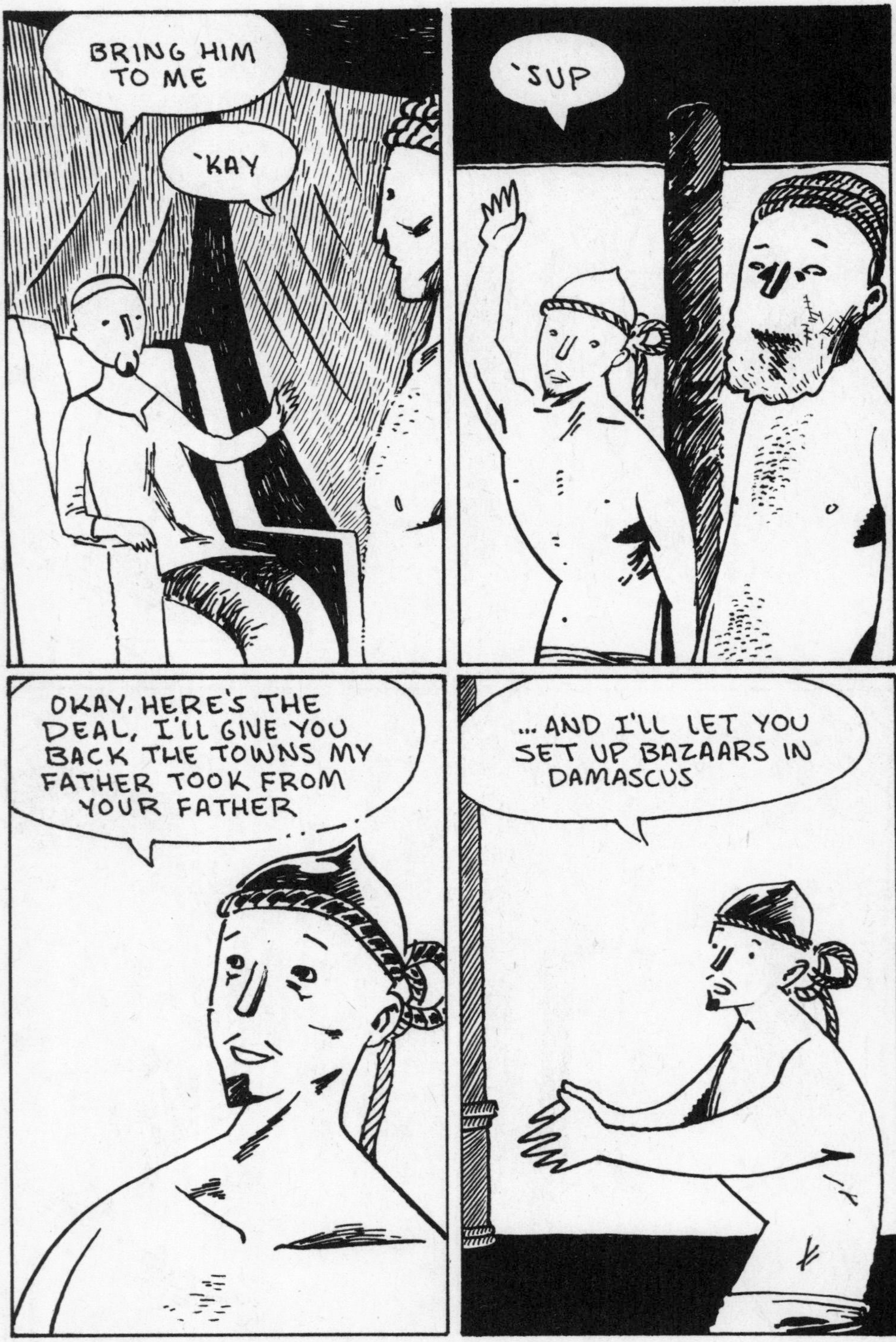
BRING HIM TO ME
`KAY
`SUP
OKAY, HERE'S THE DEAL, I'LL GIVE YOU BACK THE TOWNS MY FATHER TOOK FROM YOUR FATHER
...AND I'LL LET YOU SET UP BAZAARS IN DAMASCUS

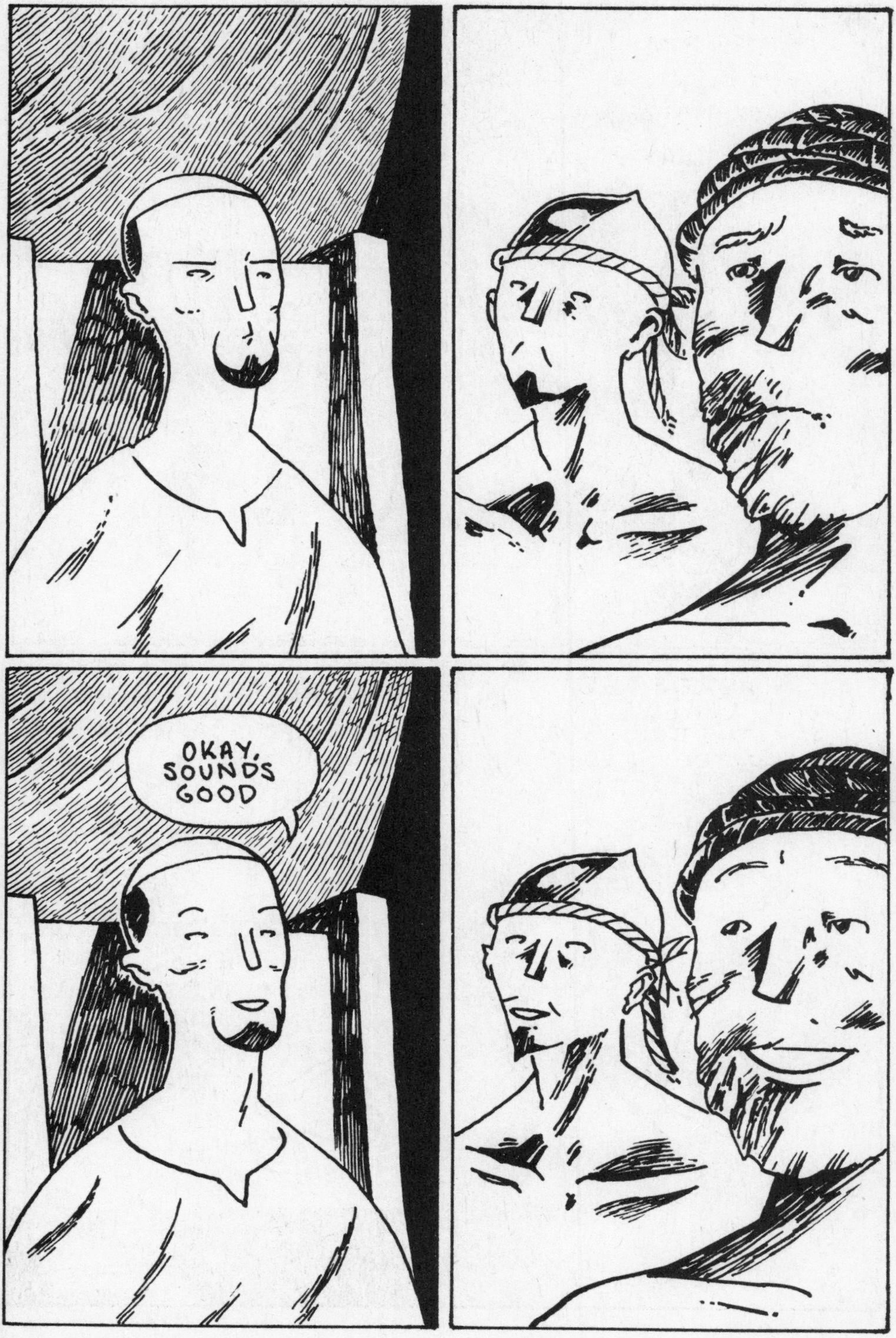
OKAY, SOUNDS GOOD

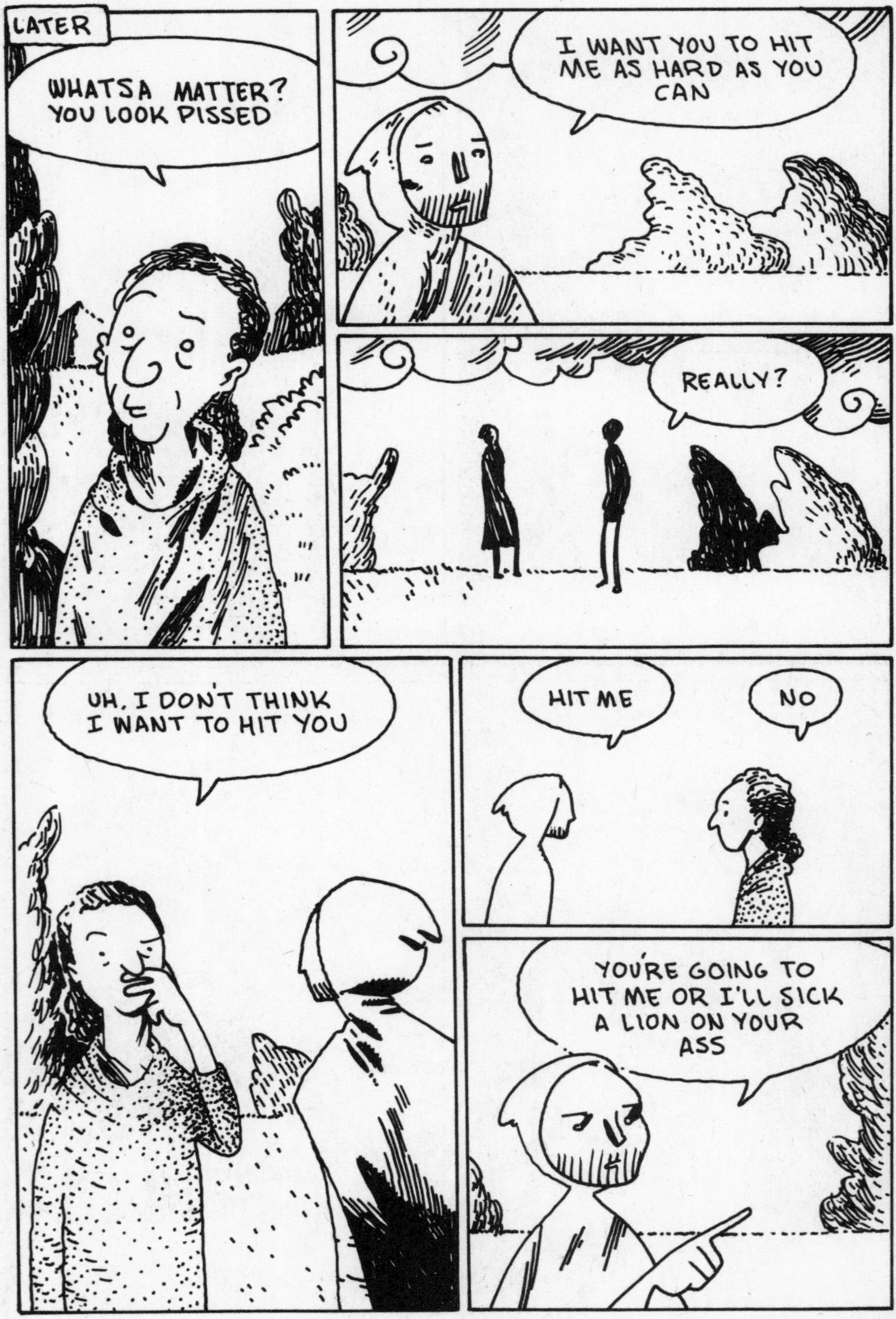
LATER
WHATSA MATTER? YOU LOOK PISSED
I WANT YOU TO HIT ME AS HARD AS YOU CAN
REALLY?
UH. I DON'T THINK I WANT TO HIT YOU
HIT ME
NO
YOU'RE GOING TO HIT ME OR I'LL SICK A LION ON YOUR ASS

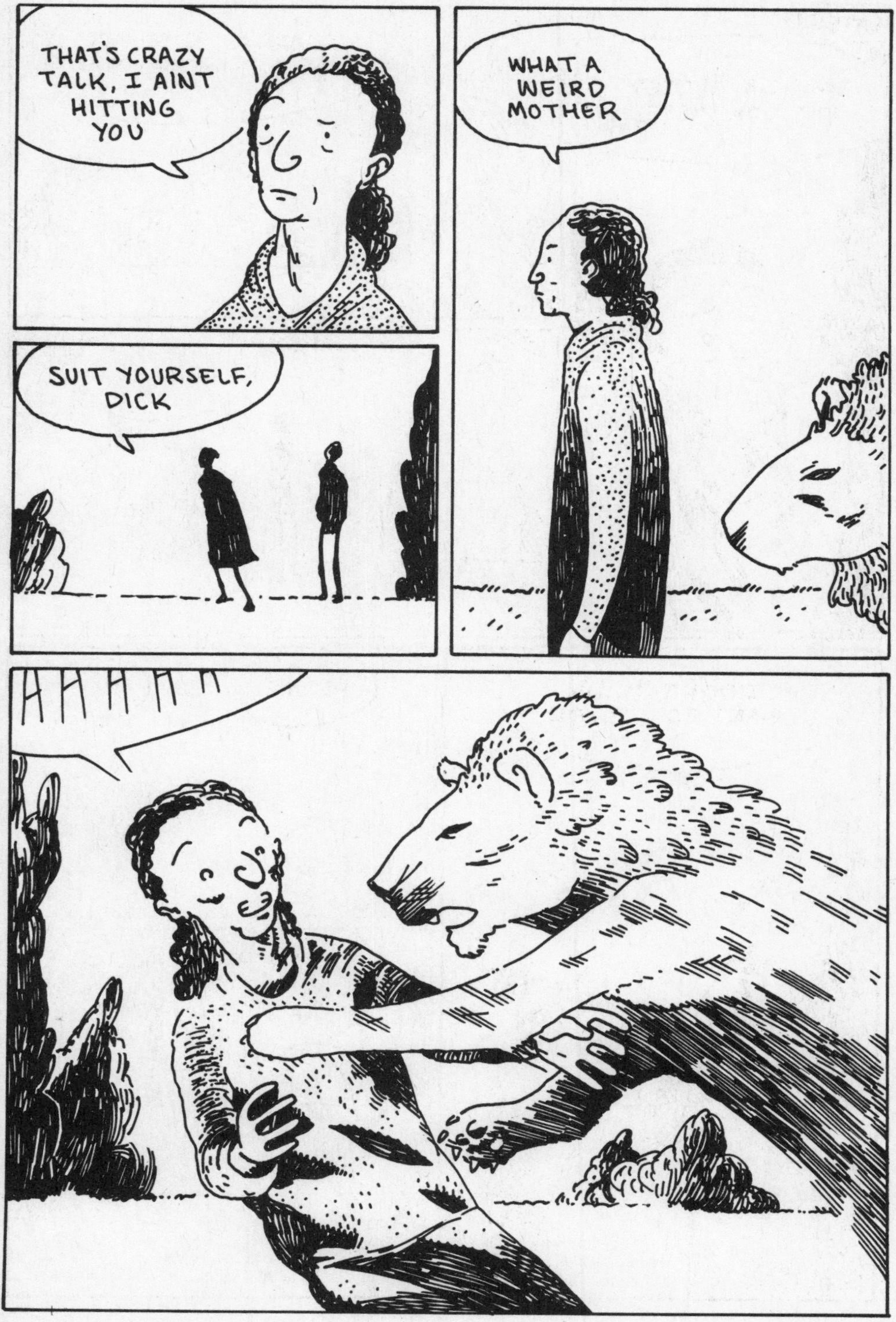
THAT'S CRAZY TALK, I AINT HITTING YOU
WHAT A WEIRD MOTHER
SUIT YOURSELF, DICK
AAAAA

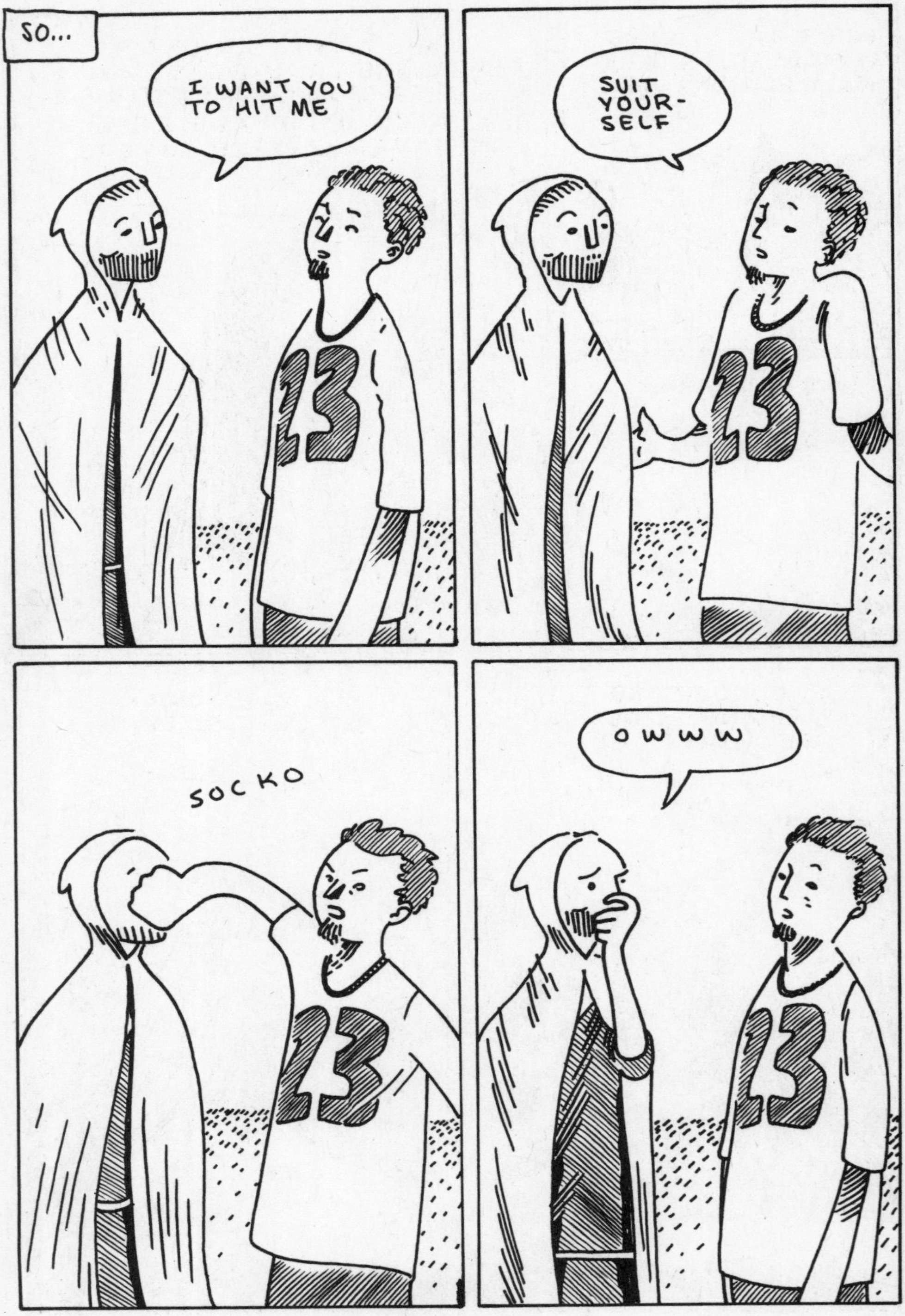
SO...
I WANT YOU TO HIT ME
SUIT YOUR-SELF
SOCKO
OWWW

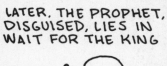

LATER, THE PROPHET, DISGUISED, LIES IN WAIT FOR THE KING

I WAS TOLD TO GUARD A PRISONER AND IF I LET HIM ESCAPE I'D BE PUNISHED OR FORCED TO PAY A FINE, THE PRISONER ESCAPED, SO HERE I AM...

HEY, WHATCHA DOING?

...WOUNDED AND BLEEDING BY THE SIDE OF THE ROAD

YOU MADE YOUR BED DUDE, SLEEP IN IT

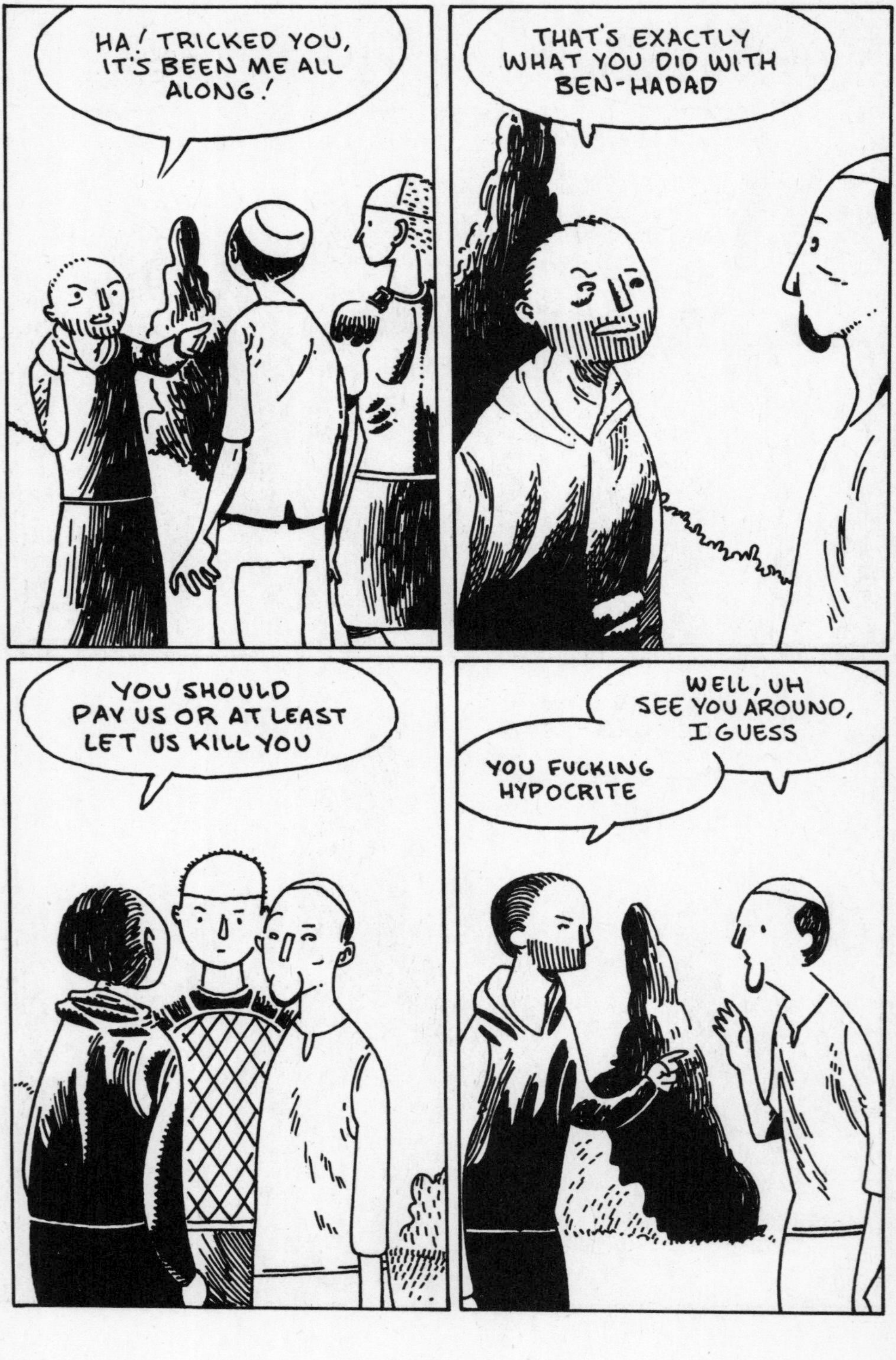
HA! TRICKED YOU, IT'S BEEN ME ALL ALONG!
THAT'S EXACTLY WHAT YOU DID WITH BEN-HADAD
YOU SHOULD PAY US OR AT LEAST LET US KILL YOU
YOU FUCKING HYPOCRITE
WELL, UH SEE YOU AROUND, I GUESS

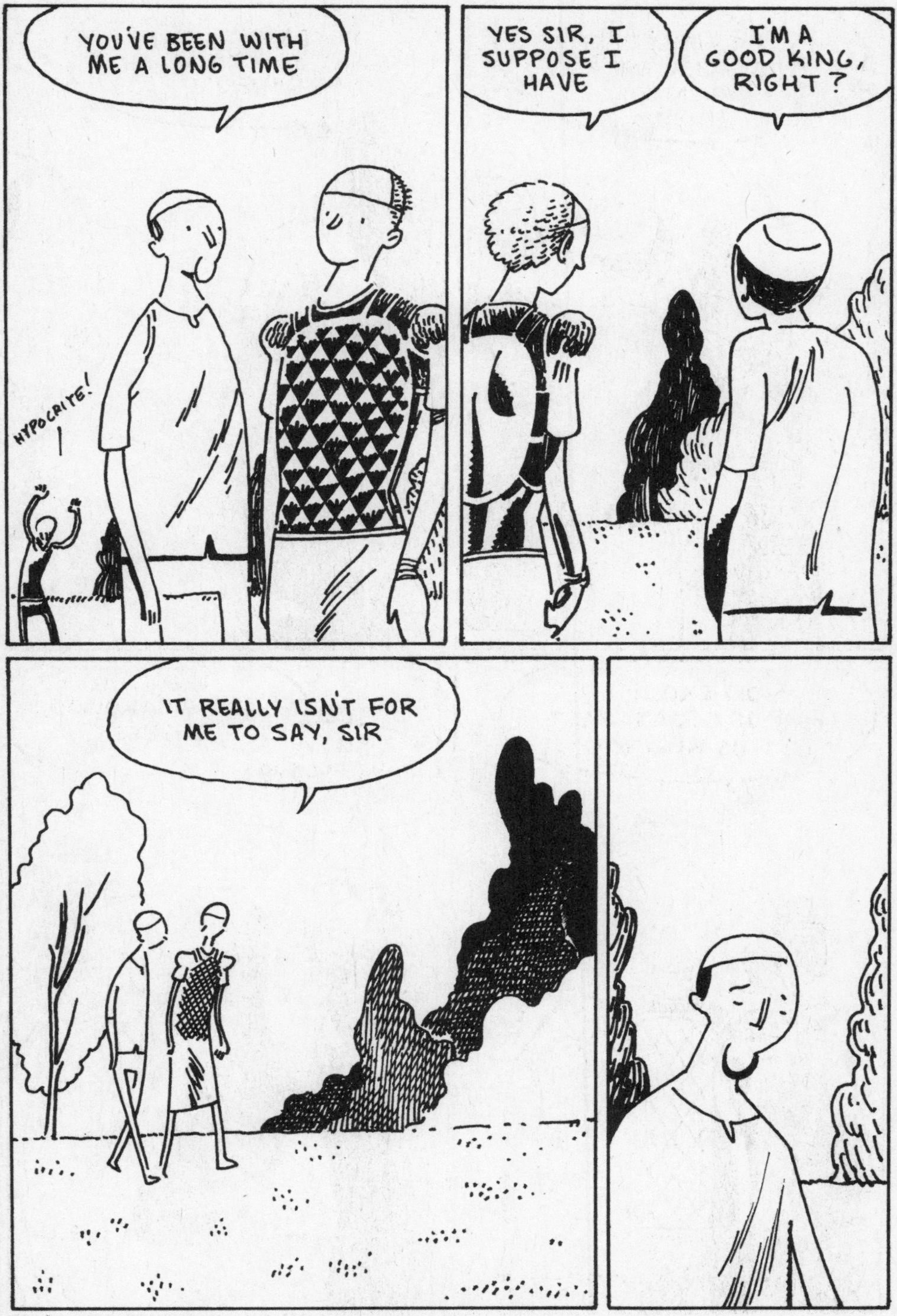
YOU'VE BEEN WITH ME A LONG TIME
HYPOCRITE!
YES SIR, I SUPPOSE I HAVE
I'M A GOOD KING, RIGHT?
IT REALLY ISN'T FOR ME TO SAY, SIR

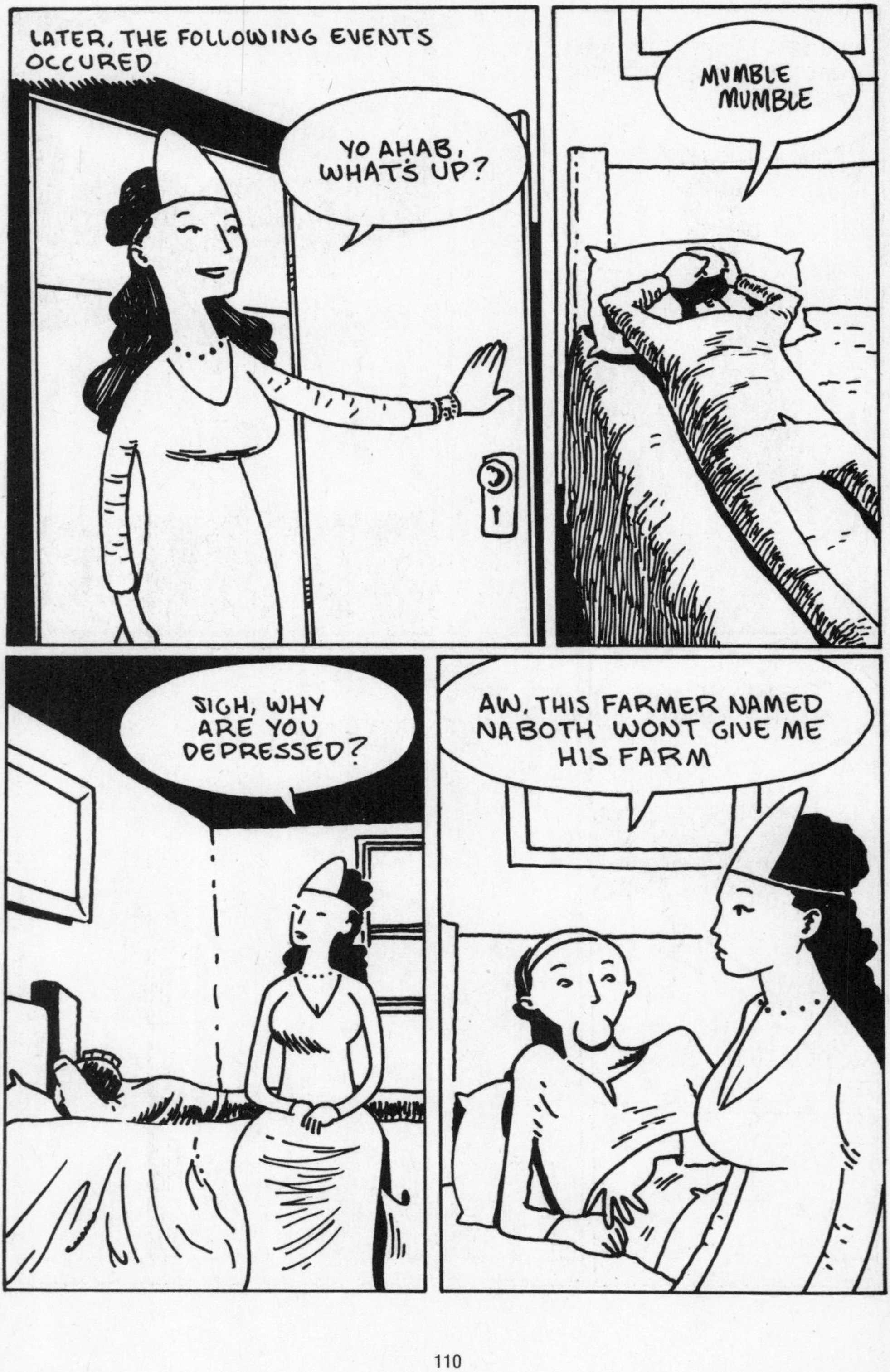
LATER, THE FOLLOWING EVENTS OCCURED
YO AHAB, WHAT'S UP?
MUMBLE MUMBLE
SIGH, WHY ARE YOU DEPRESSED?
AW, THIS FARMER NAMED NABOTH WONT GIVE ME HIS FARM

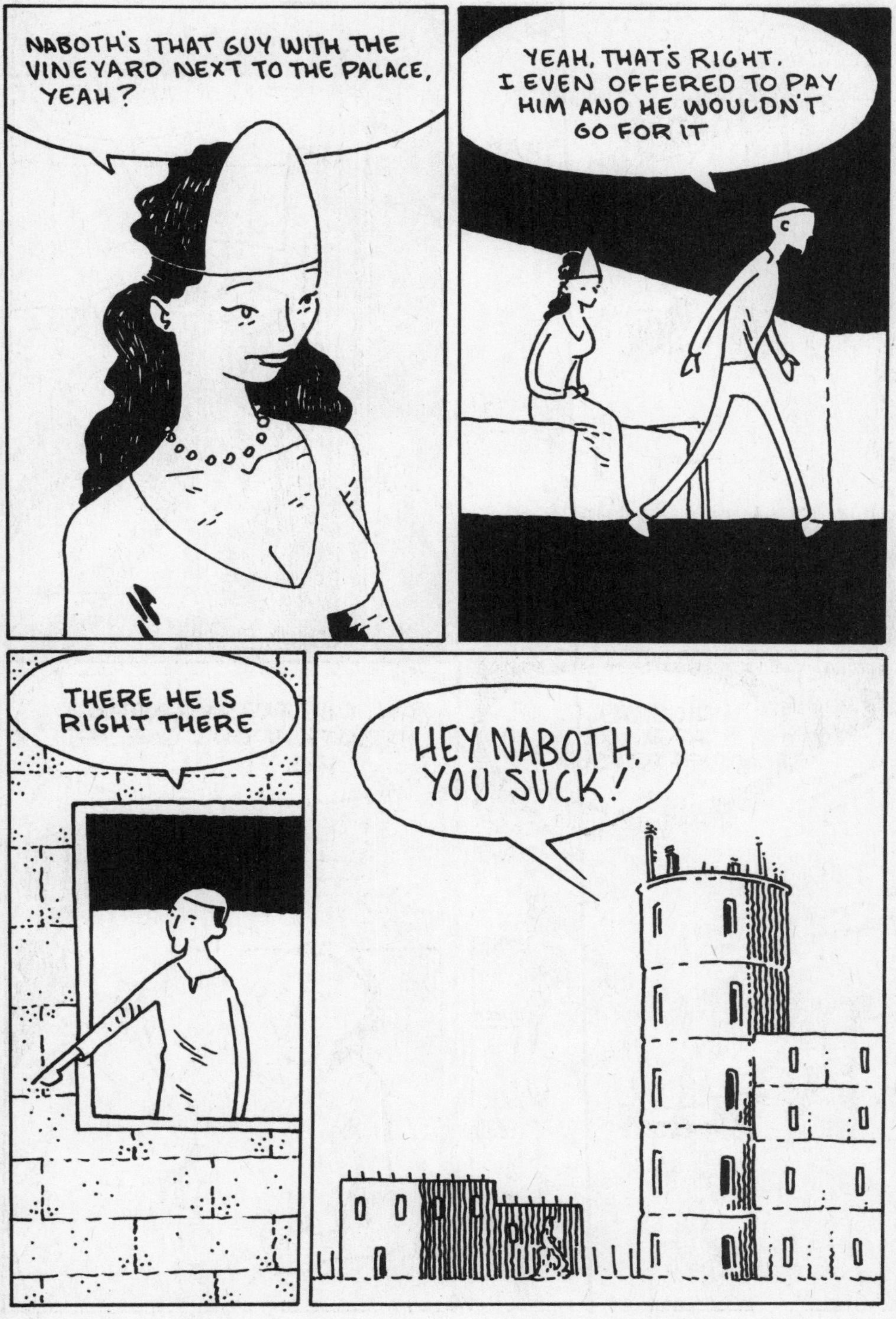
NABOTH'S THAT GUY WITH THE VINEYARD NEXT TO THE PALACE, YEAH?
YEAH, THAT'S RIGHT. I EVEN OFFERED TO PAY HIM AND HE WOULDN'T GO FOR IT
THERE HE IS RIGHT THERE
HEY NABOTH. YOU SUCK!

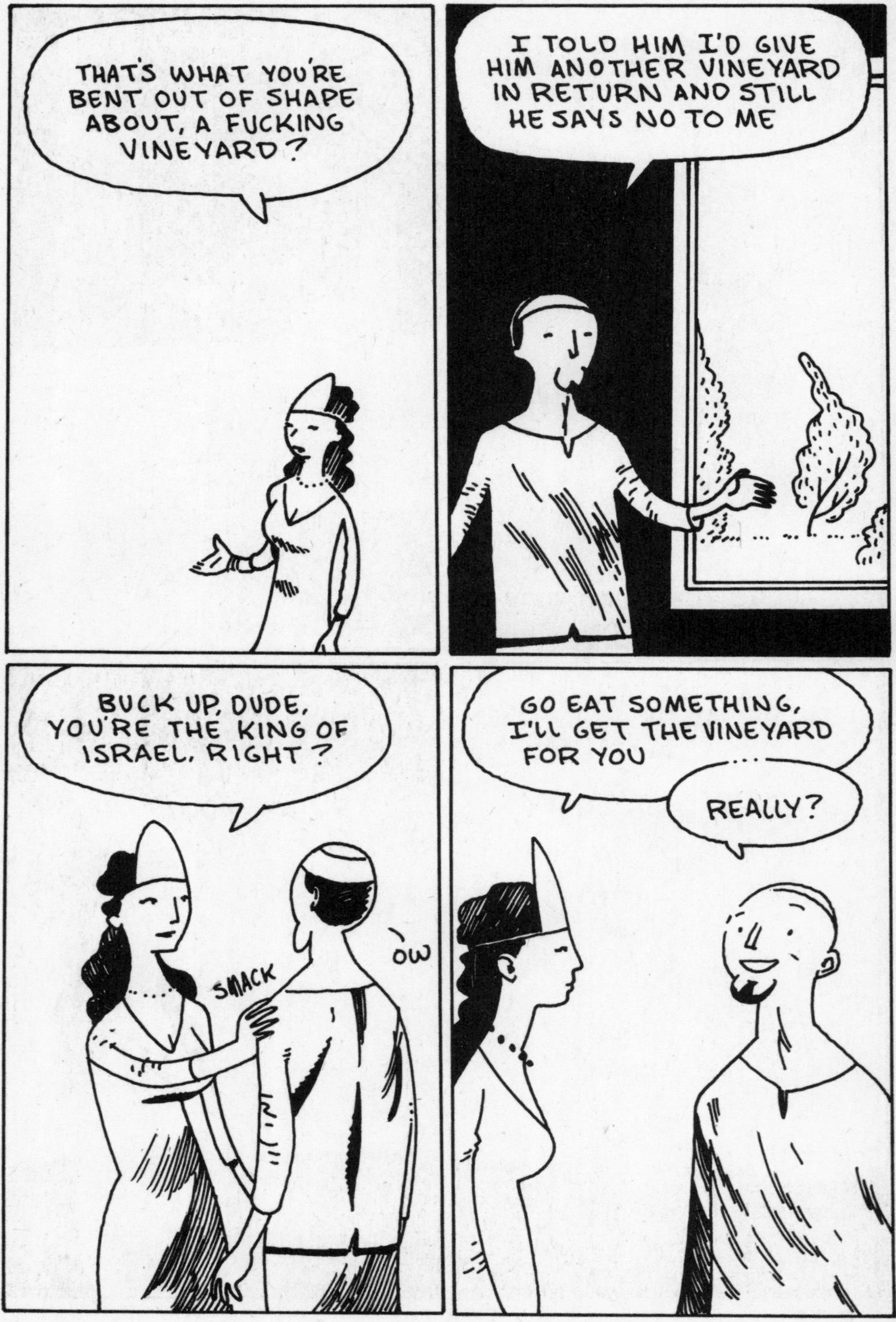
THAT'S WHAT YOU'RE BENT OUT OF SHAPE ABOUT, A FUCKING VINEYARD?
I TOLD HIM I'D GIVE HIM ANOTHER VINEYARD IN RETURN AND STILL HE SAYS NO TO ME
BUCK UP, DUDE, YOU'RE THE KING OF ISRAEL, RIGHT?
SMACK
OW
GO EAT SOMETHING, I'LL GET THE VINEYARD FOR YOU
...
REALLY?

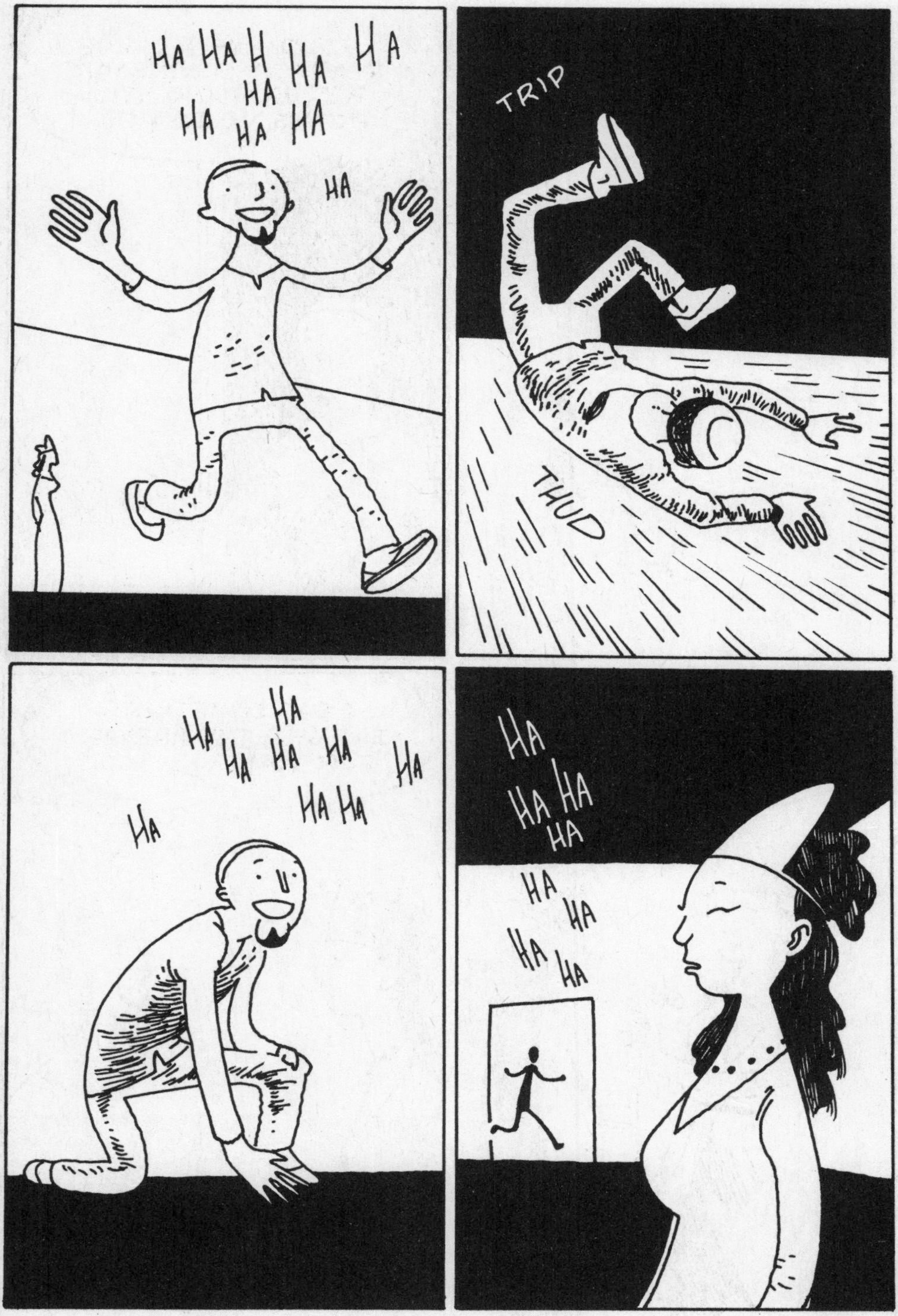
HA HA H HA H A
HA
HA HA HA
HA
TRIP
THUD
HA
HA HA HA HA HA
HA HA HA
HA
HA
HA HA
HA
HA
HA
HA HA

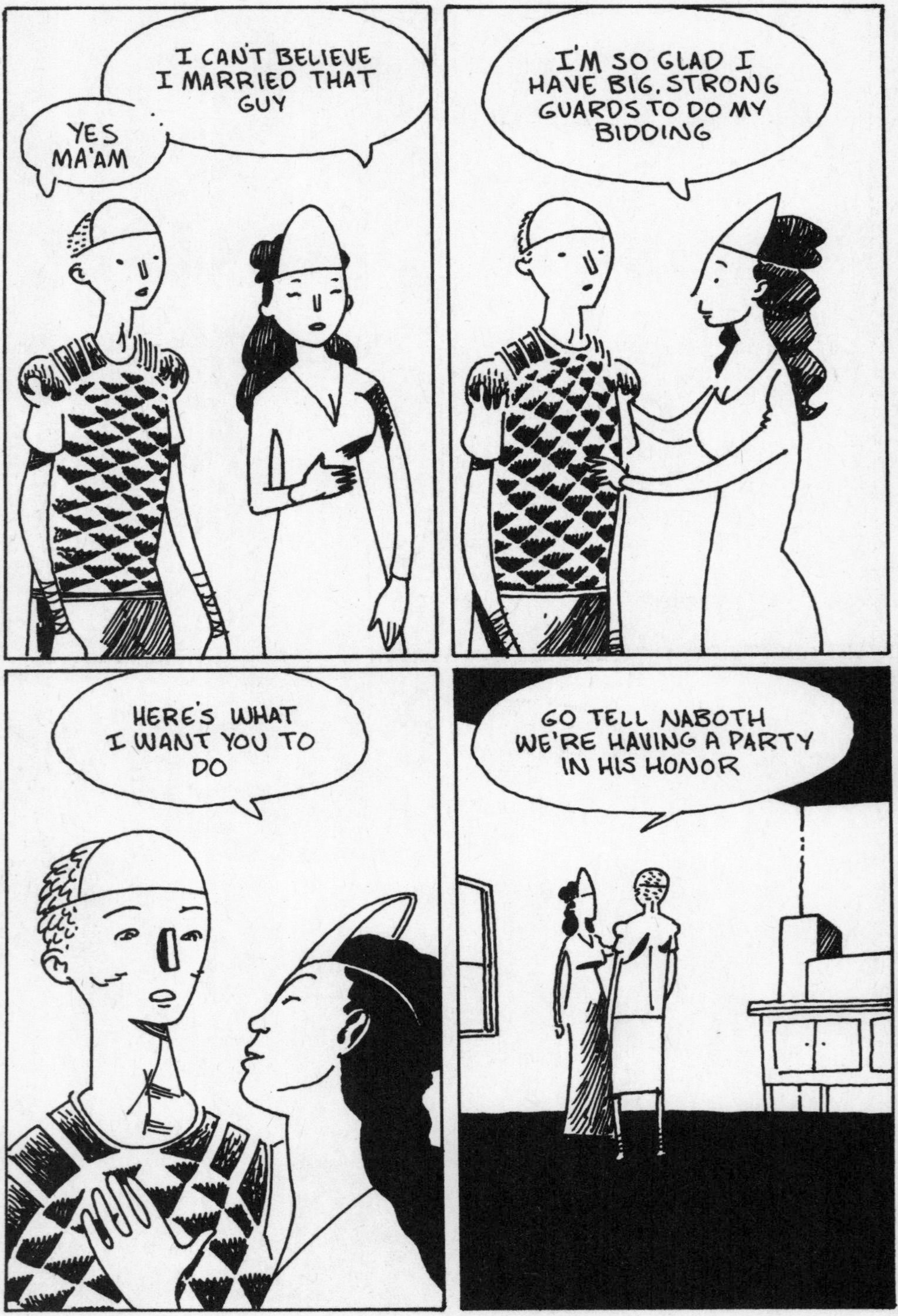
I CAN'T BELIEVE I MARRIED THAT GUY
YES MA'AM
I'M SO GLAD I HAVE BIG, STRONG GUARDS TO DO MY BIDDING
HERE'S WHAT I WANT YOU TO DO
GO TELL NABOTH WE'RE HAVING A PARTY IN HIS HONOR

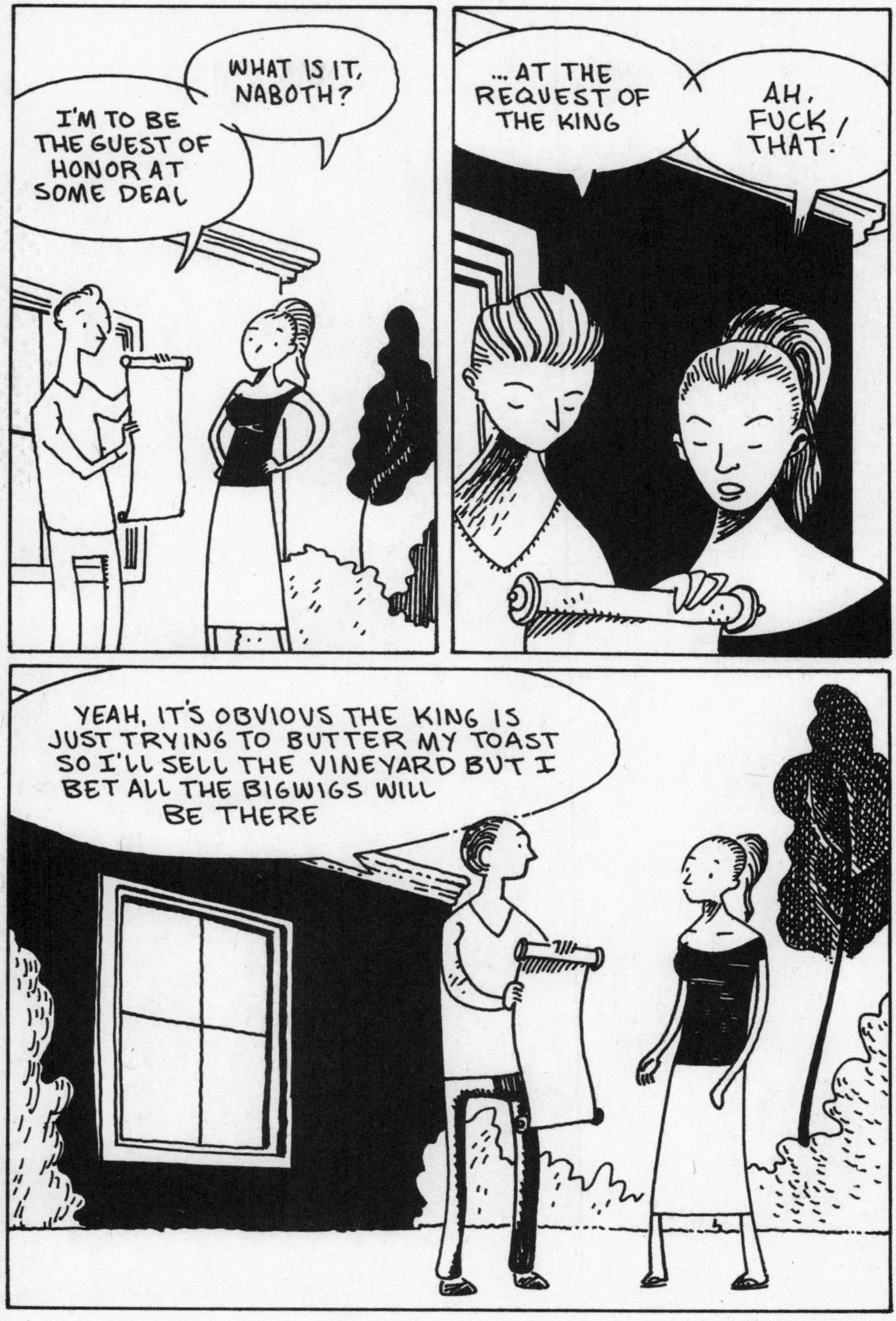
I'M TO BE THE GUEST OF HONOR AT SOME DEAL
WHAT IS IT, NABOTH?
... AT THE REQUEST OF THE KING
AH, FUCK THAT!
YEAH, IT'S OBVIOUS THE KING IS JUST TRYING TO BUTTER MY TOAST SO I'LL SELL THE VINEYARD BUT I BET ALL THE BIGWIGS WILL BE THERE

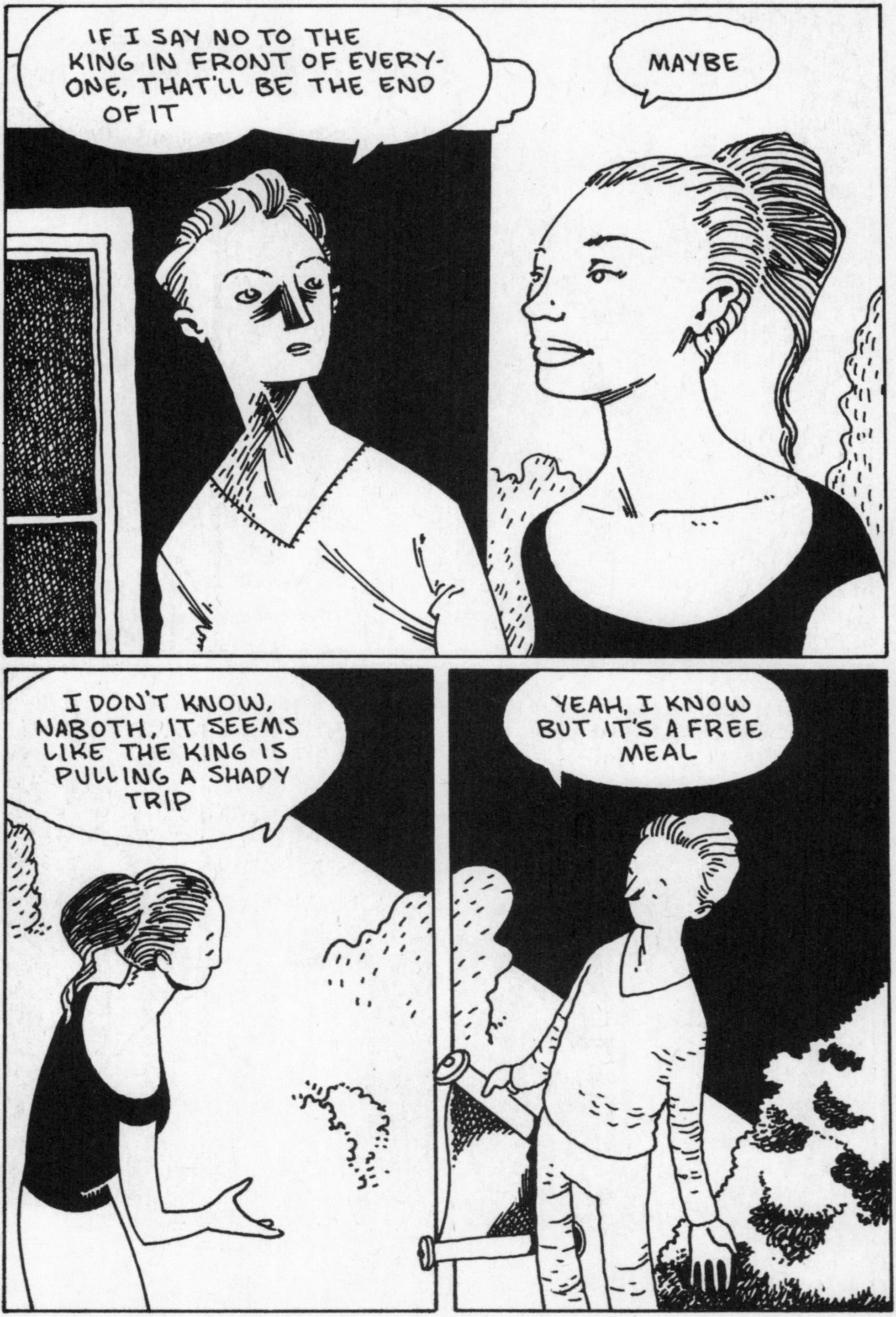
IF I SAY NO TO THE KING IN FRONT OF EVERY-ONE, THAT'LL BE THE END OF IT
MAYBE
I DON'T KNOW, NABOTH, IT SEEMS LIKE THE KING IS PULLING A SHADY TRIP
YEAH, I KNOW BUT IT'S A FREE MEAL

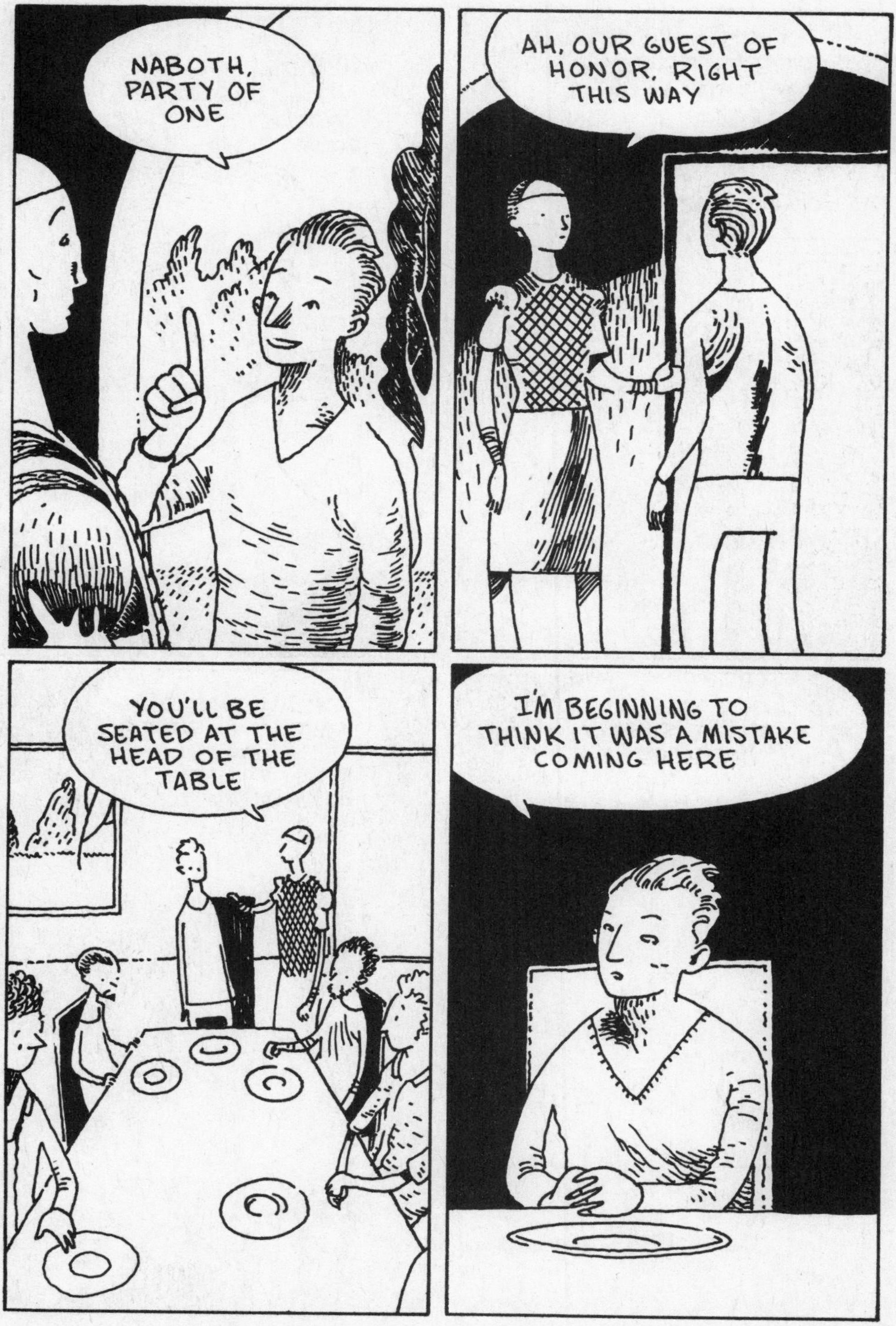
NABOTH, PARTY OF ONE
AH, OUR GUEST OF HONOR, RIGHT THIS WAY
YOU'LL BE SEATED AT THE HEAD OF THE TABLE
I'M BEGINNING TO THINK IT WAS A MISTAKE COMING HERE

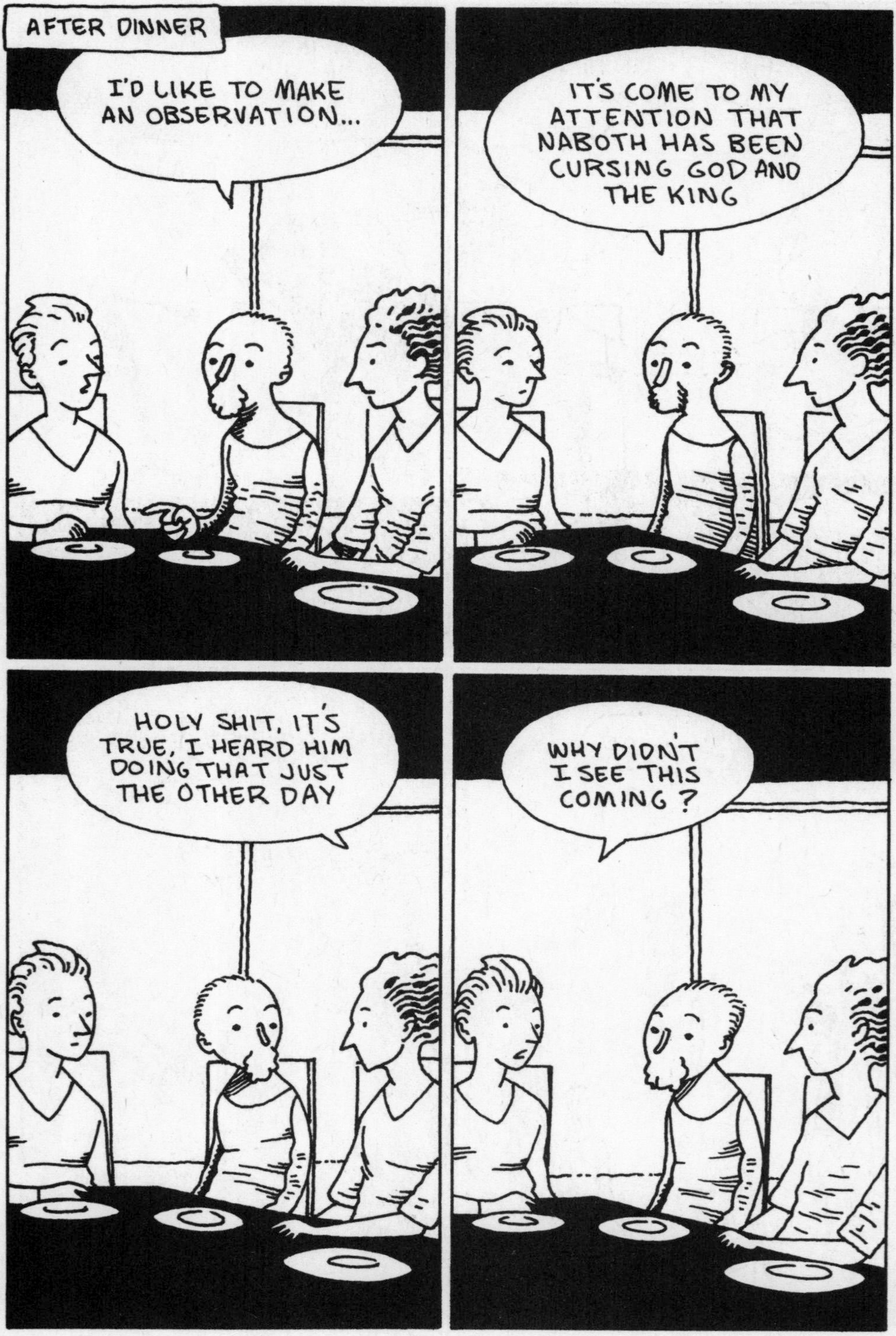
AFTER DINNER
I'D LIKE TO MAKE AN OBSERVATION...
IT'S COME TO MY ATTENTION THAT NABOTH HAS BEEN CURSING GOD AND THE KING
HOLY SHIT, IT'S TRUE, I HEARD HIM DOING THAT JUST THE OTHER DAY
WHY DIDN'T I SEE THIS COMING?

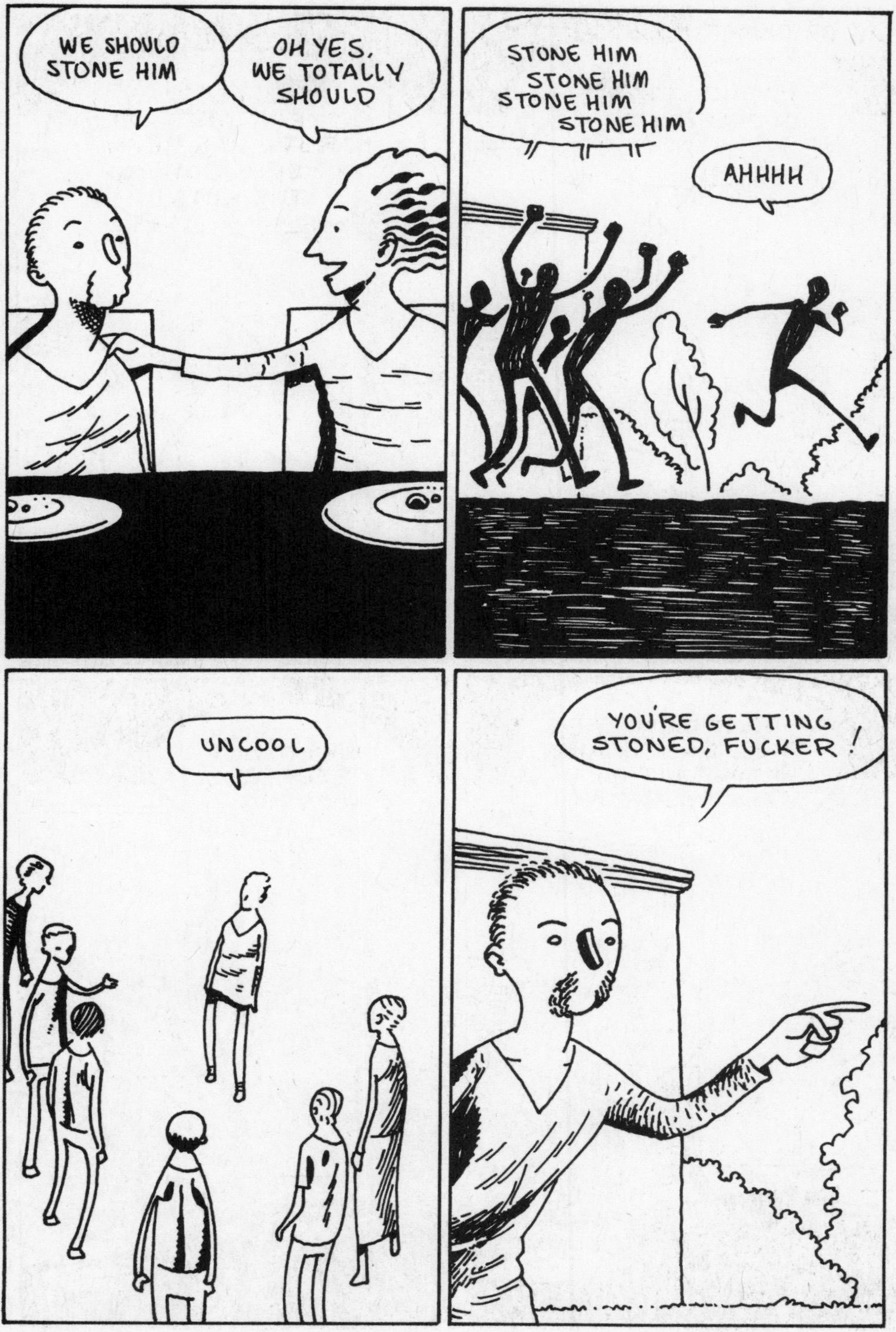
WE SHOULD STONE HIM
OH YES, WE TOTALLY SHOULD
STONE HIM STONE HIM STONE HIM STONE HIM
AHHHH
UNCOOL
YOU'RE GETTING STONED, FUCKER!

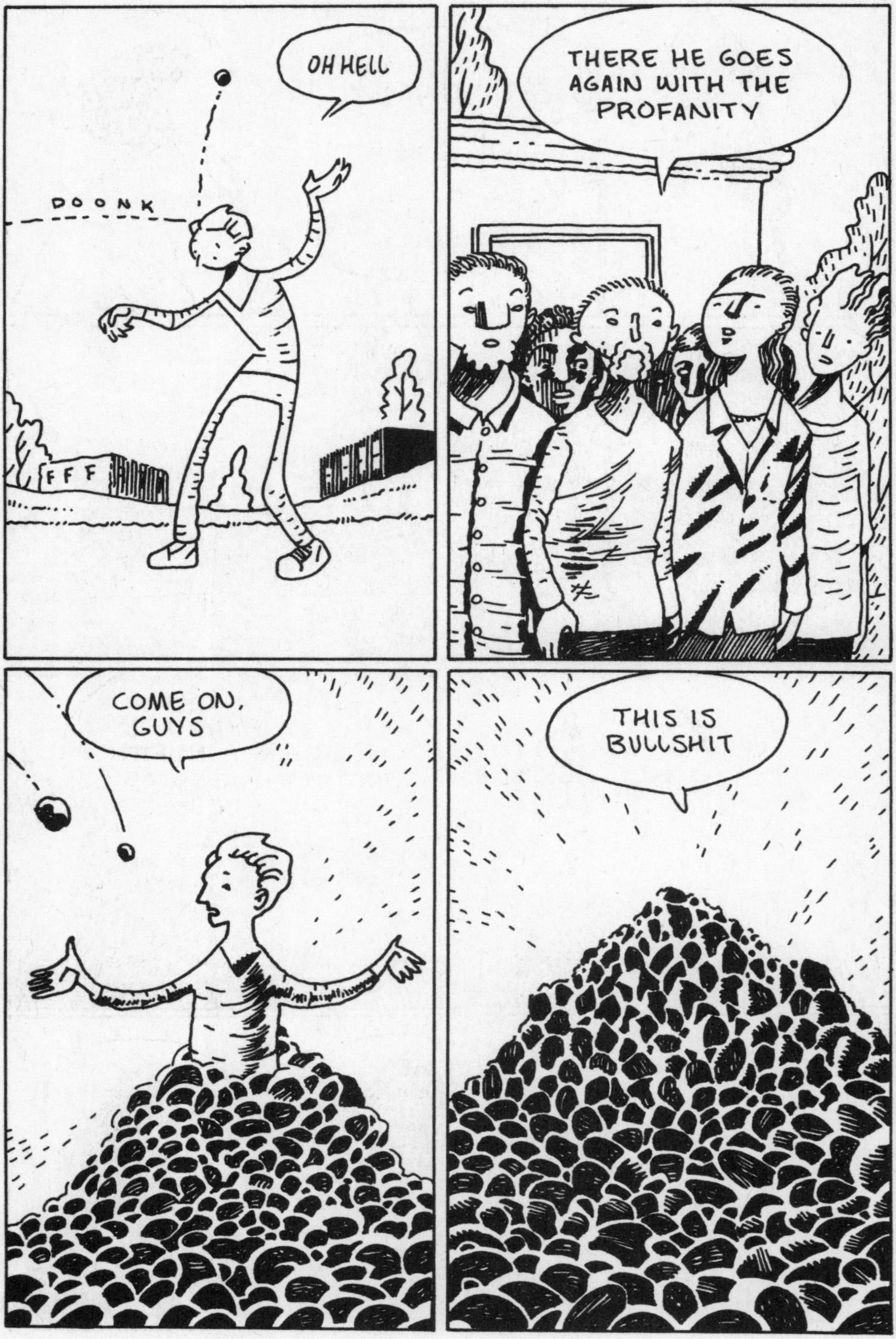
OH HELL
DOONK
FFF
THERE HE GOES AGAIN WITH THE PROFANITY
COME ON, GUYS
THIS IS BULLSHIT

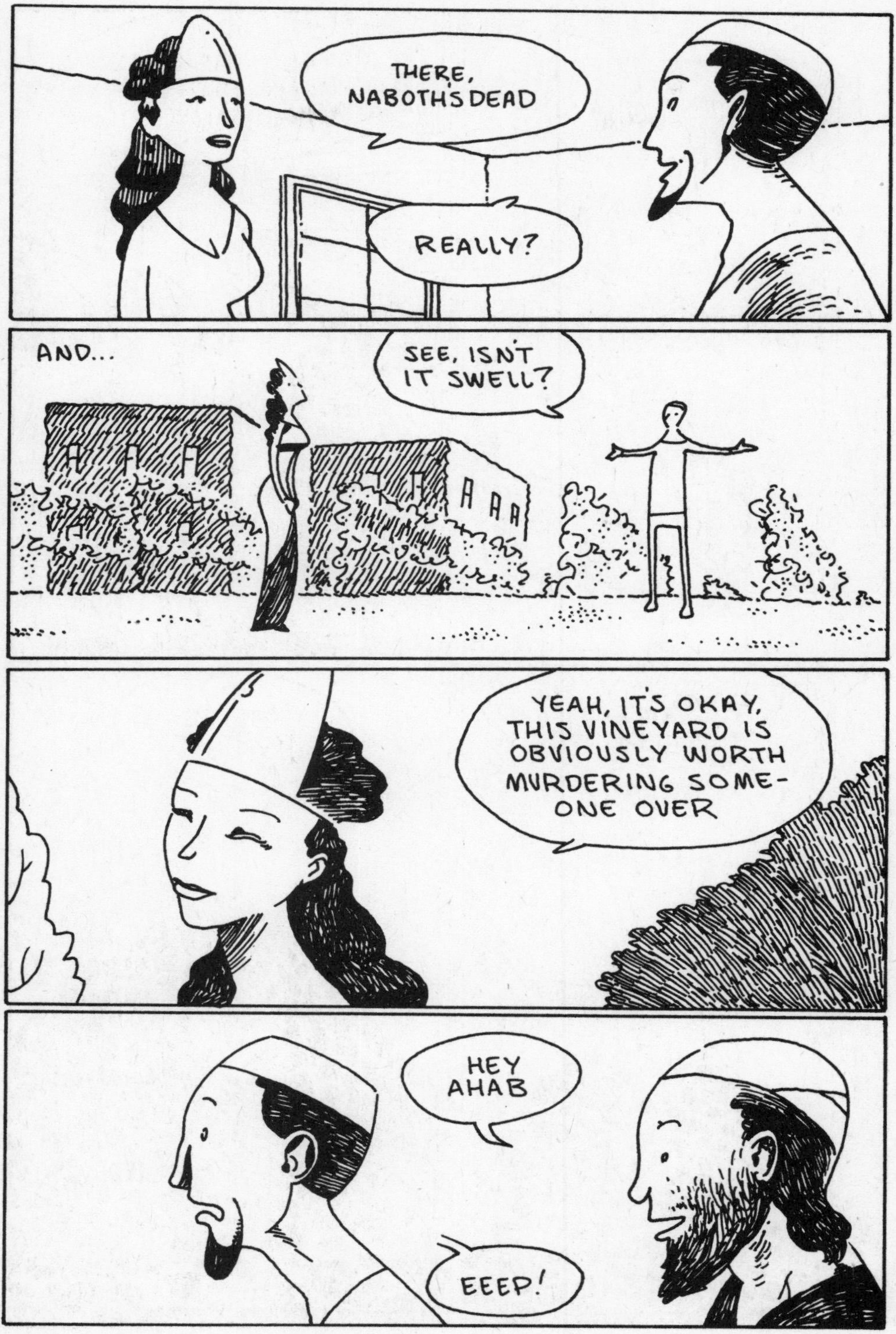
THERE, NABOTH'S DEAD
REALLY?
AND...
SEE, ISN'T IT SWELL?
YEAH, IT'S OKAY, THIS VINEYARD IS OBVIOUSLY WORTH MURDERING SOME-ONE OVER
HEY AHAB
EEEP!

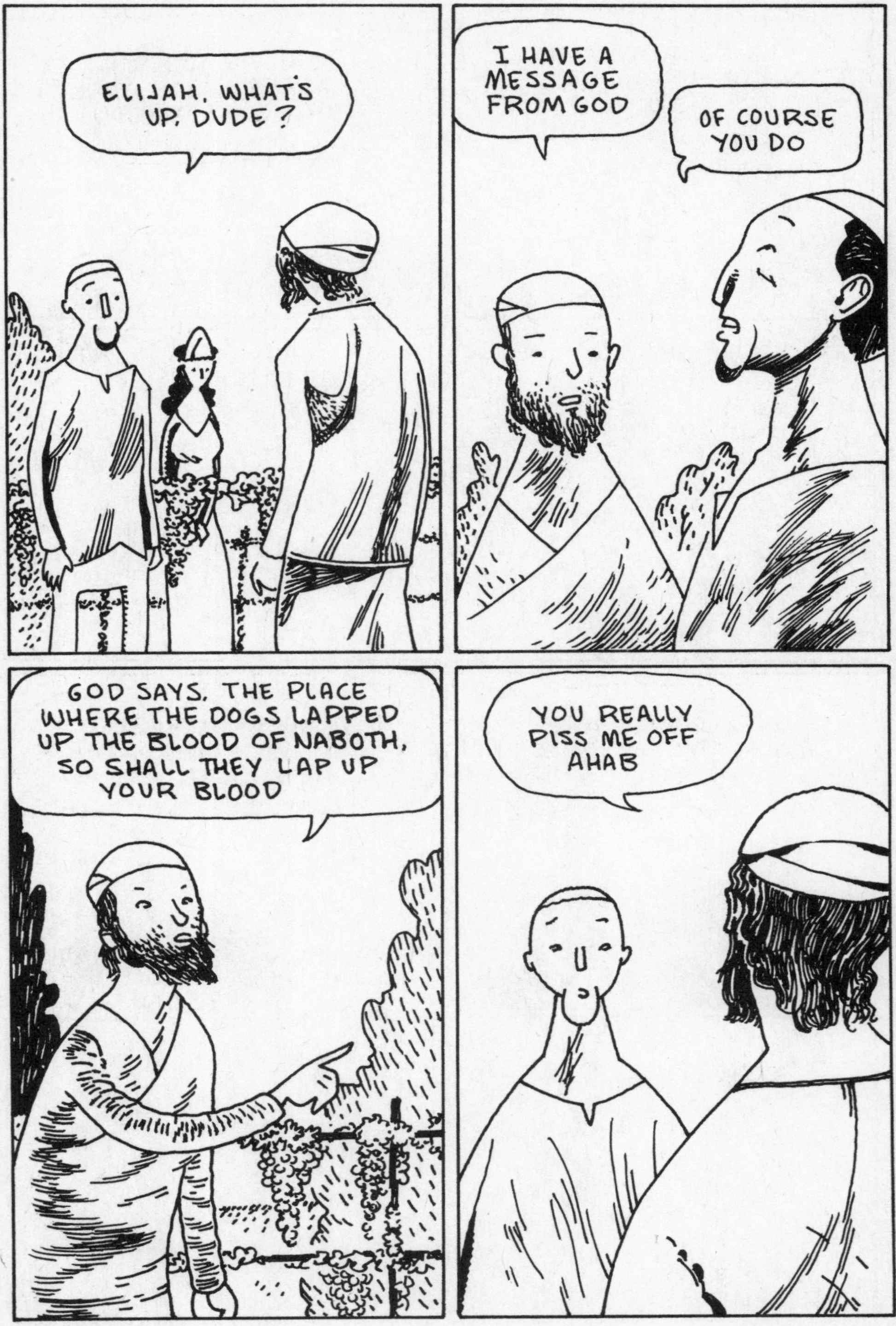
ELIJAH, WHAT'S UP, DUDE?
I HAVE A MESSAGE FROM GOD
OF COURSE YOU DO
GOD SAYS, THE PLACE WHERE THE DOGS LAPPED UP THE BLOOD OF NABOTH, SO SHALL THEY LAP UP YOUR BLOOD
YOU REALLY PISS ME OFF AHAB

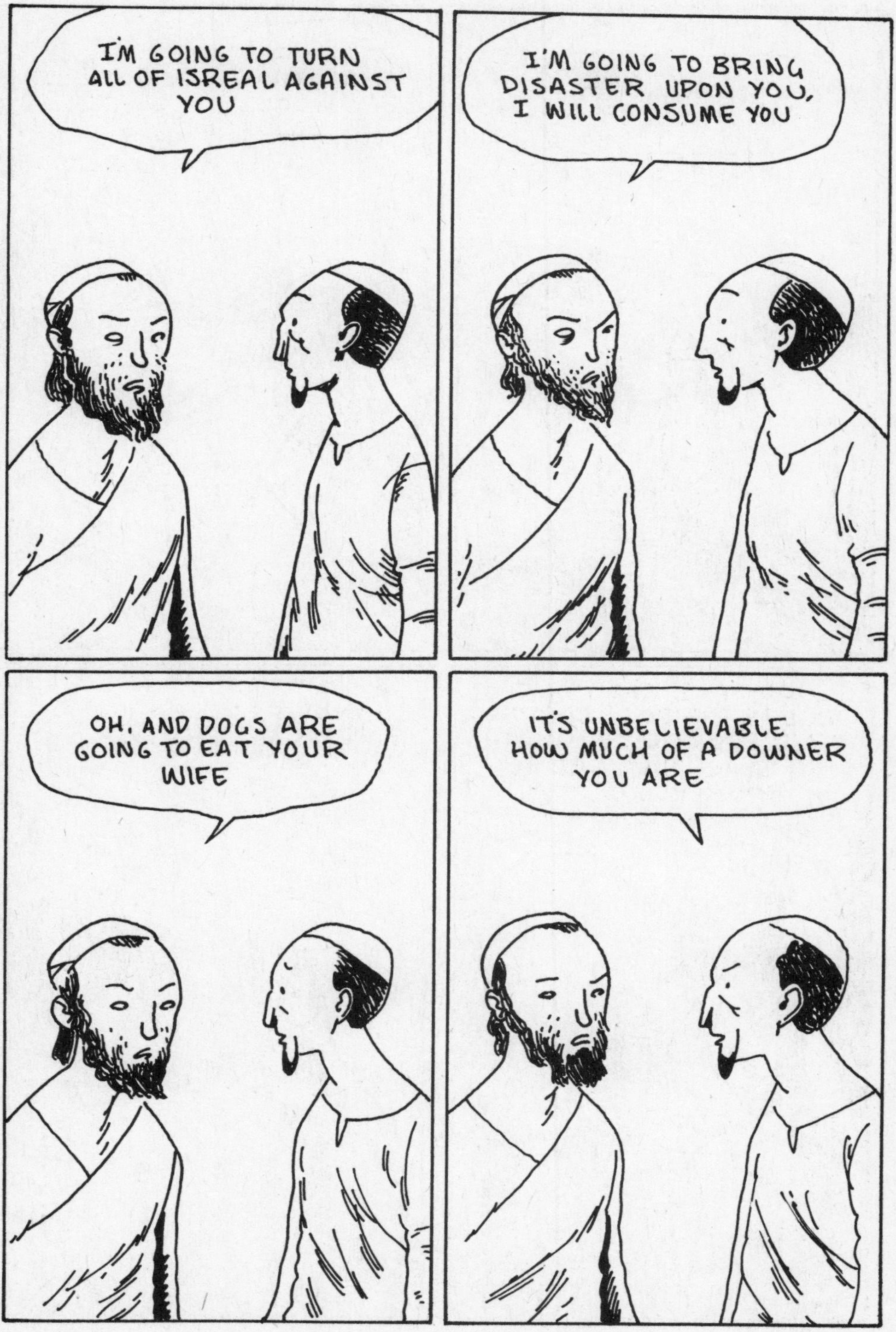
I'M GOING TO TURN ALL OF ISREAL AGAINST YOU
I'M GOING TO BRING DISASTER UPON YOU, I WILL CONSUME YOU
OH, AND DOGS ARE GOING TO EAT YOUR WIFE
IT'S UNBELIEVABLE HOW MUCH OF A DOWNER YOU ARE

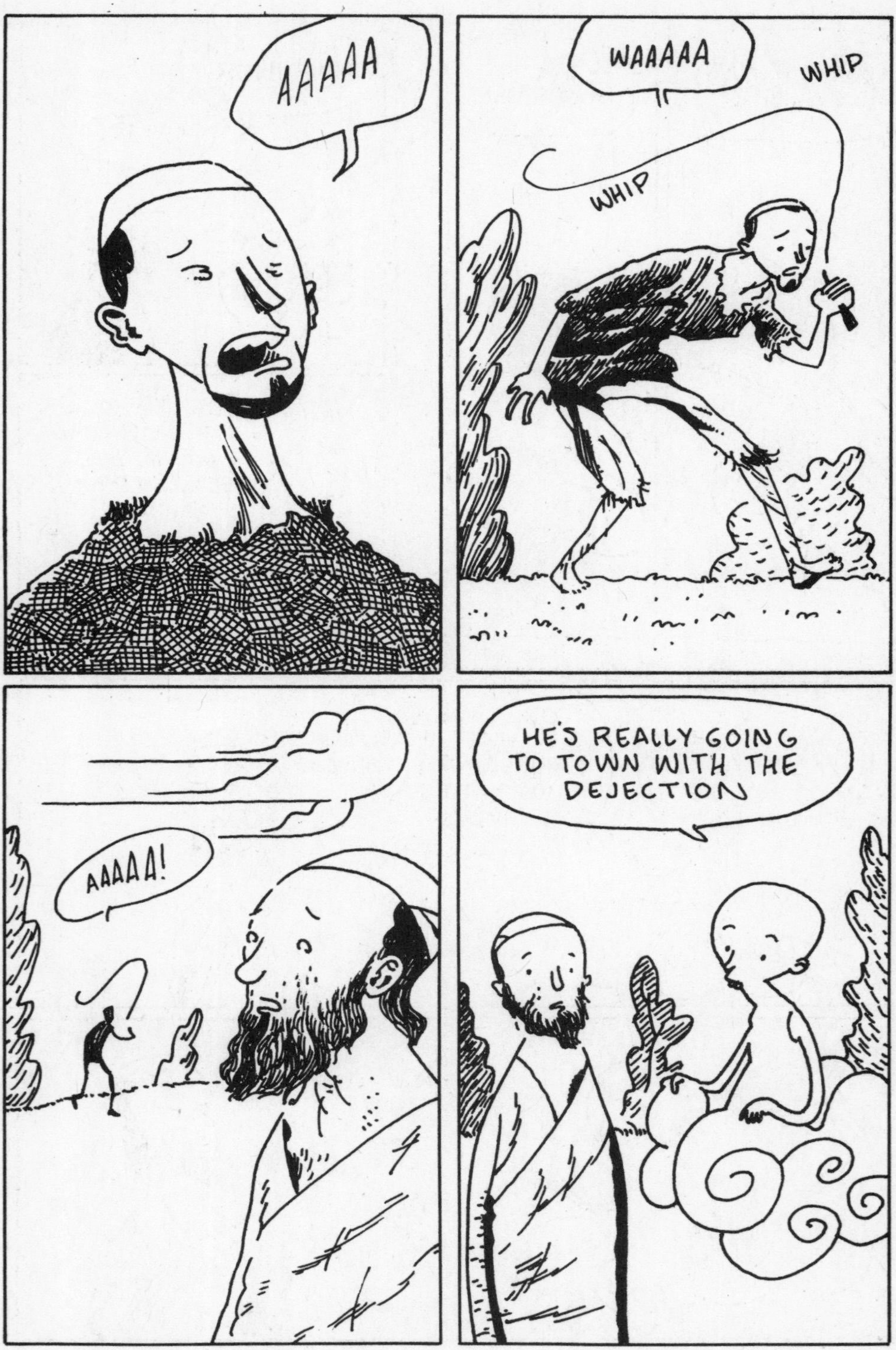
AAAAA
WAAAAA
WHIP
WHIP
AAAAA!
HE'S REALLY GOING TO TOWN WITH THE DEJECTION

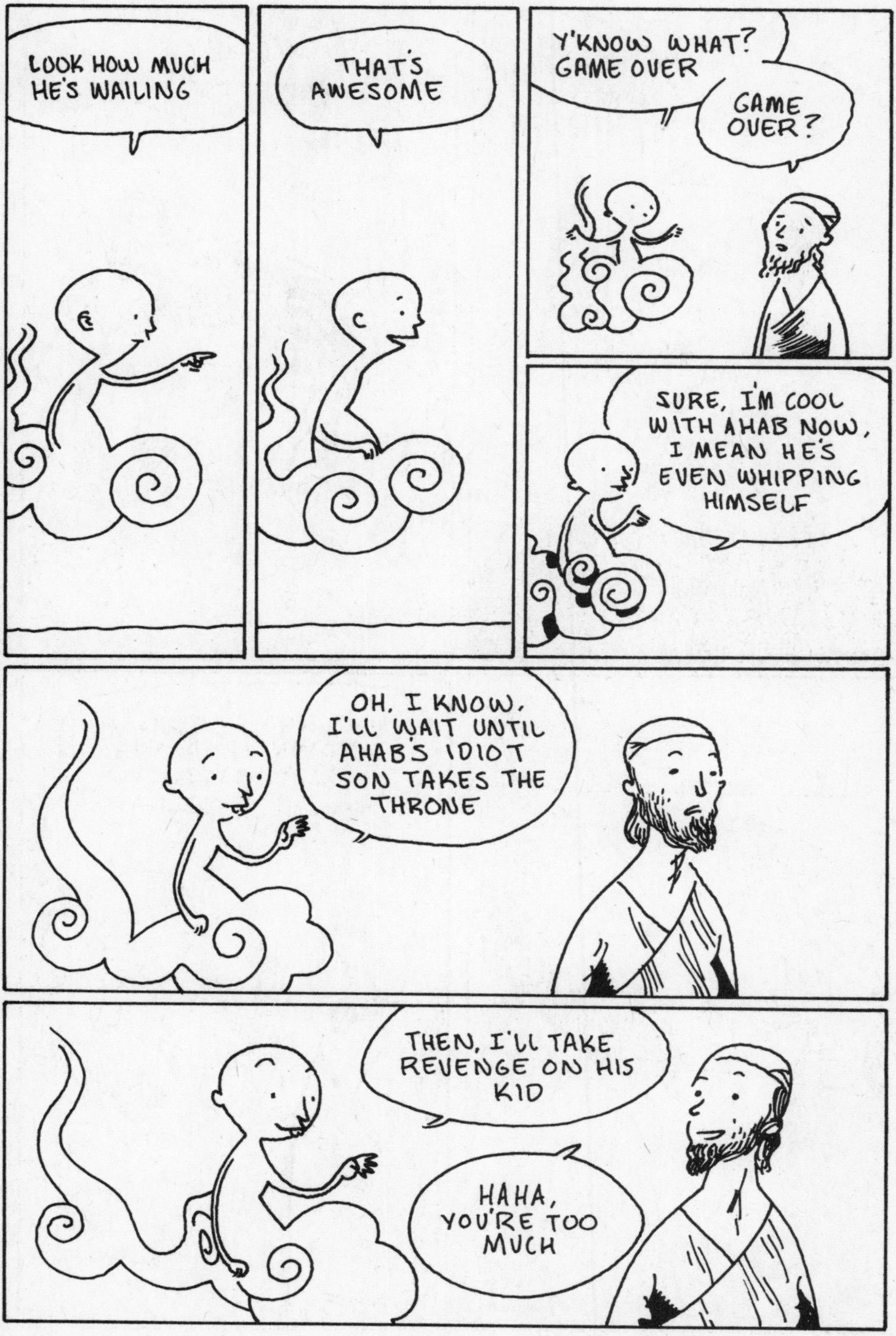
LOOK HOW MUCH HE'S WAILING
THAT'S AWESOME
Y'KNOW WHAT? GAME OVER
GAME OVER?
SURE, I'M COOL WITH AHAB NOW, I MEAN HE'S EVEN WHIPPING HIMSELF
OH, I KNOW. I'LL WAIT UNTIL AHAB'S IDIOT SON TAKES THE THRONE
THEN, I'LL TAKE REVENGE ON HIS KID
HAHA, YOU'RE TOO MUCH

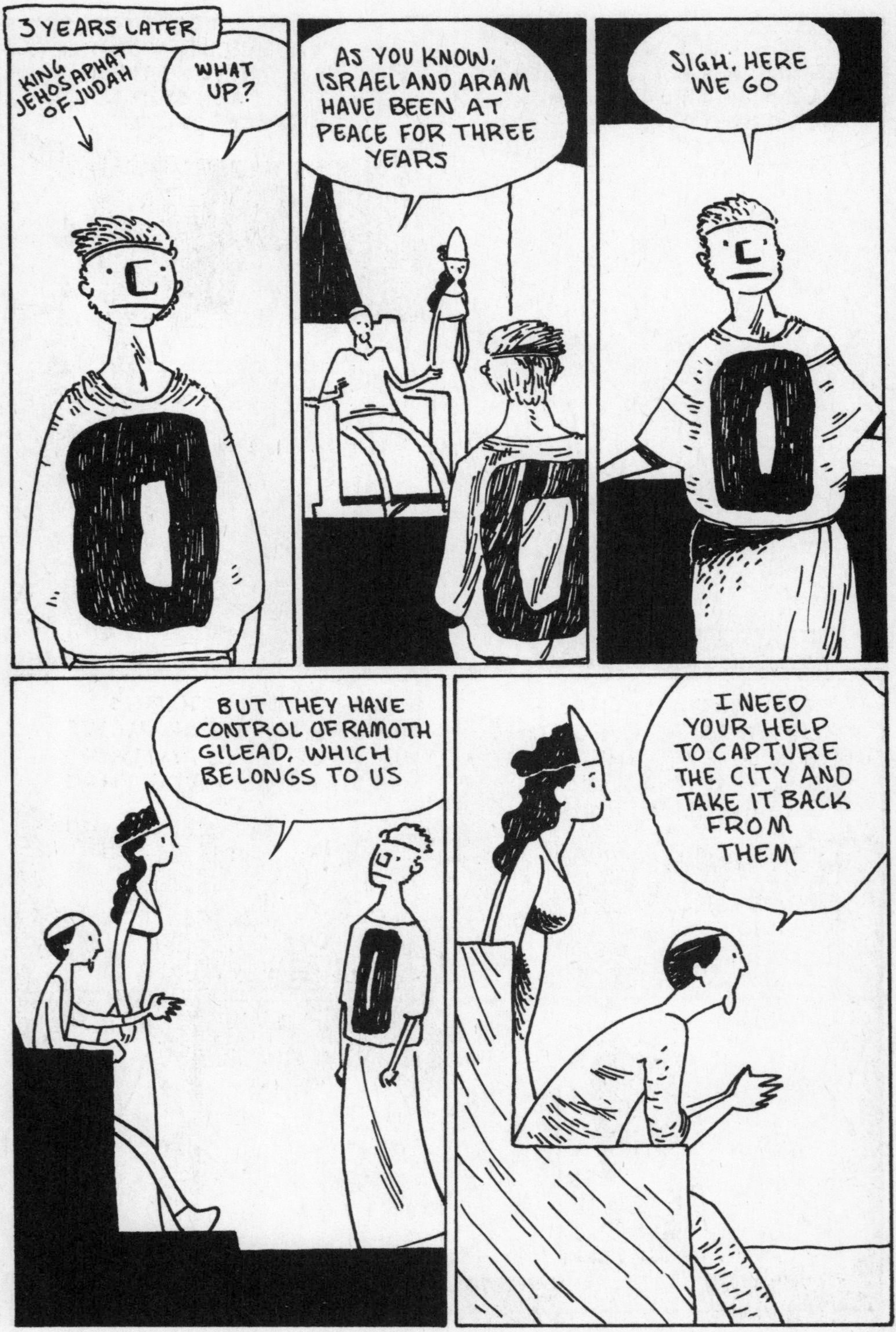
3 YEARS LATER
KING JEHOSAPHAT OF JUDAH
WHAT UP?
AS YOU KNOW, ISRAEL AND ARAM HAVE BEEN AT PEACE FOR THREE YEARS
SIGH, HERE WE GO
BUT THEY HAVE CONTROL OF RAMOTH GILEAD, WHICH BELONGS TO US
I NEED YOUR HELP TO CAPTURE THE CITY AND TAKE IT BACK FROM THEM

LOOK DUDE, MI ARMY ES SU ARMY, Y'KNOW? BUT MAYBE WE SHOULD GET A SECOND OPINION

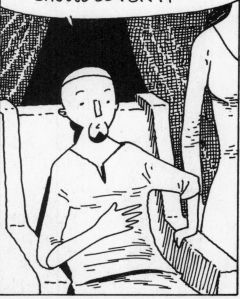

I GOT LIKE, FOUR HUNDRED PROPHETS TOGETHER AND THEY ALL SAID I SHOULD GO FOR IT

YEAH BUT ALL THOSE PROPHETS ARE FUCKING NUTS, AREN'T THERE ANY REAL PROPHETS WE CAN TALK WITH?

YEAH, I GUESS THERE'S MICAIAH BUT HE'S A DICK, HE NEVER SAYS ANYTHING POSITIVE... I HATE THAT GUY

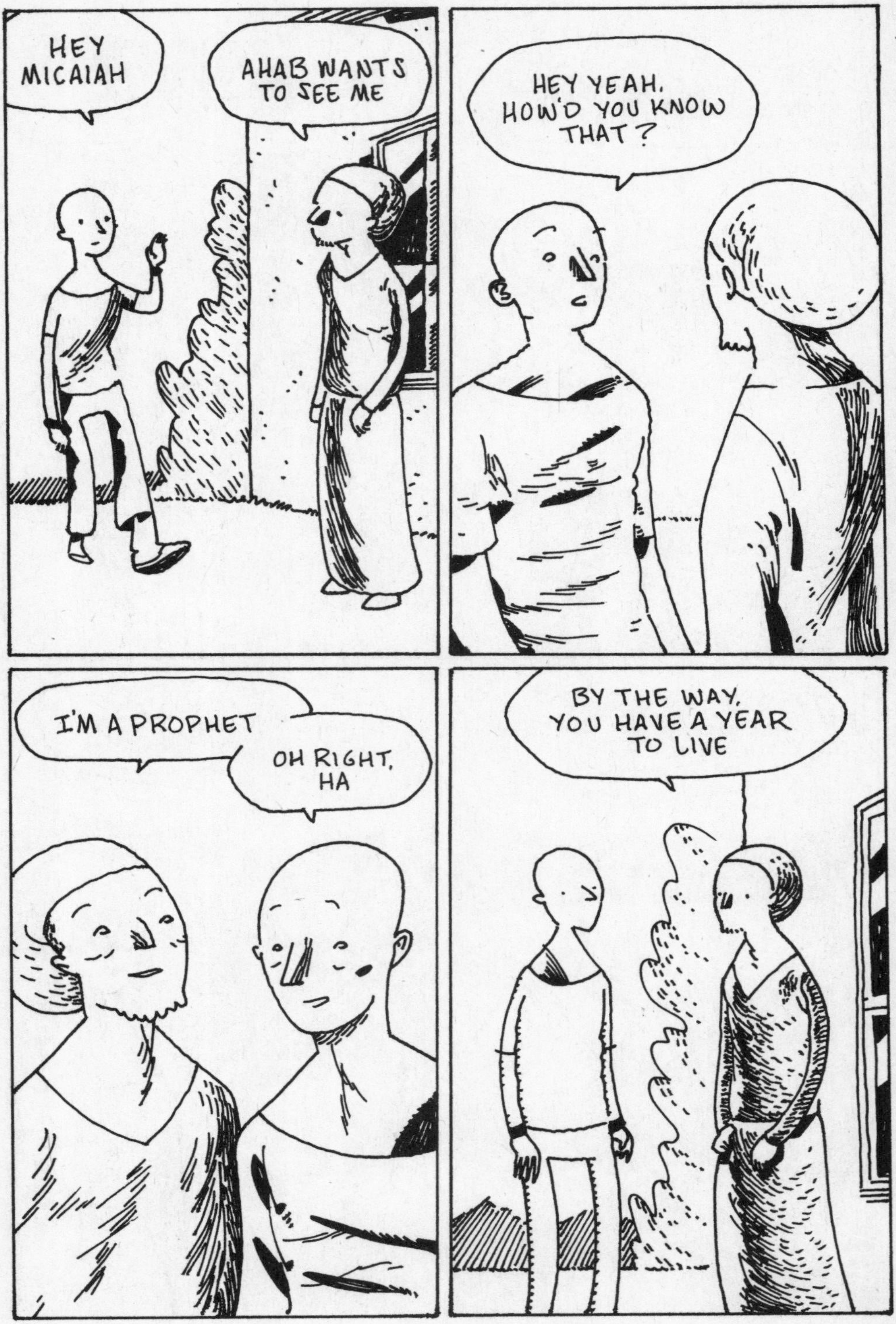
HEY MICAIAH
AHAB WANTS TO SEE ME
HEY YEAH. HOW'D YOU KNOW THAT?
I'M A PROPHET
OH RIGHT, HA
BY THE WAY, YOU HAVE A YEAR TO LIVE

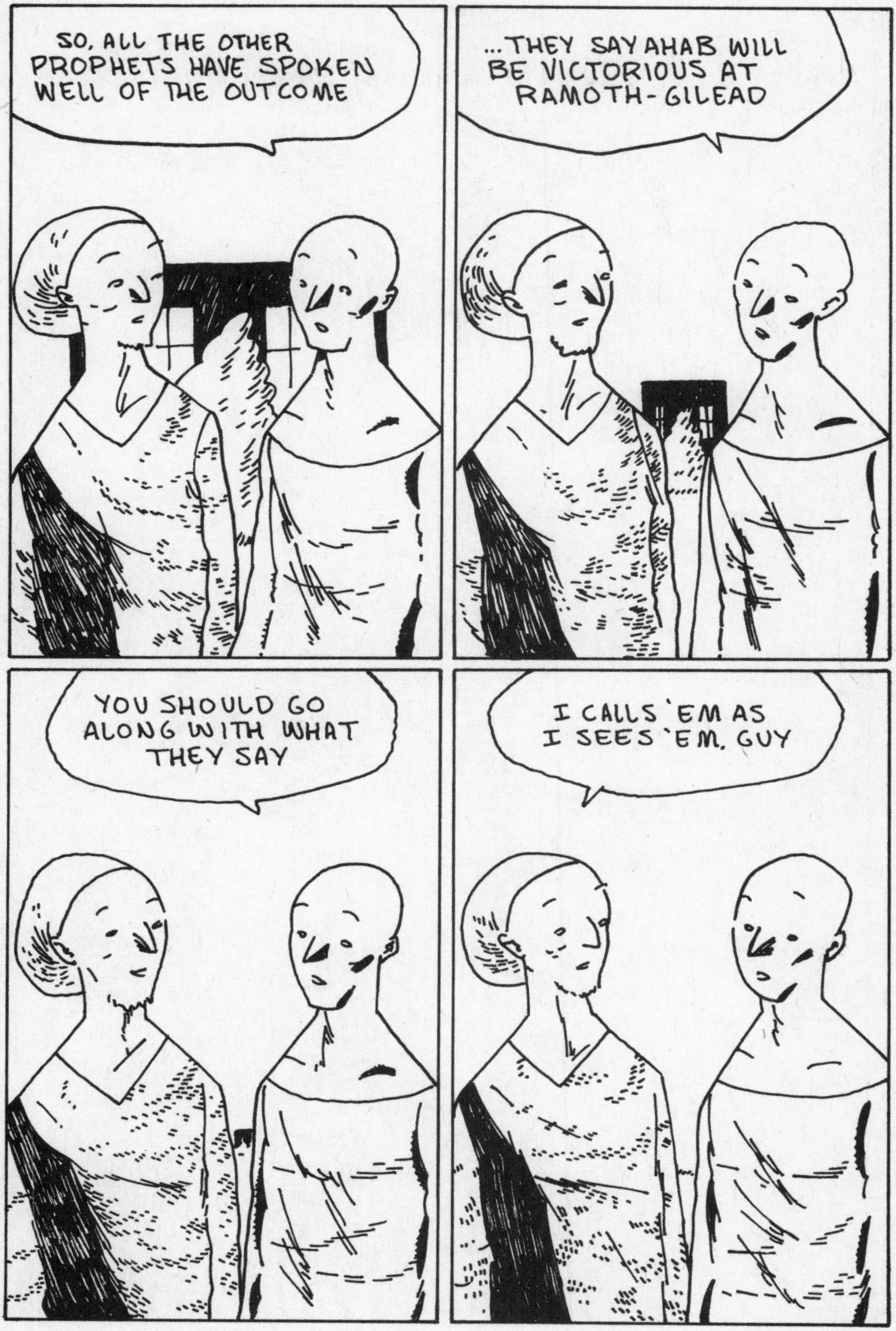
SO, ALL THE OTHER PROPHETS HAVE SPOKEN WELL OF THE OUTCOME
...THEY SAY AHAB WILL BE VICTORIOUS AT RAMOTH-GILEAD
YOU SHOULD GO ALONG WITH WHAT THEY SAY
I CALLS 'EM AS I SEES 'EM, GUY

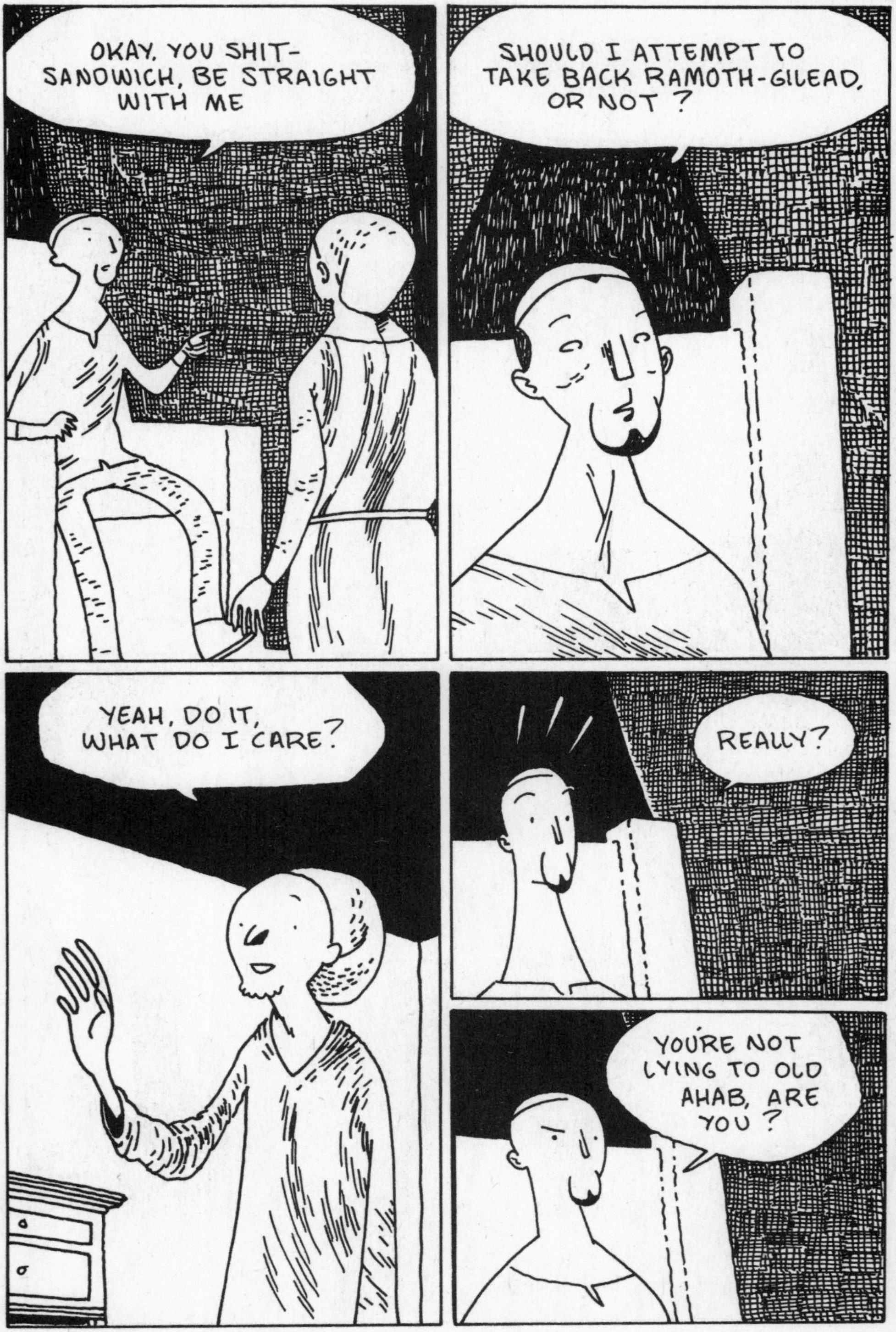
OKAY, YOU SHIT-SANDWICH, BE STRAIGHT WITH ME
SHOULD I ATTEMPT TO TAKE BACK RAMOTH-GILEAD, OR NOT ?
YEAH, DO IT, WHAT DO I CARE?
REALLY?
YOU'RE NOT LYING TO OLD AHAB, ARE YOU ?

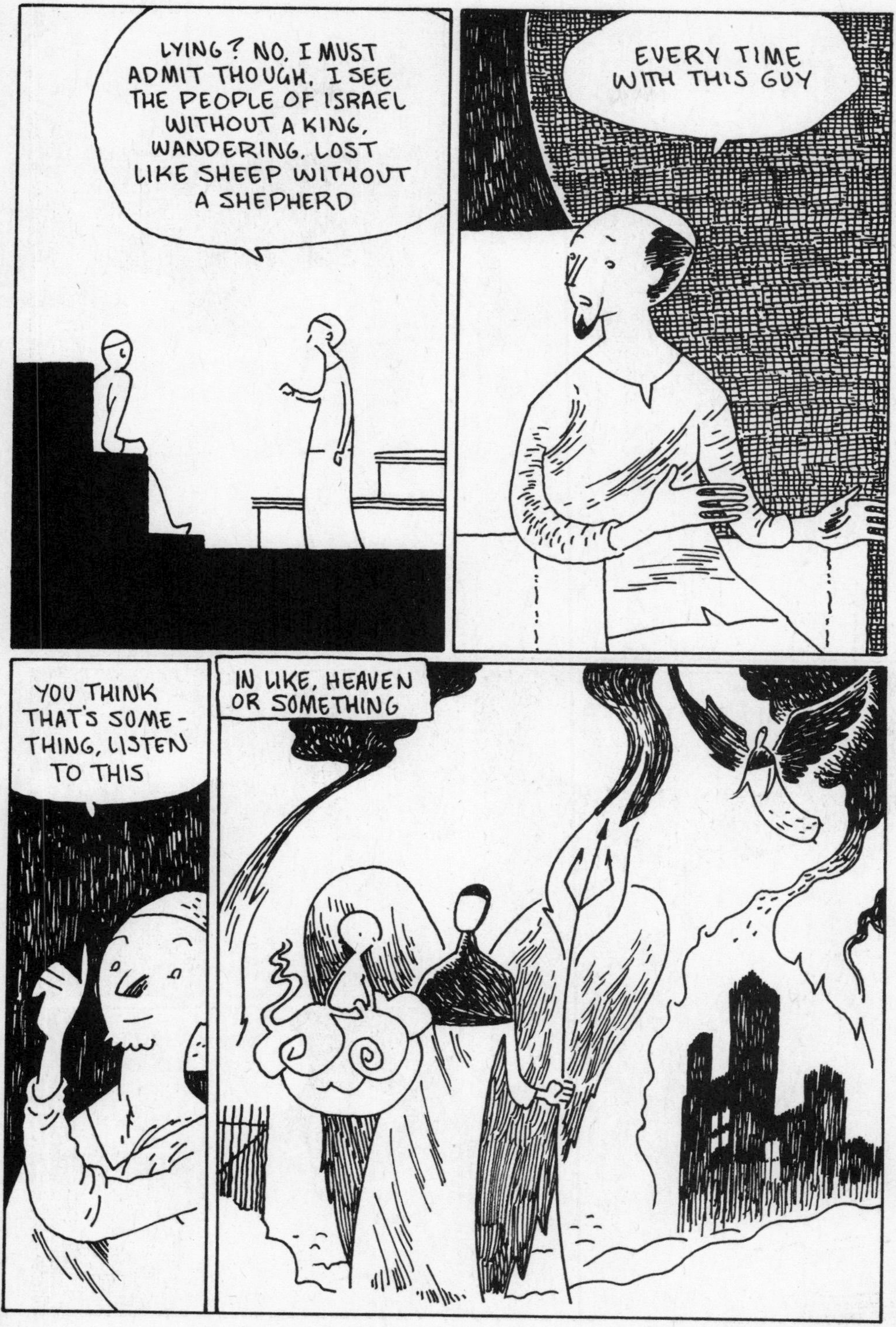
LYING? NO, I MUST ADMIT THOUGH, I SEE THE PEOPLE OF ISRAEL WITHOUT A KING, WANDERING, LOST LIKE SHEEP WITHOUT A SHEPHERD
EVERY TIME WITH THIS GUY
YOU THINK THAT'S SOME-THING, LISTEN TO THIS
IN LIKE, HEAVEN OR SOMETHING

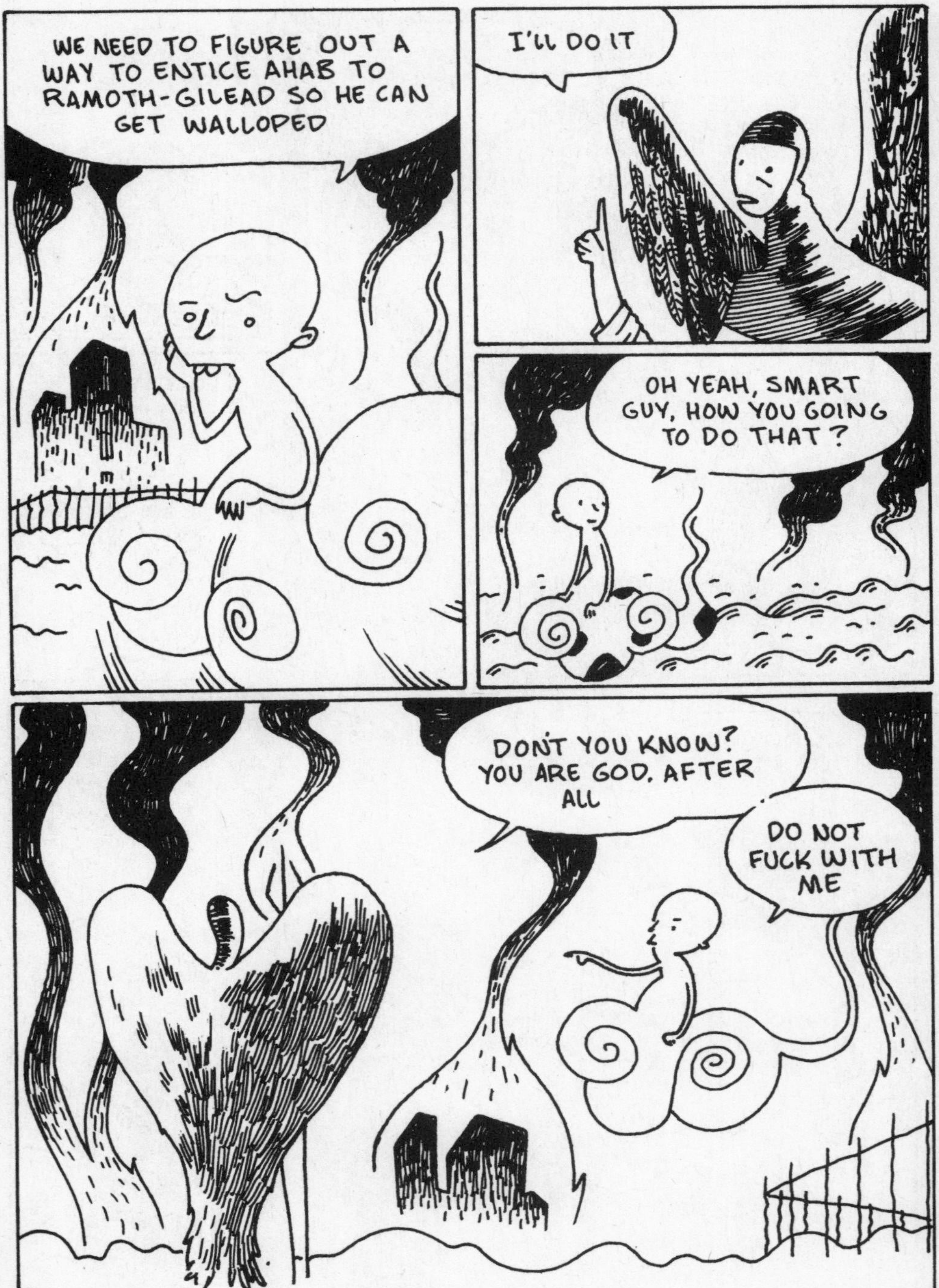
WE NEED TO FIGURE OUT A WAY TO ENTICE AHAB TO RAMOTH-GILEAD SO HE CAN GET WALLOPED
I'LL DO IT
OH YEAH, SMART GUY, HOW YOU GOING TO DO THAT?
DON'T YOU KNOW? YOU ARE GOD. AFTER ALL
DO NOT FUCK WITH ME

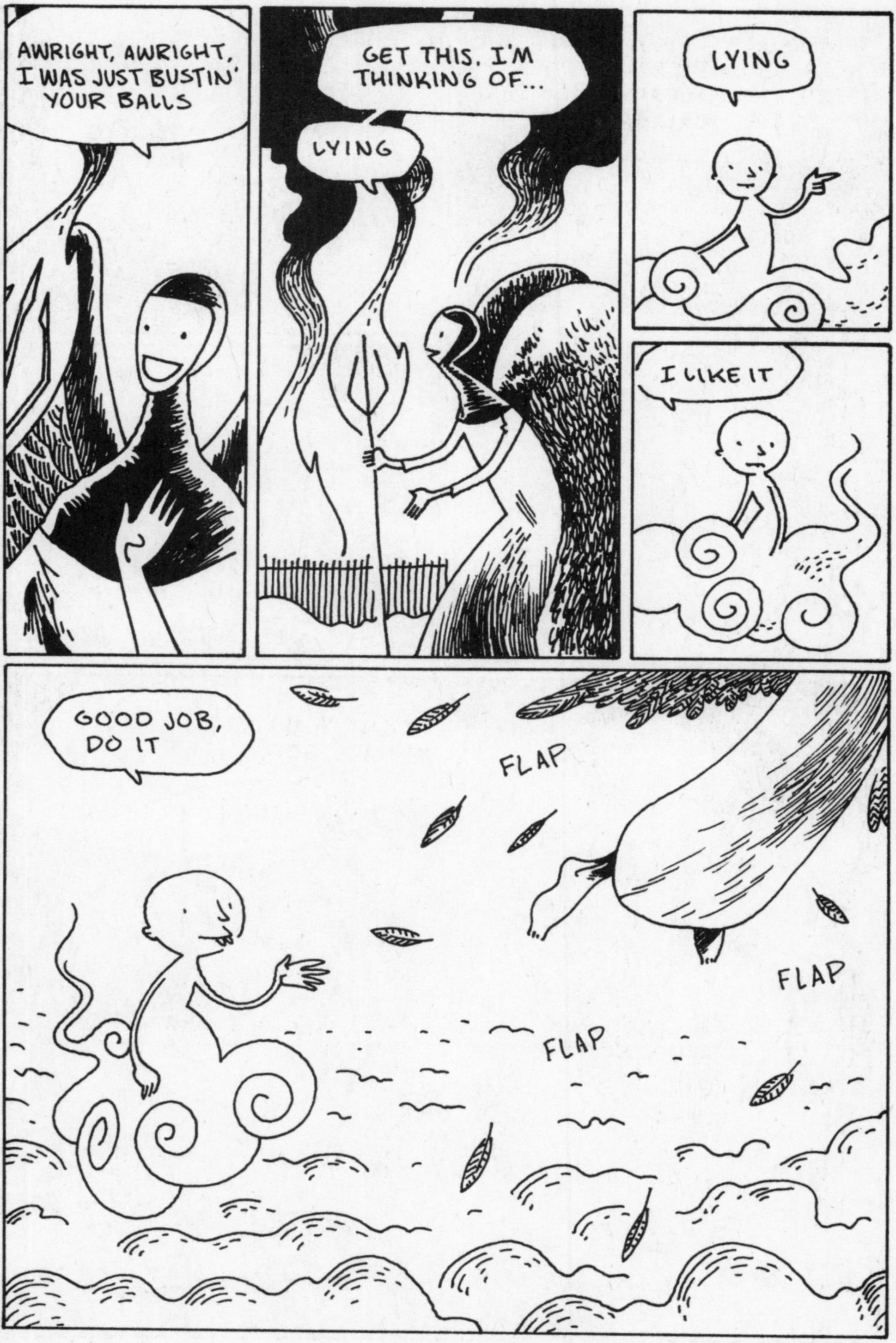
AWRIGHT, AWRIGHT, I WAS JUST BUSTIN' YOUR BALLS
GET THIS. I'M THINKING OF...
LYING
LYING
I LIKE IT
GOOD JOB, DO IT
FLAP
FLAP
FLAP

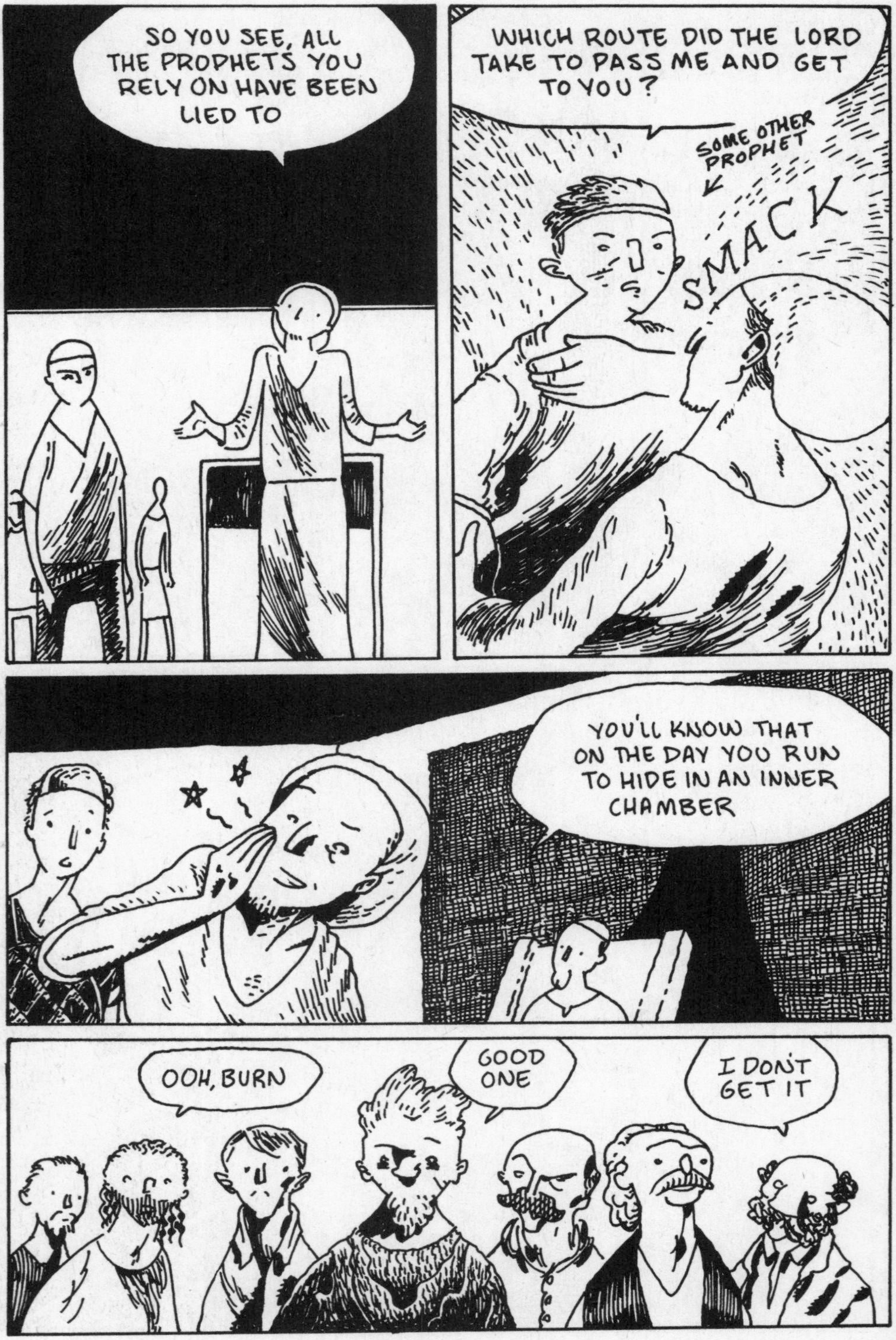
SO YOU SEE, ALL THE PROPHETS YOU RELY ON HAVE BEEN LIED TO
WHICH ROUTE DID THE LORD TAKE TO PASS ME AND GET TO YOU?
SOME OTHER PROPHET
SMACK
YOU'LL KNOW THAT ON THE DAY YOU RUN TO HIDE IN AN INNER CHAMBER
OOH, BURN
GOOD ONE
I DON'T GET IT

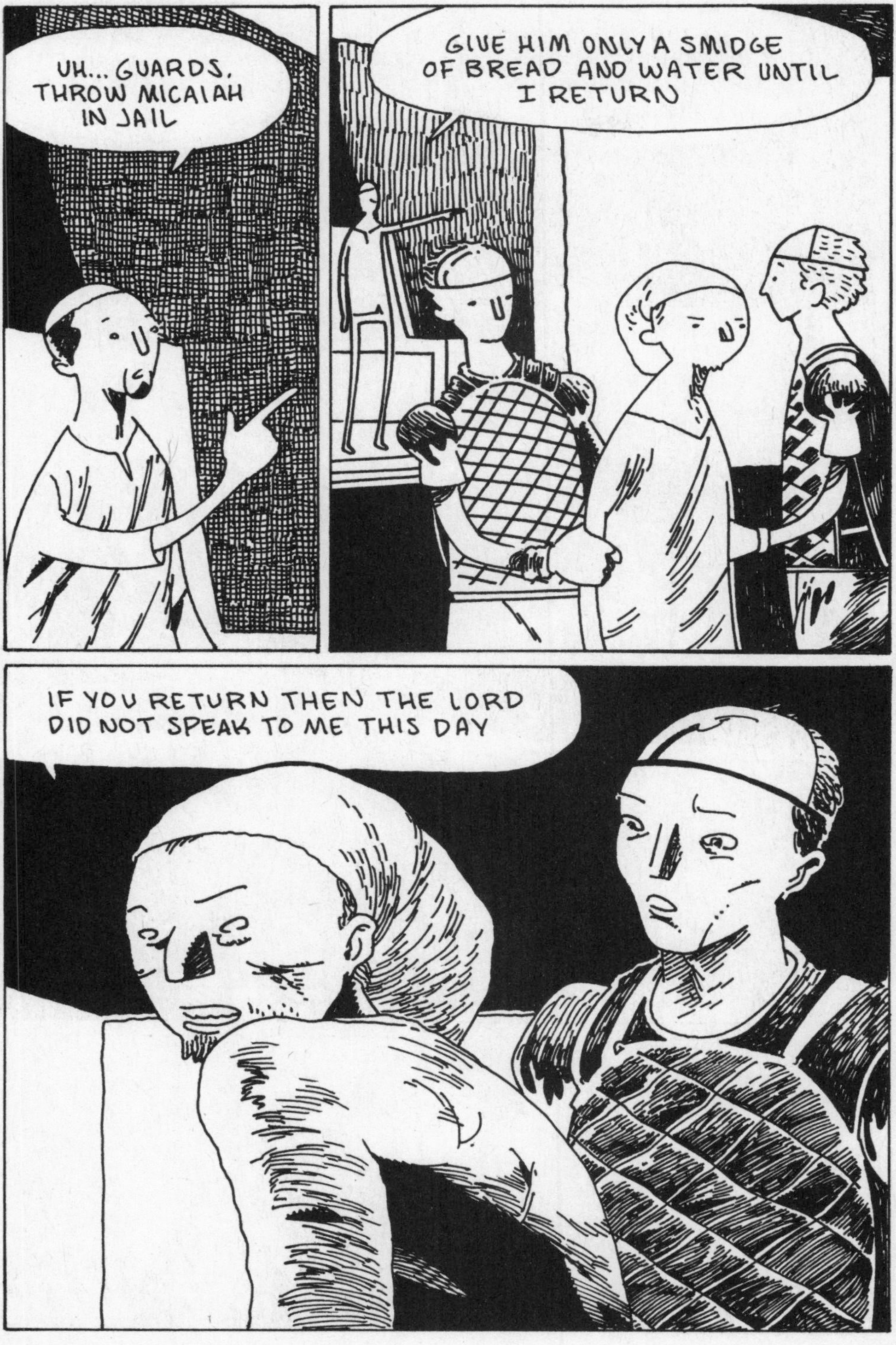
UH... GUARDS, THROW MICAIAH IN JAIL
GIVE HIM ONLY A SMIDGE OF BREAD AND WATER UNTIL I RETURN
IF YOU RETURN THEN THE LORD DID NOT SPEAK TO ME THIS DAY

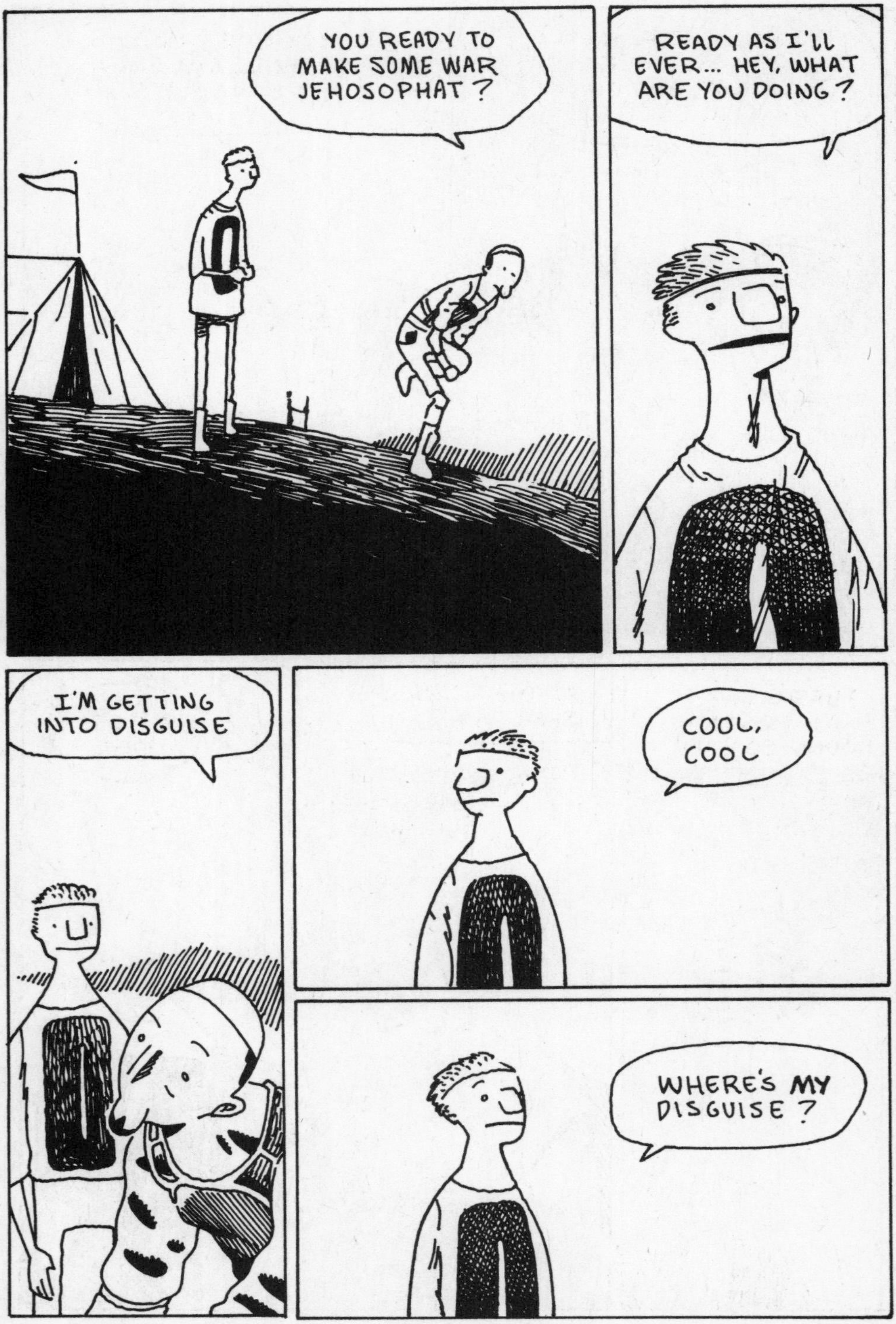
YOU READY TO MAKE SOME WAR JEHOSOPHAT?
READY AS I'LL EVER... HEY, WHAT ARE YOU DOING?
I'M GETTING INTO DISGUISE
COOL, COOL
WHERE'S MY DISGUISE?

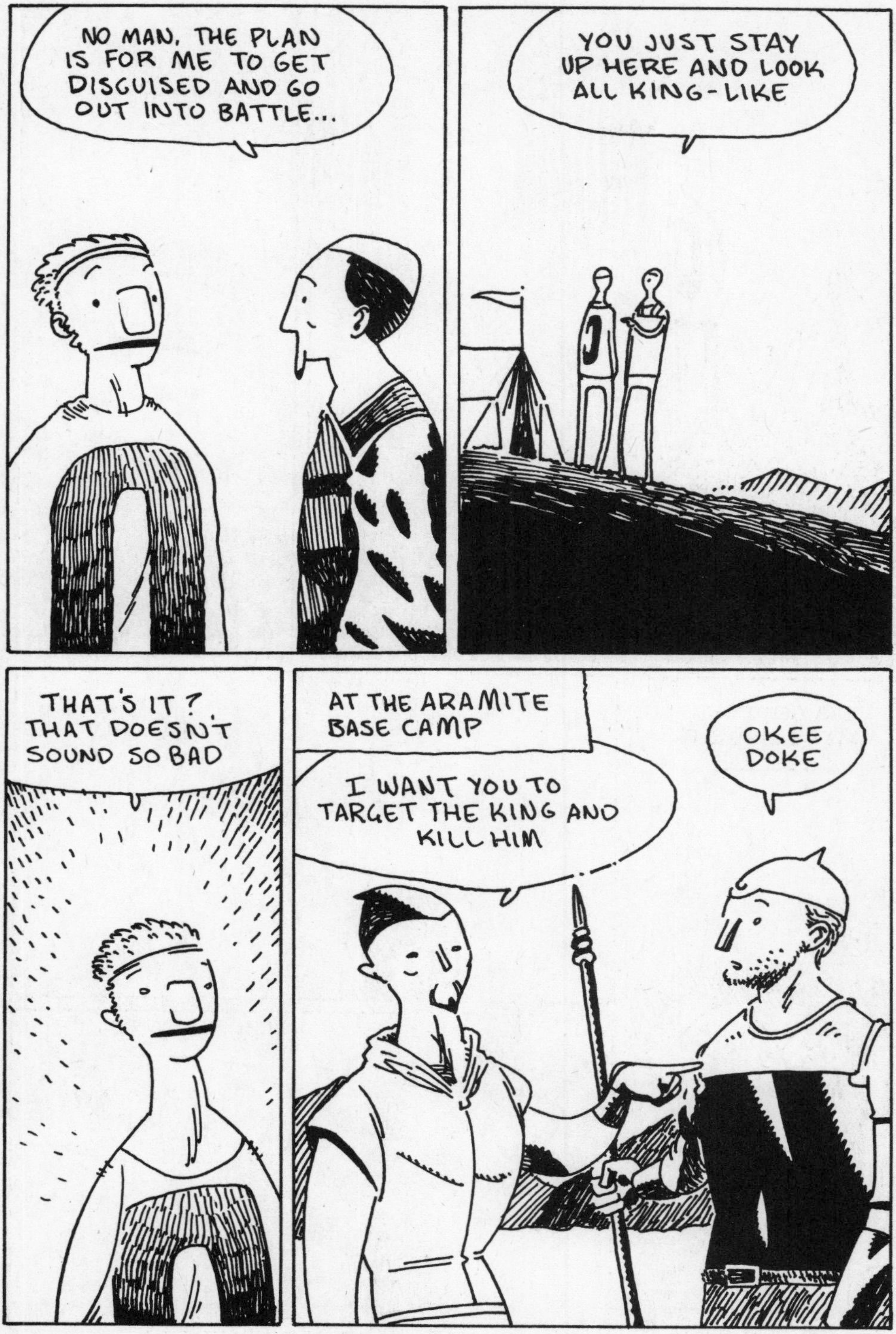
NO MAN, THE PLAN IS FOR ME TO GET DISGUISED AND GO OUT INTO BATTLE...
YOU JUST STAY UP HERE AND LOOK ALL KING-LIKE
THAT'S IT? THAT DOESN'T SOUND SO BAD
AT THE ARAMITE BASE CAMP
I WANT YOU TO TARGET THE KING AND KILL HIM
OKEE DOKE

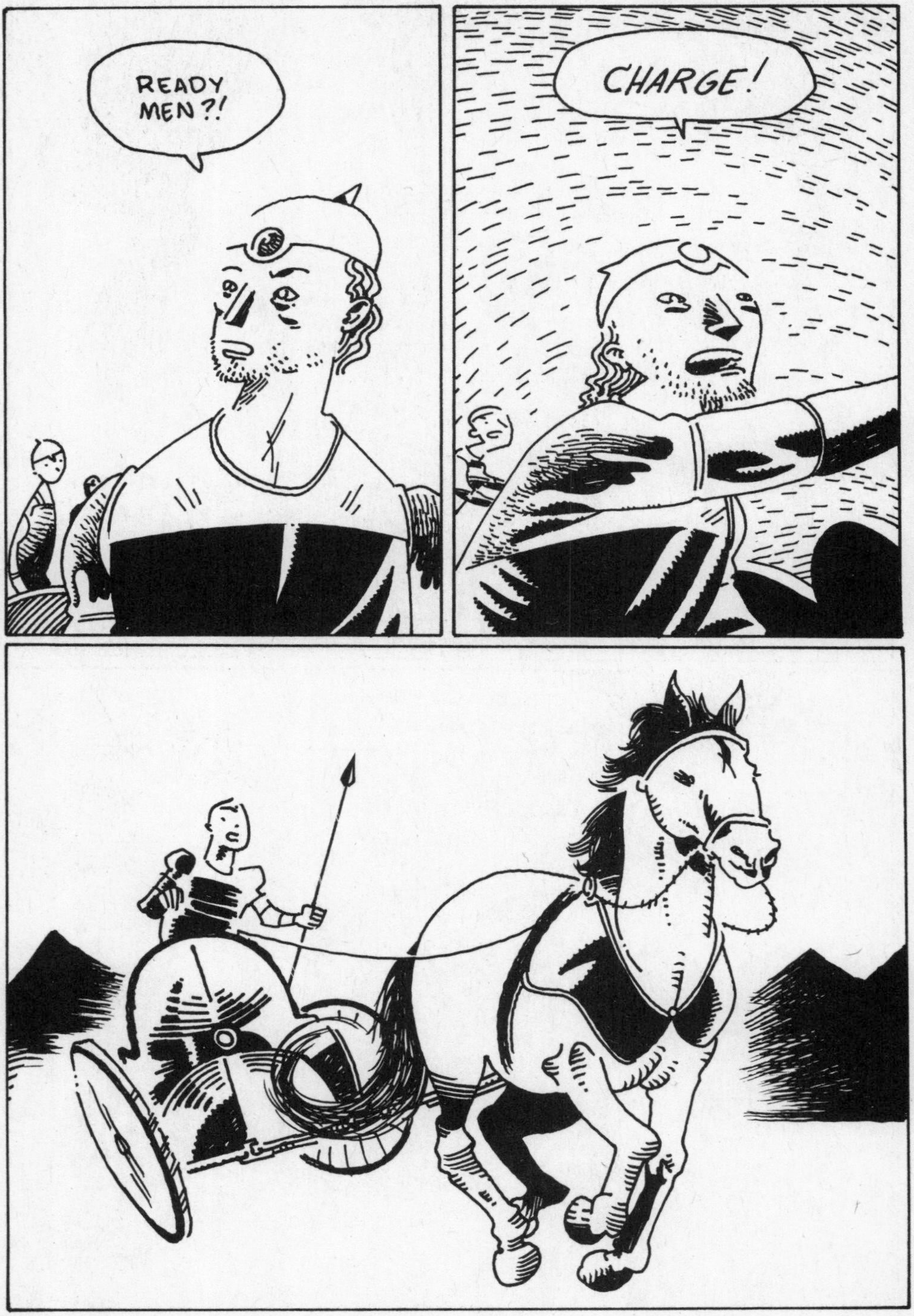
READY MEN?!
CHARGE!

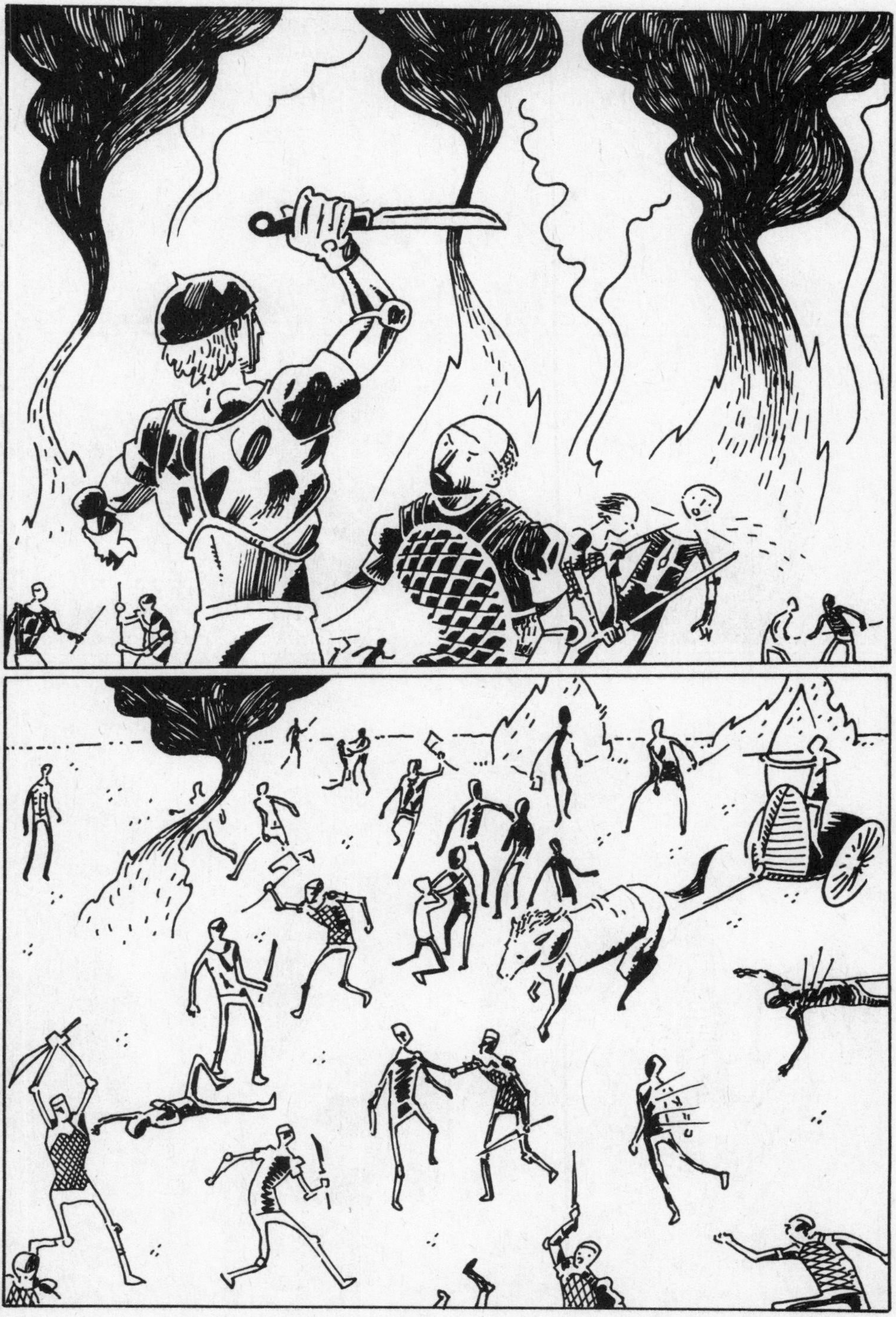

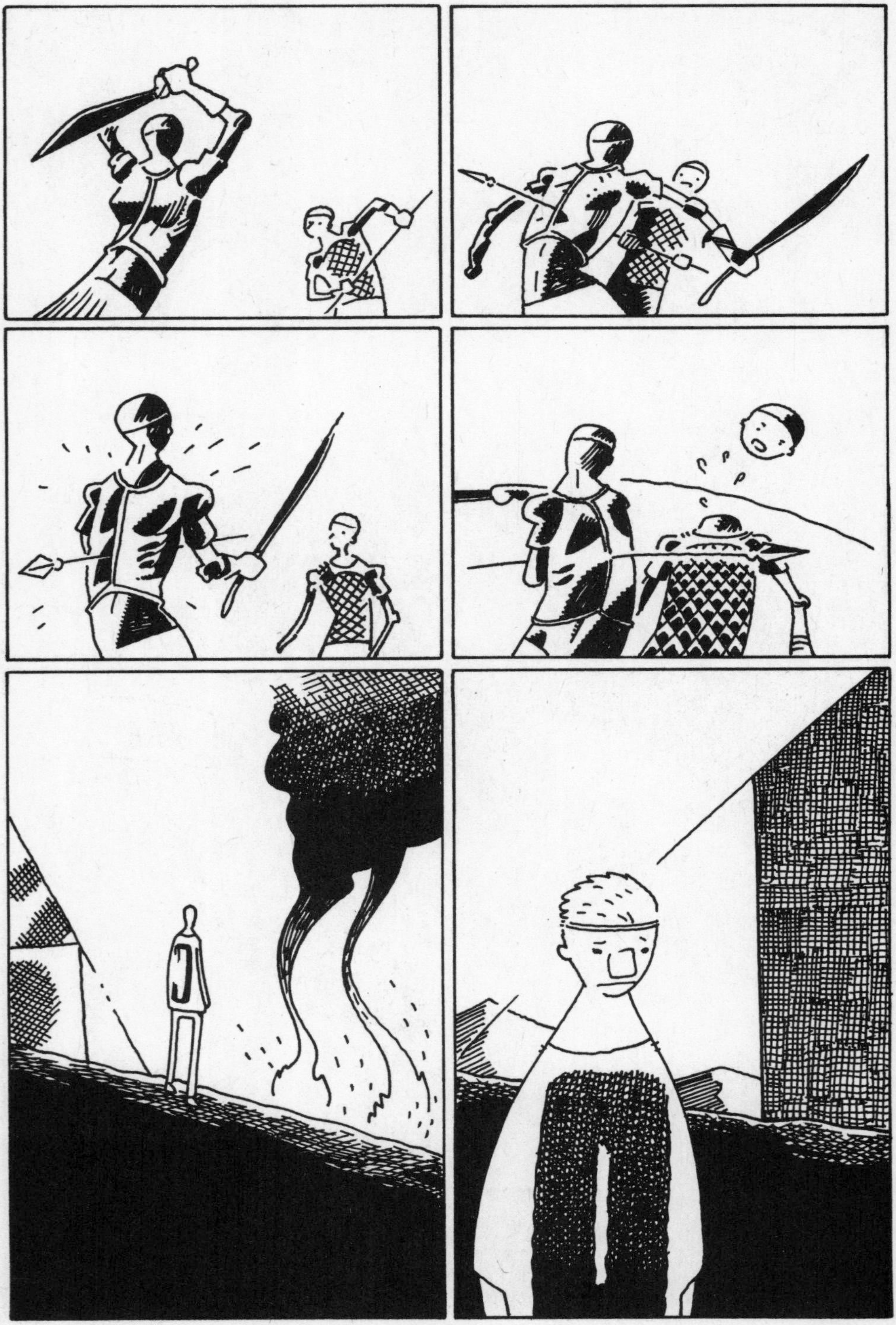

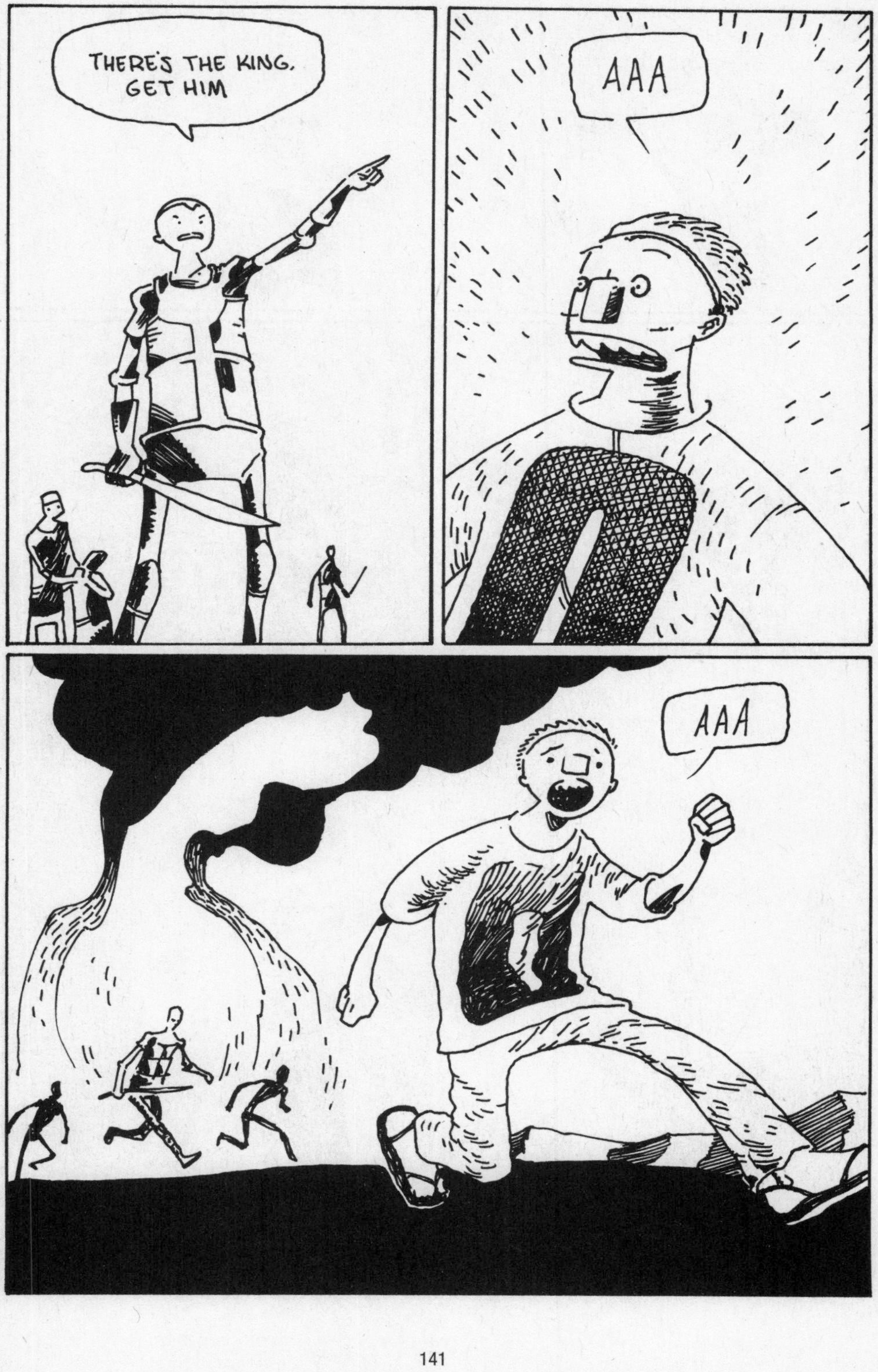
THERE'S THE KING.
GET HIM
AAA
AAA

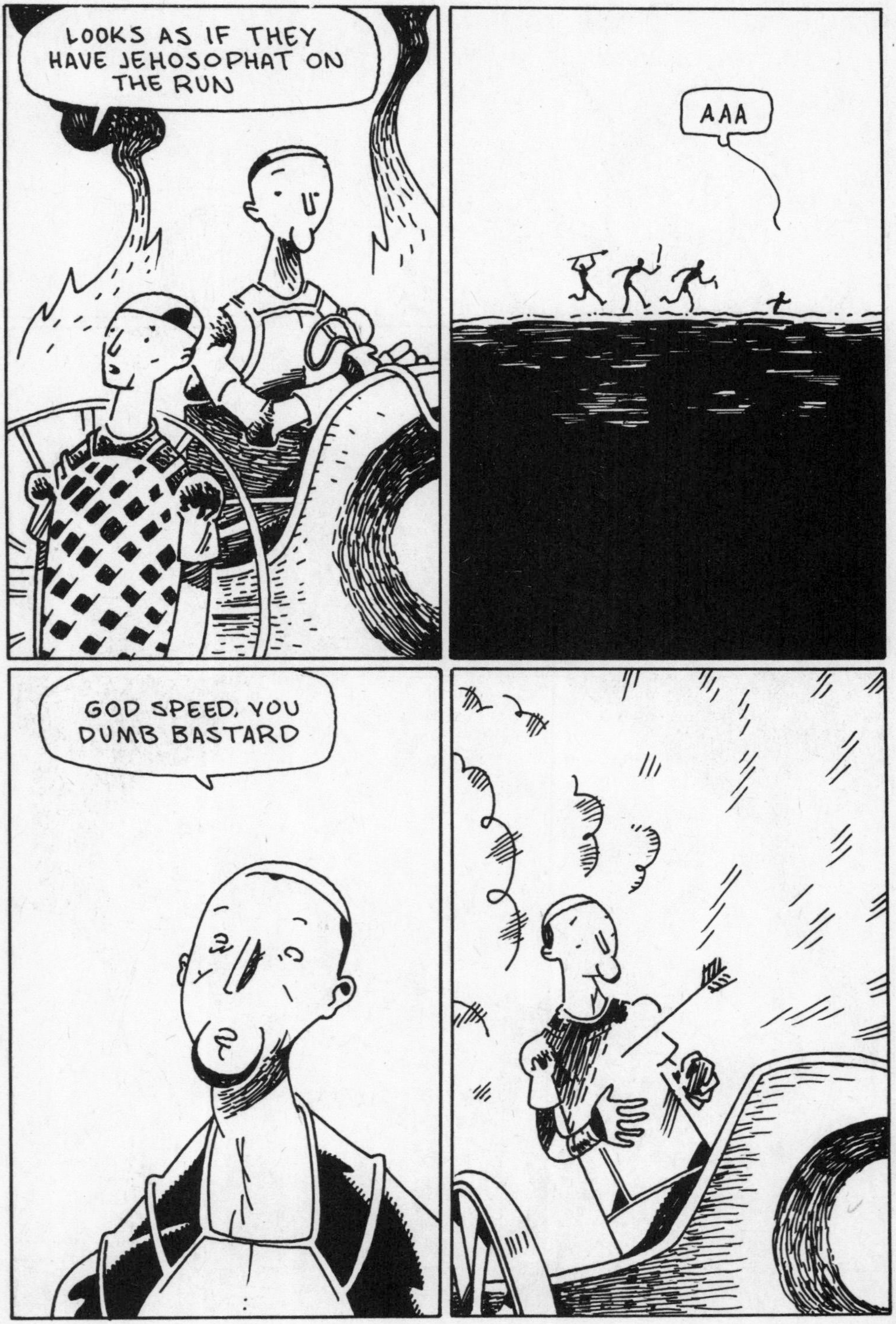
LOOKS AS IF THEY HAVE JEHOSOPHAT ON THE RUN
AAA
GOD SPEED, YOU DUMB BASTARD

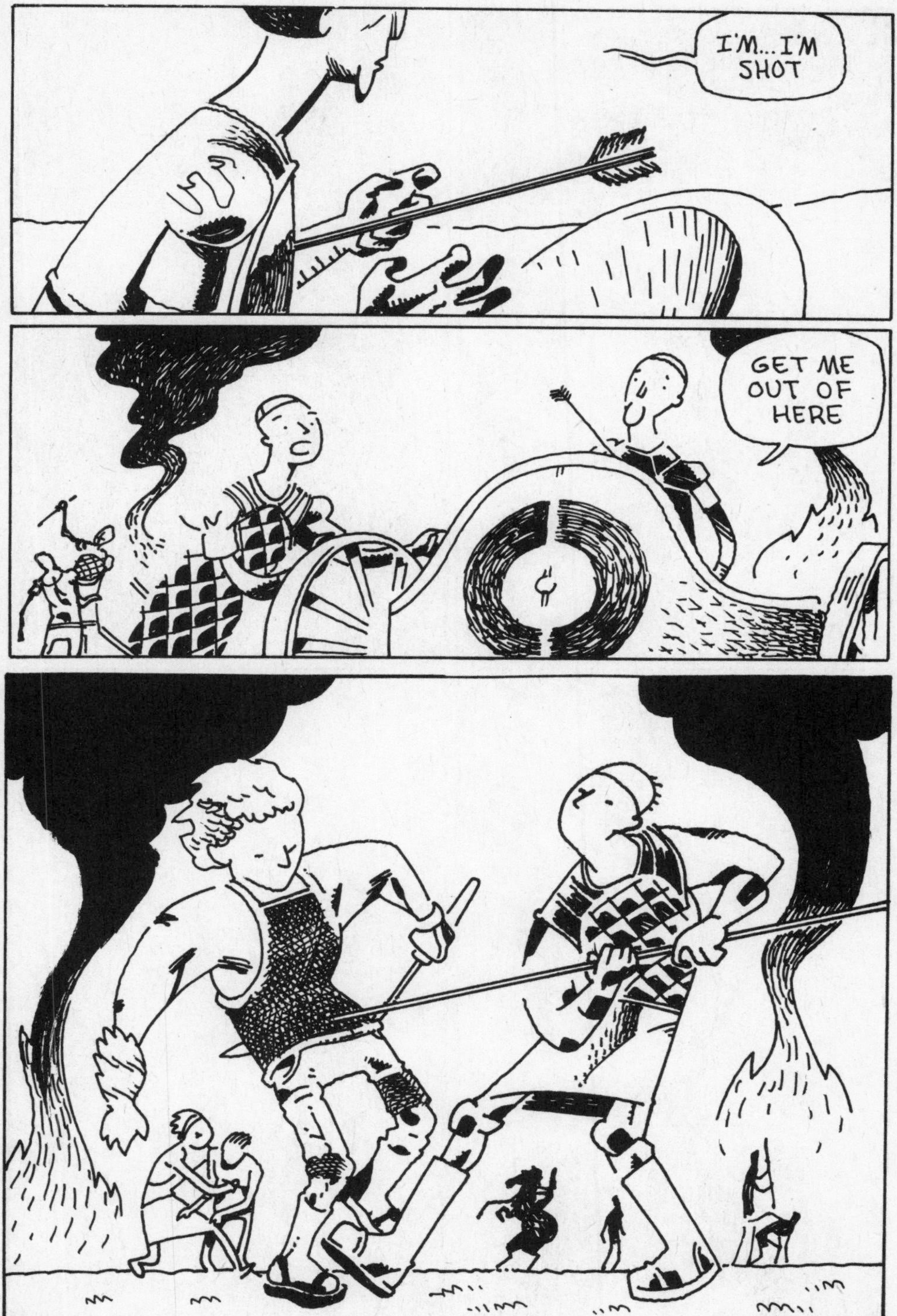
I'M... I'M SHOT
GET ME OUT OF HERE

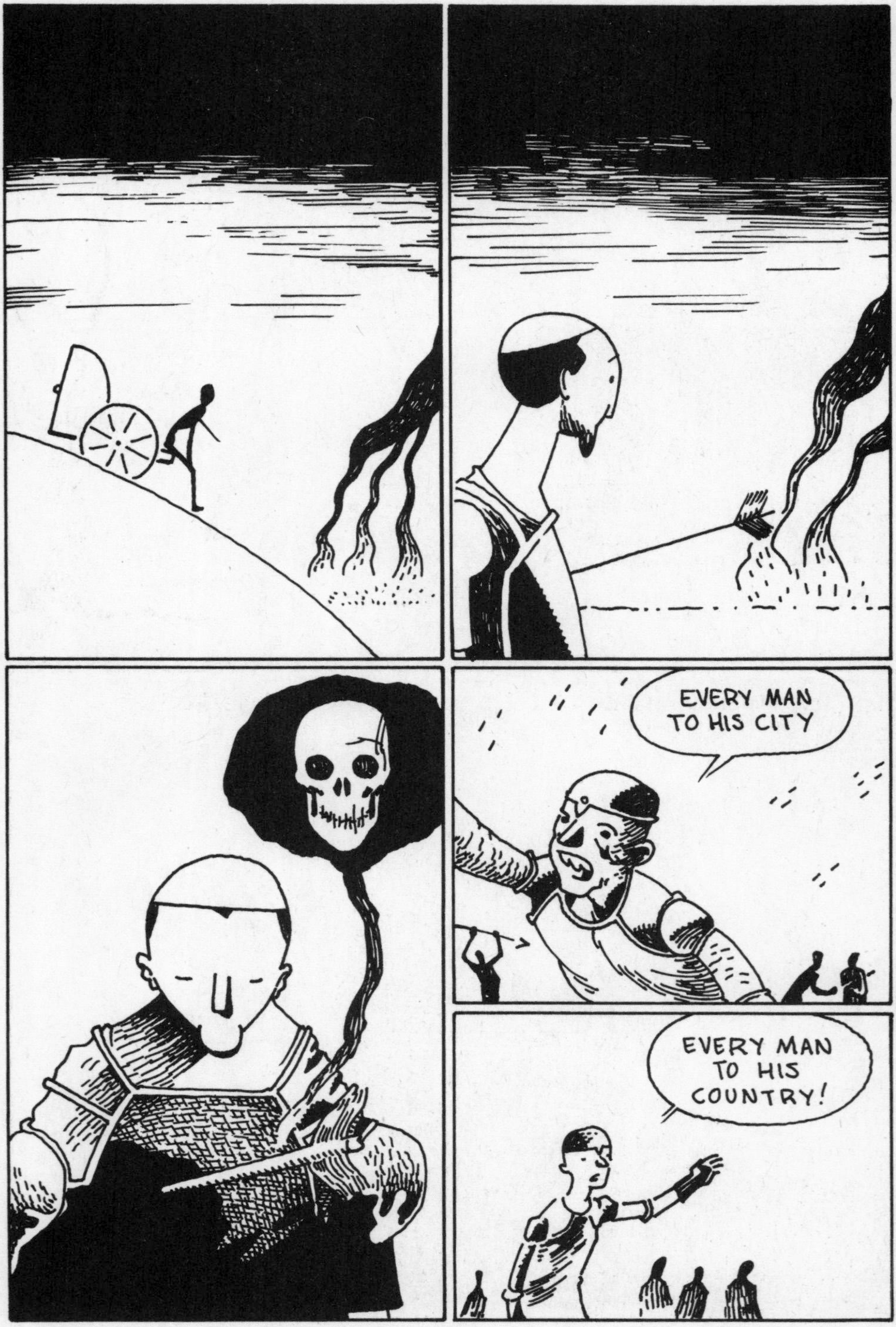
EVERY MAN TO HIS CITY
EVERY MAN TO HIS COUNTRY!

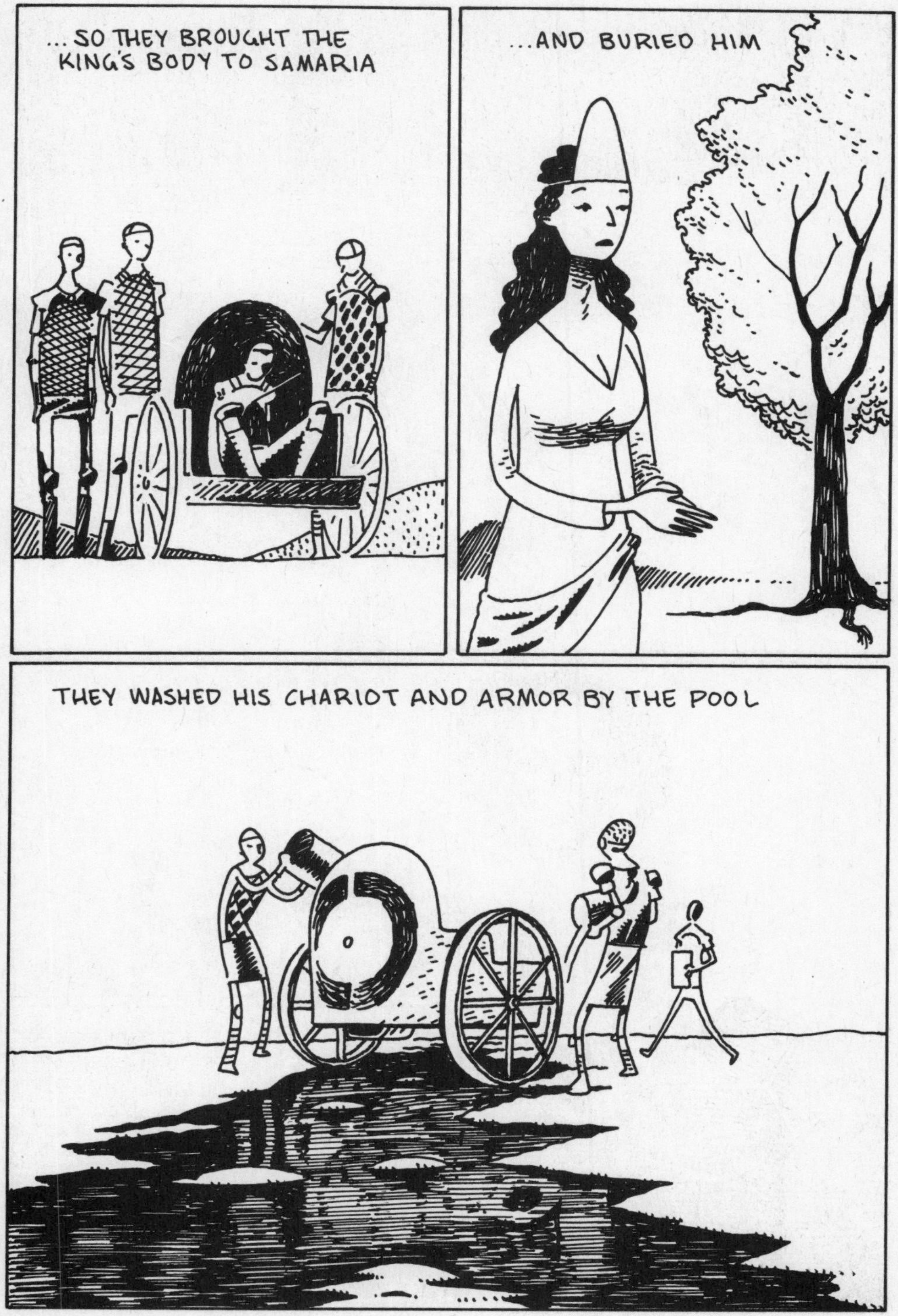
...SO THEY BROUGHT THE KING'S BODY TO SAMARIA
...AND BURIED HIM
THEY WASHED HIS CHARIOT AND ARMOR BY THE POOL

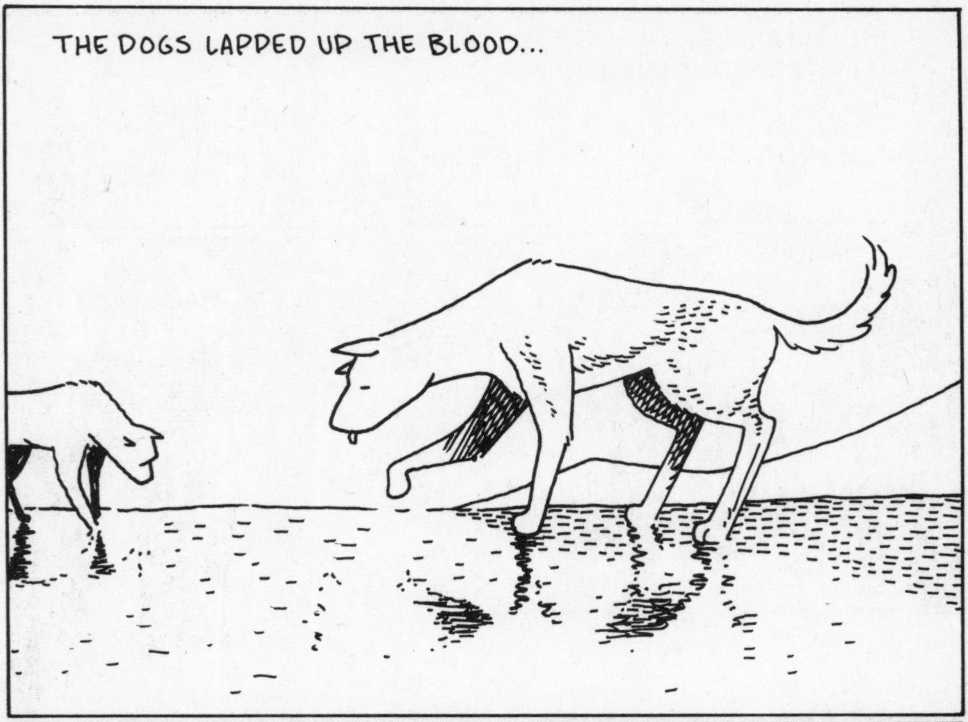
THE DOGS LAPPED UP THE BLOOD...

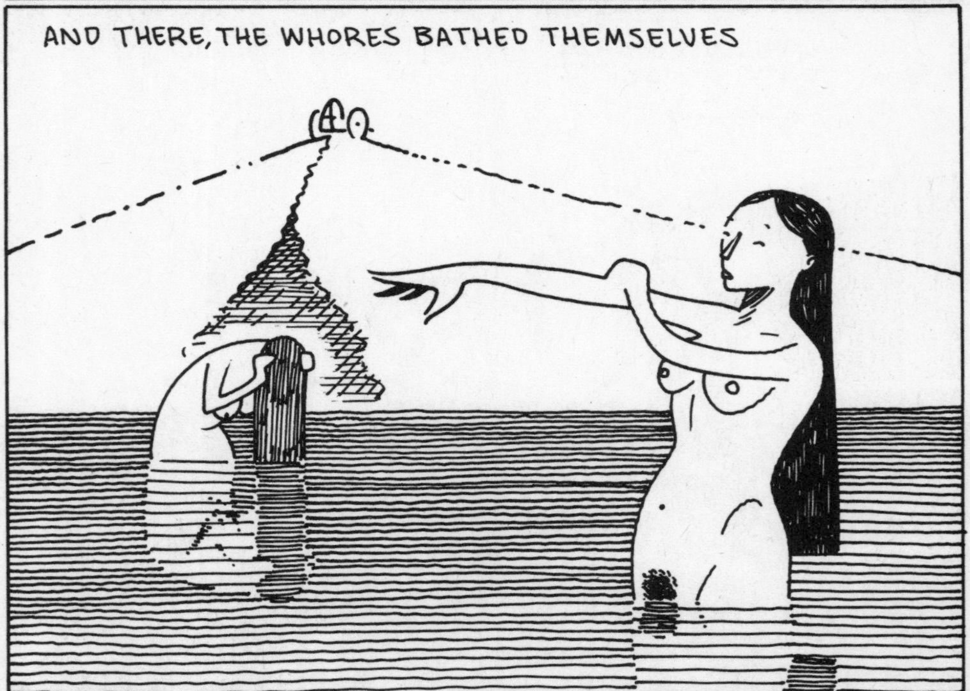
AND THERE, THE WHORES BATHED THEMSELVES

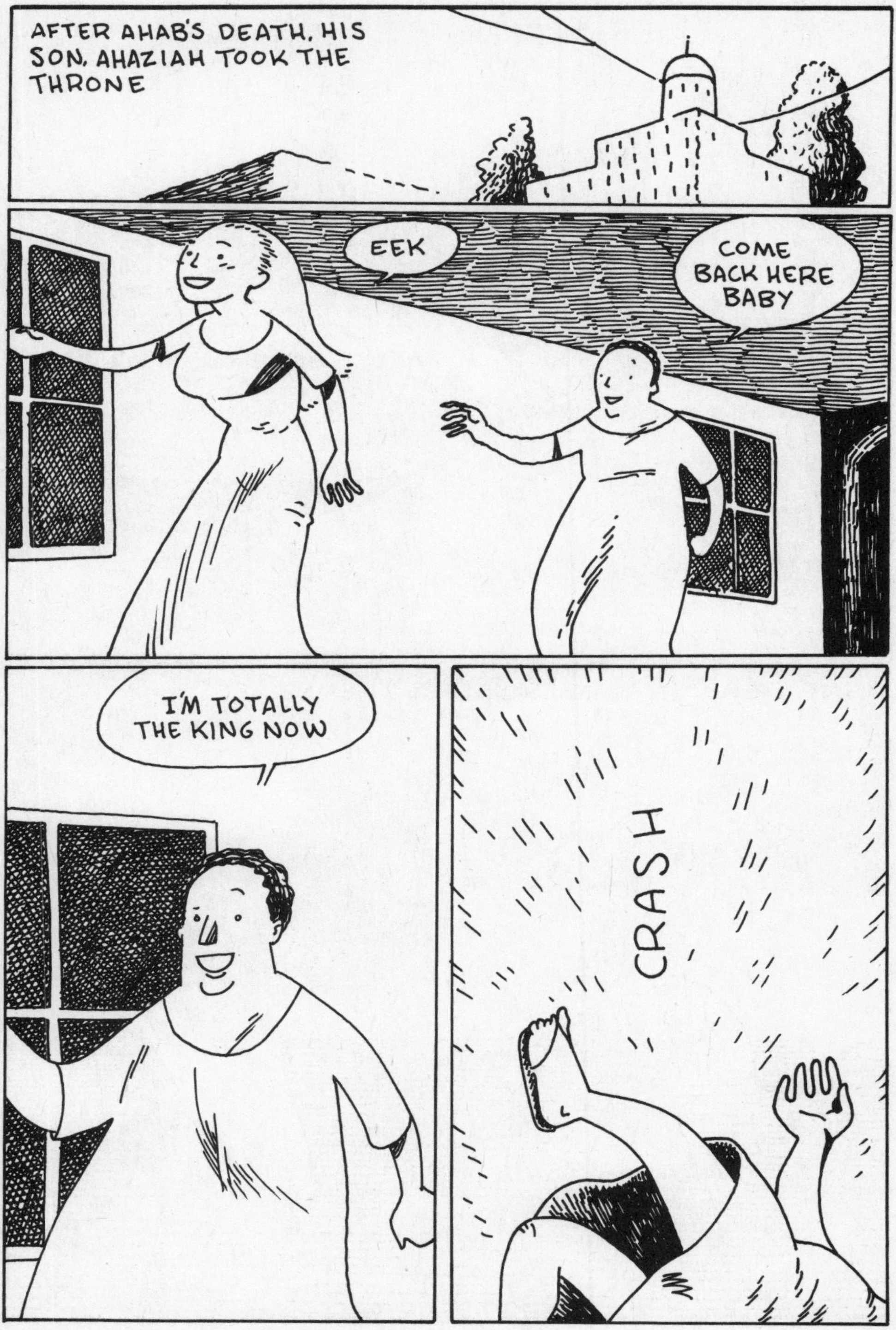
AFTER AHAB'S DEATH, HIS SON, AHAZIAH TOOK THE THRONE
EEK
COME BACK HERE BABY
I'M TOTALLY THE KING NOW
CRASH

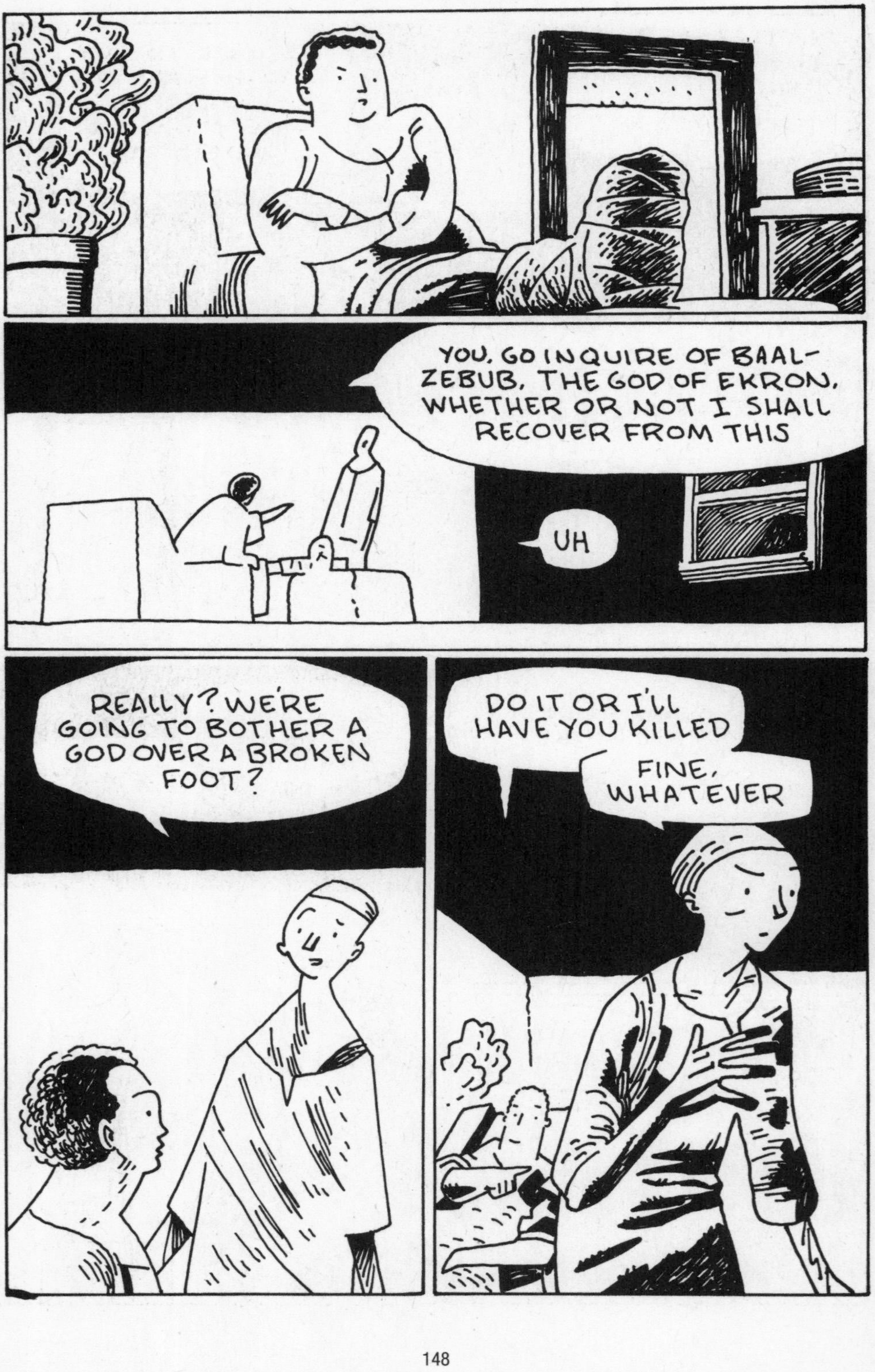
YOU, GO INQUIRE OF BAAL-ZEBUB, THE GOD OF EKRON, WHETHER OR NOT I SHALL RECOVER FROM THIS
UH
REALLY? WE'RE GOING TO BOTHER A GOD OVER A BROKEN FOOT?
DO IT OR I'LL HAVE YOU KILLED
FINE, WHATEVER

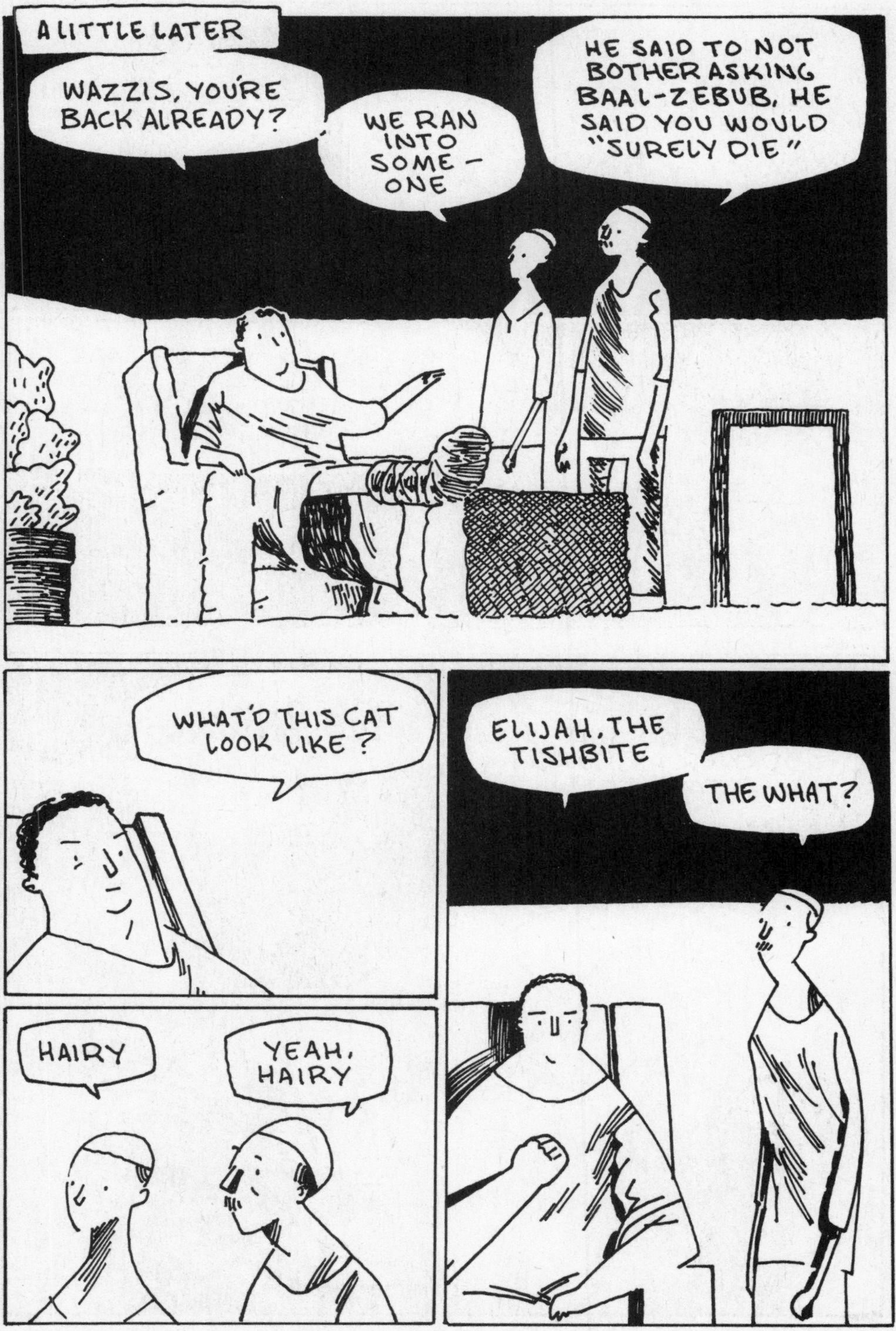
A LITTLE LATER
WAZZIS, YOU'RE BACK ALREADY?
WE RAN INTO SOME-ONE
HE SAID TO NOT BOTHER ASKING BAAL-ZEBUB, HE SAID YOU WOULD "SURELY DIE"
WHAT'D THIS CAT LOOK LIKE?
HAIRY
YEAH, HAIRY
ELIJAH, THE TISHBITE
THE WHAT?

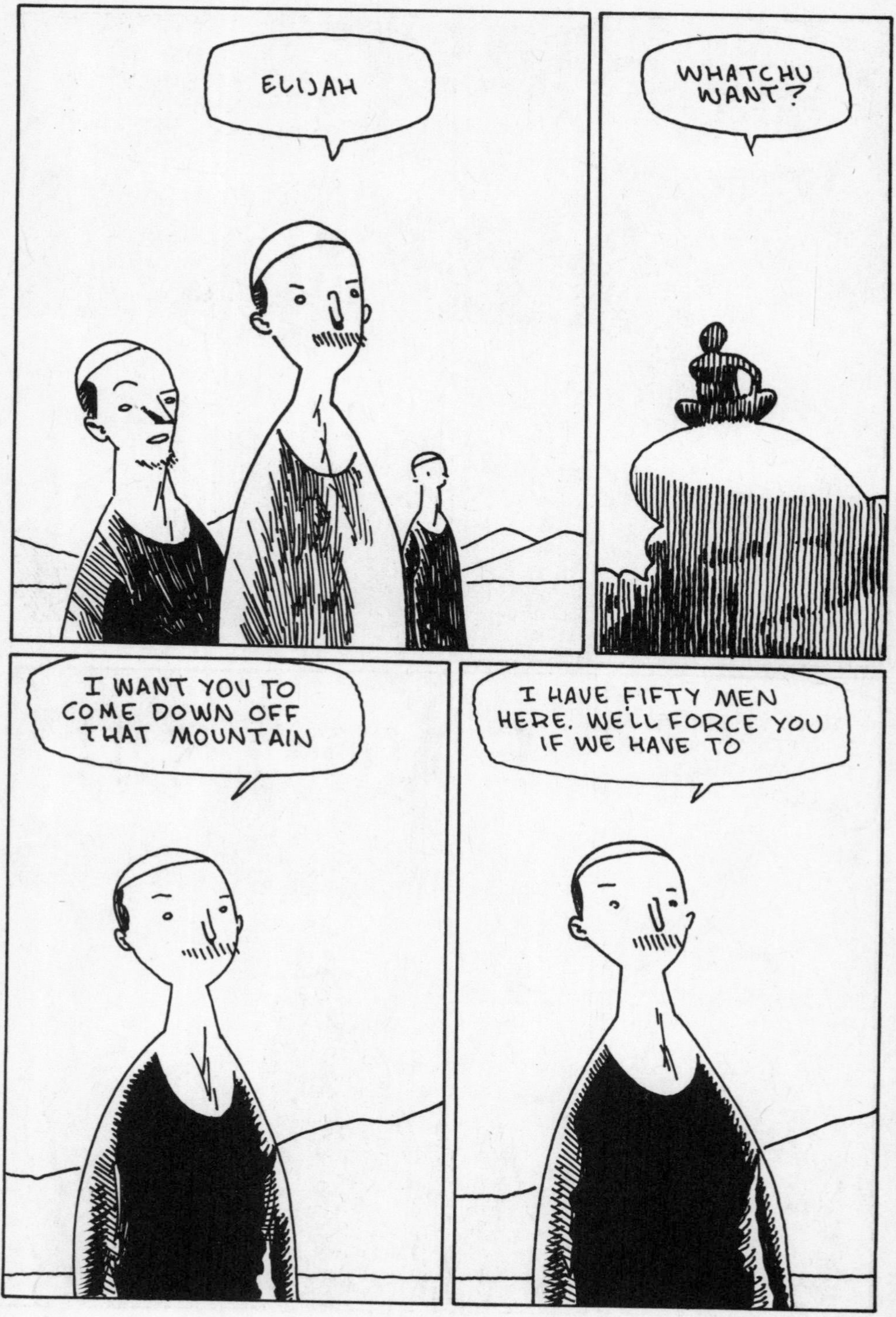
ELIJAH
WHATCHU WANT?
I WANT YOU TO COME DOWN OFF THAT MOUNTAIN
I HAVE FIFTY MEN HERE. WE'LL FORCE YOU IF WE HAVE TO

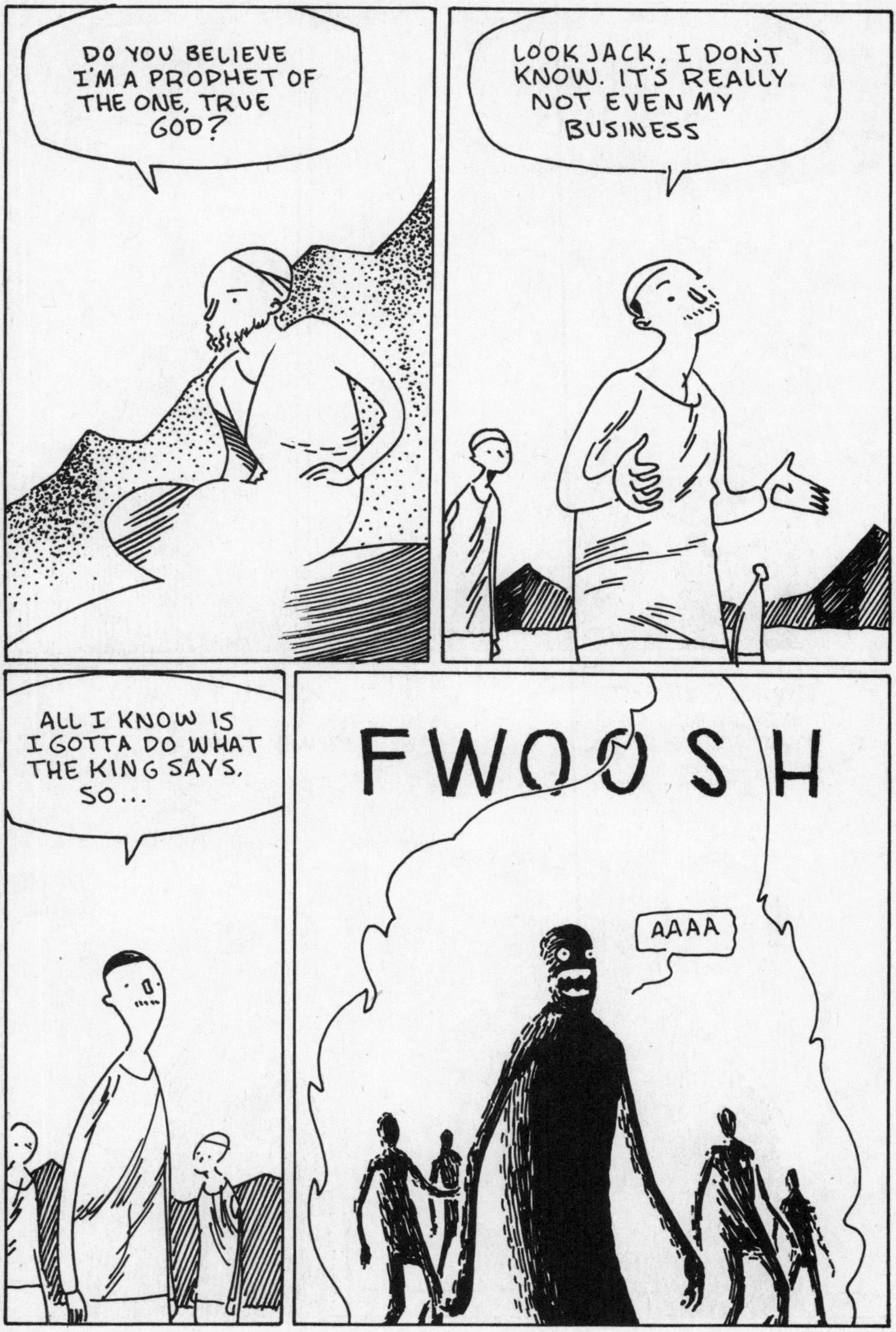
DO YOU BELIEVE I'M A PROPHET OF THE ONE, TRUE GOD?
LOOK JACK, I DON'T KNOW. IT'S REALLY NOT EVEN MY BUSINESS
ALL I KNOW IS I GOTTA DO WHAT THE KING SAYS, SO...
FWOOSH
AAAA

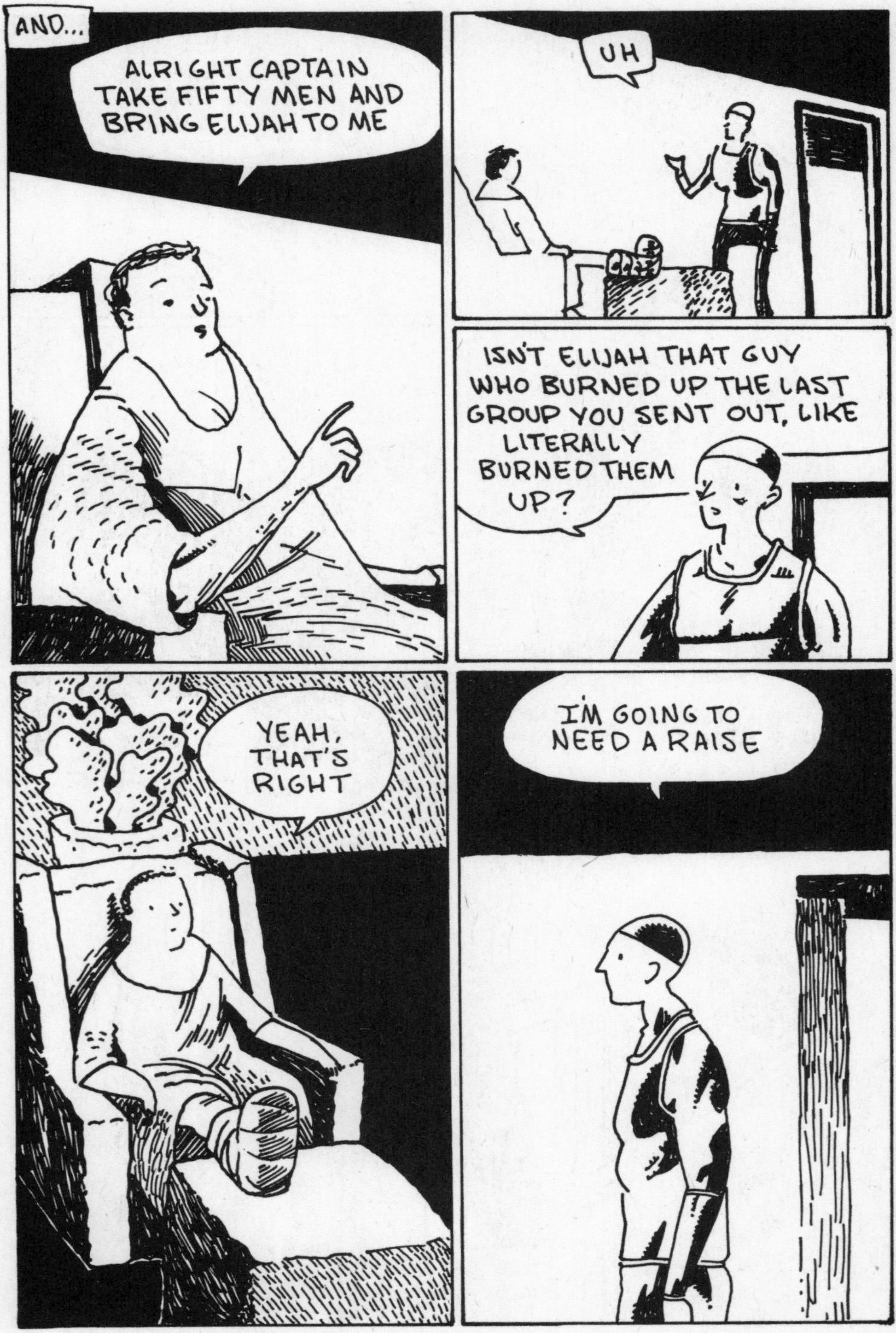
AND...
ALRIGHT CAPTAIN TAKE FIFTY MEN AND BRING ELIJAH TO ME
UH
ISN'T ELIJAH THAT GUY WHO BURNED UP THE LAST GROUP YOU SENT OUT, LIKE LITERALLY BURNED THEM UP?
YEAH, THAT'S RIGHT
I'M GOING TO NEED A RAISE

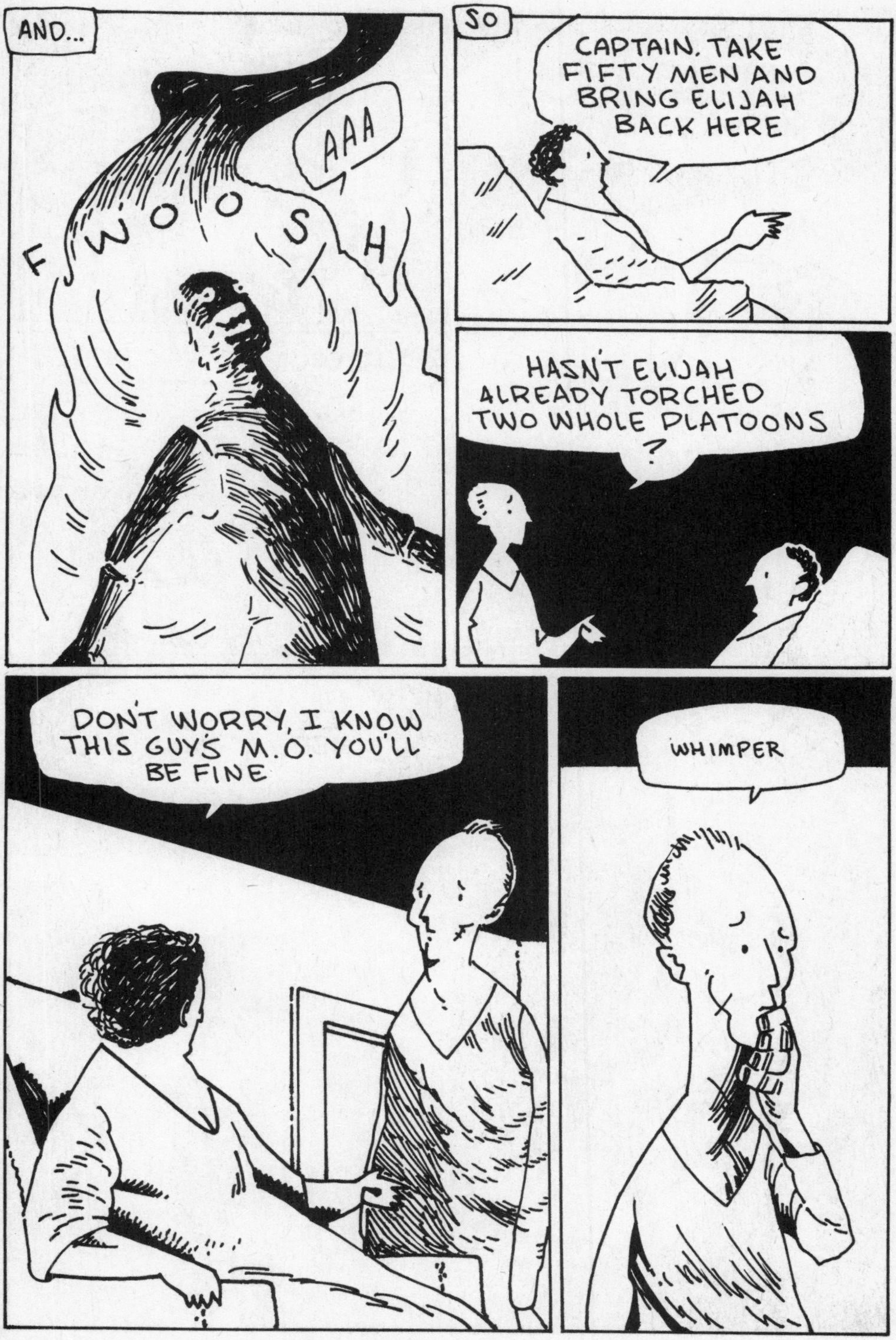
AND...
AAA
FWOOSH
SO
CAPTAIN. TAKE FIFTY MEN AND BRING ELIJAH BACK HERE
HASN'T ELIJAH ALREADY TORCHED TWO WHOLE PLATOONS ?
DON'T WORRY, I KNOW THIS GUY'S M.O. YOU'LL BE FINE
WHIMPER

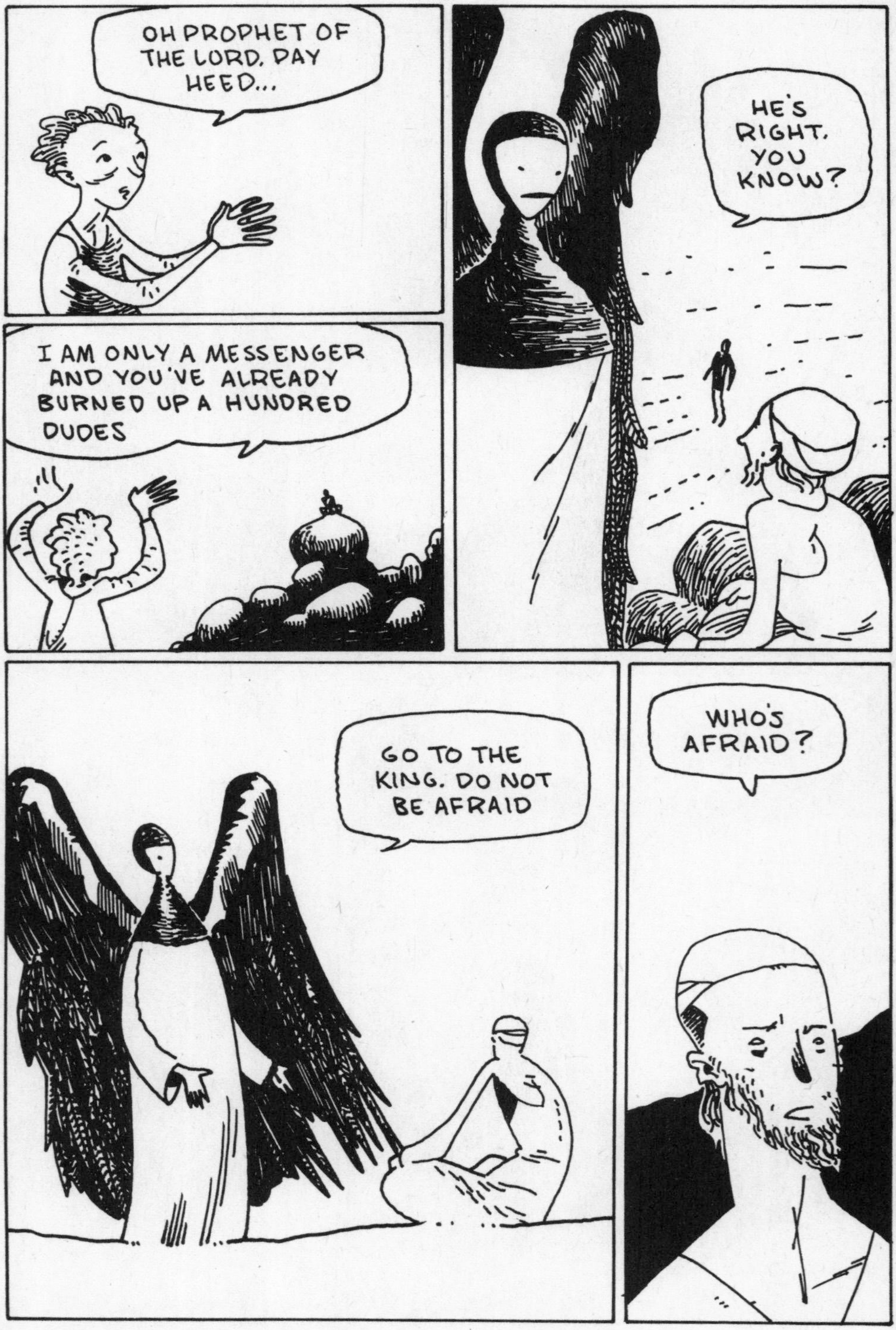
OH PROPHET OF THE LORD, PAY HEED...
I AM ONLY A MESSENGER AND YOU'VE ALREADY BURNED UP A HUNDRED DUDES
HE'S RIGHT, YOU KNOW?
GO TO THE KING. DO NOT BE AFRAID
WHO'S AFRAID?

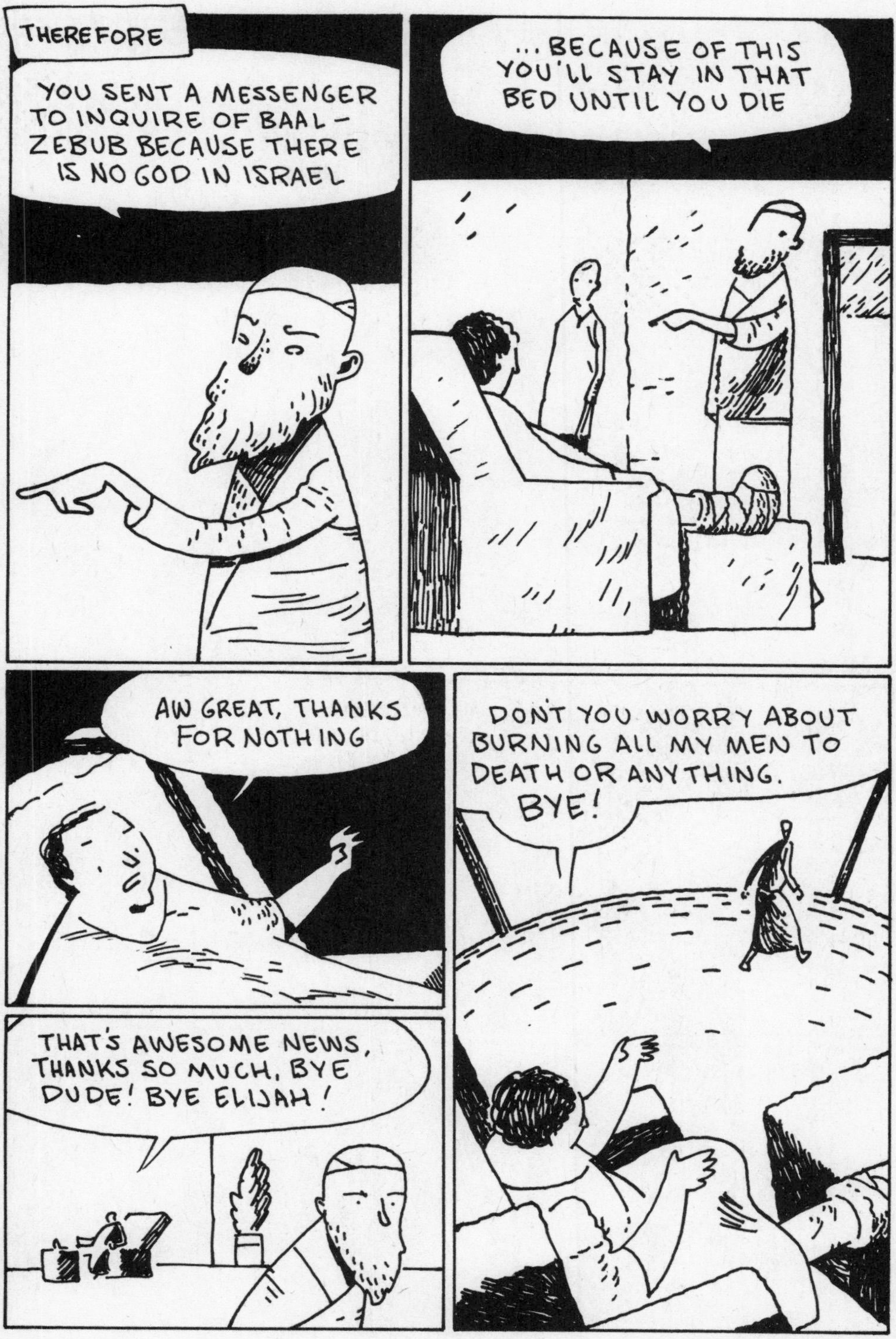
THEREFORE
YOU SENT A MESSENGER TO INQUIRE OF BAAL-ZEBUB BECAUSE THERE IS NO GOD IN ISRAEL
... BECAUSE OF THIS YOU'LL STAY IN THAT BED UNTIL YOU DIE
AW GREAT, THANKS FOR NOTHING
THAT'S AWESOME NEWS, THANKS SO MUCH, BYE DUDE! BYE ELIJAH!
DON'T YOU WORRY ABOUT BURNING ALL MY MEN TO DEATH OR ANYTHING.
BYE!

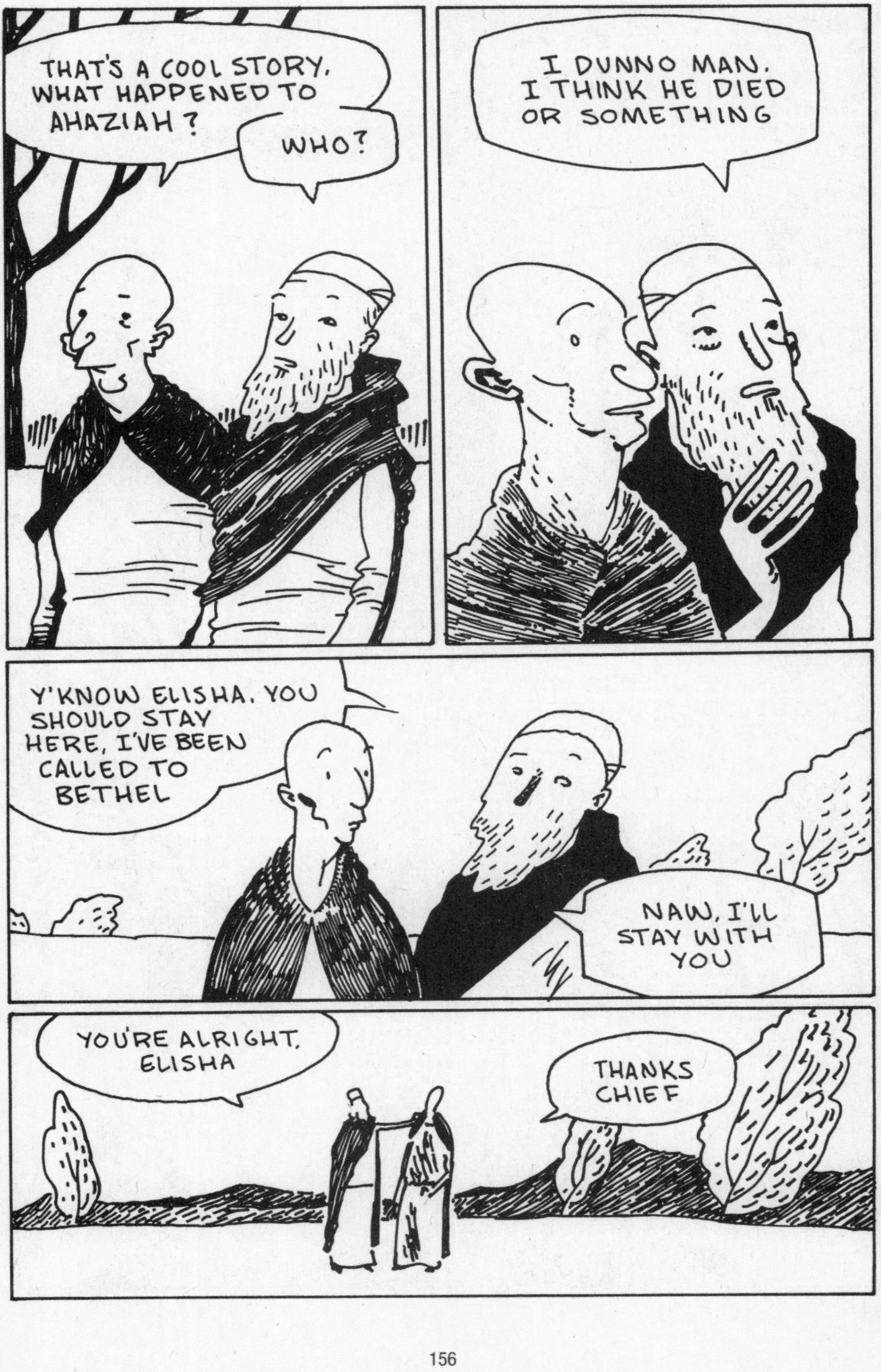
THAT'S A COOL STORY. WHAT HAPPENED TO AHAZIAH?
WHO?
I DUNNO MAN. I THINK HE DIED OR SOMETHING
Y'KNOW ELISHA. YOU SHOULD STAY HERE, I'VE BEEN CALLED TO BETHEL
NAW, I'LL STAY WITH YOU
YOU'RE ALRIGHT, ELISHA
THANKS CHIEF

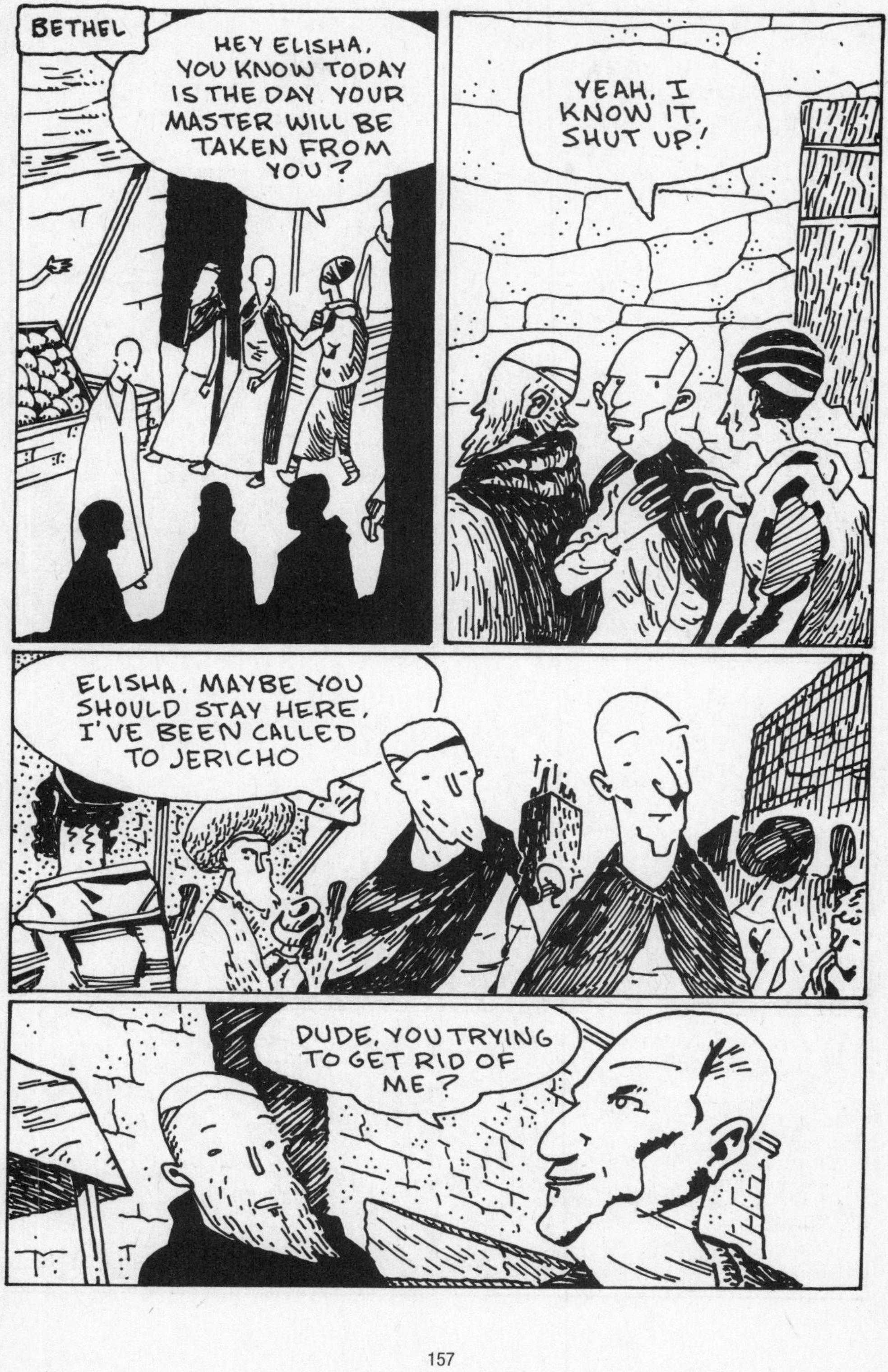
BETHEL
HEY ELISHA, YOU KNOW TODAY IS THE DAY YOUR MASTER WILL BE TAKEN FROM YOU?
YEAH, I KNOW IT, SHUT UP!
ELISHA. MAYBE YOU SHOULD STAY HERE. I'VE BEEN CALLED TO JERICHO
DUDE, YOU TRYING TO GET RID OF ME?

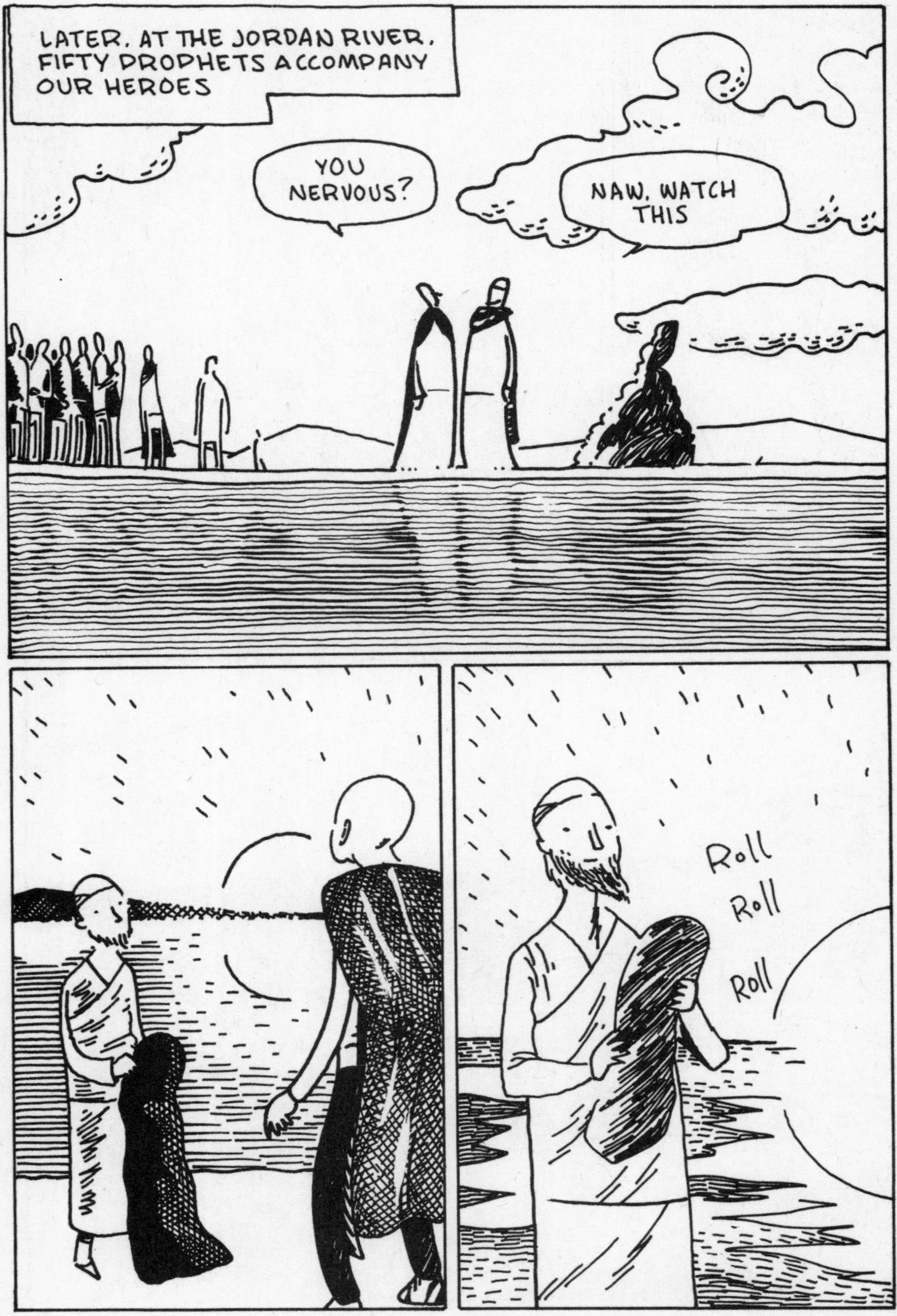
LATER. AT THE JORDAN RIVER. FIFTY PROPHETS ACCOMPANY OUR HEROES
YOU NERVOUS?
NAW. WATCH THIS
Roll
Roll
Roll

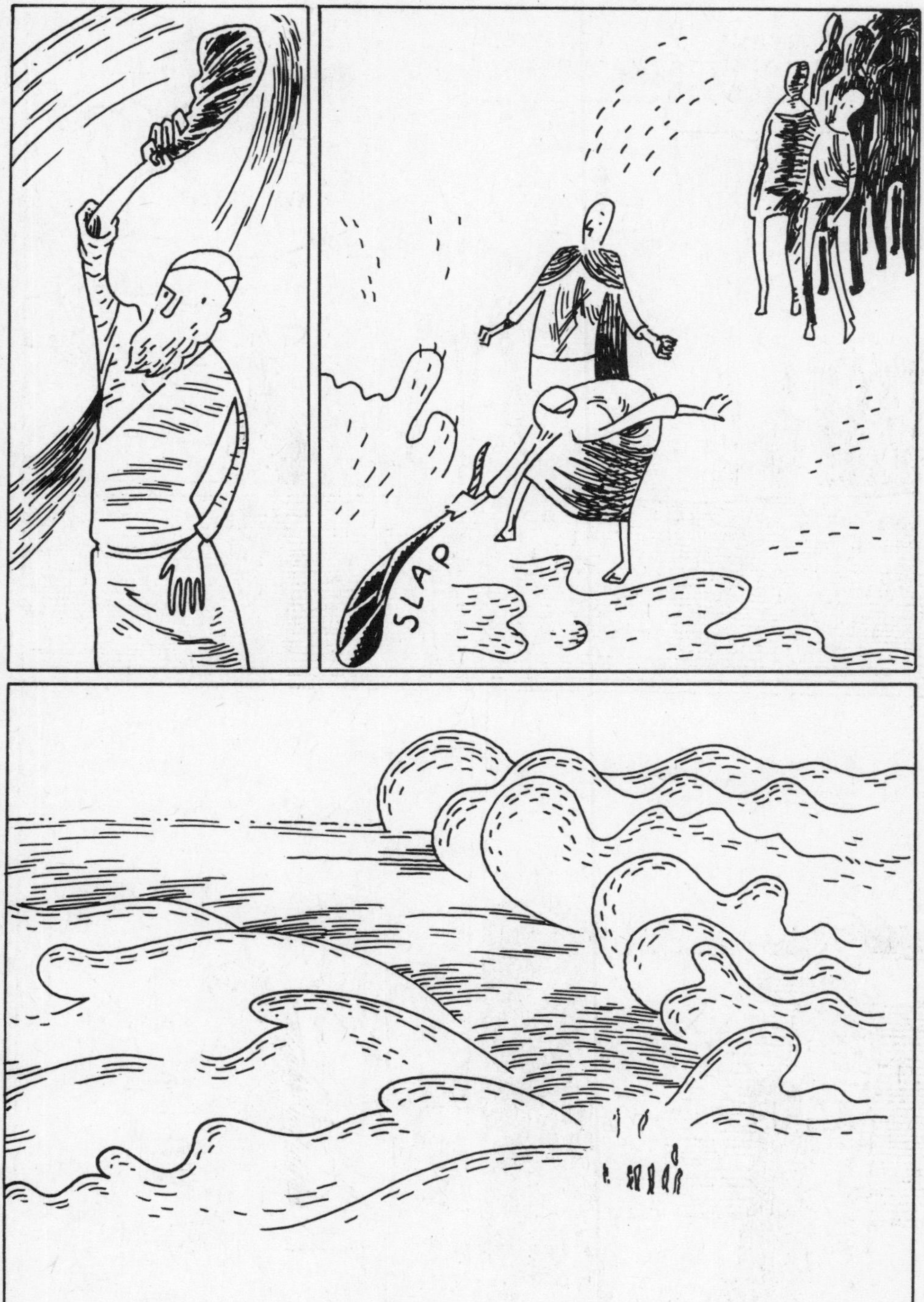
SLAP

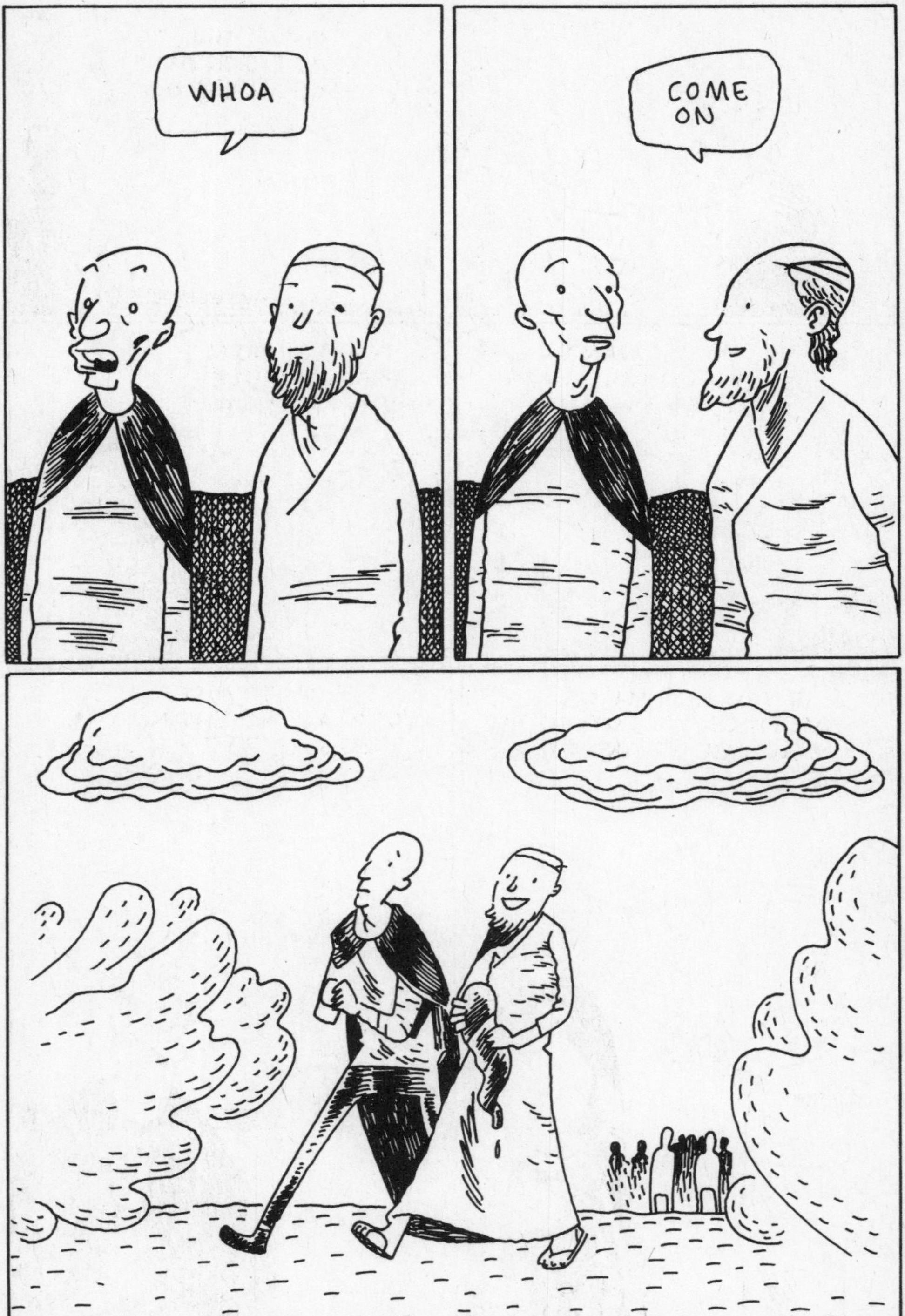
WHOA
COME ON

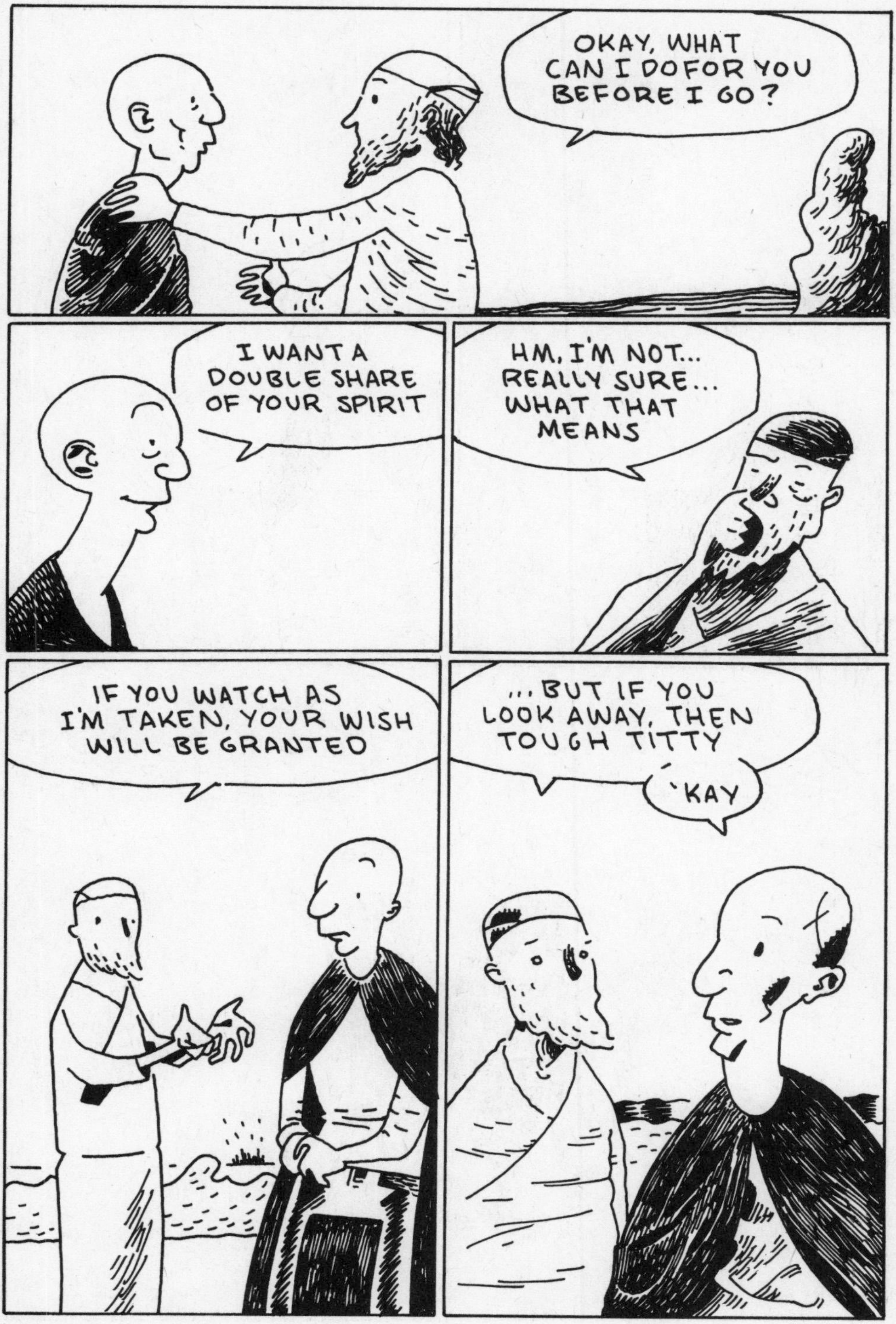
OKAY, WHAT CAN I DO FOR YOU BEFORE I GO?
I WANT A DOUBLE SHARE OF YOUR SPIRIT
HM, I'M NOT... REALLY SURE... WHAT THAT MEANS
IF YOU WATCH AS I'M TAKEN, YOUR WISH WILL BE GRANTED
...BUT IF YOU LOOK AWAY, THEN TOUGH TITTY
'KAY

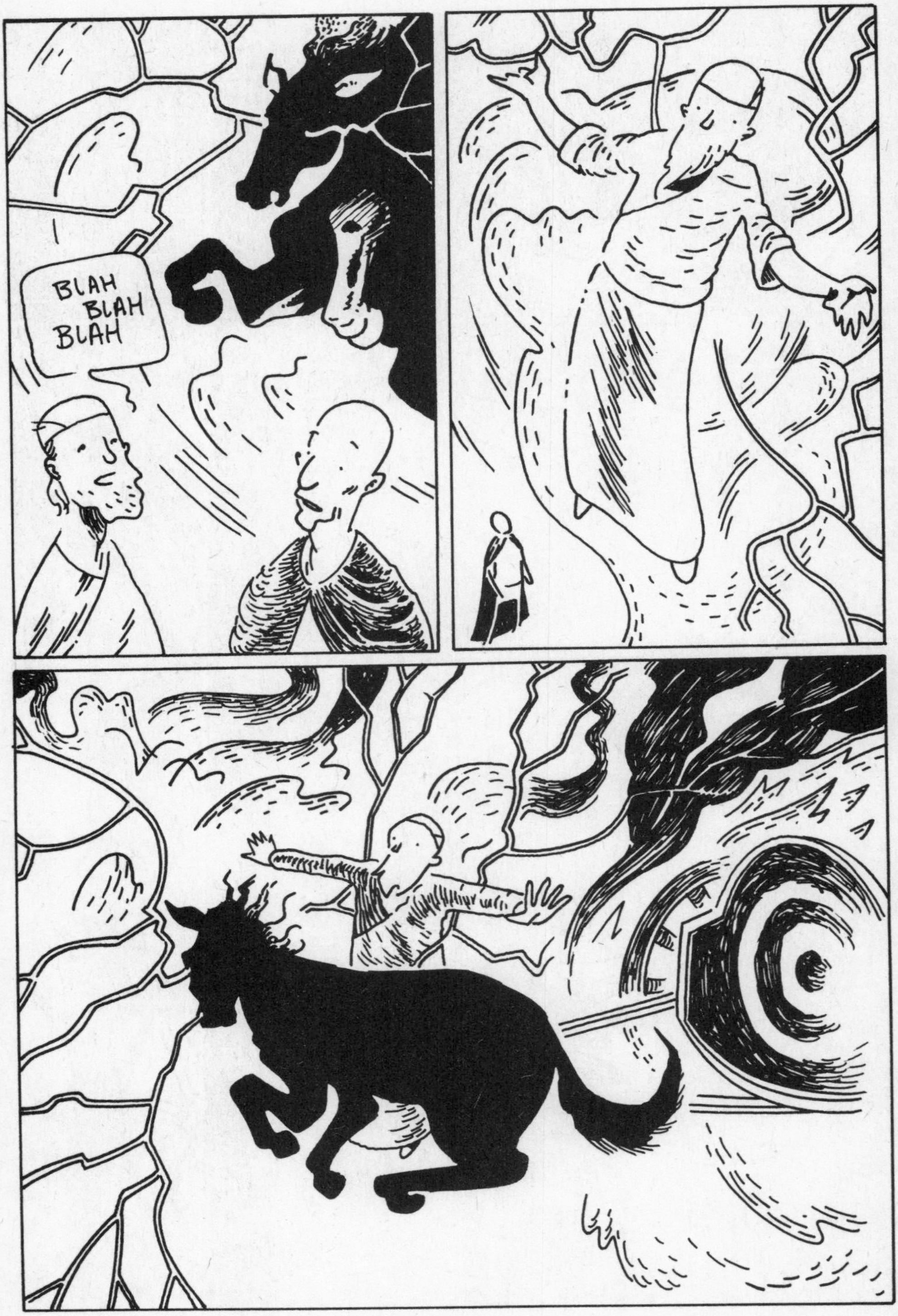
BLAH BLAH BLAH

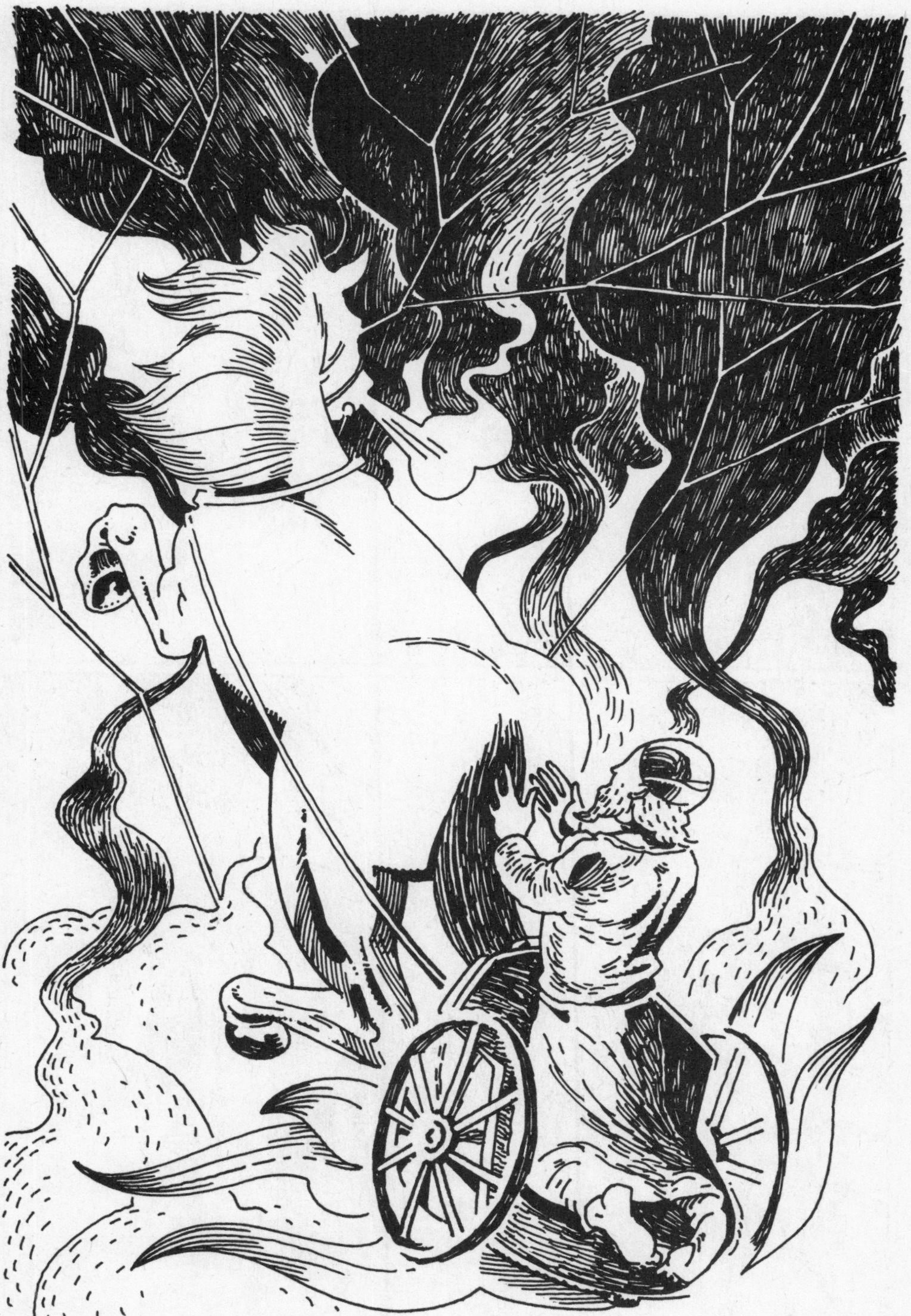

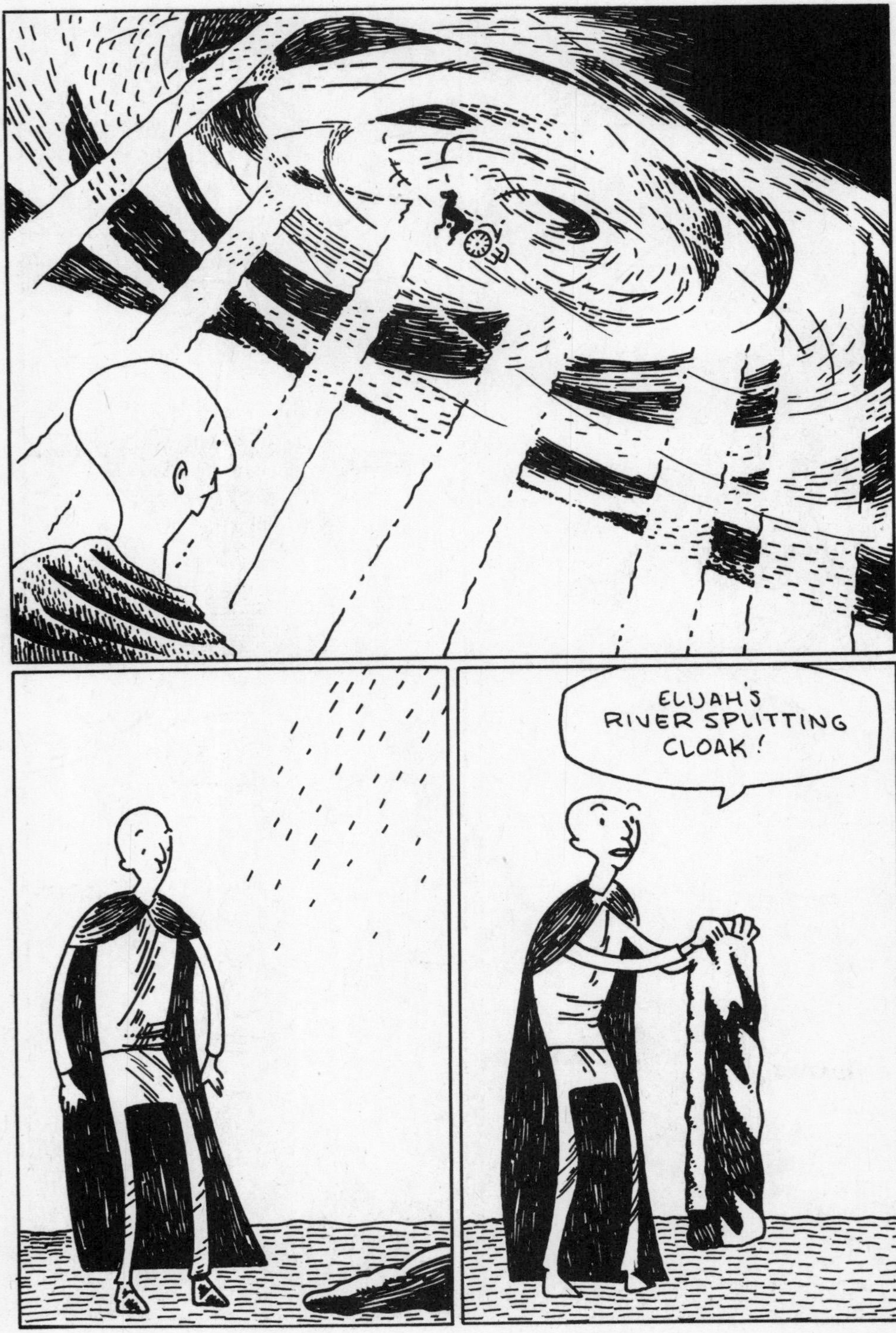
ELIJAH'S RIVER SPLITTING CLOAK!

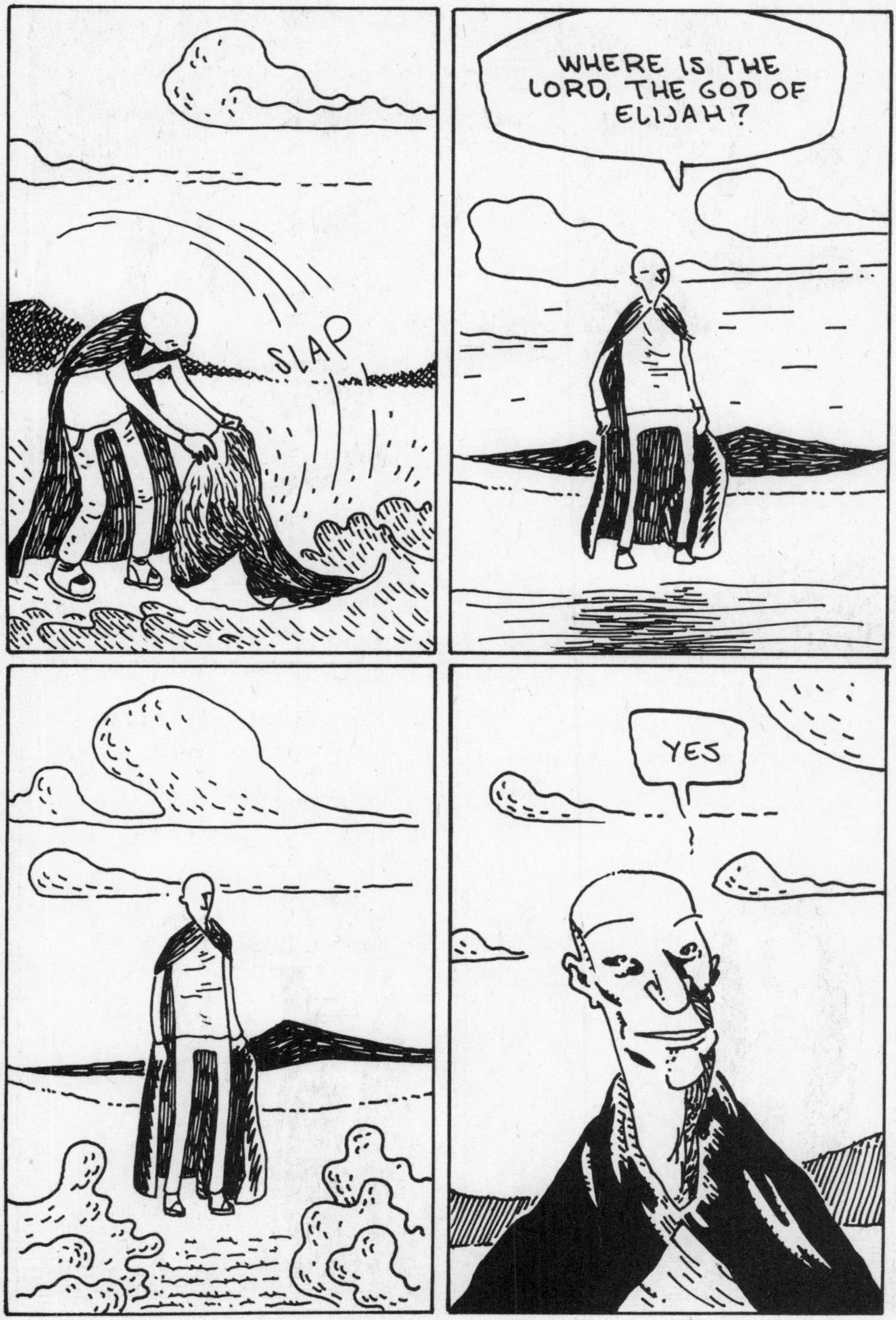
SLAP
WHERE IS THE LORD, THE GOD OF ELIJAH?
YES

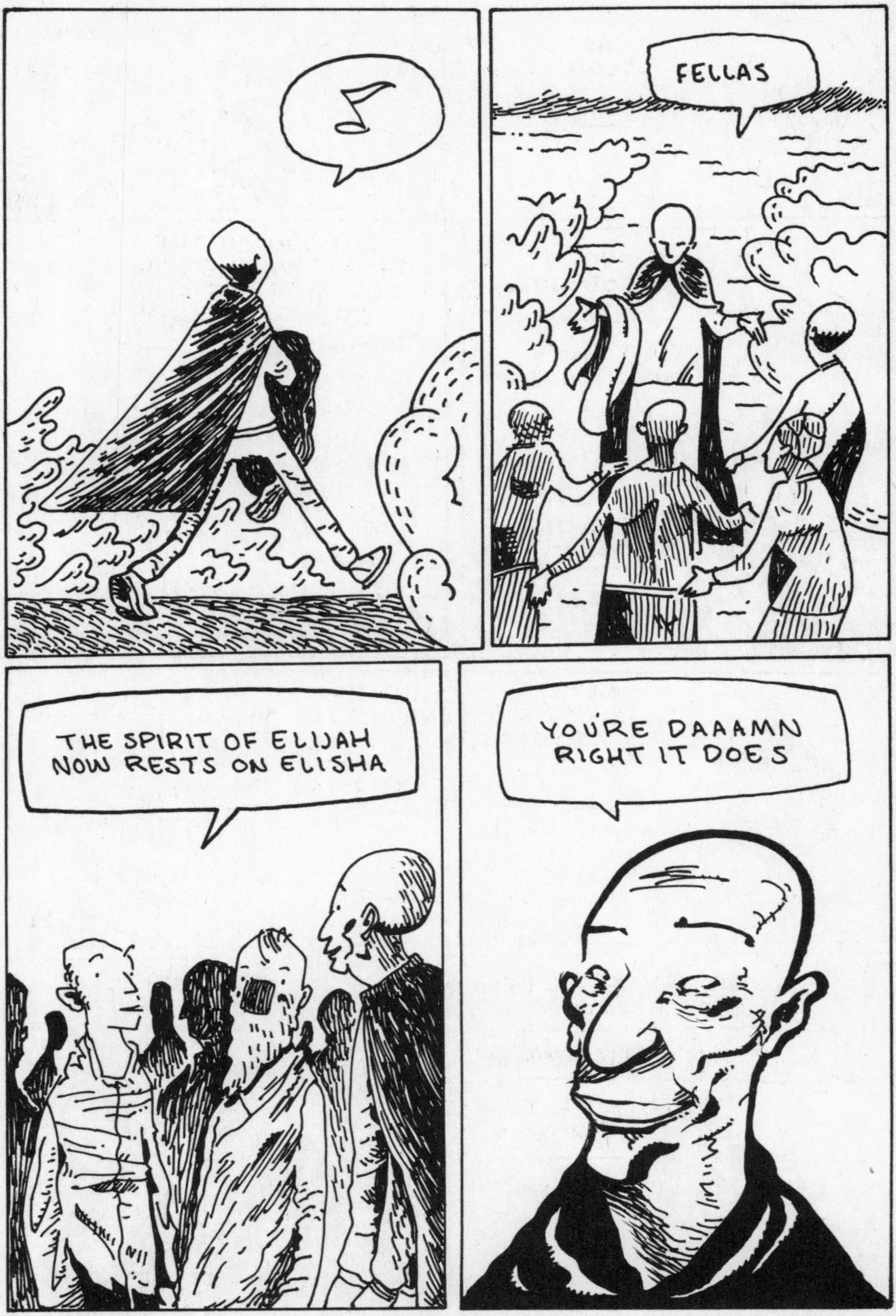
FELLAS
THE SPIRIT OF ELIJAH NOW RESTS ON ELISHA
YOU'RE DAAAMN RIGHT IT DOES

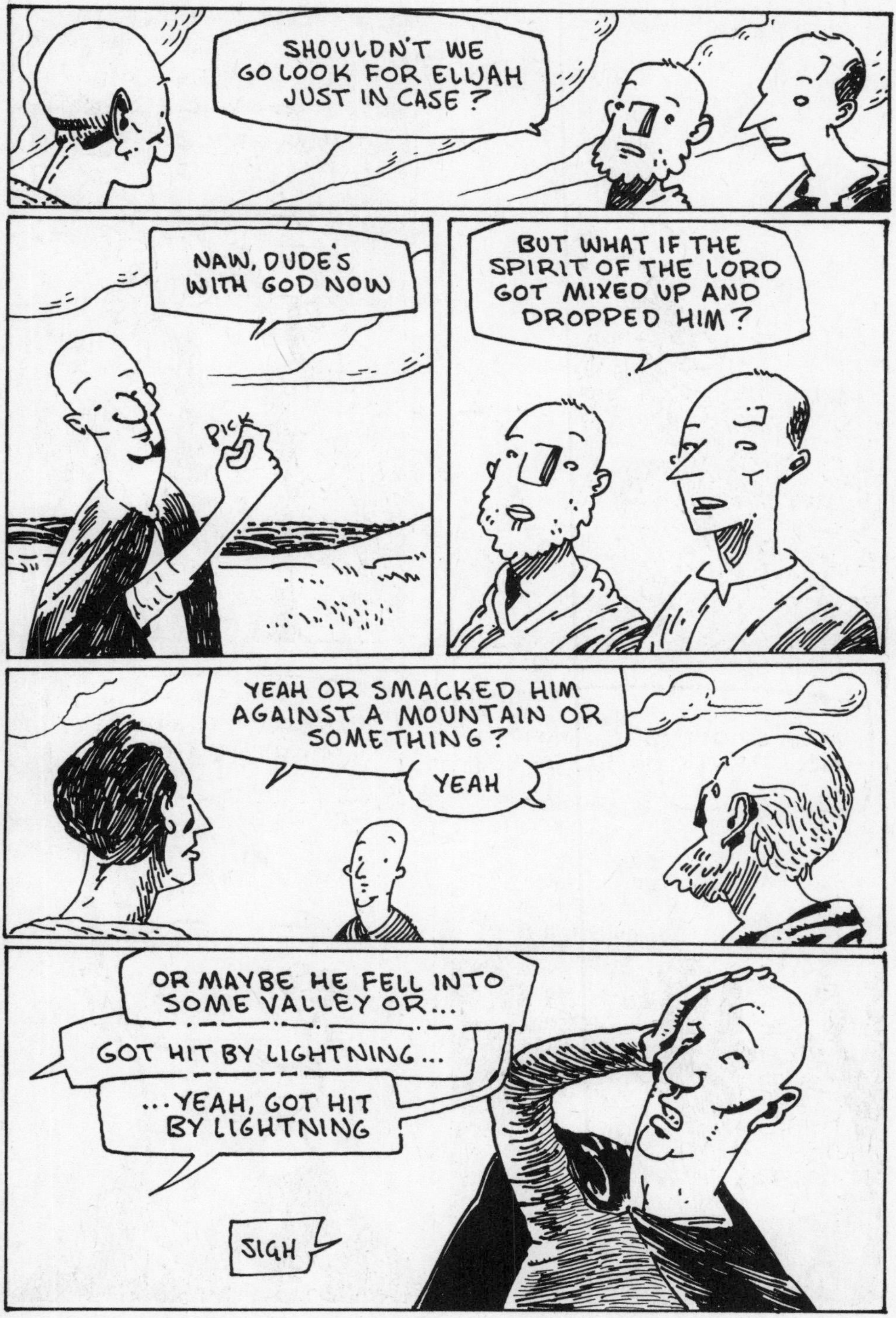
SHOULDN'T WE GO LOOK FOR ELIJAH JUST IN CASE?
NAW, DUDE'S WITH GOD NOW
PICK
BUT WHAT IF THE SPIRIT OF THE LORD GOT MIXED UP AND DROPPED HIM?
YEAH OR SMACKED HIM AGAINST A MOUNTAIN OR SOMETHING?
YEAH
OR MAYBE HE FELL INTO SOME VALLEY OR...
GOT HIT BY LIGHTNING...
...YEAH, GOT HIT BY LIGHTNING
SIGH

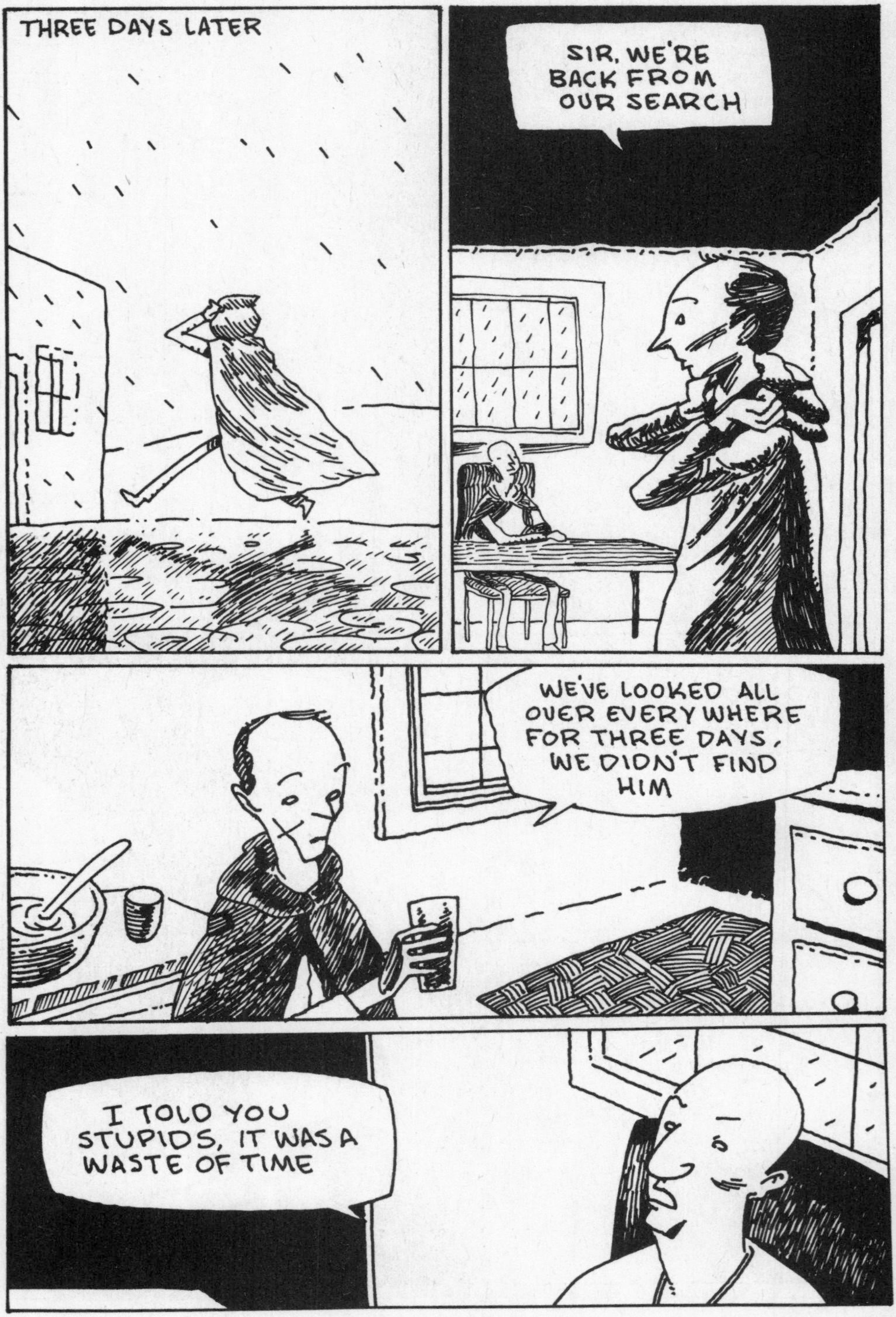
THREE DAYS LATER
SIR, WE'RE BACK FROM OUR SEARCH
WE'VE LOOKED ALL OVER EVERY WHERE FOR THREE DAYS, WE DIDN'T FIND HIM
I TOLD YOU STUPIDS, IT WAS A WASTE OF TIME

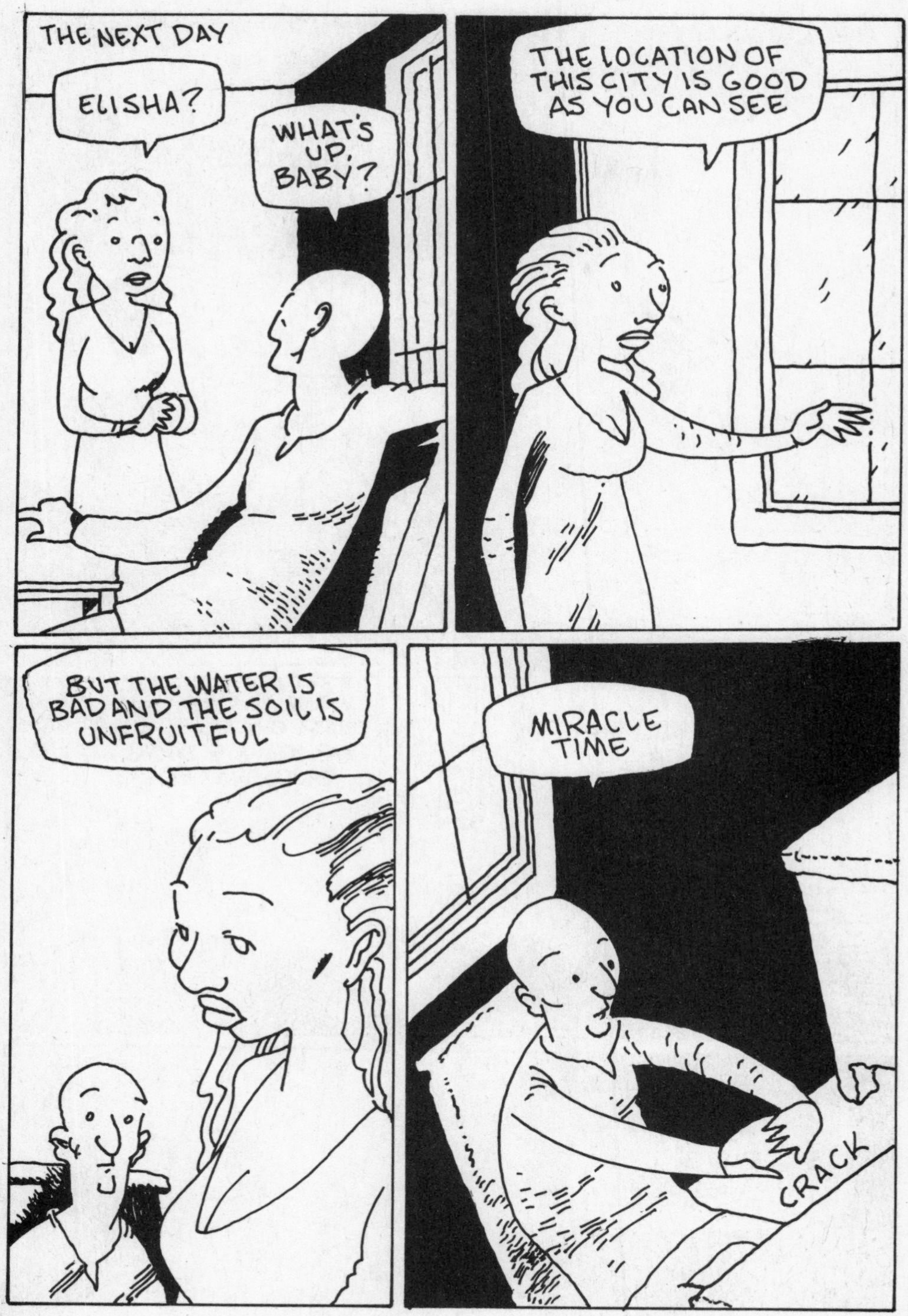
THE NEXT DAY
ELISHA?
WHAT'S UP, BABY?
THE LOCATION OF THIS CITY IS GOOD AS YOU CAN SEE
BUT THE WATER IS BAD AND THE SOIL IS UNFRUITFUL
MIRACLE TIME
CRACK

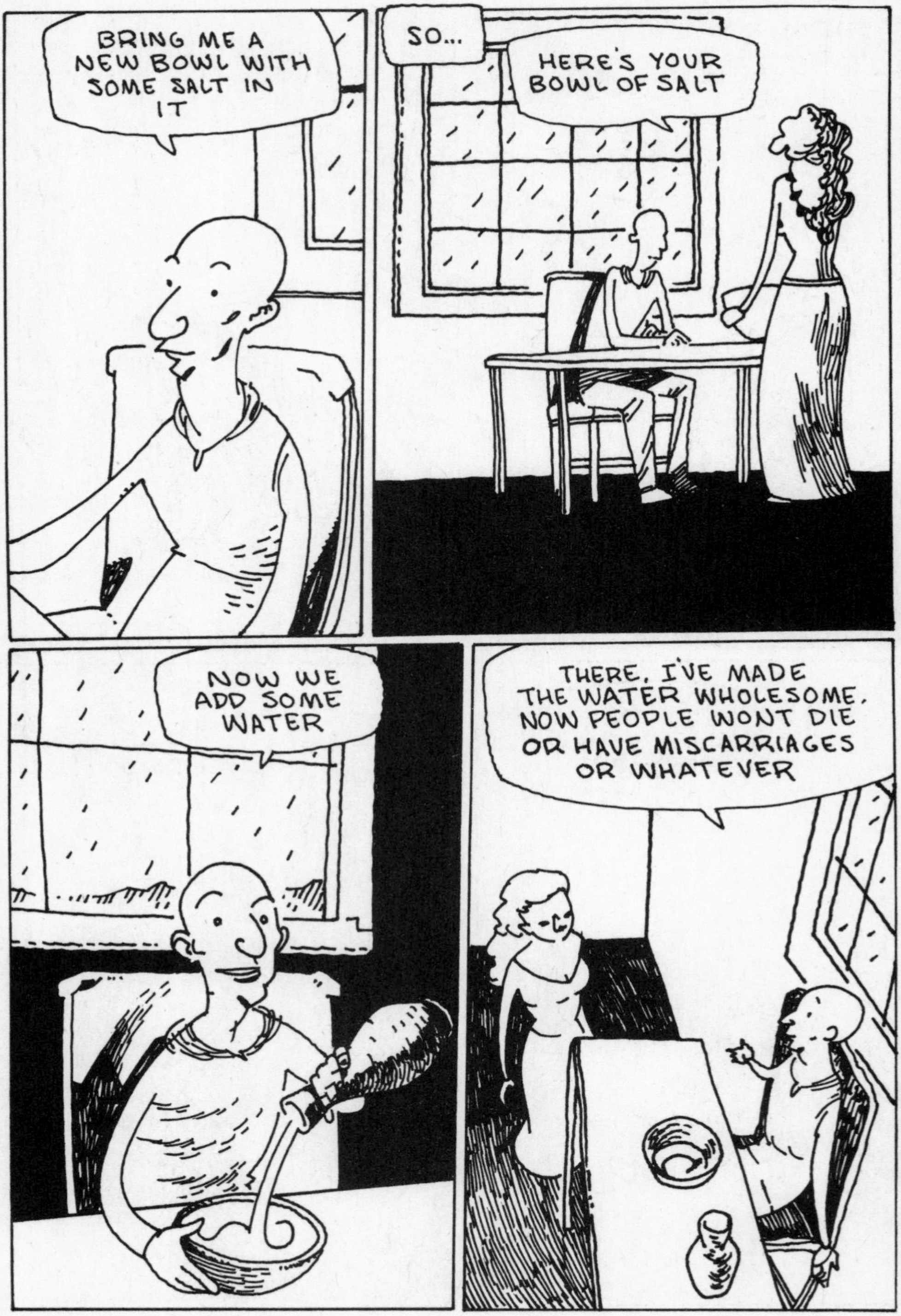
BRING ME A NEW BOWL WITH SOME SALT IN IT
SO...
HERE'S YOUR BOWL OF SALT
NOW WE ADD SOME WATER
THERE, I'VE MADE THE WATER WHOLESOME. NOW PEOPLE WONT DIE OR HAVE MISCARRIAGES OR WHATEVER

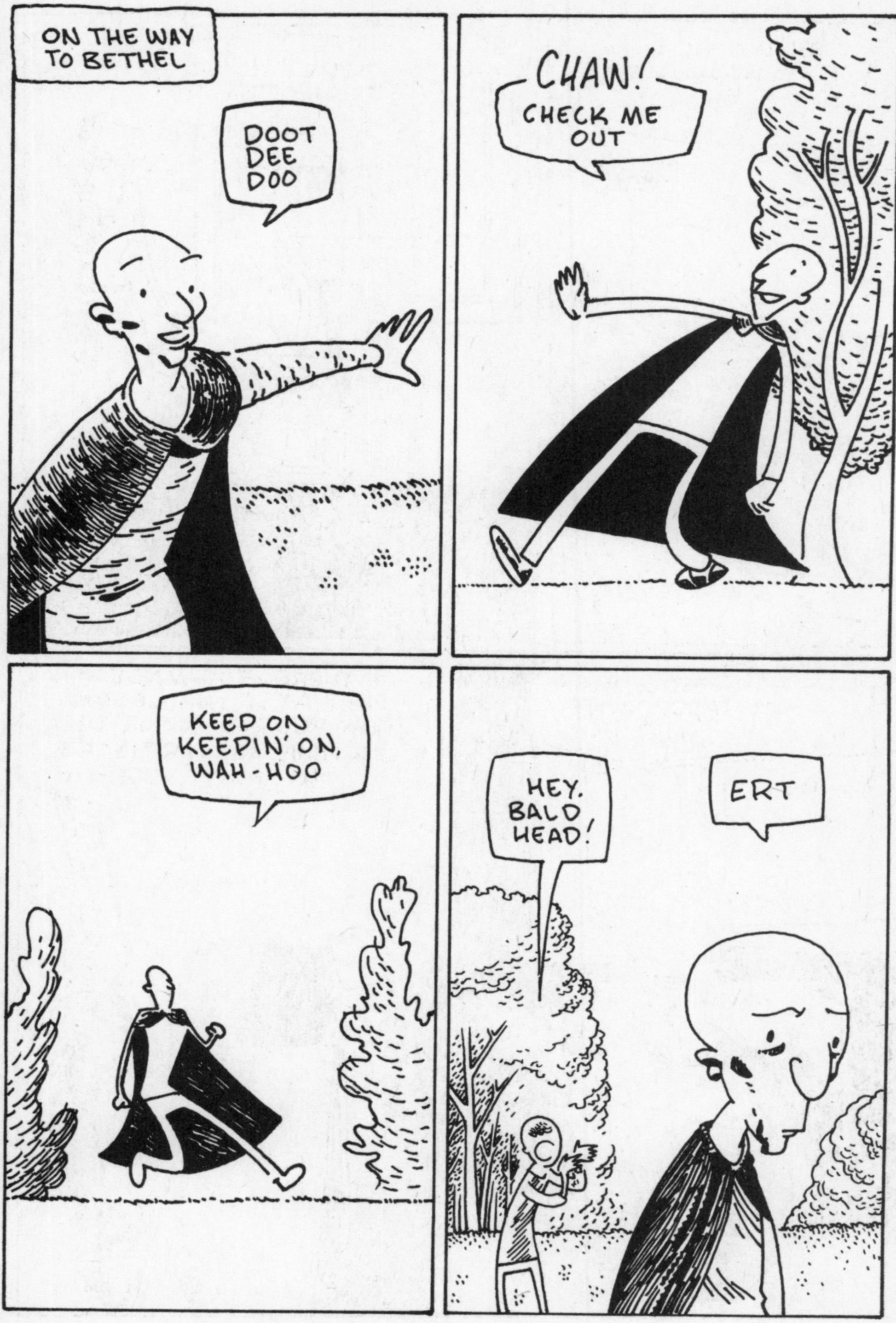
ON THE WAY TO BETHEL
DOOT DEE DOO
CHAW! CHECK ME OUT
KEEP ON KEEPIN' ON, WAH-HOO
HEY. BALD HEAD!
ERT

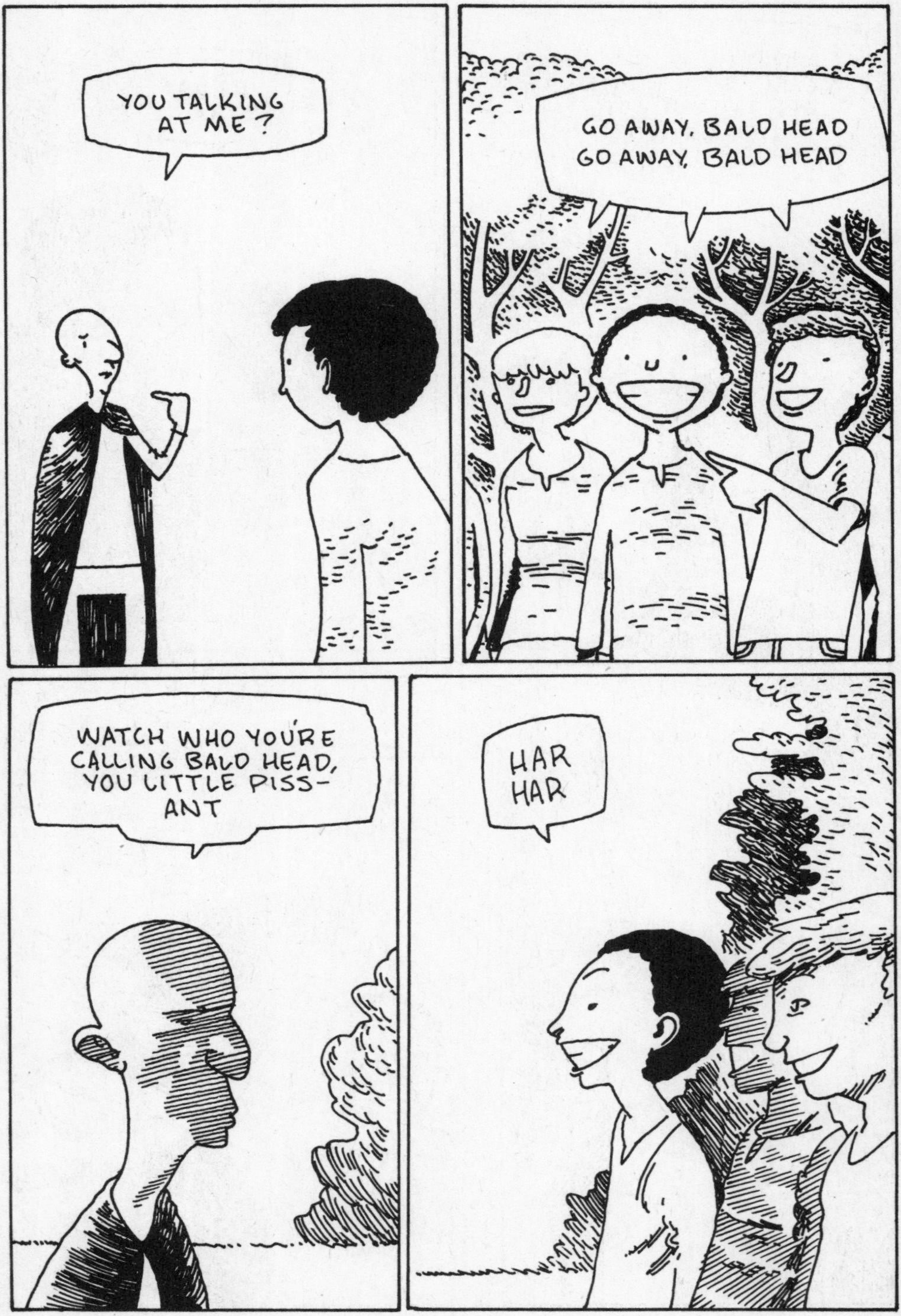
YOU TALKING AT ME?
GO AWAY, BALD HEAD GO AWAY, BALD HEAD
WATCH WHO YOU'RE CALLING BALD HEAD, YOU LITTLE PISS-ANT
HAR HAR

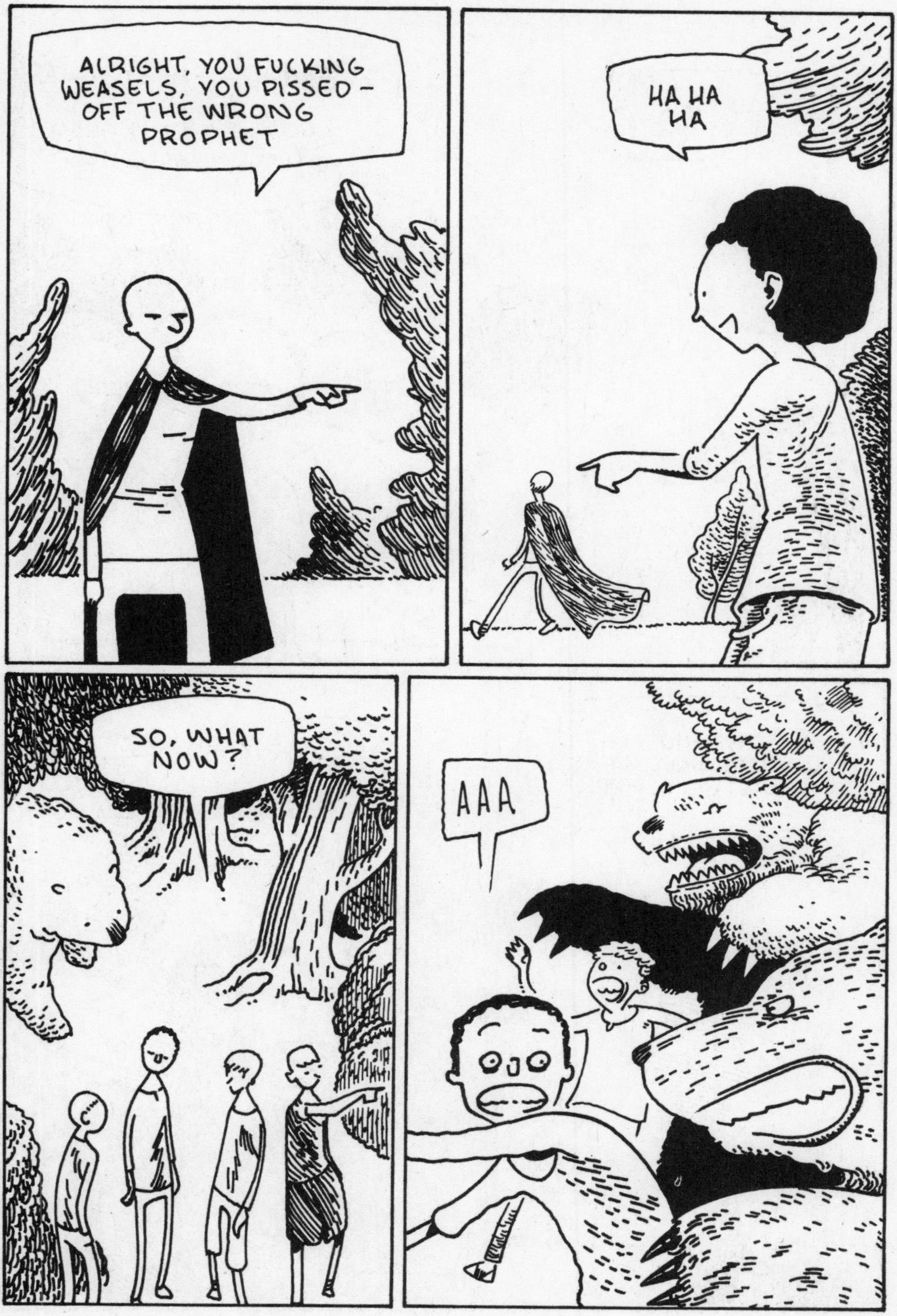
ALRIGHT, YOU FUCKING WEASELS, YOU PISSED-OFF THE WRONG PROPHET
HA HA HA
SO, WHAT NOW?
AAA

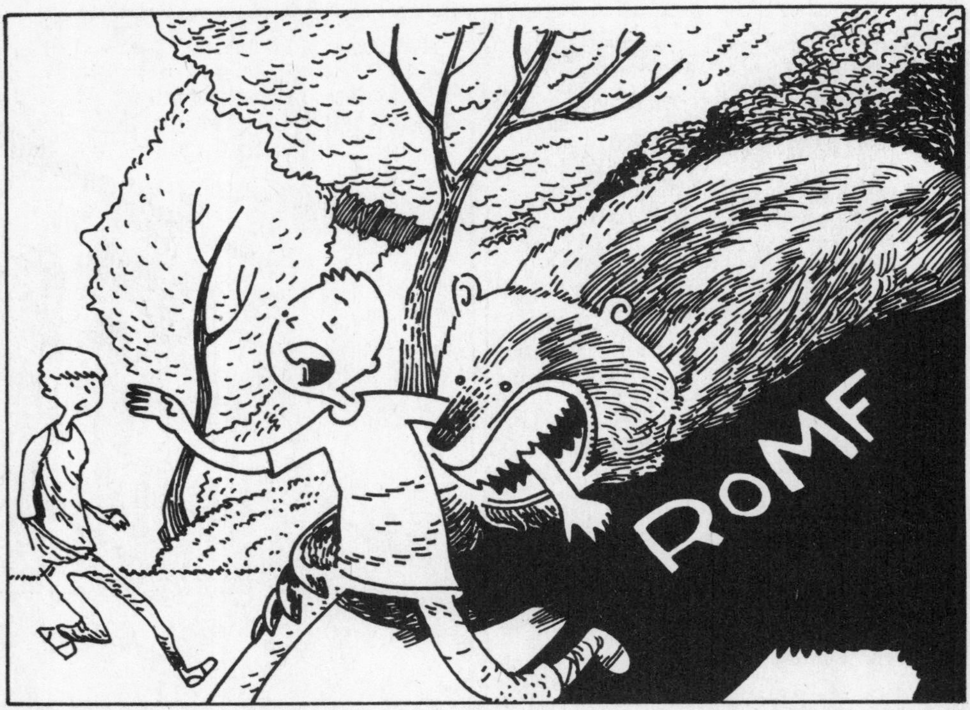
ROMF

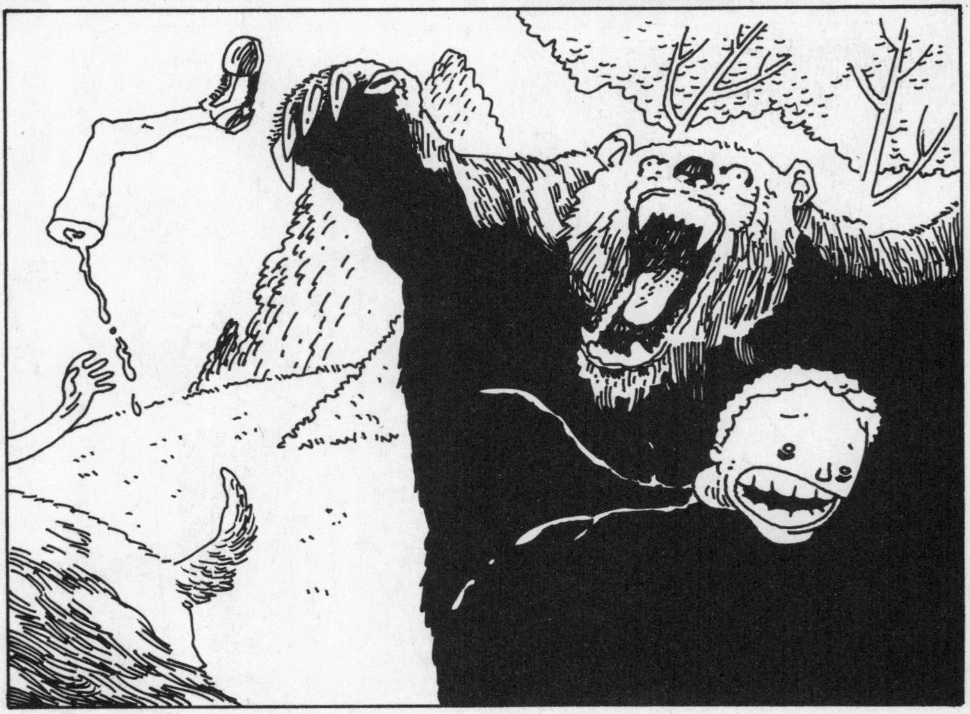

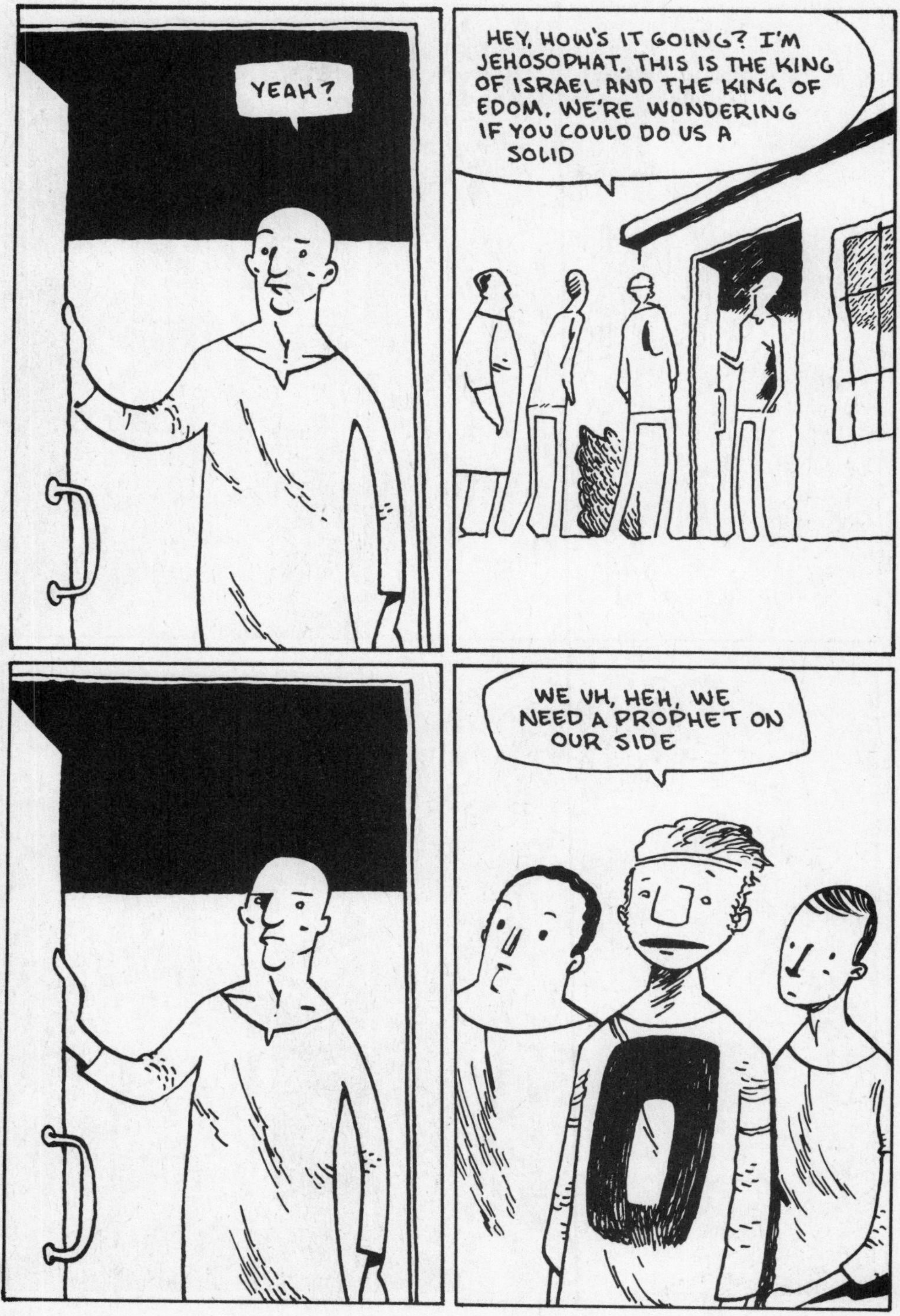
YEAH?
HEY, HOW'S IT GOING? I'M JEHOSOPHAT, THIS IS THE KING OF ISRAEL AND THE KING OF EDOM. WE'RE WONDERING IF YOU COULD DO US A SOLID
WE UH, HEH, WE NEED A PROPHET ON OUR SIDE

SEE, WE'RE GOING TO BATTLE WITH KING MESHA OF MOAB, IT'S SORT OF OVER A BUNCH OF SHEEP, LONG STORY
WE JUST NEED TO KNOW IF WE'RE GOING TO SURVIVE ALL THIS, DIG?
AND WE KNOW YOU USED TO HANG OUT WITH ELIJAH, AND THAT GUY HAD IT GOING ON

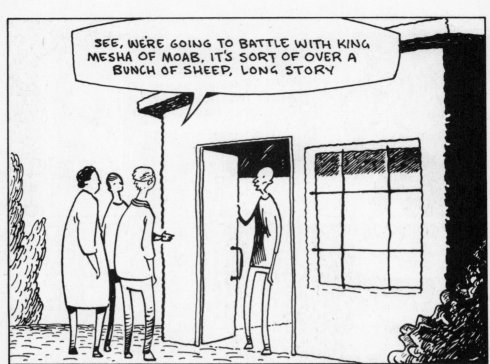

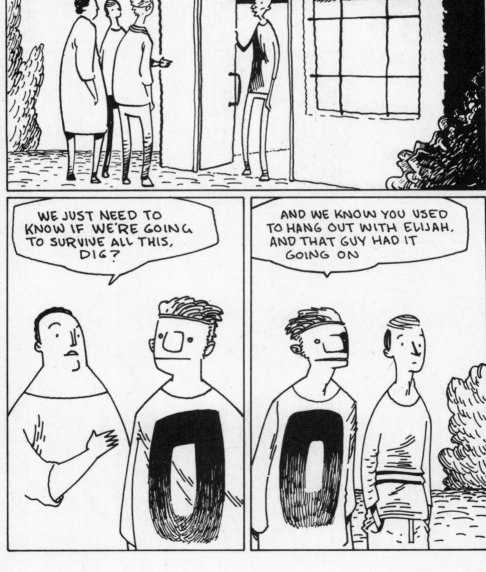

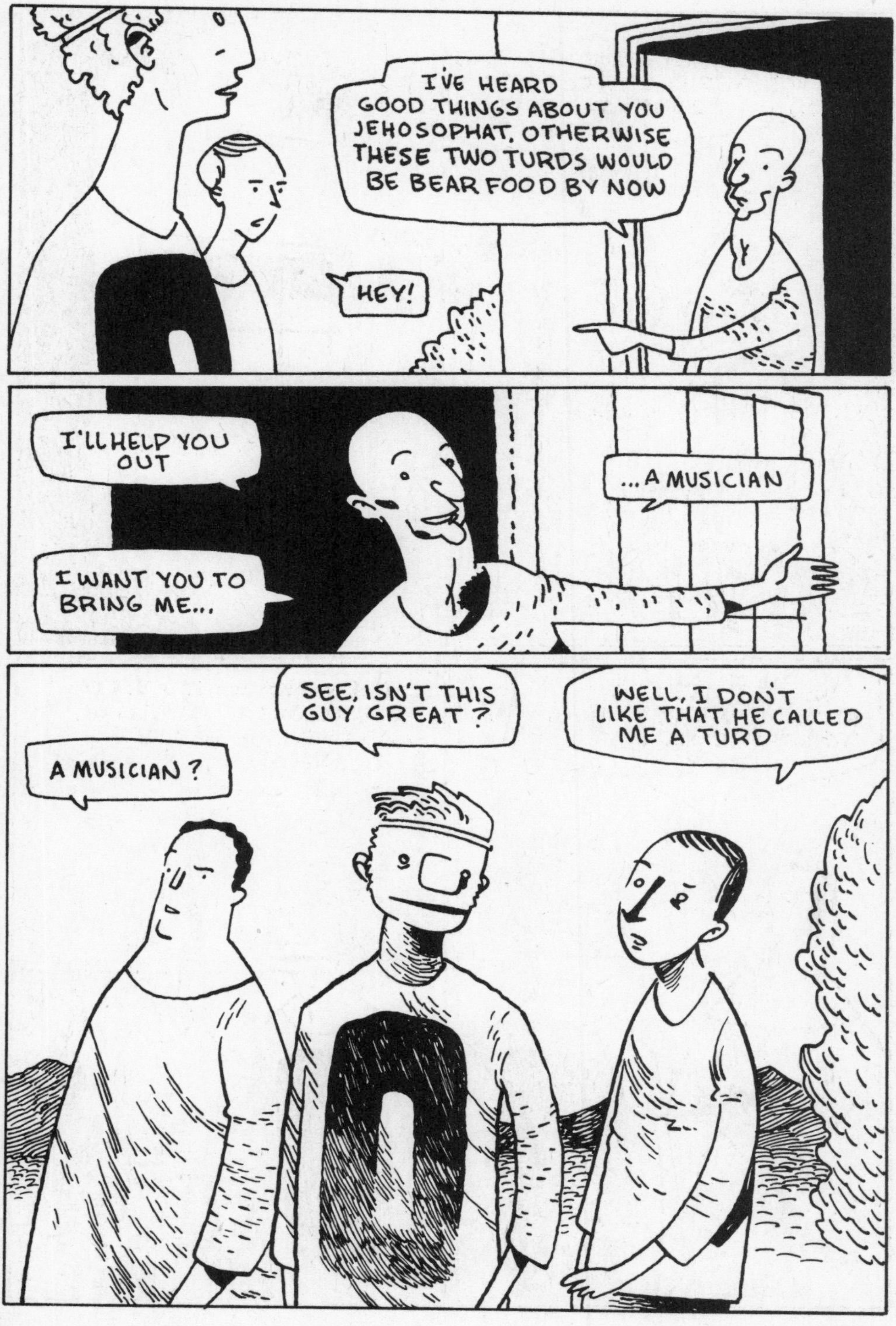
I'VE HEARD GOOD THINGS ABOUT YOU JEHOSOPHAT. OTHERWISE THESE TWO TURDS WOULD BE BEAR FOOD BY NOW
HEY!
I'LL HELP YOU OUT
I WANT YOU TO BRING ME...
...A MUSICIAN
A MUSICIAN?
SEE, ISN'T THIS GUY GREAT?
WELL, I DON'T LIKE THAT HE CALLED ME A TURD

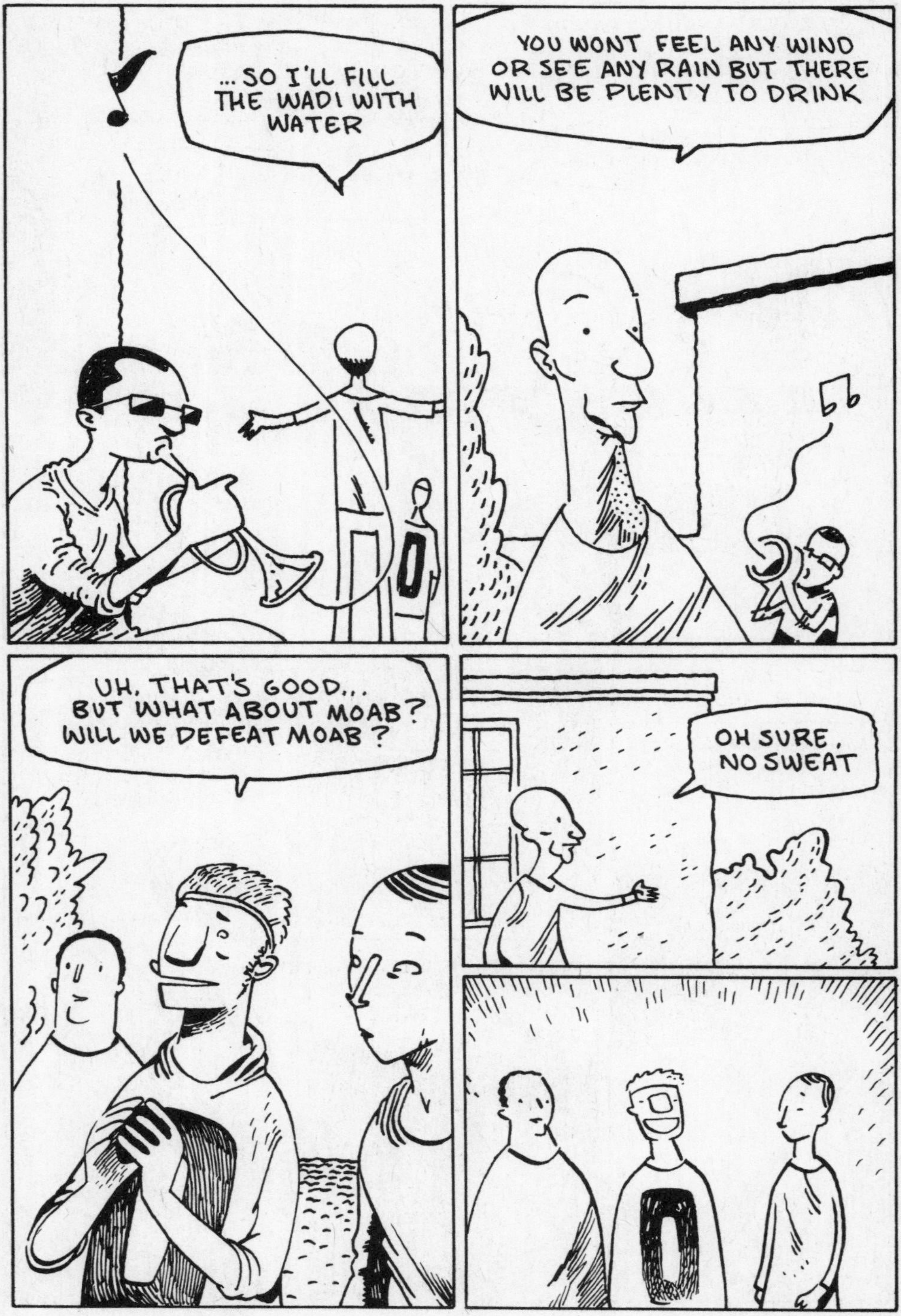
...SO I'LL FILL THE WADI WITH WATER
YOU WONT FEEL ANY WIND OR SEE ANY RAIN BUT THERE WILL BE PLENTY TO DRINK
UH, THAT'S GOOD... BUT WHAT ABOUT MOAB? WILL WE DEFEAT MOAB?
OH SURE, NO SWEAT

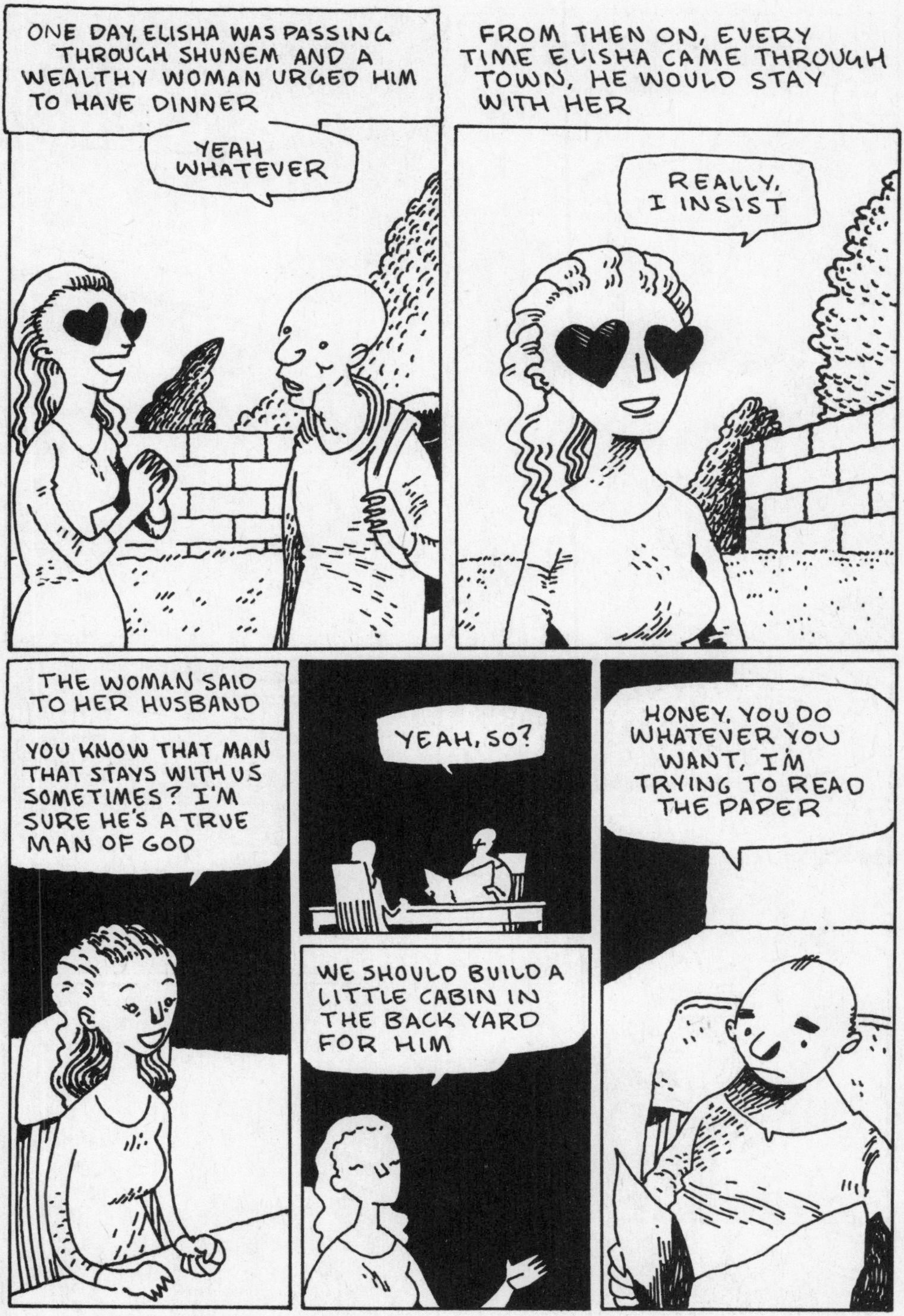

ONE DAY, ELISHA WAS PASSING THROUGH SHUNEM AND A WEALTHY WOMAN URGED HIM TO HAVE DINNER
YEAH WHATEVER
FROM THEN ON, EVERY TIME ELISHA CAME THROUGH TOWN, HE WOULD STAY WITH HER
REALLY, I INSIST
THE WOMAN SAID TO HER HUSBAND
YOU KNOW THAT MAN THAT STAYS WITH US SOMETIMES? I'M SURE HE'S A TRUE MAN OF GOD
YEAH, SO?
WE SHOULD BUILD A LITTLE CABIN IN THE BACK YARD FOR HIM
HONEY, YOU DO WHATEVER YOU WANT, I'M TRYING TO READ THE PAPER

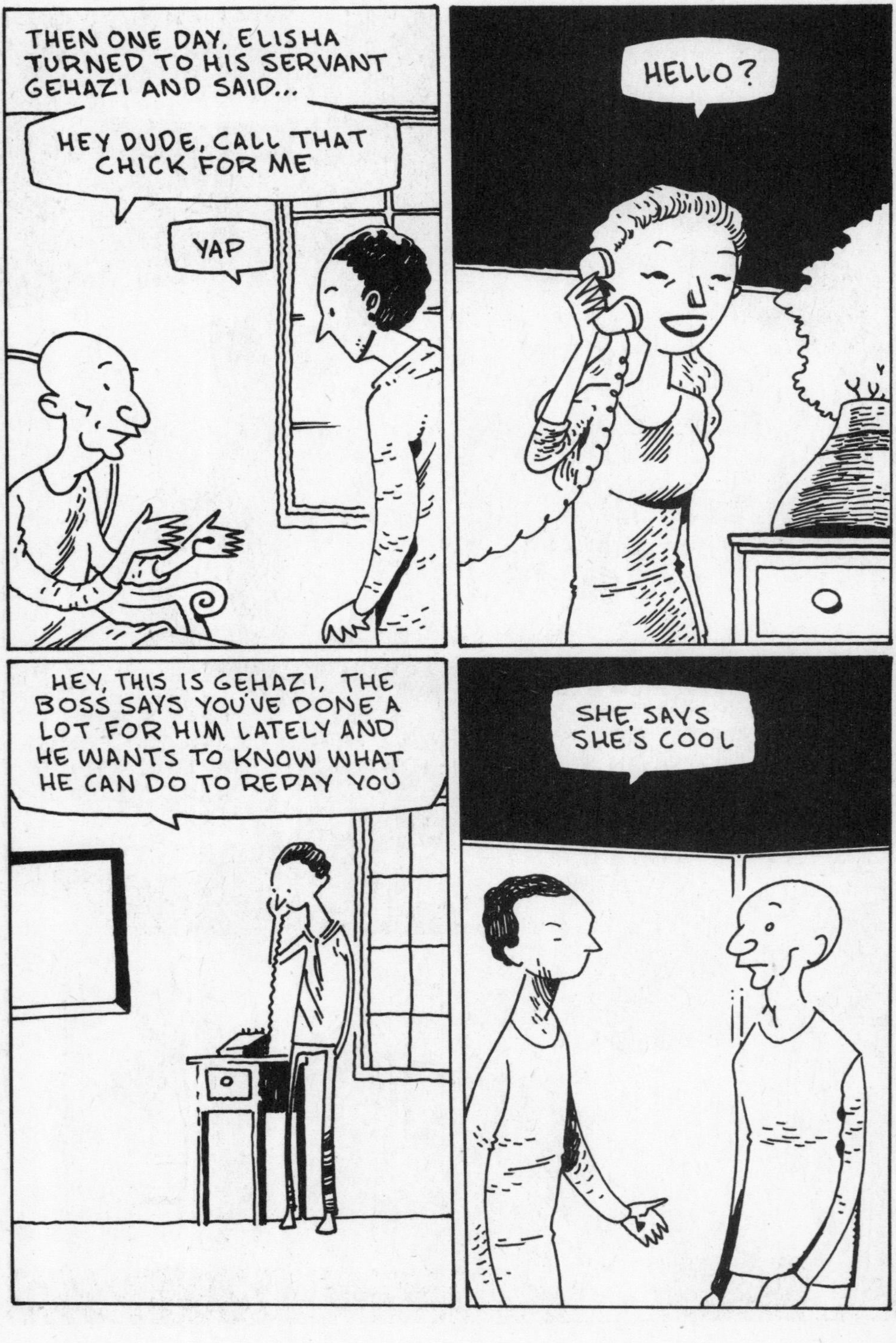
THEN ONE DAY, ELISHA TURNED TO HIS SERVANT GEHAZI AND SAID...
HEY DUDE, CALL THAT CHICK FOR ME
YAP
HELLO?
HEY, THIS IS GEHAZI, THE BOSS SAYS YOU'VE DONE A LOT FOR HIM LATELY AND HE WANTS TO KNOW WHAT HE CAN DO TO REPAY YOU
SHE SAYS SHE'S COOL

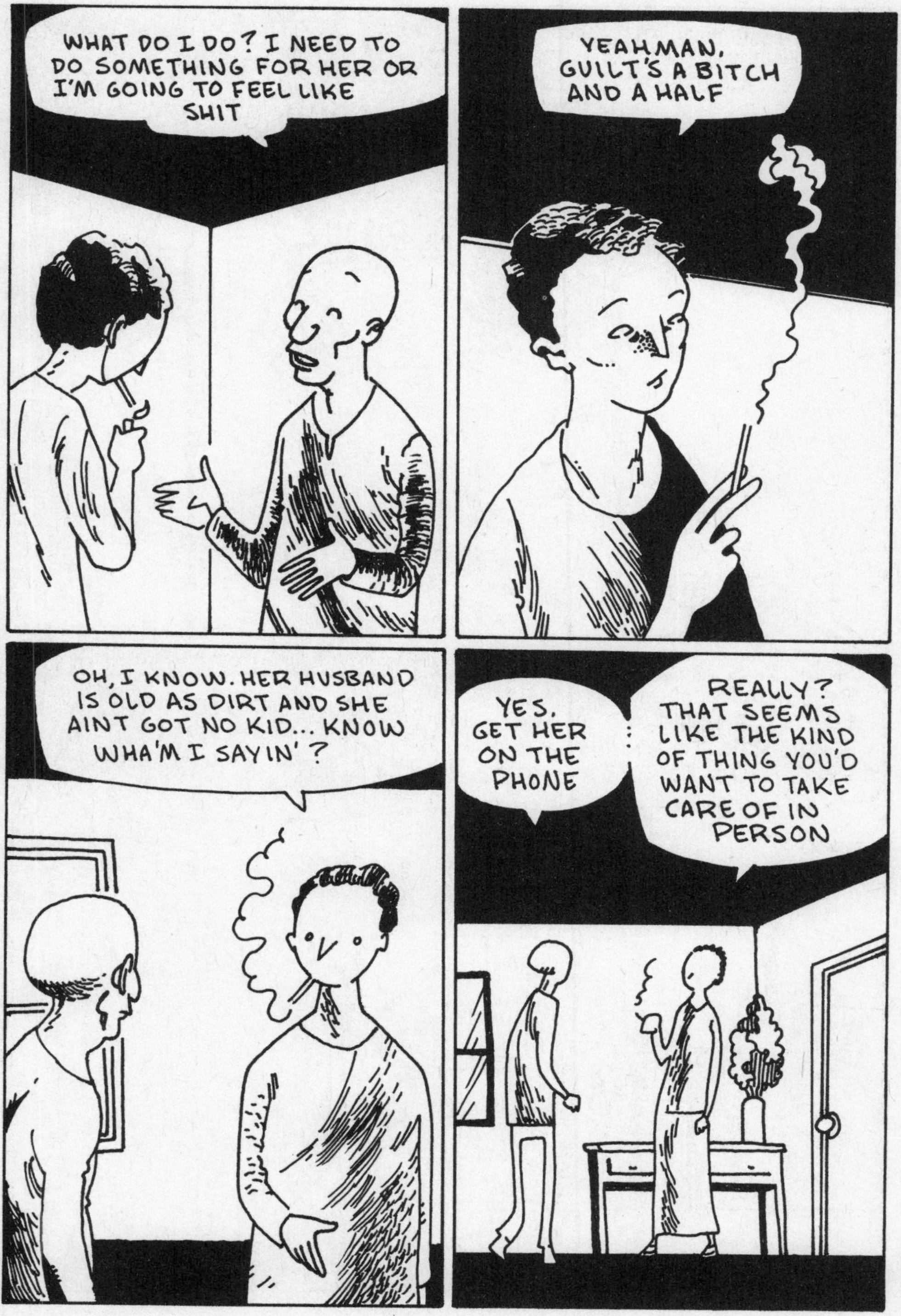
WHAT DO I DO? I NEED TO DO SOMETHING FOR HER OR I'M GOING TO FEEL LIKE SHIT
YEAH MAN. GUILT'S A BITCH AND A HALF
OH, I KNOW. HER HUSBAND IS OLD AS DIRT AND SHE AINT GOT NO KID... KNOW WHA'M I SAYIN'?
YES. GET HER ON THE PHONE
REALLY? THAT SEEMS LIKE THE KIND OF THING YOU'D WANT TO TAKE CARE OF IN PERSON

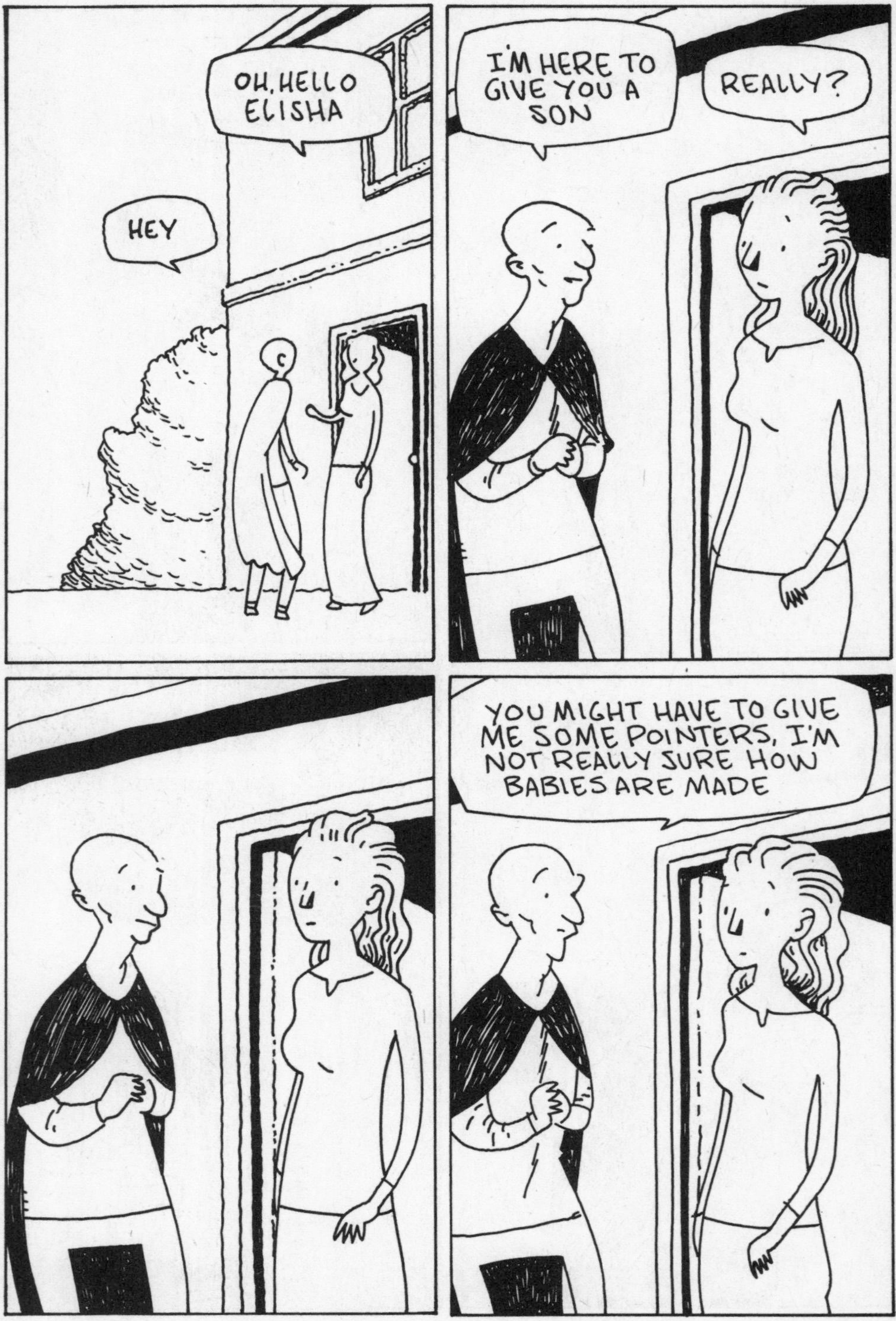
OH, HELLO ELISHA
HEY
I'M HERE TO GIVE YOU A SON
REALLY?
YOU MIGHT HAVE TO GIVE ME SOME POINTERS, I'M NOT REALLY SURE HOW BABIES ARE MADE

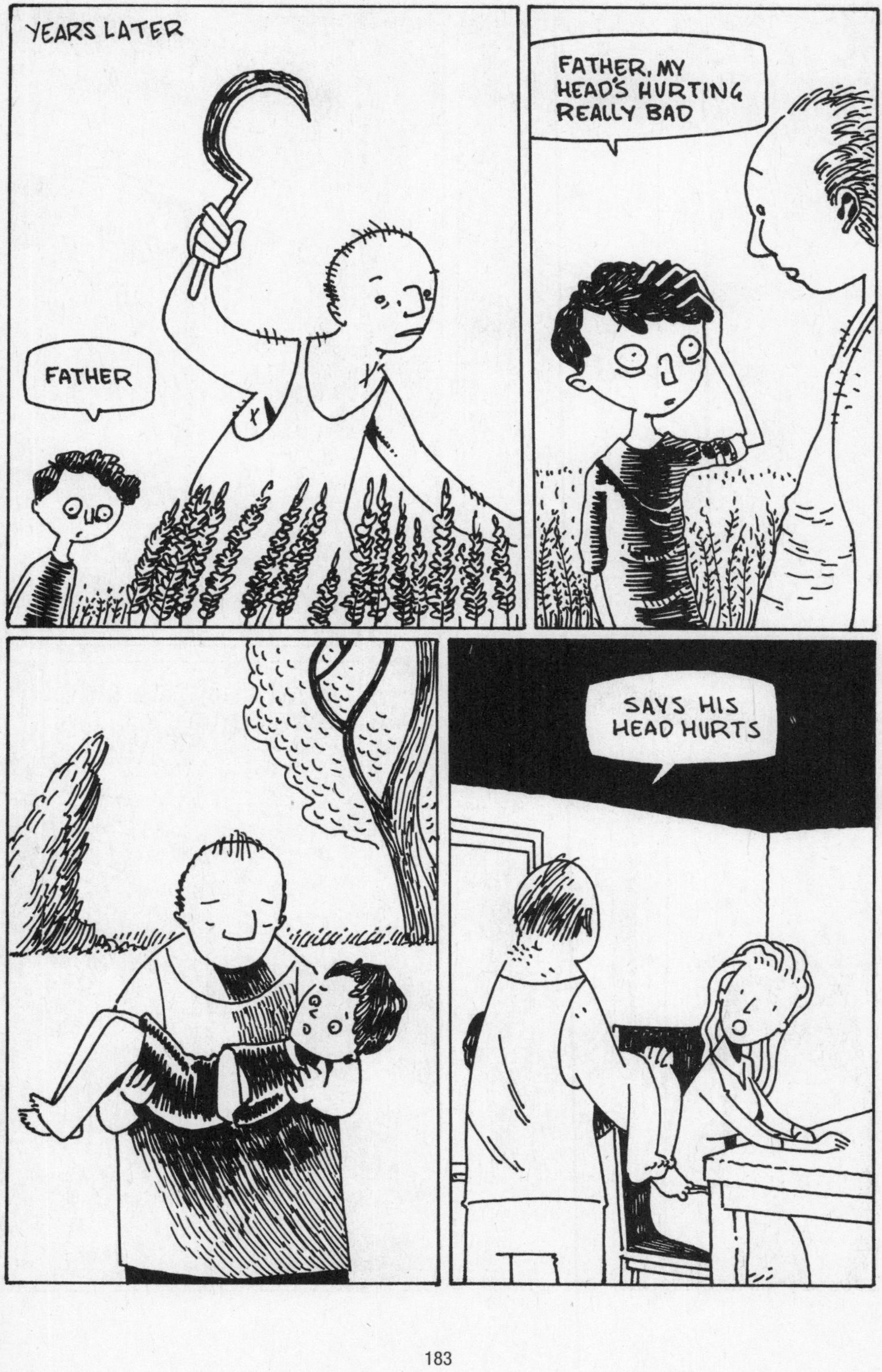
YEARS LATER
FATHER
FATHER, MY HEAD'S HURTING REALLY BAD
SAYS HIS HEAD HURTS

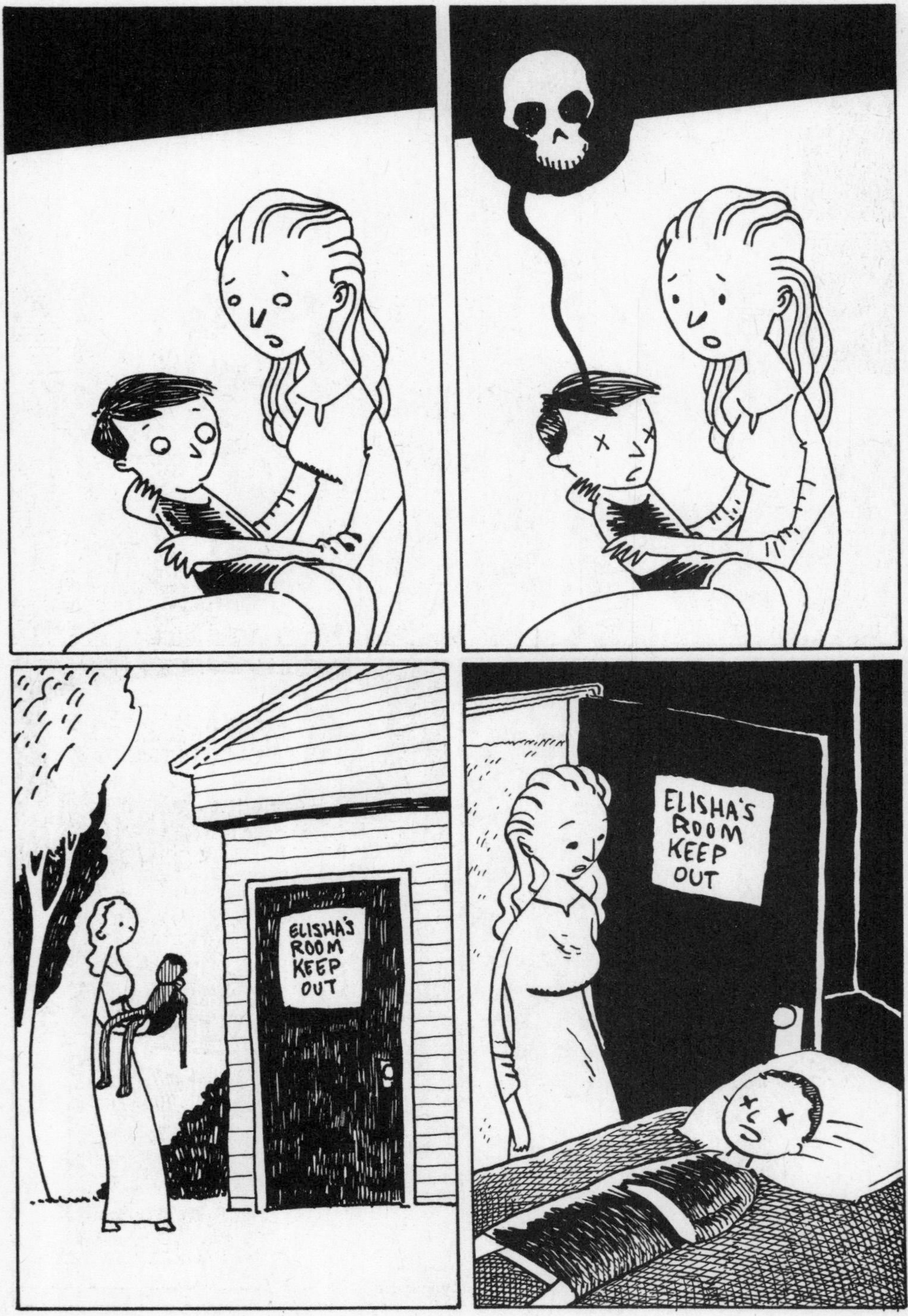
ELISHA'S
ROOM
KEEP
OUT
ELISHA'S
ROOM
KEEP
OUT

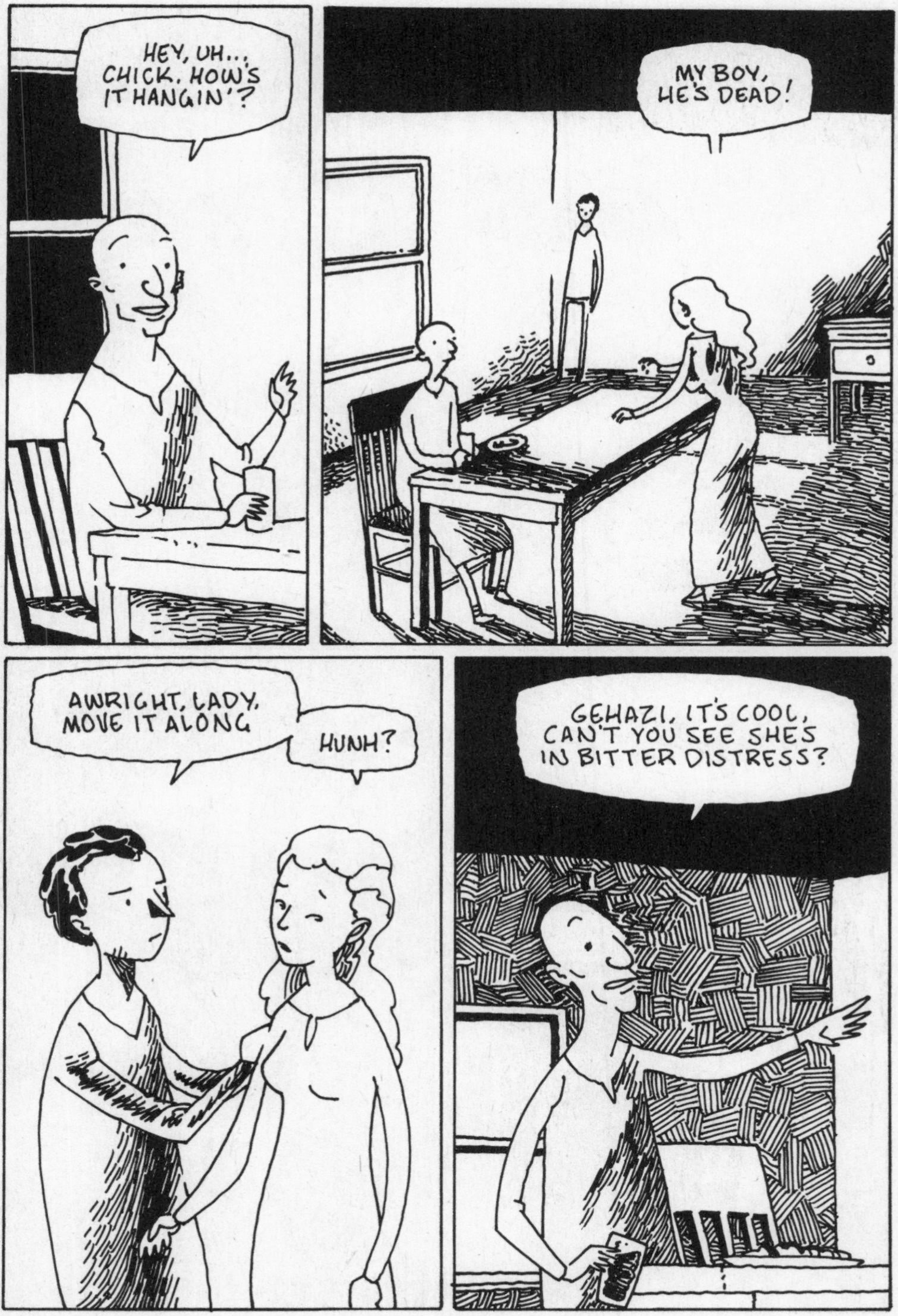
HEY, UH... CHICK. HOW'S IT HANGIN'?
MY BOY, HE'S DEAD!
AWRIGHT, LADY, MOVE IT ALONG
HUNH?
GEHAZI, IT'S COOL, CAN'T YOU SEE SHE'S IN BITTER DISTRESS?

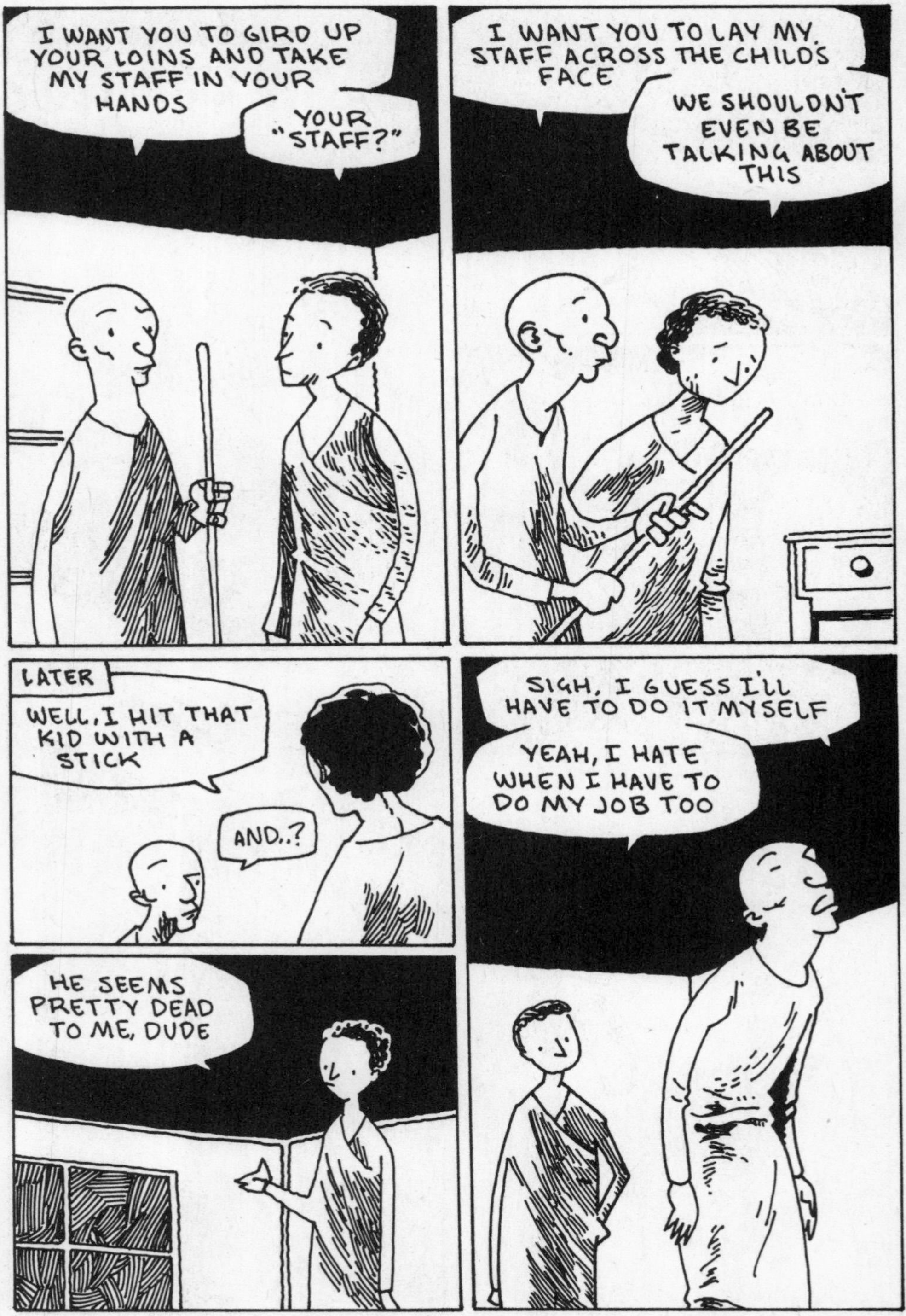
I WANT YOU TO GIRD UP YOUR LOINS AND TAKE MY STAFF IN YOUR HANDS
YOUR "STAFF?"
I WANT YOU TO LAY MY STAFF ACROSS THE CHILD'S FACE
WE SHOULDN'T EVEN BE TALKING ABOUT THIS
LATER
WELL, I HIT THAT KID WITH A STICK
AND..?
SIGH, I GUESS I'LL HAVE TO DO IT MYSELF
YEAH, I HATE WHEN I HAVE TO DO MY JOB TOO
HE SEEMS PRETTY DEAD TO ME, DUDE

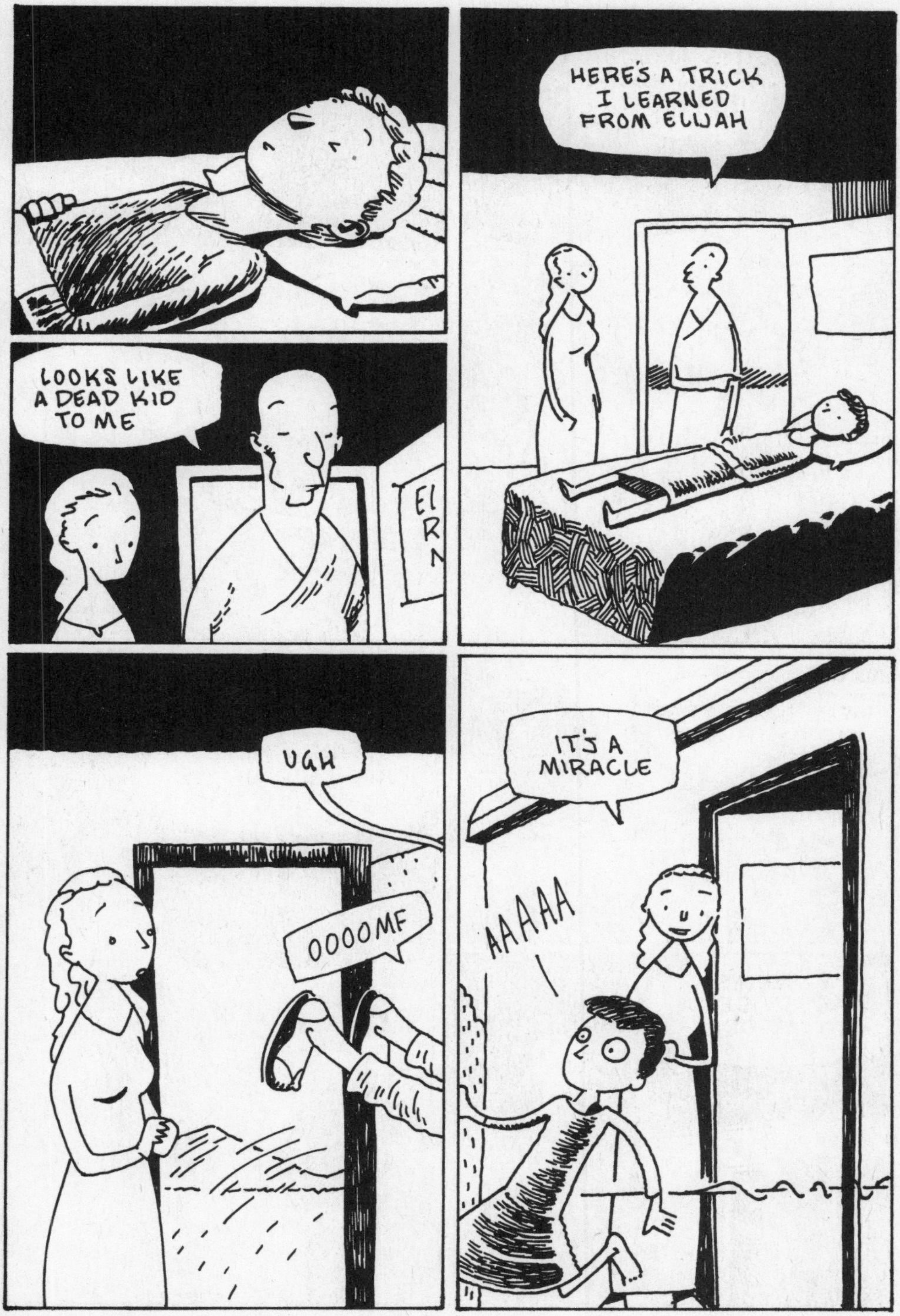
HERE'S A TRICK I LEARNED FROM ELIJAH
LOOKS LIKE A DEAD KID TO ME
UGH
OOOOMF
IT'S A MIRACLE
AAAAA

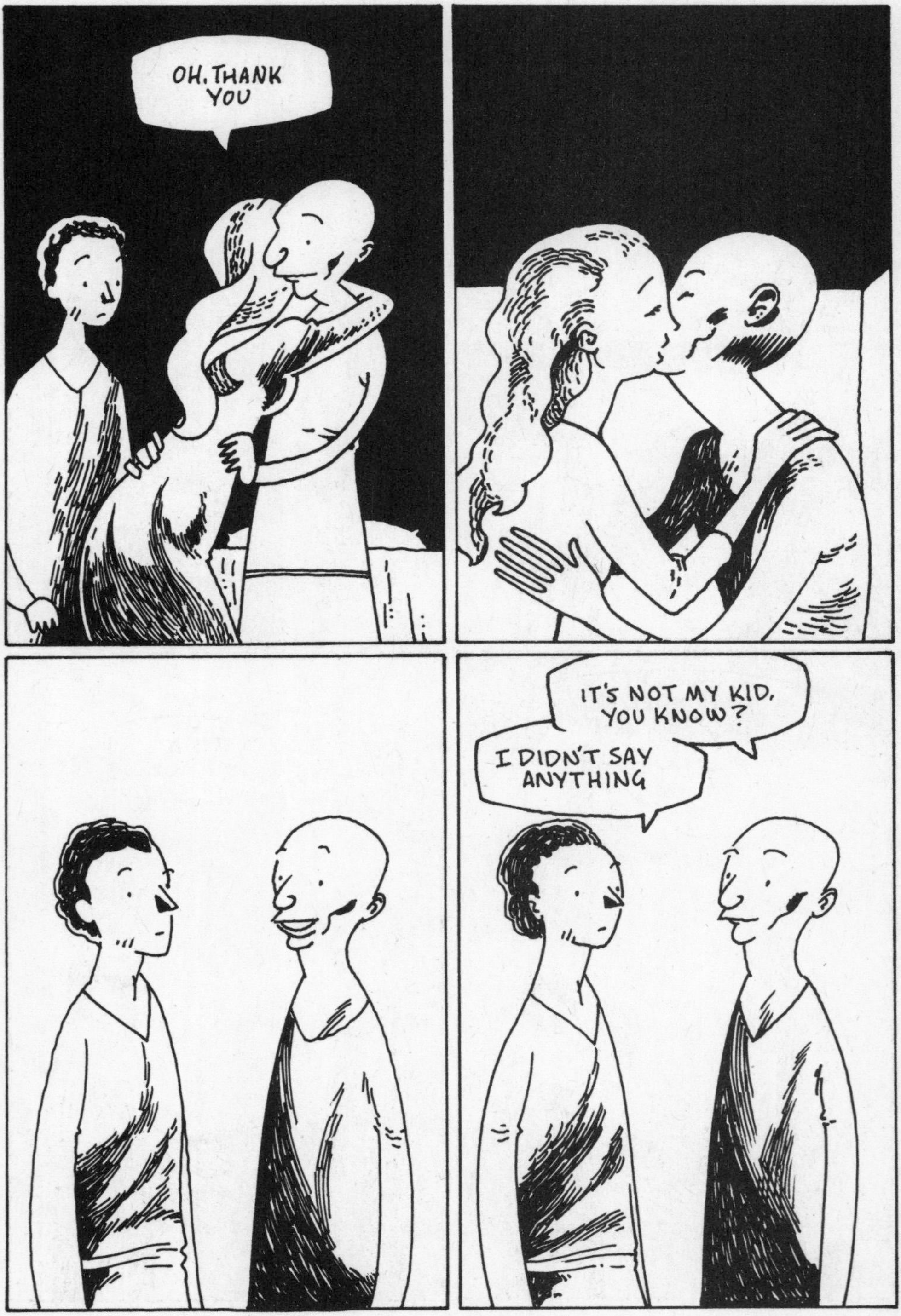
OH, THANK YOU
IT'S NOT MY KID, YOU KNOW?
I DIDN'T SAY ANYTHING

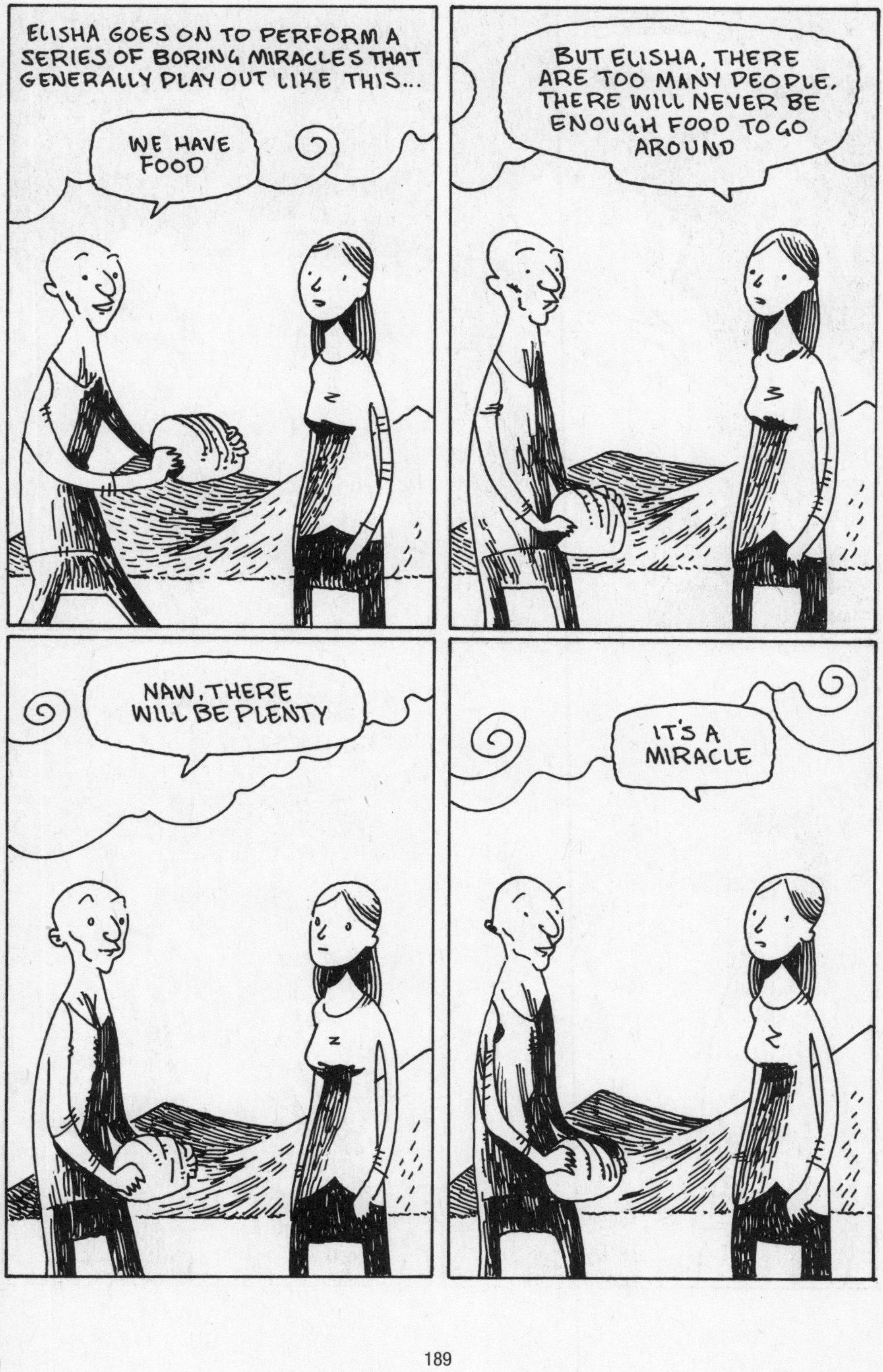
ELISHA GOES ON TO PERFORM A SERIES OF BORING MIRACLES THAT GENERALLY PLAY OUT LIKE THIS...
WE HAVE FOOD
BUT ELISHA, THERE ARE TOO MANY PEOPLE. THERE WILL NEVER BE ENOUGH FOOD TO GO AROUND
NAW, THERE WILL BE PLENTY
IT'S A MIRACLE

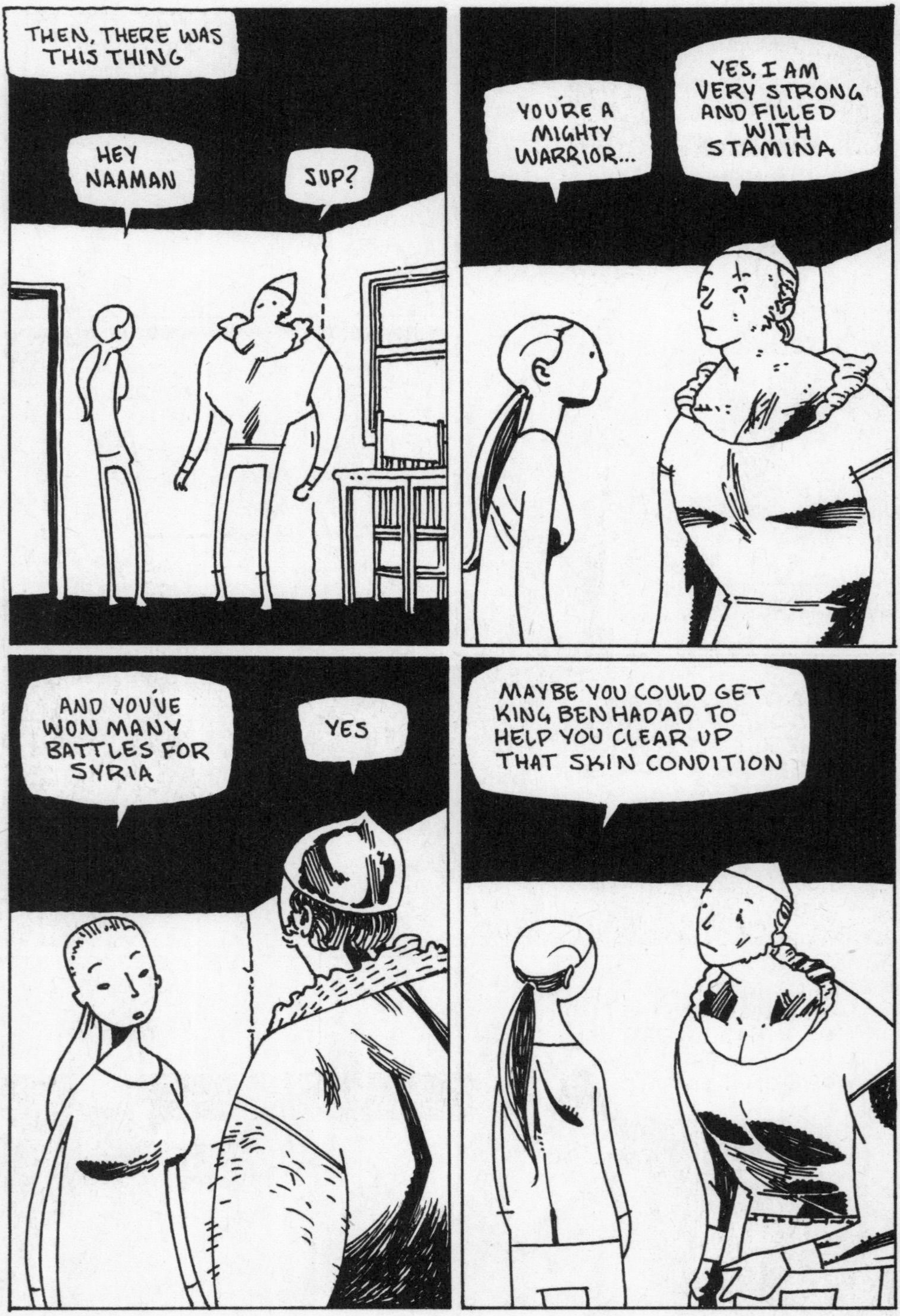
THEN, THERE WAS THIS THING
HEY NAAMAN
SUP?
YOU'RE A MIGHTY WARRIOR...
YES, I AM VERY STRONG AND FILLED WITH STAMINA
AND YOU'VE WON MANY BATTLES FOR SYRIA
YES
MAYBE YOU COULD GET KING BEN HADAD TO HELP YOU CLEAR UP THAT SKIN CONDITION

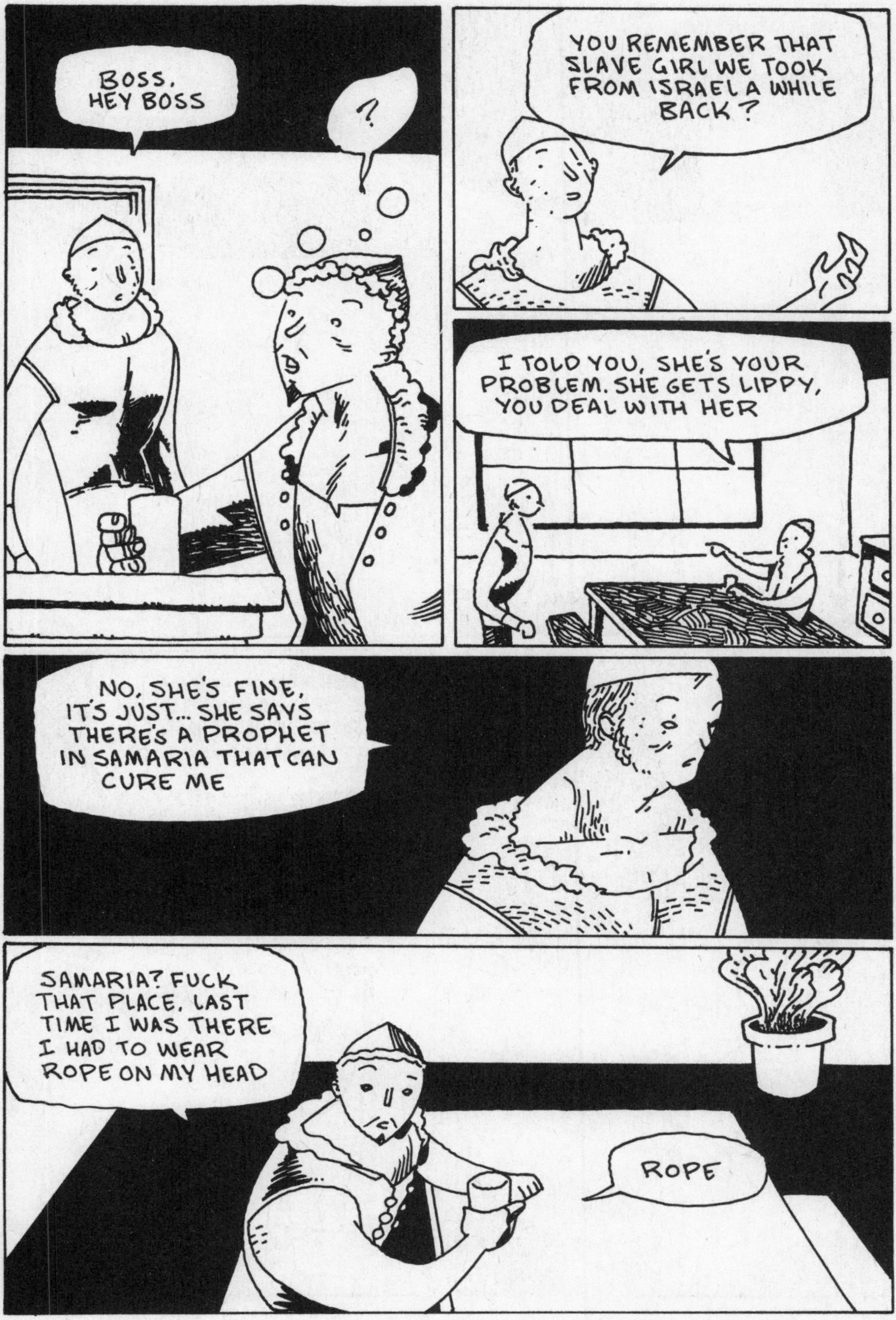

BOSS.
HEY BOSS
?
YOU REMEMBER THAT SLAVE GIRL WE TOOK FROM ISRAEL A WHILE BACK?
I TOLD YOU, SHE'S YOUR PROBLEM. SHE GETS LIPPY, YOU DEAL WITH HER
NO. SHE'S FINE, IT'S JUST... SHE SAYS THERE'S A PROPHET IN SAMARIA THAT CAN CURE ME
SAMARIA? FUCK THAT PLACE. LAST TIME I WAS THERE I HAD TO WEAR ROPE ON MY HEAD
ROPE

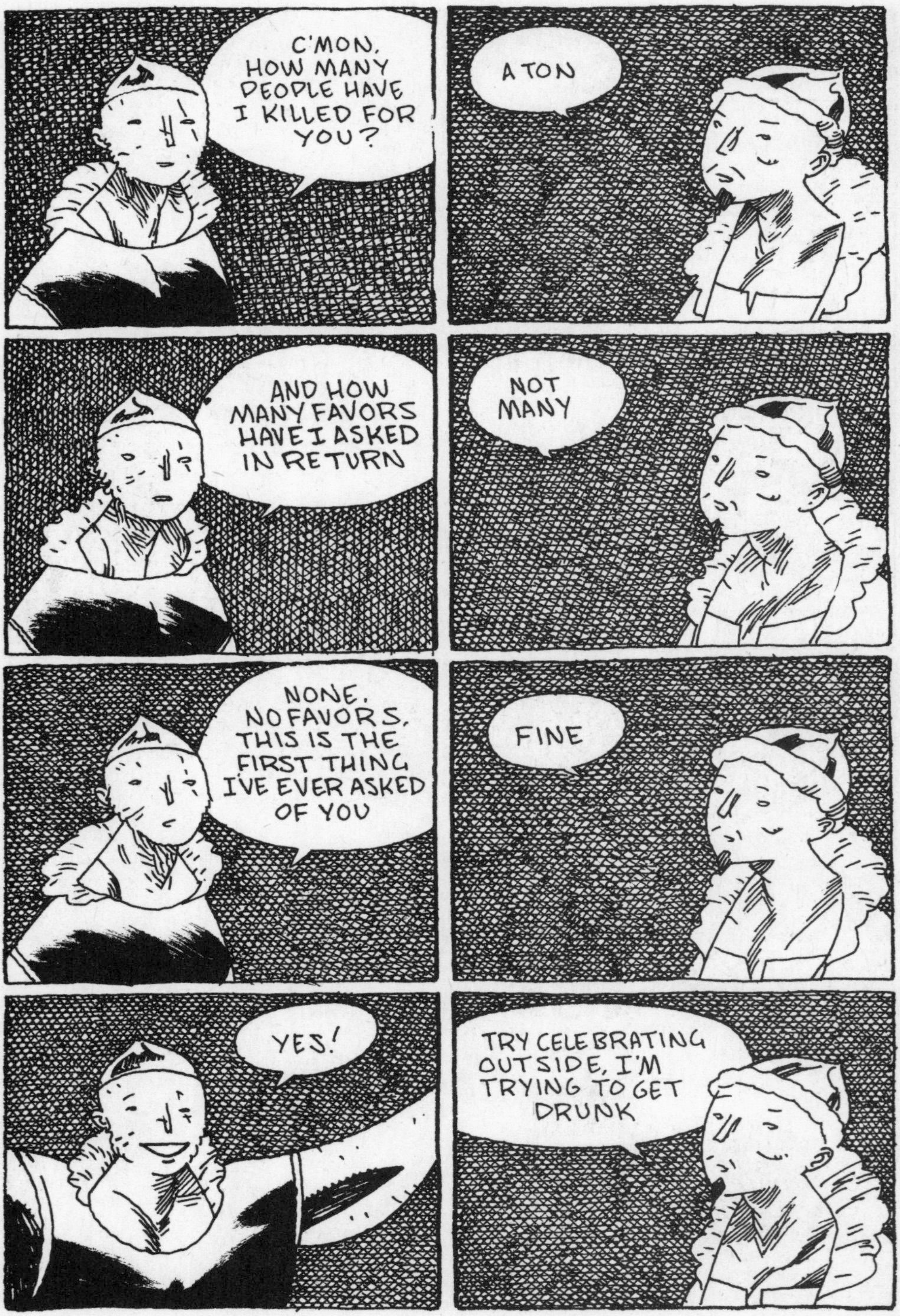
C'MON, HOW MANY PEOPLE HAVE I KILLED FOR YOU?
A TON
AND HOW MANY FAVORS HAVE I ASKED IN RETURN
NOT MANY
NONE. NO FAVORS. THIS IS THE FIRST THING I'VE EVER ASKED OF YOU
FINE
YES!
TRY CELEBRATING OUTSIDE, I'M TRYING TO GET DRUNK

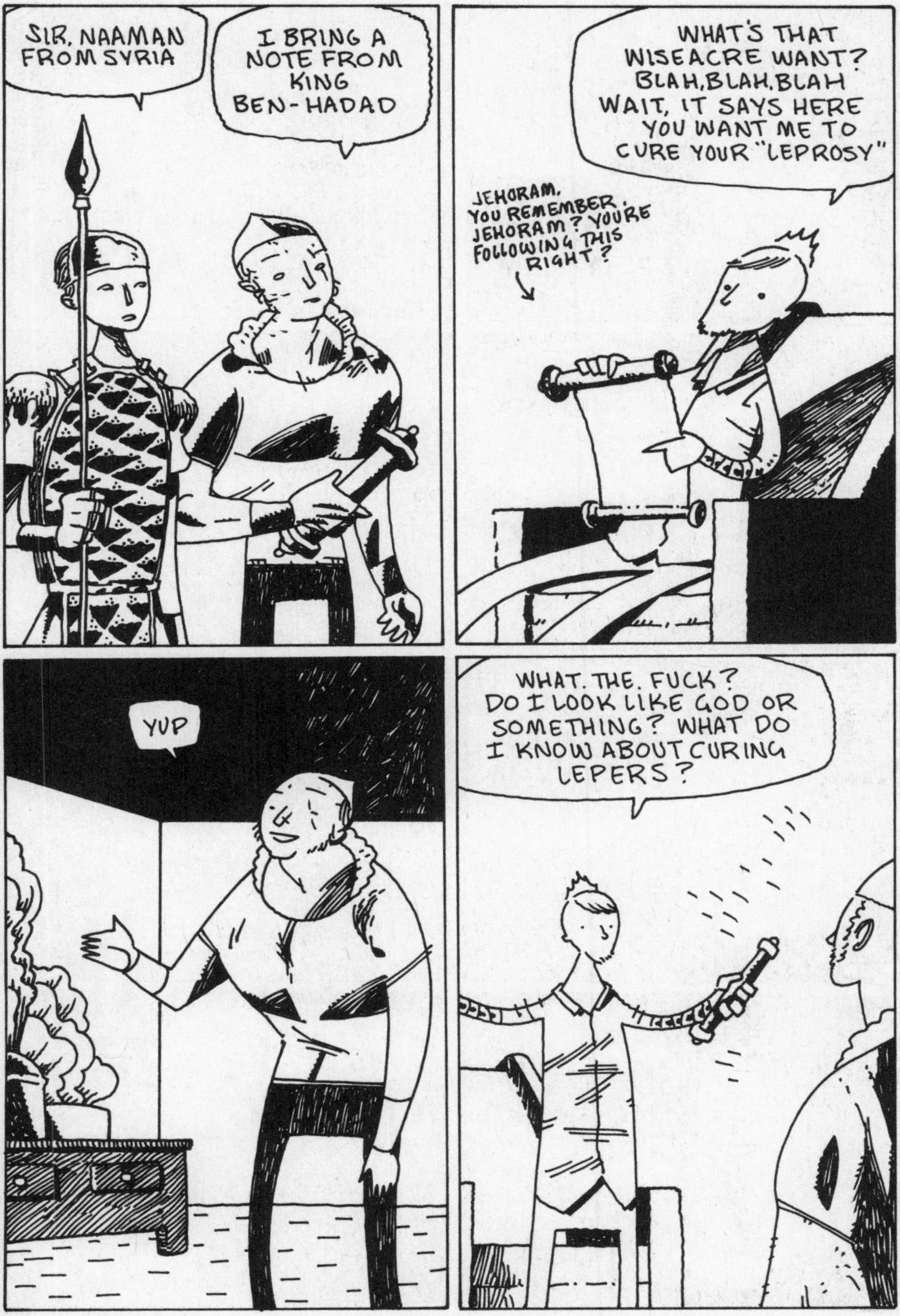
SIR, NAAMAN FROM SYRIA
I BRING A NOTE FROM KING BEN-HADAD
WHAT'S THAT WISEACRE WANT? BLAH, BLAH, BLAH WAIT, IT SAYS HERE YOU WANT ME TO CURE YOUR "LEPROSY"
JEHORAM. YOU REMEMBER. JEHORAM? YOU'RE FOLLOWING THIS RIGHT?
YUP
WHAT. THE. FUCK? DO I LOOK LIKE GOD OR SOMETHING? WHAT DO I KNOW ABOUT CURING LEPERS?

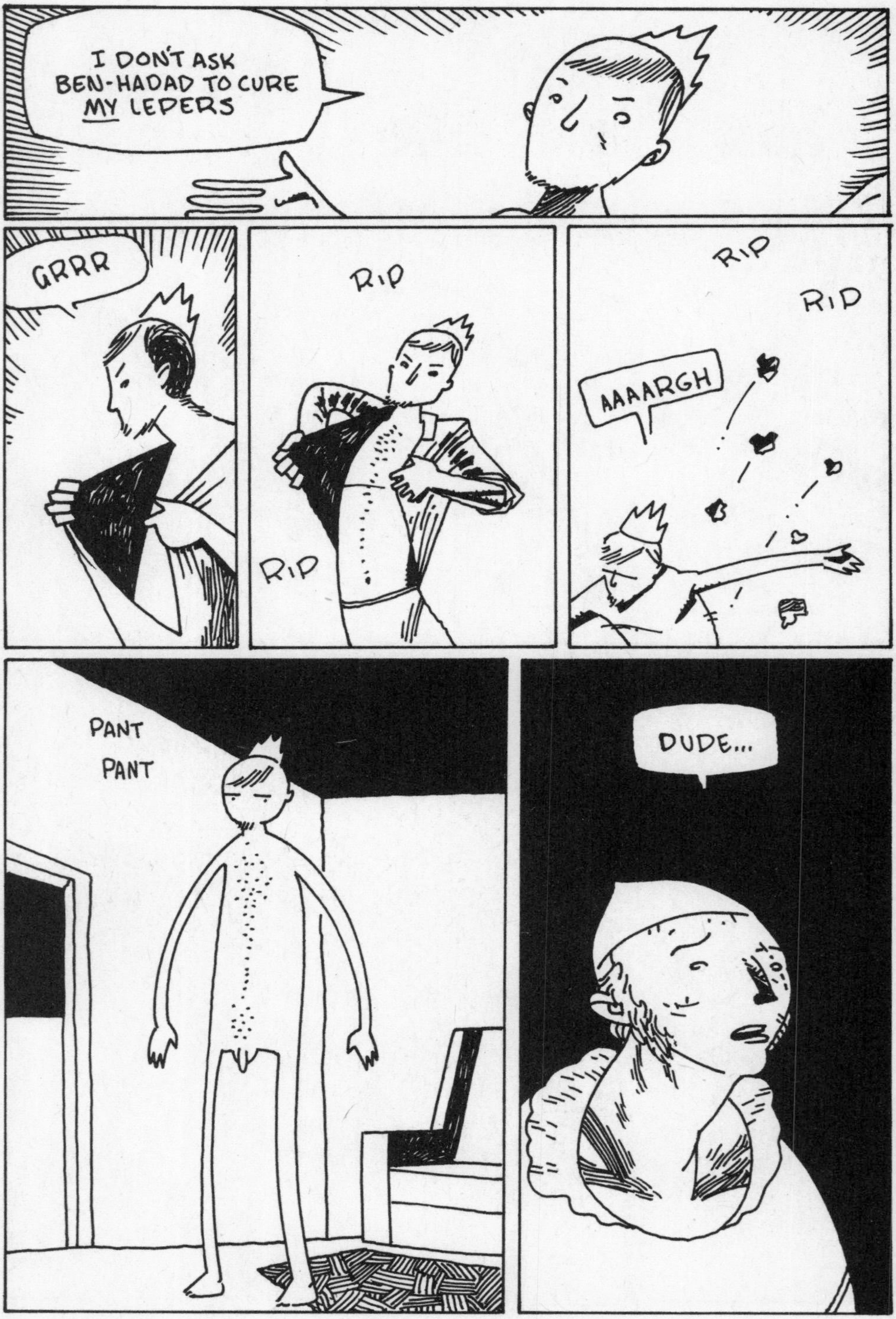
I DON'T ASK BEN-HADAD TO CURE MY LEPERS
GRRR
RIP
RIP
RIP
RIP
AAAARGH
PANT
PANT
DUDE...

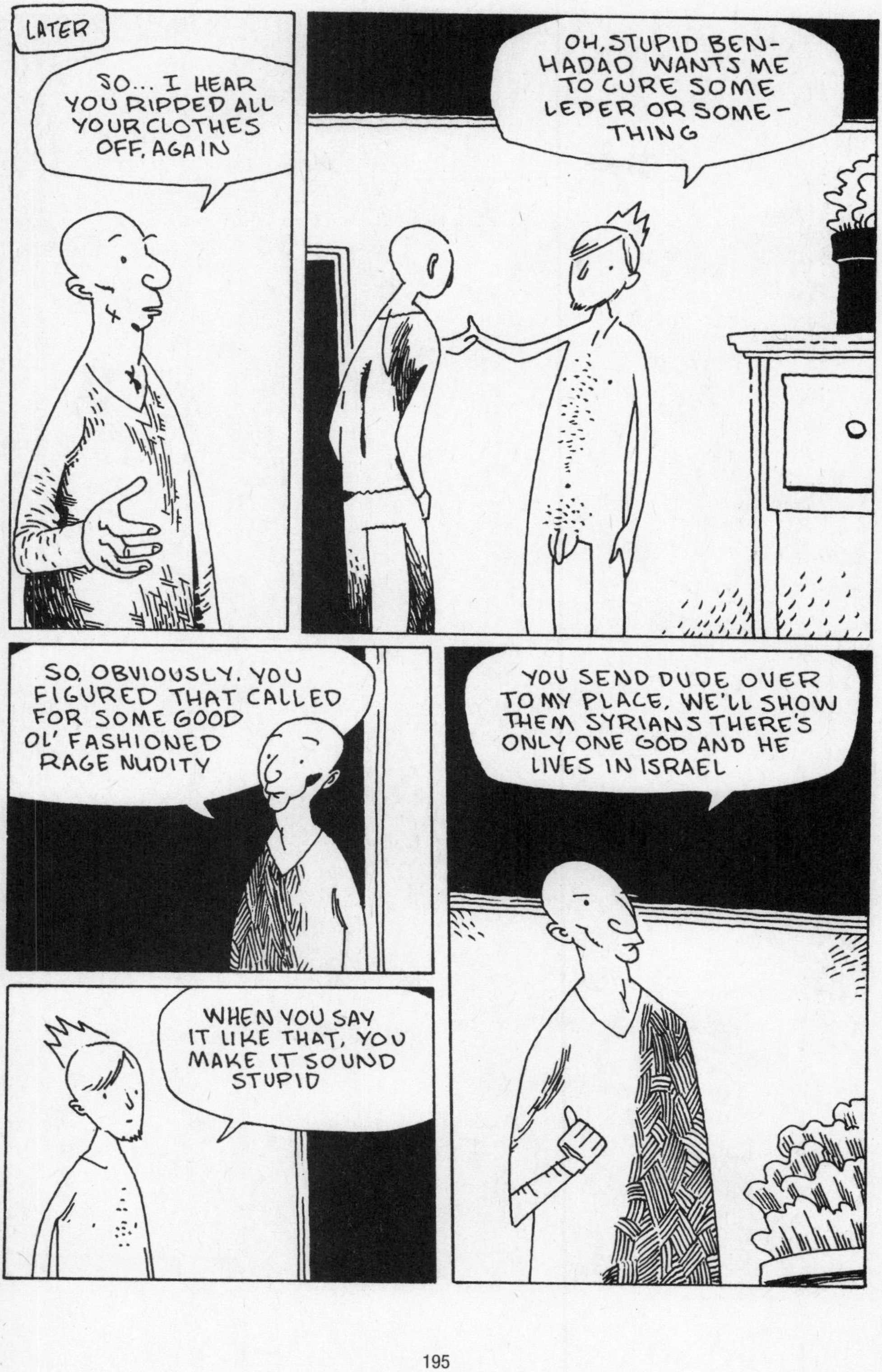
LATER
SO... I HEAR YOU RIPPED ALL YOUR CLOTHES OFF, AGAIN
OH, STUPID BEN-HADAD WANTS ME TO CURE SOME LEPER OR SOME-THING
SO, OBVIOUSLY, YOU FIGURED THAT CALLED FOR SOME GOOD OL' FASHIONED RAGE NUDITY
WHEN YOU SAY IT LIKE THAT, YOU MAKE IT SOUND STUPID
YOU SEND DUDE OVER TO MY PLACE. WE'LL SHOW THEM SYRIANS THERE'S ONLY ONE GOD AND HE LIVES IN ISRAEL

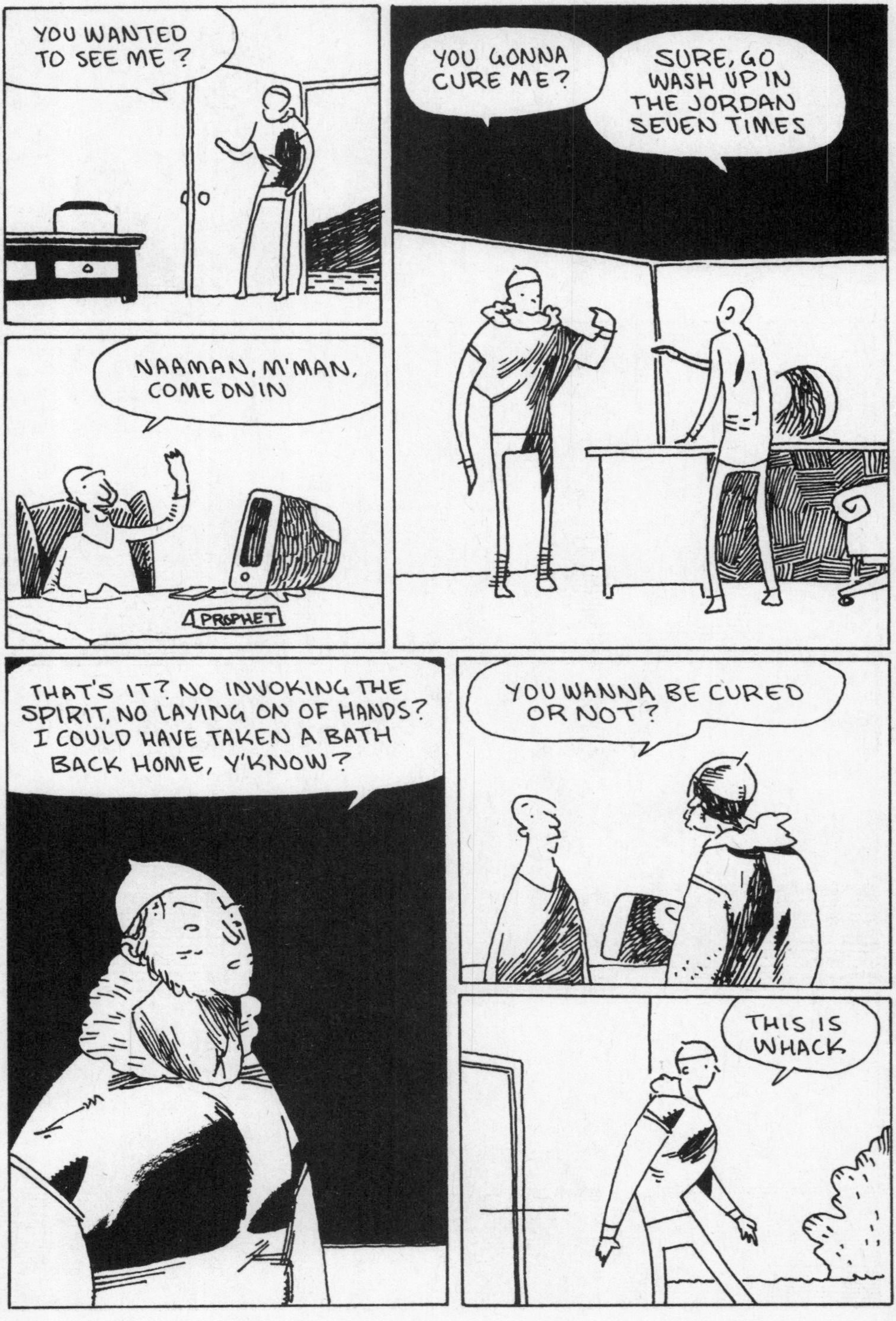
YOU WANTED TO SEE ME?
NAAMAN, M'MAN, COME ON IN
PROPHET
YOU GONNA CURE ME?
SURE, GO WASH UP IN THE JORDAN SEVEN TIMES
THAT'S IT? NO INVOKING THE SPIRIT, NO LAYING ON OF HANDS? I COULD HAVE TAKEN A BATH BACK HOME, Y'KNOW?
YOU WANNA BE CURED OR NOT?
THIS IS WHACK

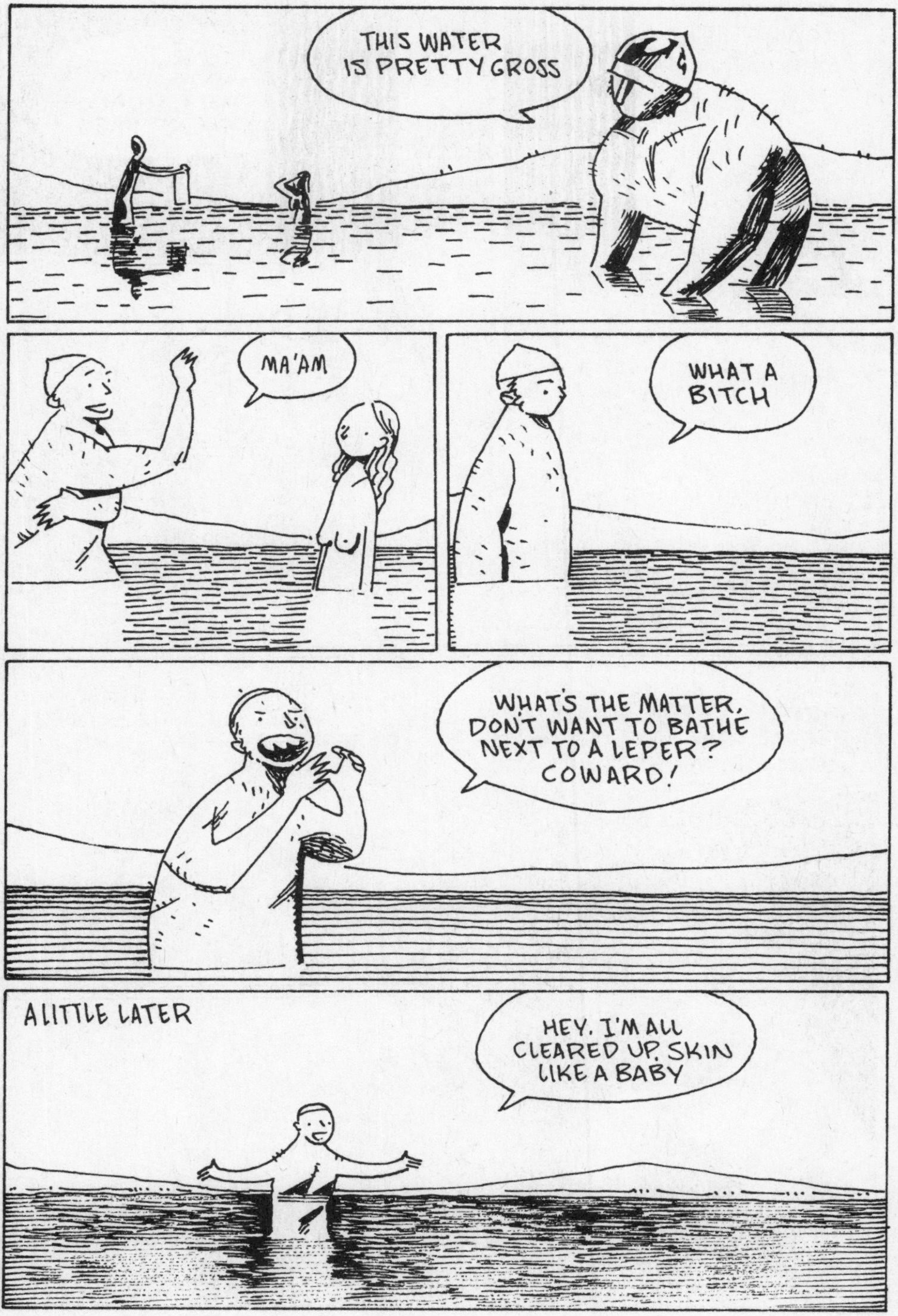
THIS WATER IS PRETTY GROSS
MA'AM
WHAT A BITCH
WHAT'S THE MATTER, DON'T WANT TO BATHE NEXT TO A LEPER? COWARD!
A LITTLE LATER
HEY. I'M ALL CLEARED UP. SKIN LIKE A BABY

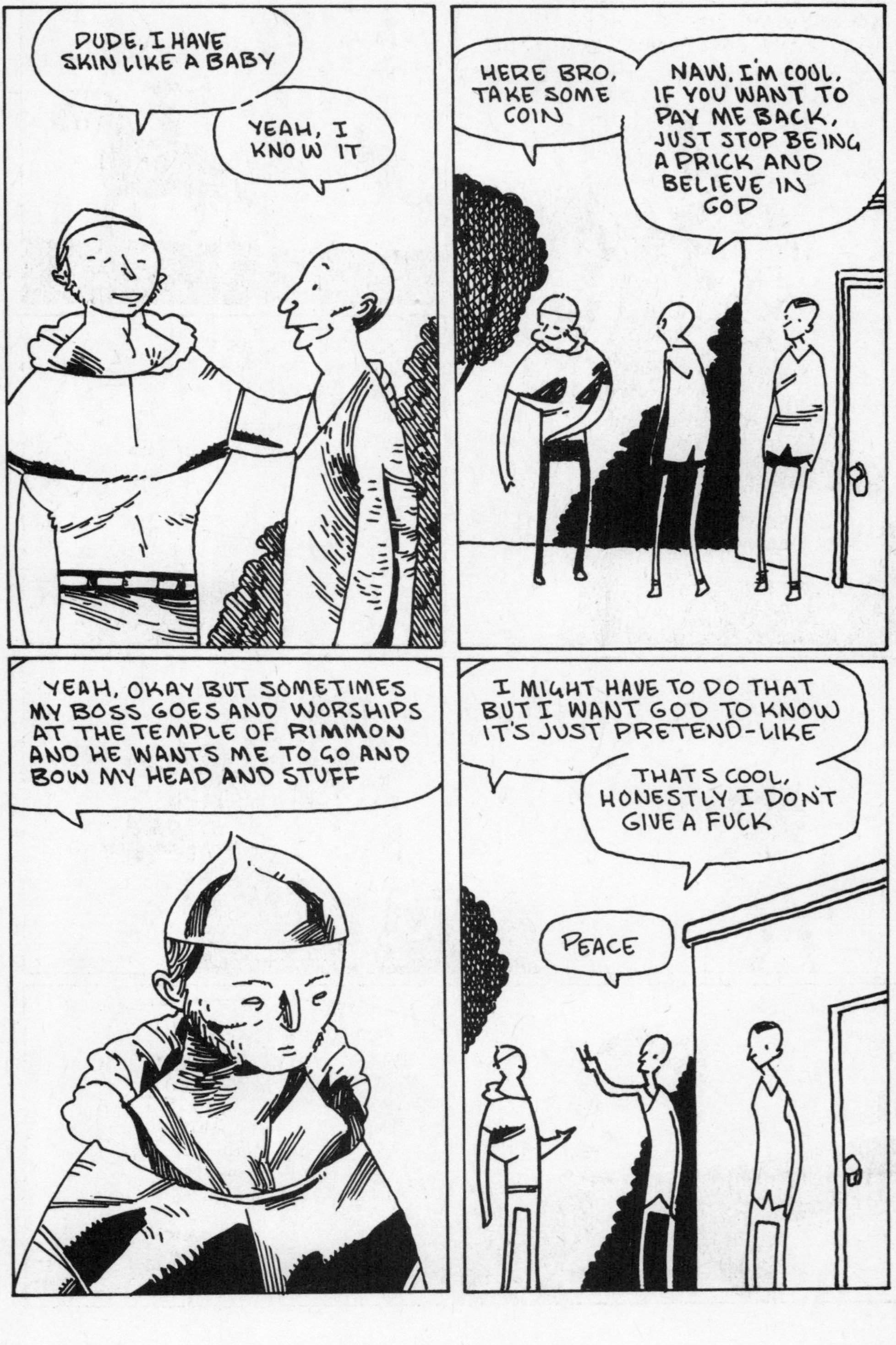
DUDE, I HAVE SKIN LIKE A BABY
YEAH, I KNOW IT
HERE BRO, TAKE SOME COIN
NAW, I'M COOL, IF YOU WANT TO PAY ME BACK, JUST STOP BEING A PRICK AND BELIEVE IN GOD
YEAH, OKAY BUT SOMETIMES MY BOSS GOES AND WORSHIPS AT THE TEMPLE OF RIMMON AND HE WANTS ME TO GO AND BOW MY HEAD AND STUFF
I MIGHT HAVE TO DO THAT BUT I WANT GOD TO KNOW IT'S JUST PRETEND-LIKE
THATS COOL, HONESTLY I DON'T GIVE A FUCK
PEACE

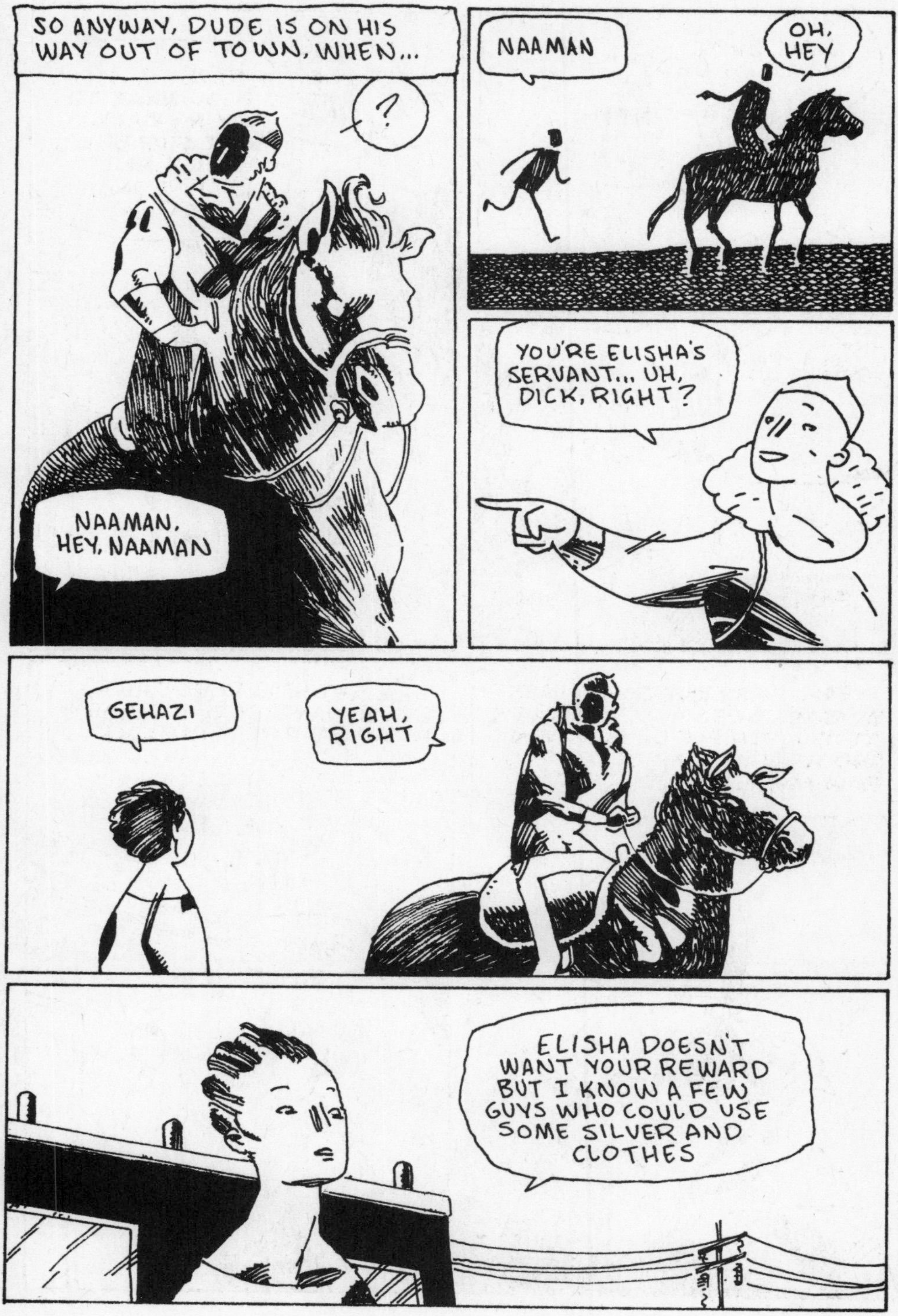
SO ANYWAY, DUDE IS ON HIS WAY OUT OF TOWN, WHEN...
?
NAAMAN, HEY, NAAMAN
NAAMAN
OH, HEY
YOU'RE ELISHA'S SERVANT... UH, DICK, RIGHT?
GEHAZI
YEAH, RIGHT
ELISHA DOESN'T WANT YOUR REWARD BUT I KNOW A FEW GUYS WHO COULD USE SOME SILVER AND CLOTHES

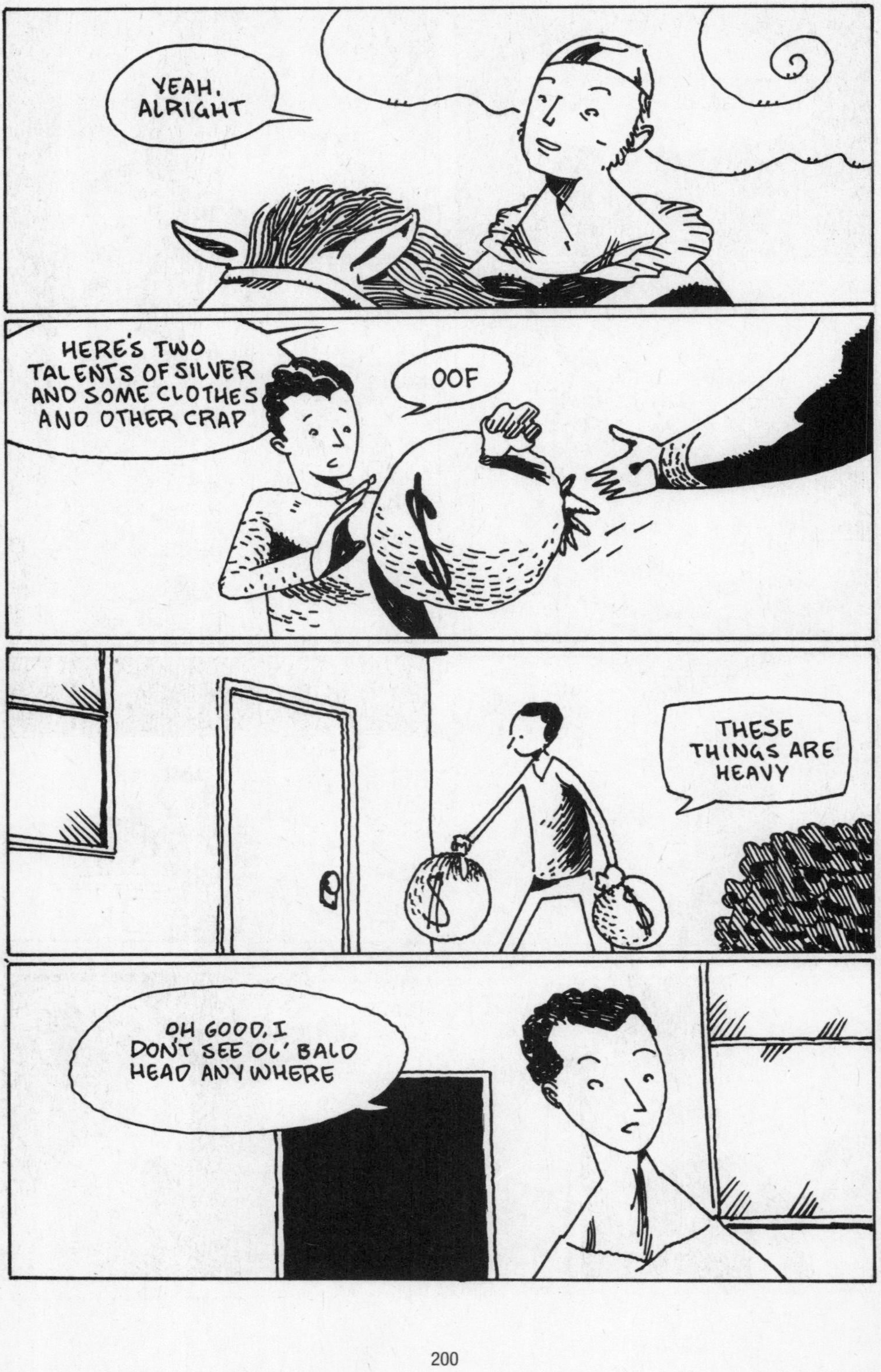
YEAH. ALRIGHT
HERE'S TWO TALENTS OF SILVER AND SOME CLOTHES AND OTHER CRAP
OOF
THESE THINGS ARE HEAVY
OH GOOD. I DON'T SEE OL' BALD HEAD ANYWHERE

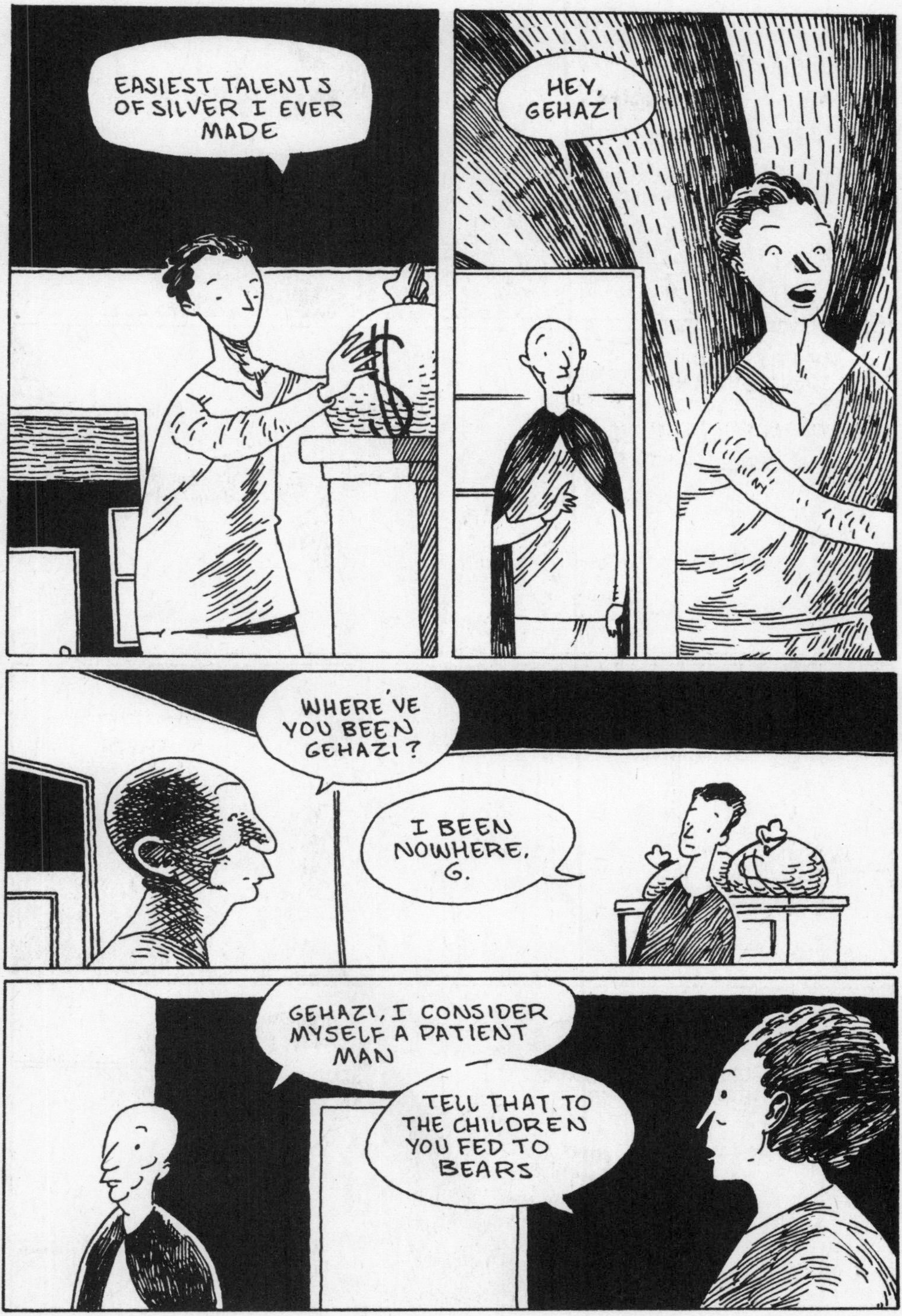

EASIEST TALENTS OF SILVER I EVER MADE
HEY, GEHAZI
WHERE'VE YOU BEEN GEHAZI?
I BEEN NOWHERE, G.
GEHAZI, I CONSIDER MYSELF A PATIENT MAN
TELL THAT TO THE CHILDREN YOU FED TO BEARS

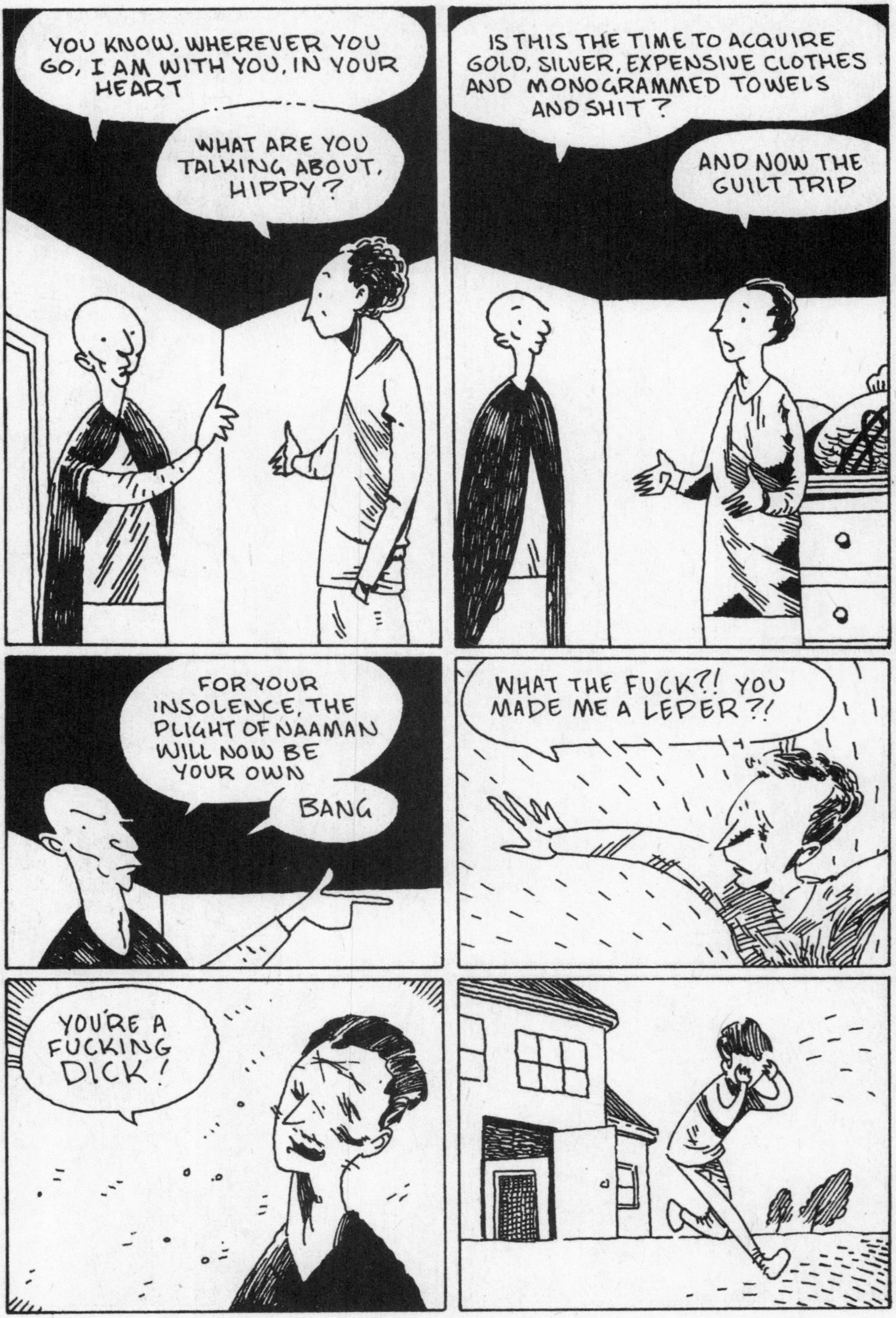
YOU KNOW, WHEREVER YOU GO, I AM WITH YOU, IN YOUR HEART
WHAT ARE YOU TALKING ABOUT, HIPPY?
IS THIS THE TIME TO ACQUIRE GOLD, SILVER, EXPENSIVE CLOTHES AND MONOGRAMMED TOWELS AND SHIT?
AND NOW THE GUILT TRIP
FOR YOUR INSOLENCE, THE PLIGHT OF NAAMAN WILL NOW BE YOUR OWN
BANG
WHAT THE FUCK?! YOU MADE ME A LEPER?!
YOU'RE A FUCKING DICK!

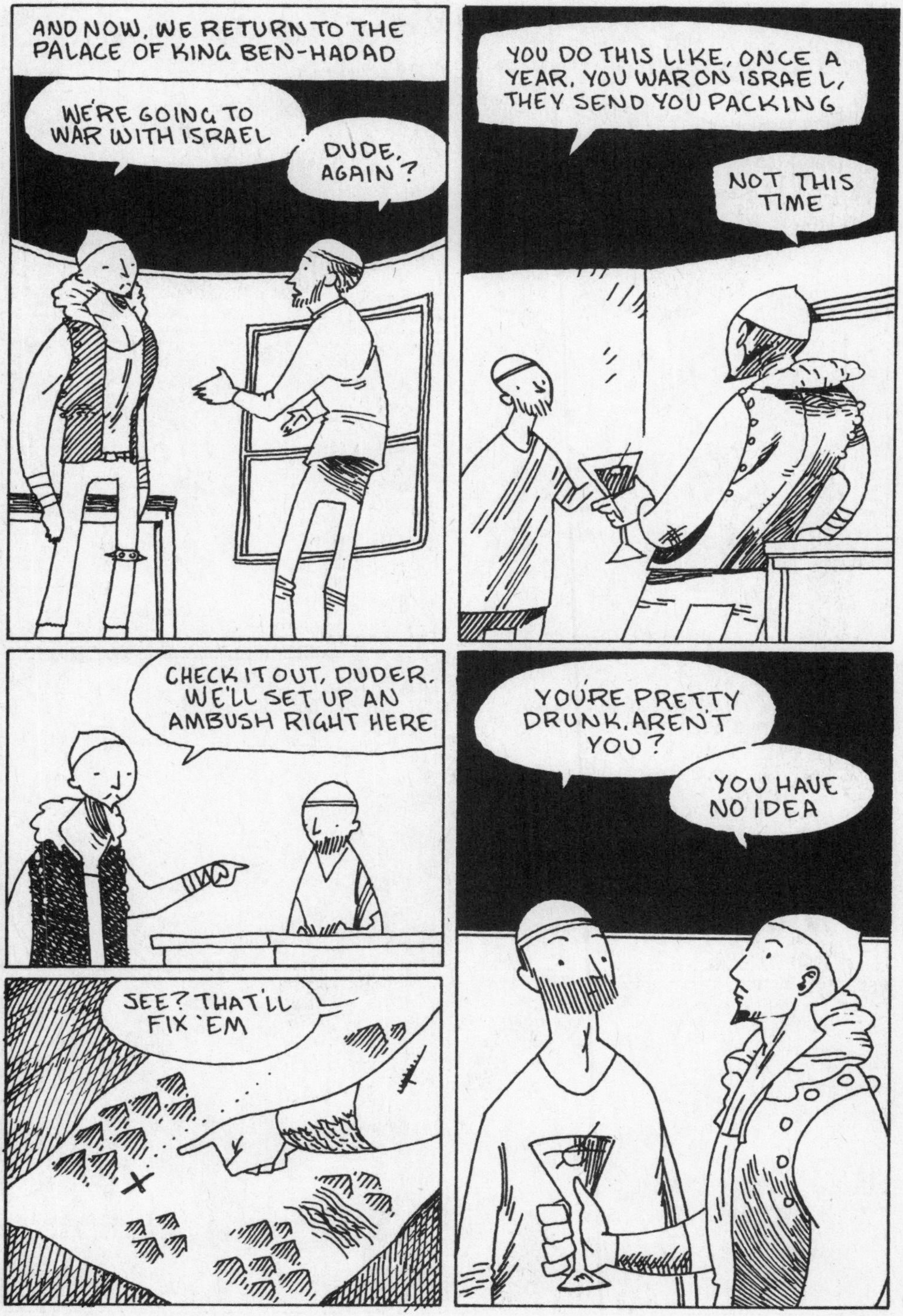
AND NOW, WE RETURN TO THE PALACE OF KING BEN-HADAD
WE'RE GOING TO WAR WITH ISRAEL
DUDE, AGAIN?
YOU DO THIS LIKE, ONCE A YEAR. YOU WAR ON ISRAEL, THEY SEND YOU PACKING
NOT THIS TIME
CHECK IT OUT, DUDER. WE'LL SET UP AN AMBUSH RIGHT HERE
SEE? THAT'LL FIX 'EM
YOU'RE PRETTY DRUNK, AREN'T YOU?
YOU HAVE NO IDEA

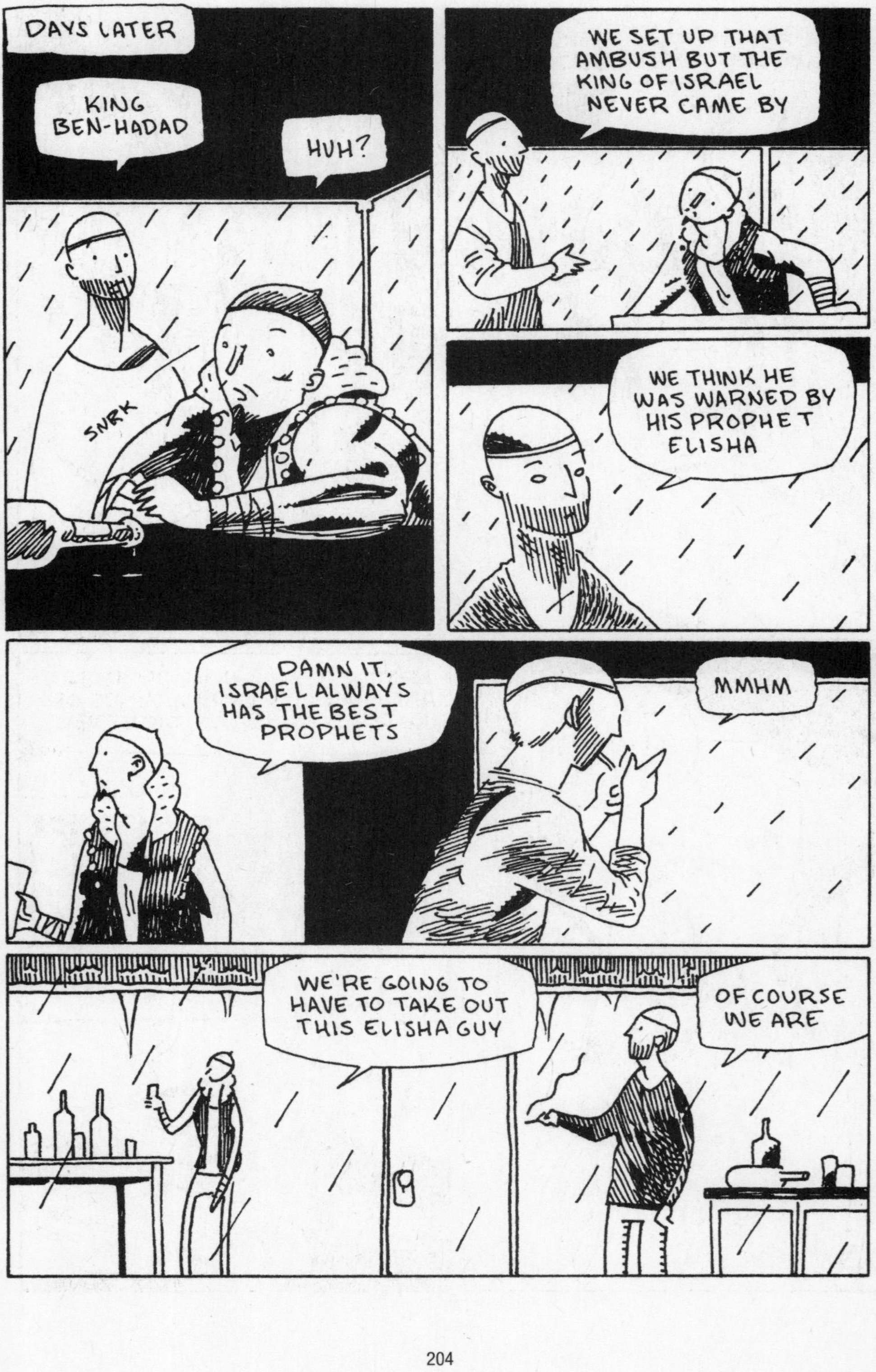
DAYS LATER
KING BEN-HADAD
HUH?
SNRK
WE SET UP THAT AMBUSH BUT THE KING OF ISRAEL NEVER CAME BY
WE THINK HE WAS WARNED BY HIS PROPHET ELISHA
DAMN IT. ISRAEL ALWAYS HAS THE BEST PROPHETS
MMHM
WE'RE GOING TO HAVE TO TAKE OUT THIS ELISHA GUY
OF COURSE WE ARE

BEN-HADAD SENT HORSES AND CHARIOTS THAT CAME BY NIGHT AND COMPASSED THE CITY ABOUT

THAT MORNING

HOLY FLIPPIN' SHIT!

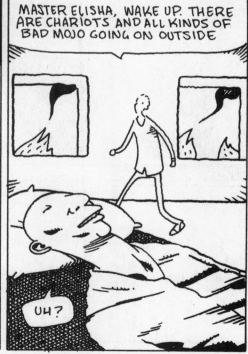

MASTER ELISHA, WAKE UP. THERE ARE CHARIOTS AND ALL KINDS OF BAD MOJO GOING ON OUTSIDE

UH?

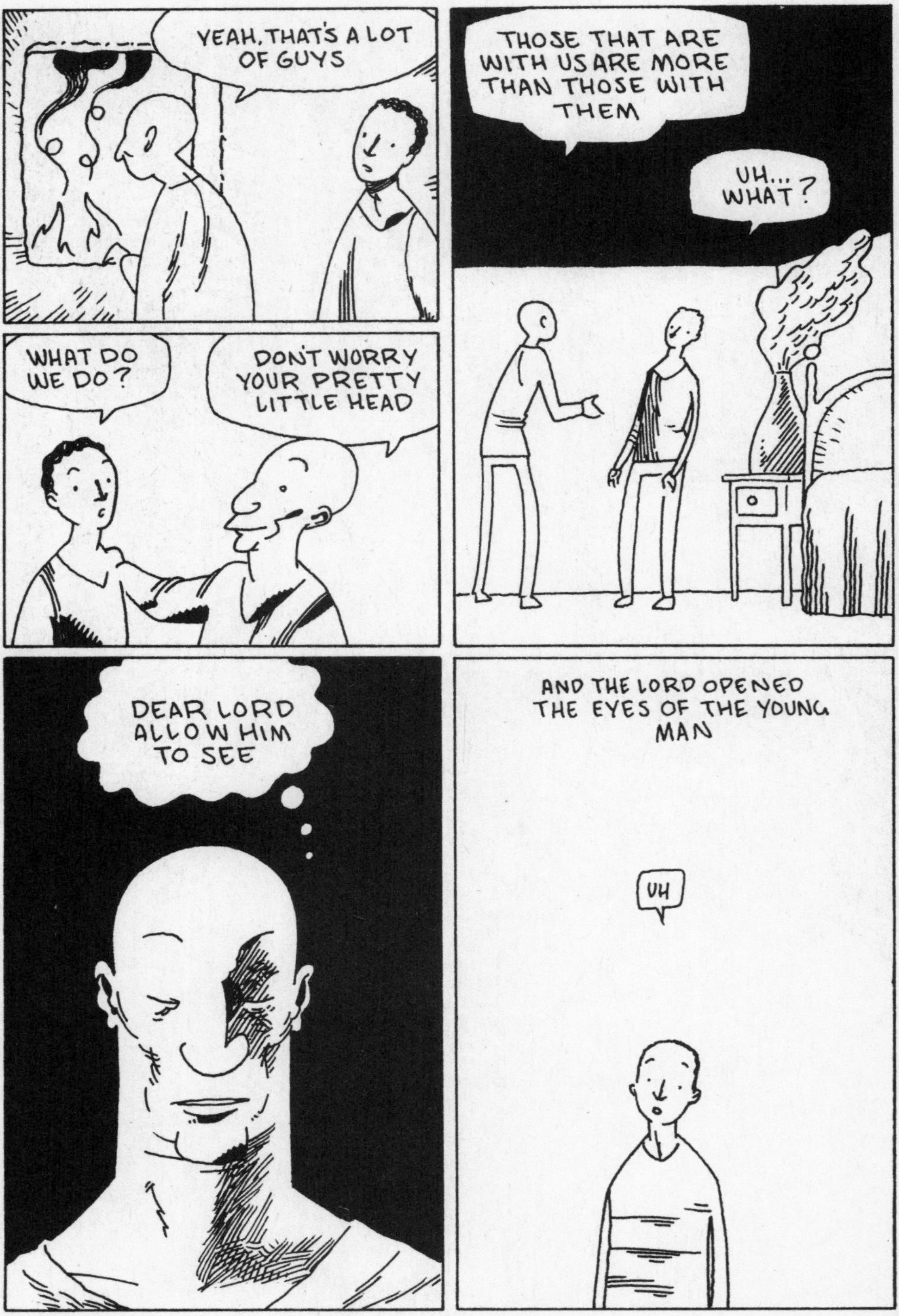
YEAH, THAT'S A LOT OF GUYS
THOSE THAT ARE WITH US ARE MORE THAN THOSE WITH THEM
UH... WHAT?
WHAT DO WE DO?
DON'T WORRY YOUR PRETTY LITTLE HEAD
DEAR LORD ALLOW HIM TO SEE
AND THE LORD OPENED THE EYES OF THE YOUNG MAN
UH

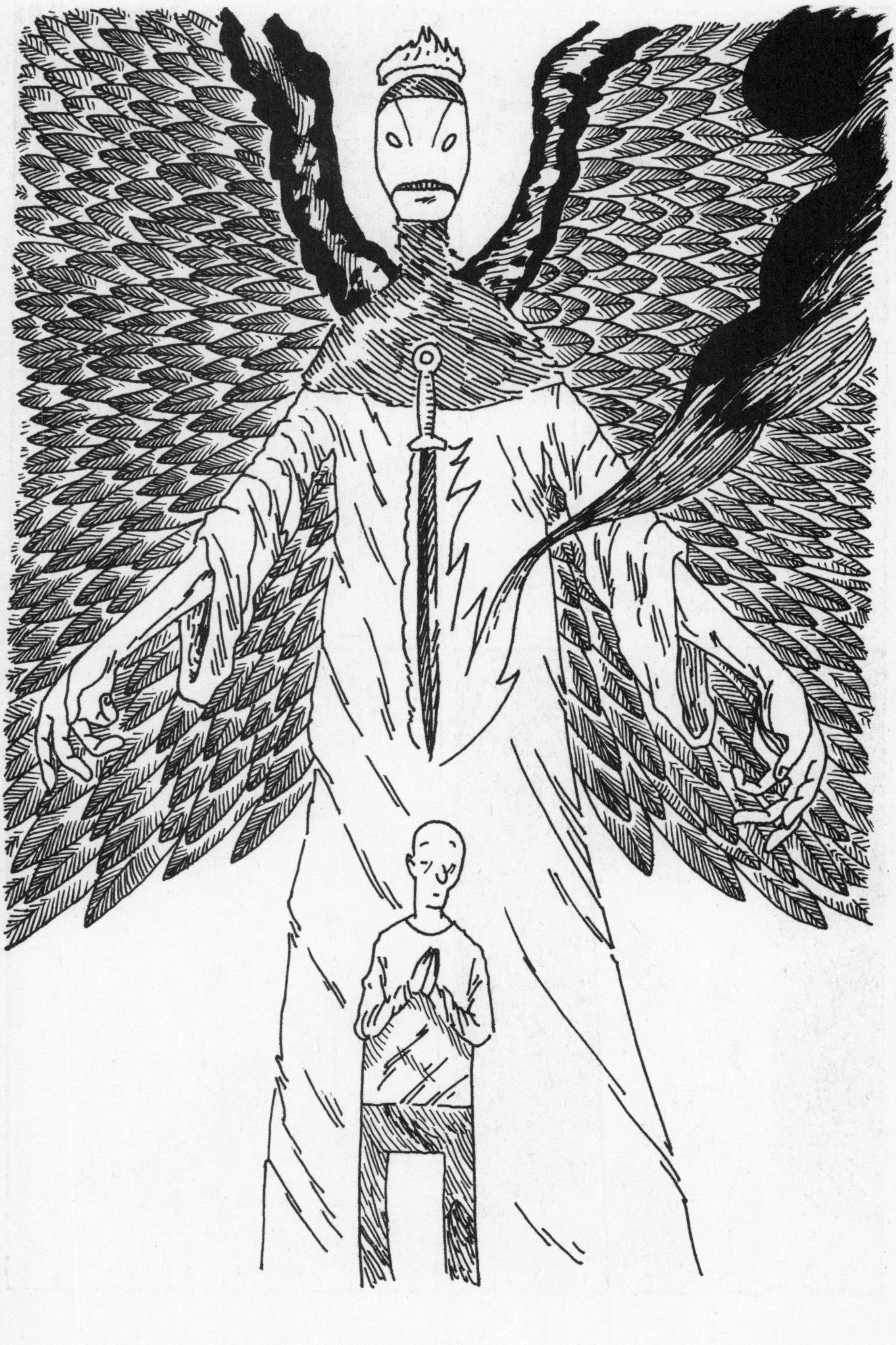

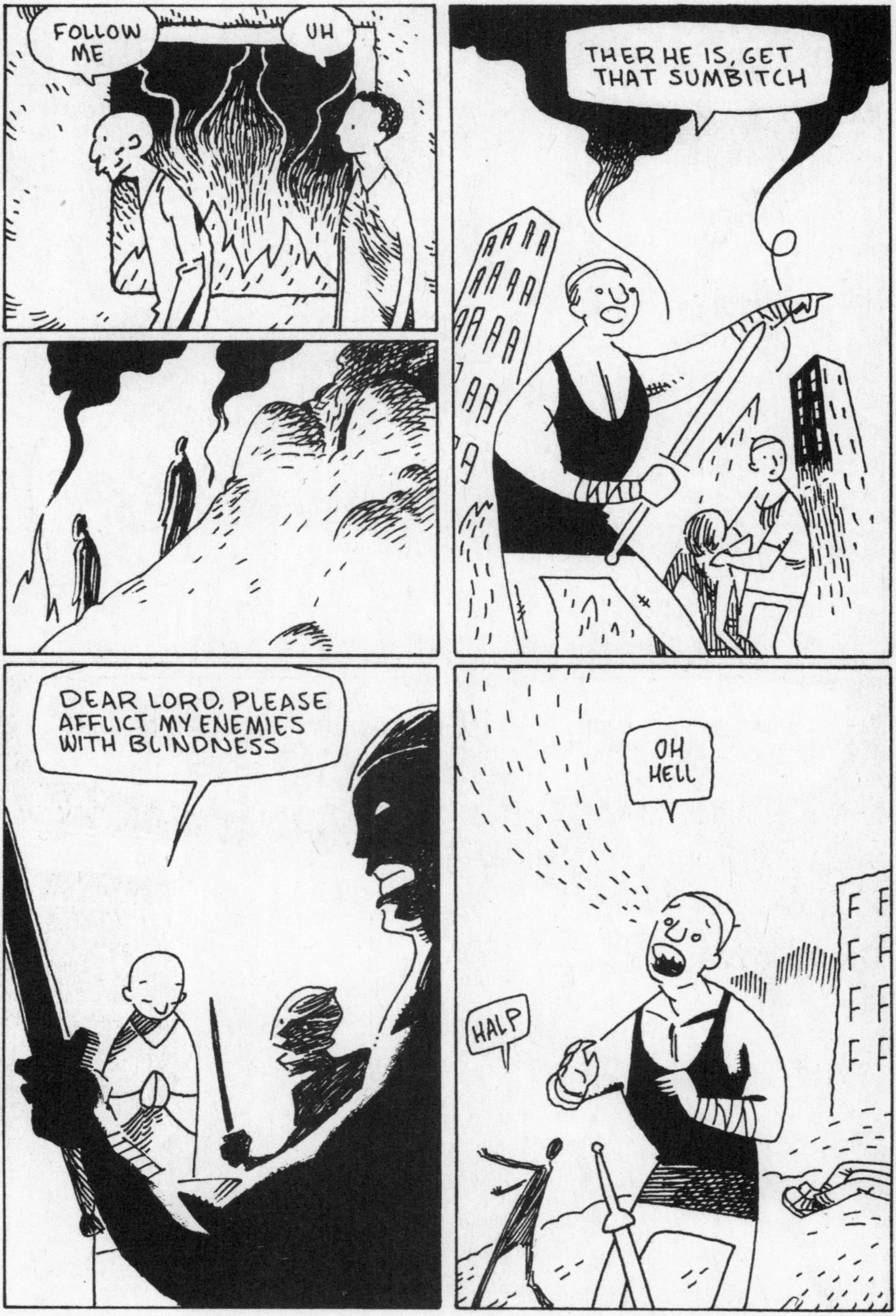
FOLLOW ME
UH
THER HE IS, GET THAT SUMBITCH
DEAR LORD, PLEASE AFFLICT MY ENEMIES WITH BLINDNESS
OH HELL
HALP

THERE YOU GO, YOU BLIND FUCKS, HOW DOES IT FEEL?

A LITTLE LATER, ELISHA WORKS WITH THE KING OF ISRAEL

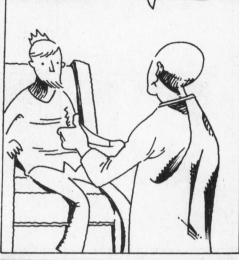

I HAVE A TON OF BLIND PRISONERS OUT BACK

WHAT SHOULD I DO? SHOULD I JUST KILL 'EM?

NO, IDIOT. YOU TREAT THE AS PRISONERS OF WAR, FEED THEM, GIVE THEM SHELTER

AND SYRIAH NEVER BOTHERED ISRAEL AGAIN...

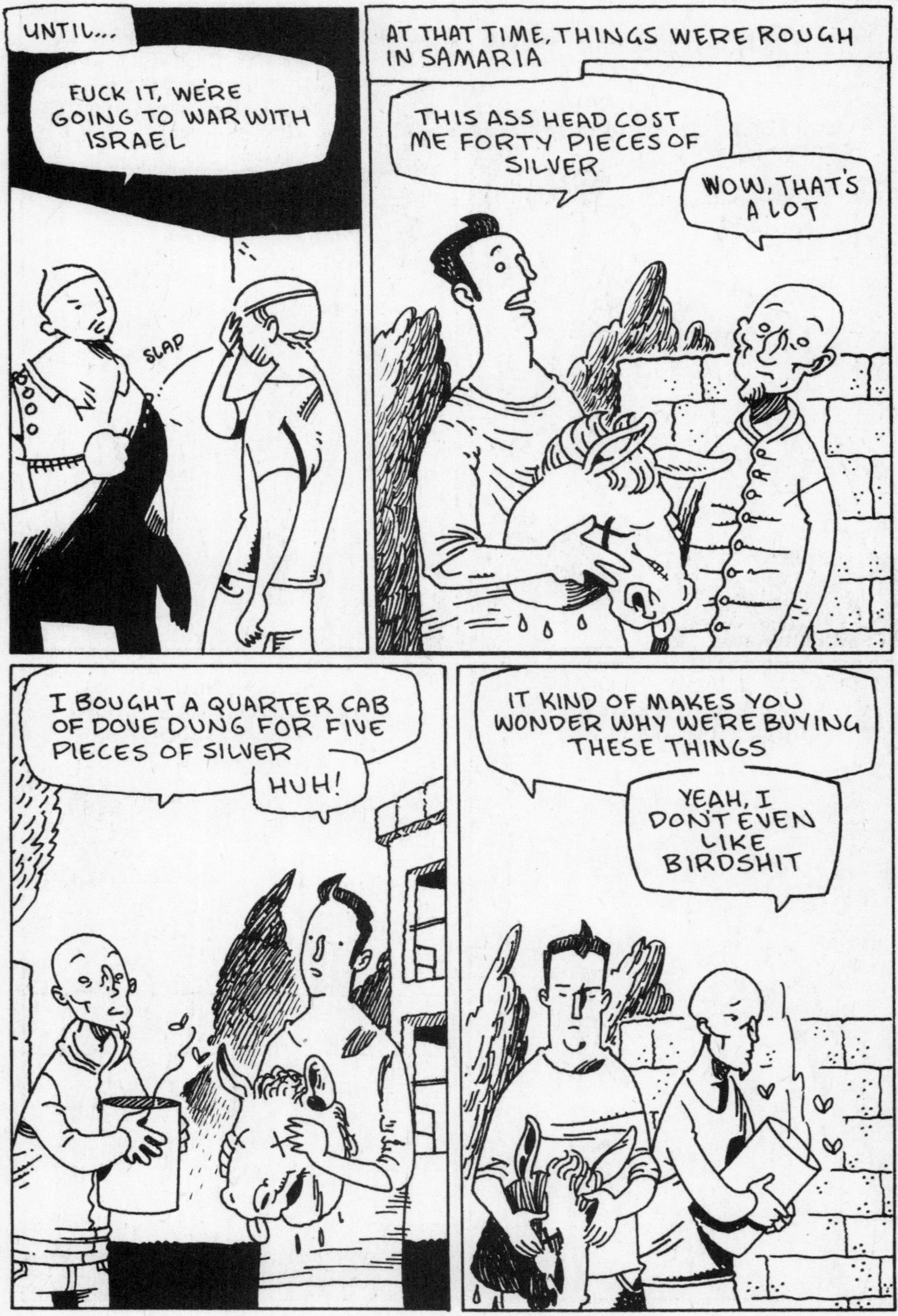
UNTIL...
FUCK IT, WE'RE GOING TO WAR WITH ISRAEL
SLAP
AT THAT TIME, THINGS WERE ROUGH IN SAMARIA
THIS ASS HEAD COST ME FORTY PIECES OF SILVER
WOW, THAT'S A LOT
I BOUGHT A QUARTER CAB OF DOVE DUNG FOR FIVE PIECES OF SILVER
HUH!
IT KIND OF MAKES YOU WONDER WHY WE'RE BUYING THESE THINGS
YEAH, I DON'T EVEN LIKE BIRDSHIT

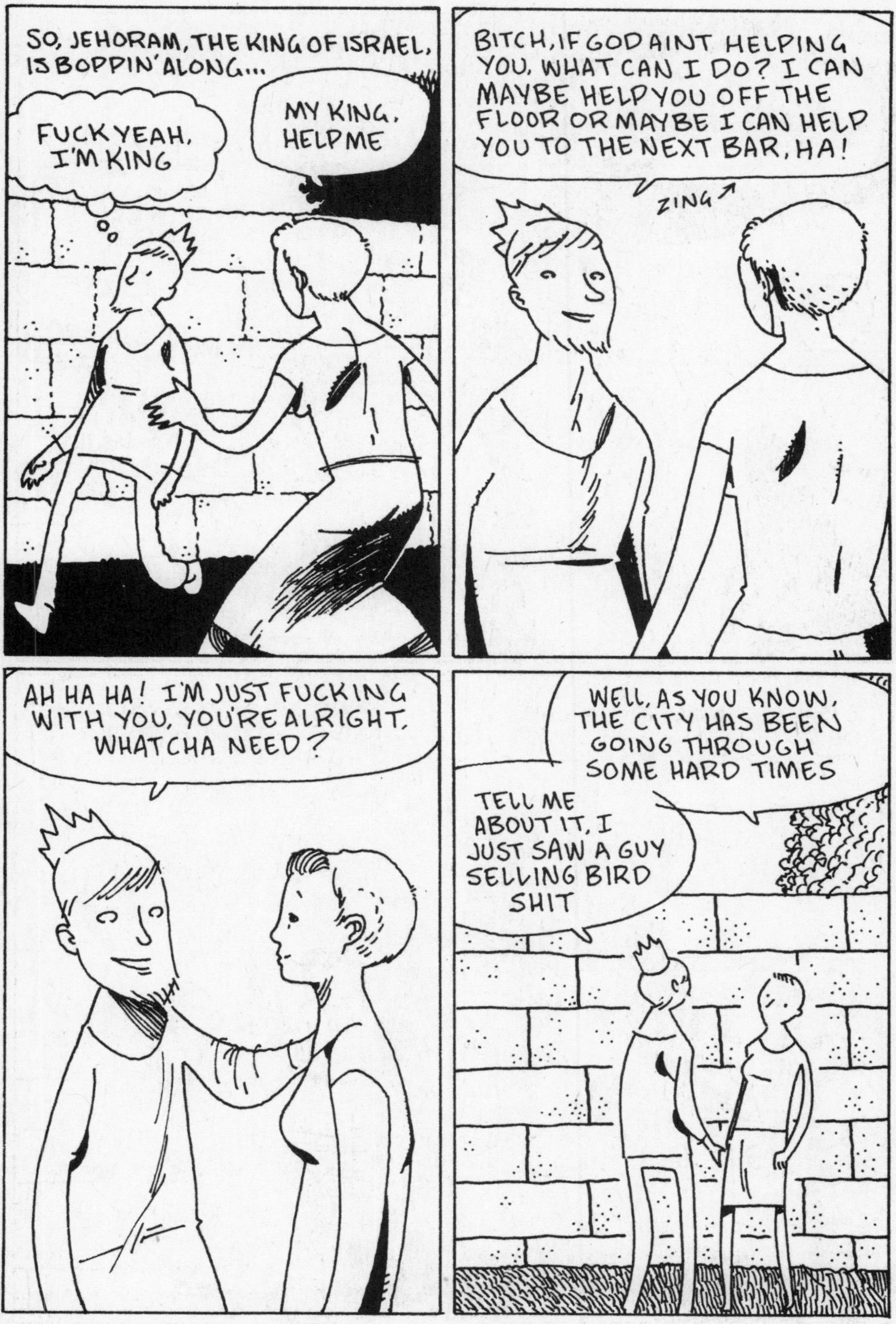
SO, JEHORAM, THE KING OF ISRAEL, IS BOPPIN' ALONG...
FUCK YEAH, I'M KING
MY KING, HELP ME
BITCH, IF GOD AINT HELPING YOU, WHAT CAN I DO? I CAN MAYBE HELP YOU OFF THE FLOOR OR MAYBE I CAN HELP YOU TO THE NEXT BAR, HA!
ZING
AH HA HA! I'M JUST FUCKING WITH YOU, YOU'RE ALRIGHT, WHATCHA NEED?
WELL, AS YOU KNOW, THE CITY HAS BEEN GOING THROUGH SOME HARD TIMES
TELL ME ABOUT IT, I JUST SAW A GUY SELLING BIRD SHIT

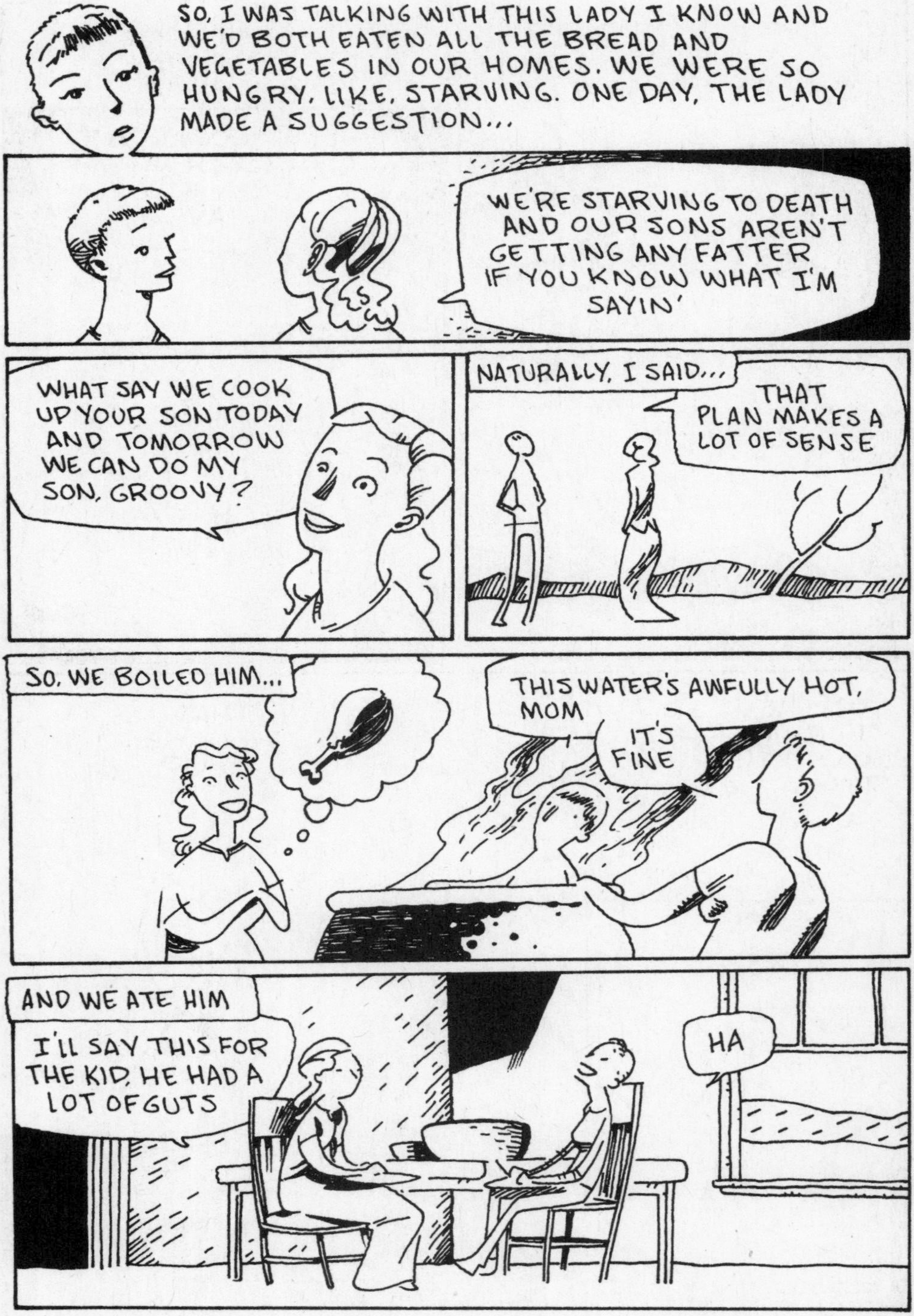
SO, I WAS TALKING WITH THIS LADY I KNOW AND WE'D BOTH EATEN ALL THE BREAD AND VEGETABLES IN OUR HOMES. WE WERE SO HUNGRY. LIKE, STARVING. ONE DAY, THE LADY MADE A SUGGESTION...
WE'RE STARVING TO DEATH AND OUR SONS AREN'T GETTING ANY FATTER IF YOU KNOW WHAT I'M SAYIN'
WHAT SAY WE COOK UP YOUR SON TODAY AND TOMORROW WE CAN DO MY SON, GROOVY?
NATURALLY, I SAID...
THAT PLAN MAKES A LOT OF SENSE
SO, WE BOILED HIM...
THIS WATER'S AWFULLY HOT, MOM
IT'S FINE
AND WE ATE HIM
I'LL SAY THIS FOR THE KID, HE HAD A LOT OF GUTS
HA

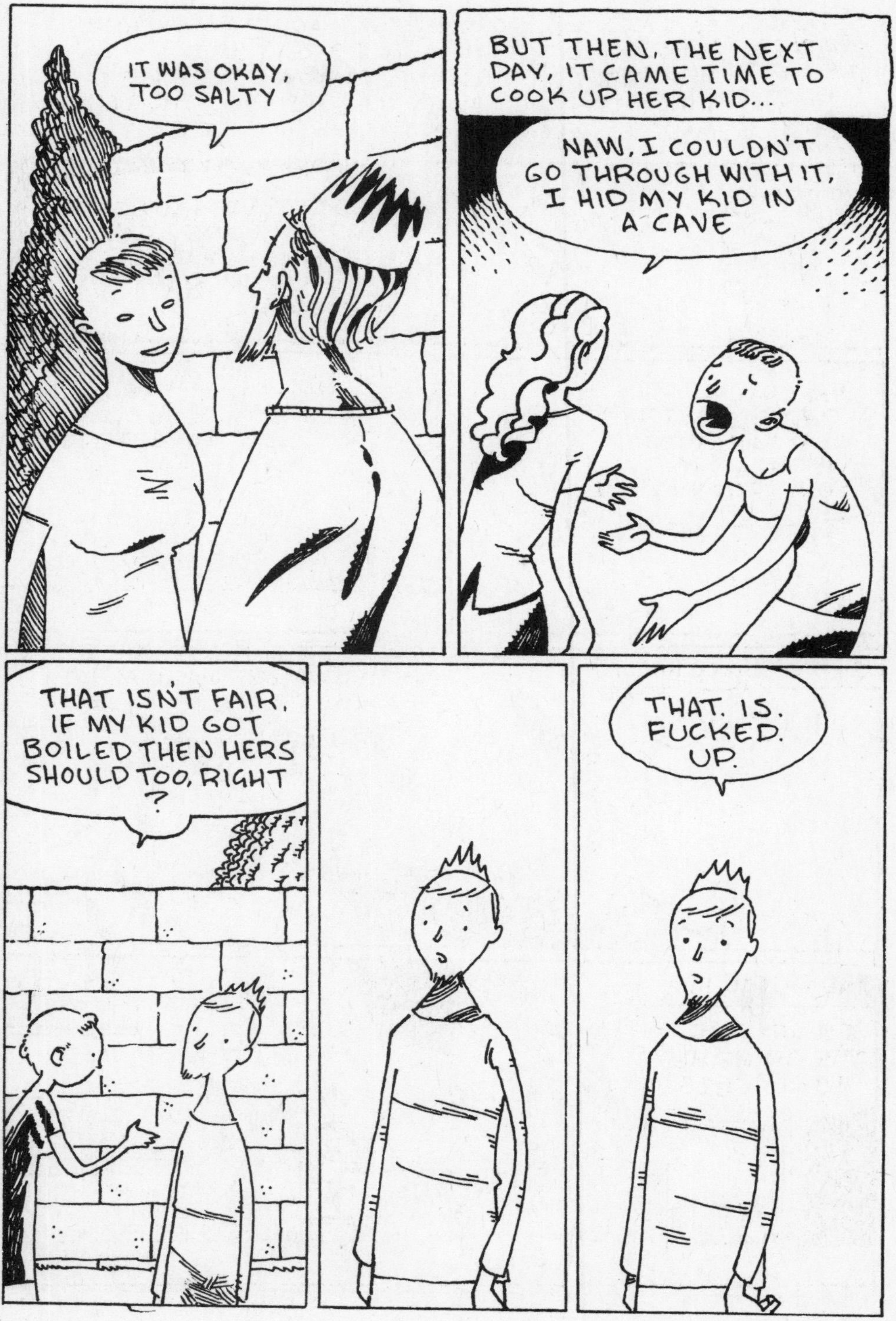
IT WAS OKAY, TOO SALTY
BUT THEN, THE NEXT DAY, IT CAME TIME TO COOK UP HER KID...
NAW, I COULDN'T GO THROUGH WITH IT, I HID MY KID IN A CAVE
THAT ISN'T FAIR, IF MY KID GOT BOILED THEN HERS SHOULD TOO, RIGHT ?
THAT. IS. FUCKED. UP.

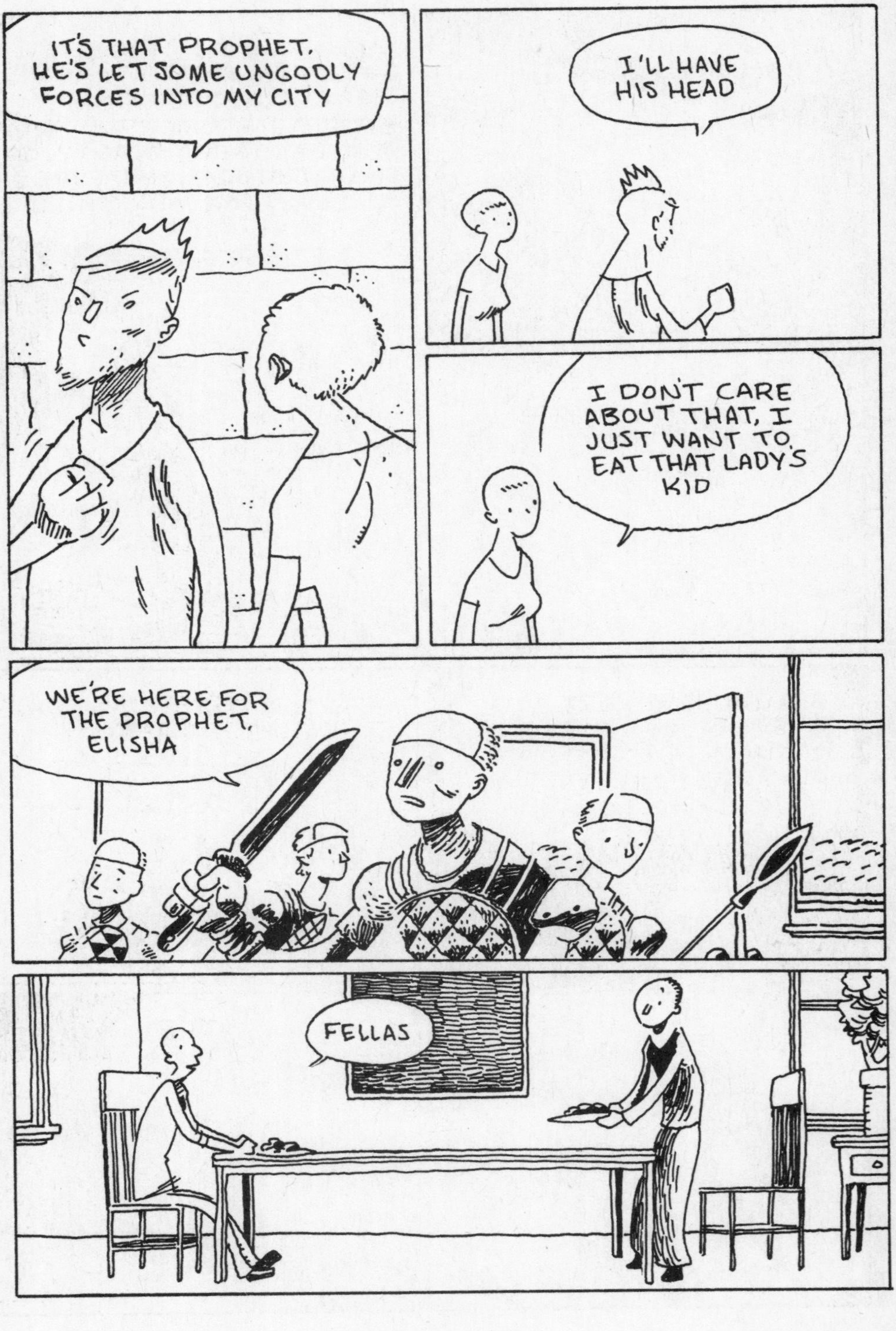
IT'S THAT PROPHET. HE'S LET SOME UNGODLY FORCES INTO MY CITY
I'LL HAVE HIS HEAD
I DON'T CARE ABOUT THAT, I JUST WANT TO, EAT THAT LADY'S KID
WE'RE HERE FOR THE PROPHET, ELISHA
FELLAS

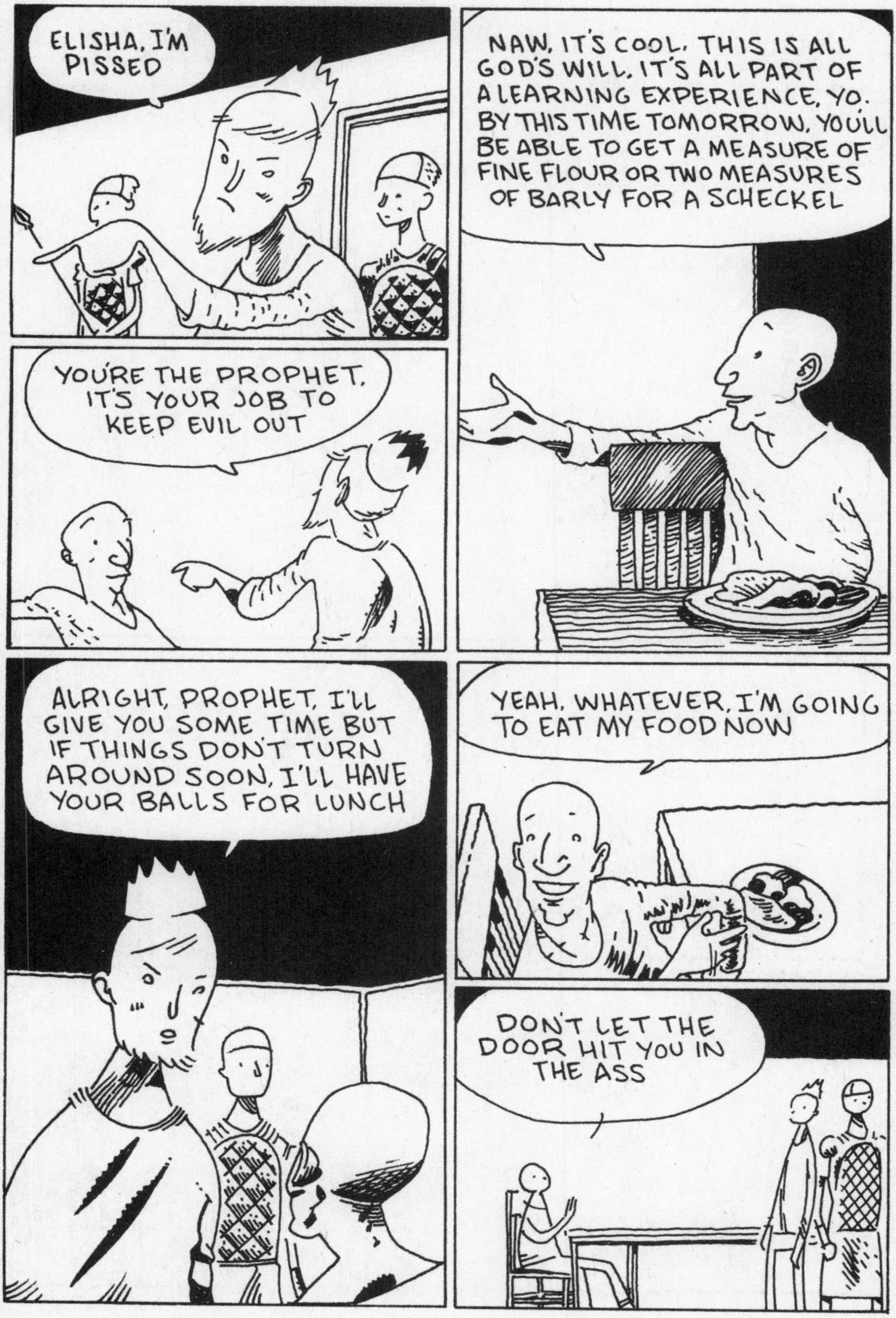
ELISHA, I'M PISSED
NAW, IT'S COOL. THIS IS ALL GOD'S WILL. IT'S ALL PART OF A LEARNING EXPERIENCE, YO. BY THIS TIME TOMORROW, YOU'LL BE ABLE TO GET A MEASURE OF FINE FLOUR OR TWO MEASURES OF BARLY FOR A SCHECKEL
YOU'RE THE PROPHET. IT'S YOUR JOB TO KEEP EVIL OUT
ALRIGHT, PROPHET, I'LL GIVE YOU SOME TIME BUT IF THINGS DON'T TURN AROUND SOON, I'LL HAVE YOUR BALLS FOR LUNCH
YEAH, WHATEVER. I'M GOING TO EAT MY FOOD NOW
DON'T LET THE DOOR HIT YOU IN THE ASS

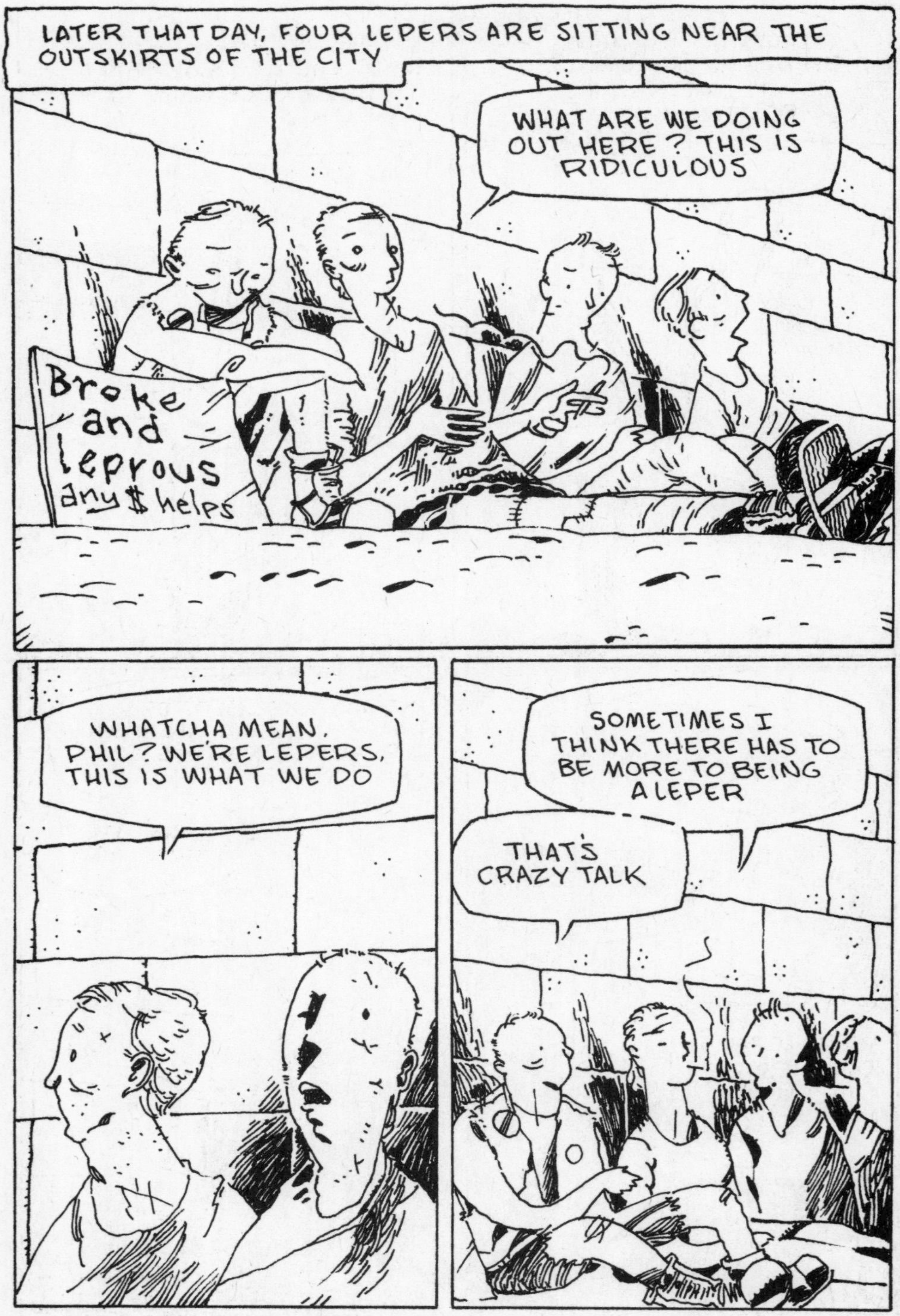
LATER THAT DAY, FOUR LEPERS ARE SITTING NEAR THE OUTSKIRTS OF THE CITY
WHAT ARE WE DOING OUT HERE? THIS IS RIDICULOUS
Broke and leprous any $ helps
WHATCHA MEAN, PHIL? WE'RE LEPERS, THIS IS WHAT WE DO
SOMETIMES I THINK THERE HAS TO BE MORE TO BEING A LEPER
THAT'S CRAZY TALK

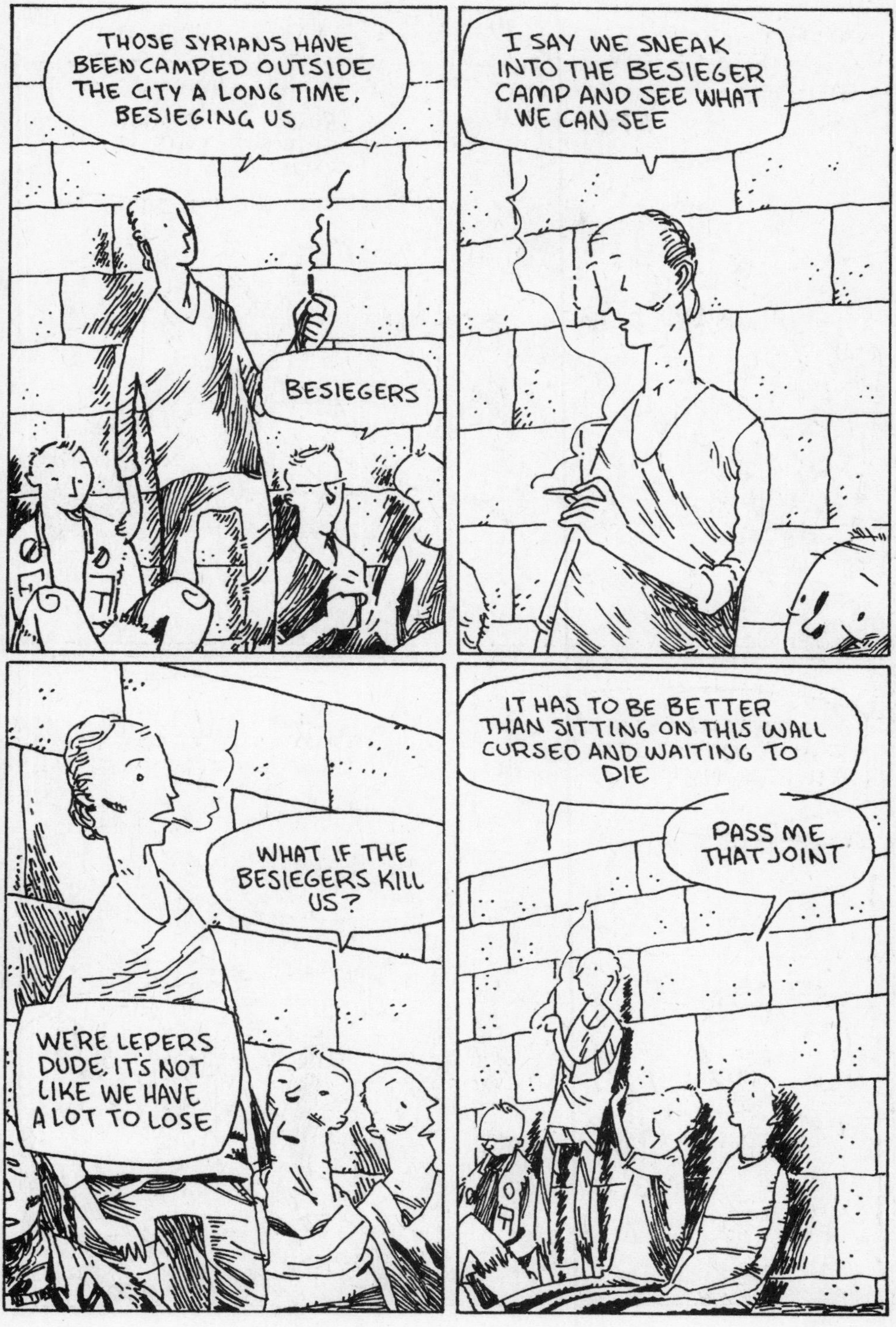
THOSE SYRIANS HAVE BEEN CAMPED OUTSIDE THE CITY A LONG TIME, BESIEGING US
BESIEGERS
I SAY WE SNEAK INTO THE BESIEGER CAMP AND SEE WHAT WE CAN SEE
WHAT IF THE BESIEGERS KILL US?
WE'RE LEPERS DUDE. IT'S NOT LIKE WE HAVE A LOT TO LOSE
IT HAS TO BE BETTER THAN SITTING ON THIS WALL CURSED AND WAITING TO DIE
PASS ME THAT JOINT

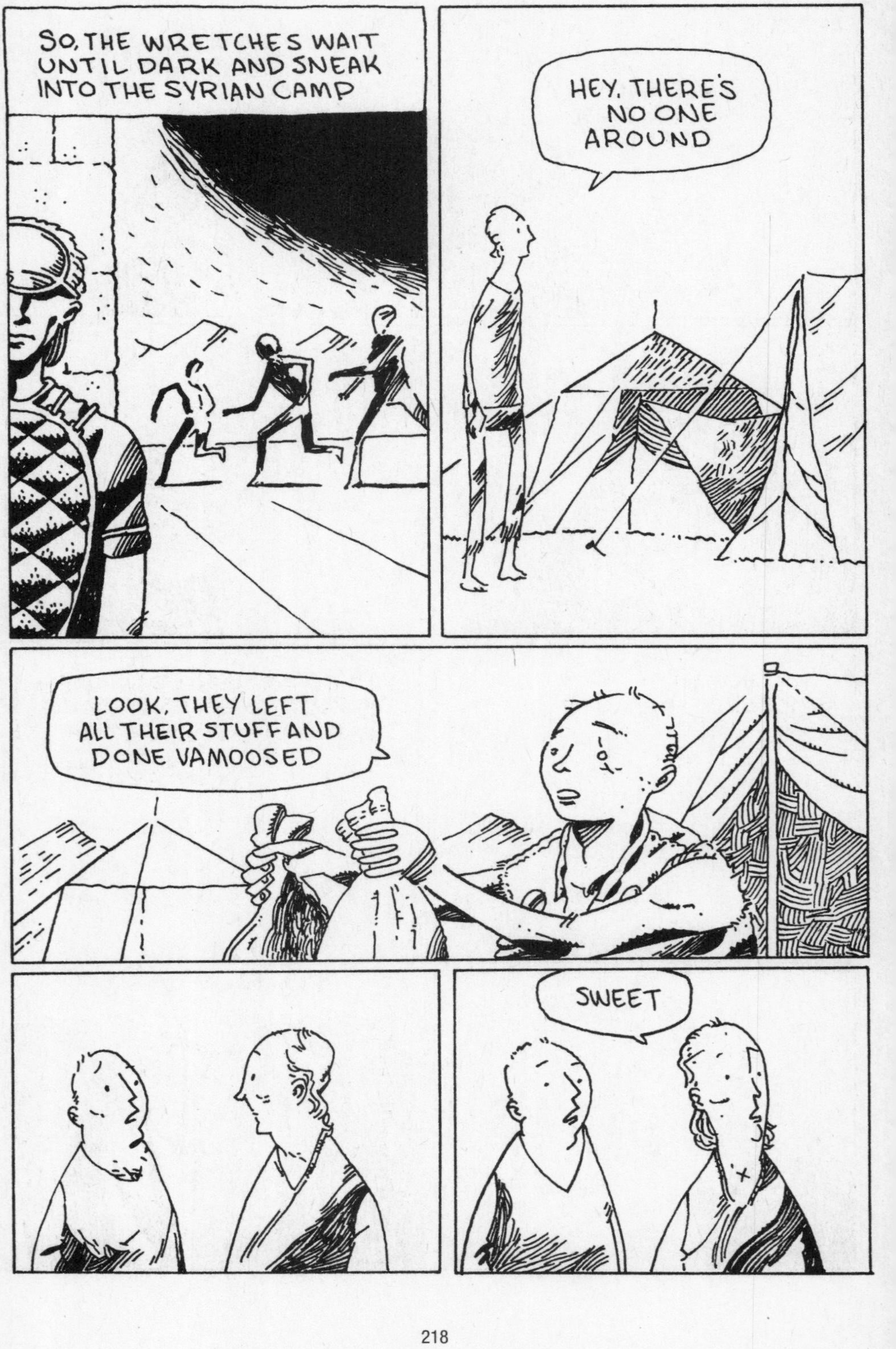
SO, THE WRETCHES WAIT UNTIL DARK AND SNEAK INTO THE SYRIAN CAMP
HEY, THERE'S NO ONE AROUND
LOOK, THEY LEFT ALL THEIR STUFF AND DONE VAMOOSED
SWEET

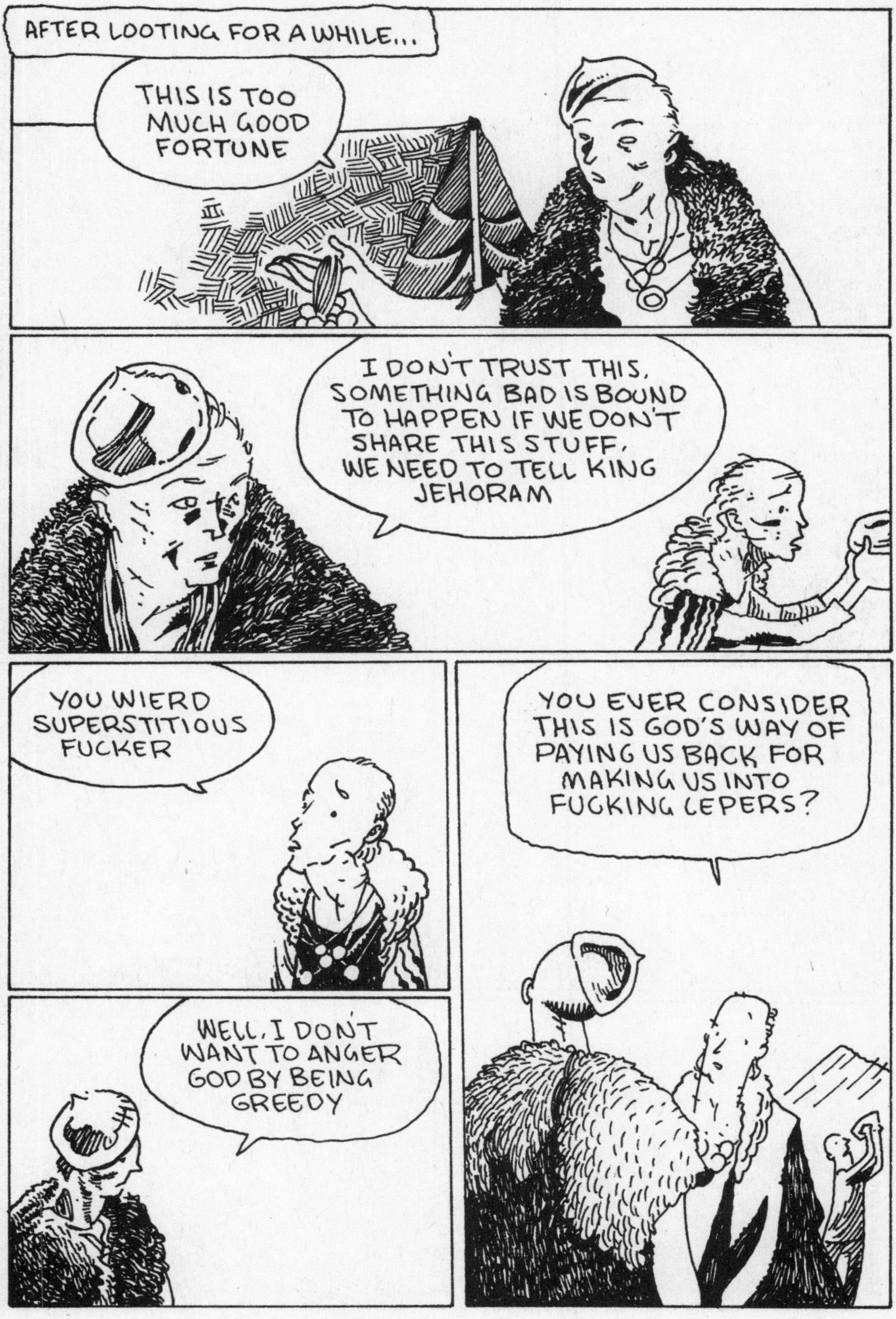
AFTER LOOTING FOR A WHILE...
THIS IS TOO MUCH GOOD FORTUNE
I DON'T TRUST THIS. SOMETHING BAD IS BOUND TO HAPPEN IF WE DON'T SHARE THIS STUFF. WE NEED TO TELL KING JEHORAM
YOU WIERD SUPERSTITIOUS FUCKER
YOU EVER CONSIDER THIS IS GOD'S WAY OF PAYING US BACK FOR MAKING US INTO FUCKING LEPERS?
WELL, I DON'T WANT TO ANGER GOD BY BEING GREEDY

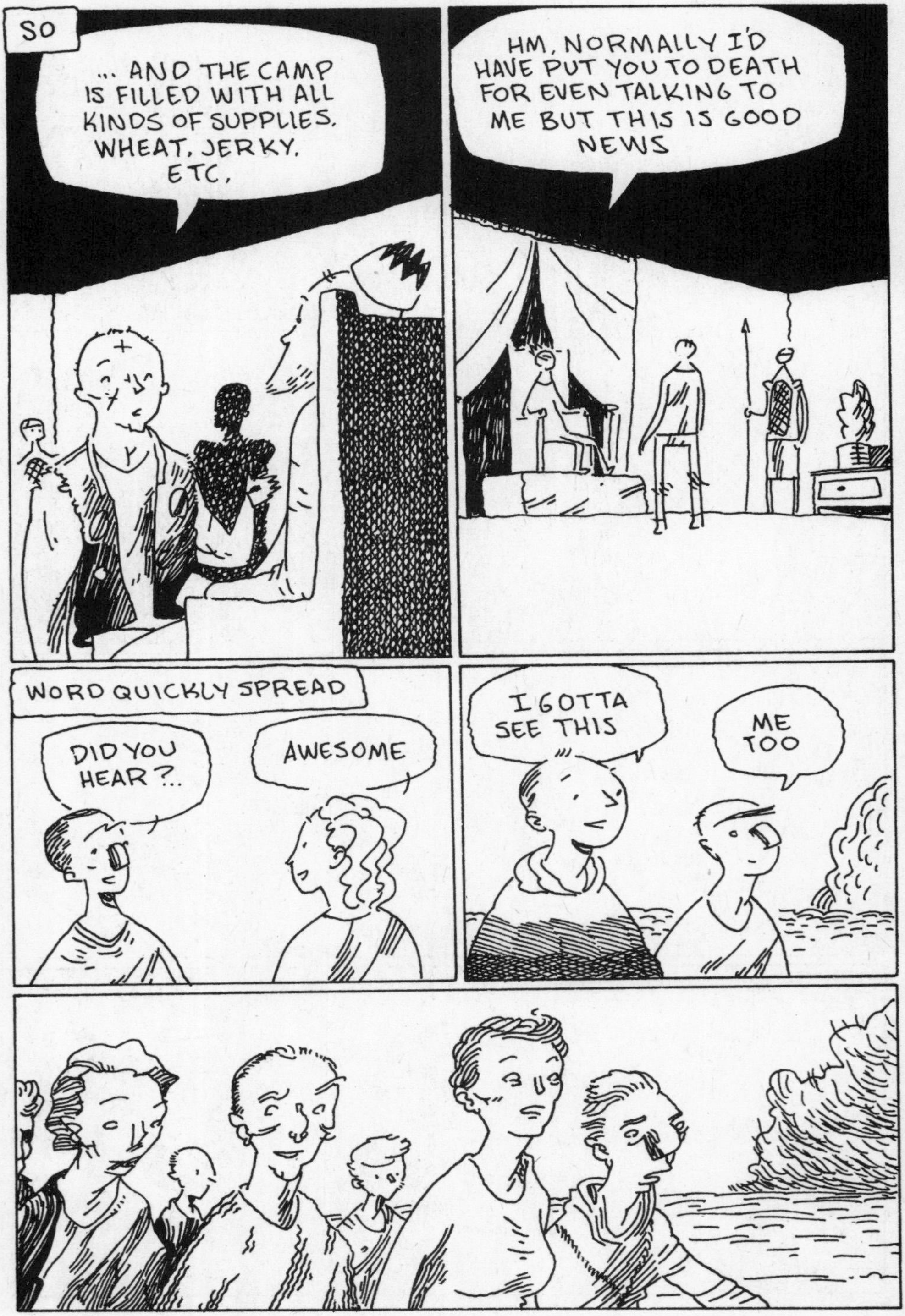
SO
... AND THE CAMP IS FILLED WITH ALL KINDS OF SUPPLIES. WHEAT, JERKY, ETC.
HM, NORMALLY I'D HAVE PUT YOU TO DEATH FOR EVEN TALKING TO ME BUT THIS IS GOOD NEWS
WORD QUICKLY SPREAD
DID YOU HEAR?...
AWESOME
I GOTTA SEE THIS
ME TOO

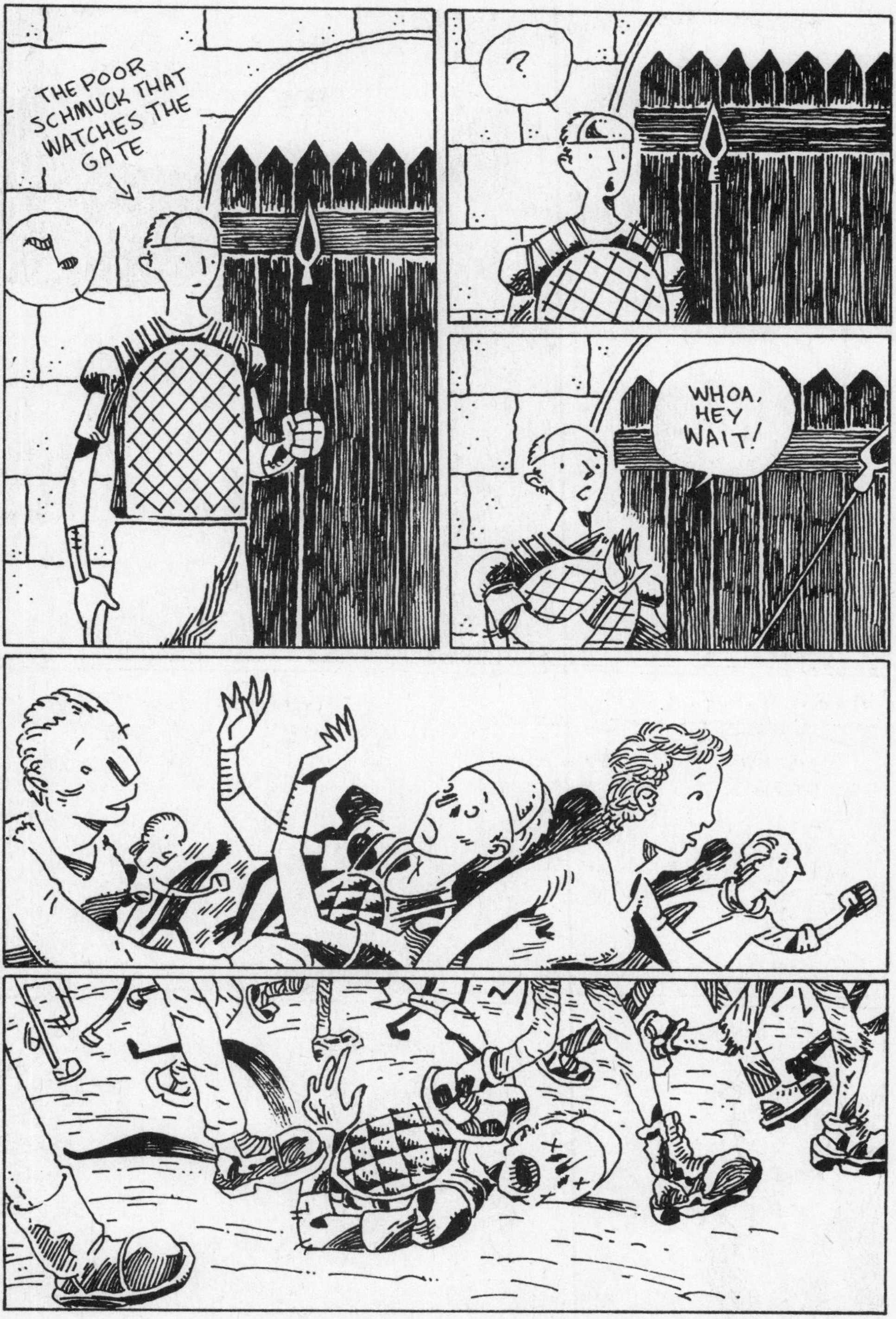
THE POOR SCHMUCK THAT WATCHES THE GATE
?
WHOA, HEY WAIT!

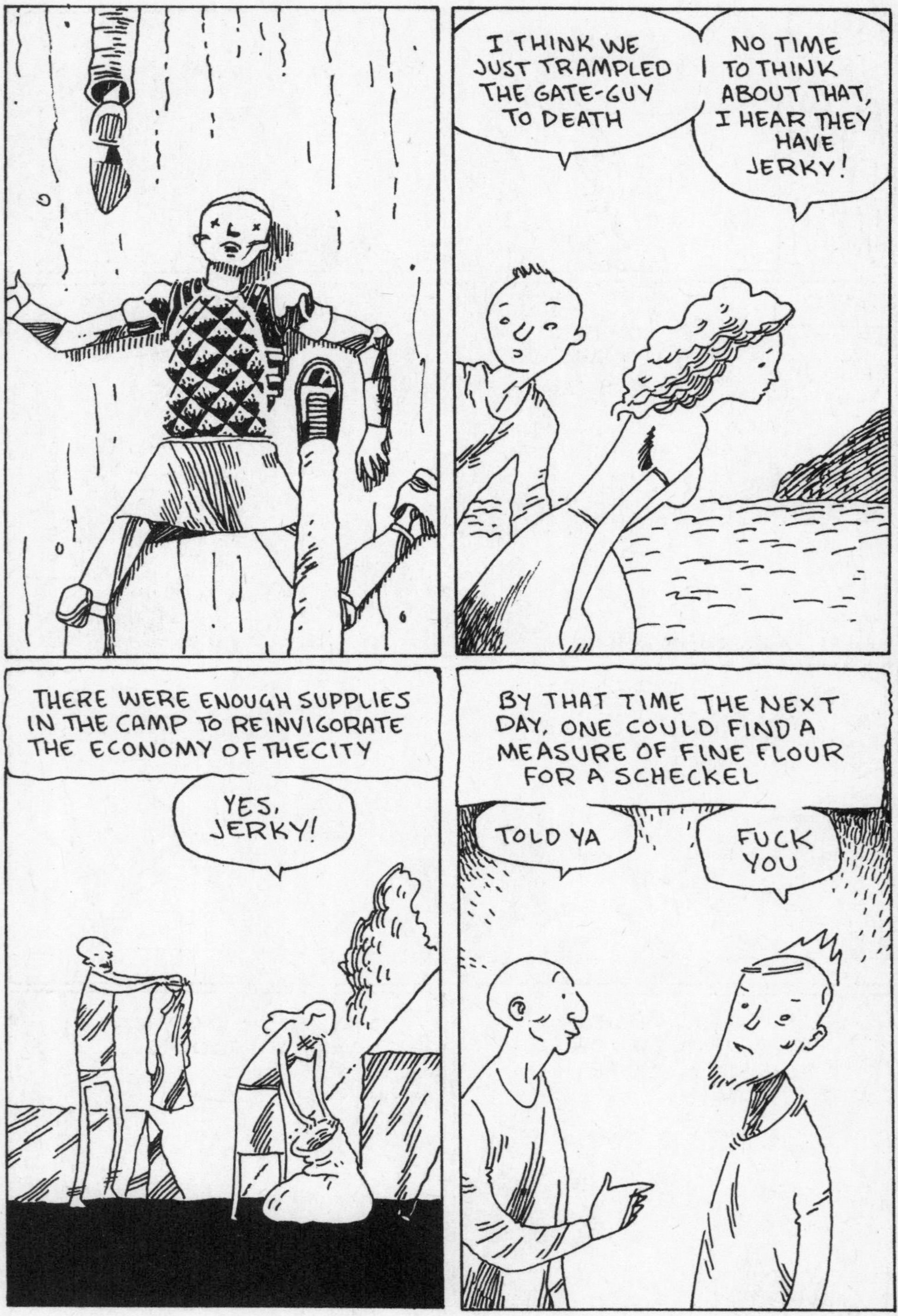
I THINK WE JUST TRAMPLED THE GATE-GUY TO DEATH
NO TIME TO THINK ABOUT THAT, I HEAR THEY HAVE JERKY!
THERE WERE ENOUGH SUPPLIES IN THE CAMP TO REINVIGORATE THE ECONOMY OF THECITY
YES, JERKY!
BY THAT TIME THE NEXT DAY, ONE COULD FIND A MEASURE OF FINE FLOUR FOR A SCHECKEL
TOLD YA
FUCK YOU

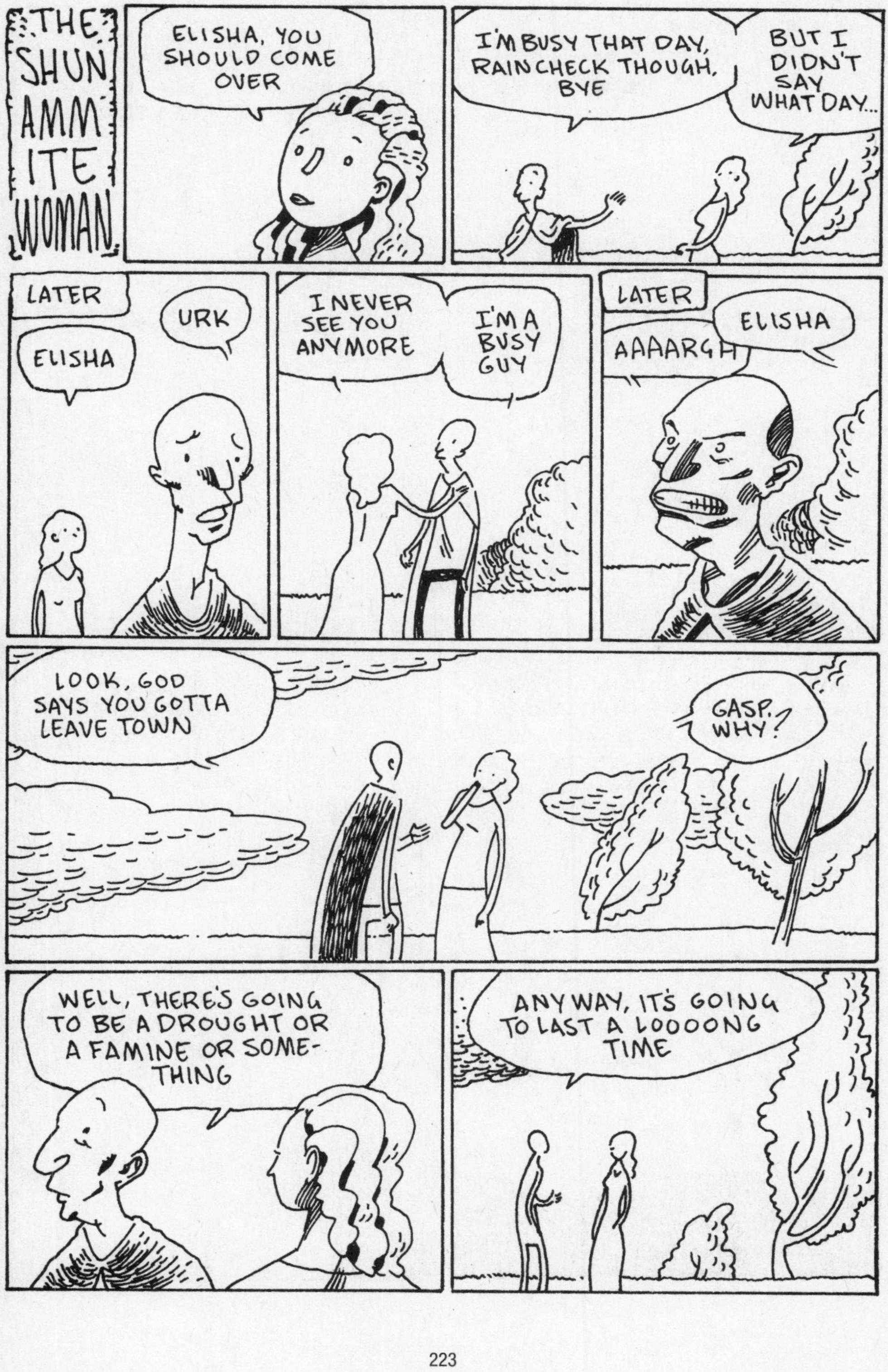
THE SHUNAMMITE WOMAN
ELISHA, YOU SHOULD COME OVER
I'M BUSY THAT DAY, RAINCHECK THOUGH, BYE
BUT I DIDN'T SAY WHAT DAY...
LATER
ELISHA
URK
I NEVER SEE YOU ANYMORE
I'M A BUSY GUY
LATER
ELISHA
AAAARGH
LOOK, GOD SAYS YOU GOTTA LEAVE TOWN
GASP. WHY?
WELL, THERE'S GOING TO BE A DROUGHT OR A FAMINE OR SOMETHING
ANYWAY, IT'S GOING TO LAST A LOOOONG TIME

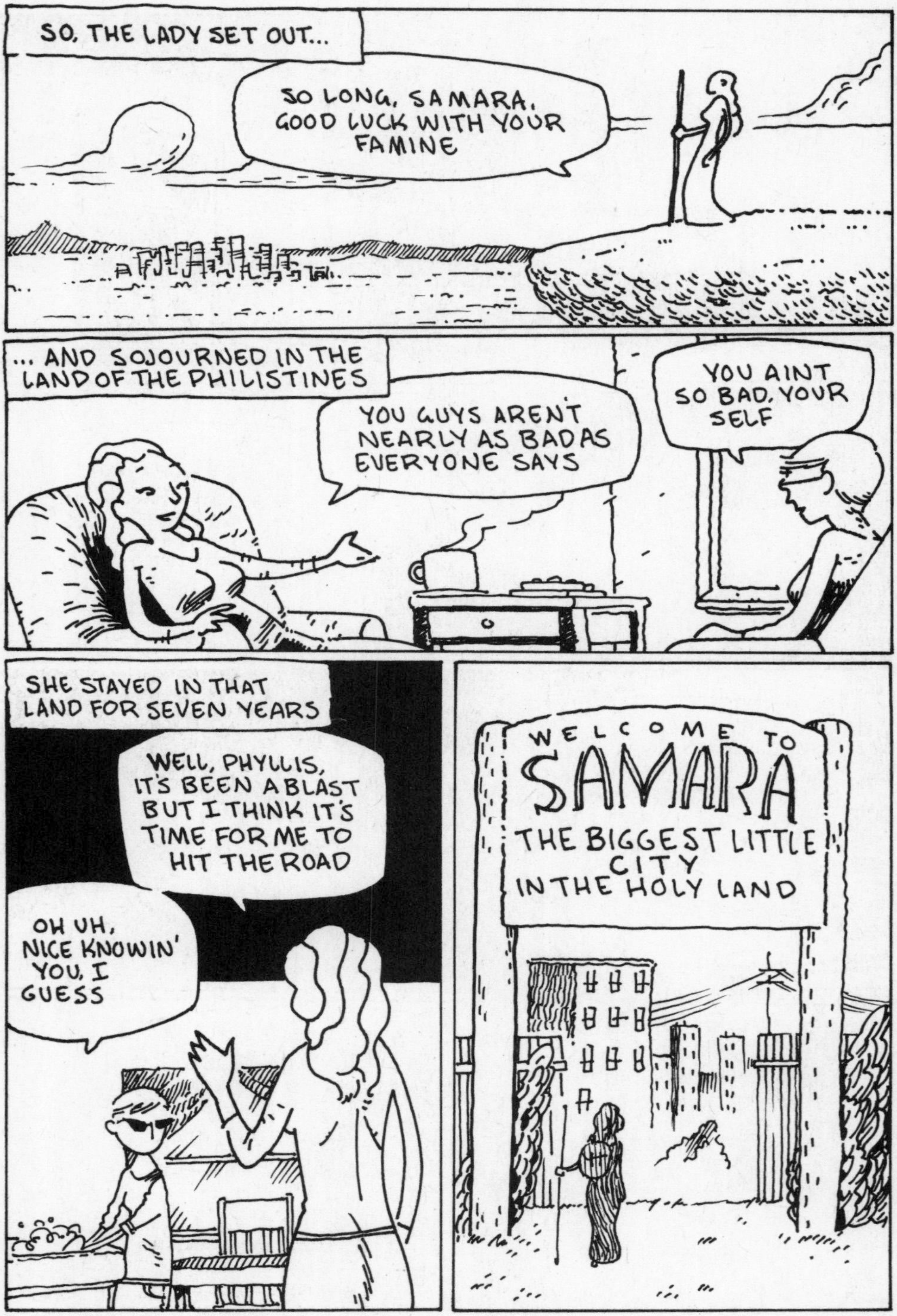
SO, THE LADY SET OUT...
SO LONG, SAMARA. GOOD LUCK WITH YOUR FAMINE
... AND SOJOURNED IN THE LAND OF THE PHILISTINES
YOU GUYS ARENT NEARLY AS BAD AS EVERYONE SAYS
YOU AINT SO BAD, YOUR SELF
SHE STAYED IN THAT LAND FOR SEVEN YEARS
WELL, PHYLLIS, IT'S BEEN A BLAST BUT I THINK IT'S TIME FOR ME TO HIT THE ROAD
OH UH, NICE KNOWIN' YOU, I GUESS
WELCOME TO SAMARA THE BIGGEST LITTLE CITY IN THE HOLY LAND

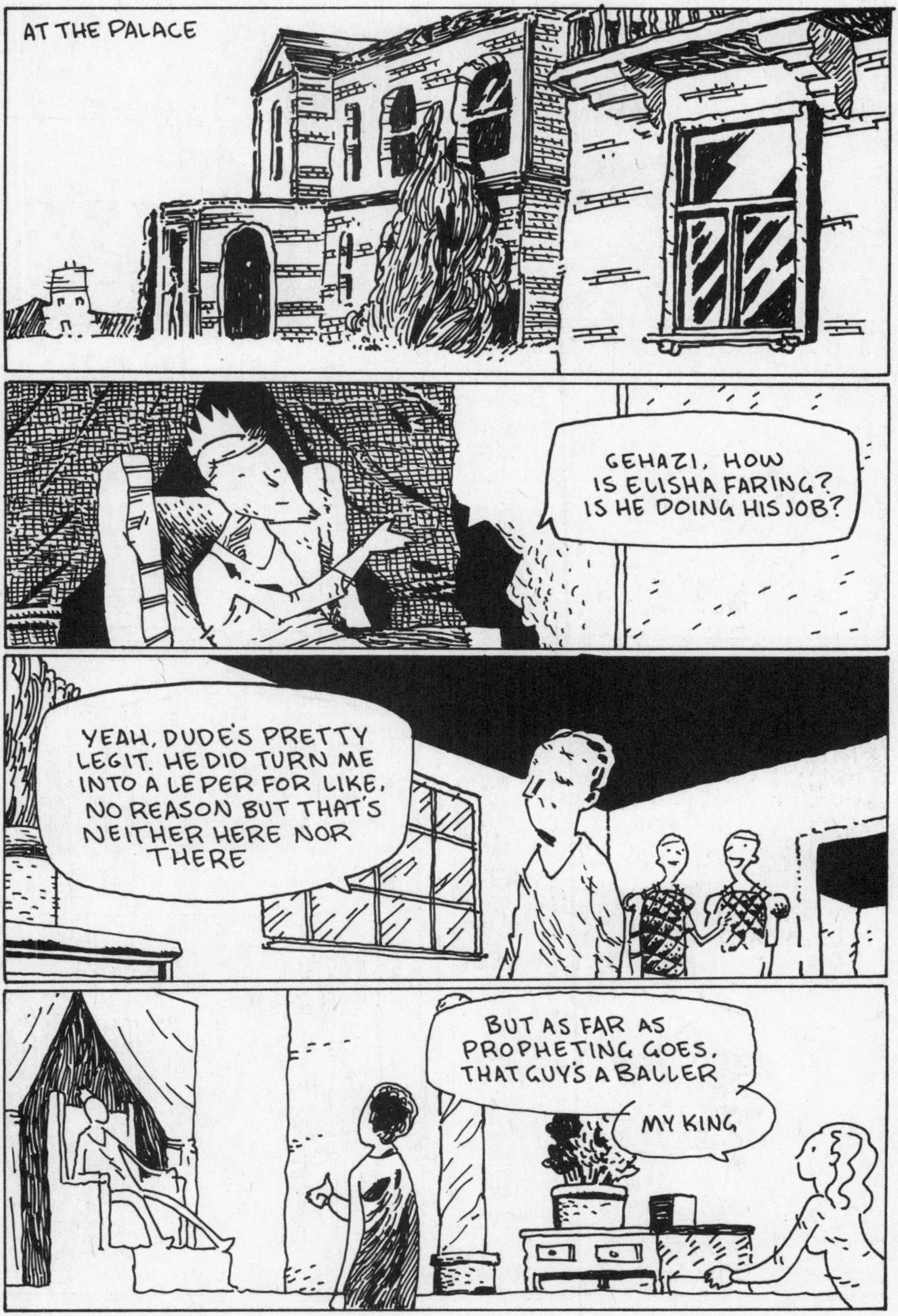
AT THE PALACE
GEHAZI, HOW IS ELISHA FARING? IS HE DOING HIS JOB?
YEAH, DUDE'S PRETTY LEGIT. HE DID TURN ME INTO A LEPER FOR LIKE, NO REASON BUT THAT'S NEITHER HERE NOR THERE
BUT AS FAR AS PROPHETING GOES, THAT GUY'S A BALLER
MY KING

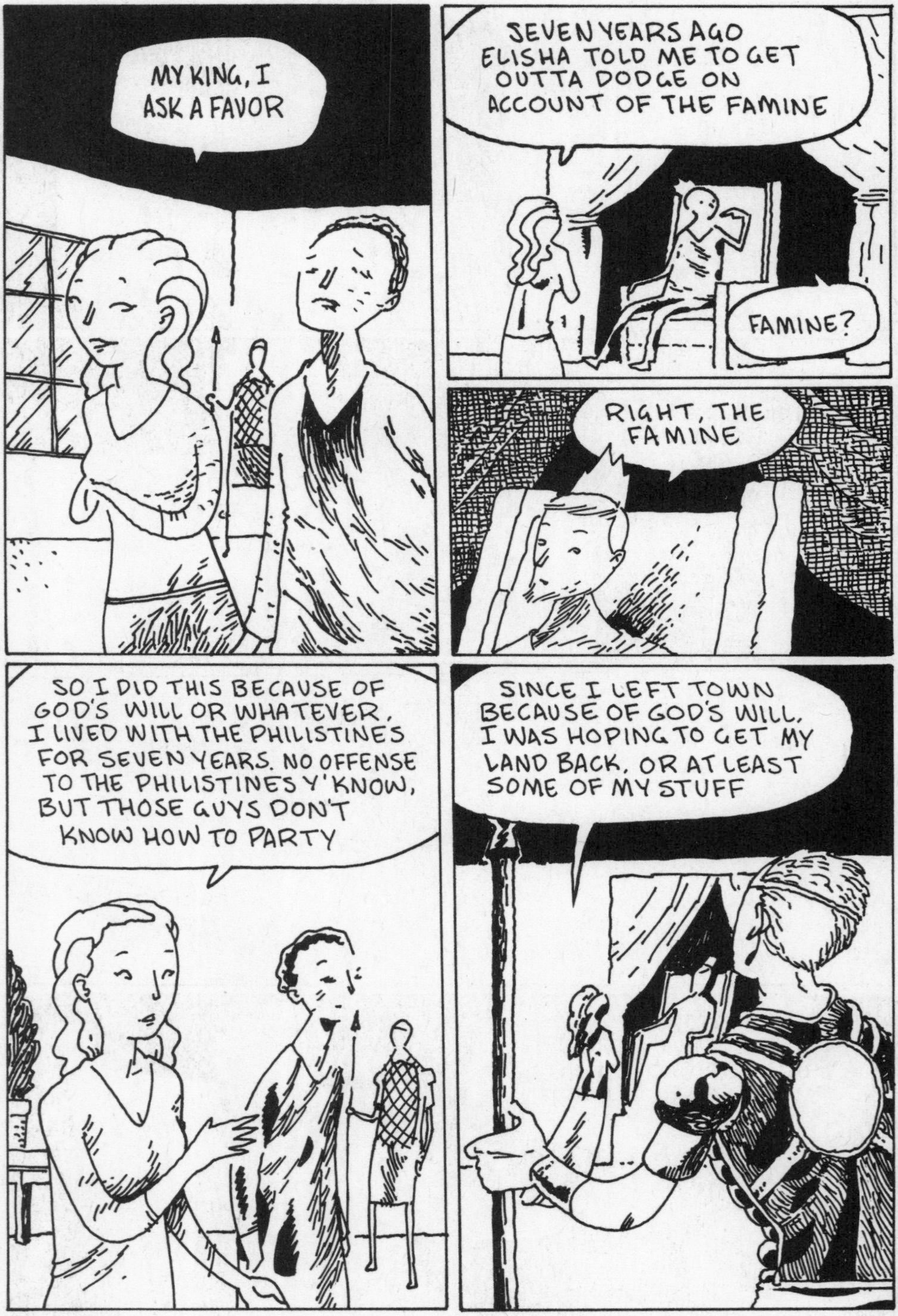
MY KING, I ASK A FAVOR
SEVEN YEARS AGO ELISHA TOLD ME TO GET OUTTA DODGE ON ACCOUNT OF THE FAMINE
FAMINE?
RIGHT, THE FAMINE
SO I DID THIS BECAUSE OF GOD'S WILL OR WHATEVER, I LIVED WITH THE PHILISTINES FOR SEVEN YEARS. NO OFFENSE TO THE PHILISTINES Y'KNOW, BUT THOSE GUYS DON'T KNOW HOW TO PARTY
SINCE I LEFT TOWN BECAUSE OF GOD'S WILL, I WAS HOPING TO GET MY LAND BACK, OR AT LEAST SOME OF MY STUFF

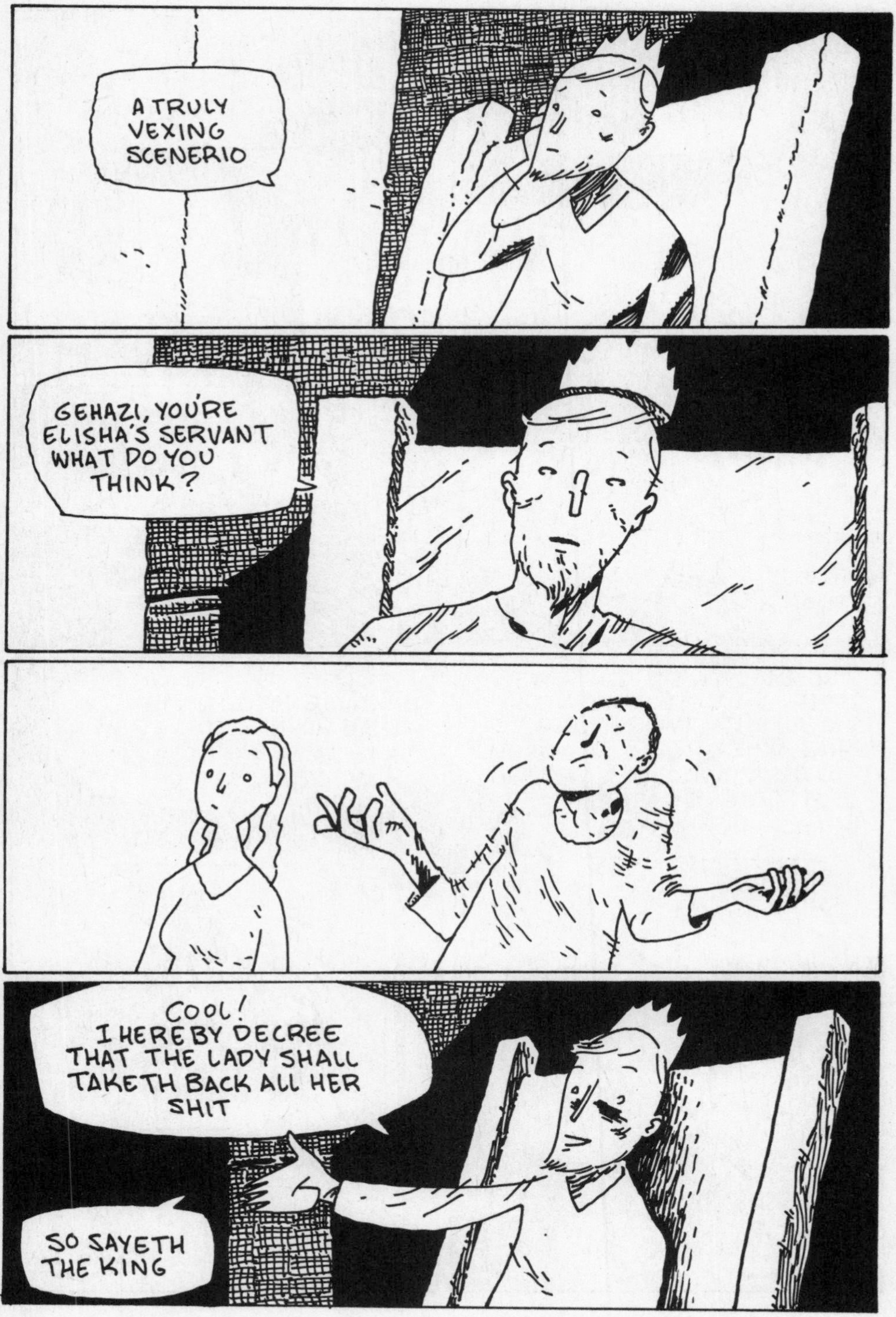
A TRULY VEXING SCENERIO
GEHAZI, YOU'RE ELISHA'S SERVANT WHAT DO YOU THINK?
COOL! I HEREBY DECREE THAT THE LADY SHALL TAKETH BACK ALL HER SHIT
SO SAYETH THE KING

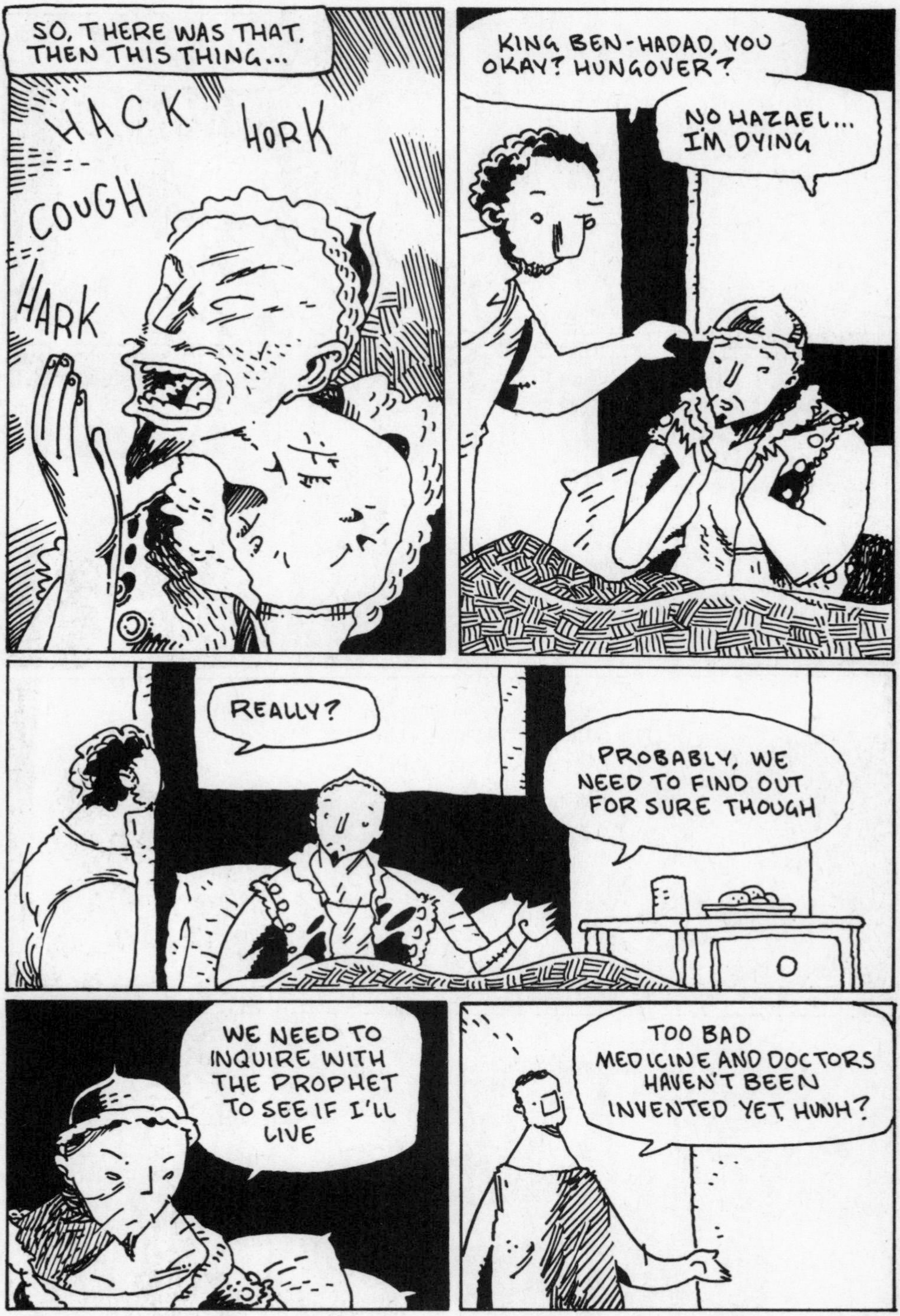
SO, THERE WAS THAT, THEN THIS THING...
HACK
HORK
COUGH
HARK
KING BEN-HADAD, YOU OKAY? HUNGOVER?
NO HAZAEL... I'M DYING
REALLY?
PROBABLY, WE NEED TO FIND OUT FOR SURE THOUGH
WE NEED TO INQUIRE WITH THE PROPHET TO SEE IF I'LL LIVE
TOO BAD MEDICINE AND DOCTORS HAVEN'T BEEN INVENTED YET, HUNH?

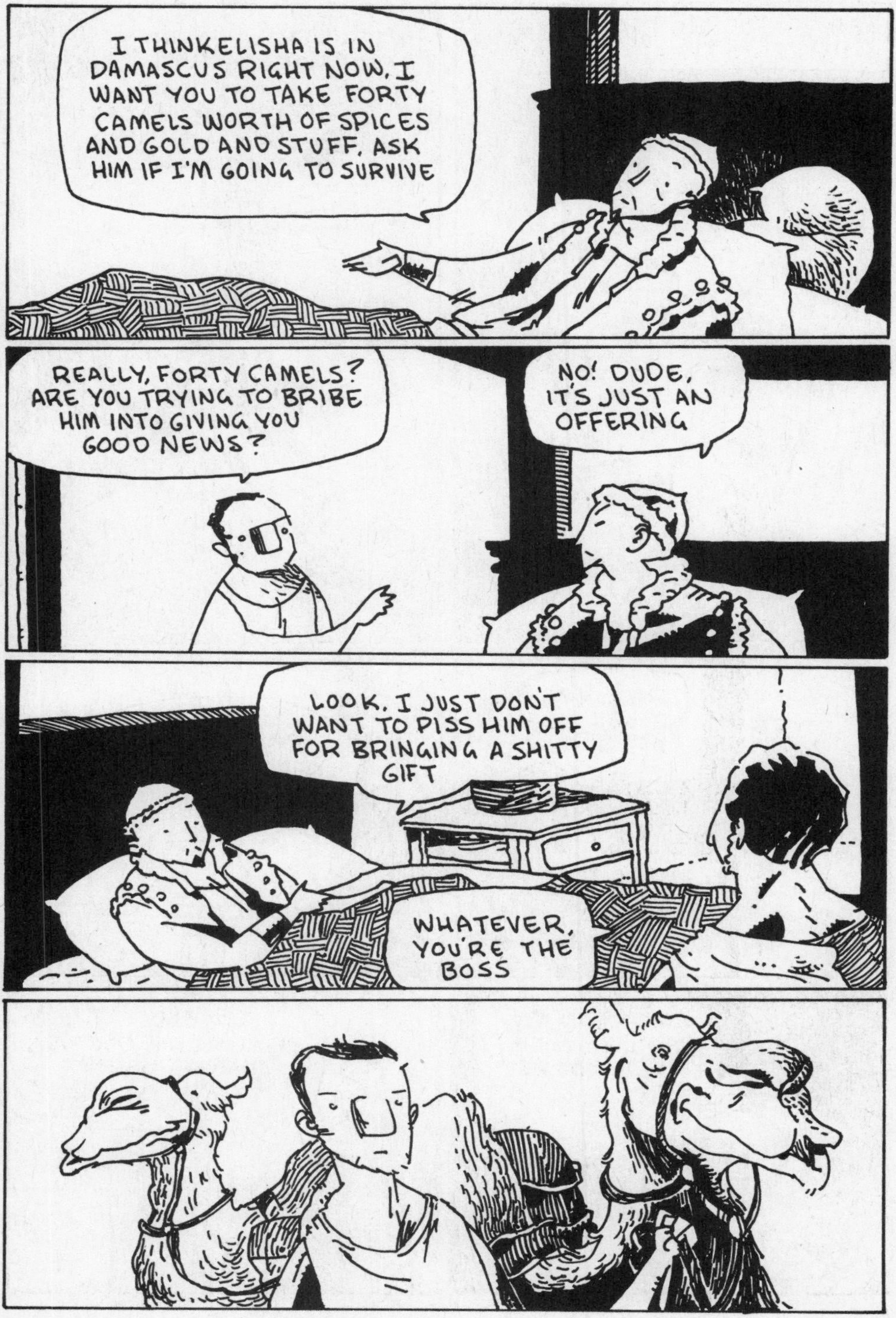
I THINKELISHA IS IN DAMASCUS RIGHT NOW. I WANT YOU TO TAKE FORTY CAMELS WORTH OF SPICES AND GOLD AND STUFF. ASK HIM IF I'M GOING TO SURVIVE
REALLY, FORTY CAMELS? ARE YOU TRYING TO BRIBE HIM INTO GIVING YOU GOOD NEWS?
NO! DUDE, IT'S JUST AN OFFERING
LOOK, I JUST DON'T WANT TO PISS HIM OFF FOR BRINGING A SHITTY GIFT
WHATEVER, YOU'RE THE BOSS

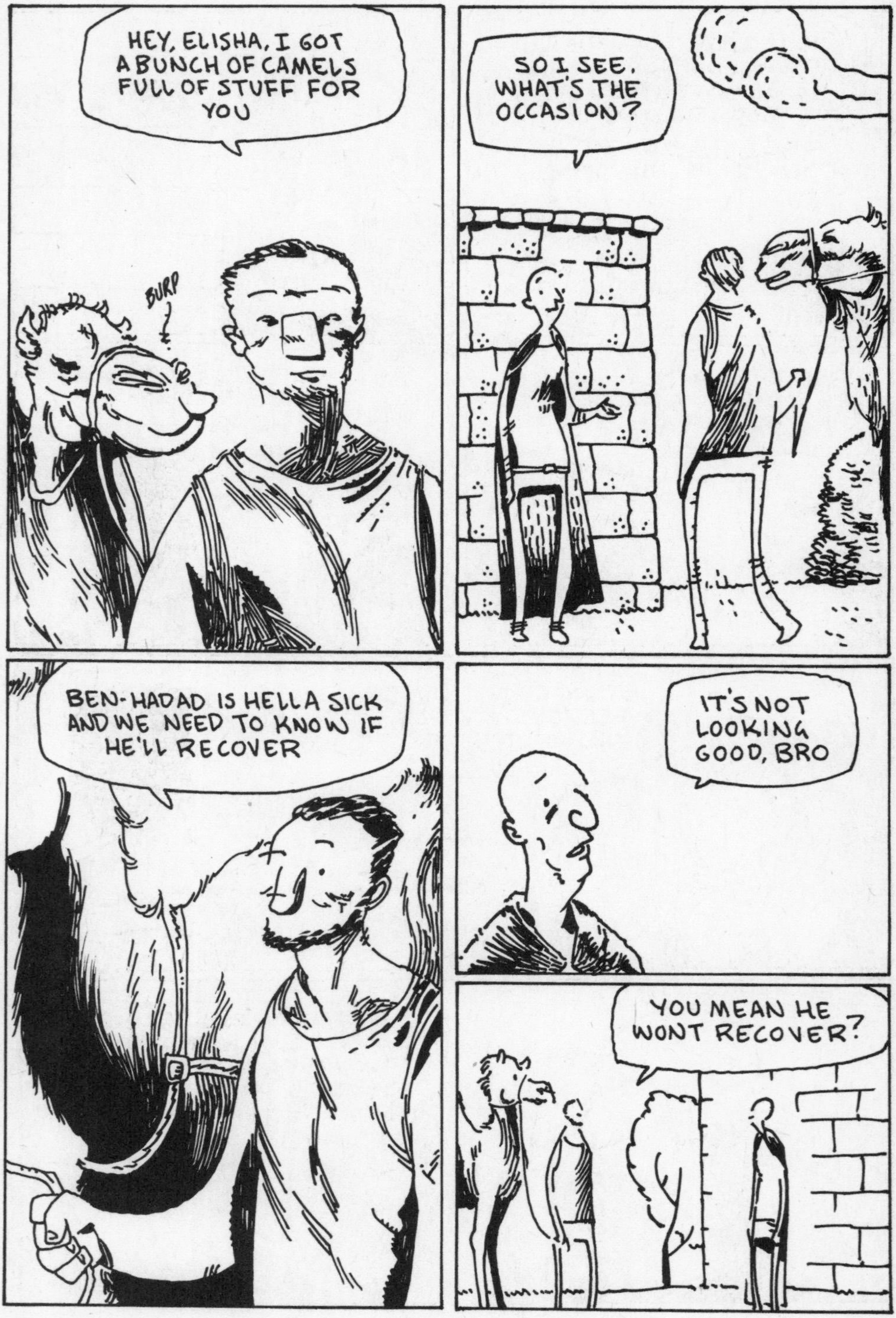
HEY, ELISHA, I GOT A BUNCH OF CAMELS FULL OF STUFF FOR YOU
BURP
SO I SEE. WHAT'S THE OCCASION?
BEN-HADAD IS HELLA SICK AND WE NEED TO KNOW IF HE'LL RECOVER
IT'S NOT LOOKING GOOD, BRO
YOU MEAN HE WONT RECOVER?

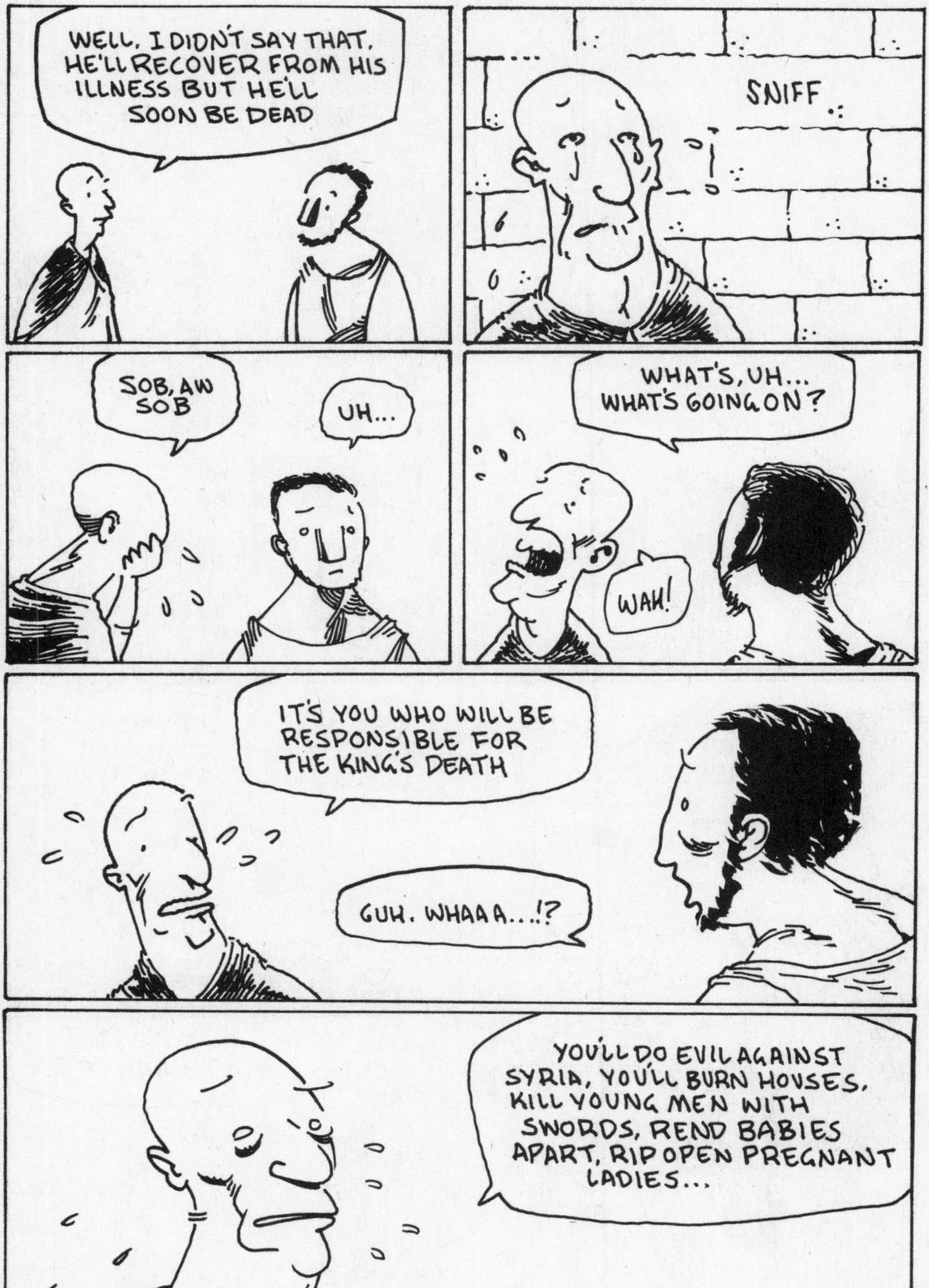
WELL, I DIDN'T SAY THAT. HE'LL RECOVER FROM HIS ILLNESS BUT HE'LL SOON BE DEAD
SNIFF
SOB, AW SOB
UH...
WHAT'S, UH... WHAT'S GOING ON?
WAH!
IT'S YOU WHO WILL BE RESPONSIBLE FOR THE KING'S DEATH
GUH. WHAAA...!?
YOU'LL DO EVIL AGAINST SYRIA, YOU'LL BURN HOUSES, KILL YOUNG MEN WITH SWORDS, REND BABIES APART, RIP OPEN PREGNANT LADIES...

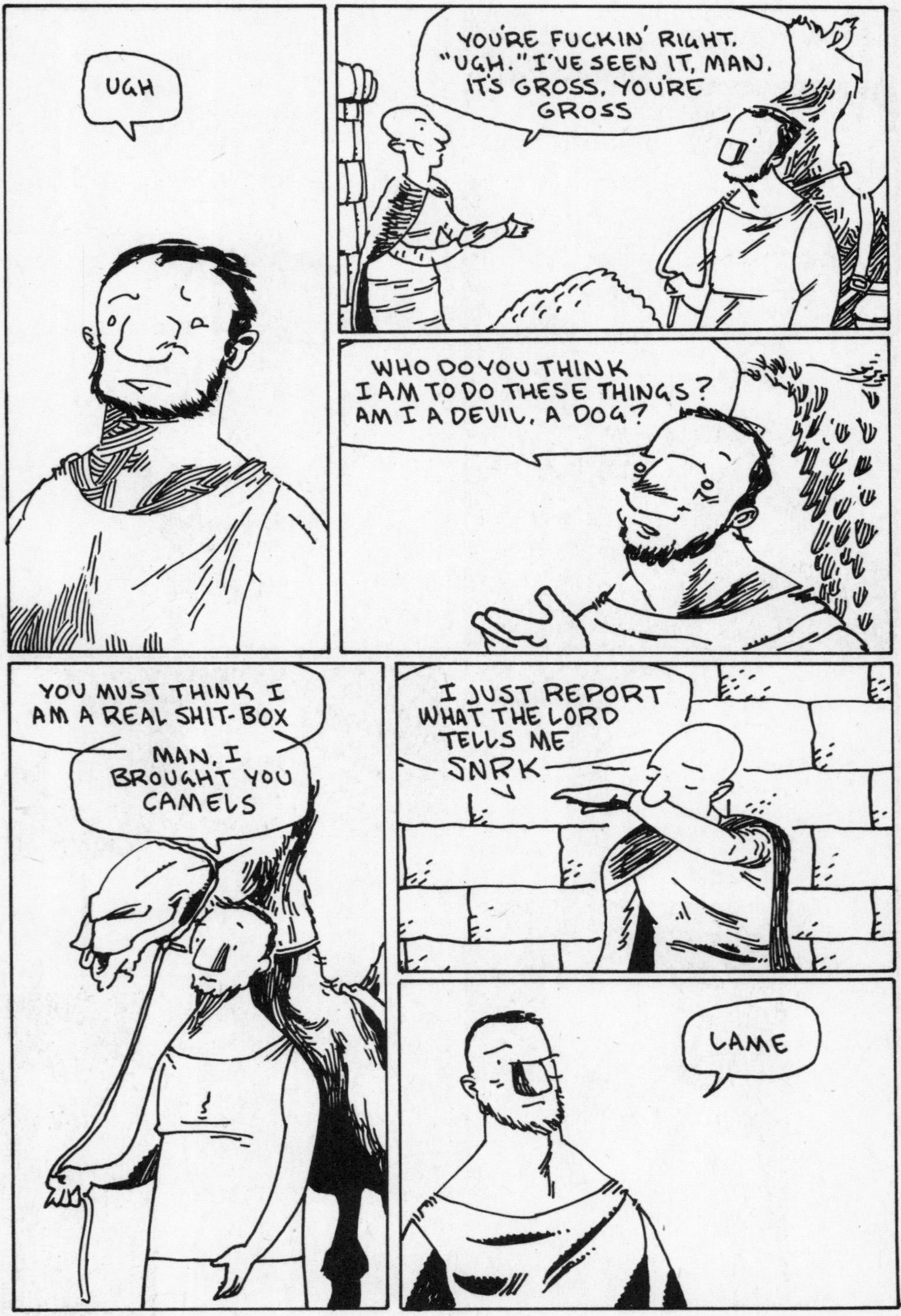
UGH
YOU'RE FUCKIN' RIGHT. "UGH." I'VE SEEN IT, MAN. IT'S GROSS. YOU'RE GROSS
WHO DO YOU THINK I AM TO DO THESE THINGS? AM I A DEVIL, A DOG?
YOU MUST THINK I AM A REAL SHIT-BOX
MAN, I BROUGHT YOU CAMELS
I JUST REPORT WHAT THE LORD TELLS ME
SNRK
LAME

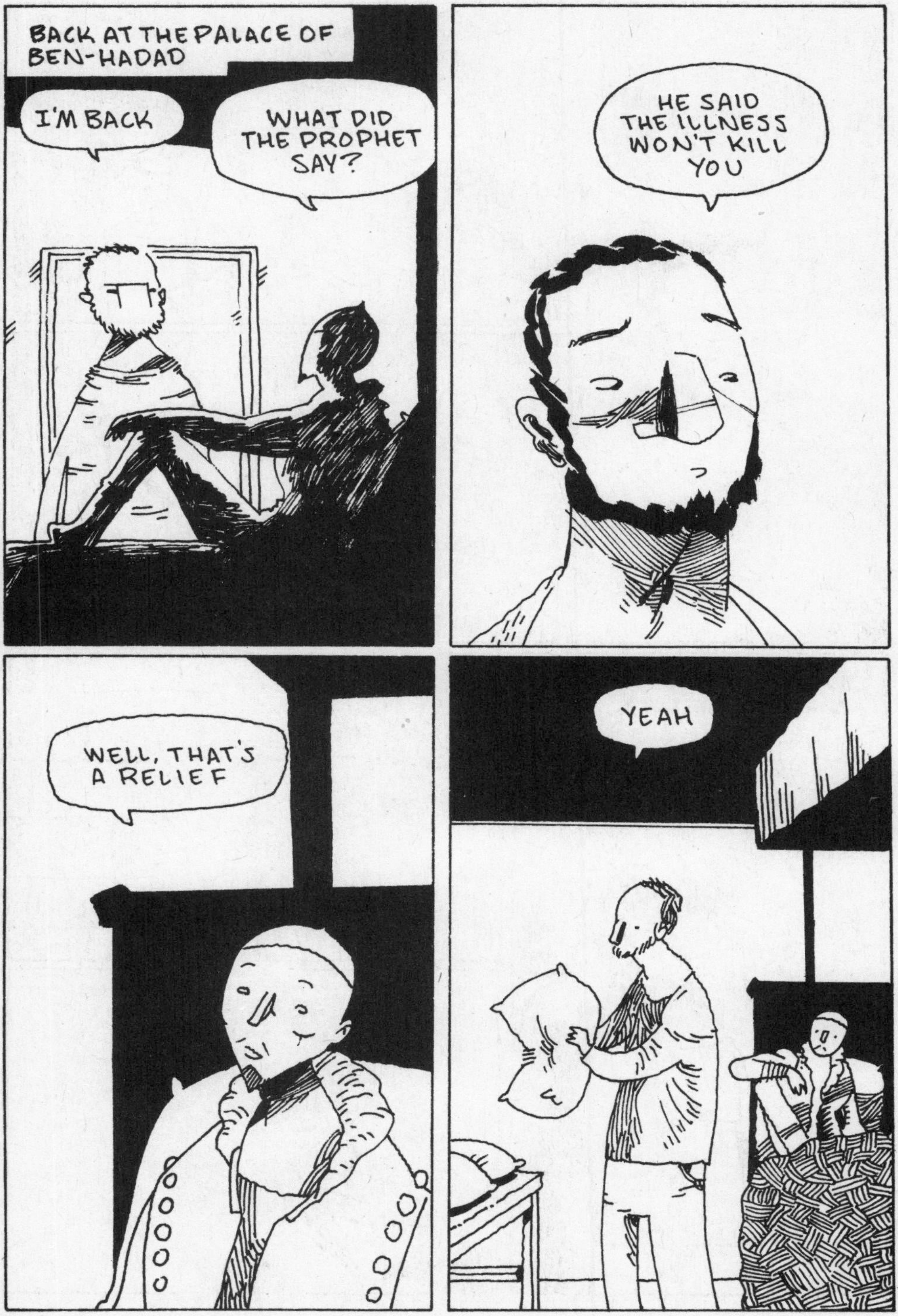
BACK AT THE PALACE OF BEN-HADAD
I'M BACK
WHAT DID THE PROPHET SAY?
HE SAID THE ILLNESS WON'T KILL YOU
WELL, THAT'S A RELIEF
YEAH

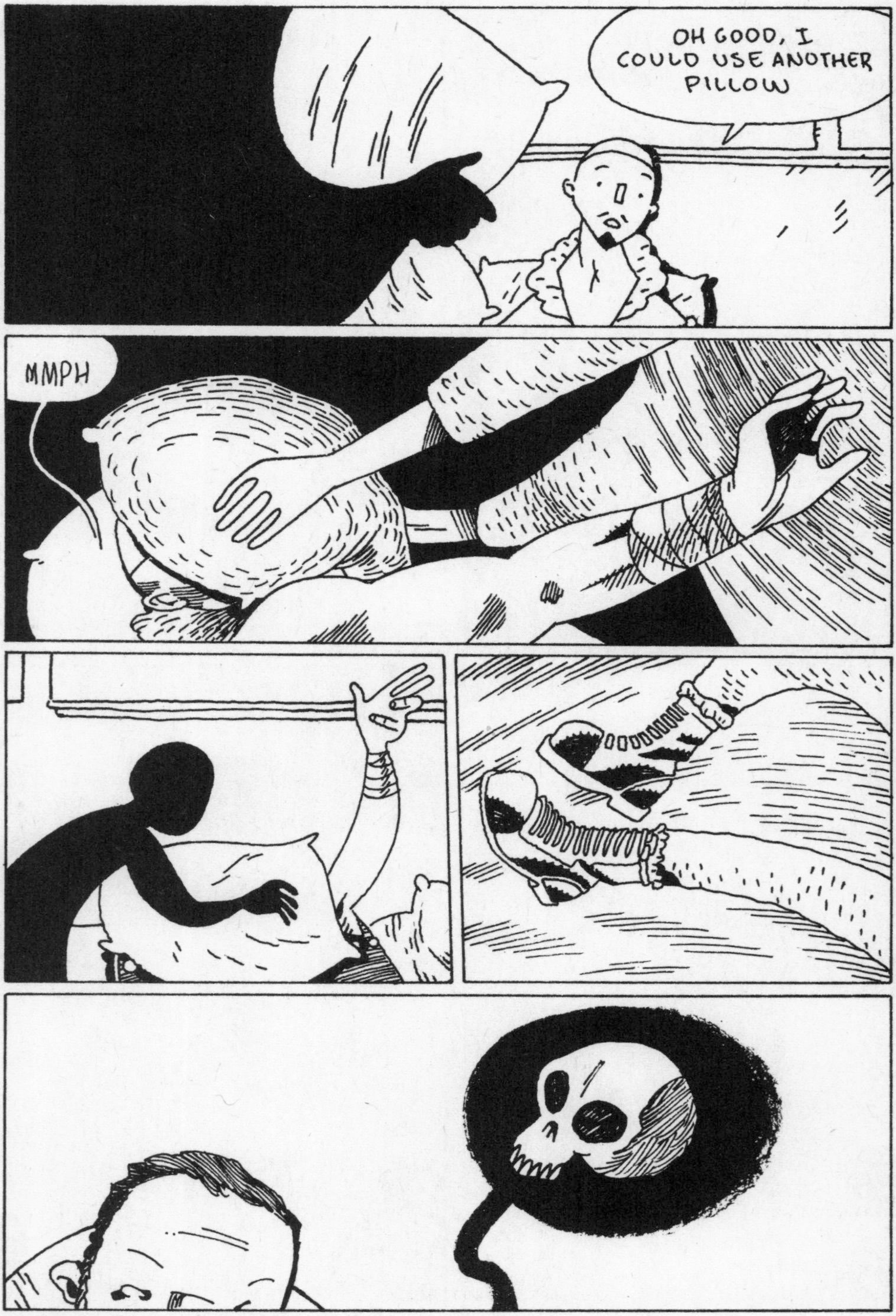
OH GOOD, I COULD USE ANOTHER PILLOW
MMPH

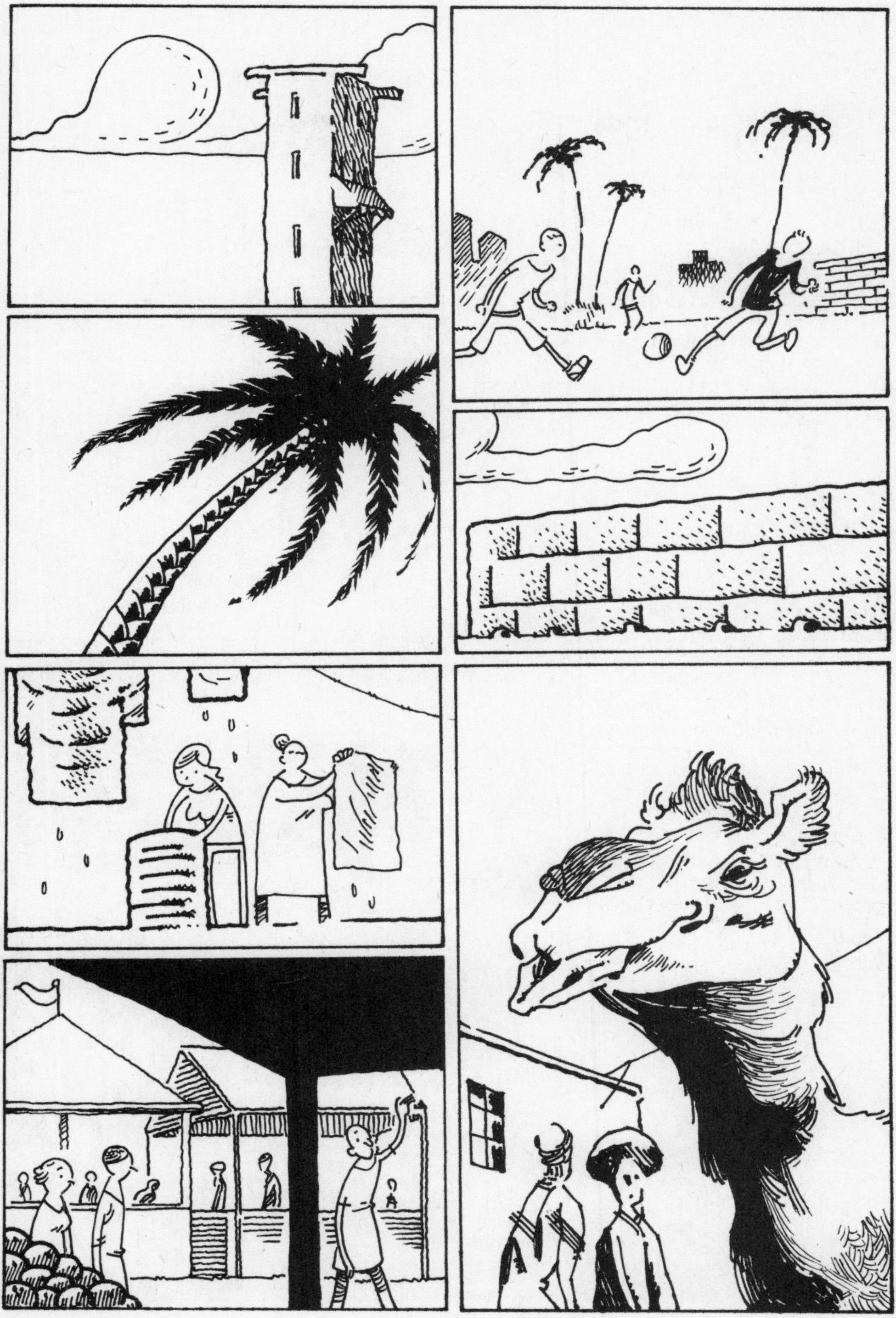

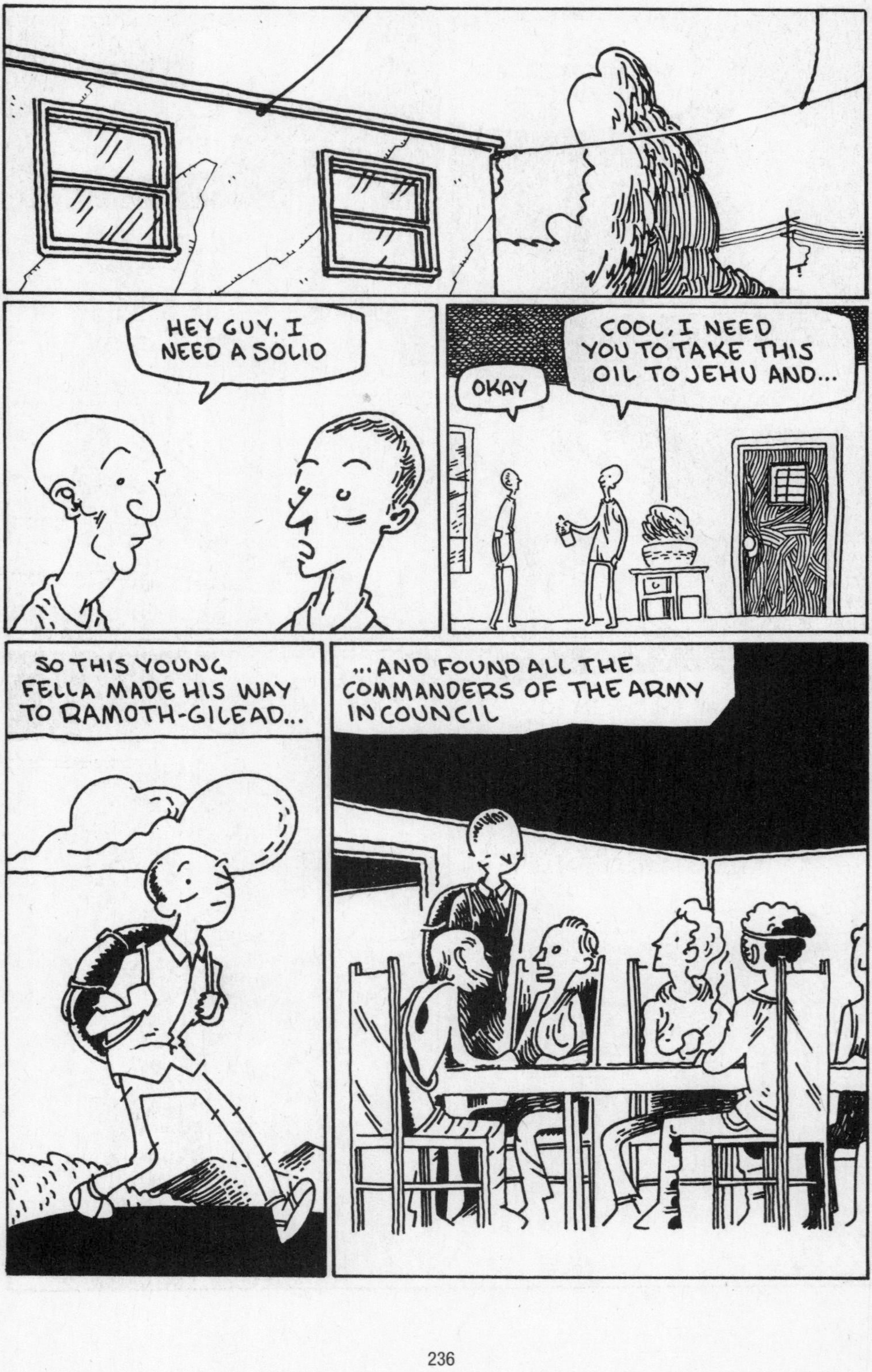
HEY GUY. I NEED A SOLID
OKAY
COOL, I NEED YOU TO TAKE THIS OIL TO JEHU AND...
SO THIS YOUNG FELLA MADE HIS WAY TO RAMOTH-GILEAD...
...AND FOUND ALL THE COMMANDERS OF THE ARMY IN COUNCIL

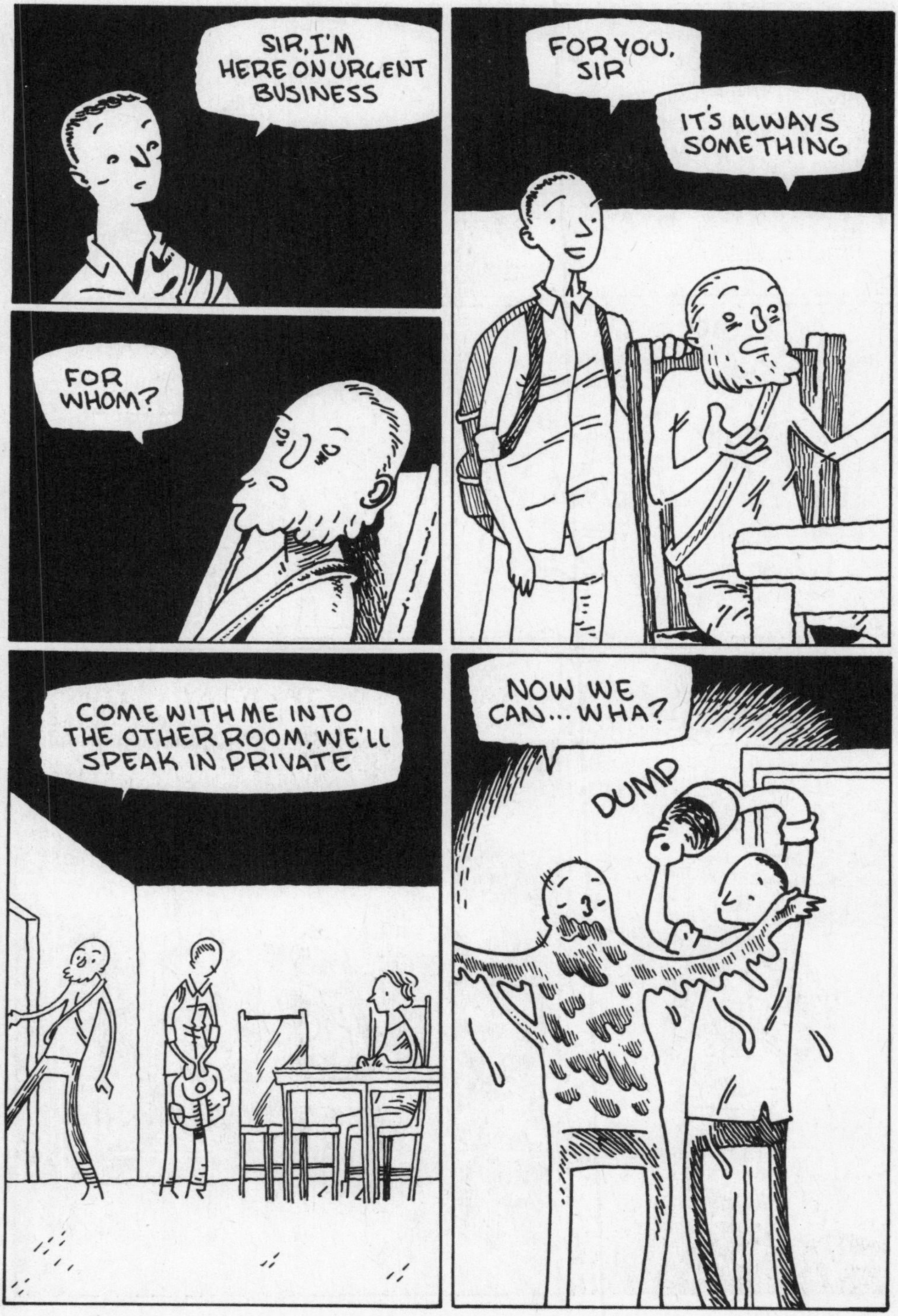
SIR, I'M HERE ON URGENT BUSINESS
FOR YOU, SIR
IT'S ALWAYS SOMETHING
FOR WHOM?
COME WITH ME INTO THE OTHER ROOM, WE'LL SPEAK IN PRIVATE
NOW WE CAN... WHA?
DUMP

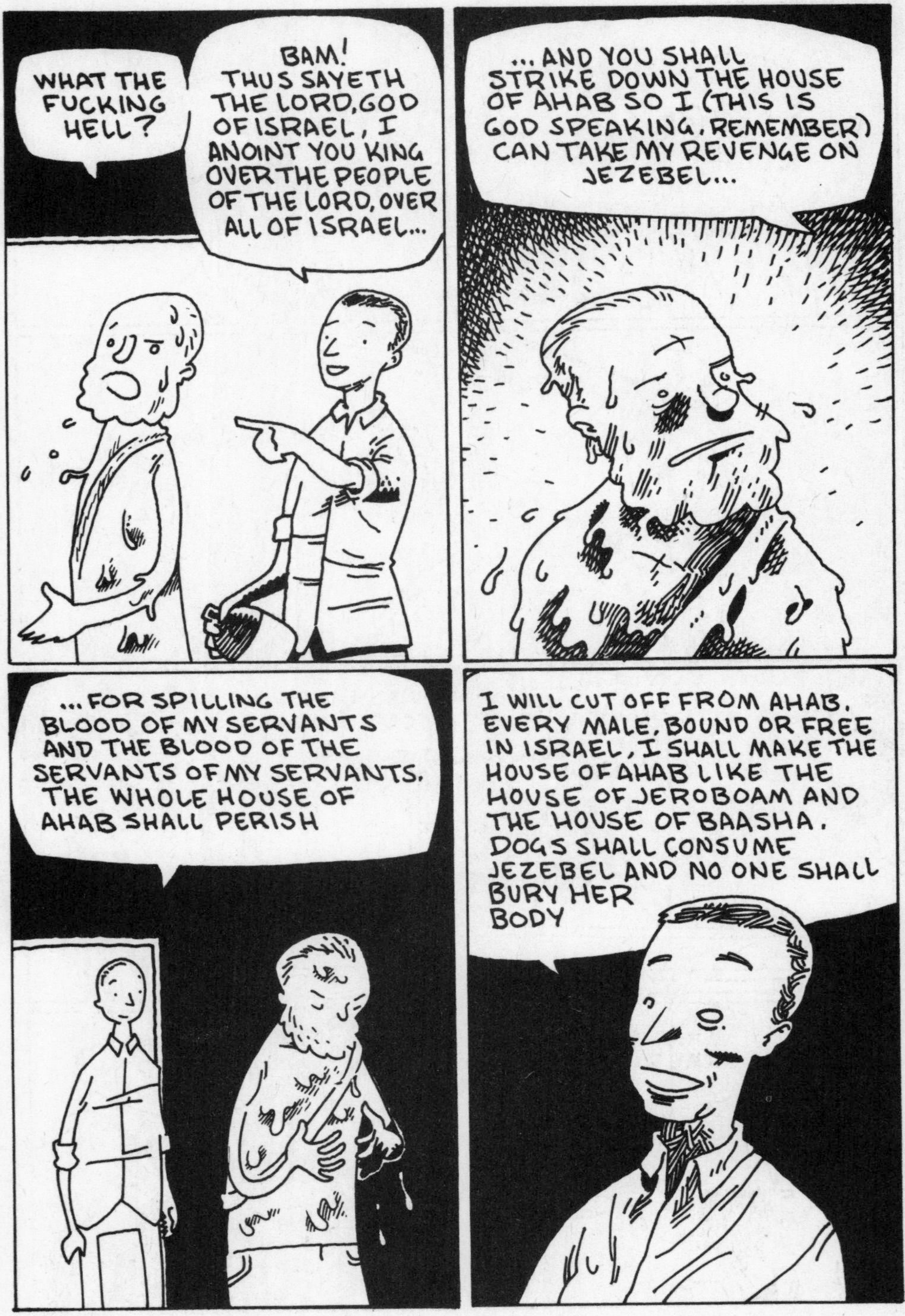
WHAT THE FUCKING HELL?
BAM! THUS SAYETH THE LORD, GOD OF ISRAEL, I ANOINT YOU KING OVER THE PEOPLE OF THE LORD, OVER ALL OF ISRAEL...
...AND YOU SHALL STRIKE DOWN THE HOUSE OF AHAB SO I (THIS IS GOD SPEAKING, REMEMBER) CAN TAKE MY REVENGE ON JEZEBEL...
...FOR SPILLING THE BLOOD OF MY SERVANTS AND THE BLOOD OF THE SERVANTS OF MY SERVANTS. THE WHOLE HOUSE OF AHAB SHALL PERISH
I WILL CUT OFF FROM AHAB, EVERY MALE, BOUND OR FREE IN ISRAEL, I SHALL MAKE THE HOUSE OF AHAB LIKE THE HOUSE OF JEROBOAM AND THE HOUSE OF BAASHA. DOGS SHALL CONSUME JEZEBEL AND NO ONE SHALL BURY HER BODY

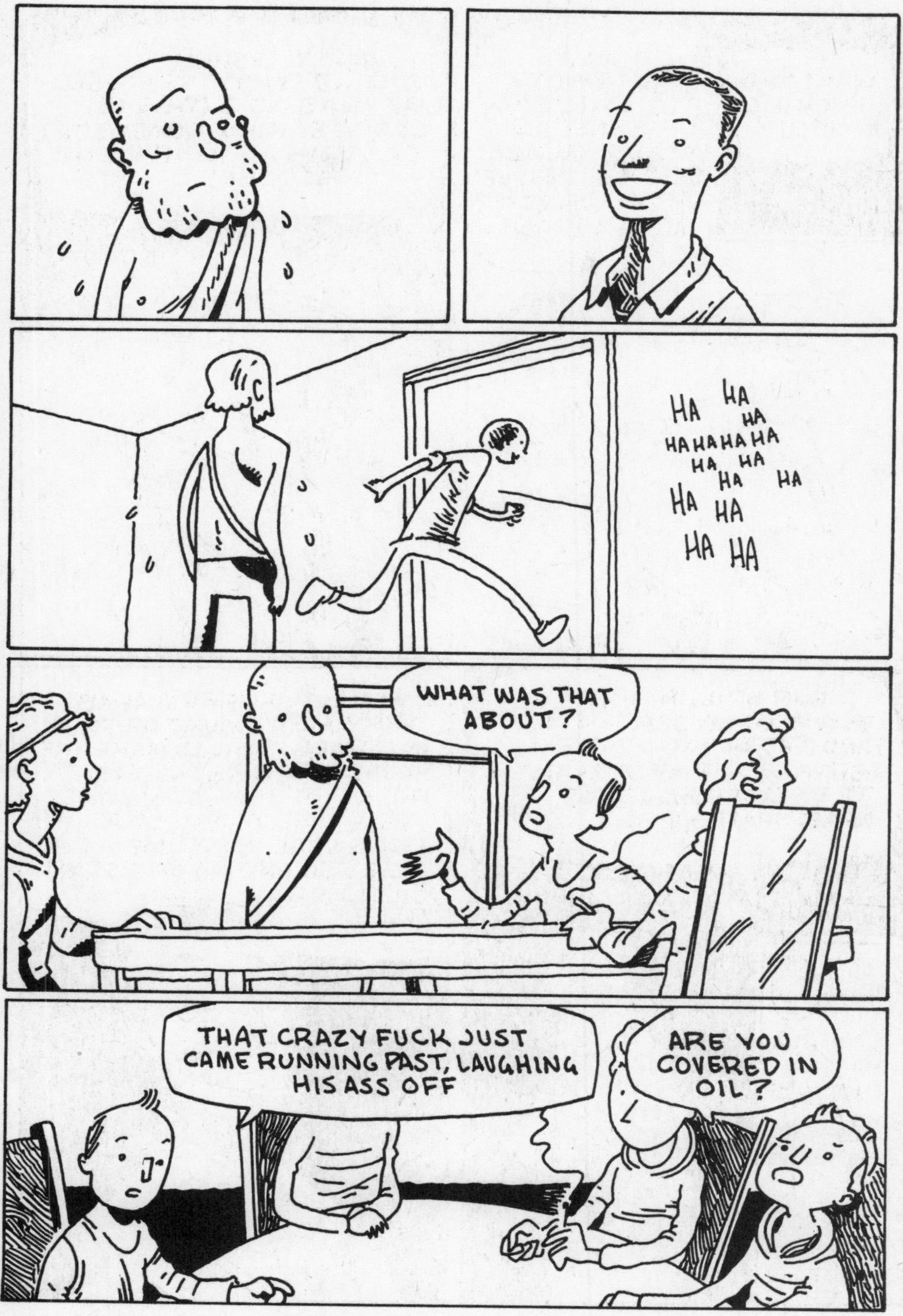
HA HA HA HAHAHAHAHA HA HA HA HA HA HA HA HA
WHAT WAS THAT ABOUT?
THAT CRAZY FUCK JUST CAME RUNNING PAST, LAUGHING HIS ASS OFF
ARE YOU COVERED IN OIL?

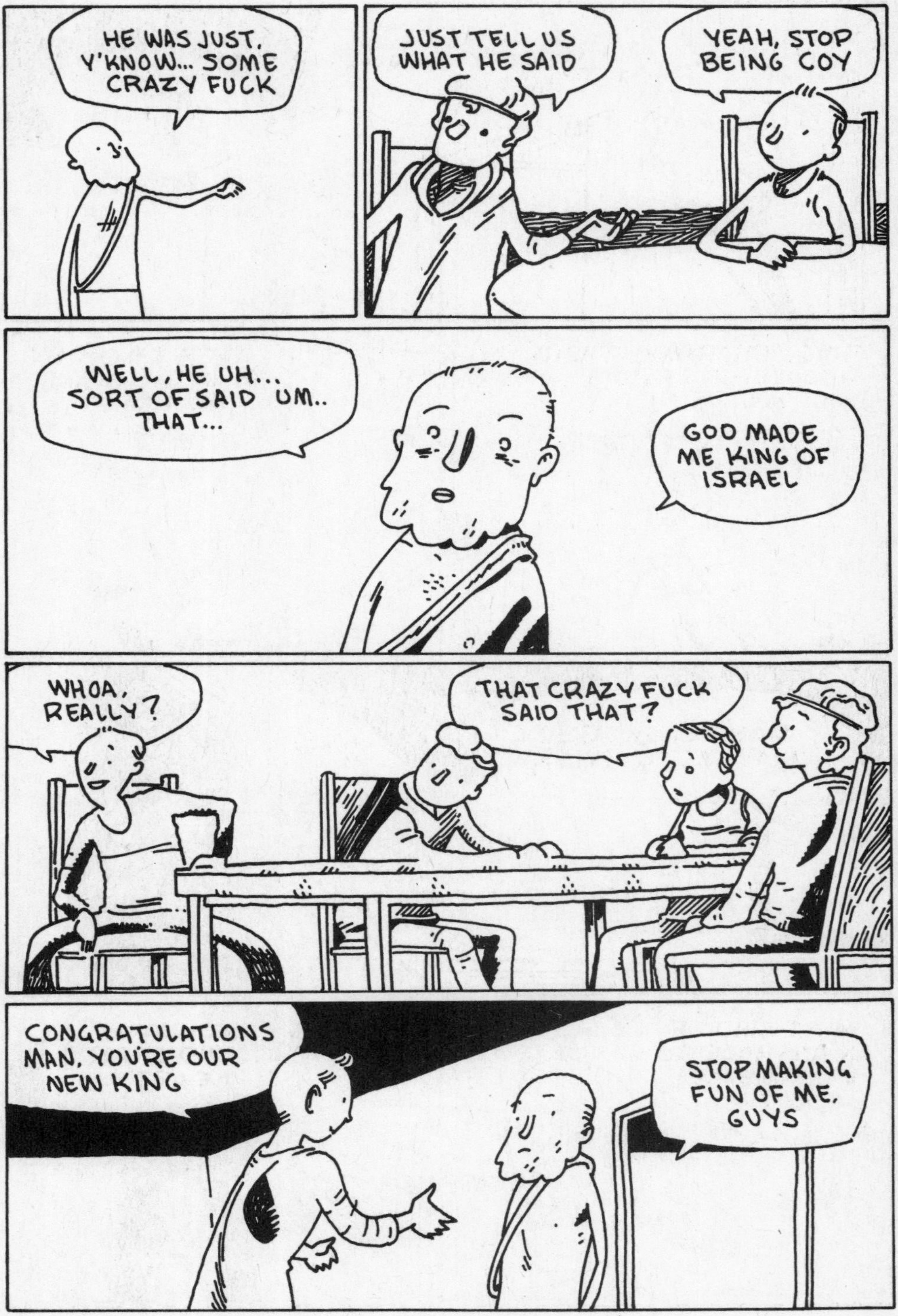
HE WAS JUST, Y'KNOW... SOME CRAZY FUCK
JUST TELL US WHAT HE SAID
YEAH, STOP BEING COY
WELL, HE UH... SORT OF SAID UM.. THAT...
GOD MADE ME KING OF ISRAEL
WHOA, REALLY?
THAT CRAZY FUCK SAID THAT?
CONGRATULATIONS MAN, YOU'RE OUR NEW KING
STOP MAKING FUN OF ME, GUYS

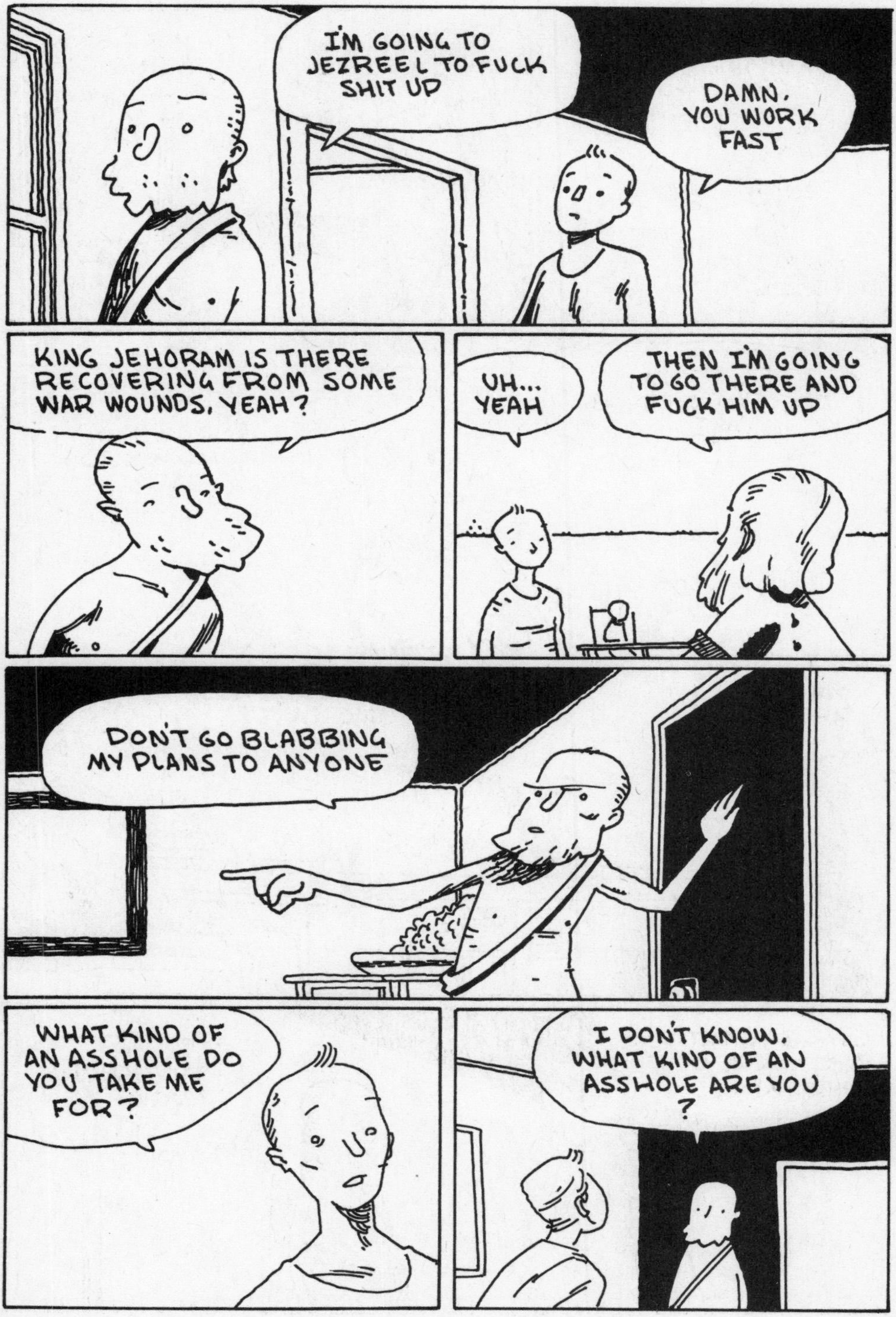
I'M GOING TO JEZREEL TO FUCK SHIT UP
DAMN. YOU WORK FAST
KING JEHORAM IS THERE RECOVERING FROM SOME WAR WOUNDS, YEAH?
UH... YEAH
THEN I'M GOING TO GO THERE AND FUCK HIM UP
DON'T GO BLABBING MY PLANS TO ANYONE
WHAT KIND OF AN ASSHOLE DO YOU TAKE ME FOR?
I DON'T KNOW. WHAT KIND OF AN ASSHOLE ARE YOU ?

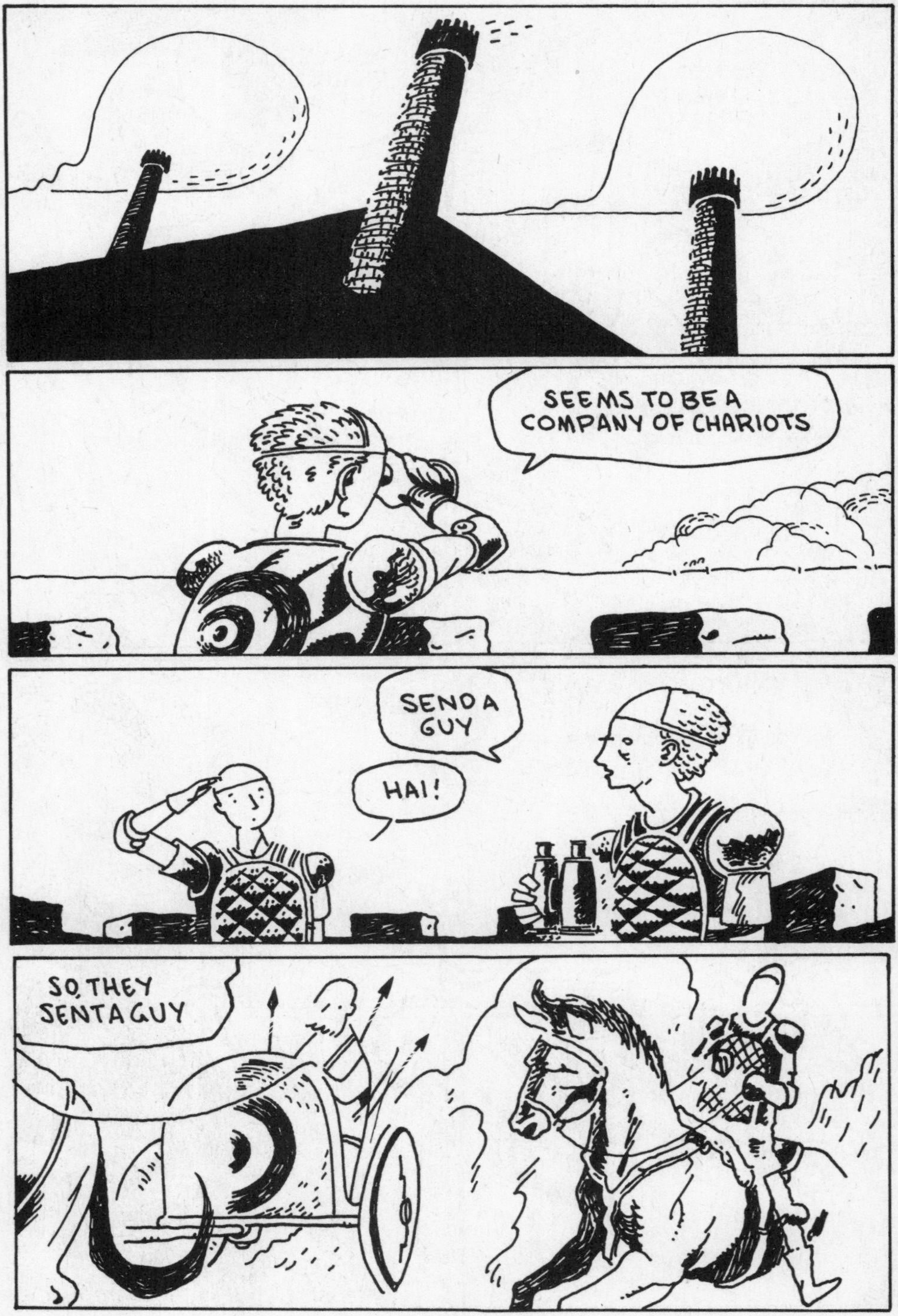
SEEMS TO BE A COMPANY OF CHARIOTS
SEND A GUY
HAI!
SO, THEY SENT A GUY

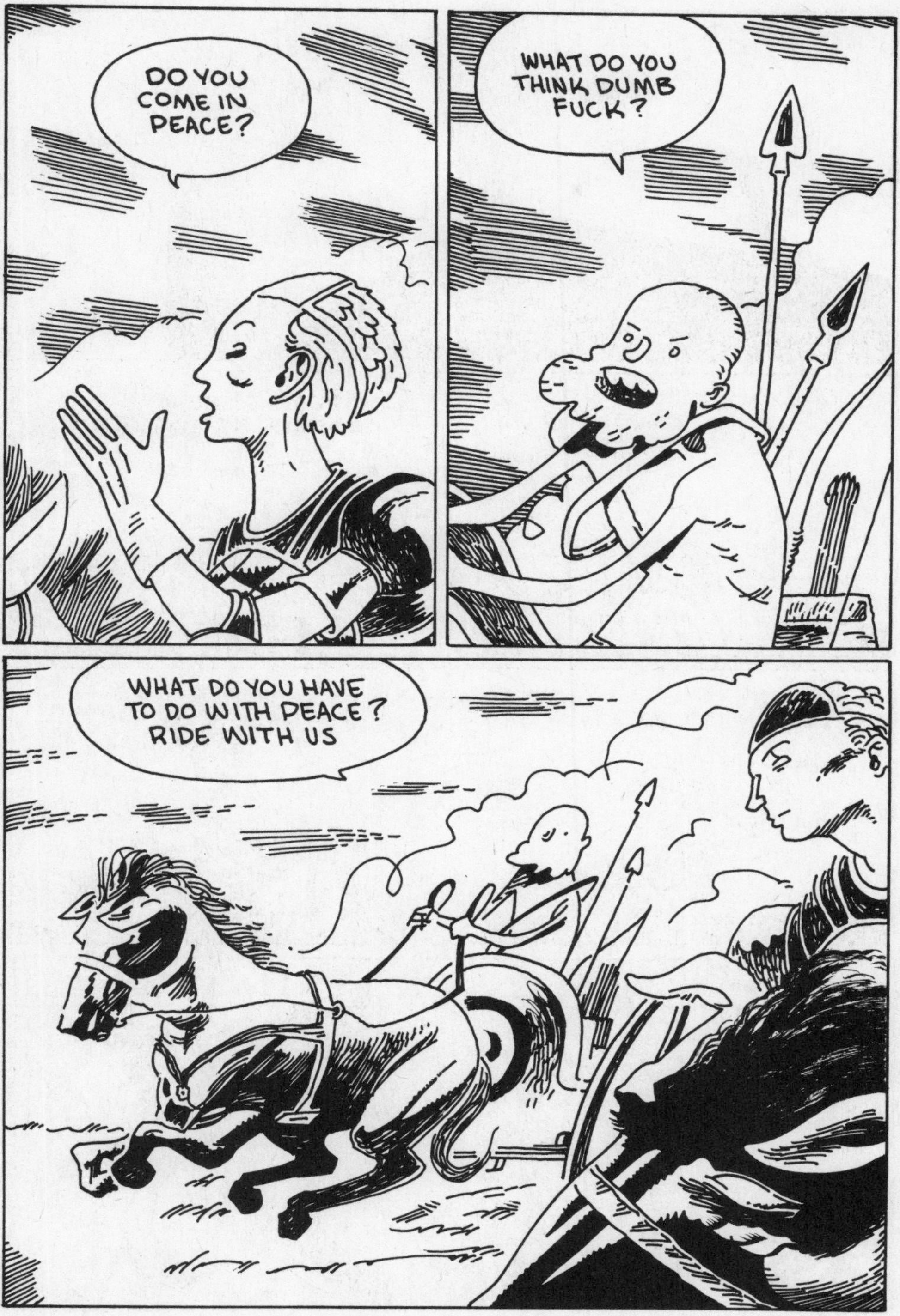
DO YOU COME IN PEACE?
WHAT DO YOU THINK DUMB FUCK?
WHAT DO YOU HAVE TO DO WITH PEACE? RIDE WITH US

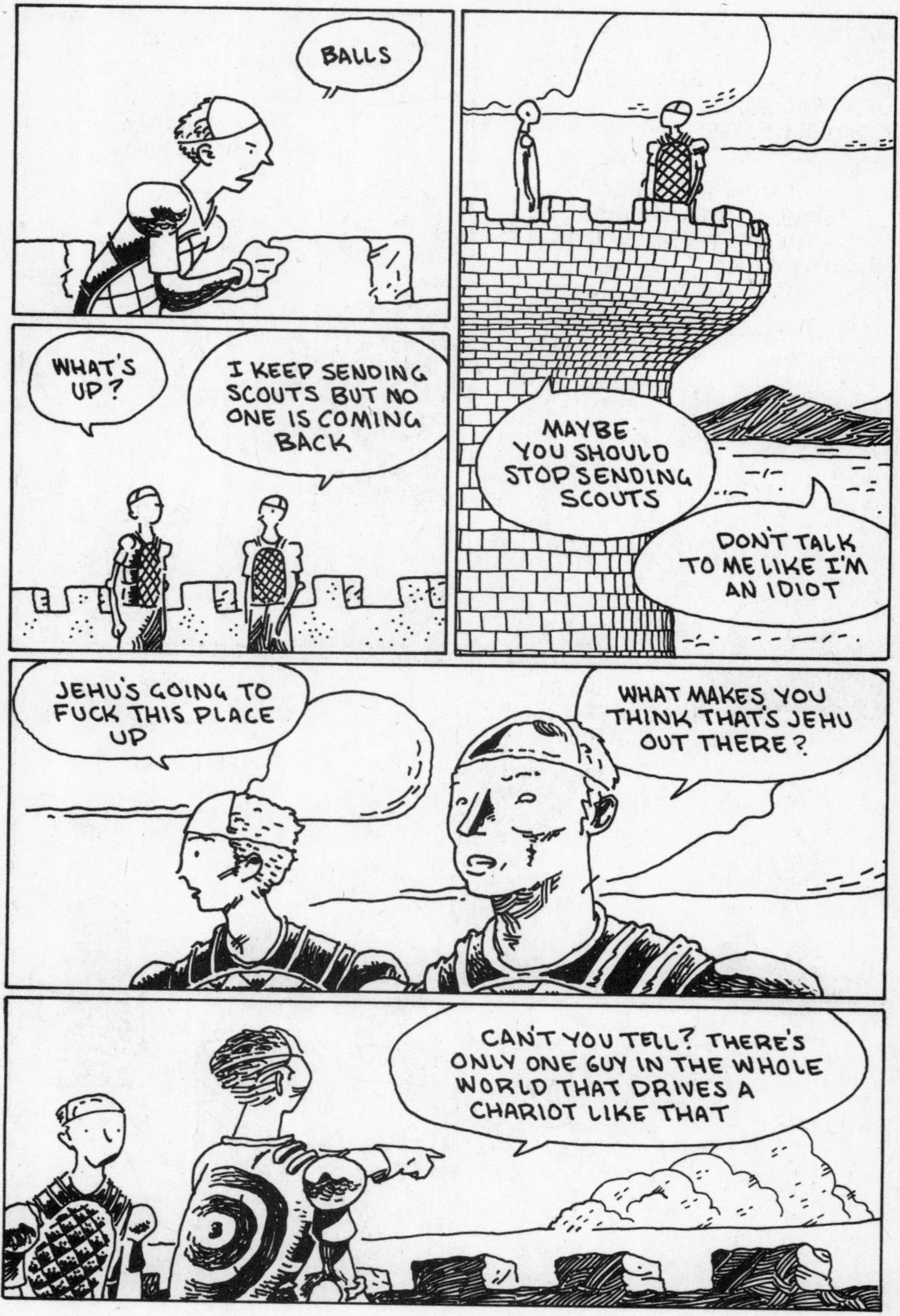
BALLS
WHAT'S UP?
I KEEP SENDING SCOUTS BUT NO ONE IS COMING BACK
MAYBE YOU SHOULD STOP SENDING SCOUTS
DON'T TALK TO ME LIKE I'M AN IDIOT
JEHU'S GOING TO FUCK THIS PLACE UP
WHAT MAKES YOU THINK THAT'S JEHU OUT THERE?
CAN'T YOU TELL? THERE'S ONLY ONE GUY IN THE WHOLE WORLD THAT DRIVES A CHARIOT LIKE THAT

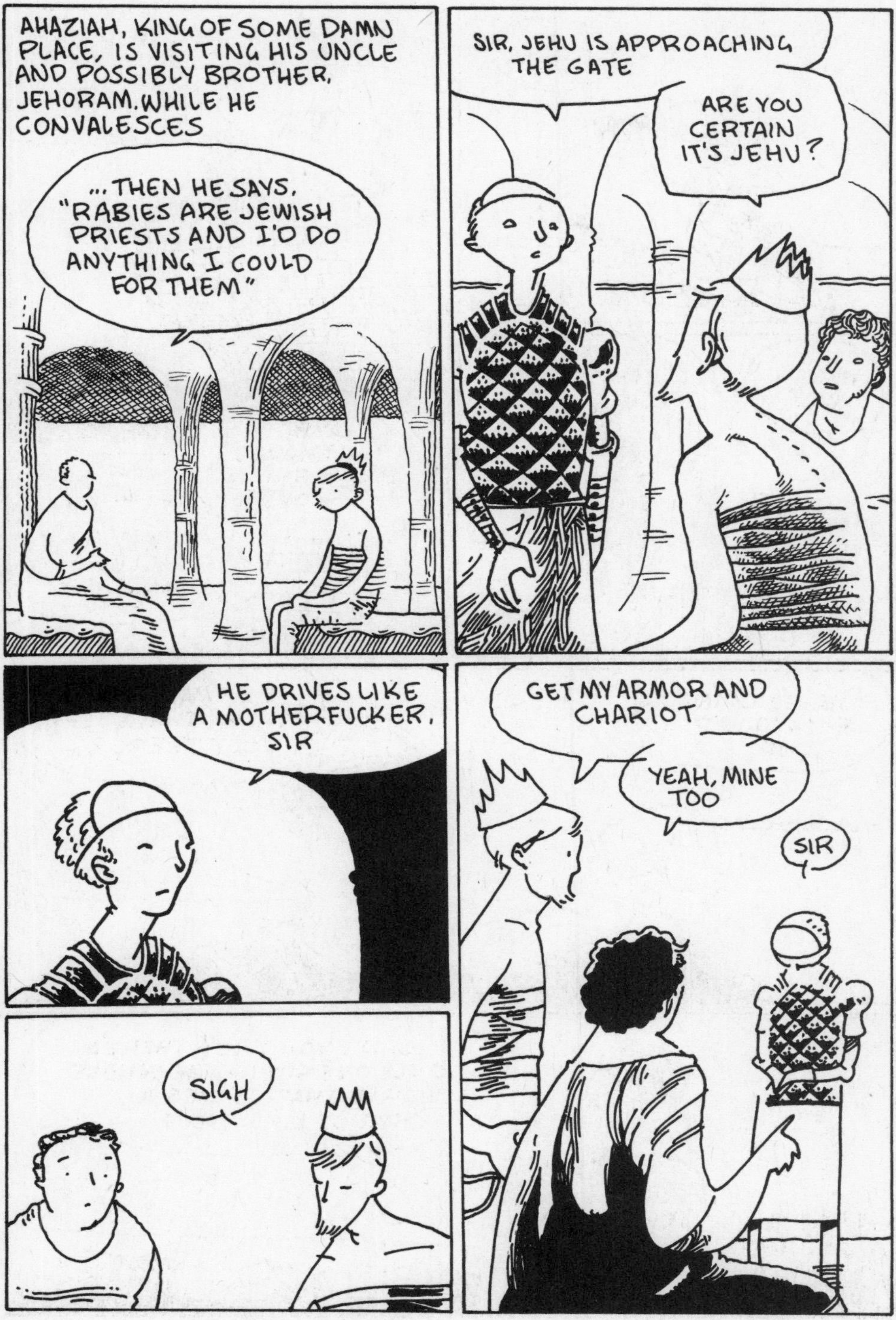
AHAZIAH, KING OF SOME DAMN PLACE, IS VISITING HIS UNCLE AND POSSIBLY BROTHER, JEHORAM. WHILE HE CONVALESCES
...THEN HE SAYS, "RABIES ARE JEWISH PRIESTS AND I'D DO ANYTHING I COULD FOR THEM"
SIR, JEHU IS APPROACHING THE GATE
ARE YOU CERTAIN IT'S JEHU?
HE DRIVES LIKE A MOTHERFUCKER, SIR
SIGH
GET MY ARMOR AND CHARIOT
YEAH, MINE TOO
SIR

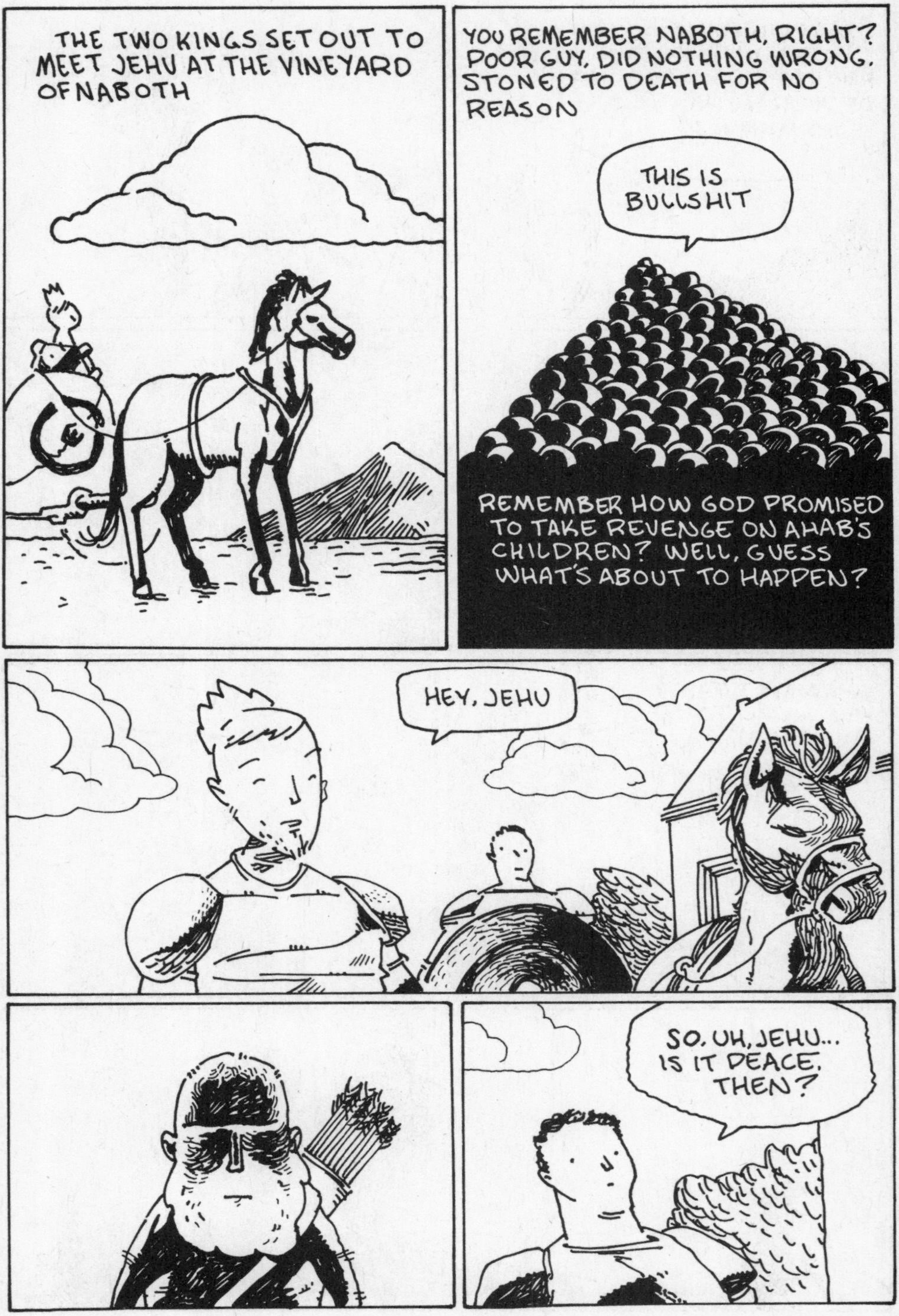
THE TWO KINGS SET OUT TO MEET JEHU AT THE VINEYARD OF NABOTH
YOU REMEMBER NABOTH, RIGHT? POOR GUY, DID NOTHING WRONG. STONED TO DEATH FOR NO REASON
THIS IS BULLSHIT
REMEMBER HOW GOD PROMISED TO TAKE REVENGE ON AHAB'S CHILDREN? WELL, GUESS WHAT'S ABOUT TO HAPPEN?
HEY, JEHU
SO, UH, JEHU... IS IT PEACE, THEN?

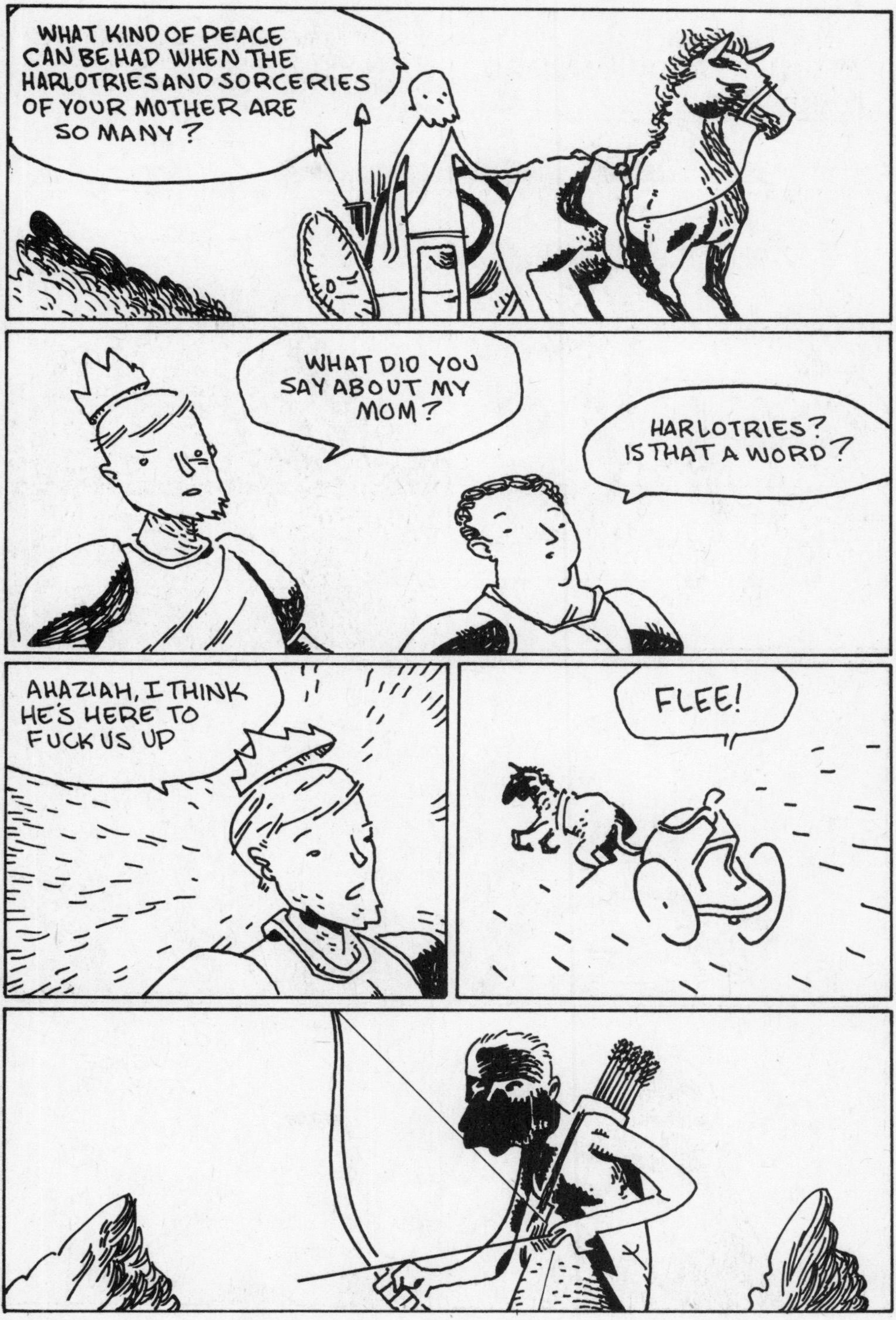
WHAT KIND OF PEACE CAN BE HAD WHEN THE HARLOTRIES AND SORCERIES OF YOUR MOTHER ARE SO MANY?
WHAT DID YOU SAY ABOUT MY MOM?
HARLOTRIES? IS THAT A WORD?
AHAZIAH, I THINK HE'S HERE TO FUCK US UP
FLEE!

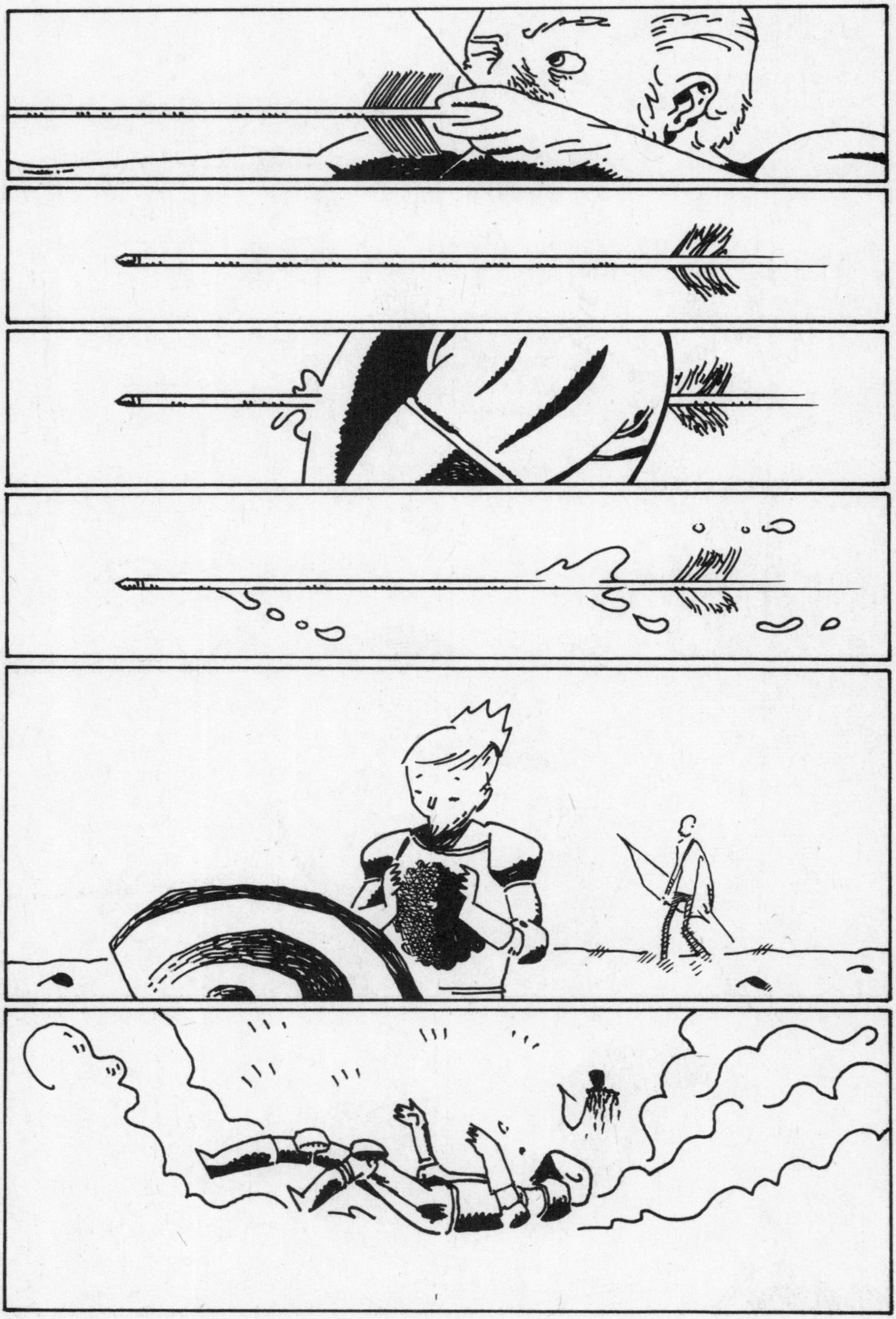

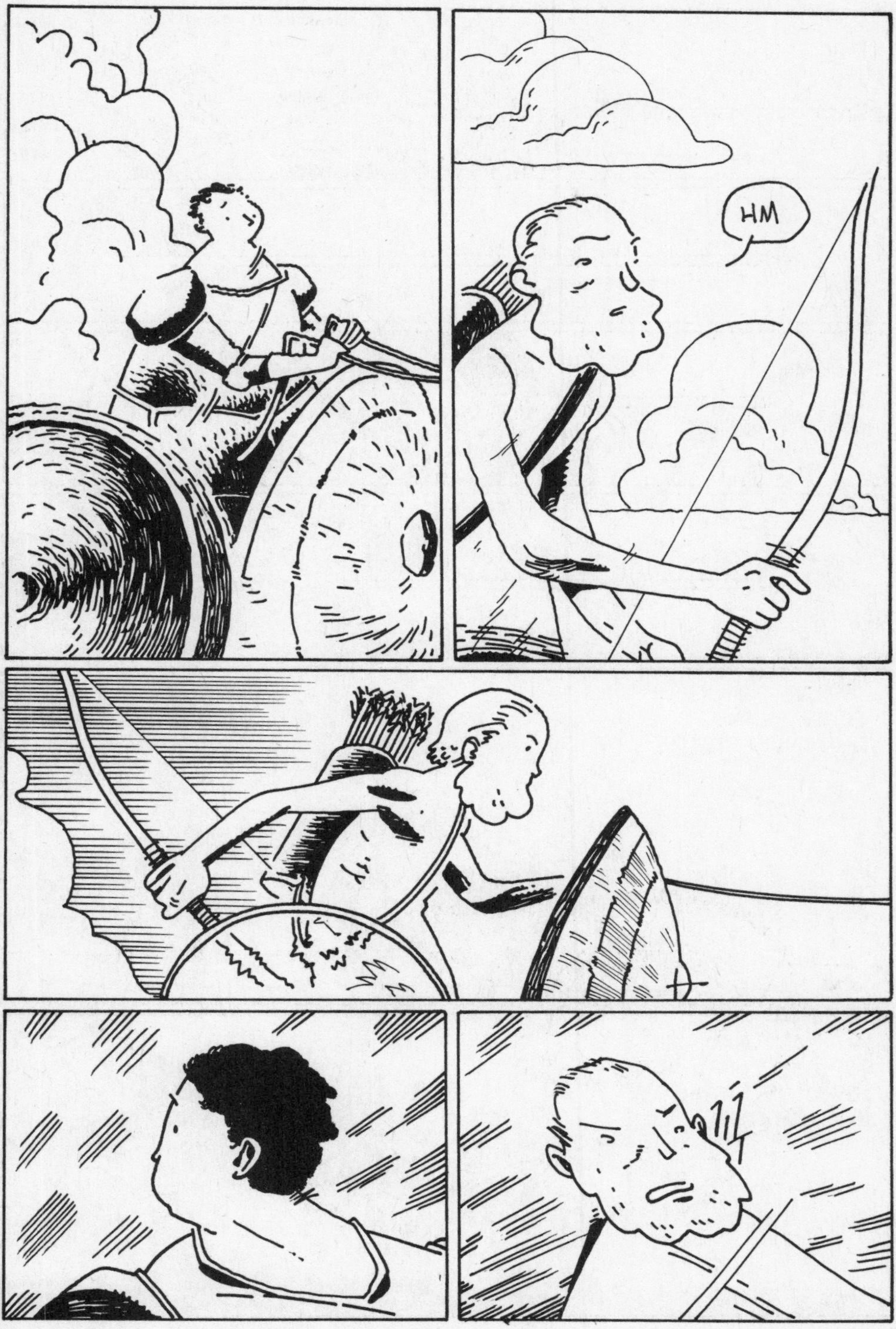
HM

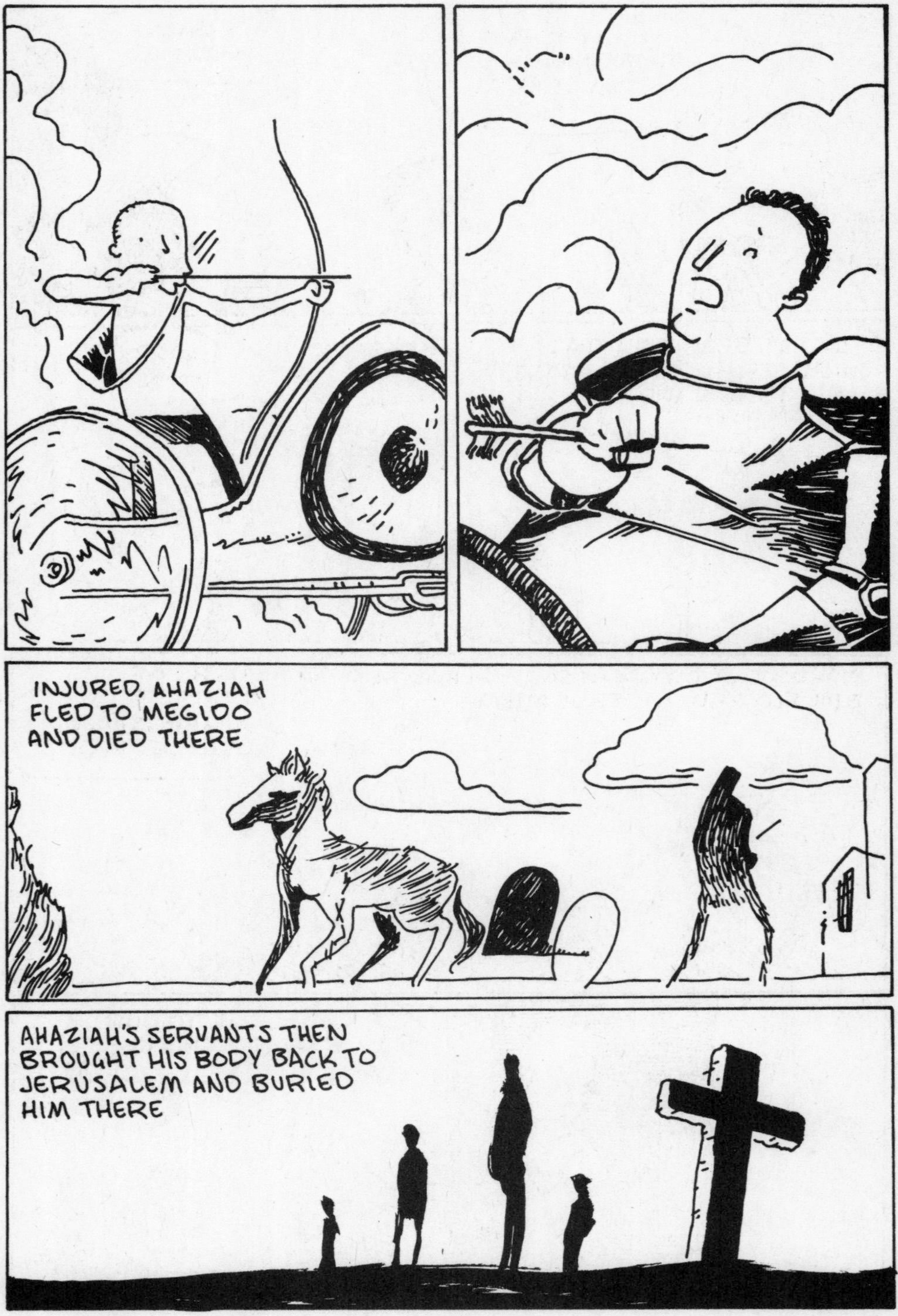
INJURED, AHAZIAH
FLED TO MEGIDO
AND DIED THERE
AHAZIAH'S SERVANTS THEN
BROUGHT HIS BODY BACK TO
JERUSALEM AND BURIED
HIM THERE

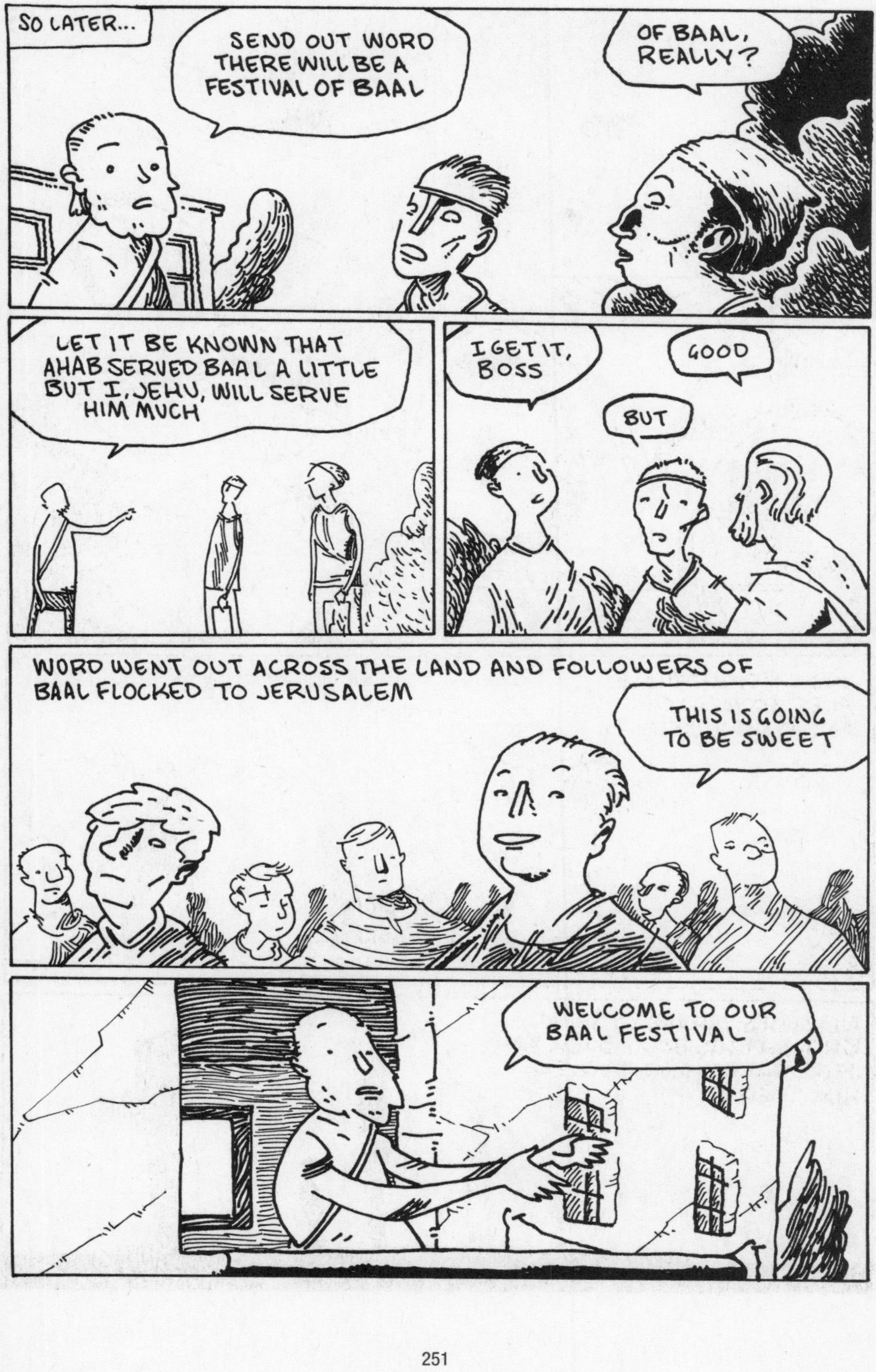
SO LATER...
SEND OUT WORD THERE WILL BE A FESTIVAL OF BAAL
OF BAAL, REALLY?
LET IT BE KNOWN THAT AHAB SERVED BAAL A LITTLE BUT I, JEHU, WILL SERVE HIM MUCH
I GET IT, BOSS
GOOD
BUT
WORD WENT OUT ACROSS THE LAND AND FOLLOWERS OF BAAL FLOCKED TO JERUSALEM
THIS IS GOING TO BE SWEET
WELCOME TO OUR BAAL FESTIVAL

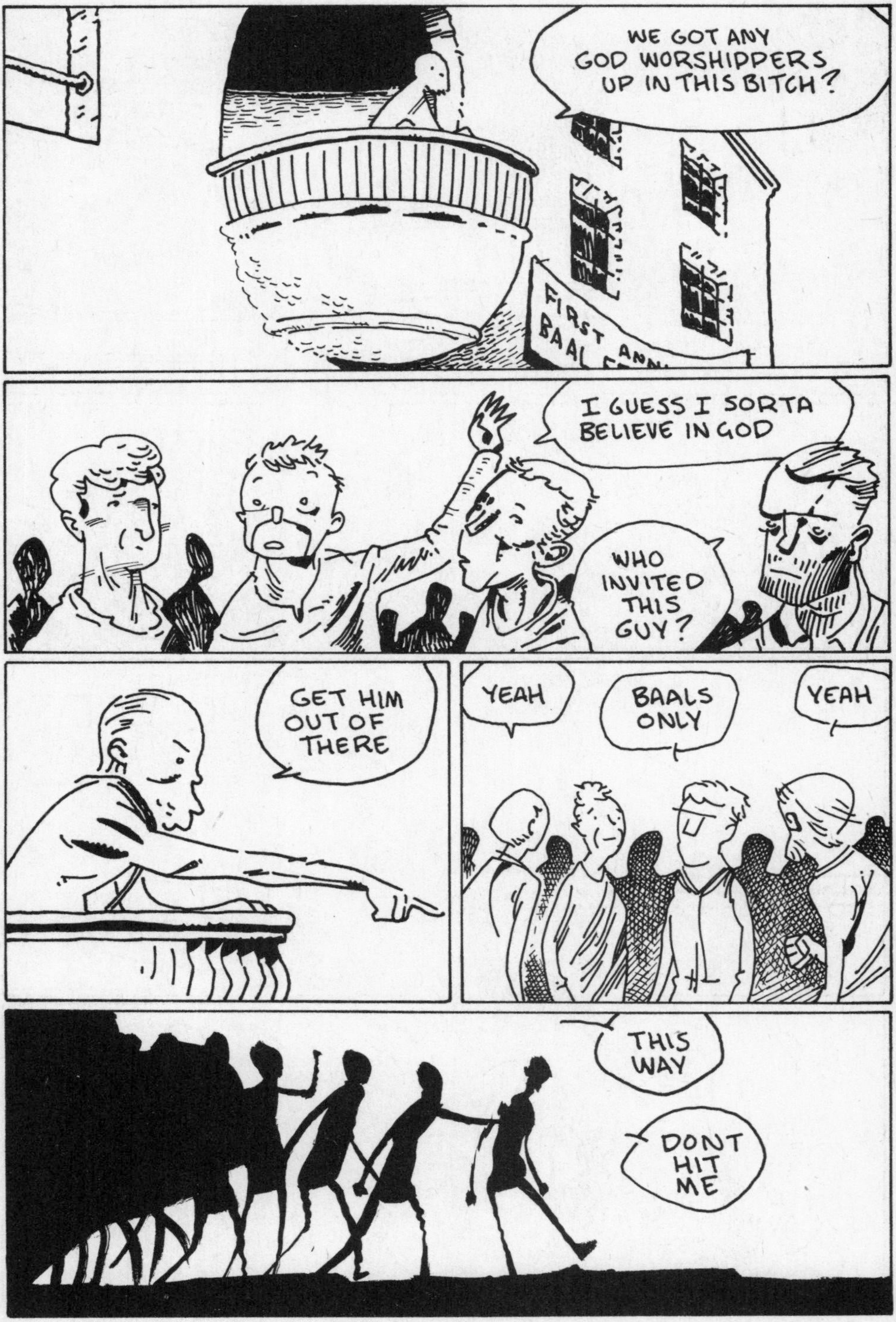
WE GOT ANY GOD WORSHIPPERS UP IN THIS BITCH?
FIRST ANN
BAAL
I GUESS I SORTA BELIEVE IN GOD
WHO INVITED THIS GUY?
GET HIM OUT OF THERE
YEAH
BAALS ONLY
YEAH
THIS WAY
DONT HIT ME

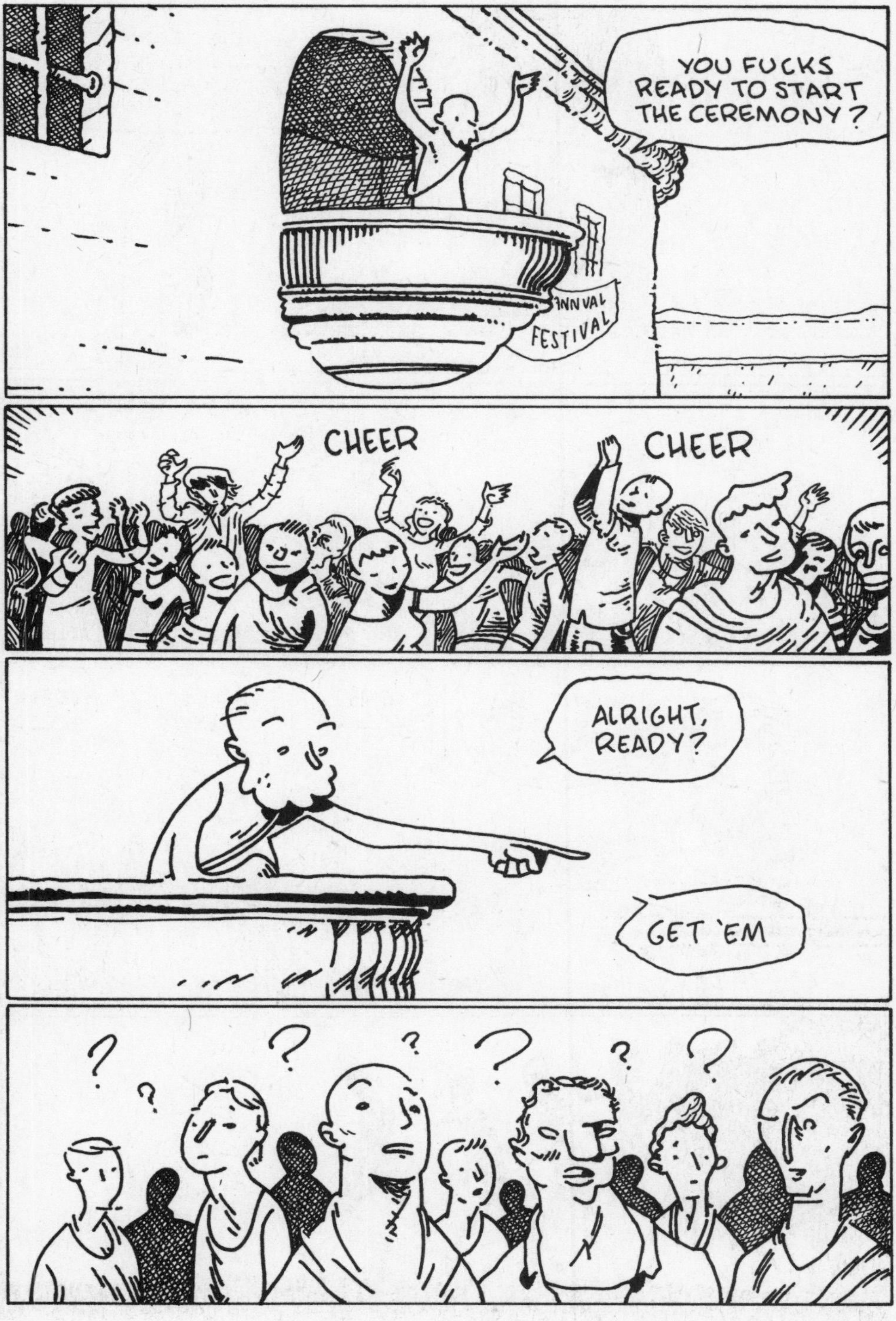
YOU FUCKS READY TO START THE CEREMONY?
ANNUAL FESTIVAL
CHEER
CHEER
ALRIGHT, READY?
GET 'EM
?
?
?
?
?
?
?

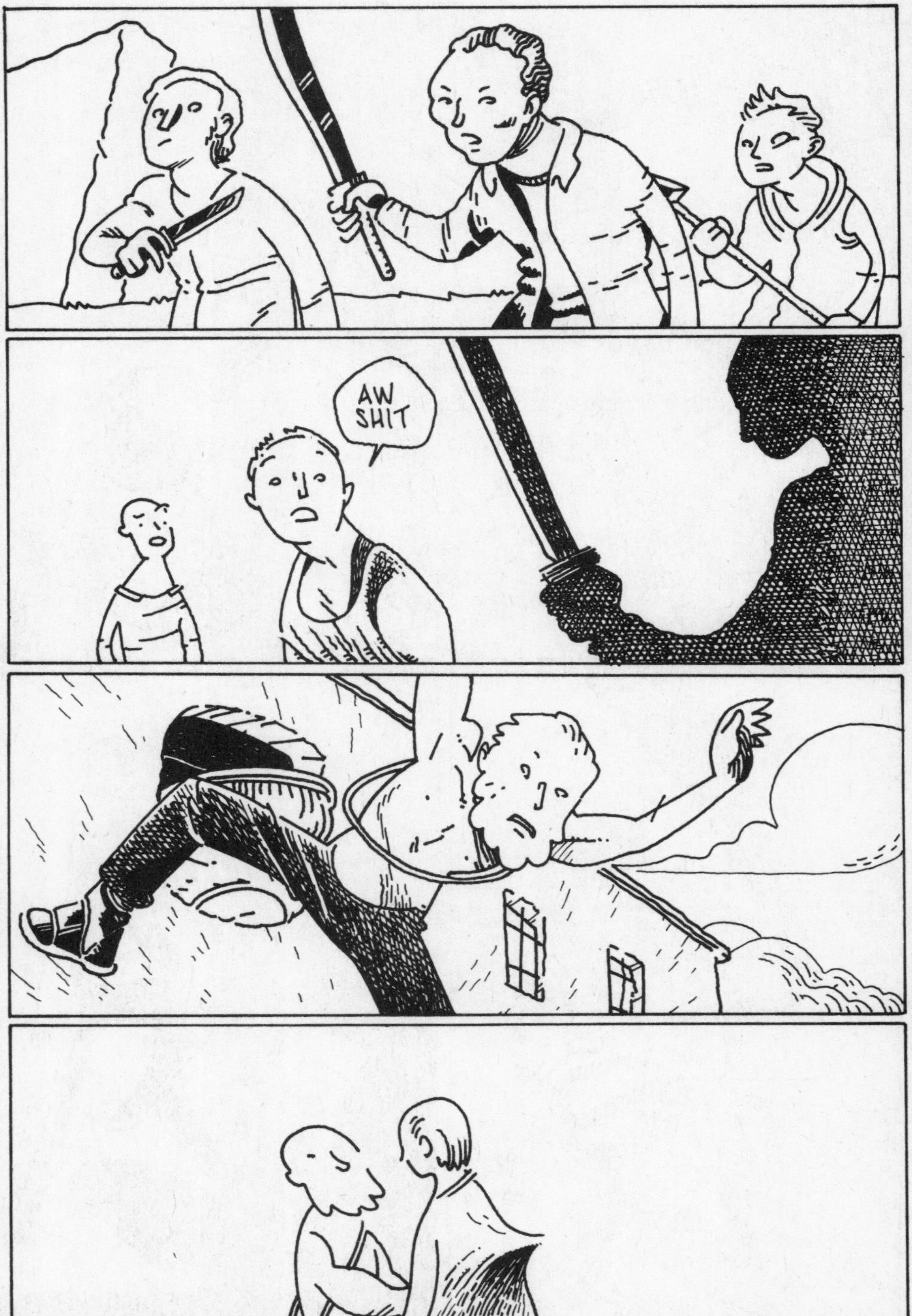
AW SHIT

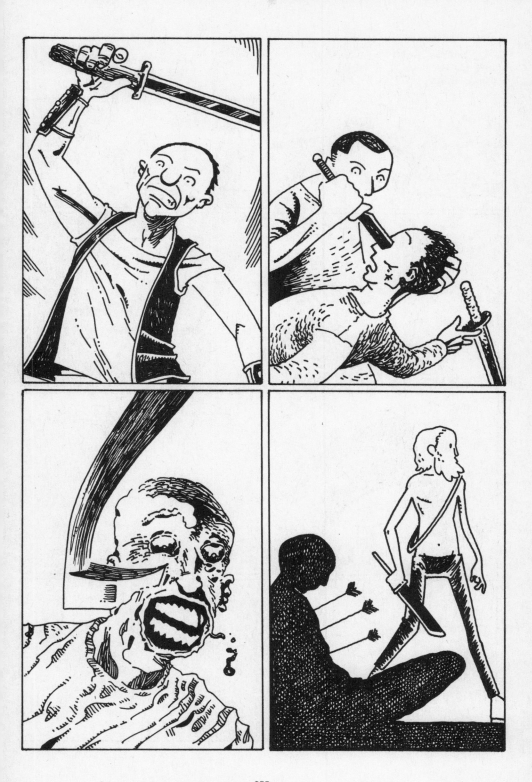

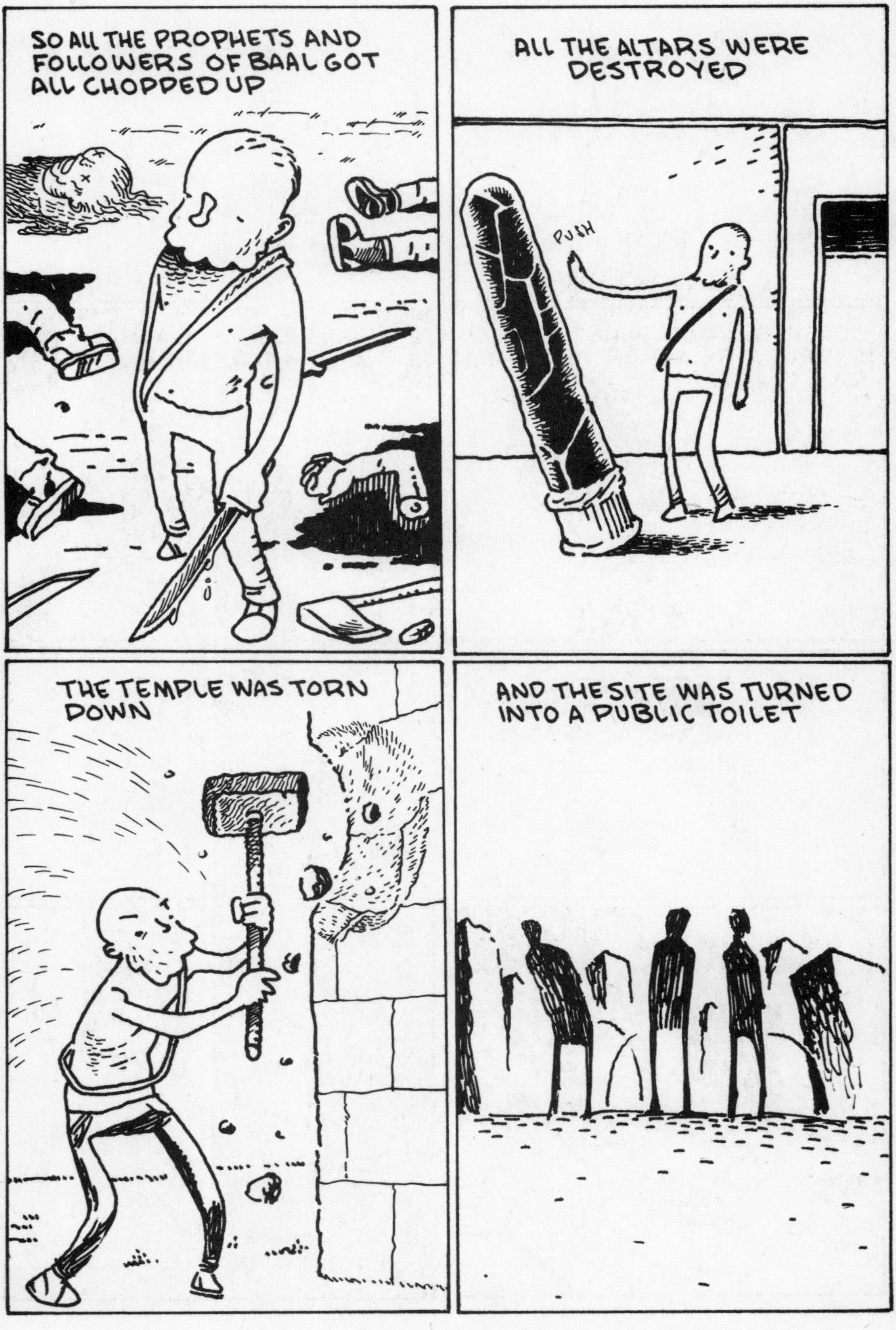
SO ALL THE PROPHETS AND FOLLOWERS OF BAAL GOT ALL CHOPPED UP
ALL THE ALTARS WERE DESTROYED
PUSH
THE TEMPLE WAS TORN DOWN
AND THE SITE WAS TURNED INTO A PUBLIC TOILET

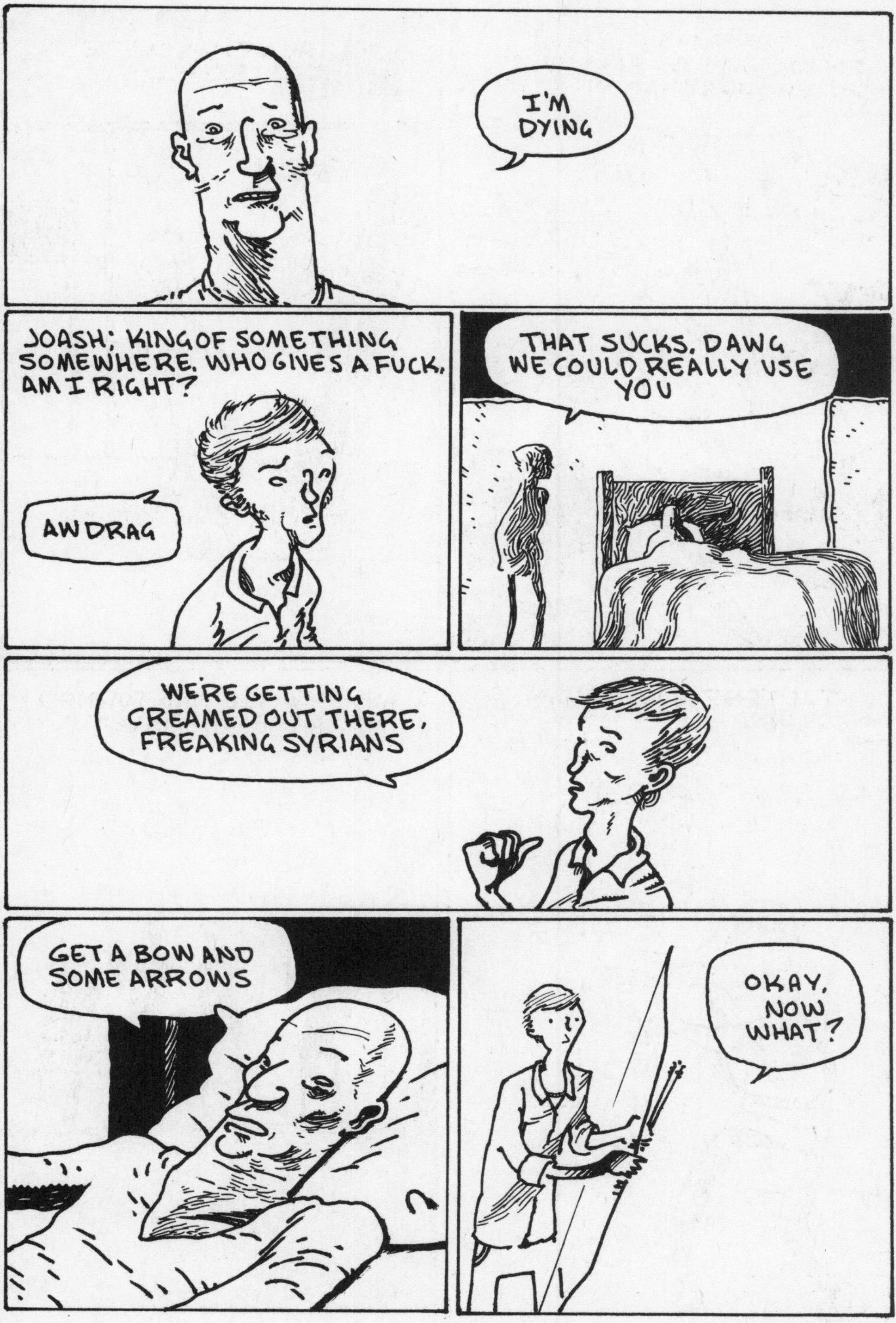
I'M DYING
JOASH; KING OF SOMETHING SOMEWHERE. WHO GIVES A FUCK. AM I RIGHT?
AW DRAG
THAT SUCKS. DAWG WE COULD REALLY USE YOU
WE'RE GETTING CREAMED OUT THERE, FREAKING SYRIANS
GET A BOW AND SOME ARROWS
OKAY, NOW WHAT?

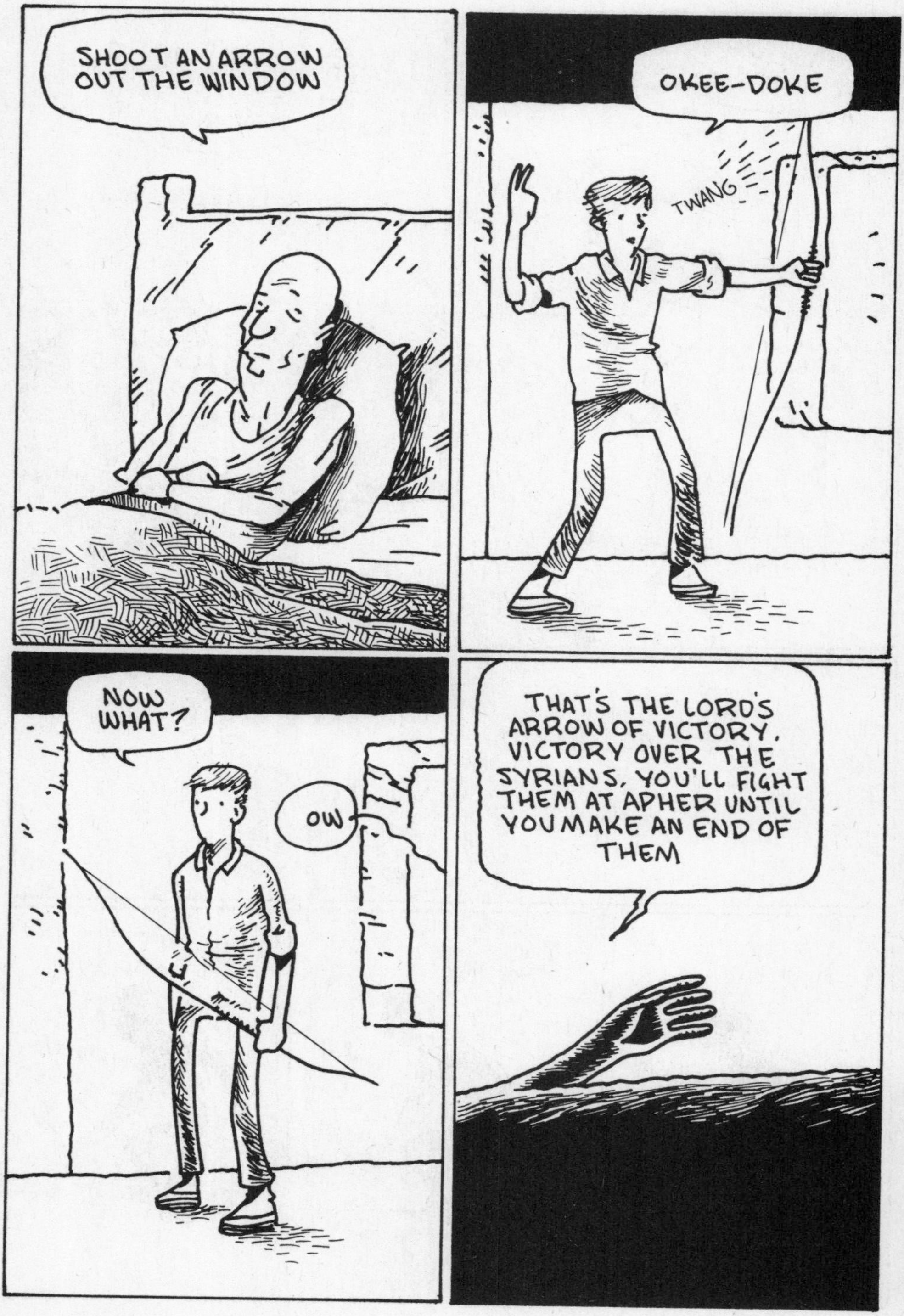
SHOOT AN ARROW OUT THE WINDOW
OKEE-DOKE
TWANG
NOW WHAT?
OW
THAT'S THE LORD'S ARROW OF VICTORY, VICTORY OVER THE SYRIANS, YOU'LL FIGHT THEM AT APHER UNTIL YOU MAKE AN END OF THEM

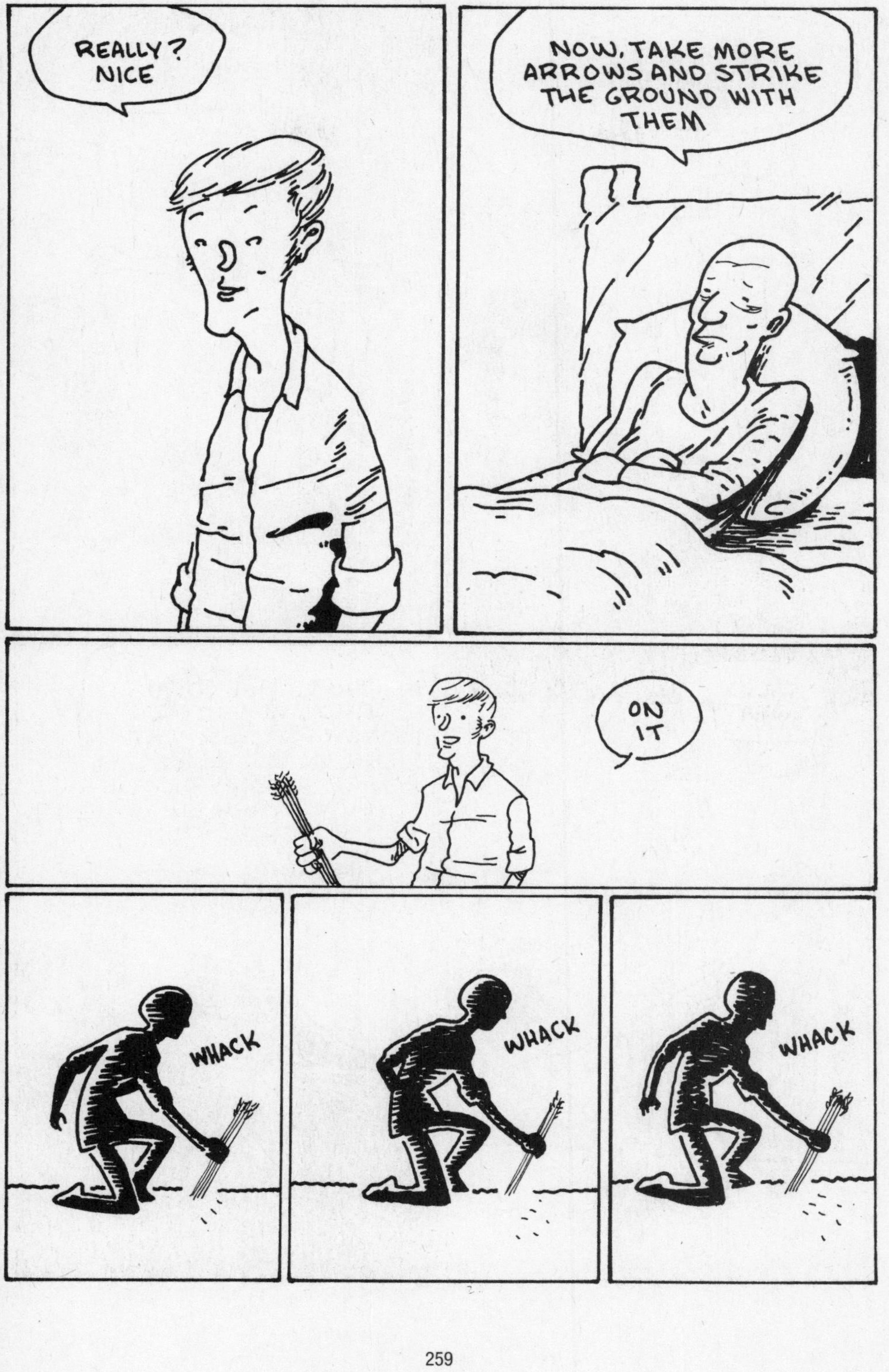
REALLY? NICE
NOW, TAKE MORE ARROWS AND STRIKE THE GROUND WITH THEM
ON IT
WHACK
WHACK
WHACK

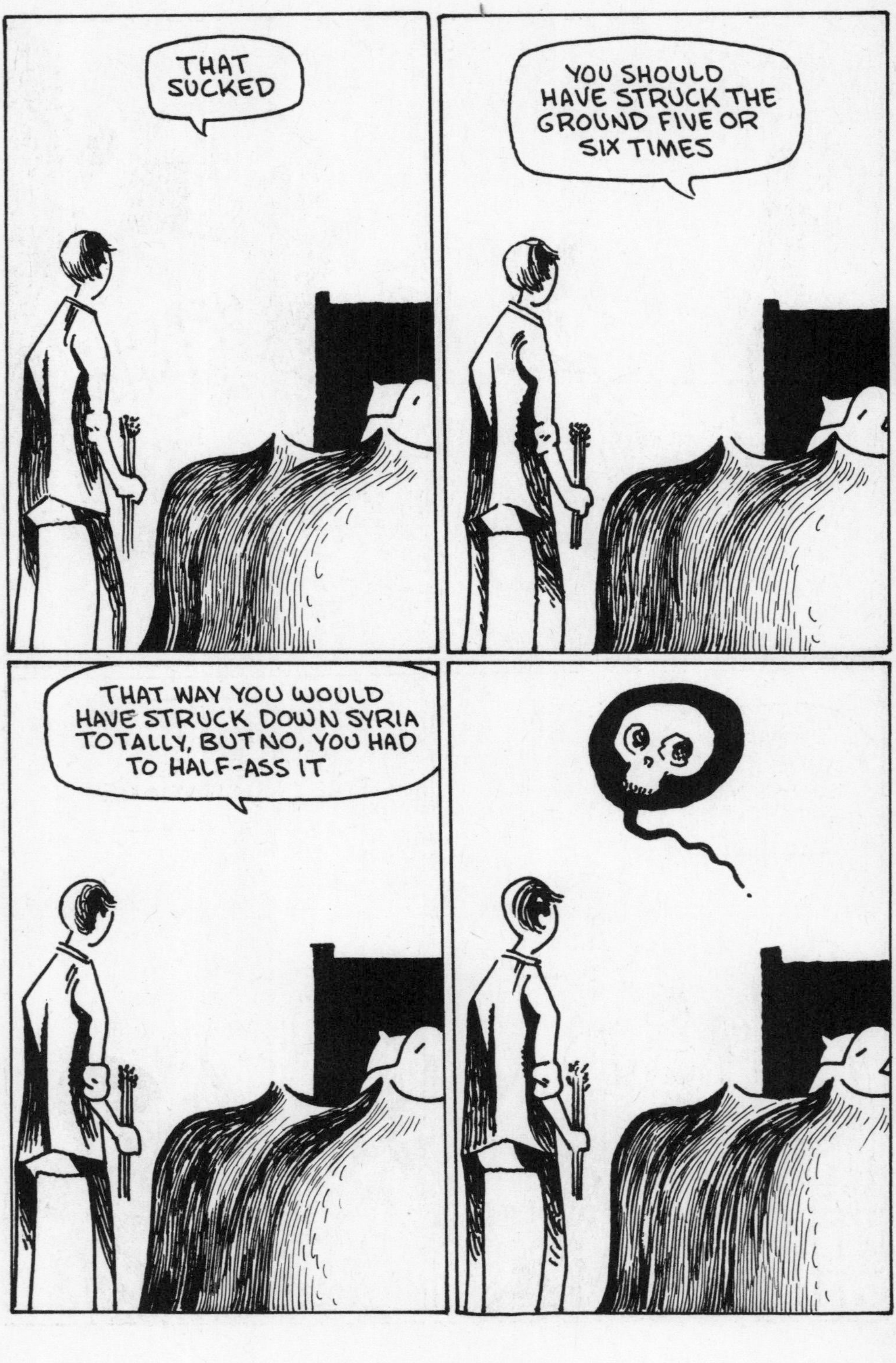
THAT SUCKED
YOU SHOULD HAVE STRUCK THE GROUND FIVE OR SIX TIMES
THAT WAY YOU WOULD HAVE STRUCK DOWN SYRIA TOTALLY, BUT NO, YOU HAD TO HALF-ASS IT

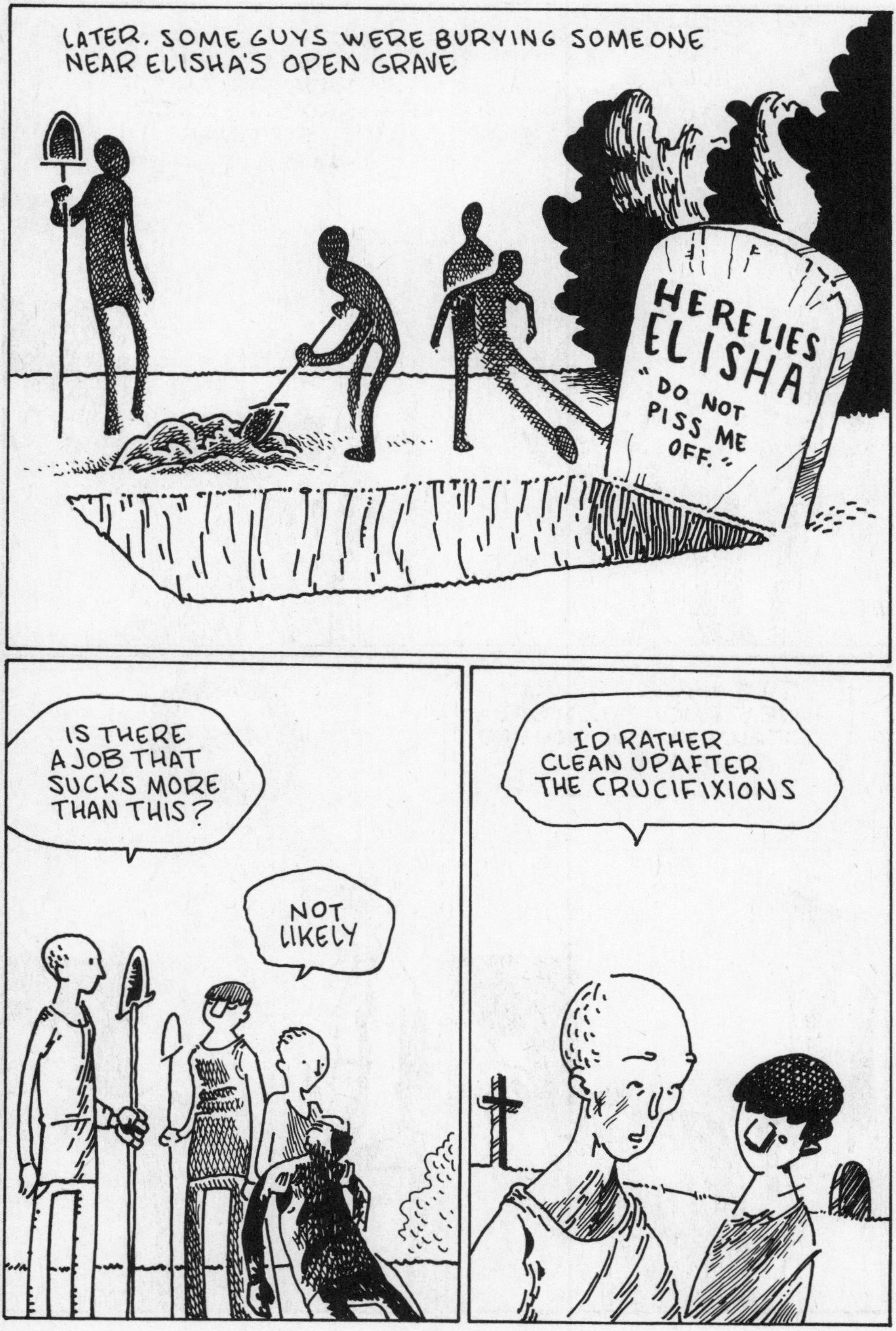
LATER, SOME GUYS WERE BURYING SOMEONE NEAR ELISHA'S OPEN GRAVE
HERE LIES ELISHA "DO NOT PISS ME OFF."
IS THERE A JOB THAT SUCKS MORE THAN THIS?
NOT LIKELY
I'D RATHER CLEAN UP AFTER THE CRUCIFIXIONS

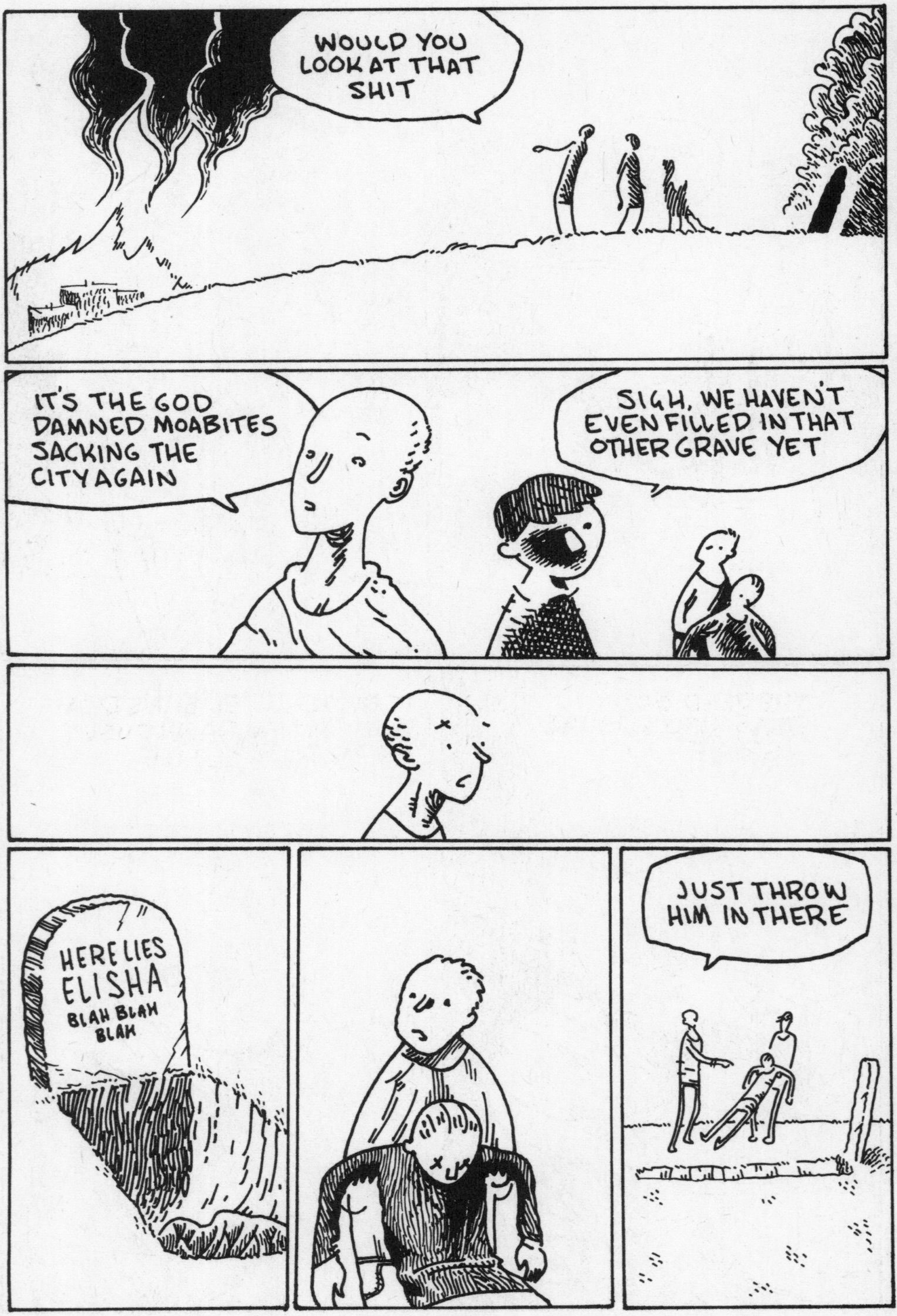
WOULD YOU LOOK AT THAT SHIT
IT'S THE GOD DAMNED MOABITES SACKING THE CITY AGAIN
SIGH, WE HAVEN'T EVEN FILLED IN THAT OTHER GRAVE YET
HERE LIES ELISHA BLAH BLAH BLAH
JUST THROW HIM IN THERE

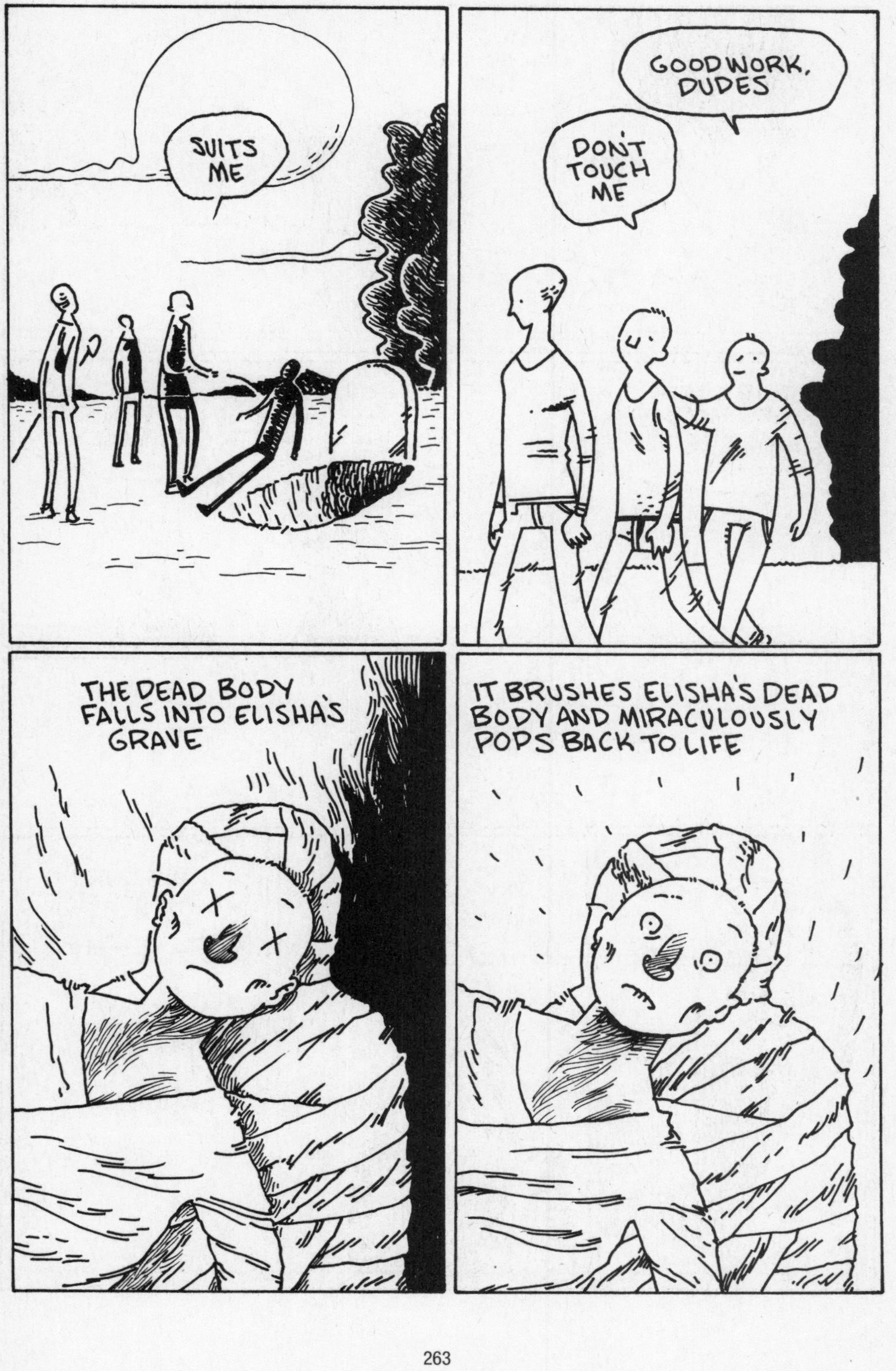
SUITS ME
GOODWORK, DUDES
DON'T TOUCH ME
THE DEAD BODY FALLS INTO ELISHA'S GRAVE
IT BRUSHES ELISHA'S DEAD BODY AND MIRACULOUSLY POPS BACK TO LIFE

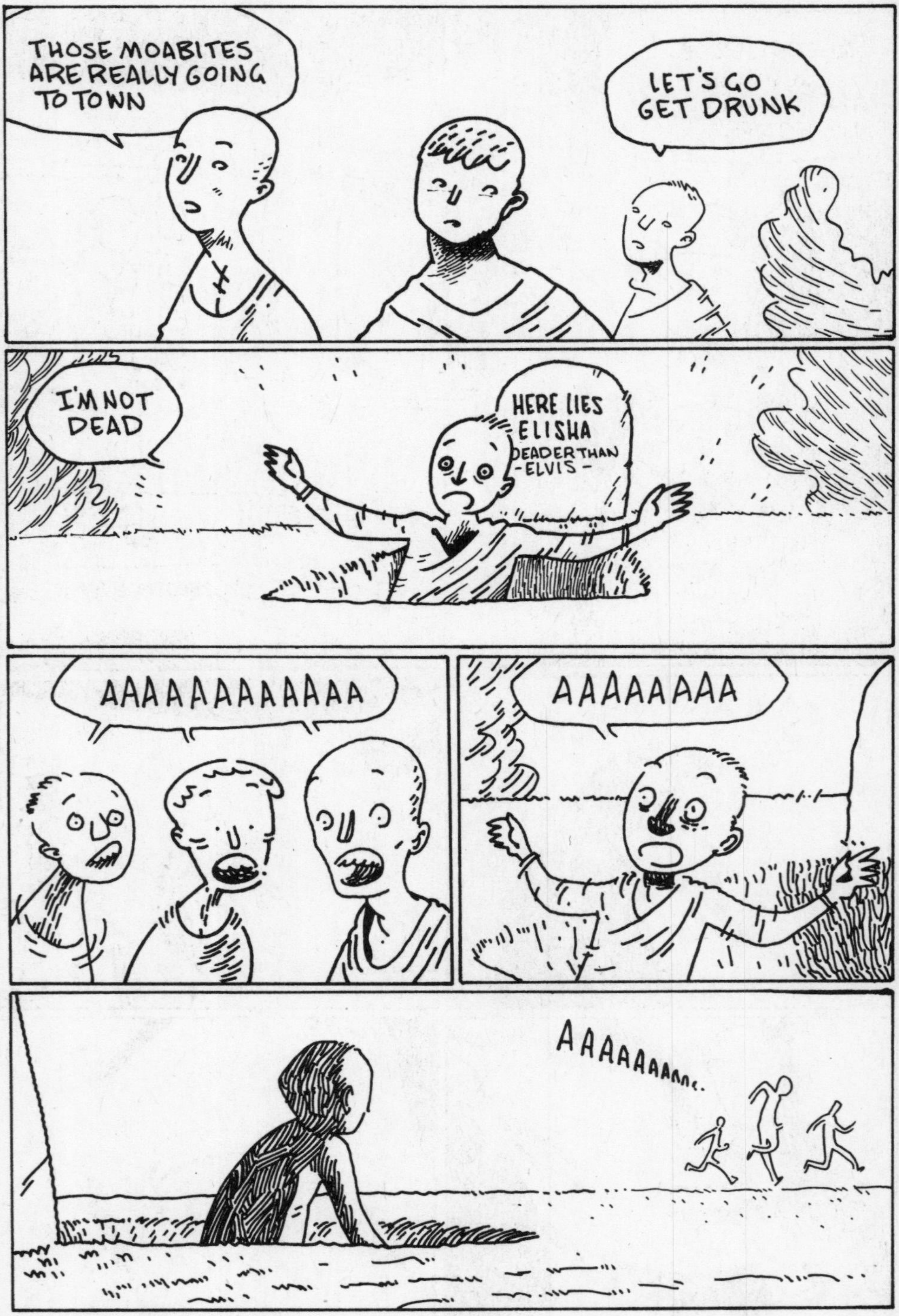
THOSE MOABITES ARE REALLY GOING TO TOWN
LET'S GO GET DRUNK
I'M NOT DEAD
HERE LIES ELISHA DEADER THAN -ELVIS-
AAAAAAAAAAAA
AAAAAAAA
AAAAAAAAA...

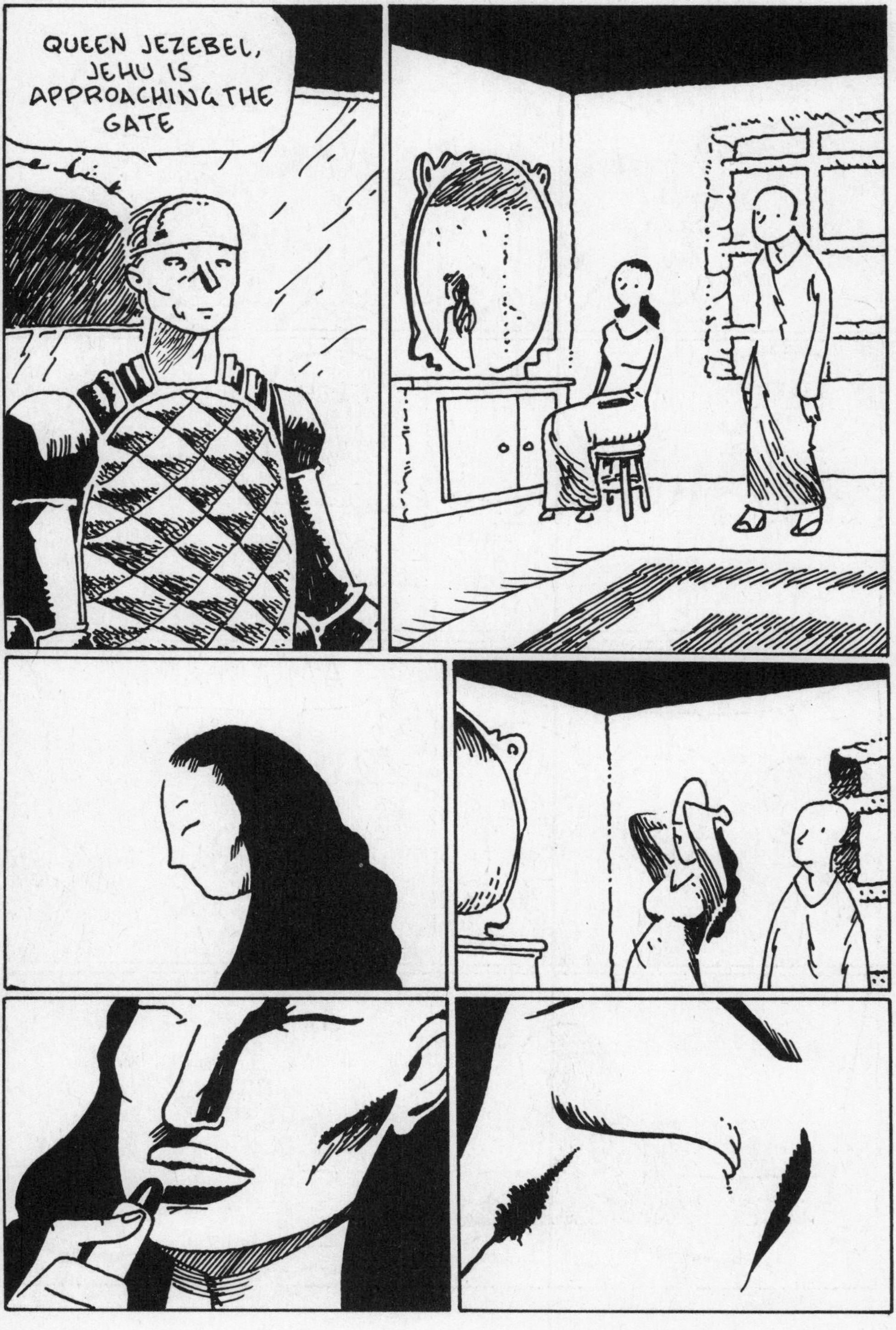
QUEEN JEZEBEL, JEHU IS APPROACHING THE GATE

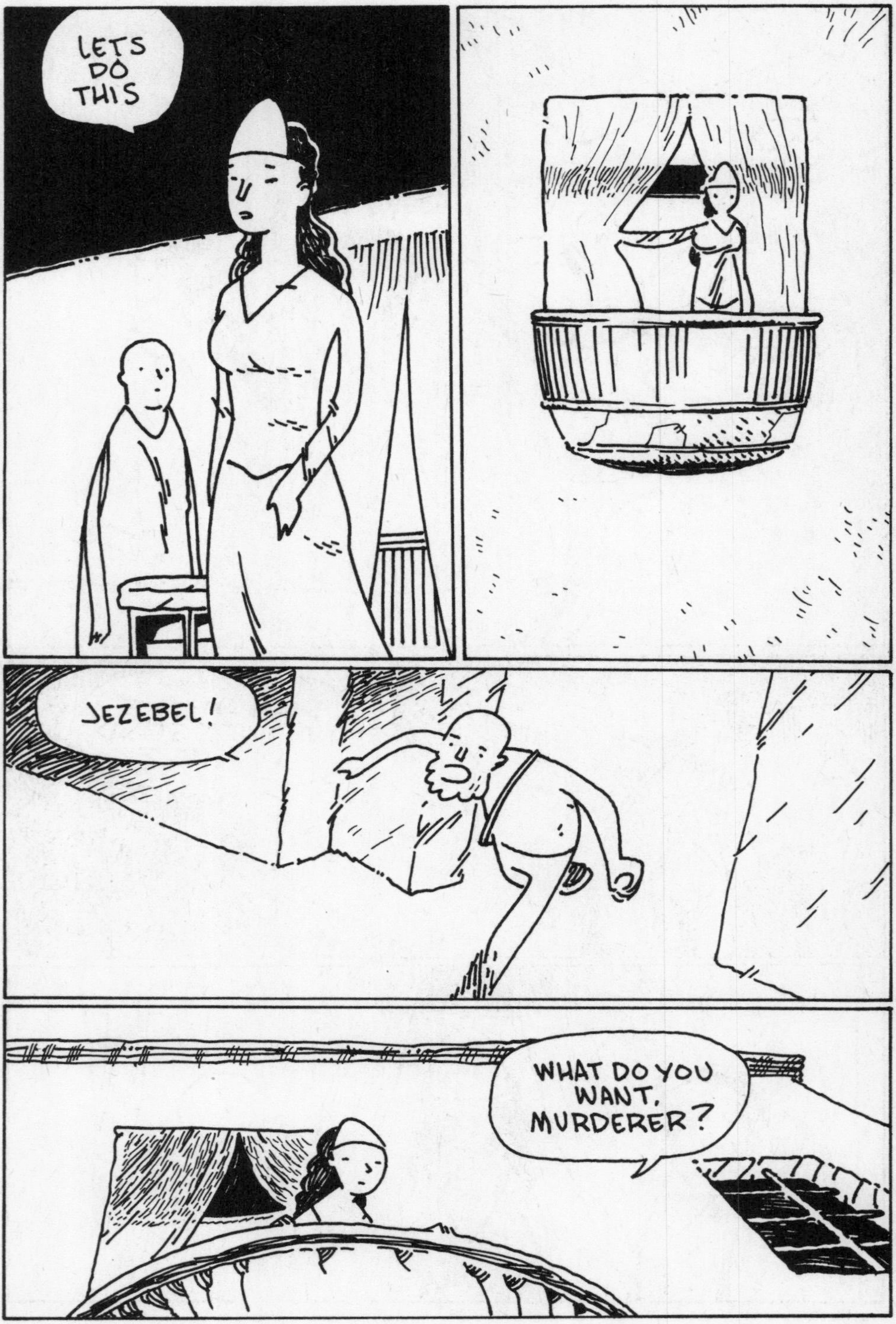
LETS DO THIS
JEZEBEL!
WHAT DO YOU WANT, MURDERER?

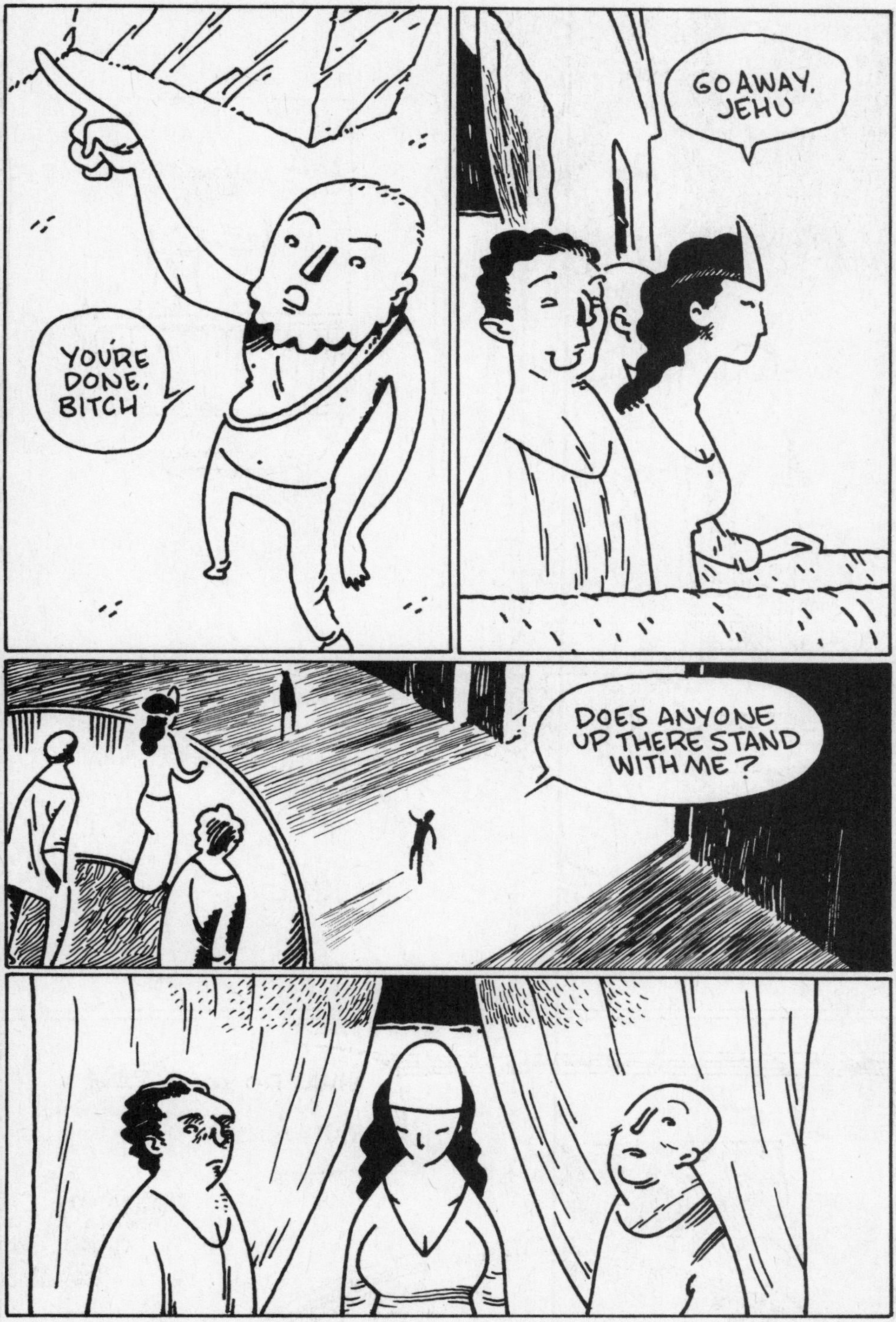
YOU'RE DONE, BITCH
GO AWAY, JEHU
DOES ANYONE UP THERE STAND WITH ME?

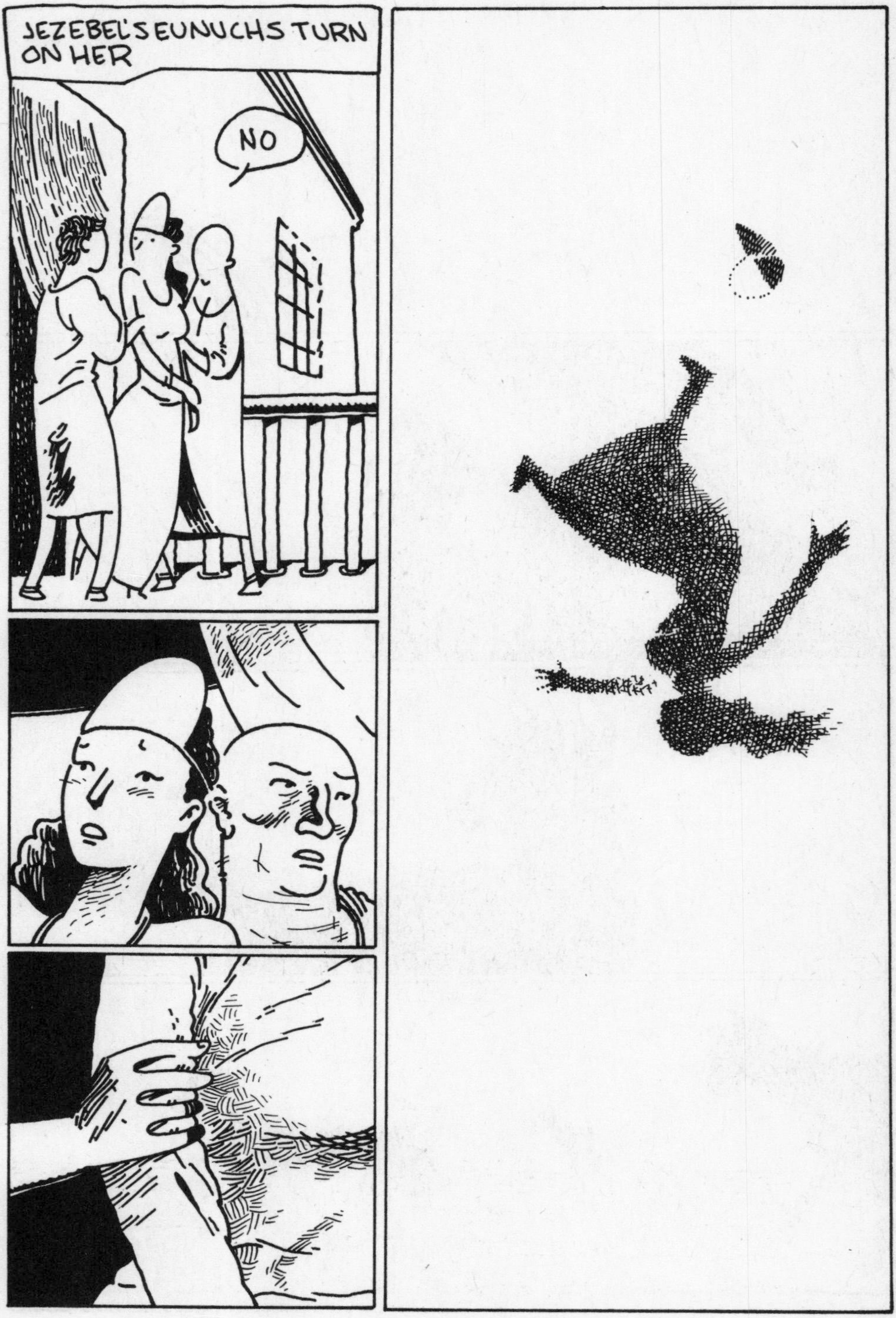
JEZEBEL'S EUNUCHS TURN ON HER
NO

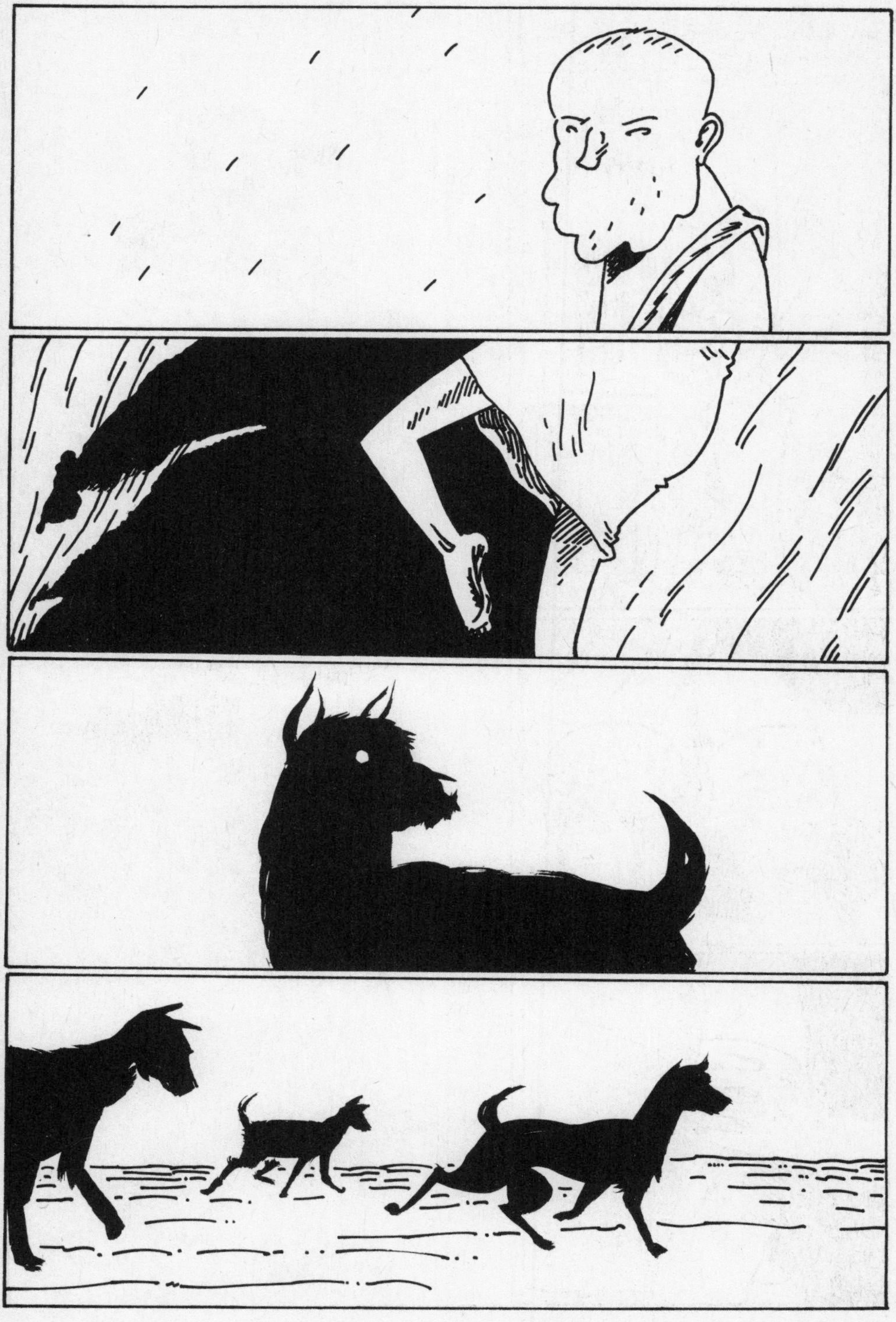

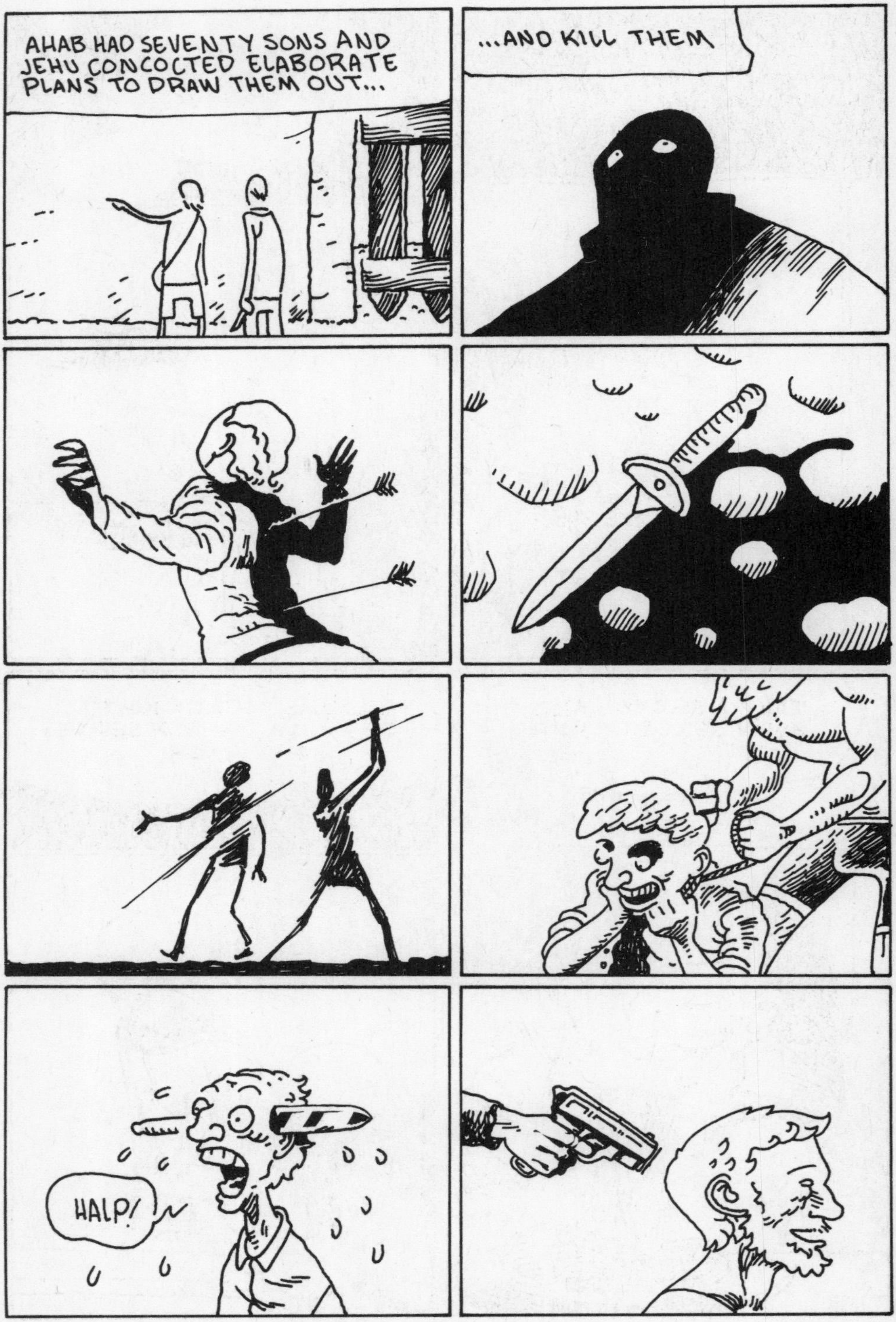
AHAB HAD SEVENTY SONS AND JEHU CONCOCTED ELABORATE PLANS TO DRAW THEM OUT...
...AND KILL THEM
HALP!

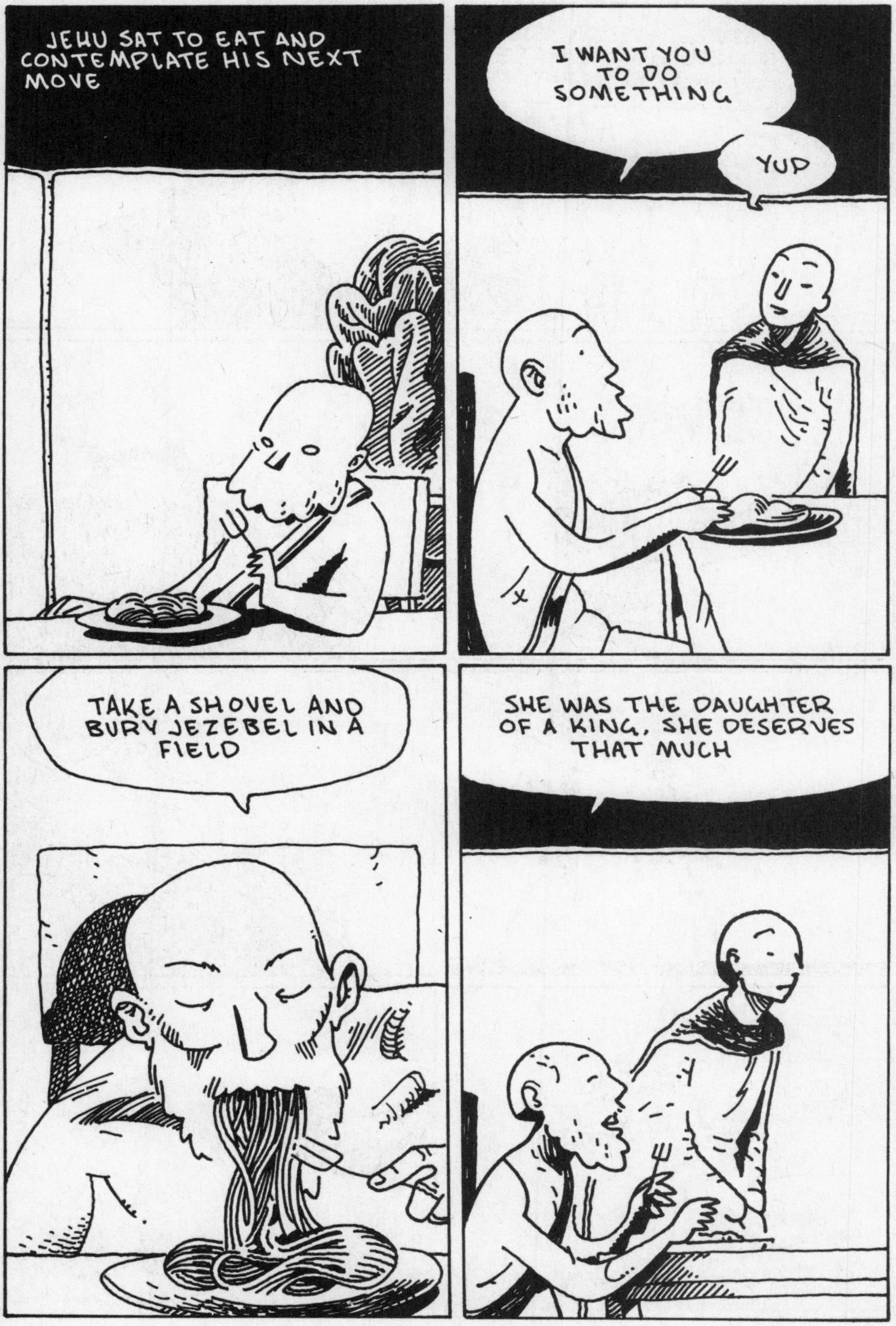
JEHU SAT TO EAT AND CONTEMPLATE HIS NEXT MOVE
I WANT YOU TO DO SOMETHING
YUP
TAKE A SHOVEL AND BURY JEZEBEL IN A FIELD
SHE WAS THE DAUGHTER OF A KING, SHE DESERVES THAT MUCH

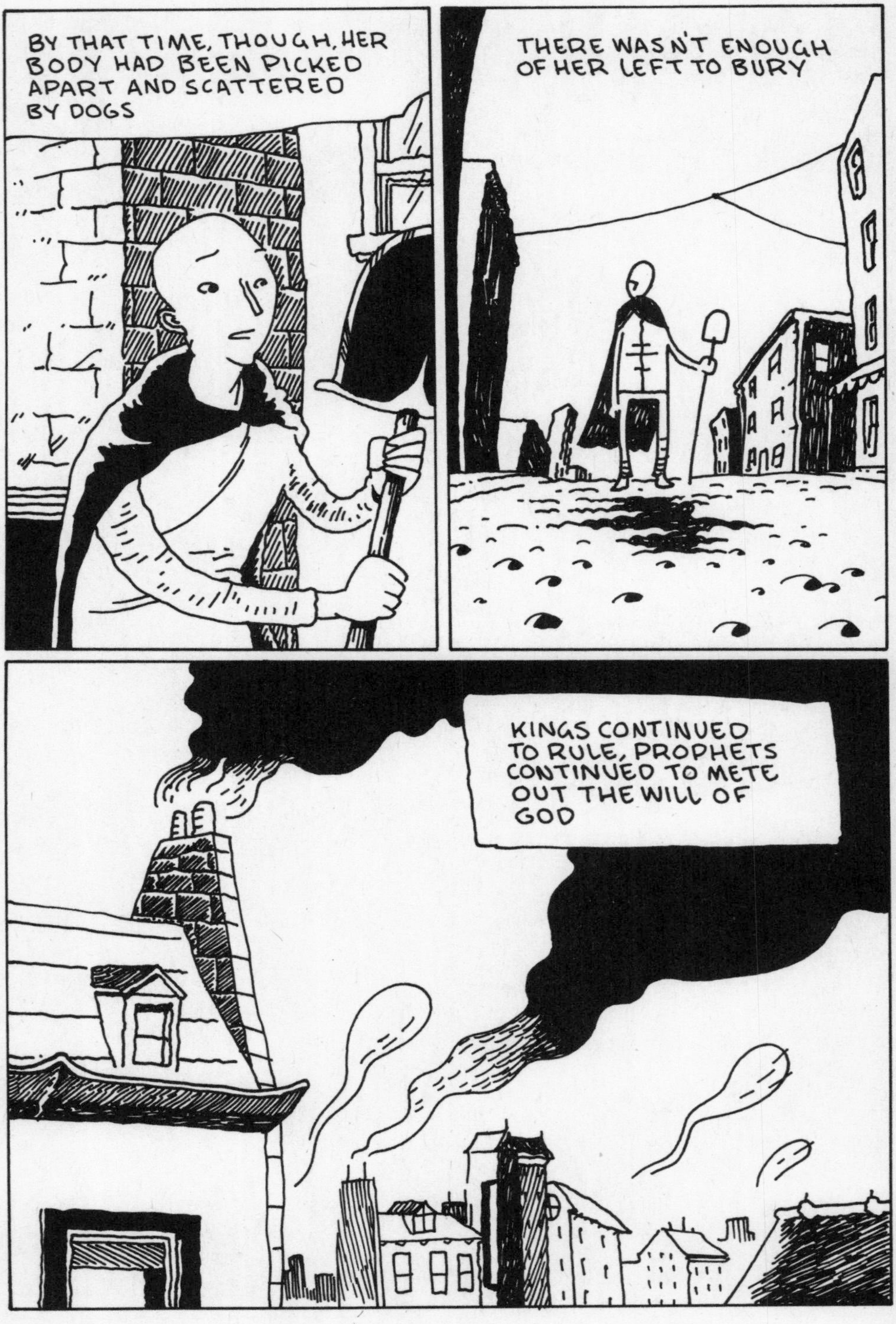
BY THAT TIME, THOUGH, HER BODY HAD BEEN PICKED APART AND SCATTERED BY DOGS
THERE WASN'T ENOUGH OF HER LEFT TO BURY
KINGS CONTINUED TO RULE, PROPHETS CONTINUED TO METE OUT THE WILL OF GOD

UNCIVILIZED BOOKS CATALOGUE

Everything is Flammable by Gabrielle Bell

An Iranian Metamorphosis by Mana Neyestani

The Voyeurs & *Truth is Fragmentary* by Gabrielle Bell

Incidents in the Night Books 1 & 2 by David B.; Translated by Brian Evenson

Amazing Facts & Beyond by Kevin Huizenga & Dan Zettwoch

It Never Happened Again & New Construction by Sam Alden

Jacob Bladders and the State of the Art by Roman Muradov

War of Streets and Houses by Sophie Yanow

Sammy The Mouse Book 1 & 2 by Zak Sally

The Whistling Factory by Jesse McManus

Houses of the Holy by Caitlin Skaalrud

Eel Mansions by Derek Van Gieson

Plans We Made by Simon Moreton

True Swamp 1 & 2 by Jon Lewis

Pascin by Joann Sfar

Borb by Jason Little

ODOD BOOKS CATALOGUE

Musnet Vol. 1-4 by Kickliy

That Night a Monster by Marzena Sowa & Berenika Kołomycka

Over the Wall by Peter Wartman

CRITICAL CARTOONS SERIES:

Brighter Than You Think by Alan Moore & Marc Sobel

Ed vs. Yummy Fur by Brian Evenson

Carl Bark' Duck by Peter Schilling Jr.

uncivilizedbooks.com